STUDY GUIDE

BUSINESS LAW

STUDY GUIDE
Ramona Atkins
Allan Hancock College

BUSINESS LAW
Fifth Edition

Henry Cheeseman

PEARSON

Prentice
Hall

Upper Saddle River, New Jersey 07458

Editor-in-Chief: PJ Boardman
Executive Editor: Mac Mendelsohn
Assistant Editor: Sam Goffinet
Manager, Print Production: Christy Mahon
Production Editor & Buyer: Wanda Rockwell
Printer/Binder: Courier, Bookmart Press

10 9 8 7 6 5 4 3 2
ISBN 0-13-146096-X

Contents

DEDICATION

To my wonderful family

Kurt Hamblet, Monica Hamblet and Karissa Hamblet

my inspiration and motivation

ACKNOWLEDGMENTS

The creation of this study guide has been a very interesting as well as positive experience. Several individuals played significant roles in assuring its completion. Professor Cheeseman's vast knowledge as well as organization of the main text is applauded, as it was crucial and insightful in developing the exercises contained herein. Additionally, the patience, support and professionalism of Assistant Editors Ashley Keim and Sam Goffinet were greatly appreciated. The votes of confidence and encouragement from Lori Sullivan, our Prentice Hall Representative, Dr. Marie Comstock, Department Chair of Allan Hancock College's Business Department and colleague Mr. Robert Bryant were also invaluable. Finally, I would like to give special thanks to my husband Kurt Hamblet and daughters, Monica and Karissa for their understanding of the amount of time and dedication involved in generating a study guide of this size.

Ramona A. Atkins, J.D.
Associate Faculty of Business Law
Allan Hancock College, Business Education
Santa Maria, California
hamblet4@gte.net

Chapter 1

LEGAL BUSINESS AND E-COMMERCE ENVIRONMENT

Chapter Overview

This chapter provides a detailed look at the concept of law and its functions in our society. Even though the meaning of law is vast, law in general is a set of standards and rules that we justify our actions by and which is the basis of consequences as well as sanctions. The philosophy of law, various schools of thought on its development and the importance of flexibility in its application are also examined. The history and development of our laws and courts along with interpretation as it pertains to technology, growth of commerce and the standards of society are what bring about changes and new laws.

Objectives

Upon completing the exercises that follow, you should be able to:
1. To describe law based upon its function.
2. To recognize and compare the major schools of jurisprudence.
3. To understand and appreciate the history of American law.
4. To differentiate between a law court, equity court and a merchant court.
5. To recognize the sources of modern law in the United States.
6. To understand and recognize key terminology when briefing a case.
7. To understand how to recognize legal and ethical issues when briefing a case.
8. To have a broader understanding of legal history as well as business developments in cyberspace.

Practical Application

You should be able to understand the need for law as well as flexible interpretation and the framework by which laws are established.

Helpful Hints

You should read each chapter and complete or read the corresponding study sheet. Next, a Refresh Your Memory exercise will determine what materials you need to place more emphasis on. The Critical Thinking exercise that follows will help to assess your ability to analyze and apply the legal concepts you have learned to the facts. Finally, a Sample Quiz consisting of true/false, multiple choice and short answer questions is provided as a means of assessing your mastery of the chapter.

Essentials For a Well-Written Critical Thinking Exercise

Critical Thinking Exercises should be approached in a methodical way. Each exercise should be read twice, the first time to get a feel for the facts and determine what is being asked of you, and the second to spot the issues presented. Once you know what the question is asking you to do, you can mark up the facts with a pen and place possible applicable legal terms from the chapter you have just studied next to the fact it pertains to. In order to stay organized, it's best to outline the answer to the exercise. State your issues to be discussed and place them in the order that they will be presented. Demonstrate how the facts in your exercise meet the requirements of the legal principle(s) you are discussing.

Remember, every story has two sides, as does every argument. When applicable, give reasoning for both sides. Also, if you are applying case law that you have studied, be sure to show how the case(s) apply to the facts you've been given, based upon the similarity of both scenarios. Further, if the case is not supportive of your analysis, you may indicate this point with a brief explanation and continue with the issues you have strong support for.

Finally, make sure that you have utilized all of the relevant facts and applied the pertinent law in analyzing these facts. Remember, it is your reasoning and application of the main objectives of the chapter that will help to determine your competency of the information given to you. If you approach these types of exercises as challenging, fun and practical, you will begin to appreciate their usefulness in your every day life. A sample answer is given at the end of the chapter and is to be used as a guide. Answers will vary based on the law and analysis applied by individual students.

Study Tips

Law is a set of standards and rules that we justify our conduct and actions by and that, which is subject to consequences and sanctions.
Functions of the law include the following:
- To shape moral standards.
- To maintain the status quo.
- To facilitate planning.
- To maximize individual freedom.
- To keep the peace.
- To promote social justice.
- To facilitate orderly change.
- To provide a basis for compromise.

Various scholars have stated their philosophies on the development of the law. There are several schools of jurisprudential thought. You can remember the main ones by the following mnemonic:
A cranky squirrel commands natural history!

A - The Analytical School asserts that the law is formed by logic.
C - The Critical Legal Studies School does not believe in rules for settling disputes, but applying rules of fairness to each circumstance.
S - The Sociological School believes that law is a way to form social behavior and attain sociological goals.
C - The Command School espouses that the law changes when the ruler changes.
N - The Natural Law School maintains that the basis of law should be on morality and ethics.
H - The Historical School believes that changes in societal norms are eventually demonstrated in the law. These scholars rely on precedent to solve modern problems.

Foundation of American Law
The American common law was derived from England and its laws. It is helpful to understand a brief history of how our laws developed.

English Common Law
These laws developed from judge issued opinions that became precedent for other judges to decide similar cases.

Law Courts
The judges issued their opinions in cases that later set the precedent for deciding the same types of cases.

Equity Courts
A court that is based on fairness when deciding cases

Merchant Courts
A court that dealt with just the law of merchants. Eventually this court was combined with the regular court system.

Sources of Law

- Constitution - The supreme law of the land that provided for the structure of the federal government. This structure established the legislative, executive and judicial branches of government.

- Treaties - Compacts or agreements between two or more nations.

- Statutes - A set of state or federal laws that describes conduct that must be followed by those the statute was designed to protect.

- Ordinances - Laws that are created and enforced by local governments including counties, school districts and municipalities.

- Executive Orders - These are laws that are made by the President or state governors.

- Judicial Decisions - Federal and state issued decisions about individual lawsuits.

The Doctrine of Stare Decisis

A rule of law set forth by higher courts, which becomes precedence for lower court decisions. In addition to the benefit of helping to establish uniformity of law, this doctrine makes it easier for individuals and businesses to determine what the law is.

Key Terms

Plaintiff is the one who originally brings the lawsuit

Defendant is the party who is being sued or whom the suit is brought against.

Petitioner or Appellant is the party (plaintiff or defendant) who has appealed the decision of the lower court or trial court.

Respondent or Appellee is the party (or person) who must answer the appeal brought by the petitioner or appellant. The respondent or appellee may be either the plaintiff or defendant based on which party is the petitioner.

Essentials for briefing a case

> Case name, citation and the court
> Important case facts briefly and concisely stated
> Issues presented to the court
> Rules of law
> Analysis of the facts with incorporation of the law
> Conclusion or holding of the court hearing the case

Refresh Your Memory:

The following exercise will give you the opportunity to test your memory of the principles given in this chapter. Read the question twice and place your answer in the blanks provided. Review the chapter material for any question that you are unable to answer or remember.

1. Sidney has been given a set of rules and consequences for breaking those rules if he does not follow them. These legally binding guidelines are referred to as the _____.

2. Morality and ethics are the basis for this jurisprudential school of thought. _____

3. What jurisprudential philosophy would you apply if you based your decisions on the principle of fairness rather than established rules? _____

4. An agreement between two or more nations is known as a _____.

5. A law that states you may not mow your lawn before a certain time in the morning is called an _____.

6. If the President of the United States commanded that all encrypted technology be banned from high profile, terrorist inhabited countries, this would be an example of _____.

7. The supreme law of the land is known as the _____.

8. What is the type of court that is bases its decisions on fairness? _____

9. If George is the party bringing a lawsuit against Henry, what is George's title in the lawsuit? _____

10. If Henry decides to appeal the case brought by George, what legal term describes Henry in his appeal? _____

11. George is served with the appellate lawsuit brought by Henry. What term describes George's role in this suit? _____

12. Which court dealt primarily with merchants? _____

13. A legal scholar who basis his or her thought on logic would follow which legal school of thought? _____

14. The doctrine that helped establish uniformity of law is known as _____ _____.

15. A case is briefed by determining the issues, and _____ applying the law to the facts.

Critical Thought Exercise

Following the genocide, torture, rape, and murder of thousands of civilians in Rwanda in 1994, sixty-three individuals were tried for genocide and crimes against humanity. Numerous persons were sentenced to life sentences.

Many of those prosecuted objected to being tried outside Rwanda for acts committed within Rwanda. The accused further objected to being prosecuted for acts that were not deemed criminal by their own leaders or national laws.

You are asked to address a large convention sponsored by a nationalist group that argues against any person ever being subjected to criminal punishment by an international court for acts committed within their home country.

Your argument should address the following issues while trying to explain whether or not you feel prosecutions by an international body are lawful and justified:

1. What law is being violated when someone commits a crime against humanity?
2. Who has the authority to enforce laws against genocide and crimes against humanity?
3. Should a citizen of a sovereign nation be subjected to punishment by an international tribunal for acts committed within their home country?
4. Who is responsible for the prosecution of these crimes?

Answer. _____

_____
_____
_____
_____
_____
_____
_____
_____
_____
_____
_____
_____

_____
_____
_____
_____
_____
_____
_____
_____
_____
_____
_____
_____
_____
_____
_____
_____
_____
_____
_____
_____
_____

Practice Quiz

True/False:

1. _____ Laws consist of rules that govern the conduct of individuals, businesses and organizations that function with it. [p 3]

2. _____ Businesses are not like individuals and as such owe no duty to society. [p 3]

3. _____ Since the law cannot be written in advance to predict every potential dispute, general concepts and principles are developed for courts to apply. [p 5]

4. _____ The government may prohibit speech when it increases the chance of an unlawful act being committed at some indefinite future time. [p 6]

5. _____ The Analytical School of jurisprudence is based upon what is morally and ethically correct. [p 7]

6. _____ Legal philosophers who use past legal decisions to solve contemporary problems follow the beliefs of the Historical School of jurisprudence. [p 7]

7. ____ The English Common Law served as a basis from which many of our laws were developed. [p 9]

8. ____ An equity court emphasizes the procedure of a case versus the merits of a case. [p 9]

9. ____ A merchant court is one that administers rules to resolve commercial disputes among merchants. [p 9]

10. ____ The Chancellor's remedies were called legal remedies because they were shaped to emphasize legal procedure. [p 9]

11. ____ Any local, state or federal law which conflicts with the U.S. Constitution is unenforceable. [p 10]

12. ____ The structure of the United States federal government is comprised of the legislative, executive and prejudicial branches, each of which have been granted certain powers. [p 10]

13. ____ The federal and state courts must follow the precedent established by lower courts. [p 13]

14. ____ The doctrine of stare decisis promotes uniformity of law within a court system. [p 13]

15. ____ Executive orders can regulate the exportation of U.S. encryption technology. [p 12]

Multiple Choice:

16. Some of the primary functions of the law in our country are: [p 4]
    a. promoting social justice, encouraging legal decisions, and interpreting judicial decisions.
    b. facilitating change, providing a basis for compromise and developing legal reasoning.
    c. keeping the peace, shaping moral standards, minimizing individual freedom.
    d. none of the above.

17. The Sociological School of Jurisprudence maintains that [p 7]
    a. the law is a set of rules enforced by the ruling party and the law changes when the ruler changes.
    b. the rules of law are unnecessary and subjective decisions made be judges are permissible.
    c. the purpose of law is to achieve, advance and shape social behavior.
    d. the law is an evolutionary process.

18. The term codified law refers to [p 11]
    a. statutes enacted by the legislative branches of state and federal governments that are arranged by topic in code books.
    b. a written agreement made between the United States and another nation.
    c. administrative rules and regulations.
    d. all of the above.

19. The term stare decisis means: [p 13]
    a. to interpret statutes and make a decision.
    b. to predict the legal decision in a case.
    c. to stand by the decision.
    d. to adopt and regulate the conduct of others.

20. Provisions of state established constitutions are valid unless [p 11]
    a. they are patterned after the U.S. Constitution .
    b. they have an executive branch of their governments.
    c. they apply to evolving social, technological and economic conditions.
    d. they conflict with the U.S. Constitution or any valid federal law.

21. Which of the following is often referred to as the "fourth branch" of government? [p 12]
    a. the legislative branch.
    b. the judicial branch.
    c. the executive branch.
    d. administrative agencies.

22. The theory that the main goal of decision-making should be to promote market efficiency is derived from: [p 8]
    a. the Command School.
    b. the Law and Economics School.
    c. the Jurisprudence School.
    d. the Marketing and Advertising School.

23. Traffic laws, local building codes and zoning laws are examples of [p 11]
    a. Indian gaming regulations.
    b. federal government regulations.
    c. ordinances.
    d. state administrative orders.

24. The feminist legal theory is based upon [p 6]
    a. the premise that both men and women have the same perspective.
    b. the female perspective in developing, interpreting and applying the law.
    c. the enforcement of constraints against women.
    d. all of the above.

25. The law of the United States is mainly based on: [p 9]
    a. Federal Law
    b. Roman Civil Law
    c. English Business Law
    d. English Common Law

Short Answer:

26. What was the primary example that was set in the case of *Brown v. Board of Education?* [p 5]
    _____

27. Distinguish between a law court and a Chancery (equity) court. [p 9] _____
    _____

28. Give several examples of federal statutes. [p 11] _____
    _____

29. Give several examples of state statutes. [p 11] _____
_____

30. Define the meaning of jurisprudence. [p 7] _____
_____

31. Why will treaties become increasingly more important to business? [p 11] _____
_____

32. Administrative agencies are created to enforce and interpret statutes. Give two examples of these types of agencies. [p 12] _____

33. Which state bases its law on the French Civil Code? [p 9] _____

34. What is a judicial decision? [p 13] _____
_____

35. What do state constitutions establish? [p 11] _____

36. What are the two qualities of law as they pertain to the American legal system? [p 5]
_____ and _____

37. What type of court emphasized legal procedure over merits? [p 9] _____

38. What is critical thinking? [p] _____
_____

39. What jurisprudential school of thought do realists follow? [p 7] _____

40. What types of agencies are the Securities and Exchange Commission and the Federal Trade Commission? [p 12] _____

41. When briefing a case, what does the case name usually contain? [p 14] _____
_____

42. When stating the summary of the facts of a case you are briefing, what should be omitted? [p 14]
_____

43. How should issues that are presented in a case to be briefed be asked? [p 14] _____
_____

44. What is the holding in a case? [p 15] _____

45. What should the holding state? [p 15] _____

46. What is an appellate court or supreme court's decision called? [p 15] _____

47. What may the rationale for the court's decision be based upon? [p 15] _____
_____

48. What is a statute? [p 11] _____

49. What is an executive order? [p 12] _____

50. What powers does the judicial branch of the federal government have? [p 10] _____
_____

Answers to Refresh Your Memory

1. law [p 4]
2. Natural School of Law [p 7]
3. critical legal studies [p 8]
4. treaty [p 11]
5. ordinance [p 11]
6. executive order [p 12]
7. the Constitution [p 10]
8. equity court [p 8]
9. plaintiff [p 14]
10. appellant or petitioner [p 14]
11. respondent or appellee [p 14]
12. merchant court [p 9]
13. analytical [p 7]
14. stare decisis [p 13]
15. analytically [p 14]

Critical Thought Exercise Model Answer

The Origins of Law

In its most basic form, law is comprised of the rules created by the controlling authority of a society, usually its government. These rules are given legal force and effect and control the actions of the individuals within the society. Most law is created by each society within a country and is referred to as national law. Law that is created by way of treaties, customs, and agreements between nations is international law.

For most countries, national law finds its foundation in the philosophies of legal positivism, which assumes that there is no law higher than the laws created by the government, and legal realism, which stresses a realistic approach that takes into account customary practices and present day circumstances.

In the area of international law, the philosophy of natural law plays an important role. Natural law holds that there is a universal law that is applicable to all human beings that is higher than any law created by an individual society or government. Certain conduct, such as genocide and crimes against humanity are deemed to be without any possible moral justification, regardless of the existence or nonexistence of any national law concerning these types of acts.

When a nation or segment of a society within a nation engages in conduct that violates natural law, it is no defense to this conduct that the government or society advocates or condones the conduct.

Justification For International Criminal Tribunals and an International Criminal Court

The nations of the world have collectively agreed for over 50 years that international courts capable of resolving disputes and addressing crimes against humanity are needed. This need has been filled by the United Nations.

The members of the United Nations consent to the jurisdiction of the international courts as a way to advance their rights in the international arena. Until 1998, The International Court of Justice (ICJ) was the principal judicial organ of the United Nations. The ICJ, located in The Hague, Netherlands, began operating in 1946. The prior court had been in the same location since 1922. In 1998, The International Criminal Court (ICC) was also created.

The ICJ operates under a Statute that is part of the Charter of the United Nations. The ICJ lacks power to address situations such as the Holocaust and genocide in Cambodia because it can only hear cases between states. It has no jurisdiction over individuals.

Prior to the formation of the ICC, the United Nations members formed criminal tribunals to address war crimes and crimes against humanity that have been committed during specific periods of time. These tribunals were given authority to prosecute individuals who were responsible for these severe criminal acts.

The overall purpose of these tribunals was to pursue peace and justice in the affected areas. The International Criminal Tribunal for Rwanda was established for the prosecution of persons responsible for genocide and other serious violations of international humanitarian law committed in the territory of Rwanda between 1 January 1994 and 31 December 1994. The tribunal was also authorized to prosecute Rwandan citizens responsible for genocide and other such violations of international law committed in the territory of neighboring States during the same period.

An international criminal court has been called the missing link in the international legal system. The International Court of Justice at The Hague handles only cases between States, not individuals. Without an international criminal court for dealing with individual responsibility as an enforcement mechanism, acts of genocide and egregious violations of human rights often go unpunished. No one was held accountable for the over 2 million people killed by the Khmer Rouge in Cambodia in the 1970s. The same was true for murders of men, women and children in Mozambique, Liberia, El Salvador and other countries.

Defining International Crimes

When each instance of genocide or crimes against humanity has taken place, a specific statute had to be created which not only set up the tribunal, but defined the crimes that were to be prosecuted. The jurisdiction of the tribunal only extended to those crimes and that time period covered in the statute.

In the statute establishing the International Criminal Tribunal for Rwanda, specific definitions for genocide, crimes against humanity, and violations of the Geneva Convention were set forth in detail. To address crimes against humanity, the ICTR statute established "...the power to prosecute persons responsible for the following crimes when committed as part of a widespread or systematic attack against any civilian population on national, political, ethnic, racial or religious grounds: (a) Murder; (b) Extermination; (c) Enslavement; (d) Deportation; (e) Imprisonment; (f) Torture; (g) Rape; (h) Persecutions on political, racial and religious grounds; (i) Other inhumane acts." (ICTR Stat.ute, Article 3.)

Need For International Prosecution

Without the international tribunals, those responsible could easily flee to other countries and avoid being held accountable for their acts of genocide. This was particularly true in the case of Rwanda, where the perpetrators simply went across the border into neighboring countries to hide when pursued. They would then reenter Rwanda and continue the killing when they were able. Rwanda was unable to handle the apprehension and prosecution of those responsible because the government of Rwanda had broken down and lacked the power to enforce peace. The need for international prosecution also arises when the controlling government and its leaders are the actual perpetrators, such as in the case of Yugoslavia. The government in power may actually mandate that the criminal acts be carried out as part of an "ethnic cleansing." This was true in both Nazi Germany and in Yugoslavia in the 1990s.

Deterrence and Responsibility For Prosecutions in the Future

Nations agree that criminals should normally be prosecuted by national courts in the countries where the crimes are committed. When the national governments are either unwilling or unable to act to restore peace and seek justice, there needs to be an institution in place to address the horrors of genocide and crimes against humanity. In the past, perpetrators had little chance of being caught, much less prosecuted. The new ICC seeks to create a deterrent effect. Those responsible for murder, terrorism, genocide, and violations of the Geneva Convention will know that they will be pursued throughout the world. Additionally, the loopholes inherent in the tribunal process will be eliminated. The ineffective nature of the ICTR is shown by the fact that the murder of thousands of people from 1995-1999 will go unpunished because the ICTR was only authorized to prosecute those crimes committed in 1994.

Without an international institution to address crimes such as those committed in Rwanda, the perpetrators of the worst crimes in history would go unpunished. The members of the United Nations have decided that they desire the protection afforded by an international criminal court.

Answers to Practice Quiz:

True/False:

1. True Laws consist of rules that govern the conduct of individuals, businesses and organizations that function within it.
2. False Businesses are not like individuals and as such owe no duty to society.
3. True Specific laws cannot be written to cover every possible situation.
4. False The government may prohibit speech when it increases the chance of an unlawful act being committed at some indefinite future time.
5. False The Natural School of jurisprudence is based upon what is morally and ethically correct.
6. True Legal philosophers who use past legal decisions to solve contemporary problems follow the beliefs of the Historical School of jurisprudence.
7. True Our laws were developed using the English Common Law as a foundation.
8. False The Chancery (Equity) Courts inquired into the merits of the case as opposed to placing emphasis on legal procedure. The Equity Court was a place where a person could go if a law court could not give an appropriate remedy.
9. True A Merchant Court is one that was developed to solve the disputes of merchants who traveled through Europe and England.
10. False The Chancellor's remedies were called equitable remedies because they were shaped to emphasize the merits of a case.
11. True If a local, state or federal law conflict with the United States Constitution, it is unenforceable.
12. False The structure of the United States Government is comprised of the Legislative, Executive and Presidential branches each of which have been granted certain powers.
13. False Lower courts such as all federal and state courts must follow the precedents established by higher courts such as the U.S. Supreme Court.
14. True The term stare decisis means "to stand by the decision" which would logically promote uniformity of law within a court system, as businesses and individuals do not have to guess what the law is since the decision has been made.
15. True The Clinton administration used its express and implied powers drafted an executive order prohibiting the exportation of United States developed encryption technology.

Multiple Choice:

16. C Some of the primary functions of the law in our country are keeping the peace, shaping moral standards, and maintaining individual freedom. A is incorrect because even though we would like for legal decisions to be made, it is not a main function of law. B is incorrect as compromise comes as a result of negotiation as opposed to a function of law. Further, legal reasoning is not a function of the law, but is developed by applying the law to facts. Therefore, C is the best answer.

17. C The Sociological School maintains that the law is an avenue of attaining and advancing certain sociological goals. A is incorrect as this premise asserts the belief of the Command School. B is incorrect as this belief coincides with the Critical Legal Studies School. D is incorrect as this premise is maintained by the Historical School.

18. A This is the correct definition of codified law. B is incorrect as this is a definition of a treaty. C is incorrect as administrative rules and regulations assist in interpreting the statutes that the administrative agencies are authorized to enforce. D is incorrect for the reasons stated above.

19. C C is correct, as this is the true meaning of this Latin phrase. Answers A, B, and D are wrong as the meaning is incorrectly stated.

20. D Many state constitutions mirror the United States Constitution. Therefore, answer A is incorrect. Answer B is incorrect as state constitutions establish an executive branch of government. Answer C is a correct statement as it refers to the law and its flexibility toward evolving technological, social, and economic conditions. However, it is incorrect to say that the law is invalid because of these changes. Answer D is correct as the Constitution is the supreme law of the land. The states must follow it as opposed to creating conflicting provisions in their constitutions.

21. D Answers A, B, and C are incorrect as these are the original three branches of government that exist in the federal and state governments. Answer D is correct as the executive and legislative branches of state and federal governments are authorized to establish administrative agencies to interpret and follow through with the statutory provisions created by federal and state legislatures. This empowerment has given these administrative agencies the unofficial title of the "fourth branch" of government.

22. B Answer is correct as those such as U.S. Court of Appeals Judge Richard Posner support the theory that when making decisions in business related cases, illegalities should be found only if it causes the entire market to be less efficient. Answer A is incorrect as the Command School believes that the law changes when the ruling party changes. Answer C is incorrect as jurisprudence is a philosophy or science about how the law was developed. It is within this philosophy that the different major schools were developed. Answer D is incorrect as it has no bearing on the goal of decision-making as it pertains to the law.

23. C C is the correct answer as these are examples of ordinances that can be made by local government bodies including municipalities, cities, etc. Answer A is incorrect as Indian gaming regulations are enacted pursuant to the power of the federal government under the Indian Gaming Regulatory Act of 1988. Answer B is incorrect as the examples given are not examples of laws made by the federal government. Answer D is incorrect as the state legislature delegates the authority to make ordinances such as those posed in the question. Traffic laws, codes and zoning laws are not orders, but laws.

24. B B is the correct answer as feminist jurisprudence scholars believe that a woman's perspective in certain areas of the law such as in battered women's cases, rape, and sexual harassment, might differ from that of a male and as such it should be taken into account when making legal decisions. Answer A is incorrect as it defeats the entire premise upon which the feminist legal theory is based. Answer C is incorrect as the feminist legal theory wants more flexibility in interpreting the law based upon a female's perspective. The enforcement of constraints against women would defeat the feminist legal theory.

25.   D   D is the correct answer as the law of the United States is primarily based upon English Common Law.   A is incorrect as federal law developed from various laws including English Common Law.

Short Answer:

26.   This case demonstrates the law leading the people as well as the law's response to social changes by overturning the "separate but equal doctrine." This doctrine approved of separate schools for black and white children.
27.   The only relief available for a law court was an award of money for damages. An equity court inquired as to the merits of the case. Also, the remedies in an equity court were based on fairness with equity courts taking precedence over law courts.
28.   Examples of federal statutes include antitrust laws, securities laws, labor, bankruptcy, and environmental protection laws.
29.   Examples of state statutes include consumer protection laws, partnership laws, worker's compensation laws and the Uniform Commercial Code.
30.   Jurisprudence is defined as the philosophy or science of law.
31.   As more agreements are reached between nations, economic relations between these nations will also increase, thereby increasing their importance to business.
32.   The Securities and Exchange Commission (SEC) and the Federal Trade Commission (FTC) are two examples of administrative agencies.
33.   Louisiana.
34.   A judicial decision is a court issued statement of the holding of the case and the basis for reaching the decision in the case.
35.   State constitutions establish state governments and enumerate or specify their powers.
36.   Fairness and flexibility.
37.   Law court.
38.   The identification of essential facts and applicable law which is applied to specific issues presented in a case in order to reach a conclusion that resolves the given issues.
39.   The Sociological School.
40.   Administrative agencies.
41.   The names of the parties in the lawsuit.
42.   Extraneous facts and facts of minor importance.
43.   Issues should be asked in a one-sentence question that is only answerable by a yes or no.
44.   The decision reached by the court.
45.   The holding should state which party won the lawsuit.
46.   An opinion.
47.   Specific facts, public policy, prior law or other matters.
48.   Statutes are written laws with descriptions of behavior that must be followed by covered parties.
49.   An order issued by an executive branch member of the government.
50.   The power to interpret or translate and determine the validity or legality of the law.

Chapter 2

JUDICIAL AND ALTERNATIVE DISPUTE RESOLUTION

Chapter Overview

This chapter examines and compares the state court systems and the federal court system. It also provides a clear overview of the types of cases the various courts can hear as well as jurisdictional issues that web site operators face. Emphasis is also placed on the importance of a cost-benefit analysis when bringing, maintaining and defending a lawsuit. The pre-trial litigation process, court use of e-filings and the stages of a trial are thoroughly explained along with the nonjudicial alternatives of arbitration and medication.

Objectives

After completing the exercises that follow, you should be able to:
1. Compare the state court systems and the federal court system.
2. To analyze various factors when conducting a cost-benefit analysis in deciding whether to bring or defend a lawsuit.
3. To recognize jurisdictional issues and their application to state and federal court.
4. To understand jurisdictional issues web site operators face.
5. To understand the pre-trial litigation process.
6. To comprehend the stages of a trial.
7. To be aware of the nonjudicial alternatives of arbitration and mediation.

Practical Application

You should be able to be familiar with the costs and benefits of bringing and defending a lawsuit. You should be able to know which is the proper court and system to hear particular cases as well as be able to decide whether the benefits outweigh the costs of litigation. Additionally, you should have a broader understanding of the pre-trial litigation process and the various procedural requirements. Finally, you should be able to understand the sequence of events associated with a trial and be aware of the nonjudicial alternatives available to you.

Helpful Hints

This chapter may be a little confusing, as there appear to be so many different types of courts, all of which hear different types of cases. It is recommended that you diagram the state and federal court systems, branching each of the various courts off of the applicable state or federal court system. Page 2-3 of your text gives an example of how one diagram can be utilized.
You should also place two to four main points next to each type of court. For example, if you are working on the state court systems, in particular the limited-jurisdiction trial court, you may want to note

that they are sometimes called inferior trial courts, hear matters that are specialized and list some of the examples of the types of cases that are heard in this type of court. As you proceed in this manner, you will find that you have created a flow chart of the courts that will be easy to visualize when determining the answers to text and real life situations. Next, review this chapter's study sheet, complete the Refresh Your Memory exercise followed by the Critical Thought Exercise and Sample Quiz.

Study Tips

The laws and their development that you became familiar with in Chapter One as well as the court systems you are learning about in this chapter are analogous to the base layer of a specialty cake. It is by knowing the appropriate law and court within the proper court system that you will be able to apply the correct legal principles to situations as they occur. The areas of law in the chapters that follow will provide the upper layers and frosting to this unique cake. The essential ingredients of adhering to the proper time and procedural requirements along with satisfying the essential substantive elements for various legal actions are what provide balance to this legally created pastry if you will.

Litigation as you know is the process of bringing, maintaining and defending a lawsuit. The question to be answered however is where should litigation take place? There are two main court systems to choose from in the United States, the federal and the state court systems. It is important to know which court system has the proper jurisdiction to hear the case that has been prepared. The following list breaks down each court system highlighting some important points to remember about each court system as well as the courts within each system.

State Court Systems

A general fact about the state court systems is that every state as well as the District of Columbia has one. Additionally the majority of states have at least four types of state court systems that are discussed below.

Limited *-Jurisdiction Trial Court (Inferior Trial Courts)*. These trial courts in most cases can hear specialized cases such as those involving family law, probate, traffic matters, juvenile issues, misdemeanors, and civil cases that do not exceed a set dollar amount. An attorney trying a case in this type of court may introduce evidence and illicit testimony. If the case does not result in a favorable outcome for one of the parties to the lawsuit, that party may appeal his/her case to an appellate court or a general-jurisdiction court. Many states also have a small claims court wherein a party on his/her own behalf brings a civil case worth a small dollar amount. If a party in a small claims case loses, then that party may also appeal to the general-jurisdiction trial court or an appellate court.

General-*Jurisdiction Trial Court*. A general-jurisdiction trial court can be found in every state. The trial testimony and evidence that is preserved on record allow these courts to be called the courts of record. This court hears felonies, cases above a certain dollar amount and cases not heard by the inferior trial courts.

Intermediate Appellate Court. This court hears appeals from trial courts and decides if the trial court erred thereby justifying a reversal or modification of the decision. The entire trial court record or just the important parts of the record may be reviewed. At this level of the court system, a party may not introduce new evidence or testimony. The decision of this appellate court may be appealed to the highest state court.

Highest State Court. The majority of states have a supreme court, which is the highest court in the state court system. The job of a state supreme court is to hear appeals from the intermediate appellate court. Once again, no new evidence or testimony is allowed. Once this court has made its decision, it becomes fine. However, if there is a question of law, then the state supreme court's decision Mt be granted review by the U.S. Supreme Court.

Federal Court System

The United States Constitution states that the federal government's judicial power lies with the Supreme Court. In addition to this judicial power, Congress was allowed to establish inferior, or special courts that include the U.S. District court and the U.S. courts of appeal.

Special Federal Courts. The nature of these courts is to hear limited types of cases such as those involving federal tax laws, law suits against the United States, international commercial disputes and cases involving bankruptcy.

U.S. District Courts. These courts are the federal courts general jurisdiction courts.

U.S. Courts of Appeal. These courts are the intermediate appellate courts of the federal court system. The U.S. Courts of Appeals hear appeals from the cases already heard by the U.S. District Courts. As with the state court systems, no new evidence or testimony may be introduced by a party.

Court of Appeals for the Federal Cir*cuit.* Even though this is a United States Appellate Court, its jurisdiction is special as it is able to review the decisions made in the Patent and Trademark Office, the Court of International Trade and the Claims Court.

The U.S. Supreme Court. This high court of our land is administered by a president appointed chief justice and is made up of nine nominated justices. This court hears cases from the federal circuit courts of appeals, from some federal district and special federal courts as well as the highest state courts. A special note of interest is that a petition for certiorari must be made to the Supreme Court if a petitioner wants his/her case reviewed. If the court decides to review the case, then a writ of certiorari is issued provided there is a constitutional or other important issue involved in the case. Remember, no new evidence or testimony may be introduced at this level.

Federal and State Courts Jurisdiction

In order for a federal court to hear a case, the case must involve a federal question, or diversity of citizenship. It's important to distinguish these two concepts. A case involving a federal question deals with treaties, federal statutes and the U.S. Constitution. Also, there need not be a set dollar amount to bring this type of case. Compare this to cases involving diversity of citizenship whereby the cases need to be between citizens of different states or a citizen of a country and a citizen of a state or a citizen of a state and a foreign country with the foreign country acting as the plaintiff in a law suit. These types of cases require that the controversy exceed $75,000.00. If the dollar amount isn't met, then the appropriate state court must hear the case.

Court Jurisdiction to Hear a Case

In order to bring a lawsuit, a person must have a stake in the outcome of the lawsuit. This is known as standing.

The court must also have the proper jurisdiction to hear the case. You must be familiar with *subject matter jurisdiction, in personam, in rem,* and *quasi in rem* jurisdiction. Finally you must be familiar with the use of the *long-arm statutes* and when they are permitted over nonresidents.

Which court is the proper venue to hear my case?

The law mandates that lawsuits be heard by the court with jurisdiction that is closest to where the incident happened or where the parties live.

What are the advantages and disadvantages of bringing and defending a lawsuit?

It is very important to consider all of the factors involved when deciding to sue or defend a lawsuit. This is known as the cost-benefit analysis. This is a common sense decision that can be made by weighing how much money will be won or lost in light of your chances of winning or losing against the costs to litigate, expenses associated with employees being released from work, as well as pre-judgment interest provided by the law. Other emotional considerations such as the impact on the relationship of the parties and their reputations as well as the mental aggravation and turmoil that may manifest itself should also be factored in. Further, a caveat of the potential for error in the legal system must not be discarded in balancing whether or not it is wise to bring or defend a lawsuit.

When can a lawsuit be brought?

This refers to federal and state government time limitations regarding the period of time the plaintiff has the right to sue a defendant. Statutes of limitations will vary depending on the type of lawsuit involved.

What is involved in the pretrial litigation process?

The pretrial litigation process is an essential ingredient in the foundational layer of the legal process. You must be familiar with the various important pleadings of complaint, answer, cross-complaint and reply when initiating and responding to a lawsuit. Additionally, you will need to know about the different types of discovery and what activities both parties may participate in to discover facts of the case from one another as well as witnesses before trial. The primary types of discovery are depositions, interrogatories, production of documents and physical and mental examinations. Also, a familiarity with the pretrial motions of judgment on the pleadings, and motion for summary judgment should be developed to create an understanding that some lawsuits in whole or in part should not go to trial. Finally, you should be aware of the purpose of a settlement conference and realize that if a settlement is not forthcoming, this tool is important in identifying the main trial issues.

What are the stages of a trial?

A legal trial is much like a performance at a theater. There are those who are performing the case in a methodical fashion from beginning to end. In using this comparison, the program of a trial would read in the following order: jury selection, opening statements, the plaintiff's case, the defendant's case, rebuttal, rejoinder, closing arguments, jury instructions, with the jury deliberation and the entry of judgment acting as the end of the show. The sequel to the trial in a civil case is the appeal, which can be brought be either the plaintiff or the defendant. In a criminal trial, the appeal can only be brought by the defendant. Opening and responding briefs may be filed with the court. The drama of this performance is in the appellate court finding an error of law in the record, in which case the lower court decision will be reversed.

What other choices does a person have?

Sometimes using the court system to resolve disputes results in a great expenditure of money and time. In order to alleviate these concerns, alternative dispute resolution methods are being utilized to resolve disputes rather than using litigation. Some of the alternatives that are available include mediation, conciliation, mini-trial, fact-finding, and a judicial referee.

Refresh Your Memory

The following exercise will enable you to refresh your memory on the rules and principles presented to you in this chapter. Read each question twice and place your answer in the blanks provided. Review the chapter material for any question you miss or are unable to remember.

1. Define the term litigation. _____.

2. What are the two major court systems in the United States? The _____ and _____.

3. A state limited-jurisdictional trial court is known as an _____ _____ _____.

4. What types of cases do general-jurisdiction trial courts hear? _____.

5. What types of cases do appellate courts hear? _____.

6. If Sam Smith loses on appeal within a state court system, where can he appeal the appellate court decision? _____

7. What do most states call their highest court? _____

8. What is a petition for certiorari? _____

9. Name four types of decisions that the United States Supreme Court can issue. _____, _____, _____, _____.

10. What types of questions can federal courts hear? _____and _____

11. Fred sees George, a stranger, kicked by Sam while Fred is walking by. Fred is very polite and knows that Sam's actions were wrong. What must Fred show before he brings a lawsuit against Sam for kicking George? _____.

12. What is the usual means for accomplishing service of process of the summons and complaint? _____ _____ .

13. In order to invoke a state's long-arm statute, what must the nonresident have with the forum state? _____ _____ .

14. A concept that requires lawsuits to be heard by the court with jurisdiction that is nearest the location in which the incident occurred or where the parties reside is known as _____ .

15. Garth Hanson, the mayor of Ordinanceville has been charged with embezzlement of city funds. The local radio station has been providing continuous coverage ever since the story became known. Garth's attorney wants a change of venue. Tell why it should or should not be granted. _____
_____

16. What are the four major pleadings in a lawsuit? _____ , _____ , _____ , and _____

17. What happens if a defendant does not answer the complaint that is served upon him or her? _____

18. What is a statute of limitations? _____

19. What must an appellate court find in order to reverse a lower court decision? _____
_____

20. What is the most common form of alternative dispute resolution? _____

Critical Thought Exercise

You are a District Manager of marketing for Intestine Smart, Inc., a California corporation, makers of Colon Grenade, a colon-cleansing drug. You have negotiated the sale of over 4 million dollars worth of this product from Prescript Co, another California corporation, which operates pharmacies under the names of Col On, Goodstuff Co. and Drugs 2 Go. These pharmacies are located primarily in California, but Prescript Co has now expanded into 22 states including Utah.

Enticed by a Goodstuff add in the Utah Free Press for Colon Grenade, Alice Thinstone bought the drug at Goodstuff Co. and used it. Within a week, Thinstone suffered a ruptured colon. Alleging that the injury was caused by Colon Grenade, Thinstone sued Prescript Co and Intestine Smart in a Utah state court.

You have received a letter from the CEO of Intestine Smart, Ms. Sheila Snob, threatening to fire you and demanding to know why Intestine Smart is being subjected to a lawsuit in Utah, since she has never been informed of any sales of the product to companies outside of California.

Your assigned task is to *draft a memo to your boss*, Ms. Snob, and explain to her whether Intestine Smart must respond to the suit and defend against it in Utah. Explain the legal theory and the reasons for your opinion.

Answer: _____
_____
_____

_____
_____
_____
_____
_____
_____
_____
_____
_____
_____
_____
_____
_____
_____
_____
_____
_____
_____
_____
_____
_____
_____
_____
_____
_____

Practice Quiz

True/False:

1. ____ When parties are involved in a lawsuit, it is required that a lawyer represent them. [p 22]

2. ____ If a lawsuit proves to be too costly, a party may choose an alternative means to resolve the dispute he/she is involved in. [p 22]

3. ____ Limited-jurisdiction court decisions may not be appealed. [p 22]

4. ____ Every state except for Delaware has a general-jurisdiction trial court. [p 22]

5. ____ In order for the state supreme court to fairly decide the appeals that it hears from the intermediate state courts, it must take all of the evidence from the former trial along with any new evidence or testimony into consideration before rendering its decision. [p 23]

6. ___ A state supreme court's decision is final, unless an appealable question of law is involved. [p 23]

7. ___ The limited jurisdiction of special federal courts include cases involving federal tax laws, cases against the United States, bankruptcy and international commercial disputes. [p 24]

8. ___ Most states have a federal district court, however the states with smaller populations do not. [p 24]

9. ___ The Court of Appeals for the Federal Circuit has special appellate jurisdiction to review the decisions of the Patent and Trademark Office as well as the Court of International Trade and the Claims Court. [p 25]

10. ___ If new evidence is shown at the Supreme Court level, there is a chance that the lower court decision will be overturned. [p 25]

11. ___ A judge who disagrees with the outcome of a case, but not the reason given by the other justices, can issue a concurring opinion that explains his or her reasons for deciding the case. [p 27]

12. ___ Federal and state courts have exclusive jurisdiction to hear cases involving federal crimes, antitrust, bankruptcy, patent and copyright cases as well as suits against the United States and admiralty cases. [p 28]

13. ___ Long-arm statutes extend a state's jurisdiction to nonresidents who were not served a summons within the forum state. [p 30]

14. ___ A forum-selection clause states that any court may hear any dispute concerning the nonperformance of a contract. [p 30]

15. ___ The aggravation as well as psychological costs associated with a lawsuit should be taken into consideration when performing a cost-benefit analysis of the lawsuit. [p 32]

16. ___ A cross-complaint is a legal pleading filed by the plaintiff once the defendant has answered the plaintiff's original complaint. [p 34]

17. ___ If several lawsuits are brought as a result of the same fact situation against the same defendant, the court can consolidate the cases into one if it does not prejudice the parties. [p 34]

18. ___ A plaintiff will lose his or her right to sue if a lawsuit is not filed within the statute of limitations established for the particular type of lawsuit being brought. [p 35]

19. ___ A court cannot order another party to submit to a mental or physical examination prior to trial as this would constitute an invasion of privacy. [p 37]

20. ___ A motion for summary judgment alleges that if all of the facts presented in the pleadings are true, the party making the motion would win the lawsuit when the proper law is applied to these facts. [p 38]

21. ___ After the trial has been presented, each of the parties attorneys submit documents to

the judge that contain legal support for their side of the case. [p 39]

22. ___ When the defendant's attorney calls additional witnesses and introduces other evidence, this is known as rebuttal. [p 39]

23. ___ In a civil case, either party can appeal the trial court's decision prior to the final judgment being entered. [p 40]

24. ___ The Uniform Arbitration Act promotes arbitration of disputes at the state level. [p 42]

25. ___ Conciliation is a form of mediation in which the parties select an interested third party to be a mediator. [p 43]

Multiple Choice:

26. State jurisdiction is limited to [p 28]
    a. bankruptcy cases.
    b. antitrust cases.
    c. matters not subject to federal jurisdiction.
    d. suits against the United States.

27. A party who disputes the jurisdiction of a court can [p 30]
    a. enter a claim in the forum state's small claims court to recover expenses of the dispute.
    b. make a special appearance in that court to argue against imposition of jurisdiction.
    c. appeal to the state supreme court and ask that the suit be dismissed.
    d. be served a complaint if he or she makes a special appearance in the court to argue against imposition of jurisdiction.

28. The bringing, maintaining, and defense of a lawsuit is known as [p 32]
    a. discovery
    b. litigation
    c. a cross-complaint
    d. a summons

29. A law that establishes the period within which a plaintiff must bring a lawsuit against the defendant is known as [p 35]
    a. a statute of limitations
    b. a complaining period
    c. an e-filing of pleadings
    d. all of the above

30. A deposition is [p 36]
    a. written testimony given by a party or witness prior to trial
    b. oral testimony given by a party or witness prior to trial
    c. a pleading alleging ultimate allegations of fact
    d. all of the above

31. The production of documents refers to [p 37]

    a. written questions submitted by one party to a lawsuit to another party

    b. physical and mental concerns of the condition of a party to the lawsuit

    c. the assembly of legal documents

    d. one party to a lawsuit requesting that the other party produce all documents that are relevant to the case prior to trial.

32. The term rejoinder refers to [p 39]

    a. when the plaintiff's attorney calls witnesses and puts forth evidence to rebut the defendant's case

    b. the making of a closing argument by each party's attorney

    c. the reading of jury instructions to the jury

    d. the calling of additional witnesses and introduction of other evidence to counter the plaintiff's rebuttal

33. When a court overturns a verdict based on bias or jury misconduct, this is known as [p 40]

    a. a judgment on the pleadings

    b. an entry of judgment

    c. a judgment notwithstanding the verdict

    d. all of the above.

34. The responding party in an appeal is known as [p 40]

    a. the respondent

    b. the appellant

    c. the defendant

    d. the plaintiff

35. When the parties choose an impartial third party to hear and decide a dispute, this is known as [p 43]

    a. mediation

    b. a minitrial

    c. arbitration

    d. a judicial referee

36. One of the provisions of the Federal Arbitration Act is [p 42]

    a. to reenact the arbitration agreements that existed in English common law

    b. to eliminate arbitration agreements that call for resolution of disputes that arise under federal statutes

    c. to provide that arbitration agreements involving commerce are valid, irrevocable, and enforceable contracts, unless some ground exist at law or equity.

    d. to prohibit parties from obtaining court orders that compel arbitration if the other party has failed, neglected, or refused to comply with an arbitration agreement

37. The role of a judicial referee is to [p 44]

    a. conduct a private trial and render a judgment

    b. report his or her findings to the adversaries and recommend a basis for settlement

    c. act as an interested third party, a conciliator

    d. to referee judicial sports activities involving court personnel

38. One means of eliminating the burden of paper pleadings, interrogatories, and other legal

documents would be to implement [p 35]

    a. a shorter statute of limitations thereby requiring those who were serious about filing a lawsuit to do so in a more expeditious manner

    b. technology for electronic filing including CD-ROMs to manage e-filings of court documents.

    c. shorter forms that would take up less space

    d. all of the above

Short Answer:

39.   Explain the meaning of discovery. [p 36] _____

_____

40.   What are interrogatories? [p 37] _____

41.   The request by one party to another party to produce all documents relevant to the case prior to trial is known as the _____ of _____. [p 37]

42.   A motion a party can make to try to dispose of all or part of a lawsuit prior to trial is known as a _____ _____. [p 38]

43.   The jury in a jury trial and the judge where there is not a jury trial is known as the _____ of _____. [p 39]

44.   A person chosen as a neutral third party who acts as a conveyor of information between the parties and helps them to try and reach a settlement of the dispute is known as a _____. [p 43]

45.   A process whereby the parties hire a neutral person to investigate the dispute is known as a _____ _____. [p 43]

46.   Give at least five differences between the American and Japanese legal systems. [p 44]

    (1) _____

    _____

    (2) _____

    _____

    (3) _____

    _____

    (4) _____

    _____

    (5) _____

    _____

47.   State and federal courts have concurrent jurisdiction to hear cases that involve _____ of _____ and _____ _____. [p 28]

48.   A plaintiff must have _____ to sue before he/she can bring a lawsuit. [p 29]

49.   When a court has jurisdiction over the property of a lawsuit, it has _____ _____ jurisdiction. [p 30]

50. If other persons are interested in becoming part of a lawsuit, they may _____ and become parties to a lawsuit. [p 34]

51. Give at least three factors that should be considered when performing a cost-benefit analysis of whether to bring or defend a lawsuit. _____, _____, and _____ [p 32]

52. Under a _____fee arrangement, the lawyer receives a percentage of the amount recovered for the plaintiff upon settling or winning the lawsuit. [p 32]

53. A _____ is issued once a complaint has been filed with the court. [p 33]

54. The defendant must file an _____once he/she is served with the complaint. [p 33]

55. The defendant may assert _____ _____ when answering the plaintiff's complaint. [p 33]

Answers to Refresh Your Memory

1. The process of bringing, maintaining and defending a lawsuit. [p 32]
2. The federal court system and the court systems of the 50 states and the District of Columbia. [p 22
3. inferior trial courts. [p 22]
4. Cases that are not within the jurisdiction of the limited-jurisdiction trial courts, such as felonies, civil cases over a certain dollar amount. [p 22]
5. They hear appeals from trial courts. [p 23]
6. Sam can appeal the appellate court decision to the state's highest court. [p 23]
7. The supreme court. [p 23]
8. A petition asking the Supreme Court to hear one's case. [p 26]
9. unanimous decision, majority decision, plurality decision, tie decision [p 27]
10. federal questions and diversity of citizenship [p 28]
11. Fred must show he has standing or a stake in the outcome before he can sue Sam. [p 29]
12. personal service [p 30]
13. minimum contact [p 30]
14. venue [p 31]
15. If the pretrial publicity may prejudice jurors located in the proper venue, then a change of venue may be requested in order to find a more impartial jury in light of the continuous radio station coverage. [p 31]
16. complaint, answer, cross-complaint and reply [p 34]
17. A default judgment is entered against him or her [p 33]
18. A period during which a plaintiff must bring a lawsuit against a defendant [p 35]
19. an error of law [p 40]
20. arbitration [p 41]

Model Answer to Critical Thought Exercise

To: Ms. Snob
From: Student, District Manager, Intestine Smart Inc.

Re: Response to Lawsuit in Utah State Court

This is a question involving jurisdiction. Jurisdiction is the authority of a court to hear a case. There are three types of jurisdiction: 1) *In personam* whereby the court has jurisdiction over the parties to a lawsuit; 2) *In rem* jurisdiction which is when the court has jurisdiction to hear a case because of jurisdiction over the property involved in the lawsuit; and 3) *quasi in rem* jurisdiction; where jurisdiction is allowed a plaintiff who obtains a judgment in one state to try to collect the judgment by attaching the property of the defendant located in another state.

Even though you were never informed of any sales of Colon Grenade outside of the state of California, we may be required to respond to the suit and defend against it in Utah based on the following reasons:

1) Even though our company wasn't physically located in Utah when Alice Thinstone suffered a ruptured colon, she may apply the principles surrounding the theory set forth in *International Shoe Co. v. Washington,* 326 U.S. 310 wherein the court said that "the Due Process Clause permits jurisdiction over a defendant in any state in which the defendant has 'certain minimum contacts' such that the maintenance of the suit does not offend traditional notions of fair play and substantial justice." Arguably by selling our product to Prescript Co., which operates in 22 states, including Utah, we are receiving the benefit of increased sales, albeit indirectly from Utah resident Alice Thinstone. Further, as was expressed in the court's ruling in *Calder v. Jones,* 465 U.S. 783, 104 S.Ct. 1482, 79 L.Ed.2d 804 (1984), Intestine Smart should "reasonably anticipate being hauled into court" in Utah as it is reasonably foreseeable that colon grenade would be sold in different states given the fact that Prescript Co. operates in 22 states, with Utah being one of them. If it is found that Intestine Smart, Inc. had sufficient minimum contacts with the forum State of Utah and that the sale of its product there afforded Intestine Smart the benefits of the laws of the forum state, then we will be required to defend ourselves in a suit in Utah state court.

2) It may be argued that we assumed the risk that our product would be sold to an out-of-state resident as we knowingly and voluntarily negotiated the sale of the Colon Grenade product with Prescript Co., a business operating in several states. Also, we should not be allowed to reap only the benefits of profit from our sales and shirk our corporate ethical responsibility to not harm those to whom our product is sold.

In conclusion, Ms. Snob, it would be in our best interest to respond to the lawsuit filed against us. If we are able to show that there was some other intervening act (such as improper use of Colon Grenade by Ms. Thinstone, some other medical condition that could have had the same result, etc.) responsible for Ms. Thinstone's ruptured colon and that Colon Grenade in no way caused her injury, we may be successful in defending against the suit. We could really secure a feather in our cap if we could demonstrate that despite an alleged forseeability of the injury alleged, the use of Colon Grenade could not have possibly caused the result complained of by Ms. Thinstone. *(Note: A higher degree of understanding is demonstrated by a student who incorporates the reasoning given in this paragraph, as this material is not addressed until later in the text.)*

Answers to Practice Quiz

True/False:

1.   False   It is not required that a lawyer represent parties, though most people when involved

		In a lawsuit do hire a lawyer to represent them.
2.	True	A party may choose one of several types of nonjudicial dispute resolution in response to the costs and difficulty of bringing a lawsuit.
3.	False	The limited-jurisdiction court decisions can be appealed to a general-jurisdiction court or an appellate court.
4.	False	Every state, even Delaware has a general-jurisdiction trial court.
5.	False	Even though the function of a state supreme court is to hear appeals from intermediate state courts and certain trial courts, no new evidence or testimony is heard.
6.	True	When a question of law is involved, then a decision of the state supreme court may be appealable to the U.S. Supreme Court. Otherwise, state supreme court decisions are final.
7.	True	Congress established special limited jurisdiction courts including the U.S. tax court, U.S. claims court, U.S. Court of International Trade and the U.S. Bankruptcy Court.
8.	False	Each state has at least one federal district court, as does the District of Columbia. The more populated states have more than one district court.
9.	True	The Court of Appeals for the Federal Circuit was established to provide uniformity in the application of federal law.
10.	False	The Supreme Court hears appeals from the federal circuit of appeals and reviews the lower court record. However, no new evidence or testimony is heard.
11.	False	Concurring opinions are issued when a justice agrees with the outcome of a case, but not the reason given by other justices. These concurring opinions explain his/her reasons for deciding the case.
12.	False	Only federal court have exclusive jurisdiction to hear cases involving federal crimes, antitrust, bankruptcy, patent and copyright cases as well as suits against the United States and admiralty cases.
13.	True	This is a true statement of law. Additionally the nonresident must have had some minimum contact with the forum state and jurisdiction over the nonresident must not violate traditional notions of fair play and substantial justice.
14.	False	A forum-selection clause is an agreed upon contract provision that states a certain court will hear any dispute concerning the nonperformance of the contract. The case of *Carnival Cruise Lines v. Shute* at page 2-10 in your text illustrates this concept.
15.	True	The aggravation as well as psychological costs associated with a lawsuit are only two of several factors that should be weighed before bringing or settling a lawsuit. Other factors to examine include the odds of winning or losing, the money that is to be won or lost, managerial time off as well as loss of time by personnel, the effect on the relationship between the parties, the law's provision for prejudgment interest, and the chance of error in the law.
16.	False	A cross-complaint is a legal pleading filed by the defendant who believes that he or she has been injured by the plaintiff. The defendant can file a cross-complaint against the plaintiff at the same time he or she files an answer to the plaintiff's complaint.
17.	True	The court may consolidate several cases into one when there are several plaintiffs who have filed separate lawsuits resulting from the same set of facts against the defendant.
18.	True	A statute of limitations sets forth the time period within which a plaintiff must bring a lawsuit against the defendant. If the plaintiff fails to bring his or her suit within the set time frame, he or she will lose his or her right to sue.
19.	False	A court can order another party to submit to a physical or mental examination prior to trial as this is part of the legal process known as discovery. In cases involving the physical or mental condition of a party, the court may order the party to submit to an exam to assess the extent of the party's injuries or condition.
20.	False	A motion for summary judgment alleges that there are no factual disputes to be

decided by the jury and that the judge should apply the relevant law to the undisputed facts to decide the case. The question as presented describes a motion for judgment on the pleadings.

21. False The statement as presented is incorrect as the parties usually present trial briefs to the judge that have legal support for their case at the time of trial, not after the trial has been presented.

22. False It is after the defendant's attorney is through calling witnesses, that the plaintiff's attorney can call witnesses and present evidence to rebut the defendant's case. The answer given pertains more to the concept of rejoinder wherein the defendant's attorney can call additional witnesses and introduce other evidence to counter the rebuttal.

23. False Though it is true that either party can appeal the trial court's decision in a civil case, it must be done once a final judgment is entered, not prior to the final judgment.

24. True Approximately half of the states have adopted the Uniform Arbitration Act.

25. True The statement given is one definition for conciliation.

Multiple Choice:

26. C Bankruptcy, antitrust cases and suits against the United States are matters that the federal courts have exclusive jurisdiction over. Answer C is correct because states have exclusive jurisdiction over matters not subject to federal jurisdiction.

27. B A party may make a special appearance to dispute jurisdiction and service of process may not take place during this appearance. Answer A makes no sense, as a party who suffers expenses of a lawsuit would ask for the appropriate remedy in his/her prayer for relief of his/her complaint. Further, expenses to the lawsuit may or may not be allowed depending upon the cause(s) of action being brought. Answer C is incorrect as the function of the state supreme court is to hear appeals from intermediate state courts. The facts do not indicate that the issue of jurisdiction was one that had been tried and that a judgment against the party had been made at an intermediate court level. Answer D is incorrect, as a party may not be served with a complaint in court when the purpose of the party being in court is to dispute jurisdiction.

28. B Litigation is the process of bringing, maintaining, and defending a lawsuit. Answer A is incorrect as discovery is a detailed pretrial procedure that allows both parties to discover facts of the case from the other party and witnesses before trial. Answer C is incorrect as a cross-complaint is a pleading usually filed by a defendant who is now suing a plaintiff who filed the original complaint against him/her. The cross-complaint is usually filed at the same time as the defendant's answer to the plaintiff's complaint. Answer D is incorrect, as a summons is a court order indicating that the defendant must appear before the court and answer the complaint against him/her.

29. A A statute of limitations is a law that establishes the time period which a plaintiff must bring a lawsuit against the defendant. Answer B in incorrect as there is no such thing as a complaining period. Answer C is incorrect as an e-filing of pleadings refers to the technology that is currently available for electronic filing of pleadings and other legal documents as they pertain to a lawsuit.

30. B Answer B gives the correct definition of a deposition. Answer A is incorrect as it tries to confuse you by incorporating the written aspect of interrogatories with the oral facet of testimony which is associated with depositions. Answer C is incorrect as it is referring to the pleading known as a complaint. Answer D is incorrect for the reasons given above.

31. D Answer D states the correct explanation of the discovery form known as production of

documents. Answer A is incorrect as this is the definition for interrogatories. Answer B is incorrect as this is the explanation for discovery requesting a party to submit to a physical or mental examination. Answer C is incorrect, as it does not make sense as applied to the legal aspect of discovery.

32. D Answer D gives the correct explanation for the term rejoinder. The important aspect to remember is that rejoinder is a term that is used when the defendant is attempting to counter the plaintiff's rebuttal of the defendant's case. Answer A is incorrect as this explains the term rebuttal. Answer B is incorrect as this in an incorrect explanation of the term. Answer C is incorrect as the reading of jury instructions refers to the aspect of the trial that occurs once the closing arguments by each party are completed.

33. C Answer C gives the correct terminology for a verdict overturned based on bias or jury misconduct. Answer A is incorrect as a motion for judgment on the pleadings is made once the pleadings are complete. In essence it is asking for the judge to dispose of all or part of the lawsuit before trial as compared to overturning a verdict after the trial as in a judgment notwithstanding the verdict. Answer B is incorrect as the entry of judgment refers to the court's official decision of the successful party based upon the verdict, not on overturning the verdict.

34. A Answer A is correct, as the responding party in an appeal is known as the respondent and is also referred to as the appellee. Answer B is incorrect as the appellant is the party who is bringing the appeal. The appellant is also known as the petitioner. Answer C is incorrect as the term respondent is usually used at the appellate level whereas the term defendant is used at the trial court level. Answer D is incorrect as the plaintiff is the party to the original lawsuit who has initiated the action against the defendant.

35. C Answer C is correct, as arbitration is the term that is defined in the question. Answer A is incorrect as a mediator is chosen as a neutral third party to convey information between the parties in an effort to reach a settlement, however, the mediator does not make a decision or an award like an arbitrator does. Answer B is incorrect as the explanation for a minitrial is one in which the attorneys for both parties present their cases to representatives of each party who have been given authority to settle the dispute. Answer D is incorrect as a judicial referee is usually an appointed retired judge who conducts a private trial and then renders a judgment.

36. C Answer C gives one of the correct provisions of the Federal Arbitration Act. Answer A is incorrect as one of the reasons the Federal Arbitration Act was developed was to reverse hostility toward arbitration agreements that were present at English common law. Answer B is incorrect as another purpose of the Federal Arbitration Act was to enforce arbitration agreements that call for the resolution of disputes arising under federal statutes. Answer D is also incorrect as it is contrary to another provision of the Federal Arbitration Act that allows a party to obtain a court order to compel arbitration if the other party has failed, neglected, or refused to comply with an arbitration agreement.

37. A Answer A is correct as the court appointed judicial referee conducts a private trial and then gives his/her judgment. Answer B is incorrect as this gives the definition of a fact finder. Answer C is incorrect as a conciliator is a person who acts as a mediator in a process referred to as conciliation. Answer D is incorrect, as it does not make any sense.

38. B Answer B is correct, as technology is now available for providing electronic filings of pleadings, briefs and other legal documents. Answer A is incorrect; as even though it may be true that some people would file their claims in a more efficient manner, it would also hamper the time frame that others may need in preparing, filing and serving their claims thereby denying their right to be heard. Answer C is incorrect as shorter forms are not feasible in certain types of pleadings, such as interrogatories. Answer D is incorrect based upon the reasons given above.

Short Answer:

39. Discovery is the process of engaging in various activities to discover facts of the case from the other party and witnesses prior to trial in order to prevent surprise, prepare for trial, preserve evidence, save court time and encourage the settlement of cases.
40. Interrogatories are written questions given by one party to a lawsuit to another party.
41. production of documents
42. motion for summary judgment
43. trier of fact
44. mediator
45. fact finder
46. The Japanese avoid confrontation compared to the American culture that is open to conflict. The Japanese do not allow class actions or permit contingency fee arrangements   whereas the American system does allow for both of these. The plaintiffs in Japan are   required to pay their attorneys an upfront fee of up to eight percent of the damages and a   non-refundable filing fee of one-half of one percent of the damages. Also, discovery is not   permitted. In the American system, these specific upfront fees and court filing fees based   on a percentage of the damages do not exist. Further, discovery is encouraged in the

    American system. There is only one place in Japan to become an attorney as compared to   the vast variety of choices the American system provides for its legal education. Finally, the Japanese are prejudice against resolving disputes in the courtroom and places more   value on the long-term relationships of the parties involved as well as saving time and   money. The American system is not as concerned with the personal relationship aspect of   the parties and many parties are willing to expend as much money and time as it takes in   order to be heard in a courtroom atmosphere.
47. diversity of citizenship and federal questions
48. standing
49. in rem
50 intervene
51. lawyers' fees and the costs of litigation, loss of time by managers and other personnel, the unpredictability of the legal system and the possibility of error.
52. contingency
53. summons
54. answer
55. affirmative defenses

Chapter 3

CONSTITUTIONAL AUTHORITY
TO REGULATE BUSINESS

Chapter Overview

This chapter provides a solid overview of the legal framework that our government operates under. As you read through this chapter, you will gain a better understanding of the concept of federalism as well as separation of powers and the federal government's power to regulate foreign, interstate and even local commerce. Additionally, you will become familiar with the First Amendment on the Internet. The concepts of substantive and procedural due process, equal protection and the constitutional limits on e-commerce are also analyzed.

Objectives

Upon completion of this chapter's exercises, you should be able to:
1. Recognize the function of the powers granted to the state and federal government.
2. Understand the importance of the supremacy clause and its application.
3. Understand the federal government's authority and rationale for regulating interstate commerce.
4. Understand the protection speech is afforded under the First Amendment.
5. Apply the first amendment freedom of speech protection to situations involving the Internet.
6. Understand the restrictions placed upon the government regarding the Freedom of Religion.
7. Be aware of the constitutional limits on e-commerce.
8. Analyze and understand substantive and procedural due process.
9. Understand the constitutional standards applicable in equal protection cases.

Practical Application

You should be able to understand the importance of the commerce clause as well as the government's reasoning behind regulation of commerce. You should also be able to understand what types of speech are protected as well as the limitations on speech. Finally, you should be able to understand and apply the various standards of review in equal protection cases.

Helpful Hints

This chapter should be approached in a manner much like you would approach the weighing as well as need for various elements in a scientific laboratory. The chapter begins with a discussion on the powers given to the federal government and those that are reserved for the states. Next, the chapter discusses the creation, need and function of balancing the three branches of government. The impact of the commerce clause on the government and its role in business are also emphasized. Further, the limitations on the First Amendment Freedom of Speech based on the type of speech as well as restrictions on the government concerning Freedom of Religion are also discussed. The important balancing of classification as set forth in a government regulation against governmental standards in equal protection cases are carefully examined as well. As you review the study tips section followed by the various chapter exercises, it is helpful as well as beneficial to weigh the governmental interest against what is being protected.

Study Tips

Federalism

This refers to our countries form of government. The states and the federal government share powers. Sometimes the federal law and state law conflict. When this happens, the federal law prevails.

Branches of the Federal Government

You should familiarize yourself with the legislative, executive and judicial branches of government and know what function each branch serves, as well as how each affects one another.

State and Local Government Regulation of Business – "Police Power"

States are able to regulate intrastate and a large amount of interstate business that takes place within its borders. The police power given to the states allows the states to make laws that protect or promote the health, safety, morals and welfare of its citizens.

Bill of Rights

You should know that the Bill of Rights is the ten amendments to the United States Constitution. Also, the two rights that are heavily emphasized are the Freedom of Speech and the Freedom of Religion as per the First Amendment.

Freedom of Speech

It is important to realize that this freedom extends only to speech and not conduct. You should also familiarize yourself with the types of speech. It is helpful to list them and place the protection each is given next to them. The following demonstrates an easy way to do this.

Political Speech – fully protected

Commercial Speech – An example would be advertising. Speeches used by businesses are subject to time, place and manner restrictions.

Offensive Speech – Speech that is offensive to a lot of people is also subject to time, place and manner restrictions.

Unprotected Speech includes: dangerous speech, fighting words, defamatory language, child pornography, and obscene speech.

Note that with obscene speech, the states can define the meaning of obscene speech. It has been stated that obscene is where the average person's prurient interest is appealed to, and the work is patently offensive thereby describing the sexual conduct in accordance with the state law and the work is in need of serious literary, artistic, political or social value.

Freedom of Religion

The Constitution mandates that the local, state and federal governments be neutral regarding religion.

The two religion clauses in the First Amendment that you should know the difference between are the Establishment Clause, which prohibits the government from establishing a state religion or promoting one religion over another and the Free Exercise Clause. The Free Exercise Clause prevents the government from making laws that inhibit or prohibit people from participating in or practicing their chosen religion.

Commerce

This is a very important term to know. As you may recall, the Commerce Clause of the Constitution has the greatest impact on business than any other clause. In order to fully appreciate as well as understand this importance, you need to know the following:

- The difference between interstate and intrastate commerce is that interstate involves instrumentalities of trade moving across state borders. Compare this to intrastate where commerce is moving within the state.

- The traditional role of government in regulating interstate commerce was to regulate only commerce that moved in interstate commerce. Whereas modernly the federal government may regulate local commerce if it has an impact on commerce as a whole.

- If state law burdens interstate commerce, then the law is declared void and unconstitutional.

The Equal Protection Clause

This clause of the Fourteenth Amendment states that a state cannot, "deny to any person within its jurisdiction the equal protection of the laws." Though it primarily applies to state and local governments, it also applies to federal government action as well. You must know the three standards for review of equal protection cases. They are:

1. *Strict Scrutiny*, which is applied when there is a classification that is a suspect class such as race.
2. *Intermediate Scrutiny*, which is applied when the classification is based on a protected class that is not race, such as age and sex.
3. Finally, the *Rational Basis Test* is applied when neither a suspect nor protected class is involved. All that is needed is a justifiable reason for the law trying to be enacted.

The Due Process Clause

This clause is provided for in the Fifth and Fourteenth Amendments as both have a due process clause. The Fifth Amendment applies to the federal government whereas the fourteenth amendment applies to state and local government. The crux of this clause is that no individual shall be deprived of life, liberty or property without due process of law. There are two types of due process, substantive and procedural. Substantive refers to the content of the law. It must be clear, not too broad and worded in such a way that a "reasonable person" could understand the law in order to obey it. The procedural aspect requires a person be given notice and an opportunity to be heard before his/her life, liberty or property is taken. Note, within this aspect is the Just Compensation Clause, which states the government, must pay to the owner just compensation for taking an individual's property.

Privileges and Immunities Clause

This clause prohibits states from enforcing laws that unduly favor their own residents thereby resulting in discrimination against residents of other states.

Refresh Your Memory

The following exercise will enable you to refresh your memory of the main principles given to you in this chapter. Read each question twice and placed your answer in the blank(s) provided. If you do not remember, go to the next question and come back to the one you did not answer. It is also helpful to look over the section(s) in the study tips again, and then try to answer what you may be having difficulty with.

1. Our country's type of government is known as _____ .

2. The powers delegated to the federal government by the states ratification of the Constitution   are known as _____ _____ .

3. The _____ _____ establishes that the federal Constitution, treaties, federal laws, and federal regulations are the supreme law of the land.

4. The United States Constitution's system of _____ and _____ prevents any one of the three branches of the federal government from becoming too powerful.

5. The _____ Clause has a greater impact on business than any other provision of the Constitution.

6. _____ commerce refers to commerce that moves between states or that affects commerce between the states.

7. The power given to the states to regulate both private and business activity within their borders is known as _____ _____ .

8. The first ten amendments to the United States Constitution are known as the _____ of _____ .

9. Under the incorporation doctrine, many of the fundamental guarantees set forth in the Bill of Rights are also applied to _____ and _____ government action.

10. The First Amendment's Freedom of Speech Clause protects _____ and not conduct.

11. _____ speech offends many individuals in society and is subject to time, place, and manner restrictions.

12. The regulation of telecommunications, including the Internet is effectuated through the _____ Act.

13. A clause that prohibits the government from establishing a state religion or promoting one religion over another is the _____ _____ .

14. The _____ _____ prohibits the government from enacting laws that either prohibit or inhibit individuals from participating or practicing their chosen religion.

15. Which clause provides that a state cannot "deny to any person within its jurisdiction the equal protection of the laws?" The _____ _____ clause.

Critical Thought Exercise

Larry Brown is a very religious person and is very active in the anti-abortion movement. While Brown travels the streets of his hometown of Westerfield, Illinois, he plays taped sermons and spiritual music that support his religious and political views. The City of Westerfield enacted an ordinance that prohibited the playing of car sound systems at a volume that would be "audible" at a distance greater than fifty feet. Brown was arrested and convicted for violating the ordinance. Brown appealed his conviction on the grounds that the ordinance violated his right to free speech and free exercise of his religious beliefs. The City of Westerfield countered that noise coming from Brown's car could pose a hazard if he and other drivers were unable to hear emergency vehicles as they approached, and as such, the ordinance was a proper exercise of the police power possessed by the State of Illinois.

Was the playing of sermons by Brown protected by the Free Speech and Free Exercise Clauses of the First Amendment to the United States Constitution?

Answer. _____

_____

_____

_____

_____

_____

_____

_____

_____

_____

_____

_____

_____

_____

_____

_____

_____

_____

_____

_____

_____

_____

Practice Quiz

True/False:

1. ____   The fundamental law of the United States is the Constitution. [p 49]

2. ____   The part of the government that consists of Congress is the executive branch. [p 50]

3. ____   When federal law takes precedence over state or local law, this is often called

preemption. [p 50]

4. ___ If a state or local law directly or substantially conflicts with a valid federal law, that state or local law is preempted under the Supremacy Clause. [p 50]

5. ___ The federal government has always had the authority to regulate activities that affect interstate commerce. [p 53]

6. ___ The federal government can regulate intrastate and interstate activity if it has an affect on interstate commerce [p 53]

7. ___ A state can regulate an area that the federal government has chosen not to regulate regardless of the burden caused on interstate commerce. [p 55]

8. ___ The federal government has exclusive power to regulate commerce with foreign nations. [p 57]

9. ___ The Bill of Rights also applies to corporations [p 57]

10. ___ Symbolic speech is protected by the First Amendment. [p 58]

11. ___ A law that is enacted that forbids citizens from not agreeing with those presently in office does not violate the Freedom of Speech. [p 58]

12. ___ The government cannot limit the time, place and manner of speech. [p 58]

13. ___ A statute authorizing a one-minute period of silence in school for meditation or voluntary prayer is invalid as it violates the Establishment Clause. [p 63]

14. ___ The Fourteenth Amendment does not prohibit discriminatory and unfair action by the government. [p 63]

15. ___ Under the rational basis test, the court's standard of review is whether the government classification is "reasonably related" to a legitimate government purpose. [p 65]

16. ___ The standard for review in an equal protection case involving sex or age is that the government classification will be found to be unconstitutional as sex and age are suspect classes. [p 65]

17. ___ The Fourteenth and Fifth Amendments of the United States Constitution both contain a Due Process Clause. [p 66]

18. ___ Procedural due process is the only classification that the government must follow. [p 67]

19. ___ Substantive due process mandates that the laws, statutes, ordinance and regulations be clear, and not too broad. [p 66]

20. ___ The Due Process Clause of the Fifth Amendment applies to state and local action. [p 66]

Multiple Choice:

21. Enumerated powers are [p 49]
    a. the part of the government that consists of the Supreme Court and other federal courts.
    b. sequentially numbered laws.
    c. powers delegated to the federal government by the states.
    d. None of the above.

22. The Commerce Clause is intended to [p 52]
    a. deregulate commerce with foreign nations.
    b. foster development of a national market and free trade among the states.
    c. authorize state governments to authorize trade with the Indian tribes.
    d. be the supreme law of the land.

23. The concept of federal law taking precedence over state or local law is called [p 50]
    a. the supremacy clause.
    b. interstate commerce regulation.
    c. the preemption doctrine.
    d. All of the above

24. Intrastate commerce refers to [p 55]
    a. commerce that crosses state borders.
    b. commerce that occurs within a state.
    c. commerce that occurs across state borders and within a state.
    d. commerce that occurs only in a limited local area.

25. Political speech is an example of [p 58]
    a. speech that is given limited protection.
    b. speech that has time, place and manner restrictions.
    c. speech that will incite the overthrow of the government.
    d. speech that is fully protected.

26. Procedural due process requires the government to give [p 67]
    a. proper notice and a hearing.
    b. clear laws and not be overly broad in what they cover.
    c. punitive damages.
    d. minimal compensation for the taking of property.

27. The privileges and immunities clause prohibits [p 68]
    a. states from giving the same privileges to out-of-state residents.
    b. prevents out-of-state residents from owning property in other states
    c. the government from enacting laws that unduly discriminate in favor of their own residents.
    d. federal government from regulating commerce that moves in interstate commerce.

28. One of the purposes of punitive damages is to [p 67]
    a. deter the defendant from similar conduct in the future.
    b. punish the defendant.
    c. set an example for others.
    d. All of the above.

29. Laws that a reasonable person could not understand and be able to comply with are usually [p 66]

    a. declared void for vagueness.
    b. placed in the language of a reasonable person.
    c. constitutional and in compliance with the state's police power.
    d. part of the privileges and immunities clause.

30. Which of the following would not be considered unprotected speech? [p 59]
    a. dangerous speech
    b. defamatory speech
    c. political speech
    d. obscene speech

Short Answer:

31. Speech that is not protected by the First Amendment and may be forbidden by the government is known as [p 59] _____ _____.

32. When federal statutes do not provide for exclusive jurisdiction, state and local governments have [p 50] _____ _____.

33. A test that is applied to classifications based on protected classes other than race is known as the [p 65] _____ _____ test.

34. What does the Computer Decency Act provide? [p 62] _____

35. The Rational Basis test is used in reviewing Equal Protection cases that do not involve a [p 65] _____ or _____ class.

36. Offensive speech is subject to _____, _____, and _____ restrictions. [p 59]

37. Direct and indirect regulation of foreign commerce by local or state commerce is _____. [p 57]

38. Which clause prohibits states from enacting laws that unduly discriminate in favor of their residents? The _____ and _____ Clause. [p 68]

39. Under which clause must the government pay the owner for taking his or her property? The _____ _____ Clause. [p 67]

40. What authority does the judicial branch have? [p 50] _____

41. The states police power enables the states to enact laws that promote the public _____, _____, _____ and _____ welfare. [p 55]

42. Which branch of the government can enter into treaties with foreign governments only with the advice and consent of the senate? The _____ branch. [p 50]

43. Give two examples of things that the legislative branch of the government is authorized to do. [p 50]
    _____

44. The FTA prohibits state and local governments from blocking freedom of entry into the
    _____ industry. [p 56]

45. Under the Supremacy Clause of the United States Constitution, the FTA _____ any state or local law that conflicts with its provisions. [p 56]

46. The purpose of enacting the Federal Telecommunications Act was to _____
    _____. [p 56]

47. Advertising is an example of _____ speech. [p 59]

48. Give three types of unprotected speech. _____, _____, and
    _____ [p 58]

49. The First Amendment's two separate religion clauses are the _____ Clause and the
    _____ _____ Clause. [p 63]

50. Punitive damages are awarded in addition to _____ _____. [p 67]

Answers to Refresh Your Memory

1. federalism [p 49]
2. enumerated powers [p 49]
3. Supremacy clause [p 50]
4. checks and balances [p 50]
5. commerce clause [p 52]
6. interstate commerce [p 53]
7. police power [p 55]
8. Bill of Rights [p 57]
9. state, local [p 57]
10. speech [p 58]
11. Offensive [p 59]
12. Telecommunication [p 62]
13. Establishment Clause [p 63]
14. Free Exercise Clause [p 63]
15. Equal Protection Clause [p 65]

Critical Thought Exercise Model Answer

States possess police powers as part of their inherent sovereignty. These powers may be exercised to protect or promote the public order, health, safety, morals, and general welfare. Free Speech that has political content, such as the speech being used by Brown, has traditionally been protected to the fullest extent possible by the courts. Free speech includes the right to effective free speech. Amplification systems can be used as long as the speech does not harass or annoy others in the exercise of their privacy rights at an inappropriate time or in an inappropriate location. Thus, Brown would have greater leeway to play his sermons in a commercial district during the day than he could to blast then in a residential neighborhood at midnight. The Free Exercise Clause provision in the First Amendment to the Constitution prohibits Congress from making a law "prohibiting the free exercise" of religion. The free exercise clause guarantees that a person can hold any religious belief that he or she wants. When religious practices are at odds with public policy and the public welfare, the government can act. Brown has the absolute right to listen to his sermons and preach them to others. However, he cannot engage in this activity if it causes a danger to the safety of others. The question that is not answered by the facts is whether the distance of fifty feet is to prevent annoyance or a danger to drivers upon the streets and highways. Without a showing by Westerfield that music and speech that is audible from fifty feet is actually dangerous to drivers, Brown is free to play his sermons and spiritual music in manner that is annoying to others.

Answers to Practice Quiz

True/False:

1. True   The Unites States Constitution is the basis of individual and business rights.
2. False   The part of government that is comprised of Congress is the legislative branch. The executive branch is made up of the President and Vice-President.
3. True   The preemption doctrine allows for federal law to take precedence over state and local law.
4. True   Local and state laws are unconstitutional if they conflict with valid federal law.
5. False   Initially, the courts translated the Commerce Clause to mean that only commerce that moved in interstate commerce could be regulated. It is the modern interpretation that allows the federal government to regulate the activities that affect interstate commerce.
6. True   The effects on interstate commerce test allows the federal to regulate both intrastate and interstate activity if it has an effect on interstate commerce.
7. False   State and local laws that unduly burden interstate commerce are unconstitutional as they violate the Commerce Clause.
8. True   The Commerce Clause of the Constitution provides for the federal government's regulation of commerce with foreign nations.
9. True   The Bill of Rights not only guarantees particular rights to natural individuals, but also apply to corporations (artificial persons) as well.
10. True   The First Amendment Freedom of Speech protects the right to engage in written, oral, and symbolic speech.
11. False This is an example of political speech, which is fully protected, and not subject to government regulation or prohibition.
12. False The government can limit certain types of speech such as commercial speech and offensive speech to a proper time, place and manner, thereby giving these types of speech limited protection.
13. True   This type of statute has been held to be invalid as it endorses religion and it violates the Establishment Clause.
14. False The Fourteenth Amendment specifically prohibits unfair and discriminatory practices by the government.
15. False Under the rational basis test, the courts will hold the government regulation as being valid and long as there is a justifiable reason for the regulation. Note that it is the intermediate scrutiny test that the courts determine whether the government classification is "reasonably related" to a legitimate government purpose.
16. False Sex and age are protected classes and as such the standard for review of these protected classes is the intermediate scrutiny test whereby the courts decide whether the government classification is "reasonably related" to a legitimate government

purpose. Compare this to race, which is a suspect class that is subject to the strict scrutiny test that finds classifications based on race to be unconstitutional.

17. True   The Due Process Clause of the Fifth Amendment pertains to federal government action and the Due Process Clause of the Fourteenth Amendment pertains to state and local government action.

18. False   The government must follow procedural as well as substantive due process. The procedural refers to the government giving proper notice and a hearing of the legal action before an individual is deprived of life, liberty or property, whereas the substantive requires that the government make laws that are clear and not too broad.

19. True   Substantive due process has been achieved if a "reasonable person" could understand the law and be able to comply with it. This is accomplished by the laws' clarity and not being overly broad in their scope.

20. False   The Fifth Amendment Due Process Clause applies to federal government action whereas the Fourteenth Amendment Due Process Clause applies to state and local government action.

Multiple Choice

21. C   Answer C is correct as the states delegated powers to the federal government when they ratified the Constitution thereby calling them enumerated powers. Answer A is incorrect as this refers to the legislative branch of the government. Answer B is incorrect, as it does not make any sense. Answer D is incorrect for the reasons given above.

22. B   Answer B is correct as the Commerce Clause has a greater impact on business than any other clause in the Constitution. Answer A is incorrect as Congress has the authority to regulate commerce with foreign nations under the Commerce Clause. Answer C is incorrect as Congress regulates commerce with the Indian tribes, not the state. Answer D is incorrect as the Constitution is the supreme law of the land.

23. C   Answer C is correct as the question provides the definition of the preemption doctrine. Answer A is incorrect as the Supremacy Clause provides that federal regulations, federal laws, treaties and the federal Constitution are the supreme law of the land. Answer B is incorrect as the regulation of interstate commerce is only one aspect of permissible regulation under federal law and does not embody an entire concept of priority over various types of state laws. Answer D is incorrect for the reasons given above.

24. B   Answer B is correct, as intrastate commerce is commerce that moves within a state. Answer A is incorrect as this refers to interstate commerce. Answer C is incorrect as it combines the concepts of interstate and intrastate commerce. Answer D is incorrect as it is an incorrect statement of law.

25. D   Answer D is correct, as political speech is an example of speech that the government cannot prohibit or regulate. Answer A is incorrect as political speech is given full protection whereas offensive speech and commercial speech are given limited protection and are subject to time, place and manner restrictions. Answer B is incorrect based on the same reasoning why answer A was incorrect. Answer C is incorrect as speech that will incite the overthrow of the government is an example of unprotected speech that is not protected under the First Amendment.

26. A   Answer A is correct, as the reasoning behind this form of process is fairness. The government must give proper notice and a hearing of the legal action before there is a liberty or property is required. Answer B is incorrect as this refers to substantive due process and how the government's statutes, ordinances, laws and regulations are written. Answer C is incorrect as punitive damages are a type of remedy enforced in cases where punishment is being sought or there is a lesson for the defendant to learn. Answer D is incorrect as the Just Compensation Clause of the Fifth Amendment provides that the

government must pay the owner just not minimal compensation for taking an individual's property. Minimal compensation would violate all notions of fairness.

27. C   Answer C is correct, as this is the main premise of the Privileges and Immunities Clause. Answer A is incorrect as the Privileges and Immunities Clause encourages nationalism and favor states giving other states the same privileges as its own residents enjoy and benefit from. Answer B is incorrect, as it would unduly discriminate in favor of the states own residents owning property, which would defeat the concept of nationalism. Answer D is incorrect as the Privileges and Immunities Clause is not applicable to regulation of   interstate commerce.

28. D   Answer D is correct, as answers A, B, and C are all purposes of punitive damages.

29. A   Answer A is correct as substantive due process require that government regulations, laws, statutes and ordinances are clear on their face and not too broad. Answer B is incorrect as it only partially states what is required in order to comply with substantive due process. In addition to writing the laws in language a reasonable person could understand, the individual must also be able to comply with it. Answer C is incorrect as it is an incorrect statement of law. Answer D is incorrect, as substantive due process applies to all laws, not just the Privileges and Immunities Clause. Further, if a reasonable person could not understand and be able to comply with a law involving privileges and immunities, the law would probably be declared void for vagueness.

30. C   Answer C is correct, as answers A, B, and D are all examples of unprotected speech.

Short Answers:

31.   unprotected speech
32.   concurrent jurisdiction
33.   intermediate scrutiny
·34.   It is one of two parts of the federal Telecommunication Act that makes it a felony to   knowingly make "indecent" or "patently offensive" materials available on computer systems, including the Internet, to persons less than 18 years of age.
35.   suspect or protected
36.   time, place and manner
37.   unconstitutional
38.   Privileges and Immunities
39.   Just Compensation
40.   It has the authority to examine the acts of the legislative and judicial branches of government and determine whether these acts are constitutional.
41.   health, safety, morals and general
42.   executive
43.   It can create federal courts and determine their jurisdiction as well as enact statutes that   change judicially made law.
44.   telecommunications
45.   preempts
46.   increase competition within the telecommunications industry.
47.   commercial
48.   dangerous speech, fighting words, defamatory speech
49.   Establishment and Free Exercise
50.   actual damages

Chapter 4

INTENTIONAL TORTS
AND NEGLIGENCE

Chapter Overview

This chapter provides a good understanding of the intentional torts against persons as well as property. Additionally, the tort of negligence as well as applicable defenses to this cause of action is explained in a very methodical fashion. The special negligence doctrines such as negligence per se, negligent infliction of emotional distress and res ipsa loquitur are also examined. Further, the torts of unfair competition, disparagement and fraud are also discussed. Finally, the issue of punitive damages and the doctrine of strict liability are reviewed as well.

Objectives

Upon completion of this chapter's exercises, you should be able to:
1. Differentiate between the different types of intentional torts against persons and against property.
2. Understand the elements that are necessary in a cause of action based on negligence and apply those elements to given fact situations.
3. Be familiar with the defenses associated with a negligence action.
4. Understand the special negligence doctrines and how they differ from one another.
5. Understand the business torts of unfair competition and disparagement.
6. Understand the elements of fraud.
7. Understand the purposes of punitive damages and the application of punitive damages in lawsuits involving the tort of bad faith.
8. Understand the doctrine of strict liability and its application.

Practical Application

You should be able to identify the different types of intentional torts as well as negligence and apply the elements associated with each to real life as well as hypothetical situations. Additionally, you should have a greater understanding of the concept of strict liability as well as why and when punitive damages are asked for.

Helpful Hints

This chapter lends itself towards organization in that you can sort the intentional torts by their application to individuals, property or business. Also, the elements of the tort of negligence are easily remembered if you list the elements vertically and diagram causation horizontally. This is displayed for you in the study tips section of this chapter. Further, the tort of misrepresentation is easily remembered by using the mnemonic given under the study tips section. Once you have these organizational skills mastered for the main sections in this chapter, the other information given is very easy to remember. Many of the cases you will review in this chapter will be easy for you to understand as they pertain to many companies that you may be familiar with.

Study Tips

The first organizational step you should take is to learn the intentional torts based upon their application. You should also be cognizant of some of the fine nuances associated with some of these torts. It is often easier to list the elements of the tort rather than state its technical definition. Student learning styles will vary, and as such, both methods are given. The pages that follow will assist you in studying the torts that are discussed in this chapter.

Tort
A tort is a civil wrong for which an individual or business may compensation for the injuries that have been caused. Compensation for these injuries may include damages for mental distress, loss of wages, pain and suffering, past and future medical expenses and in some situations, punitive damages. In a tort situation where the victim dies, a wrongful death action may also be an option.

Intentional Torts Against Persons

Assault – The intentional threat of immediate harm or offensive contact or any action that arouses reasonable apprehension of imminent harm.

Assault list of elements with special nuances
- *intentional*
- *placing of another*
- *in immediate* – Note that future threats are not actionable.
- *apprehension* –The victim must be fearful of what appears to be an inevitable contact. The victim must be aware of the tortuous act. The victim's reaction must be one of fear as opposed to laughter which would negate the element of apprehension.
- *of harmful or offensive contact*

Battery – The intentional, unauthorized harmful or offensive touching of another without consent or legal privilege.

Battery list of elements with special nuances
- *intentional*
- *unauthorized*
- *harmful* or *offensive* – A kiss may be considered offensive by some
- *touching* – The touching of an accessory such as a purse that is attached to the victim may be enough to satisfy this element.
- *of another*
- *without consent* or *legal privilege* – You should be aware of the merchant's protection statutes, which sometimes have a role in the privilege arena of this tort.

Other interesting notations on battery are that the victim does not have to be aware of the battery in order for the tort to occur. Also, the victim may be sleeping when it happens or have his or her back turned when the battery occurs. Battery and assault can occur together, however, the victim would need to show awareness in order to fully prove the elements of assault.

Transferred Intent Doctrine - When one individual intends to injure one person but instead injures another individual, the law transfers the perpetrator's intent from the person the harm was originally meant for to the actual victim. The actual victim may then bring a lawsuit against the wrongdoer.

False Imprisonment – The intentional mental or physical confinement of another without consent or legal privilege.

False Imprisonment list of elements with special nuances:
- *intentional*
- *mental* or *physical* – An example of mental confinement may be through an assertion of legal authority or by one in a superior position. Physical confinement may include barriers or threats of physical harm.
- *confinement* – Be careful with this element as future threats or moral pressure does not satisfy this element. Also, if there is a reasonable means of escape, this element may be difficult to prove.
- *of another*
- *without consent* or *legal privilege* – This element will be difficult to establish if a merchant is involved. This aspect of tort law is discussed below.

Merchant Protection Statutes - Since many merchants lose thousands of dollars every year from shoplifters, many states have enacted statutes to protect them. These statutes are often referred to as shopkeeper's privilege. There are three important aspects of this type of statute that will absolve a merchant from liability of false imprisonment allegations.

Merchant Protection Statutes nuances
- There must be reasonable grounds for detaining and investigating the shoplifter.
- The suspected shoplifter can be detained for only a reasonable time.
- The investigations must be conducted in a reasonable manner.

Defamation of Character- This tort involves an intentional or accidental untrue statement of fact made about an individual to a third party.

Defamation of Character list of elements with special nuances
- *intentional* or *accidental* – may be overheard accidentally
- *untrue statement of fact* – Be careful as truth is always a defense.
- *published to a third party* – The third party can see or hear the untrue statement.

You should be aware of some of the other important aspects of defamation of character. For example, libel is written defamation and slander is oral defamation. Some types of media such as television and radio broadcasts come under the category of libel, as the courts view them as permanent in nature since the original scripts were composed prior to broadcasting the defamatory content. Also, opinions are not actionable, as it is not considered to be an untrue statement of fact. Finally, public figures such as movie stars, celebrities and other famous people must show that the statement was knowingly made or with reckless disregard of the statement's falsity. In other words, malice must be shown.

Misappropriation of the Right to Publicity – This tort is an attempt by another to appropriate a living person's name or identity for commercial purposes. A classic example of this would be individuals who sell cheaper versions of a famous performer's concert merchandise.

Invasion of the Right to Publicity
- A violation
- of an individual's
- right to live his/her life
- without unwarranted or undesired
- publicity

Truth is not a defense to this tort, as the fact does not have to be untrue. If the fact is one of public record, this tort cannot be claimed. Examples include wiretapping, reading hand delivered as well as the e-mail of another.

Intentional Infliction of Emotional Distress
- intentional or reckless
- extreme and outrageous conduct – The conduct must go beyond the bounds of decency.
- by one individual
- against another
- that causes severe emotional distress – Many states require a physical injury, illness or discomfort. However, states that are more flexible in their interpretation of this element have found that humiliation, fear and anger will satisfy this element. Some states no longer require that the severity of the emotional distress be shown.

Negligent Infliction of Emotional Distress
Though this is not an intentional tort, it is being placed here as it is a tort that is not only against individuals, but is one that some courts are recognizing when defendant's negligent conduct causes the plaintiff to suffer severe emotional distress. This tort requires the plaintiff's relative was injured or killed and that plaintiff suffered the severe distress at the same time he or she observed the accident. Some jurisdictions require the plaintiff suffer some sort of physical injury while other states do not mandate this element.

Intentional Torts Against Property

The two torts in this area are trespass to land, which is real property, and the trespass to personal property, which involves those items that are movable. The tort of conversion is also discussed along with trespass to personal property.

Trespass to Land
- *intentional* – It is not intentional if someone else pushes an individual onto someone else's land
- *entry*
- *onto the land*
- *of another*
- *without consent* or *legal privilege* –Rescuing someone from danger is not considered trespass. By the same token, remaining on someone's land after the invitation has expired is trespass.

Trespass to Personal Property
- *intentional*
- *injury* or *interference with* – An example of this would be breaking someone else's glass vase.
- *another's enjoyment*
- *of his or her personal property*

Conversion of Personal Property
- *intentionally*
- *depriving* – Note that the failure to return borrowed property can satisfy this element.
- a true *owner*
- of the *use and enjoyment*
- *of his or her personal property*

The rightful owner can bring a cause of action to get the property back. If the property is destroyed or lost, the true owner can recover the property's value.

Negligence

In order to be successful in a negligence cause of action, one must show that a duty of care was owed to the plaintiff, that the defendant breached this duty, that the defendant was the actual and proximate cause of plaintiff's injuries and that the plaintiff suffered damages.

Duty of Care

You should know the general duty of care which states that we all owe one another a duty of due care so as to not subject others to an unreasonable risk of harm. This duty is based on the reasonable person standard. An example of when this general duty of care is owed is the situation involving an invitee. An invitee is one who is invited onto the land of another for the mutual benefit of both people. The duty of ordinary care is also owed to licensees. A licensee is one who with consent comes onto the land of another for his or her own benefit. An example of a licensee would be an encyclopedia salesperson. Note, an owner does not owe a general duty of care to a trespasser; however, an owner of property does owe a duty not to willfully or wantonly injure a trespasser. Also, children are measured against other children of similar age and experience.

There are certain situations however where a higher standard of care is owed. They involve the professionals, innkeepers, common carriers, tavern and bartenders, social hosts and paying Passengers riding in a vehicle of another.

Professionals are held to the standard of a reasonable professional. Liability is known as malpractice. You should be cognizant of the medical professional who acts as a good Samaritan. Medical professionals are relieved of liability for injury caused by their ordinary negligence when rendering aid to victims in need of emergency care.

Innkeepers owe a duty of utmost care and have to provide security for their guest.

Common carriers also owe a duty of utmost care for their guests.

Tavern and bartenders are liable to third parties who are injured by a patron who was served too much alcohol or who was served alcohol when he/she was already intoxicated. Social Hosts are held liable for injuries caused by guests who are served too much alcohol.

The Danger Invites Rescue Doctrine allows those who are injured while going to someone's rescue to sue the person who caused the dangerous situation. Compare this to the Fireman's Rule where the fireman who is injured while putting out a fire may not sue the person who caused the fire as not only does the job imply that injury may occur, but people would be reluctant to call for help if they thought they might be sued in doing so.

Breach of Duty
If a duty, albeit general and or special has been established and it is found that the defendant has not acted as a reasonable person would, the court may find a breach of the duty of care.

Causation
It is important to remember that the plaintiff must show that the defendant was the actual (factual) and proximate (legal) cause of the plaintiff's injuries. Further, the defendant must be the direct cause of the plaintiff's injuries. If this cannot be established, plaintiff must show that the injuries that occurred were foreseeable in that it would be the type of injury one would expect from the activity the defendant was engaged in. It is best to diagram this element horizontally in order to remember its nuances. Please see below.

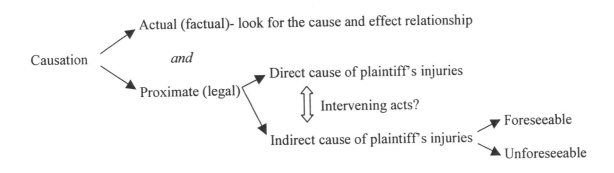

Damages
The plaintiff must nave actually suffered an injury or damages.

Defenses
Contributory negligence states that if a plaintiff is partially at fault for causing his or her own injuries, then the plaintiff is barred from recovering damages.

Comparative negligence doctrines assess damages by the plaintiff's percentage of fault. This is nown as pure comparative negligence. If however, the plaintiff is in a jurisdiction that adopts The partial comparative negligence doctrine, then plaintiff must be less than fifty percent negligent in causing his or her injuries. If the plaintiff is over fifty percent negligent, then recovery is barred and the defendant is not liable.

Assumption of the Risk is a defense that states that a defendant may assert indicating that the plaintiff knowingly and voluntarily entered into a risky activity that resulted in injury.

Special Negligence Doctrines

Negligence per se and **res ipsa loquitur** are special negligence doctrines that are important to be aware of as they are special in their establishment of the element of duty as well as assisting in the plaintiff's burden of proof in a negligence case.

Negligence Per Se – This doctrine involves the violation of a statute that proximately causes the plaintiff's injuries. There must be a statute that was enacted to prevent the type of injury suffered by the plaintiff and the plaintiff must be within the class of persons the statute was designed to protect.

Res Ipsa Loquitur – This doctrine means, "the thing speaks for itself." This is an important doctrine as there is a presumption of negligence where the plaintiff proves that the defendant had exclusive control of the instrumentality or circumstances that caused the plaintiff's injuries and the injury that the plaintiff suffered wouldn't have ordinarily occurred, "but for" someone's negligence.

Business Torts

Entering into a business or profession without a license can subject the violator to civil and criminal penalties.

Unfair Competition – This tort is also known as palming off whereby one company tries to "palm off" its products as those of a rival. Plaintiff must show the defendant used the plaintiff's symbol, trademark, logo, etc and that there is a likelihood of confusion as to the product's origin.

Disparagement – This tort involves an untrue statement made by a person or business about another business' reputation, services, products, etc. This tort is also known as product disparagement or trade libel. The defendant must have made the statement intentionally to a third party knowing that what he or she was saying was not true.

False Advertising – When companies use untruthful comparative advertising to compare the qualities of their products to those of their competitors, this is known as false advertising. False and misleading advertising is a violation of part of the federal statute known as the Lanham Act.

Intentional Misrepresentation (Fraud) – This tort lends itself nicely towards a mnemonic that will assist you in remembering its elements. The mnemonic is MIS JD.
M   Misrepresentation of material fact that was false in nature
I   Intentionally made to an innocent party
S   Scienter (knowledge) of the statement's falsity by the wrongdoer
J   Justifiable Reliance on the false statement by the innocent party
D   Damages were suffered by the injured party

Intentional Interference With Contractual Relations – There must be a valid and enforceable contract that a third party knows about. The third party induces one of the contracting parties to breach the contract with the other party.

Breach of Implied Covenant of Good Faith and Fair Dealing – Parties to a contract must adhere to the express terms of a contract and also to the implied term of "good faith." When a party to a contract acts in bad faith, this gives rise to the tort of Breach of Implied Covenant of Good Faith and Fair Dealing.

Punitive Damages – These types of damages are recoverable in torts involving fraud, intentional conduct and are in addition to actual damages. Punitive damages are awarded not only to set an example for others, but to prevent the defendant from the same or similar conduct in the future and to punish the defendant for his or her actions.

Strict Liability – This is a tort that involves liability without fault if the activity that the defendant is engaged in places the public at risk of injury despite reasonable care being taken. Examples of activities that qualify for this categorization include fumigation, storage of explosives, and blasting. Punitive damages are also recoverable in strict liability cases.

Refresh Your Memory

The following exercise will enable you to refresh your memory on the rules and principles presented to you in this chapter. Read each question twice and place your answer in the blanks provided. Review the chapter material for any question you miss or are unable to remember.

1. What does the word tort mean? _____

2. The main purpose that punitive damages are awarded is to _____ the defendant.

3. The tort of assault requires reasonable _____ of imminent harm.

4. Which doctrine places the perpetrator's intent from the target to the actual victim of the act? The doctrine of _____ _____.

5. Public officials cannot recover for defamation unless they can show the defendant acted with _____ _____.

6. Another name for an oral defamatory statement is _____.

7. The tort of appropriation is also known as _____ of the right to _____.

8. Reading someone else's e-mail is an example of the tort of _____ of the right to _____.

9. Interference with an owner's right to exclusive possession of land constitutes the tort of _____ to _____.

10. _____ of care refers to the obligation not to cause any unreasonable harm or risk of harm to others.

11. When proving causation in a negligence action, what are the two types of causation that must be proved before the plaintiff may prevail? _____ in fact and _____ _____.

12. The liability of a professional who breaches his or her duty of ordinary care is known as _____ _____.

13. The term res ipsa loquitur means the _____ _____ ____ _____.

14. Under which doctrine may a rescuer sue the person who caused the dangerous situation that the rescuer has gone to? The _____ _____ _____ doctrine.

15. An original negligent party may raise a _____ event as a defense to liability.

16. The tort of unfair competition is also known as _____ _____.

17. The Lanham Act prohibits _____ and _____ advertising.

18. The tort of disparagement is also known as product disparagement, trade _____ or _____ of title.

19. _____ _____ imposes liability without the defendant being at fault having been at fault.

20. The tort of bad faith is also known as the _____ of _____ Covenant of _____ _____ and Fair Dealing.

Critical Thought Exercise

Chip North is a 22-year-old racing enthusiast who went to a car race at Trona International Speedway. North was excited because he had obtained a seat close to the track near the finish line. North's ticket came with five others in a sealed envelope that was imprinted in a large font with the following:

"WARNING!
Your seating for this event is in a very
DANGEROUS AREA
Debris and fluids from race cars may be ejected or sprayed from the
race surface into your seating area in the event of a crash or malfunction
of a race vehicle. Please ask to change your seating if you do not desire to
ASSUME THE RISK OF SERIOUS INJURY."

The envelope is opened by North's younger brother, who does not pay any attention to the envelope and discards it after removing the tickets. During the race a car crashes into the wall in front of North's seat and sprays him with burning gasoline, causing severe injuries. North sues Trona Speedway for negligence for subjecting him to a known danger by seating him and others so close to the racetrack. Trona Speedway denies any liability based upon the warning on the envelope and the known risk that spectators take when attending a race.

At trial, which side should prevail?

Answer. _____
_____
_____
_____
_____
_____
_____
_____
_____
_____
_____
_____
_____
_____
_____
_____
_____
_____
_____

Practice Quiz

True/False

1. ___ Fred can sue Sam for assault for threatening to beat him to a pulp tomorrow. [p 74]

2. ___ Direct physical harm between the perpetrator and the victim is needed when proving the tort of battery. [p 74]

3. ___ Truth is an absolute defense to a charge of defamation. [p 75]

4. ___ An attempt by another person to use a living person's name or identity for commercial purposes is not actionable. [p 76]

5. ___ Many states provide that the right to publicity does not survive a person's death and may not be enforced by the deceased's heirs. [p 76]

6. ___ The tort of conversion can happen when someone who initially was given possession of personal property fails to return it. [p 79]

7. ___ A person who is the cause of a car accident because he or she fell asleep while driving is not liable for any resulting injuries caused by his or her carelessness as his or her actions were not intentional. [p 80]

8. ___ Under the reasonable person standard, the courts try to determine how a subjective, careful, and conscientious person would have acted in the same circumstances, and then measure the defendant's conduct against this standard. [p 80]

9. ___ Forseeability is the general test of proximate cause. [p 83]

10. ___ Since there have been an increase in malpractice law suits, almost all states have abolished the Good Samaritan laws that relieve medical professionals from liability for injury caused by their ordinary negligence in such circumstance. [p 87]

11. ___ Dram Shop Acts hold tavern and bartenders civilly liable for injuries caused to or by patrons who are served too much alcohol. [p 88]

12. ___ The fireman's rule provides that a fireman may sue the party whose negligence caused the fire for any resulting injuries from putting out the fire. [p 88]

13. ___ Under the social host liability rule, a social host is not liable for injuries caused by guests who are served alcohol at a social function. [p 88]

14. ___ Common carriers and innkeepers owe a duty of ordinary care to their passengers and guests. [p 89]

15. ___ If a plaintiff knows of and involuntarily enters into or participates in a risky activity that results in injury, the law acknowledges that the plaintiff assumed the risk involved. [p 89]

16. ___ Under a jurisdiction that adopts the doctrine of partial comparative negligence, a plaintiff may recover damages that are apportioned according to his or her fault. [p 91]

17. ___ A disparaging statement is a true statement made by one person or business about the products, services, property, or reputation of another business. [p 92]

18. ___ The tort of intentional misrepresentation is also known as fraud or deceit. [p 92]

19. ___ Fred has a contract with Harry to provide pizza crusts to Harry's Italian Restaurant. Bella tells Harry that she will give him a good deal on pizza sauce if he buys his pizza crust from her instead of Fred. Fred can sue Bella for intentionally interfering with the contract between him and Harry even if Bella did not know there was a contract between Fred and Harry. [p 93]

20. ___ Liability without fault is known as strict liability. [p 95]

Multiple Choice:

21. A tort that states that a person whose extreme and outrageous conduct intentionally or recklessly causes severe emotional distress is known as [p 78]
    a. intentional infliction of emotional distress.
    b. res ipsa loquitur.
    c. extreme negligence.
    d. invasion of right to privacy.

22. When one person injures another person's personal property or interferes with that person's enjoyment of his or her personal property, this is known as the tort of [p 79]
    a. false imprisonment.
    b. trespass to personal property.
    c. stinginess.
    d. negligence.

23. Depriving a true owner of the use and enjoyment of his or her personal property by taking over such property and exercising ownership rights would be considered to be the tort of [p 79]
    a. trespass to personal property.
    b. conversion of personal property.
    c. trespass to land.
    d. strict liability.

24. In determining the standard of care owed by an accountant, the court will measure the defendant's conduct against [p 81]
    a. a reasonable person.
    b. a reasonable brain surgeon.
    c. a reasonable accountant.
    d. a reasonable child.

25. A breach of duty of care is [p 81]
    a. a fulfillment to act as a reasonable person under the same or similar circumstances.
    b. an expectation in certain circumstances.
    c. the failure to act as a reasonable person would.
    d. immaterial in assessing liability.

26. If two or more individuals are liable for negligently causing the plaintiff's injuries, both or all can be held liable to the plaintiff if each of their acts is a [p 83]
    a. proximate cause of plaintiff's injuries.
    b. substantial factor in causing the plaintiff's injuries.
    c. inconsequential cause of plaintiff's injuries.
    d. None of the above.

27. A bystander who witnesses the injury or death of a loved one that is caused by another's negligent conduct may bring a cause of action against that individual for [p 85]
    a. negligent death.
    b. intentional infliction of emotional distress.
    c. battery.
    d. negligent infliction of emotional distress.

28. Liability for a professional who braches the reasonable professional standard of care is known as [p 86]
    a. negligence per se.
    b. res ipsa loquitur.
    c. professional malpractice.
    d. social host liability.

29. Violation of a statute that proximately causes an injury is referred to as [p 86]
    a. negligence per se.
    b. negligent infliction of emotional distress.
    c. the "Danger Invites Rescue" doctrine.
    d. unfair competition.

30. If Dr. Goodman sees Sally D. Victim laying helplessly in the line of traffic and decides to render aid, but, in doing so causes her ankle to be bruised, which statute will relieve him of liability for Sally's injuries? [p 87]
    a. Assumption of the risk
    b. Dram shop acts
    c. Good Samaritan law
    d. Strict liability

31. Guest statutes in many states provide [p 88]
    a. a rescuer who is injured while going to a guest's rescue can sue the person who caused the dangerous situation.
    b. a fireman may not sue the party whose negligence caused the fire he was injured in.
    c. social hosts are liable for injuries caused by guests who become intoxicated at a social function.
    d. that if a driver voluntarily and without compensation gives a ride in a vehicle to another person, the driver is not liable to the passenger for injuries caused by the driver's ordinary negligence.

32. If you invite a friend over for dinner, this person would be considered an [p 88]
    a. old acquaintance.
    b. invitee.
    c. interested licensee.
    d. intervening event.

33. A person who has no permission or right to be on another's property is known as a [p 89]
    a. family member.
    b. licensee.
    c. trespasser.
    d. common carrier.

34. Under the doctrine of pure comparative negligence, [p 91]
    a. the plaintiff must be less than 50 percent responsible for causing his or her own injuries in order to recover damages.
    b. the plaintiff is barred from recovery of damages.
    c. the plaintiff's damages are apportioned according to fault.
    d. the plaintiff's damages are assessed if the plaintiff did not assume the risk.

35. Damages that are awarded to deter the defendant from similar conduct in the future, and to set an example for others as well as punish the defendant are known as [p 94]
    a. compensatory damages.
    b. nominal damages.
    c. actual damages.
    d. punitive damages.

36. What must a plaintiff suffer in order to recover monetary damages for the defendant's negligence? [p 81]
    a. Ordinary negligence
    b. Personal injury or damage to his or her property
    c. Emotional distress
    d. Extreme and outrageous conduct

37. A person who sells magazines from door to door would be considered a [p 88]
    a. very industrious person.
    b. guest.
    c. trespasser.
    d. licensee.

38. Public figures must show actual malice when bringing a cause of action for defamation. Which definition best describes what actual malice is? [p 76]
    a. Ordinary negligence
    b. Intent to make a false statement
    c. Knowing and with reckless disregard for the statement's falsity
    d. A breach of the duty of care

39. If an individual uses someone else's logo to place on his or her product and the public becomes confused with regard to the source of the product, the individual may bring a cause of action for [p 92]
    a. slander.
    b. libel.
    c. shopkeeper's privilege.
    d. palming off.

40. The intentional mental or physical confinement of another without consent or legal privilege defines which tort? [p 74]
    a. Shopkeeper's privilege
    b. False imprisonment
    c. Defamation
    d. Misrepresentation

Short Answer:

41. What does a plaintiff need to prove in a lawsuit involving defamation of character? [p 75]
    _____
    _____

42. Briefly describe the difference between real property and personal property. [p 78]
    _____
    _____

43. What are the necessary elements that a plaintiff must prove in order to establish a cause of action for negligence? [p 79] _____
    _____
    _____

44. What is the difference between actual cause and proximate cause? [p 83] _____
    _____
    _____

45. What is the difference between slander and libel? [p 75] _____
    _____

46. List the elements for the tort of Intentional Misrepresentation. [p 92] _____
    _____
    _____

47. What must a plaintiff show in order to succeed in a cause of action for disparagement?
    [p 92] _____
    _____

48. Briefly explain the doctrine of transferred intent. [p 74] _____
    _____
    _____

49. In order to establish a case based on res ipsa loquitur, what elements must be met? [p 86]
    _____
    _____

50. What elements must be shown in a cause of action for Intentional Interference with Contractual Relations? [p 93] _____
    _____
    _____

Answers to Refresh Your Memory

1. wrong [p 74]
2. punish [p 74]
3. apprehension [p 74]
4. Transferred Intent [p 74]
5. actual malice [p 76]
6. slander [p 74]
7. misappropriation, publicity [p 76]
8. invasion, right, privacy [p 77]
9. trespass, land [p 79]
10. duty [p 80]
11. causation in fact, proximate cause [p 83]
12. professional malpractice [p 86]
13. thing speaks for itself [p 86]
14. Danger Invites Rescue [p 88]
15. superceding [p 89]
16. palming off [p 92]
17. false, misleading [p 92]
18. libel, slander [p 92]
19. strict liability [p 95]
20. Breach of Implied, Good Faith [p 94]

Critical Thought Exercise Model Answer

The tort of negligence occurs when someone suffers injury because of another's failure to exercise the standard of care that a reasonable person would exercise in similar circumstances. The operator of a facility where a sporting event takes place has a duty to provide safe seating for the spectators unless the risk of injury is assumed and accepted by the spectators. Spectators at a baseball game assume the risk that a ball may be hit into the stands and strike them. Spectators at a hockey game do not assume this same risk because pucks are not usually hit high enough over the protective glass to strike spectators. A plaintiff, who voluntarily enters into a risky situation, knowing the risk involved, will not be allowed to recover. This is the defense of assumption of risk. The requirements of this defense are (1) knowledge of the risk and (2) voluntary assumption of the risk. If North had actually been given knowledge of the risk, he may have voluntarily assumed that risk by sitting close to the racetrack. However, six tickets were placed in one envelope that was opened by someone other than North. Trona speedway cannot argue that North voluntarily assumed a risk for which he was not given notification. The knowledge of risk may be implied from the general knowledge of spectators at a particular type of event, such as baseball. There is no indication that North or any other spectator would know of the danger associated with sitting in a seat for which a ticket was sold. Because North did not assume the risk of being injured by burning gasoline while a spectator at the race, Trona is still liable for negligence.

Answers to Practice Quiz

True/False

1. False   Future threats are not actionable, as they do not create immediate apprehension.
2. False   There does not have to be direct physical contact between the victim and the perpetrator.

3. True   Since defamation by its very definition involves an untrue statement, truth is an absolute defense to a defamation allegation.
4. False Misappropriating a living person's name or identity for commercial gain is actionable under the tort of misappropriation of the right to publicity.
5. False The majority of states allow the right to publicity to survive a person's death and may in fact be enforced by the deceased's heirs.
6. True   When the true owner of property is deprived of the use and enjoyment of his or her personal property by another taking over such property and exercising ownership rights over it, this is known as conversion of personal property. The failure to return borrowed property is also considered conversion.
7. False The unintentional tort of negligence basis liability for harm on that which is a foreseeable consequence of his or her actions. Therefore, it is foreseeable that injuries may result from a driver who is asleep at the wheel. Under the doctrine of negligence, intent has no applicability.
8. False The courts use an objective standard to measure the defendant's standard against. The defendant's subjective intent has no bearing in determining liability.
9. True   Proximate cause is determined by forseeability, which places a limitation on liability.
10. False Nearly all states have passed Good Samaritan laws that relieve medical professionals from liability for injury caused by their ordinary negligence in such circumstances.
11. True   The bartender and tavern are liable to third parties injured by the patron and for the injuries suffered by the patron.
12. False A fireman may not sue a party whose negligence caused the fire he or she was injured in while putting out the fire.
13. False A social host is liable for injuries caused by guests who are served alcohol at a social function.
14. False Common carriers and innkeepers owe a duty of utmost care to their passengers and guests.
15. False The plaintiff must know and voluntarily enter into or participate in a risky activity that causes injury before the court will find that the plaintiff assumed the risk involved.
16. False The doctrine of partial comparative negligence states that a plaintiff must be less than fifty percent responsible for causing his or her injuries in order to recover under this theory.
17. False A disparaging statement is an untrue statement of which is the basis of the tort of disparagement which is also referred to as product disparagement, trade libel or slander of title.
18. True   The statement as written is true.
19. False The tort of intentional interference with contractual relations requires that there be a valid, enforceable contract between the contracting parties, that a third-party had knowledge of this contract and that third party induced one of the original contracting parties to breach the contract. Since Bella did not know there was a contract between Fred and Harry, all of the elements are not met thereby negating the cause of action under this tort.
20. True   Since certain activities can by their very dangerous nature cause a risk to the public, the law holds those responsible liable without fault. This is the doctrine of strict liability.

Multiple Choice:

21. A   A is the correct answer as the statement given is the definition of intentional infliction of emotional distress. Answer B is incorrect as res ipsa loquitur involves an instrumentality that is in the exlusive control of the defendant and would not have occurred but for someone's negligence. Answer C is incorrect as there is no such thing as extreme negligence. Answer D is incorrect as the question gives an incorrect definition of invasion of the right to privacy.
22. B   Answer B is the correct answer as trespass to personal property involves one person's interference with another person's personal property. Answer A is incorrect as false

imprisonment is the intentional mental or physical confinement of another without consent or legal privilege. Answer C is incorrect as stinginess is not a tort. Answer D is incorrect as trespass to property is an intentional tort, not one involving negligence.

23. B   Answer B is the correct answer as the question's conversion of personal property. Answer A is incorrect as the tort of trespass to personal property involves the interference of a person's use and enjoyment of his or her property whereas conversion involves this along with exercising ownership rights over the property. Answer C is incorrect as trespass to land involves real property as opposed to the personal property referred to in the question. Answer D is incorrect as strict liability is liability without fault that is often utilized in cases involving abnormally dangerous activities.

24. C   Answer C is correct as defendants who have a particular expertise or competence are measured against a reasonable professional standard which in this case would be that of a reasonable accountant. Answer A is not the best answer as the reasonable person standard is usually used in circumstances where a general duty of care is owed and professionals or those having a special duty are not involved. Answer B is incorrect as measuring an accountant's duty against that of a brain surgeon would not accurately indicate the conduct of a reasonable accountant in the field. Answer D is incorrect as comparing an accountant to a child would not be an indicator of the conduct of another accountant of similar expertise or competence.

25. C   Answer C is correct as the duty of care is measure against how an objective, careful and conscientious person would act in similar circumstances. As such the breach of the duty of care is the failure to act as a reasonable person would. Answer A is incorrect as the concept of breach and fulfillment are not synonymous with one another as breach connotes failure. Answer B is incorrect as breach does not imply expectation regardless of the circumstances. Answer D is incorrect as it is an untrue statement, as the breach of duty is what helps to begin the process of proof in a negligence cause of action.

26. B   Answer B is the correct answer as two or more individuals can be held liable to the plaintiff if each of their negligent acts is a substantial factor in causing the plaintiff's injuries. Answer A is incorrect as proximate cause is only one of the two types of causation that must be shown before liability can be established. Answer C is incorrect as it is an untrue statement. Answer D is incorrect for the reasons given above.

27. D   Answer D is correct as some jurisdictions have allowed the tort of emotional distress to include the negligent infliction of emotional distress of which the question addresses emotional distress as a result of a negligent act. Answer A is incorrect as death may result from a negligent act, however, there is no such thing as negligent death. Answer B is incorrect as negligent conduct is involved and not intentional. Answer C is incorrect as battery is an intentional tort and the facts indicate that negligent conduct is involved.

28. C   Answer C is correct, as the breach of the reasonable professional standard of care is known as professional malpractice. Answer A is incorrect as negligence per se involves the violation of a statute that was designed to prevent the type of injury suffered. Answer B is incorrect as res ipsa loquitor refers to an instrumentality that was in the control of the defendant that negligently caused another's injuries. Answer D is incorrect as this rule allows for social host liability for injuries caused by guests who are served too much alcohol at a social function.

29. A   Answer A is correct as negligence per se is a special negligence doctrine that establishes the duties owed by one person to another be use of a statute that is enacted to prevent the type of injury suffered. Note, the injured individual must have been within the class of individuals that the statute was designed to protect. Answer B is incorrect as negligent infliction of emotional distress is not what constitutes a violation of statute that proximately causes the injuries of an individual. Answer C is incorrect as the Danger Invites Rescue doctrine speaks to liability in terms of the person who caused the dangerous situation. Note, that the individual injured in a dangerous situation may not be afforded protection of a statute. Answer D is incorrect as unfair competition refers to the palming off of one product or service as that of another thereby creates confusion in the consumer.

30. C   Answer C is correct, as most states have passed Good Samaritan laws that relieve professionals of liability for injuries caused by their ordinary negligence. If the court finds that Sally's bruised ankle was a result of Dr. Goodman's ordinary negligence, then he will be relieved of liability. Answer A is incorrect as the defense of assumption of the risk has no applicability as Sally did not knowingly and voluntarily assume the risk that her ankle would be bruised by Dr. Goodman. Answer B is incorrect as dram shop acts refer to the civil liability that can be assessed to tavern and bartenders for injuries caused to or by patrons who are served too much alcohol. Answer D is incorrect as strict liability refers to liability without fault. Dr. Goodman's actions would not be considered a hazardous activity to be able to qualify under a strict liability theory.

31. D   Answer D is correct as it provides what may state laws include when a non-paying guest in an automobile is injured as a result of the driver's ordinary negligence. Answer A is incorrect as this refers to the Danger Invites Rescue doctrine, not the law under a guest statute. Answer B is incorrect as even though it is a true statement under the Fireman's Rule, it has no applicability under a guest statute. Answer C is incorrect this refers to liability under the Social Host Liability rule and not under a guest statute.

32. B   Answer B is correct as an invitee is one who has been expressly or impliedly invited onto the owner's premises for the mutual benefit of both parties of which dinner would qualify as such. Answer A is incorrect as there are no legal definitions to determine the status of an old acquaintance. Answer C is incorrect as an invitee is one who for his or her own benefit enters onto the property of another with the express or implied consent of the owner. Answer D is incorrect as an intervening event is not a proper description of an individual who has been invited for dinner.

33. C   Answer C is correct, as a trespasser is an individual who does not have consent or legal privilege to enter onto the land of another. Answer A is incorrect as there is not any indication by the vague description weather or not the member had permission to be on the premises. Answer B is incorrect as a licensee usually has express or implied permission to enter onto the land of another. Answer D is incorrect as a common carrier is not an individual and therefore is not applicable to the question.

34. C   Answer C is correct as it pure comparative negligence apportions the plaintiff's damages according to the percentage that he or she was at fault. Answer A is incorrect as this defines partial comparative negligence. Answer B is incorrect as this refers to contributory negligence. Answer D is incorrect as the plaintiff's assumption of the risk is a separate defense from comparative negligence.

35. D   Answer D is correct as the question addresses punitive damages. Answer A is incorrect as compensatory damages are given to make the individual whole again. Answer B is incorrect as nominal damages are given as a matter of principle. Answer C is incorrect as actual damages are assessed in terms of what the plaintiff's true injuries were.

36. B   Answer B is correct since even though a defendant's act may have breached a duty of care that was owed to the plaintiff, the plaintiff still needs to show that he or she has suffered an injury. Answer A is incorrect as an individual may not suffer ordinary negligence. Answer C is incorrect as emotional distress is not a requisite in a negligence action. Answer D is incorrect as extreme and outrageous conduct is not an element in a negligence action. However, it may be required in a cause of action for emotional distress.

37. D   Answer D is correct as a magazine salesperson would be considered a licensee since he or she enters onto others land for his or her own benefit. Though answer A may be true, it is incorrect as there is no basis in law or fact for this answer. Answer B is incorrect as a guest would be an invitee who enters onto another's land for the mutual benefit of both parties. Answer C is incorrect as a trespasser has no implied invitation whereas a licensee does.

38. C   Answer C is correct as it provides the correct definition of malice which defines the required behavior as being more than a mere intentional untrue statement about the plaintiff. Answer A is incorrect as malice has the facet of knowledge associated with it as opposed to negligence, which does not. Answer B is incorrect as a public figure must show a reckless disregard for a

statement's falsity, not just a mere intent to make a false statement as would be the case in someone who is not a famous figure or personality. Answer D is incorrect as a breach of the duty of care is an element required in a negligence action not a defamation cause of action.

39. D Answer D is correct as palming off is another way of phrasing unfair competition, which is what the question describes. Answer A is incorrect as slander is oral defamation, which has nothing to do with the question presented. Answer B is incorrect as libel is written defamation that also has nothing to do with the question presented. Answer C is incorrect as shopkeepers privilege concerns reasonable grounds, reasonable time and a reasonable manner for detaining someone on a business premises.

40. B Answer B is correct as the question provides the correct definition for false imprisonment. Answer A is incorrect as the shopkeeper's privilege may be asserted as a defense to a false imprisonment cause of action not as a definition of false imprisonment as given in the question. Answer C is incorrect as defamation concerns the publishing of a false statement to a third party about another individual, not the mental or physical confinement of another without consent or legal privilege. Answer D is incorrect as misrepresentation is fraud which is associated with the intentional misrepresentation of material fact that is made with knowledge of the statement's falsity and thereafter relied upon by the individual to whom the statement was made.

Short Answer:

41. A plaintiff needs to show that the defendant made an untrue statement of fact about the plaintiff and the statement was accidentally or intentionally published to a third party.

42. Real property involves land and personal property concerns tangible, moveable items such as a car or personal belongings.

43. A plaintiff must establish the following elements in a cause of action for negligence:
    a) The defendant must owe the plaintiff a duty of care.
    b) The defendant must have breached that duty to the plaintiff.
    c) The defendant was the actual (factual) as well as proximate (legal) cause of plaintiff's injuries.
    d) Damages.

44. Actual cause is the factual cause of plaintiff's injuries whereas proximate cause is the legal cause of the plaintiff's injuries. Proximate cause is based on forseeablity of the injury based upon the defendant's actions.

45. Slander is oral defamation, or a defamatory statement that is heard. Libel is written defamation, or what is seen.

46. The elements for the tort of intentional misrepresentation are given below.
    a) A misrepresentation of a material fact is made to the plaintiff.
    b) This misrepresentation was intentionally made.
    c) The defendant had knowledge of the statement's falsity when he or she made it.
    d) The plaintiff justifiably relied upon the misrepresentation.
    e) The plaintiff suffered damages as a result of the misrepresentation.

47. In order to be successful in a cause of action for disparagement, the plaintiff must show:
    a) The defendant made an untrue statement about the plaintiff's products or services, etc.;
    b) the defendant published this untrue statement to another individual; and
    c) the defendant knew the statement that was made was false; and
    d) the defendant made the statement maliciously intending to hurt the plaintiff.

48. The doctrine of transferred intent transfers the wrongdoer's intent from the original target to the actual victim of the act.

49. The plaintiff must show that the defendant had exclusive control of the instrumentality or situation that caused the plaintiff's injury and the injury would not have ordinarily occurred "but for" someone's negligence.

50. The following elements must be shown in order to be successful in a cause of action for Intentional Interference with Contractual Relations:

    a) An enforceable, valid contract between the contracting parties.

    b) The third party must know about the contract.

    c) The third party induced the breach of the contract.

Chapter 5

PRODUCT AND
STRICT LIABILITY

Chapter Overview

This chapter discusses the multiple tort principles that are available to injured parties as a result of defectively made products. The causes of action that are available include negligence, misrepresentation, and strict liability. Many individuals including purchasers, users, lessees and even innocent bystanders who are injured by a defective product may seek recovery under the legal theory called products liability. This chapter will help you understand how manufactures, sellers, lessors and others involved with the defective product may be held liable for the injuries caused to others who were injured by the product.

Objectives

When you have completed the exercises in this chapter, you should be able to:
1. Differentiate between the different legal theories surrounding product liability.
2. Discuss what strict liability is.
3. Determine which parties may be held liable for injuries that are a result of a defective product.
4. Compare and contrast the difference between a manufacture, design and packaging defect.
5. Compare and contrast defects associated with a failure to warn and a failure to provide sufficient instructions.
6. Recognize and be able to state applicable defenses in product liability lawsuits.
7. State and understand what damages are available in a product liability action.
8. Differentiate between contributory and comparative negligence.
9. Discuss the doctrine of market share liability.
10. Understand Japan's product liability law.

Practical Application

You should be able to identify the different types of legal theories as well as their elements when establishing a basis for a product liability lawsuit. Additionally you should be able to identify the proper party to assess liability against, identify and apply potential defenses and be familiar with the types of damages that are available.

Helpful Hints

This chapter is not only a good chapter for reviewing the concepts of negligence and misrepresentation that you learned in the last chapter, but it is also one that you can utilize to build upon your knowledge of torts. It is important to learn the duties that are owed by those who manufacture as well as sell or lease products that are defectively made so that you will be able to select the appropriate cause of action to bring against the proper party. In the Study Tips section that follows, the necessary elements for the causes of action in a product liability lawsuit as well as the proper parties whom suit should be brought against are listed under the same. By studying the causes of action in this manner, it will assist you in committing the entire concept of liability to memory.

Study Tips

Negligence
In order to be successful in a negligence action based on products liability, the plaintiff must first establish that a duty was owed and thereafter breached by the defendant. There are several types of duties that are owed, any of which can be breached alone or in combination with the others. These duties as well as who owes the duty (which is listed in parenthesis) include:

✓ the duty to assemble the product safely. (the manufacturer)
✓ the duty to properly design the product. (the manufacturer)
✓ the duty to inspect or test the product. (the manufacturer)
✓ the duty to properly package the product. (the manufacturer)
✓ the duty to warn of any dangerous propensities that the product may have. (the manufacturer and possibly the retailer and/or wholesaler)

Of course a breach of any of these duties gives rise to a negligence cause of action of which the plaintiff must demonstrate that the defendant was the actual as well as proximate cause of his or her injuries. The interesting part of this aspect is that there may be more than one defendant who is being sued for negligence, and as such, each may assert that the other was a supervening act that breaks the chain of proximate causation thereby making he or she the indirect cause of the plaintiff's injuries.

✓ The plaintiff will have a difficult time in proving a negligence cause of action based upon product liability as it is often a challenge determining who was negligent. Any one of the parties that suit will be brought against could have caused the plaintiff's injuries. The potential parties in a negligence cause of action may include the manufacturer, the retailer, a possible wholesaler, and maybe even a repairperson. Any one of these parties could singly or together have caused the plaintiff's injuries.

Misrepresentation
A plaintiff bringing a lawsuit based on misrepresentation will do so because of the fraud associated with the quality of the product. Only those who relied on the misrepresentation and thereafter suffered injury may bring a cause of action under this tort.

✓ Though misrepresentation is not the most common cause of action of which to base a product liability action on, it can be utilized if the plaintiff shows the seller or lessor made a misrepresentation concerning the product's quality or did not reveal a defect in the product. Manufacturers, sellers and lessors are potential defendants for this type of cause of action.

Strict Liability
The basis behind strict liability is to impose liability regardless of whose fault it is. As you learned in the previous chapter, strict liability is often imposed when a defendant is engaged in an ultrahazardous activity. Strict liability is also imposed upon lessors and sellers who are in the business of leasing and selling products. Casual sellers are exempt from the facet of being in the business of leasing and selling products. A casual seller is someone who is not a merchant.

✓   Be careful as strict liability involves products and not services. If the situation involves both, the court will look at the prevalent element in order to determine whether or not strict liability applies.

✓   Who may be liable under a strict liability theory?
All manufacturers, distributors, wholesalers, retailers, lessors, manufacturers of sub-components may be held strictly liable for the injuries caused by the product. Note that if one or more of the parties in the chain of distribution are held liable in a strict liability lawsuit, the parties may seek indemnification by bringing a separate cause of action against the negligent party.

✓   Special notation concerning entrepreneur liability for a defective product - Entrepreneurs may avoid the concern of being named in a product liability lawsuit by taking the cautionary measure of purchasing a products liability insurance policy. This will help minimize or eliminate the costs associated with such a lawsuit. Note that any amount of damages above and beyond what the policy covers will be the responsibility of the business.

✓   Elements in a Strict Liability cause of action
First , a defect must be shown. Several types of defects exist.

Manufacturing defect – A failure on the manufacturer' part to properly assemble, test or check the product's quality.

Design defect – This defect involves the application of a risk-utility analysis. The court will weigh the gravity of the danger from the design, the likelihood that injury will result from the design and the availability as well as expense of producing a safer different design against the utility of the design. The crashworthiness doctrine falls under this category of defect, as the court have held that automobile manufacturers have a duty when designing automobiles to take into account the possibility of a second collision from within the automobile. A failure to protect occupants from foreseeable dangers may result in a lawsuit based upon strict liability.

Packaging defect – A manufacturer has a duty to design and provide safe packages for their products so that they are either tamperproof or indicate if they have been tampered with. This type of defect has particular application in the pharmaceutical industry.

Failure to warn is viewed as a defect – Manufacturers as well as sellers have a duty to warn users about the dangerous aspects. The warning must be clear and conspicuous on the product. A failure to warn may subject those in the chain of distribution to a lawsuit based on strict liability.

Miscellaneous defects – There are other defects that can give rise to a strict liability cause of action, included of which are the failure to safely assemble a product, failure to provide adequate instructions for the safe use or assembly of a product, failure to adequately test a product or select proper component parts or materials, and failure to properly certify the product.

✓   Defenses to a Product Liability Lawsuit
There are many *defenses* that may have applicability in a product liability lawsuit.

Supervening Event- No liability exists if the product is materially altered or modified after it leaves the sellers possession and the modification or alteration causes the injury.

Generally Known Dangers – If a product is generally known to be dangerous and a seller fails to warn of this, then liability may attach. However, placing a safety feature on a generally known dangerous product may assist in limiting or absolving liability.

Government Contractor Defense – A Government contract must show that the government provided precise specifications for the product and the contract did in fact conform to those specifications. Further that the government was warned by the contractor of any known product defects or dangers.

Assumption of the Risk – Even though a defendant may utilize this defense by showing that the plaintiff knew and appreciated the risk involved and voluntarily assumed the risk, this defense is not widely used.

Misuse of Product – The main aspect the defendant must prove is that the plaintiff has abnormally misused the product and that such misuse was unforeseeable. If the misuse was foreseeable, the seller of the product will remain liable.

Statute of Limitations and Repose – A failure to bring a cause of action within the allowed time frame will relieve the defendant of liability. Many jurisdictions state that the statute of limitations begins to run when the plaintiff suffers an injury. Other states feel this is unfair to the seller and have created statutes of repose that limit the liability a seller has by setting a time frame in terms of years from when the product was initially sold.

Contributory and Comparative Negligence – If a person is found to have been negligent in contributing to his or her own injuries, this will not prevent him or her from recovering in a strict liability cause of action as it would under an ordinary negligence cause of action. Further, the courts have also applied the defense of comparative negligence thereby apportioning the damages based upon the negligence of each of the parties.

✓ Damages in a strict liability action include
- personal injury with some jurisdictions limiting the dollar amount of the award.
- property damage, which is recoverable in most jurisdictions.
- lost income which is recoverable in some jurisdictions.
- punitive damages are recoverable if the plaintiff can show that the defendant intentionally injured him or her or acted maliciously for his or her safety.

✓ Compare to Product Liability in Japan
- Japan has very few product liability cases. The reasons for the lack of cases are given below.
- The plaintiff must show that the company was negligent.
- Japan does not recognize the doctrine of strict liability.
- Japan does not allow the use of discovery in order to strengthen and build one's case.
- Losers and winners of a lawsuit must both pay a percentage of the requested damages as well as court fees, and therefore the damage requests are low.
- Japanese court granted awards are small and punitive damages are not available.

Refresh Your Memory

The following exercise will enable you to refresh your memory on the rules and principles presented to you in this chapter. Read each question twice and place your answer in the blanks provided. Review the chapter material for any question you miss or are unable to remember.

1. Strict liability involves _____ not services.

2. It is wise for an entrepreneur to purchase a _____ _____ _____ policy to help minimize or eliminate the costs associated with a product liability lawsuit.

3. When examining a design defect, the court will apply the _____ _____ analysis.

4. Manufacturers as well as sellers of a product have a duty to _____ users about the dangerous propensities associated with a product.

5. The defense of misuse of product requires the defendant to show that the product misuse was _____.

6. In most jurisdictions, a statute of limitations begins to run when the plaintiff suffers an _____.

7. A statute of _____ limits a seller's liability by setting a time frame in terms of years from when the product was originally sold.

8. Contributory negligence by the plaintiff _____ _____ bar recovery.

9. A defense that apportions damages based upon the negligence of each of the parties is known as _____ _____.

10. Liability may attach to a seller if a product is generally known to be dangerous and the seller fails to _____ of this danger.

11. In Japan, cases involving product liability are not awarded _____ damages.

12. Japan does not recognize _____ _____ in cases involving product liability.

13. Automobile manufacturers have a duty to take into account the possibility of a second collision within the automobile. This is known as the _____ doctrine.

14. If a product is materially altered or modified after it leaves the seller's possession, then the defense of _____ _____ would be applicable.

15. If a seller or lessor did not reveal a defect in a product, a plaintiff may bring a cause of action based on _____.

Critical Thought Exercise

Bruce Owens bought a Chevrolet Suburban from General Motors Corp. (GMC). Four years later, Owens crashed into the rear of another car while commuting to work. The speed of Owens' vehicle at the time of the crash was estimated to be less than 35 miles per hour. A properly functioning seatbelt will restrain the driver from impacting the steering wheel and the windshield during a crash at 40 miles per hour. During the crash, the seatbelt that Owens was properly wearing broke away from its anchor, causing Owens to be thrust against the steering wheel and into the windshield. Owens received a fractured skull, broken ribs, and a fractured left ankle. Owens sued GMC, Chevrolet, and the dealership that sold the vehicle to him. Owens claimed in his suit that because the seat belt broke, the defendants were strictly liable for his injuries. Investigation determined that the seatbelt anchor was both inadequate to sustain the forces involved in restraining a person during a crash, and had been installed in a manner that increased the likelihood of failure during a crash.

Are the defendants strictly liable to Owens?

Answer. _____

_____

_____

_____

_____

_____

_____

_____

_____

_____

_____

_____

_____

_____

_____

_____

Practice Quiz

True/False

1. ___ If a person is injured by a defective product, her or she may bring a cause of action for negligence against the negligent party. [p 103]

2. ___ Since most respectable manufacturers, sellers and lessors do not purposefully misrepresent the quality of their products, misrepresentation is not used very often as a basis for a product liability lawsuit. [p 103]

3. ___ Most states have adopted the doctrine of strict liability in tort as a foundation for product liability actions. [p 104]

4. ___ Strict liability, like negligence does require the injured person to prove that the defendant breached his or her duty of care. [p 105]

5. ___ In transactions involving both products and services, strict liability will be determined based upon which element dominates the transaction. [p 105]

6. ___ Not everyone in the chain of distribution of a defective product may be held strictly liable for the injuries caused by the product. [p 106]

7. ___ There must also be privity of contract between the plaintiff and the defendant in a strict liability cause of action. [p 107]

8. ___ Bystanders are also afforded the protection of strict liability. [p 108]

9. ___ A plaintiff may not recover property damage in a strict liability action. [p 108]

10. ___ All of the parties in the chain of distribution of a defective product are liable for any injury caused by the product even though some of the parties are not responsible. [p 106]

11. ___ To recover for strict liability, the injured party must not only show the product was defective but also who caused the product to become defective. [p 107]

12. ___ A defect in manufacture may occur when the manufacturer properly tests a product. [p 107]

13. ___ Cases involving toys designed with removable parts have supported strict liability cases based upon design defects. [p 108]

14. ___ A manufacturer and dealer may be subject to strict liability if there is a failure to design the automobile to protect occupants from foreseeable dangers caused by a second collision. [p 110]

15. ___ Drug manufacturers owe a duty to place their products in containers that are easier for children to open. [p 111]

Multiple Choice:

16. Manufacturers and sellers of inherently dangerous products are under a duty to [p 112]
    a. warn users about the product's dangerous propensities.
    b. warn users about the product's tamperproof packaging.
    c. alter or modify a product in order to absolve themselves of liability.
    d. enforce statute of repose.

17. The failure to bring a cause of action within a certain number of years from the time of injury is based upon complying with [p 114]
    a. the statute of repose.
    b. the correction of a product defect.
    c. the statute of limitations.
    d. reasonable notice.

18. Which of the following best describes a Japanese product liability action? [p 115]
    a. Discovery is often easy.
    b. Court awards are often higher than American product liability awards.
    c. Japan's product liability action mirrors the United States doctrine of strict liability.
    d. Regardless of winning or losing, the claimants must pay a percentage of any kind of damages requested as court fees

19. Under the doctrine of comparative negligence, a plaintiff who is contributorily negligent for his or her injuries is responsible for [p 115]
    a. a small share of the damages.
    b. a proportional share of the damages.
    c. only the property damage that may have resulted.
    d. replacement of part of the product.

20. Punitive damages are usually allowed in a strict liability action if the plaintiff can prove that [p 107]
    a. jurisdictions have judicially or statutorily extended the protection of strict liability to bystanders.
    b. property damage is recoverable in most jurisdictions.
    c. the defendant either intentionally injured him or her or acted with reckless disregard of his or her safety.
    d. sellers and lessors are liable to the ultimate user or consumer.

21. Which of the following would not be considered a defect in manufacture? [p 107]
    a. A failure to properly assemble a product.
    b. A failure to place a product in tamperproof packaging.
    c. A failure to properly test a product.
    d. A failure to adequately check the quality of the product.

22. A manufacturer that makes a defective product and thereafter discovers the defect must [p 114]
    a. notify users and purchasers of the defect and correct the defect.
    b. know and appreciate the risk and voluntarily assume the risk.
    c. file a complaint in accordance with its state's statute of limitations.
    d. prove that the plaintiff has abnormally misused the product.

23. Which doctrine establishes a duty of an automobile manufacturer to design an automobile to account for the possibility of harm from a person's body striking something inside the automobile in case of a car accident? [p 110]
    a. The collision doctrine
    b. The doctrine of res ipsa loquitur
    c. The negligence per se doctrine
    d. The crashworthiness doctrine

24. Who may be able to recover for his or her injuries as a result of a product's defect? [p 107]
    a. Sellers, lessors and manufacturers
    b. Purchasers, lessees, users or bystanders
    c. Anyone who witnesses the defect causing the injuries
    d. All of the above

25. Drug manufacturers owe a duty to [p 111]
    a. place their products on shelves out of a child's reach.
    b. provide nicely packaged containers for their drugs.
    c. properly design easy to swallow pills.
    d. place their products in containers that cannot be opened by children.

Short Answer:

26. The liability of manufacturers, sellers, lessors, and others for injuries caused by a defective product is known as _____ _____. [p 103]

27. The defense of _____ _____ bars an injured plaintiff from recovering from the defendant in a negligence action. [p 115]

28. A plaintiff who is contibutorily negligent for his or her injuries is responsible for a _____ _____ of the damages under the doctrine of comparative negligence. [p 115]

29. The doctrine of _____ _____ in tort is a basis for product liability actions. [p 105]

30. When a manufacturer fails to adequately check the quality of the product, this is considered to be a defect in _____. [p 107]

31. The gravity of the danger posed by a product's design weighed against the utility of the product is an evaluation referred to as a _____-_____ analysis. [p 108]

32. If an automobile manufacturer fails to design an automobile to protect the passengers from foreseeable dangers caused by a second collision, the _____ and the _____ are subjected to a lawsuit based on strict liability. [p 110]

33. If a manufacturer of Get Well Quick drugs places its tablets into bottles that a child could easily twist the cap off of, it may have breached the duty to provide _____ _____ for its products. [p 111]

34. If Peter leases a boat and the front end is too weighted from the materials used to construct it thereby causing it to sink its first time in the water, Peter may utilize _____ _____ laws in order to recover for the design defect. [p 105]

35. A _____ and _____ warning placed on the product protects those in the chain of distribution from strict liability. [p 112]

36. If a computer manufacturer fails to place instructions on how to put together its brand of computer, and a buyer gets injured from overloading the system due to an improperly installed plug, the consumer may claim that the product defect was the manufacturer's _____ to _____ _____ _____. [p 113]

37. What is the defense that acknowledges that certain products are inherently dangerous and are known to the general population to be so? [p 113] _____ _____ _____.

38. An abnormally misused product will _____ the seller of product liability if the use was _____. [p 114]

39. A limitation of a seller's liability to a certain number of years from the date when the product was first sold is known as a _____ of _____. [p 114]

40. If a bicycle manufacturer discovers that the front tire is not properly mounted or installed due to a bolt that is improperly made, it must _____ the purchasers and _____ of the defect and _____ the defect. [p 114]

41. Manufacturers, distributors, wholesalers, retailers, lessors and subcomponent manufacturers are referred to as the _____ of _____. [p 106]

42. A _____ _____ absolves all prior sellers in the chain of distribution from strict liability. [p 113]

43. Japan has not adopted the United States doctrine of _____ _____. [p 115]

44. Michael Lemmone is a car salesperson sold a new sport utility vehicle to Suzy Victim. He failed to tell Suzy about the vehicle being in a lot car accident that caused substantial damage to the rear axle and to the transmission. Suzy bought the vehicle relying upon Michael's statement that the vehicle she was buying was in perfect condition. She drove it home on the freeway and the transmission fell out causing Suzy to crash into a ditch on the side of the road. What cause of action may Suzy bring against Michael Lemmone? [p 103]

_____

45. Paul is a worker on an assembly line for a treadmill manufacturer where he is responsible for putting the safety handrails on each machine. The demand for the treadmills has been high and as such, the production line speed has increased dramatically. Paul becomes sloppy trying to keep up with the speed of production and fails to tighten down the safety rail on a machine that Fanny Fitness purchases. Fanny injures herself after losing her balance on the treadmill when the safety handrail detached itself from the machine. What duty has Paul breached? The duty to _____ the _____ carefully. [p 103]

46. Roger is in a hurry to leave the sewing machine factory where he works and has one more sewing machine to place the bobbin holder in. Since he is unable to find the small type of screw he usually uses, he opts to use a different, less efficient screw to put the bobbin holder in. When Patti purchases the machine and begins to sew, the screw from the bobbin holder pops out and hits Patti in the eye. What type of defect may Patti claim exists in her products liability action? [p 113]

_____

_____

47. If Marie does not bring a cause of action within the statute of limitations provided by her state, this will _____ the defendant of _____. [p 114]

48. Plaintiffs may allege _____ product _____ in one lawsuit for strict liability. [p 107]

49. Strict liability applies only to _____, not _____. [p 105]

50. Strict liability does not require the injured person prove that the defendant _____ a _____ of _____. [p 105]

Answers to Refresh Your Memory

1. products [p 105]
2. product liability insurance [p 107]

3.   risk-utility [p 108]
4.   warn [p 112]
5.   unforseeable [p 114]
6.   injury [p 114]
7.   repose [p 114]
8.   will not [p 115]
9.   comparative [p 115]
10.   warn [p 113]
11.   punitive [p 116]
12.   product liability [p 116]
13.   crashworthiness [p 110]
14.   supervening event [p 113]
15.   misrepresentation [p 103]

Critical Thought Exercise Model Answer

In order to establish strict liability, Owens must establish the following requirements:
(1) *The defendant must sell the product in a defective condition.* The anchor was unable to perform as intended because it was poorly designed and was also installed incorrectly. Either reason makes the product defective. (2) *The defendant was in the business of selling this product.* GMC, Chevrolet, and the dealership are all in the business of selling Suburbans. (3) *The product must be unreasonably dangerous to the user because of its defect.* A vehicle without a safely functioning seatbelt that can properly restrain a passenger during a crash is very dangerous. There is no valid reason for a manufacturer not to install a working seatbelt. (4) *The plaintiff must incur physical injury.* Owens was severely injured. (5) *The defective condition must be the proximate cause of the injury.* We know that Owens was propelled into the steering wheel and windshield because the seatbelt did not restrain him. The speed of the crash was within limits where the seatbelt should have worked properly. (6) *The goods must not have substantially changed from the time of sale to the time of injury.* There are no facts showing any modification to the seatbelt while owned by Owens.

All of the elements needed to establish strict liability for the defective product are present. When a product is defective, as in this case, all defendants in the chain of distribution, from the manufacturer, to the distributor, to the dealer, have joint and several liability for the injury to plaintiff. Owens may recover against all the defendants in this case.

Answers to Practice Quiz

True/False

1.   True   A successful plaintiff will have proved that the defendant breached a duty of due care to the plaintiff that caused the plaintiff's injuries. Examples of a failure to exercise due care include negligent inspection or testing of the product, negligent packaging, failure to warn of the product's dangerous propensities, negligent product design, and a failure to assemble the product carefully.
2.   True   Most manufacturers, lessors or sellers have integrity when they sell their products, and as such do not misrepresent the quality of their products thereby minimizing the use of fraud as a means of recovery for a product liability action.
3.   True   Use of strict liability as a basis for product liability actions has eliminated many of the difficulties associated with the other causes of action of products liability.
4.   False   Strict liability is imposed regardless of fault.

5. True   The court will determine whether the goods or the services were the main basis of the transaction.

6. False   All who are in the chain of distribution are strictly liable. Public policy encourages sellers and lessors to insure against the risk of a strict liability lawsuit.

7. False   Privity of contract is not required between the plaintiff and defendant because strict liability is a tort defense.

8. True   Bystanders are afforded protection in strict liability cases in most state statutes.

9. False   Property damage may be recovered in a majority of jurisdictions.

10. True   Strict liability is imposed irrespective of fault and as such applies to sellers and lessors who are in the business of selling and leasing products.

11. False   The injured party must show that the product was defective, however, he or she need not prove who caused the product to become defective.

12. False   A defect in manufacturer occurs when the manufacturer fails to properly test a product not when the manufacturer properly tests a product.

13. True   Removable parts of toys that could be swallowed by children are among the various types of design defects that have supported strict liability cases.

14. True   The fact that both the manufacturer as well as dealer are in the chain of distribution supports the liability surrounding a design defect under the crashworthiness doctrine.

15. False   Drug manufacturers owe a duty to place their products in containers that cannot be opened by children. These manufacturers are also under a duty to provide packages that are tamperproof or indicative of having been tampered with.

Multiple Choice

16. A   Answer A is correct as certain products are dangerous by their very nature and cannot be made safer and still be useful for which they are designed. Answer B is incorrect, as it makes no sense to warn a user about the product's tamperproof packaging. Answer C is incorrect as it violates public policy to encourage manufacturers to produce safe products and take responsibility for their actions. Answer D is incorrect as manufacturers and sellers are not in a position to enforce any statute, and the statute of repose involves the period of time one may have in bringing a strict liability lawsuit based pm the date of the products purchase, which has no bearing on the sellers or manufacturers duty.

17. C   Answer C is correct as the statute of limitations involves the time frame in which a party may bring a cause of action for an injury from a defective product. Answer A is incorrect as the statute of repose limits the seller's liability to a set number of years from the date that a product was first sold. Answer B is incorrect because even though the correction of a product's defect may prevent an injured individual from brining a lawsuit, this fact alone has nothing to do with refraining from bringing a cause of action within a certain period of time. Answer D is incorrect, as it makes no sense.

18. D   Answer D is correct, as it is a true statement. Answer A is incorrect, as the Japanese courts do not allow discovery thereby making it difficult to prove a product was defective. Answer B is incorrect as the Japanese court awards are small and punitive damages are not available. Answer C is incorrect as Japan is almost immune from product liability claims and the entire legal procedure of the United States is opposite that of Japan's.

19. B   Answer B is correct, as the principle behind comparative negligence is to apportion damages between the plaintiff and the defendant. Answer A is incorrect as this is presuming that the plaintiff's negligence was proportionately less than that of the defendant and that the damages would be reduced only slightly. Answer C is incorrect, as the plaintiff's liability under a comparative negligence statute would include other damages besides property damage as a result of the plaintiff's negligence. Answer D is incorrect as once again, it is under the assumption that the plaintiff's negligence was as a result of failing to replace a part of the product.

20. C   Answer C is correct punitive damages are designed to punish those who acted maliciously or with a wanton or reckless disregard for the plaintiff. Answer A is incorrect, as judicial and statutory extensions of protection have no correlation to when punitive damages are allowed. Answer B is incorrect as property damage is not the basis of punitive damages. Answer D is incorrect because punitive damages may be assessed if malice is shown. However, proving a seller or lessor's liability to an ultimate user or consumer is not equivalent to a wanton or reckless disregard for a plaintiff.

21. B   Answer B is correct as it describes a defect in packaging as opposed to a defect in manufacture. Answers A, C, and D are incorrect as all state defects in manufacture.

22. A   Answer A is correct as it reiterates what the law requires with regard to notifying consumers and users of defects discovered by the manufacturer. Answer B is incorrect has the explanation for the defense of assumption of the risk does not apply to the duties placed on a manufacturer upon discovery of a defective product it has produced. Answer C is incorrect, as the filing of a complaint by a manufacturer who discovered a defect in one of its products is not required to file a complaint as a result of its discovery. Answer D is incorrect as abnormal misuse is a potential defense in a products liability lawsuit, not a requirement of proof upon discovery of a manufacturing defect by the manufacturer.

23. D   Answer D is correct as the crashworthiness doctrine, which is also referred to as the second collision requires manufacturers to design automobiles with the possibility of a second collision. Answer A is incorrect as being crashworthy and the concept of collision by itself are not synonymous. Answer B is incorrect as res ipsa loquitur means 'the thing speaks for itself" and is helpful in establishing negligence in a variety of cases of which the duty to design an automobile taking into account the possibility of harm are contradictory to one another. Answer C is incorrect as negligence per se is also a special negligence doctrine that has its basis in statutory law that is designed to protect a described class of people against a specific type of act.

24. B   Answer B is correct as purchasers, lessees, users and bystanders are those who are protected under product liability law. Answer A is incorrect as sellers, lessors and manufacturers are in the chain of distribution of a product that makes them prone to liability for injuries resulting from a defective product. Answer C is incorrect as witnessing is not the same concept as being injured as a bystander and would therefore not be able to recover based on mere observation of the defect causing injuries. Answer D is incorrect for the reasons given above.

25. D   Answer D is correct as the drug manufacturer has a duty to package their products in tamperproof packaging. Answer A is incorrect, as even though this may be a cautionary measure on the manufacturer's part, it is not a duty that if breached would give rise to a cause of action based on product liability. Answer B is incorrect, as the marketing of a manufacturer's drug by use of nicely packaged containers is also not a duty that if reached would give rise to a cause of action based on product liability. Answer C is incorrect, as the manufacturer has no duty to properly design easy to swallow pills.

Short Answer:

26. product liability
27. contributory negligence
28. proportionate share
29. strict liability
30. manufacture
31. risk-utility
32. manufacturer and dealer
33. safe packaging
34. strict liability
35. proper and conspicuous
36. failure to provide adequate instructions

37. generally known dangers
38. relieve, unforseeable
39. statute of repose
40. notify users and correct
41. chain of distribution
42. supervening event
43. strict liability
44. misrepresentation
45. assemble product
46. inadequate selection of component parts
47. relieve liability
48. multiple defects
49. products, services
50. breach of duty of care

Chapter 6
BUSINESS AND
ONLINE CRIMES

Chapter Overview

This chapter gives an insightful presentation of business and online crimes. You will be able to know the difference between a felony and a misdemeanor as well as know how the various crimes are defined and what elements are necessary to establish liability for each. Additionally, the chapter provides a thorough overview of criminal procedure from arrest through trial. The Racketeer Influenced and Corrupt Organization Act (RICO), Foreign Corrupt Practices Act and the safeguards provided in the Fourth, Fifth, Sixth and Eighth amendments to the U.S. Constitution are also examined. Finally the law as it pertains to the computer and Internet crimes is reviewed.

Objectives

Upon completion of this chapter's exercises, you should be able to:
1. Describe the difference between a felony and a misdemeanor.
2. Discuss the elements of a crime.
3. Discuss criminal procedure beginning with the arrest and ending with the trial.
4. Differentiate between crimes against persons and property as well as those involving white-collar crimes and criminal fraud.
5. Be familiar with the Racketeer Influenced and Corrupt Organization Act (RICO), and the Foreign Corrupt Practices Act.
6. Understand the safeguards inherent in the Fourth, Fifth, Sixth and Eighth Amendments to the United States Constitution.
7. Familiarize you with the laws affecting the computer and crimes involving the Internet.

Practical Application

You should be able to identify the different types of crimes, including those involving the computer and the Internet as well as identify the elements necessary to establish liability. Further, you should be able to understand and explain the criminal process beginning with the arrest through to trial. In addition, you should be able to access the application of the safeguards that are afforded under the United States constitution.

Helpful Hints

It is helpful to distinguish between what a felony is versus a misdemeanor. This chapter lends itself toward categorization. It is easier to remember the crimes that are involved if you categorize them based on whether the crimes are against individuals, property or the computer and Internet. In order to remember the aspects of criminal procedure that accompanies the crime itself, it is helpful to draw a horizontal time line listing the various stages of the criminal process. Further, it is important to be aware of the various statutory acts such as Racketeer Influenced and Corrupt Organization Act and the Foreign Corrupt Practices Act.

Study Tips

Background Information
✓ The United States leads the world in terms of humanity and sophistication in the criminal law system.
✓ A person is presumed innocent until proven guilty.
✓ Guilt must be established beyond a reasonable doubt.
✓ The United States Constitution gives the accused certain safeguards.

Crime
A crime is a violation of a duty owed to society that has legal consequences and which requires the individual to make amends to the public.

Sources of Criminal Law
✓ Statutes are the main source
✓ Penal codes – These are detailed, well-defined criminal activities along with punishment for the same if committed.
✓ State and federal regulatory statutes.

Parties to a criminal action
✓ The government is the plaintiff in a criminal action and is represented by an attorney called a prosecutor.
✓ The accused is the defendant and is represented by a defense attorney. The government will provide a free attorney if the defendant is unable to afford representation.

Important facts to know about felonies:
✓ They are the most serious types of crimes.
✓ Crimes that are inherently evil (mala in se) are considered to be felonies.
✓ Crimes such as murder, rape, bribery and embezzlement are felonies in a majority of jurisdictions.
✓ Imprisonment is the usual punishment, however, the death penalty is imposed in some jurisdictions for the crime of first-degree murder.
✓ Federal law requires mandatory sentencing for certain crimes.
✓ Some states require mandatory sentencing for certain crimes.
✓ A number of statutes provide for the degrees of crime and the penalties for each.

Important facts to know about misdemeanors:
✓ They are less serious than felonies.
✓ Crimes that are prohibited by society (mala prohibita) are categorized as a misdemeanor.
✓ Crimes such as burglary, regulatory statute violations, and robbery are examples of misdemeanors.
✓ These types of crimes have punishments that are less severe than felonies.
✓ Punishment includes imprisonment for less than a year and/or a fine.

Violations are neither a felony nor a misdemeanor.
✓ Examples of a violation include jaywalking and traffic violations. A fine is the only punishment allowable unless a jury trial is granted.

Elements of a Crime

Two necessary elements to be shown when proving a person is guilty of a crime:

Criminal Act

- ✓ The defendant must have performed the wrongful act. The performance of the wrongful act is also known as the actus reus.
- ✓ The performing or failure to do a certain act can satisfy this element.
- ✓ A defendant's thought of doing the crime will not satisfy the criminal act element. The wrongful act must have been carried out.
- ✓ An interesting notation is that criminal acts can bring about civil law actions that have their basis in tort.

Criminal Intent

- ✓ The defendant must have the necessary state of mind (specific or general intent) when he/she performed the act. This intent is also referred to as the mens rea.
- ✓ It is important to differentiate between specific and general intent. Specific intent is demonstrated when the accused intentionally or with knowledge or purposefully performs the prohibited act. General intent is proven where there is a lesser amount of culpability.
- ✓ The jury may deduce the type of intent based upon the defendant's actions.
- ✓ There is no crime where there is no mens rea. If the act that was performed was an accident, then mens rea cannot be established.
- ✓ Strict or absolute liability for a prohibited act means that mens rea is not required. A violation of an environmental statute would be an example where absolute liability would be imposed.

Crimes Affecting Business

The most common crimes that affect business are those given below. It is important for you to be aware of the necessary elements of a particular crime in order to prove that it has or has not been committed. When you are given a certain set of facts, it is important to analyze them and determine their applicability to each of the requisite elements of the crime you are trying to prove.

Robbery

- ✓ The taking of personal property of another using fear or force.
- ✓ Note that a pickpocket does not qualify as a robbery as there is no fear or force.

Burglary

- ✓ At common law, burglary was the "breaking and entering a dwelling at night" with the intent to commit a felony therein.
- ✓ Compare the common definition to the modern expansion, which includes daytime thefts of offices and commercial buildings. Further, the breaking element is no longer a requirement in many jurisdictions. If there has been an unauthorized entry through an unlocked door or window, this will be sufficient.

Larceny

- ✓ At common law, larceny was the "wrongful and fraudulent taking of another person's personal property."
- ✓ Personal property includes trade secrets, computer programs, tangible property and other types of business property.
- ✓ Examples of larceny include automobile theft, car stereo theft and pick pocketing.
- ✓ The perpetrator need not use force or go into a building in order to commit this crime.
- ✓ Some jurisdictions categorize the larceny as either grand or petit based upon the value of the goods that were taken.

Theft
✓ In those jurisdictions that do not categorize their crimes in terms of robbery, larceny and burglary, the crimes of this nature are under the heading of theft. These jurisdictions then label the theft as petit or grand depending on the value of the goods taken.

Receiving Stolen Property
✓ If a person knowingly receives stolen property with the intent to deprive its rightful owner of that property, they may be found to have committed the crime of receiving stolen property. The stolen property may be personal property, money, stock certificates or anything tangible.
✓ An important notation is that the element of knowledge may be inferred from the circumstances.

Arson
✓ The crime of Arson at common law was defined as "the malicious or willful burning of the dwelling house of another person."
✓ Modernly, the term dwelling includes all buildings including public, commercial and private ones.

Forgery
✓ This crime involves the fraudulent making or alteration of a written document, which affects the legal liability of another person.
✓ Examples include falsifying public records and counterfeiting as well as imitating another person's signature on a check or altering the amount of the check. Note, that one spouse may sign his or her spouse's check and deposit it into a joint account without it being designated as forgery. There is no intent to defraud in this situation.

Extortion
✓ Extortion involves the obtaining of property of another with or without his or her consent by use of actual or threatened force, violence or fear.
✓ The truth or falsity of the information does not matter.
✓ Examples of extortion include when one person threatens another that a piece of information will be exposed unless money or property is given to the extortionist. This is known as blackmail.
✓ Extortion of public officials is referred to as extortion "under color of official right."

Credit-Card Crimes
✓ Many jurisdictions have made it a crime for the misappropriation and use of another person's credit cards.
✓ Some states prosecute credit-card crimes under their forgery statutes.

Bad Check Legislation
✓ A majority of jurisdictions hold that an individual who knowingly makes, draws, or presents a check for which there are insufficient funds in the individual's account to cover the amount of the check has committed a crime.
✓ Some jurisdictions require that proof of the intent to defraud be shown.

White- Collar Crimes otherwise known as Crimes Usually Committed by Businesspersons
✓ These are usually called white-collar crimes and involve deceit.
✓ Embezzlement, Criminal Fraud, and Bribery are examples of white-collar crimes.

Embezzlement
✓ A statutory crime involving the fraudulent conversion of property by a person to whom another individual's property was entrusted.

✓ Employer's representatives, agents or employees usually commit this crime.
✓ The main element to be aware of is the fact that the property was entrusted to the individual whom ultimately absconded with it.

Criminal Fraud
✓ This crime is known as false pretenses or criminal fraud or deceit as the accused obtains title to the property through trickery.
✓ Included under this crime is the crime of mail and wire fraud. The government will prosecute a suspect if the mail or wires are used to defraud another individual.
✓ It is important to be aware of the Identity Theft and Assumption Deterrence Act of 1998. This act makes it a crime the stealing of another's identity. This crime imposes a penalty of prison sentences from three to twenty-five years. The Federal Trade Commission also appoints a representative to assist in restoring victims credit and expunge the consequences of the imposter.

Bribery
✓ When one individual gives money, property, favors or anything of value to another in exchange for a favor in return, this is known as bribery. This is often referred to as a kickback or a payoff.
✓ Intent is an essential element of this crime.
✓ If the offeree accepts the bribe, he or she is then also guilty of the crime.
✓ The offeror can be guilty of the crime without the offeree accepting the bribe.
✓ The Foreign Corrupt Practices Act of 1977 requires firms to keep accurate records as they pertain to foreign transactions. Additionally, American companies may not bribe a foreign official, political party or candidate in an attempt to influence new business or retention of a continuing business. Knowledge is a key element in making the conduct as described above a crime. Punishment includes fines and imprisonment.

The Racketeer Influenced and Corrupt Organizations Act (RICO)
✓ It is a federal crime to acquire or maintain an interest in or conduct or participate in an "enterprise" through a "pattern" of "racketeering activity."
✓ Examples of racketeering activity include gambling, robbery, arson, deals involving narcotics, bribery, mail fraud, etc.
✓ Punishment includes fines, imprisonment, and forfeiture of any property or business interests that were obtained as a result of the RICO violations.
✓ The government can also seek business reorganization, dissolution, and the dissolution of the defendant's interest in an enterprise as part of civil penalties for RICO violations.

Inchoate crimes
✓ Nonparticipants commit these crimes.
✓ Conspiracy is an inchoate crime, which is defined as two or more individuals who enter into an agreement to commit a crime. An overt act in furtherance of the crime is needed.
✓ Attempt to commit a crime is a crime requiring an act in furtherance but not completion of a crime.
✓ Aiding and abetting the commission of a crime is a crime that occurs when an individual supports, assists or encourages the commission of a crime.

Corporate Criminal Liability
✓ At common law, the courts held that corporations lacked the mens rea needed to commit a crime.
✓ Modernly, corporations are being held criminally liable for the acts of their managers, employees, and agents. Since imprisonment is not feasible, they are being fined or having their franchise or license taken away.
✓ The corporate officers, employees or directors are held personally liable for crimes that they Personally commit regardless if it was done for personal gain or for the corporation. Further,

if a corporate manager fails to appropriately supervise his or her subordinate, the manager may be held criminally liable for the subordinate's criminal activities.

Criminal Procedure

There are several pretrial procedures as well as the trial itself that you need to be familiar with. The pretrial procedure involves the arrest, indictment, arraignment and plea-bargaining.

Arrest
✓ The police must have a warrant based upon probable cause before a person can be arrested. Probable cause has been defined as the existence of objective, articulated facts that would raise in the mind of a reasonable person that a crime has been committed or is about to be committed.
✓ A search without a warrant is allowed when the crime is in progress, those involved in the crime are fleeing from the scene or there is a great chance that the evidence will be destroyed. Probable cause is still required even in the absence of a warrant.
✓ After the accused is arrested, a booking take place. The booking involves the recording of the arrest as well as the standard fingerprinting.

Indictment or Information
✓ The indictment or information involves the formal charges that must be brought against the accused before being brought to trial,
✓ The government evaluates those charged with serious crimes. If there is enough evidence to hold the accused for trial, an indictment is then issued and the accused is held for trial.
✓ For crimes with a lesser magnitude, a judge will determine if there is sufficient evidence to hold the accused for trial. An information is issued upon confirmation that the evidence is sufficient and the accused is then held over for trial.

Arraignment
✓ Once an information or indictment is issued, the accused is informed of the charges against her or him and is requested to enter a plea.
✓ The accused may enter a guilty, not guilty or nolo contendere plea. If the latter is chosen, the accused does not admit guilt, but agrees to a penalty. Nolo contendere pleas may not be used later on in a civil proceeding. Acceptance of the nolo contendere pleading is optional.

Plea Bargaining
✓ This involves an agreement between the government and the accused whereby the accused admits to a lesser offense in exchange for the government's imposition of a lesser penalty.
✓ The rationale behind plea bargaining is to minimize overcrowding of prisons, avoid trial risks, and to save costs associated with trial.

The Criminal Trial
✓ All jurors must agree unanimously before the accused is found guilty.
✓ The defendant may appeal if he or she is found to be guilty.
✓ Even if one juror disagrees, the accused will not be found guilty.
✓ If the defendant is innocent, the government can not appeal.
✓ If a unanimous decision does not come to fruition, the jury will be hung in terms of what they decided. The government then has the option of retrying the case before a new jury or judge.

Constitutional Safeguards
✓ The **Fourth Amendment** plays an important role in protecting corporations and persons from

unreasonable searches and seizures by the government. "It permits people to be secure in their person, houses, papers and effects." Note that regulated businesses as well as those who are involved in hazardous industries are subject to warrantless searches.

Searches may not go beyond the area specified in the warrant. If evidence is obtained as a result of an unreasonable search or seizure, it will be considered tainted. This evidence may not be used against the accused, but can be used against other individuals.

The "good faith" exception to the exclusionary rule states that illegally obtained evidence may be used against the accused if the police officers that obtained the evidence believed in good faith that they were acting in accordance with a lawful search warrant.

✓ The **Fifth Amendment** states "no person shall be compelled in any criminal case to be a witness against himself."

The *privilege against self-incrimination* is applicable to individuals, not corporations and partnerships. Be aware though that private papers such as personal diaries of businesspersons are protected from disclosure.

✓ **Immunity from Prosecution**
The government consents to not use any evidence given by an individual against that person. Immunity is usually granted when the government wants information from an individual who has asserted his or her Fifth Amendment privilege against self-incrimination. If immunity is granted, the individual loses his or her Fifth Amendment protection.

✓ Fifth Amendment Protection Against **Double Jeopardy**
The Fifth Amendment via its double jeopardy clause states a person may not be tried twice for the same crime. Compare this to where the accused has committed several crimes. The accused may be tried for each of the crimes without being in violation of the double jeopardy rule. Also, if the acts are violations in different jurisdictions, each jurisdiction may try the accused.

The *attorney-client privilege* is provided for in the Fifth Amendment. The Fifth Amendment also recognizes the psychiatrist/psychologist-patient privilege, priest/minister/rabi-penitent privilege, spouse-spouse privilege and parent-child privilege.
✓ Sixth Amendment Right to a **Public Jury Trial**
The Sixth Amendment gives the accused the right to be tried by an impartial jury, to cross-examine witnesses against the accused, to have a lawyer's assistance and to have a speedy trial.

✓ Eighth Amendment Protection against **Cruel and Unusual Punishment**
This amendment protects the accused from abusive or torturous punishments.

✓ **Accountant-Client Privilege**
Many states have enacted statutes that have created an accountant-client privilege. This law states that an accountant may not be called as a witness against a client. Note that there is no federal law that provides for the accountant-client privilege.

Federal Antiterrorism Act of 2001
✓ Congress enacted this act to help the government in prevention and detection of terrorist activities and with the investigation and prosecution of terrorists.

✓ Special Intelligence Court – This part of the act provides authorization for the issuance of expanded wiretap orders and subpoenas.

✓ Nationwide Search Warrant- Instead of using the traditional warrant that specified certain areas that a search warrant was good for, the act now provides for a nationwide search warrant to gather evidence of terrorist activities.

✓ Roving Wiretaps- Any person suspected of involvement in terrorism may have a roving wiretap placed on the use of multiple telephones, including cellular phones in order to monitor their activities. Former law required separate permission for each telephone that was used.

✓ Sharing Information – Evidence that is obtained by the multiple government agencies such as the Federal Bureau of Investigation, Central Intelligence Agency, etc. may share with one another. Prior law restricted what information was being shared.

✓ Detention of Non-citizens – A nonresident of the United States may be detained for up to seven days if he or she is suspected of terrorist activities. If an individual is a threat to national security, he or she may be held for up to six months. Nonresidents who raise revenue to support terrorist activities and organizations may be deported.

✓ Bio terrorism Provision – Biological or chemical weapons may only be used for peaceful purposes. Possession for any other use is illegal.

✓ Anti-Money Laundering Provision – This aspect provides for the discovery, tracing and impounding of bank accounts that are being used to fund terrorist activities. The banks are required to divulge information regarding sources of large overseas bank accounts. Failure to do so will result in sanctions or forfeiture of the banks' licenses to do business.

Refresh Your Memory

The following exercise will enable you to refresh your memory on the rules and principles presented to you in this chapter. Read each question twice and place your answer in the blanks provided. Review the chapter material for any question you miss or are unable to remember.

1. A _____ is defined as any act done by an individual in violation of those duties that he or she owes to society and for the breach of which the law provides that the wrongdoer shall make amends to the public.

2. The government is represented by an attorney called the _____ in a criminal lawsuit.

3. _____ are the most serious kinds of crimes.

4. Felonies are usually punishable by _____.

5. _____ are crimes that are less serious than felonies.

6. The two elements that must be shown for a person to be found guilty of most crimes are criminal _____ and criminal _____.

7. When the police obtain an arrest warrant, it usually must be based upon _____ _____.

8. Accused persons must be _____ charged with a crime before they can be brought to trial.

9. If a grand jury determines that there is enough evidence to hold the accused for trial, it will issue an _____.

10. At a criminal trial, all jurors must _____ agree before the accused is found _____ of the crime charged.

11. _____is defined as the taking of personal property from another person by the use of fear or force.

12. The wrongful and fraudulent taking of another person's personal property is the definition for the crime of _____.

13. A criminal _____ happens when two or more persons enter into an agreement to commit a crime.

14. The Fourth Amendment protects the rights of the people from _____ _____ and seizure by the _____.

15. The _____ _____ clause of the Fifth Amendment protects persons from being tried twice for the same crime.

16. The Sixth Amendment provides the right to a _____ _____ trial.

17. The _____ Amendment protects against cruel and unusual punishment.

18. The _____ _____ _____ of 2001 assists the government in detecting and preventing terrorist activities and prosecuting businesses.

19. A plea of ____ _____means that the accused agrees to the imposition of a penalty but does not admit guilt.

20. Crimes that involve cunning and deceit and that are prone to be committed by businesspersons are referred to as _____ _____ crimes.

Critical Thought Exercise

Build-Rite Construction Company of Santa Maria, Jamaica receives a copy of an invoice for $160,000 of supplies from Hayward Lumber. Tom Cheat, owner of Build-Rite, notices that the invoice states that the company name is Build-Right Contractors and gives the company office address as Santa Maria, California. The invoice contains three different account numbers that Cheat discovers are all assigned to Build-Right. Cheat pays the invoice but does nothing to correct the account numbers.

During the next 14 months, Cheat has his employees order over $800,000 worth of materials from Hayward Lumber via the Internet, using the account numbers assigned to the California company. When the bills come due each month, Build-Right pays for the materials sent to Build-Rite, thinking that they have been shipped to one of their own construction sites. Cheat builds over 200 luxury vacation homes in Jamaica and has the funds from the sale of the homes send to his accounts in the Bahamas, where his brother runs a one-person bank. The credit of Build-Right is ruined when they discover the misuse of their account numbers and refuse to pay the balance of over $300,000 charged to their accounts. Several banks pull their funding of Build-Right projects and equipment is seized. Build-Right has to temporarily lay off 180 employees.

What crime, if any, has been committed by Tom Cheat or his company? Who may be prosecuted? What law will apply? What steps should Build-Right take to help it recover financially and prevent this from happening again in the future?

Answer. _____

_____

_____

_____

_____

_____

_____

_____

_____

_____

_____

_____

_____

_____

_____

_____

_____

_____

_____

_____

_____

_____

_____

_____

Practice Quiz

True/False:

1. ___ In a criminal lawsuit, the government is the plaintiff. [p 122]

2. ___ The actual performance of the criminal act is called the actus reus. [p 123]

3. ___ General intent is where there is a showing of a lesser degree of mental culpability or recklessness. [p 123]

4. ___ To be found guilty of a crime, the state of mind of the accused when the act was committed is irrelevant. [p 123]

5. ___ The charge of having committed a crime based on the judgment of the jury is known as an indictment. [p 125]

6. ___ If the defendant is not found guilty, he or she may appeal. [p 126]

7. ____ Larceny is defined as the forceful and fraudulent taking of another person's personal property. [p 127]

8. ____ A number of states have made laws that make the misappropriation and use of another person's credit cards a crime. [p 128]

9. ____ The crime of commercial bribery encourages the payment of bribes to private persons and businesses. [p 130]

10. ____ The fraudulent conversion of property by a person to whom the property was entrusted is known as embezzlement. [p 129]

11. ____ Individuals who provide assistance after the crime has been committed cannot be charged with aiding and abetting the commission of a crime. [p 134]

12. ____ Under the exclusionary rule, evidence that is tainted cannot be prohibited from introduction at a trial or administrative proceeding against the person searched. [p 136]

13. ____ Any confessions or statements obtained from a suspect before he or she is read his or her Miranda rights may be excluded from evidence at trial. [p 140]

14. ____ When a suspect is offered immunity from prosecution, the government agrees to use the evidence given by a person granted immunity against that person. [p 141]

15. ____ If the same criminal act violates the laws of two or more jurisdictions, each jurisdiction may try the accused. [p 142]

16. ____ One of the guarantees provided for in the Sixth Amendment is the right to confront the witnesses against the accused. [p 142]

17. ____ The Eighth Amendment prohibits capital punishment. [p 142]

18. ____ An attempt to commit a crime is not a crime by itself. [p 134]

19. ____ Protection against self-incrimination applies only to natural persons who are accused of crimes. [p 140]

20. ____ When a magistrate finds that there is enough evidence to hold the accused for trial, he or she will issue an indictment. [p 125]

21. ____ Corporate directors, officers and employees can be held individually liable for crimes that they personally commit, whether for personal benefit or on behalf of the corporation. [p 135]

22. ____ The government may deny immunity from prosecution if a suspect asserts his or her Fifth Amendment privilege against self-incrimination. [p 141]

23. ____ Under modern law, arson includes the burning of all types of private, commercial and public buildings. [p 128]

24. ____ Misdemeanors are crimes that are mala in se because of their inherently evil nature. [p 123]

25. ___ The crime of forgery has been committed if one spouse signs the other spouse's payroll check for deposit in a savings account or joint checking account at the bank. [p 128]

Multiple Choice:

26. What type of crimes are traffic violations and jaywalking? [p 123]
    a. Violations
    b. Felonies
    c. Misdemeanors
    d. Trespass

27. A magistrate who finds there is enough evidence to hold the accused for trial of a lesser crime will issue an [p 125]
    a. information.
    b. indictment.
    c. injunction.
    d. intentional tort.

28. Knowingly participating in a financial transaction involving the proceeds of some form of specified unlawful activity is a violation of which act? [p 126]
    a. Identity Theft and Assumption Deterrence Act of 1998
    b. The Racketeer Influenced and Corrupt Organization Act
    c. Money Laundering Control Act
    d. Civil False Claims Act

29. Warrantless searches are allowed only when [p 136]
    a. they are incident to an arrest.
    b. where evidence is in "plain view."
    c. where it is likely that evidence will be destroyed.
    d. all of the above.

30. Which crime means to obtain property from another, with or without his or her consent induced by actual or threatened force, violence or fear? [p 128]
    a. Forgery
    b. Extortion
    c. Receiving stolen property
    d. Larceny

31. If Samantha obtains title to June's car through deception or trickery, which crime has she committed? [p 129]
    a. Embezzlement
    b. Mail fraud
    c. False pretenses
    d. Misrepresentation

32. If Bob Builder writes a large check to Ivan, a building inspector in an effort to get Ivan to ignore exposed asbestos, a building code violation, which crime has Bob Builder committed? [p 130]
    a. Violation of the exclusionary rule
    b. Credit card fraud
    c. Criminal fraud
    d. Bribery

33. In order to be liable for the crime of criminal conspiracy, what must take place? [p 133]
    a. The harboring of one of the criminals after he or she committed the crime.
    b. An overt act in furtherance of the agreed upon crime.
    c. A wrongful and fraudulent taking of another person's personal property.
    d. Intent to permanently deprive another person of his or her personal property.

34. The Foreign Corrupt Practices Act was designed to [p 131]
    a. prevent American companies from engaging in the bribery of foreign government officials in order to obtain profitable contracts.
    b. make it a federal crime to acquire or maintain an interest in the affairs of an "enterprise" through a pattern of racketeering activity.
    c. prevent the aiding and abetting the commission of a crime.
    d. go after entities and persons involved in illegal check-cashing schemes, bribery, and insurance fraud.

35. Which amendment guarantees the right of the accused to be tried by an impartial jury of the state or district in which the accused crime was committed as well as to be able to cross-examine the witnesses against the accused, to have an attorney's assistance and to have a speedy trial? [p 142]
    a. The Fifth Amendment
    b. The Fourth Amendment
    c. The Sixth Amendment
    d. The Eighth Amendment

Short Answer:

36. What is the usual punishment for felonies that are committed? [p 122] _____
    _____

37. What are the two elements that must be proven for a person to be found guilty of most crimes? [p 123] _____

38. Why would a person injured by a criminal act not sue the criminal to recover civil damages? [p 124] _____

39. Who usually evaluates the evidence of serious crimes? [p 125] _____

40. Please tell what it means when the government grants a suspect immunity from prosecution. [p 141] _____
    _____

41. What is the definition for the crime of robbery? [p 127] _____
    _____

42. What is required for the crime of receiving stolen property? [p 127] _____
    _____

43. Mr. Sly convinces Suzy Sweet to withdraw all of her money and invest in his water well that he claims to bottle as the water of youth. He has Suzy believe that her investment will triple in a month. Mr. Sly takes her money and flees the country to live in Barbados. What crime has Mr. Sly committed? [p 129] _____

44. What does the Fourth Amendment protect persons and corporations from? [p 136] _____
_____

45. How may an accused be prosecuted twice or more without violating the double jeopardy clause of the Fifth Amendment? [p 142] _____
_____

46. What is required under the bad check legislation to make it a crime? [p 128] _____
_____

47. What is extortion of a private person referred to as? [p 128] _____

48. What is a conspiracy? [p 133] _____
_____

49. What is the good faith exception to the exclusionary rule? [p 136] _____
_____
_____

50. What is the attorney-client privilege? [p 141] _____
_____

Answers to Refresh Your Memory

1. crime [p 122]
2. prosecutor [p 122]
3. felonies [p 122]
4. imprisonment [p 122]
5. misdemeanor [p 123]
6. act, intent [p 123]
7. probable cause [p 124]
8. formally [p 125]
9. indictment [p 125]
10. unanimous, guilty [p 126]
11. robbery [p 127]
12. larceny [p 127]
13. conspiracy [p 133]
14. unreasonable search, government [p 136]
15. double jeopardy [p 142]
16. public jury [p 142]
17. Sixth [p 142]
18. Federal Antiterrorism Act of 2001 [p 143]
19. nolo contendere [p 125]
20. white collar [p 129]

Critical Thought Model Answer

Obtaining title to property through deception or trickery constitutes the crime of theft by false pretenses. This crime is commonly referred to as fraud. When the fraud is accomplished by the use of mails or wires, a federal offense has taken place. Because Cheat assumed the identity of Build-Right, the offense of identity theft may have been committed. The use of new technology, especially computers and the Internet make this offense hard to prevent and extremely damaging to the victim. To combat such fraud, Congress passed the Identity Theft and Assumption Deterrence Act of 1998. Identity theft is a federal felony punishable by a sentence of up to 25 years. The act also appoints the Federal Trade Commission to help victims restore their credit and erase the impact of the imposter.

Cheat may be both criminally and civilly liable under the Racketeer Influenced and Corrupt Organization Act (RICO). RICO makes it a federal crime to acquire or maintain an interest in, use income from, or conduct or participate in the affairs of a criminal enterprise through a pattern of racketeering activity. The commission of two or more enumerated crimes within a ten-year period establishes the pattern of activity. The enterprise can be a corporation, partnership, sole proprietorship, business, or organization. The Build-Rite construction company suffices as a criminal enterprise. The use of the Internet previously created a problem if wires were not used for transmission of the fraudulent communication. The statutes concerning wire fraud have been amended to include Internet activity within the definition of wire fraud. If the profits from the building of the condominiums had been invested in or maintained by Build-Rite, the assets would have been subject to forfeiture.

Unfortunately, the funds have been transferred to a bank in the Bahamas. The Bahamas have joined the Cayman Islands as a location where the bank secrecy laws protect the identity and amount of account deposits. The assets of Build-Rite are subject to forfeiture as are the proceeds sent to the Bahamas. Cheat is liable for multiple criminal offenses, if he can be apprehended. The employees of Build-Rite will incur criminal liability only if they knew that the account numbers were being misused. To remedy the situation, Build-Right should create a secure electronic signature for all account transactions. They can insist that all orders over a certain amount be confirmed by a separate e-mail with a password. The FTC should be consulted for advice and help in getting equipment released and credit with the banks restored.

Answers to Practice Quiz

True/False:

1. True — In a criminal lawsuit, there is not a private party. Instead the government is the plaintiff.
2. True — Actus reus means guilty act, which references the criminal nature of the act.
3. True — General intent is less than that of specific intent where an accused purposefully and intentionally or with knowledge commits a prohibited act. General intent indicates a degree of recklessness.
4. False — There is no crime if the requisite state of mind cannot be proven.
5. True — If the grand jury finds that there is enough evidence to hold the accused for trial, it will issue an indictment.
6. False — If the defendant is found not guilty, he or she would be innocent and have no need for an appeal.
7. False — Larceny is the wrongful and fraudulent taking of another person's personal property. Larceny does not have the element of force in its definition whereas robbery does require force.
8. True — Statutes have been acted to protect against the misappropriation and use of another person's credit cards.

9. False   The crime of commercial bribery prohibits, not encourages the payment of bribes to private persons and businesses.
10. True   Embezzlement is most commonly committed by an employer's employees, agents or representatives, thus to people whom property is entrusted. The embezzlement occurs when the entrusted individual(s) convert the property.
11. False   Individuals who assist, support, or encourage the commission of a crime, albeit before or after the crime has been committed may be found to have aided and abetted the commission of that crime.
12. False   Tainted evidence can be prohibited from introduction at a trial or administrative hearing if it is against the accused, however, this tainted evidence may be used against other individuals.
13. True   The Supreme Court requires that the Miranda rights be read to a criminal suspect before he or she is interrogated. The Fifth Amendment privilege against self-incrimination cannot be utilized unless a suspect is aware of this right.
14. False   When the government grants an individual immunity from prosecution, this means that the government agrees not to use any evidence given by a person granted immunity against that person.
15. True   If the laws of two or more jurisdictions are violated by the same act, each jurisdiction may try the accused.
16. True   The Sixth Amendment guarantees criminal defendants the right to cross-examine and confront witnesses against the accused.
17. False   The Eighth Amendment protects against cruel and unusual punishment but does not prohibit capital punishment.
18. False   The fact that the crime was not completed does not lessen the fact that an attempt or furtherance of the crime itself is a crime.
19. True   Artificial persons such as corporations may not assert the protection against self-incrimination, as it applies only to natural persons who are accused of crimes.
20. False   A grand jury determines if there is enough evidence and issues an indictment whereas a magistrate (a judge) will determine if there is sufficient evidence to hold the accused for trial of usually lesser crimes. Thereafter the magistrate will issue an information.
21. True   Even though the common law held that corporations did not have the criminal mind to be held criminally liable, modern courts have expanded a corporation's criminal liability for acts of their employees, agents and managers. Additionally the employees, agents, and managers can be held individually liable for crimes they personally commit.
22. False   The government may offer immunity from prosecution in cases where the suspect has asserted his or her Fifth Amendment privilege against self-incrimination. The policy behind this offer is for the government to obtain information that will lead to the prosecution of other more important criminal suspects.
23. True   At common law, the definition of arson was the malicious or willful burning of the dwelling of another person. Under the modern definition, all types of private, commercial and public buildings are included.
24. False   Misdemeanors are mala prohibita because they are not inherently evil but are prohibited by society, unlike felonies, which are mala in se because of their inherently evil nature.
25. False   Though forgery happens if a written document is fraudulently made or altered, one spouse signing another spouse's payroll for deposit into a joint savings or checking account is not forgery.

Multiple Choice:

26. A. Answer A is correct, as jaywalking and traffic violations are neither misdemeanors nor are they felonies. Answer B is incorrect as felonies are the most serious crimes of which jaywalking

and traffic violations are not included. Answer C is incorrect as misdemeanors are less serious than felonies, but, more serious than jaywalking or traffic violations. Answer D is incorrect as trespass is an intentional tort that has nothing to do with jaywalking or traffic violations.

27. A. Answer A is correct as a magistrate (judge) decides whether there is sufficient evidence to hold the accused for trial of a lesser crime and will then issue an information. Answer B is incorrect as the grand jury issues an indictment if they decide there is sufficient evidence to hold the accused for trial of a serious crime. Answer C is incorrect as an injunction is an equitable remedy that has nothing to do with the finding of evidence to hold an accused for trial. Answer D is incorrect, as a magistrate cannot issue an intentional tort or wrong. Further, torts are civil in nature and the issuance of an indictment or an information are both criminal in nature.

28. C. Answer C is correct as per the federal Money Laundering Control Act wherein narcotics activities and almost every white-collar crime are considered unlawful under this act. Answer A is incorrect as this act criminalizes identity fraud. Answer B is incorrect as this Act provides for making the participation in or maintenance of an interest, use of income or conducting affairs in a "pattern" of racketeering activity a federal crime. Answer D is incorrect as it protects against corrupt government contractors and their employees who defraud the government.

29. D. Answer D is correct as answers A, B, and C all state when warrantless searches are allowed.

30. B. Answer B is correct as extortion involves the procurement of another's property with or without their consent, induced by an improper use of actual or threatened force, fear or violence. Answer A is incorrect as forgery involves the fraudulent making or altering of a written document that alters the legal liability of another person. Answer C is incorrect as receiving stolen property is where an individual knowingly receives stolen property and intends to deprive the rightful owner of that property. Answer D is incorrect as larceny is the intentional taking and carrying away of the personal property of another without consent or legal privilege. Notice that with the crime of larceny there is no force as there can be with the crime of extortion.

31. C. Answer C is correct as false pretenses involves obtaining title to property through deception or trickery. Answer A is incorrect as embezzlement is the fraudulent conversion of property by a person to whom the property is entrusted. Answer B is incorrect as the facts do not indicate that the mail was used to defraud June. Answer D is incorrect because even though misrepresentation has an element of deceit to its cause of action, this is a tort and further, title to property is not always the result of the misrepresentation.

32. D. Answer D is correct as bribery is defined as one person giving money, property, favors or anything else of value to another for a favor in return. In this example, Bob gave Ivan a check in exchange for Ivan's non-compliance with the building code. Answer A is incorrect as the exclusionary rule pertains to tainted evidence that is inadmissible. Answer B is incorrect as credit card fraud entails the misappropriation and use of some one else's credit cards. The question has nothing to do with credit cards. Answer C is incorrect, as criminal fraud involves obtaining title to property through deception or trickery.

33. B. Answer B is correct as conspiracy is defined as two or more persons entering into an agreement for an unlawful purpose, of which an overt act must be taken in furtherance of the crime. Answer A is incorrect as this refers to aiding and abetting, of which the harboring of one of the criminals after the crime was committed would be an accessory after the fact. Answers C and D are incorrect as both refer to the crime of larceny.

34. A. Answer A is correct as American companies bribed foreign officials or procure profitable contracts. Thereafter, Congress enacted the Foreign Corrupt Practices Act of 1977. Answer B is incorrect as this refers to the Racketeer Influenced and Corrupt Organization Act (RICO). Answer C is incorrect as there is no such act to prevent aiding and abetting the commission of a crime. Answer D is incorrect as the Money Laundering Control Act makes it a crime to be involved in illegal check-cashing schemes, bribery or insurance fraud.

35. C. Answer C is correct, as the Sixth Amendment provides for an accused to be tried by an impartial jury of the state, etc. Answer A is incorrect as the Fifth Amendment provides an accused with the privilege against self-incrimination. Answer B is incorrect as the Fourth Amendment protects against unreasonable searches and seizures. Answer D is incorrect as the Eighth Amendment protects against cruel and unusual punishment.

Short Answer:

36. imprisonment.
37. A criminal act and criminal intent are the two elements that must be proven for a person to be found guilty of most crimes.
38. Because the criminal is often judgment proof and does not have the money to pay the civil judgment.
39. The grand jury usually evaluates the evidence of serious crimes.
40. Immunity from prosecution means that the government agrees not to use any evidence given by a person granted immunity against that person.
41. Robbery is the taking of personal property from another by the use of fear or force.
42. A person must knowingly receive stolen property and intend to deprive the rightful owner of that property.
43. Mr. Sly has committed criminal fraud as he obtained Suzy Sweets's money through deception by convincing her to withdraw and invest all of her money in non-existant water.
44. The Fourth Amendment protects persons and corporations from unreasonable searches and seizures by the government.
45. If the same criminal act violates the laws of two or more jurisdictions, each jurisdiction is free to prosecute the accused without violating the double jeopardy clause.
46. It is a crime for a person to draw, make or deliver a check to another knowing that there is insufficient funds in the account to be able to cover the check.
47. Extortion of a private person is called blackmail.
48. A conspiracy is when two or more persons enter into an agreement to commit a crime.
49. This exception allows illegally obtained evidence to be introduced against the accused if the police officers who conducted the unreasonable search reasonably believed that they were acting pursuant to a lawful search warrant.
50. The attorney-client privilege is invoked when a client tells his or her attorney about his or her case without fear that the attorney will be called as a witness against his or her client.

Chapter 7

ETHICS AND
SOCIAL RESPONSIBILITY
OF BUSINESS

Chapter Overview

This chapter provides a clear understanding of the moral principles that determine the conduct of individuals or a group. The five main theories of ethics are thoroughly discussed with case law providing an excellent example of each.

Objectives

Upon completion of the exercises that accompany this chapter, you should be able to:
1. Define the meaning of ethics.
2. Define and compare the five main theories of ethics.
3. Discuss the principles of conduct that are necessary for international business.
4. Compare the traditional role of social responsibility of business to the modern trend.
5. Describe corporate citizenship.
6. Describe the corporate social audit and discuss its importance in business today.
7. Apply traditional ethics principles to technology such as the Internet
8. Observe the differences in ethical standards from country to country.

Practical Application

You should be able to recognize the types of ethical behavior being utilized in business based upon your knowledge of the various ethical principles. Additionally, you will have a greater appreciation for the history of this area of the law.

Helpful Hints

It is important to become familiar with the key terms and phrases associated with ethics. Additionally, it is helpful to be familiar with a case example for the theory you are trying to remember. The study tips given below have been organized by theory accompanied by a case or an example to enforce the principles it applies to.

Study Tips

Utilitarianism
The concept behind this theory is that people have to choose or follow the rule that provides the greatest good to society.

Example of utilitarianism - The case of Charter *Township of Ypsilanti Michigan v. General Motors Corporation,* No. 161245 (Mich. App. 1993) involved a General Motors Chevrolet production plant that decided to move from Ypsilanti, Michigan to Arlington Texas. The Charter Township of Ypsilanti brought a suit against General Motors alleging that it had given the automaker $13 million dollars in tax abatements, and that without the plant 4,500 people would be out of work. The trial judge appeared to apply the concept of utilitarianism in this case by ruling that just because General Motors thinks it can make the cars cheaper elsewhere does not make it right to desert the workers and their families. Further that the tax abatements given to the automaker could have been given toward education. Unfortunately, the appellate court reversed holding that there was no quid pro quo (this for that) agreement between the parties.

Kantian Ethics
This theory of ethics is also referred to as duty ethics. In other words, "do unto others as you would have them do unto you. In terms of business under this theory, an obligated party must keep his or her part of the bargain as he or she has a moral duty to do so regardless of any detriment that the party may suffer.

Rawl's Social Justice Theory
Under this theory, each person in society is presumed to have entered into a social contract with society in an effort to promote peace and harmony. Those following this theory agree to abide by the rules as long as everyone else also keeps to the rules.

Example of Rawl's social justice theory – The Sears and Robuck Co. "bait and rip off" scheme wherein Sears distributed discount brake job coupons to consumers and upon redemption of the same would convince the consumer that he or she needed additional repairs. The customers presumed that Sears would act ethically until many became upset with being overcharged. Thereafter California officials became aware of the situation and threatened to revoke Sears auto repair license. Sears settled all lawsuits against it. In this case forty-one states voiced complaints thereby evoking anger and conflict versus peace and harmony as per this ethical theory.

Ethical Relativism
Under this moral theory, individuals have to determine what is ethical using their own intuition or feelings as to what is right or wrong. Due to the subjectivity of what the moral standard is, an individual who adopts ethical relativism cannot be criticized for the way he or she feels. Most philosophers do not find this theory a satisfactory one when it comes to applying it to morals.

Example of ethical relativism - The case of *McNeil-P.C.C. inc. v. Bristol-Meyers Squibb Co. 938F.2d 1544 (1991)* illustrates this theory as McNeil sued Bristol –Meyers based upon the theory of false advertising. Bristol Meyers had advertised that Excederin worked better than Tylenol. After testing both products, it was found that they were basically the same and that Bristol-Meyers violated the Lanham Act, which prohibits false advertising. If Bristol-Meyers were applying ethical relativism to their claims regarding their product, they may claim that in their opinion, its products is better than that of McNeil-P.C.C. and that there should be no conflict on this point based upon how they feel. Therefore, even though the court found that fraud was committed, under this theory, Bristol-Meyer's thought would in fact be ethical.

Business and its Social Responsibility

More than ever we are looking at the impact as well as the social responsibility those businesses owe to society as a whole. Traditionally all that was viewed was a cost-benefit analysis and how a business' actions affected profits. Modernly however corporations are being held responsible for their actions. The four theories of social responsibility are the maximization of profits, the moral minimum, the takeholder's interest, and corporate citizenship all of which are discussed individually.

Maximizing Profits

The traditional rule regarding a business and its social responsibility was that it should maximize its profits for the shareholders. Proponents of this theory affirm this philosophy by adding that a business should participate in activities that will increase its profits as long as long as it is without any fraud or deception.

Example of maximizing profits – The case of *Mangini v. R.J. Reynolds Tobacco Company* involved R.J. Reynolds Tobacco Company's use of Joe Camel, a cartoon character that attorney and plaintiff Janet Mangini claimed was using unfair business practices. The defendant utilized the defense of freedom of speech under the First Amendment. However the plaintiff showed that R.J. Reynold's advertising was targeted at youth who were unable to make an informed choice knowing what the health risks are. R.J. Reynold's marketing ploy was designed to make money regardless of the existing and potential harm it was causing to those it wanted to sell to. It appears that this case is a classic example of the theory of maximizing profits.

Moral Minimum

This theory states that a business' social responsibility is met as long as it either avoids or corrects any social injury it causes. In other words, a corporation may make a profit, if it does not cause harm to others while doing so.

Example of the moral minimum- The case of *In re Union Carbide Corporation Gas Plant Disaster at Bhopal, India, in December 1984, 634 F.Supp. 842 (S.D.N.Y. 1986); 804 F.2 195 (2d Cir. 1987); cert. Denied, 484 U.S. 871 (1987)* involved a leakage of Methyl isocyanate, a toxic gas used to produce pesticides. The winds blew the gas into a heavily populated residential area causing many deaths and over 200,000 people to be injured. After determining that the Indian legal system would decide the cause of the event, Union Carbide was ordered to set up a fund of $470 million dollars for the claimants. Many issues were raised in this case, however, the main ethical one appears to be, did this fund correct the injuries it caused? Opponents argue that it did not as the settlement amounted to less than a thousand dollars per claimant.

Stakeholder Interest

Businesses have to consider the impact its actions will have on its stockholder, employees, suppliers, customers, creditors and the community as a whole. All of these individuals have a stake in the business.

Example of the stakeholder interest theory - As per your text, if employees of a business were seen only as a means to acquire wealth for the stockholders, this would not take into consideration the impact it would have on those employees.

Corporate Citizenship

This theory maintains that a business has a responsibility to do well. Under this theory, Businesses are under a duty to help solve social problems that it had minimum or no association with. The rationale behind this theory is because of the social power society has given to businesses. Opponents of this theory tend to lean toward moderation as society will always have some sort of social problem that needs to be solved. Businesses have limits too.

<u>Example of corporate citizenship –</u> Corporations owe a duty to fund a cure for a local child suffering from a rare disease.

Principles for International Business
The Caux Round Table developed Principles for International Business which is a code that states the responsibilities of business beyond shareholders toward stakeholders as well as the economic and social impact of business toward innovation, justice and world community.

The Corporate Social Audit
Generally speaking, audits are usually conducted to examine the financial health of a business. However, it has been suggested that a moral check up be conducted as well. Included in the ethical check up would be an examination of employee adherence to the company's code of ethics, whether the corporation has fulfilled its duty of social responsibility, promotion of worker safety, employment opportunities, etc. An independent firm should conduct the audit in an effort to assist in determining how the company can move toward the goal of social responsibility.

Refresh Your Memory

The following exercise will enable you to refresh your memory on the rules and principles presented to you in this chapter. Read each question twice and place your answer in the blanks provided. Review the chapter material for any question you miss or are unable to remember.

1. Ethics is a set of _____ principles or _____ that governs the conduct of an individual or group.

2. The moral theory of _____ states that people must choose the actions or follow the rule that provides the greatest good to society.

3. The ethical theory that would have an individual behave according to the imperative, "Do unto others as you would have them do unto you," is known as _____ _____.

4. A theory that promulgates that each person is presumed to have entered into a social contract with all others in society to obey moral rules that are necessary for people to live in peace and harmony is known as _____ _____ _____ theory.

5. If June, a store clerk observes a Brinks security man drop a bag of cash and her first instinct is to inform him of it, she would be applying the theory of _____ _____.

6. If an oil company has an oil spill that causes damage to an entire town and the company offers to tear down the town and rebuild it, the company would be adhering to the _____ _____theory.

7. Unique principles based on transnational values and ethics can be found in a code called the _____ for _____ _____.

8. The traditional view of the social responsibility owed by businesses is that they should
   _____ .

9. If a corporation is considering the effects its actions have on other stakeholders, what theory is it utilizing? The _____ _____ theory.

10. A businesses responsibility to help solve social problems that it may not have caused would have its foundation in the theory known as _____ _____ .

11. The corporate social audit refers to an audit of the corporation's _____ health.

12. If George looks to the Bible for ethical rules or commands to guide him, he would be supporting the theory of _____ _____ .

13. Corporations have some degree of _____ _____ for their actions.

14. Those following the theory that a corporation's duty is to make a profit while avoiding causing harm to others is known as the _____ _____ theory.

15. The corporate citizenship theory of social responsibility states that businesses have a _____ to do good for society.

Critical Thought Exercise

You are an employee in the public relations department of Preciso, the luxury European automobile manufacturer. Preciso's sales have skyrocketed since the handcrafted vehicles were introduced to the United States ten years ago. Preciso's president has announced that Preciso will stop buying wood products from endangered forests following the example last year of Challenger Motor Company. Preciso will immediately stop buying wood from Canada's Great Bear Forest in British Columbia and phase out purchases of other wood from endangered forests. Instead, Preciso would like to use a "manmade wood-like product" for the interior parts (steering wheels, door panels, shifter knobs, etc.) of the autos it designs and builds.

There is no law against using wood from endangered forests and it is highly profitable to include these rare woods as part of the interiors of Preciso's cars. Shareholders are furious with the decision and are considering suing the Board of Directors and the officers of Preciso for wasting profits.

You are asked by the President of Preciso to draft a speech that she will deliver t the annual shareholders meeting which will explain the ethical business decision that was made and persuades the shareholders to not pursue a suit against the company.

Answer. _____

_____
_____
_____
_____
_____
_____
_____

_____

Practice Quiz

True/False:

1. ___ The corporate social audit should be designed to inspect the corporation's financial health. [p 160]

2. ___ The moral minimum theory states that a corporation's social responsibility is to do well and solve social problems. [p 158]

3. ___ When a person looks to an outside source such as the Koran or the Bible for ethical rules, he or she is utilizing ethical fundamentalism. [p 150]

4. ___ Under Rawl's Social Justice Theory, one must enter into a formal written contract in order to enforce rules that are necessary for people to live in peace and harmony. [p 152]

5. ___ Kantian ethics refers to an individual's own feelings as to what is right or wrong. [p 151]

6. ___ Ethical standards are different in each country. [p 155]

7. ___ Under the maximizing profits theory, the interest of others such as employees, suppliers, and local residents are not important in and of themselves. [p.7-19]

8. ___ There is no international ethics code in existence because there are too many transnational values. [p 155]

9. ___ If a corporation pollutes the waters and then gives compensation to those whom it injures, it has met its moral minimum duty of social responsibility. [p 158]

10. ___ The stakeholder interest theory is widely accepted, as it is an easy way to harmonize the conflicting interests of the stakeholders. [p 159]

11. ___ In the past, many businesses have made business decisions based only upon a cost-benefit analysis. [p 155]

12. ___ Ethical relativism would apply in the situation of one company making what it feels is an honest comparison to a competitor's product even though the comparison is invalid. [p 153]

13. ___ It is unethical for a company to purposefully create partnerships in order to appear profitable and use these partnerships in an effort to borrow money to engage in speculative business dealings. [p 150]

14. ___ Proponents of the corporate citizenship theory contend that the duty of a corporation to do good is unlimited and that business is responsible for helping solve social problems. [p 160]

15. ___ Advertising dangerous products to youth in order to realize profits from all marketing channels are not considered unethical under today's ethical standards. [p 157]

16. ___ As part of transnational corporation's code of conduct, they must adhere to socio-cultural objectives and values of the countries in which they operate. [p 161]

17. ___ One of the benefits of utilizing Kantian ethics as a basis for conduct is that it facilitates and promotes what the universal rules of conduct should be. [p 151]

18. ___ The theory of ethical fundamentalism leaves little room for individuals to decide what is right and wrong on their own. [p 150]

19. ___ The theory of utilitarianism is a favored moral theory as it assists in determining what "good" will result from different actions. [p 151]

20. ___ Consistency and reversibility are two main principles espoused in deontology's universal rules. [p 151]

Multiple Choice:

21. A moral theory that states that people must choose the actions that will provide the greatest good to society is [p 151]
    a. Kantian ethics.
    b. maximizing profits.
    c. Utilitariansim.
    d. corporate social audit.

22. Which theory proposes a social contract theory of morality? [p.7-10]
    a. Stakeholder interest
    b. Rawl's Social Justice Theory
    c. Ethical relavtivism
    d. Ethical fundamentalism

23. Which theory indicates that the use of fraud is all right if the perpetrator honestly thought it was in fact ethical? [p 153]
    a. Rawl's distributive justice theory
    b. Maximizing profits
    c. Principles for International Business
    d. Ethical relativism

24. What type of ethics have many multinational corporations around the world adopted? [p 155]
    a. Principles for International Business
    b. Moral minimum
    c. Corporate citizenship
    d. All of the above

25. Edward brought a $15.00 discount coupon off of his next oil change to Sam Slick's garage. Fred, an employee of Sam Slick's garage convinces Edward to have a variety of other services performed, which in turn causes Edward's final bill to be over $500.00. What ethical theory would Sam Slick allege if his "bait and switch" scheme is questioned? [p 150]
    a. Utilitarianism
    b. Ethical fundamentalism
    c. Ethical relativism
    d. Stakeholder interest

26. If a computer manufacturer decided to close one of its manufacturing plants in Burlington, Vermont because the employees were not assembling the computers fast enough which in turn was causing sales to drop, which ethical theory would this manufacturer be violating? [p 158]
    a. sSakeholder interest
    b. Utilitarianism
    c. Kantian ethics
    d. All of the above

27. Under which ethical theory could an individual be considered to act unethically if he or she went to extremes in following the code of conduct promulgated by this theory? [p 150]
    a. Athical fundamentalism
    b. Maximizing profits
    c. Corporate citizenship
    d. Corporate audit

28. Traditionally businesses made decisions based on [p 155]
    a. social responsibility.
    b. a cost-benefit analysis.
    c. the economic and social impact of business.
    d. the flip of a coin.

29. Which view held that the interest of employees, suppliers, and residents of the communities in which the businesses are located are not important in and of themselves? [p 156]
    a. The Milton Friedman law
    b. The Caux Round Table principles
    c. Consumer protection laws
    d. Maximizing profits

30. Which theory advocates that a corporation owes a debt to society to make it a better place and that this duty arises because of the social powers bestowed on them? [p 160]
    a. Ethical relativism
    b. Deontology's universal rules
    c. Corporate citizenship
    d. Forum non conveniens

Short Answer:

31. A set of universal rules that establishes ethical duties describes _____ ethics. [p 151]

32. Corporations that conduct _____ _____ will be more likely to prevent illegal and unethical conduct by employees, managers, and agents. [p 160]

33. What is the international ethics code that is based on transnational values from the East and West? [p 155] _____ for _____ _____

34. If Brian, a bank teller follows the commandment, "Thou shall not steal," he most likely follows _____ _____ as the basis for his conduct. [p 150]

35. If a winery uses a teenager sipping a glass of its wine while listening to a rock and roll concert in one of its ads, what ethical theory might it be utilizing? [p 156]
    The _____ theory.

36. The Environmental Safe Company promotes the safe dumping of toxic materials into our nation's waters. On one particular instance, Environmental caused the deaths of hundreds of sea lions. Its only response to the tragedy was that there are plenty of sea lines to mate with one another. Further, the population will be back in no time. If Environmental would have complied with the _____ _____ theory, it would have met its duty of social responsibility by cleaning up the waters where the toxic materials were dumped and provide for safe dumping in the future so that other marine life are saved. [p 158]

37. Which theory says that a corporation must consider the effects its actions have on individuals other than its stockholders? [p 158] The _____ _____ theory.

38. What is the code of conduct that includes the respect for national sovereignty as well as adherence to socio-cultural objectives and values called? [p 161] The _____ _____ code of conduct for _____ _____.

39. Businesses that make their decisions solely on a cost-benefit analysis owed a certain amount of _____ _____ for their actions as their decisions may have negative consequences for others. [p 155]

40. The theory of utilitarianism states that people must choose the actions or follow the rule that provides the _____ _____ __ _____. [p 151]

41. What are the two principles that deontology's universal rules are based upon? [p 151]
    _____
    _____

42. How might forum shopping be considered unethical? [p 158] _____
    _____

43. Give two reasons why social audits may be difficult to conduct. [p 160] _____
_____
_____

44. "Do unto others as you would have them do unto you," best describes _____ ethics. [p 151]

45. Give at least two principles that were developed in the international ethics code known as the Principles for International Business. [p 155] _____
_____
_____

46. When individuals decide what is ethical based on their own feelings of what is right or what is wrong, this is known as _____ _____. [p 153]

47. Give two examples of laws established by the government that establish minimum standards for conduct for business in other areas. [p 158] _____
_____

48. Compare the difference between ethical fundamentalism and ethical relativism. [p 154]
_____
_____

49. What does the moral minimum theory of corporate social responsibility state? [p 158]
_____
_____

50. What is the primary criticism of the corporate citizenship theory of social responsibility? [p.7-28]
_____
_____

Answers to Refresh Your Memory

1. moral values [p 149]
2. utilitarianism [p 151]
3. Kantian ethics [p 151]
4. Rawl's Social Justice Theory [p 152]
5. ethical relativism [p 153]
6. moral minimum [p 158]
7. Principles for International Business [p 155]
8. maximize profits [p 156]
9. stakeholder's interest [p 158]
10. corporate citizenship [p 160]
11. moral [p 160]
12. ethical fundamentalism [p 150]
13. social responsibility [p 155]
14. moral minimum [p 158]
15. responsibility [p 160]

Critical Thought Exercise Model Answer

Traditionally, it was perceived that the duty to shareholders took precedence over all other duties owed by the corporation and that the primary duty and goal of a company was to maximize profits. However, as corporations have developed global markets and society has changed, corporations have come to realize that they have several other duties that must be fulfilled. Employers have an ethical duty to employees to provide a safe workplace, to pay a decent wage, and to provide employment opportunities to present and future employees. AS society has changed, the corporation has had to take into account ethical concerns such as equal pay for equal work and the prevention of sexual harassment. The company has had to change its policies to comply with laws such as the Family Medical Leave Act and the Americans With Disabilities Act. A corporation also has a duty to the persons who use its products. We must make a safe product that is economical and gives good value to the consumer for their investment and faith in us. We have a duty to our suppliers to maintain good business relations and use good faith and fair dealing in our contracts with them. WE have a duty to the community where our facilities and offices are located. What we do as a corporation affects the tax base of the community and the quality of the schools, services, and collateral businesses in the area. Lastly, we have a duty to society at large to be the most ethical citizen possible. This means complying with environmental protection laws, preservation of scarce natural resources, and being part of the solution to very big problems instead of a cause. This corporation is in a unique position because of our wealth and power. We have a responsibility to society to use that wealth and power in socially beneficial ways. We should promote human rights, strive for equal treatment of minorities and women in the workplace, preserve and protect the environment, and not seek profits at the expense of ethics. If a corporation fails to conduct its operation ethically or respond quickly to an ethical crisis, its goodwill and reputation, along with profits, will suffer. Instead of aiming for maximum profits, we should aim for optimum profits—profits that can be realized while staying within legal and ethical limits set by government and society. For all these reasons, we have a duty to refrain from using wood from endangered forests to decorate our product. The manmade products we will substitute are more economical and will not detract from the overall look. Conversely, if we are known as the company that abuses scarce resources, consumers will support our competitors who are concerned about their corporate ethics.

Answers to Practice Quiz

True/False:

1. False   There are already audits to inspect a corporation's financial health. The corporate social audit should be designed to prevent unethical and illegal conduct by mangers, employees and agents. The purpose of the social audit is to examine a company's moral health.
2. False   The moral minimum theory contends that it is a corporation's duty to make a profit while avoiding causing harm to others.
3. True   When an individual looks to an outside source for ethical rules or commands, the individual is said to be adhering to the theory of ethical relativism.
4. False   Under Rawl's Social Justice Theory, a person is presumed to have entered into an implied social contract with all others in society to obey the moral rules that are needed for people to live in peace and harmony.
5. False   The question states the principle behind ethical relativism. Kantian ethics basic premise is that people owe more duties that are based on universal rules.
6. True   Ethics derives its purpose based upon factors such as religion, history and culture. Since these factors vary from country to country, the ethical standards also vary.

7. True   The traditional view of business and the social responsibility owed is that a business should maximize its profits for its shareholders regardless of the interests others may hold.

8. False   A group of leaders from many multinational corporations developed an international code of ethics that are based upon transnational values.

9. True   The moral minimum theory of corporate social responsibility asserts that a corporation's duty is to make a profit while avoiding harm to others. Compensation for the harm caused by the pollution meets the moral minimum as it acts as a corrective measure.

10 False   The stakeholder interest theory is criticized due to the difficulty in harmonizing the stakeholders' conflicting interests.

11. True   Traditionally the "bottom line" is all that mattered and as such the cost-benefit analysis was utilized to determine the profit that was to be made.

12. True   Ethical relativism is based on an individual's own feelings of what is right or wrong. So, even though one company is making an invalid product comparison to that of its competitor, under this theory, it would not be unethical if the company making the comparison thought it was ethical to do so despite the lack of validity.

13. True   This is a classic example of what has happened to the Enron Corporation. It would be far reaching to even apply ethical relativism to this situation in light of the fact that speculative business dealings were involved, which most business people should know are not the sort of ventures a secure company would engage itself in.

14. True   Those who promote the corporate citizenship theory content that corporations owe a duty to promote the same social goals as individual members of society and that they should make the world a better place because of the social power placed upon them.

15. False   Advertising dangerous products such as cigarettes for example to youth so that a profit can be made is considered unethical especially under today's standards.

16. True   Not only do corporations have to have respect for national sovereignty and adhere to socio-cultural objectives and values in the countries that they operate in, but they must also respect human rights and fundamental freedoms as well as abstain from corrupt practices.

17. False   Even though Kantian ethics believe that people owe moral duties based upon universal rules, it is hard to reach an agreement as to what the rules should be.

18. True   Under ethical fundamentalism involves looking to an outside source for commands or ethical rules. As such, this theory lacks flexibility to allow an individual the freedom to decide right from wrong.

19. False   Though the theory behind utilitarianism is that people must choose the actions or abide by the rule that provides the greatest good to society, it is difficult to predict the "good" that will come about as a result of different actions.

20. True   An actor must live by the rule he or she uses to judge someone else's morality based on that person's conduct and an actor must also be consistent in his or her treatment of others as well.

Multiple Choice:

21. C   Answer C is correct as utilitarianism dictates that individuals must select the actions or abide by the rule that provides the greatest good to society. Answer A is incorrect as Kantian ethics dictate that people owe moral duties based upon universal rules. Answer B is incorrect as the maximizing profit theory bases its theory upon the maximum amount of profits that business can make for its shareholders regardless if it is good or bad for others with an interest. Answer D is incorrect as the corporate social audit involves checking on a corporation's moral health.

22. B   Answer B is correct, as Rawl's Social Justice Theory believes that each person is presumed to have entered into an implied social contract with others to obey rules that are necessary for people to live in peace and harmony. Answer A is incorrect as the stakeholder interest theory contends that a corporation must consider the effects its actions have on other stakeholders. Answer C is incorrect as ethical relativism bases its theory upon an individual's feelings on whether the action

he or she is taking is right or wrong. Answer D is incorrect as those following the theory of ethical fundamentalism look to an outside source for ethical guidelines.

23. D Answer D is correct as actions that are usually viewed as unethical, such as fraud would not be considered unethical if the perpetrator thought the action taken was ethical. Under ethical relativism, individuals must decide what is ethical based on their own feelings of what is right or wrong. Answer A is incorrect as in Rawl's distributive justice theory, fairness is the crux or justice. Answer B is incorrect, as this theory is mainly concerned with the maximum amount of profits that can be made for the shareholders regardless of the effect it has on other interested parties. Answer C is incorrect, as the Principles for International Business are a code of ethics that have been adopted by many multinational corporations wherein avoidance of illicit operations, including fraud is clearly stated in one of its principles.

24. A Answer A is correct as the Principles for International Business is the international code that many multinational corporations have adopted. Answer B is is incorrect, as multinational corporations have adopted a code that provides for much more than the moral minimum, which sets forth a corporation's duty to make money without causing harm to others. Answer C is incorrect as the underlying theory of corporate citizenship contends that business has a responsibility to do good. This is only partially applicable to the ethics adopted by multinational corporations as those ethics argue that businesses should contribute to human rights, educations, welfare and vitalization of the countries in which they operate. However, this aspect is not the sole basis of the ethics of transnational corporations. Answer D is incorrect, for the reasons given above.

25. C Answer C is correct as this moral theory leaves little room for criticism if that it is subjective in nature. If Sam truly believes that Edward should have the additional auto services even though Edward came in for a discounted oil change, then Sam has met his own moral standards based on what he feels are right or wrong. Therefore, ethical relativism would be Sam's best theory to allege. Answer A is incorrect as utilitarianism involves choosing the best alternative that would provide the greatest good to society. The greatest good would b the subject of debate depending on whom you were trying to do the greatest good for, Sam or Edward. Therefore this would not be the best answer. Answer B is incorrect as ethical fundamentalism involves looking to an outside source for what is right or wrong. By finding other automotive services to convince Edward of, some might contend that Sam was stealing or "ripping off" Edward in contradiction to an outside source's commandment for example of "Thou shall not steal." Answer D is incorrect, as the stakeholder interest theory would favor Edward more as the social responsibility includes considering the interests of customers. Arguably, Edward's interests as a customer trying to save a little bit of money by using a coupon are not being considered.

26. A Answer A is correct as the stakeholder interest theory would require that the computer manufacturer considers the effects of its actions on the other stakeholders. Since the amount of sales seems to be its main concern, it appears that the only value it sees in its employees is their ability to make money. The closing of the plant and its effects on unemployment do not appear to be a factor. Answer B is incorrect as closing the plant would not provide the greatest good to society, which is the premise underlying utilitarianism. Instead, closing the plant appears to be detrimental in nature. Answer C is incorrect, as followers of Kantian ethics believe that people owe moral duties based upon universal rules. As such, even though the employees are not producing fast enough to create larger profits, the parties have a contract. Under Kantian ethics, this contract needs to be honored regardless of the drop in profits and the detriment suffered by the company's owners. Answer D is incorrect, for the reasons stated above.

27. A Answer A is correct as critics do not favor ethical fundamentalism since people take the outside source's meaning and guidelines literally which can make people go to extreme and act unethically despite the belief in an ethical principal. Answer B is incorrect, as the theory of maximizing profits was the traditional view of social responsibility whereby business should maximize its profits for the shareholders and any other interests associated with the business is not important in and of themselves. Ignoring the other interests by itself does not necessarily

constitute going to extremes that would qualify as being unethical. Answer C is incorrect as corporate citizenship involves a business' responsibility to do good and solve social problems regardless if the business caused the problems or not. The solving of social problems hardly constitutes unethical behavior. Answer D is incorrect as the corporate audit involves a moral or values check up of a business that would not be unethical in and of itself.

28. B   Answer B is correct as businesses used to make their business decisions mainly based upon a cost-benefit analysis. Answer A is incorrect as businesses made few if any decisions based on their social responsibility. Answer C is incorrect as the economic and social impact of a business' decision was not even a factor that went into deciding what they were going to do. Answer D is incorrect as this indicates that businesses just took their chances with little to no thought going into their business decisions.

29. D   Answer D is correct as the maximizing profits theory was the main philosophy businesses operated under and the effects that it had on anyone else were not even considered. Answer A is incorrect as Milton Friedman was an advocate of the maximizing profits theory as long as there was no deception or fraud involved. There is no Milton Freidman law per se. Answer B is incorrect, as the Caux Round Table Principles specifically provide for the customers, employees and shareholders by defining the responsibilities of business beyond shareholders toward stakeholders. Answer C is incorrect as consumer protection laws are geared toward the concern of those associated with products which would include employees, suppliers and residents of the communities in which the businesses are located.

30. C   Answer C is correct as the question states the definition of corporate citizenship. Answer A is incorrect as ethical relativism argues that individuals must determine what is ethical based on their own feelings as to what is right or wrong. Answer B is incorrect as deontology's universal rules refers to Kantian ethics, which espouse that people owe moral duties based on universal rules. In essence whatever a business does to society, society may do the same in return to business. This theory is somewhat contradictory to the corporate citizenship theory as further defined in the definition. Answer D is incorrect as forum non conveniens refers to an inconvenient forum in which to hear a case.

Short Answer:

31.   Kantian
32.   social audits
33.   Principles *for* International Business
34.   Kantian ethics
35.   maximizing profits
36.   moral minimum
37.   stakeholder interest
38.   United Nations, transnational corporations
39.   social responsibility
40.   greatest good to society
41.   consistency in that all cases are treated equally and reversibility, meaning that the one taking the action must follow the same rule that he or she is using in judging another's conduct.
42.   It might be considered unethical if the party choosing the forum is selecting it based upon a less stringent standard than if the party would have remained with the original forum.
43.   It might be hard to understand exactly what is being audited. Also, it might be hard to assess the results.
44.   duty (or Kantian)
45.   On principle involves business' responsibilities beyond shareholders and going toward stakeholders. Another principle involves the economic and social impact of business with an emphasis on innovation, justice and the world community.

46. ethical relativism
47. occupational safety laws and consumer protection laws
48. The theory of ethical fundamentalism believes that a person looks to an outside source for his or her ethical guidelines. Whereas, the theory of ethical relativism believes that individuals determine what is ethical based on their own feelings about what is right or wrong.
49. The moral minimum theory of social responsibility holds that business should avoid causing harm and to compensate for harm caused.
50. It puts too much of a burden on business in that there will always be problems that need solving.

Chapter 8

INTERNATIONAL AND
COMPARATIVE LAW

Chapter Overview

This chapter explores the federal government's power under the Foreign Commerce and Treaty Clauses of the U.S. Constitution as well as the sources of international law. It also details the functions and governance of the United Nations. Various economic organizations including the North American Free Trade Agreement are also examined. The other international facets that are discussed include international intellectual property rights provided by Internet treaties, sovereign immunity, the World Trade Organization's dispute resolution procedure, and the arbitration of international disputes.

Objectives

Upon completion of the exercises that follow, you should be able to:
1. Recognize the function of the federal government's power under the Foreign Commerce and Treaty Clauses of the U.S. Constitution.
2. List and differentiate between the different sources of international law.
3. Understand the functions and importance of the United Nations.
4. Be familiar with the North American Free Trade Agreement and other regional economic organizations.
5. Understand the international intellectual property rights provided by the Internet treaties.
6. Discuss how the World Trade Organization's dispute resolution procedure works.
7. Discuss the doctrine of sovereign immunity.
8. Discuss how international disputes are arbitrated.
9. Discuss international e-commerce and Internet laws.

Practical Application

You should be able to appreciate the importance of the Foreign Commerce and Treaty Clauses of the U.S. Constitution as well as the impact of sovereign immunity. Further, you should be familiar with the names and functions of the various regional organizations. Finally, you should be able to state how international disputes are arbitrated and how the World Trade Organization's dispute resolution procedure works.

Helpful Hints

One of the most helpful tools to understanding the importance of this chapter is to focus on the fact that the chapter involves the international spectrum of business. The study tips below are organized first by sources of international law, then by regional organization, followed by procedure for resolving international disputes. It is very beneficial to understand the functions of the various organizations in order to better understand the cases discussed in this chapter.

Study Tips

Background information – A legislative source of international law does not exist. A separate court for interpreting international law does not exist. Further, a world executive branch that could enforce the international laws is also non-existent. International law is very important with the increase in technology and transportation that is bringing businesses all over the world closer together.

The United States Constitution and International Affairs

Foreign Commerce Clause allows Congress to regulate commerce with foreign nations.
Treaty Clause gives the president the power to make treaties as long as two-thirds of the senators present agree. States cannot unduly burden foreign commerce. State and local laws cannot conflict with treaties, as treaties are part of the Constitution.

Sources of International Law

- **Treaties and conventions** – These are like legislations that published by the United Nations and whose subject matter involves human rights, commerce, dispute settlements, foreign aid and navigation.
- **Treaty defined**- An agreement or contract between two or more nations, formally signed and ratified by the supreme power of each nation.
- **Conventions defined**- Treaties that are sponsored by international organizations and are signed by several signatories.
- **Customs**- A separate source of international law which defines a practice followed by two or more nations when interacting with one another. Requirements for a practice to become a custom include a repetitive action by two or more nations over a long period of time and acknowledgment that the custom is followed. Special note- Customs that have been followed for a considerable amount of time may become treaties.
- **General Principles of Law** – Many countries depend on general principles of law that are used in civilized nations in order to resolve international disputes. These principles may be derived from statutes, common law, regulations or other sources.
- **Judicial Decisions or Teaching** - This fourth source of law refers to the judicial teachings and decisions of scholars from the nations in dispute. Note: There is no precedent for international courts.

International Organizations

- **The United Nations** - A very important international organization dedicated toward maintaining peace and security in the world, espousing economic and social cooperation and protecting human rights. A legislative body called the General Assembly, the Security Council and the Secretariat governs it. The General Assembly adopts resolutions and the council's duty is to maintain peace and security internationally. The United Nations is made up of several agencies including the United Nations Educational, Scientific, and Cultural Organization, the United Nations International Children's Emergency Fund and the International Monetary Fund, the World Bank International Fund for Agricultural Development.
- **The European Union** - This international regional organization used to be referred to as the European Community or Common Market. It represents more than 300 million people and is made up of several countries of Western Europe. The European Commission acts solely in the

best interests of the union. Customs duties have been abolished among member nations and customs tariffs have been enacted for European Union trade with the rest of the world.

- **Asian Economic Communities** - Several Asian countries have created the Association of South East Asian Nations (ASEAN). China and Japan are not members of this association, however, Japan has given financing for the countries that comprise this organization. China may one day become a member of ASEAN.
- **Latin, Central, and South American Economic Communities** - There are several Latin American and Caribbean countries that have founded many regional organizations to further economic development and cooperation. They are the Central American Common Market, the Mercosur Common Market, the Caribbean Community and the Andean Common Market.
- **African Economic Communities** - The economic communities that have been formed in Africa include the Economic and Customs Union of Central Africa, the Eat African Community, the Organization of African Unity, and the Economic Community of West African States.
- **Middle Eastern Economic Communities** - The Organization of Petroleum Exporting Countries is the best-known Middle Eastern economic organization. The Gulf Cooperation Council was formed to develop an economic trade area.

World Trade Organization (WTO)
- **Basic Information** - The WTO was created as part of the Uruguay Round of trade negotiations concerning the General Agreement on Tariffs and Trade. It is located in Switzerland.
- **Function of the WTO** - The function of the WTO is to hear and decide trade disputes between nations that are members. A three-member panel hears the dispute, which then generates a report that is given to the dispute settlement body. The WTO has expunged the blocking ability of member nations. There is however an appellate body to appeal the dispute settlement body. Only issues of law, not fact may be appealed.
- **Findings of Trade Agreement Violations** - If a violation of a trade agreement is found, the offending nation may be ordered to stop participating in the violating practice, as well as to pay damages to the other party. If the violating nation does not comply with the order, retaliatory trade sanctions by other nations may be assessed against the offending nation.
- **WTO Jurisdiction** - The WTO is also known as the "Supreme Court of Trade." Its jurisdiction involves the enforcement of comprehensive and important world trade agreements.

Jurisdiction of National Courts to Decide International Disputes
- **General Facts** - National courts of individual nations hear the bulk of disputes involving international law.
- **Judicial Procedure and the Problems Nations Face** - The main problems a party seeking judicial resolution of an international dispute faces are which court will hear the case and which law will be applied. Most cases are heard in the plaintiff's home country. However, many international contracts provide for a forum-selection clause as well as a choice of law clause. Dispute resolution becomes more difficult and often impossible without these two clauses.

Important Principles of International Law
- The **act of state doctrine** - This act proclaims that judges of one country cannot question the authority of an act committed by another country that occurs within that country's own borders.
- The **doctrine of sovereign immunity** - This doctrine states that countries are granted immunity from suits in courts in other countries.
- The **Foreign Sovereign Immunities Act** - This act provides a qualified or restricted immunity in two situations. The first instance in which a foreign country is not immune from lawsuits in the United States courts is if the foreign country has waived its immunity, either explicitly or by implication. The second instance is if the action is based upon a commercial activity carried on

in the United States by the foreign country or carried on outside the United States but causing a direct effect in the United States.

- **Nationalization of Private Property owed by Foreigners** - This international law allows nations to nationalize private property owned by foreigners if it is for a public purpose. This can occur by expropriation whereby the owner is paid just compensation by the government that took the property or it can be accomplished by confiscation in which case the owner either receives an insufficient payment or no payment at all for the property seized.
- Political risk insurance as per the **Overseas Private Investment Corporation** - The Overseas Private Investment Corporation was created to help insure United States businesses and citizens against losses incurred from confiscation by foreign governments. The American businesses and citizens may purchase an insurance policy to protect their property.

Ways to Resolve International Disputes

International Arbitration is a nonjudicial method of resolving disputes whereby a neutral third party decides the case. The arbitrator will issue an award, not a judgment. The award wining party may attach property of the losing party regardless of which country the property is located in.

International Criminal Prosecutions

A nation may criminally prosecute a business or individual that commits crimes within its jurisdiction or that violate the nations laws. If the wrongdoer takes refuge in another country, the person may be sent back to the country that wants to prosecute him or her. Extradition is necessary in order to punish the perpetrator.

Jewish Law and the Torah

In addition to abiding by the criminal and civil laws of their host countries, the Jews also obey the legal principles of the Torah. The Torah is an exhaustive set of religious and political rules that are formulated from Jewish principles. The base of the Torah is to determine the truth.

Islamic Law and the Koran

Saudi Arabia has Islamic law as its only law. It is mainly used in matters involving divorce, marriage and inheritance with some criminal law. One main characteristic of Islamic law is that it prohibits the making of unjustified or unearned profit.

Hindu Law

The Hindu law is religious based, using scholarly decisions that have been handed down from century to century. It embodies the doctrine of proper behavior. Note, that outside of India, Anglo-Hindu law applies in many countries with Hindu populations.

The Socialistic Law System

This system emphasizes codes that primarily are associated with public law. Since the private ownership of property is not recognized under this system, the Sino-Soviet law maintains the authority of state over property. Laws that protect property rights are replacing sino-Soviet law.

Germany as the E-Commerce Police

The European Union allows the collection and selling of consumer databases as provided for in the European Union Directive on Data Protection. This directive outlines what companies must do if they want to do business in any European Union country. Police from the European Union will conduct investigations to make sure that these companies are obeying the directive.

Refresh Your Memory

The following exercise will enable you to refresh your memory on the rules and principles presented to you in this chapter. Read each question twice and place your answer in the blanks provided. Review the chapter material for any question you miss or are unable to remember.

1. There is no individual source of _____ law.

2. Which clause of the United States Constitution gives Congress the power to regulate commerce with foreign nations? The _____ _____ _____.

3. What are the four sources of international law as listed by the Statute of the International Court of Justice? _____
_____
_____

4. What is the equivalent of legislation at the international level? _____ and _____.

5. What describes a practice followed by two or more nations when dealing with each other?
_____

6. What do courts and tribunals that decide international disputes often rely upon to make their decisions? _____ _____ of _____.

7. What is known as the fourth source of law to which international tribunals can refer? _____ _____ and _____ of the most qualified scholars of the nations that are involved in the dispute.

8. What is the International Court of Justice also known as? The _____ _____.

9. The European Union members have given a significant amount of powers to the European Union _____, which has the authority to enact _____.

10. The purpose of the North American Free Trade Agreement was to create a _____-_____ zone.

11. Which two countries, despite their large size do not belong to any major economic community? _____ and _____

12. What is one of the main functions of the World Trade Organization? _____
_____

13. Most of the cases concerning international law disputes are heard by _____ _____ of individual nations.

14. Give the name of one of the oldest principles of international law that states that countries are granted immunity from suits in courts of other countries. The _____ of _____.

15.   A foreign country may nationalize the assets of private property owned by foreigners by either
_____ or _____.

Critical Thought Exercise

Scientists at Cornell University engaged in genetic engineering and created a pear called the New York Sweetie that is resistant to bruising, browning, and insect infestation. The Sweetie grows approximately 30% larger than known pears and has both a higher water and sugar content, making the Sweetie highly desired by consumers worldwide. The only pear that can compete with the quality of the Sweetie is the Favlaka Beauty, grown exclusively in Favlaka. Favlaka is a large European nation with a population of over 300 million people. The country of Favlaka is a member of the European Union and the World Trade Organization. The residents of Favlaka consume over $1.2 billion worth of pears each year. All pears that are eaten on Favlaka are grown in Favlaka or a neighboring EU country. Favlaka will not allow the importation of fruit that has undergone any genetic engineering. The Favlaka Pear Cartel argues that the introduction of genetically engineered pears into their markets jeopardizes the Favlakan pear industry and the health of all Favlakans. They fear that future crops will become susceptible to insect infestation and attacks by mold and fungus. The United States Pear Growers argue that there is no scientific evidence that the NY Sweetie will cause damage to any other variety of pear or humans when it is grown or consumed. They further argue that the actions of the Favlakan government is banning the Sweetie are unfair trade practices under WTO agreements. It is argued that the Favlakan government is only motivated by the goal of preventing international competition for the Favlakan Beauty.

In what forum should this dispute be resolved? What procedure should be used to resolve this international dispute? What law should control the issues in this case? How should the WTO rule in this case?

Answer. _____

Practice Quiz

True/False:

1. ___ The Security Council for the United Nations is mainly responsible for maintaining international peace and security. [p 169]

2. ___ The Educational, Scientific, and Cultural Organization, the United Nations International Children's Emergency Fund and the International Monetary Fund are among the agencies that are excluded from the United Nations due to the Economic and social problems involved with these agencies. [p 169]

3. ___ Individuals and businesses that have a claim against another country may have their cases decided by the International Court of Justice. [p 170]

4. ___ The European Union treaty blocks borders for trade by providing for limited flow of capital, labor, goods and services among member nations. [p 172]

5. ___ In order to admit a new member to the European Union, there must be a unanimous vote by existing European Union members. [p 172]

6. ___ The European Court of Justice does not have any jurisdiction to enforce European Union law. [p 172]

7. ___ The European Court of Justice is the final arbiter of European Union law. [p 172]

8. ___ The North American Free Trade Agreement provides for the elimination or reduction of most of the duties, tariffs, quotas and other various trade barriers between Canada, the United States and Mexico. [p 172]

9. ___ Japan and China belong to the Association of South East Asian Nations. [p.8-10]

10. ___ Mexico has been reluctant to enter into a free trade agreement with the countries of Central America as well as Chile, Colombia, and Venezuela. [p 174]

11. ___ The most well-known Middle Eastern economic organization is the General Agreement on Tariffs and Trade. [p 174]

12. ___ An important characteristic of the World Trade Organization is the elimination of the blocking power of member nations. [p 177]

13. ___ Vietnam is not an economic partner with the United States. [p 178]

14 ___ The World Trade Organization has also been called the "Supreme Court of Trade." [p 177]

15. ___ The federal district court of the United States may hear disputes between foreign governments or parties and U.S. companies. [p 179]

16. ___ A general principle of international law is that a country has no authority over what takes place within its own territory. [p 180]

17. ___ The Foreign Sovereign Immunities Act governs suits against foreign nations in the United States, whether in federal or state court. [p 181]

18. ___ The Rabbi-judges sitting as Beis Din are more concerned with the truth than its adversarial process. [p 184]

19. ___ Islamic law prohibits the making of unearned or unjustified profit. [p 184]

20. ___ The Sino-Soviet socialist law system applies to over thirty percent of the people of the world. [p 185]

21. ___ Companies doing business prior to October 25, 1998 do not have to abide by the European Union Directive on Data Protection. [p 186]

22. ___ Companies found violating the European Union Directive on Data Protection may be prosecuted criminally for violating it. [p 186]

23. ___ A nation has the power to criminally prosecute individuals or businesses that commit crimes within its territory or that violate the nation's laws. [p 184]

24. ___ An arbitrator issues a judgment, not an award. [p 183]

25. ___ If there is no agreement providing where an international dispute will be brought, the case will usually be brought in the national court of the plaintiff's home country. [p 179]

Multiple Choice:

26. What types of matters are treaties and conventions concerned with? [p 168]
    a. Statutes banning state governments from purchasing goods and services
    b. Human rights, foreign aid, navigation, commerce and dispute settlement
    c. Consistent and recurring action by two or more nations over a long period of time
    d. General principles of law that are recognized by civilized nations

27. Custom is often defined as [p 169]
    a   an agreement between two nations.
    b. a principle of law that is common to the national law of the parties in dispute.
    c. a practice followed by two or more nations when dealing with each other.
    d. a goal to maintain peace and security in the world.

28. The European Court of Justice decides disputes concerning [p 172]
    a. the member nations' compliance with European Union law.
    b. the equivalency to the U.S. Federal Reserve Board.
    c. the best interests in the union.
    d. all of the above.

29. The European Court of First Instance purpose is to [p 172]
    a. create a free-trade zone from the Yukon to the Yucatan.
    b. acquire jurisdiction over Japan and China.
    c. provide a means of enforcing its decisions against member nations.
    d. to relieve some of the European Court's caseload.

30. Which fact describes the appellate body of the World Trade Organization? [p 177]
    a. Panels composed of three members of the appellate body hear appeals.
    b. The appeals court is made u p of seven professional justices.
    c. Appeals are limited to issues of law, not fact.
    d. All of the above.

31. Under the doctrine of sovereign immunity, [p 181]
    a. a foreign country has waived its immunity, either explicitly or by implications.
    b. the foreign sovereign is subject to suit in the United States.
    c. a nation's right to nationalize private property is recognized by international law.
    d. countries are granted immunity from suits in courts in other countries.

32. Which of the following is not a true statement? [p 166]
    a. Nations must obey international law enacted by other countries or international organizations.
    b. There is no world executive branch to enforce international laws.
    c. There is no individual world court that must interpret international laws.
    d. There is no individual legislative source of international law.

33. One of the purposes of the two World Intellectual Property Organization treaties is to [p 168]
    a. eliminate or reduce duties, tariffs and other trade barriers between Mexico and Canada.
    b. grant protection to copyright holders over the Internet and in the digital marketplace.
    c. limit copyright protection to rentals and means of distribution.
    d. exclude protection of performers and producers in renting copies of their performances.

34. A choice of forum clause in an international contract is a clause that [p 179]
    a. states that commercial disputes between the United States and foreign governments or parties may be brought in federal district court.
    b. an agreement that designates which nation's laws will be applied in deciding the case.
    c. a trade pact giving nations much easier access to the United States' marketplace.
    d. designates which nation's court has jurisdiction to hear a case arising out of the contract.

35. The act of state doctrine states that [p 180]
    a. the restraint on the judiciary is not justified under the doctrine of separation of powers.
    b. a country has no authority over what transpires within its own territory.
    c. judges of one country cannot question the strength of an act committed by another country within its own borders.
    d. the courts may sit in judgment upon the acts of the government of another, done within its own borders.

Short Answer:

36. What function does the World Intellectual Property Organization have? [p 168]

    _____

    _____

37. What countries make up the European Union? [p 172] _____

    _____

38. What are the two constitutional provisions that give power to the federal government to regulate international affairs? [p 166] The _____ _____ Clause and the _____ Clause.

39. What is the name of the international organization that was created by a multinational treaty to promote social and economic cooperation among nations and to protect human rights? [p 169]

    _____ _____

40. What is the most well known Middle Eastern economic organization? [p 174]
    The _____ of _____ _____ _____

41. Which organization has become the world's most important trade organization? [p 177] _____

    _____

42. Which court hears most of the international disputes? [p 179] The _____
    _____ of the plaintiff's home country.

43. What is the most litigated aspect of the Foreign Sovereign Immunities Act? [p 181]

    _____

44. What is the name of the United States Corporation that insures U.S. citizens and its businesses against losses incurred from a foreign government's confiscation of their assets? [p 182] The
    _____ _____ _____ Corporation.

45. What is the Sino-Soviet socialist law system based upon? [p 185] _____

    _____

46. What are the benefits of having an arbitrator decide a dispute that arises between parties to a contract? [p 183] _____

    _____

47. What law have many European nations adopted that regulates the compilation and selling of consumer databases? [p 186] The _____ _____ _____ on
    _____.

48. If Rodney had an international dispute that he needed to have resolved, which two sources of international law would he encourage the court to rely on when making its decision? [p 168]
    _____ and _____

49. If Sue, an exporter of material from the United States has an excessive tariff placed upon her goods when they enter one of the World Trade Organization's member countries, what multilateral treaty might she rely upon to help limit the tariff? [p 175] _____

    _____

50. What was the affect of the trade pact between the United States and Vietnam? [p 178]

    _____

    _____

    _____

Answers to Refresh Your Memory

1. international [p 166]
2. Foreign Commerce Clause [p 166]

3. treaties and conventions, custom, general principles of law and judicial decisions and teachings [p 167]
4. treaties and conventions [p 168]
5. custom [p 169]
6. general principles of law [p 169]
7. judicial decisions and teachings [p 169]
8. World Court [p 170]
9. Commission, legislation [p 172]
10. free-trade [p 172]
11. Japan and China [p 174]
12. To hear and decide trade disputes between member nations [p 176]
13. national courts [p 179]
14. doctrine of sovereign immunity [p 181]
15. expropriation, confiscation [p 182]

Critical Thought Exercise Model Answer

Both Favlaka and the United States are members of the United Nations (UN) and signatories to the General Agreement on Tariffs and Trade that created the World Trade Organization (WTO). The World Court in The Hague is the judicial branch of the UN. One of the functions of the WTO is to hear and decide trade disputes between member nations. Any member nation that believes a trade agreement has been breached can initiate a proceeding that is first heard by a three-member panel of the WTO. The panel issues a report that is referred to a dispute settlement body of the WTO. A seven-member appellate body hears any appeal from the dispute settlement body. The dispute between Favlaka and the United States involves a trade barrier imposed by Favlaka. A nation may protect its food sources and livestock from foreign threats that are scientifically proven to exist. A member nation cannot create a barrier that favors its domestic sources of goods over foreign sources for the sole purpose of economic advantage. Favlaka will have to show that the threat of crop destruction from the NT Sweetie is real. According to the facts, there is no scientific proof that the NY Sweetie poses any danger to the Favlaka Beauty. This issue has been decided before. Japan tried to prevent the importation of American apples into Japan by creating apple-testing regulations that acted as a form of tariff or trade barrier. The WTO ruled that the lack of scientific evidence that the American apples posed any threat to the Japanese crops meant that the apple-testing regulations were without merit and improperly impeded entry of foreign-grown apples. The situation with Favlaka is very similar. A judge would likely be compelled to follow the same reasoning and order Favlaka to receive the NY Sweetie for sale in its country.

Answers to Practice Quiz

True/False:

1. True   The Security Council of the United Nations is made up of fifteen member nations whose main responsibility is to maintain international peace as well as security. The members may also use armed forces if necessary to accomplish this goal.
2. False UNESCO, UNICEF, IMF and the IFAD are agencies that not only are a part of the United Nations, but who deal with a variety of economic as well as social problems.
3. False Only nations can have cases decided by the International Court of Justice. However, a nation may bring a claim on behalf of an individual or business that wants to seek redress against another country.

4. False   The European Union treaty opens borders for trade by providing for the free flow of capital, services, goods and labor among the member nations.

5. True   Unanimity among European Union members is required in order to admit a new member.

6. False   The European Court of Justice decides disputes involving member nations' adherence to European Union law.

7. True   Though there are many national courts that may interpret as well as enforce the European Union law, the final arbiter of this law is the European Court of Justice.

8. True   The North American Free Trade Agreement was created and signed by these three countries in order to create a free-trade zone between them.

9. False   China and Japan do not belong to any important economic community. Note though that Japan has played an important role in financing the Association of South East Asian nations.

10. False   Mexico has entered into a free trade agreement with the countries of Chile, Columbia, Venezuela, and all of the countries of Central America.

11. False   The Organization of Petroleum Exporting Countries (OPEC) is the most famous Middle Eastern economic organization.

12. True   Prior to the World Trade Organization being created, the General Agreement on Tariffs and Trade ruled over trade disputes. If a party lost under a panel report, it would vote to block the implementation of a panel's findings against it. However, with the creation of the World Trade Organization, the blocking power of member nations has been eliminated.

13. False   Vietnam and the United States signed a trade agreement that opened up one another's borders.

14. True   Many refer to the World Trade Organization as the "Supreme Court of Trade" because of the power given to it to peaceably solve trade disputes among its more than 130 member nations.

15. True   Commercial disputes between foreign governments and U.S. companies may be brought in federal district court.

16. False   A country has absolute authority over what occurs within its own territory.

17. True   The act exclusively governs suits brought against foreign nations regardless if it is brought in the United States federal or state court.

18. True   Due to the active involvement of the rabbi-judges, the Beis Din is more concerned with the truth than the adversarial process.

19. True   Making a profit from providing services or the sale of goods is allowed. However, making a profit from unearned or unjustified profit is not.

20. True   Though the Sino-Soviet socialist law system is the youngest law system of the world, it applies to thirty percent of the people of the world.

21. False   As of October 25, 1998, the compilation and selling of consumer databases is now highly regulated by the European Union. The European Union Directive on Data Protection is the law that provides for this regulation.

22. True   If the police from the European Union countries determine that companies and or individuals are not obeying the European Union Directive, then they may be prosecuted criminally for violating it.

23. True   Criminal prosecution of individuals or businesses that commit crimes within a country's borders or that violate another country's law is allowed.

24. False   An arbitrator issues an award, not a judgment.

25. True   Though the decision of which nation's courts will hear a case involving an international dispute is often a problem, if there is no agreement providing otherwise, the case will usually be brought in the national court of the plaintiff's home country.

Multiple Choice:

26. B   Answer B is correct as their provisions address such things as the settlement of disputes, human rights, foreign aid, navigation and commerce. Answer A is incorrect as treaties and conventions

both involve agreements often involving trade versus abolishing the purchase of goods and services. Further, treaties and conventions involve agreements between nations, not states. Answer C is incorrect as this indicates one of the two elements necessary to show that a practice has become a custom. Answer D is incorrect as this refers to what courts and tribunals depend on to resolve international disputes, not what treaties and conventions center around.

27. C Answer C is correct as consistent and recurring action by two or more nations over a significant period of time as well as recognition of the custom's binding affect is what is needed to show a custom exists between two or more nations. Answer A is incorrect as this is the definition of a treaty. Answer B is incorrect as a custom is not a principle of law, but rather a practice. Answer D is incorrect as this states one of the goals of the United Nations.

28. A Answer A is correct as the European Court of Justice has jurisdiction to enforce European Union law. Answer B is incorrect, as this does not make any sense. Answer C is incorrect as the court may act in the best interest of the European Union however the question states an oxymoron in that the court hears and decides disputes rather than hearing and deciding best interests. Answer D is incorrect for the reasons stated above.

29. D Answer D is correct as the European Court of First Instance is attached to the European Court, and can also hear actions brought by businesses and individuals. It was created to lessen the caseload of the European Court. Answer A is incorrect as this answer states the purpose of the North American Free Trade Agreement. Answer B is incorrect as it is an incorrect statement of fact. Answer C is incorrect, as it makes no sense.

30. D Answer D is correct as answers A, B, and C all are correct statements of fact that describe the appellate body of the World Trade Organization.

31. D Answer D is correct as countries are granted immunity from suits in other countries. Answer A is incorrect as this states an exception when a foreign country is not immune from lawsuits in U.S. courts. Answer B is incorrect as this is making reference to commercial activity being carried on by a foreign country that would be subject to suit in the United States. Answer C is incorrect as it is referring to nationalization not sovereign immunity.

32. A Answer A is correct, as nations do not have to obey international law enacted by other countries or international organizations. Answers B, C, and D are all true statements and therefore they are not the correct answers.

33. B Answer B is correct as the World Intellectual Property Organization issued two conventions, one of which was the Copyright Treaty wherein protection is granted to copyright holders over the Internet and in the digital marketplace. Answer A is incorrect, as this has nothing to do with the World Intellectual Property Organization, but rather the North American Free Trade Agreement's goal. Answer C is incorrect as the WIPO's purpose is to extend not limit copyright protection to rentals and means of distribution. Answer D is incorrect as the other convention known as the Phonogram Treaty, which is also part of the WIPO, provides protection to performers and producers in renting copies of their performances.

34. D Answer D is correct as the forum-selection clause, also known as the choice of forum clause chooses which nation's court has jurisdiction to hear a case arising out of the contract. Answer A is incorrect because even though this is a true fact, it had nothing to do with which court has jurisdiction to hear cases arising out of an international contract. Answer B is incorrect as this is referring to the choice of law clause not the choice of forum clause. Answer C is incorrect as a trade pact granting easier access to the U.S. has little or no bearing on the choice of forum to hear an international contract case.

35. C Answer C is correct based on the principle that a country has absolute authority over what transpires in its own country but, cannot question the validity of an act committed by another country within that other country's own borders. Answer A is incorrect as it is not a true statement, since the restraint on the judiciary is justified under the doctrine of separation of powers. Answer B is incorrect as a country has absolute authority over what transpires within its own territory. Answer D is incorrect, as the courts of one country will not sit in judgment upon the acts of the government of another, done within its own territory.

Short Answer:

36. To cover and expand copyright and intellectual property protection in the digital environment.
37. Many countries of Western Europe, including, France, Italy, Belgium, Luxembourg, Germany, The Netherlands, Denmark, the United Kingdom, Ireland, Greece, Spain and Portugal.
38. The Foreign Commerce Clause and the Treaty Clause
39. The United Nations
40. The Organization of Petroleum Exporting Countries
41. The World Trade Organization
42. national court
43. Determining what constitutes, "commercial activity" is the most litigated aspect of the FSIA.
44. The Overseas Private Investment Corporation
45. It is based upon the eradication of capitalism and the elimination of the private ownership of property.
46. Arbitration is faster, less formal, less expensive and more private than litigation.
47. The European Union Directive on Data Protection
48. treaties and conventions
49. She might rely on the General Agreement on Tariffs and Trade.
50. It opened up each other's borders, reduced tariffs on Vietnamese imports, eliminated the 50 percent surcharge on the importation of American products, encouraged Vietnam to adopt the WTO's standards of protection for intellectual property, and encouraged the phasing in of U.S. service industries into Vietnam.

Chapter 9

NATURE OF TRADITIONAL
AND E-COMMERCE CONTRACTS

Chapter Overview

There are a variety of situations in which an individual will enter into a contractual situation in his or her lifetime. This chapter will provide you with a broad overview of the different types of contracts, the requirements for contract formation, the sources of contract law and technology's role in contract law.

Objectives

Upon completion of the exercises in this chapter, you should be able to:
1. Define what a contract is.
2. Describe the necessary elements to form a valid contract.
3. Differentiate between a bilateral and unilateral contract.
4. Differentiate between an implied-in-fact contract and an express contract.
5. Describe and distinguish the difference between an executed and executory contract.
6. Describe the difference between a valid, void, voidable and unenforceable contract.
7. Define what a quasi-contract is and when it applies.
8. Discuss equity and its applicability to contracts.
9. Recognize the important role that the Uniform Computer Information Transaction Act plays in the creation and enforcement of cyberspace contracts and licenses.
10. Discuss the importance of the United Nations Convention on Contracts for the Sale of International Goods (CISG).

Practical Application

You should be able to recognize whether or not a contract has been formed, as well as the type of contract that is involved. You should also be able to recognize whether or not equity will play a role in the situation you are assessing. Finally, you should be more aware of the difficulties that individuals face when entering into electronic contracts and the licensing of computer information as well as the importance of the Uniform Computer Information Transaction Act in these matters.

Helpful Hints

This chapter lends itself toward organization. As you attempt to learn the area of contract law, it is first helpful to know what a contract is as well as the necessary requisites for its formation. Then it is beneficial to list the various types of contracts along with an example of each to help you remember and differentiate between them. As you study various fact situations, it is especially important in contract law that you read the hypotheticals and or cases line by line being careful to examine the facts as they may or may not be controlled by the contract principles that you have learned. In contract law, slight variations in wording or sequence of events can change the outcome.

Study Tips

The following study tips have been organized in a manner that will assist you in easily learning the concepts involved in this chapter.

Contract

- <u>Defined</u>: An agreement between two or more parties that is enforceable in equity or a court of law.

- <u>Parties to a contract</u>: The offeror whom is the one making the offer, and the offeree who is the individual to whom the offer is made.

- <u>Requirements to have a valid contract:</u> In order to have a valid contract, there must be:
    1. An offer and acceptance, both of which equate to an agreement.
    2. Consideration that is a legally sufficient bargained-for- exchange. Be careful with this element, as gift promises, moral obligations, past consideration and illusory promises are considered insufficient consideration.
    3. Contractual capacity to enter into the contract. This is another area to watch for issues in, as minors, intoxicated individuals and those who have been adjudged insane may not have the requisite capacity to understand the nature of the transaction they are entering into.
    4. Lawful object. Contracts to accomplish illegal goals are contrary to public policy and are void. An example of this would be a contract entered into to kill another individual in order to receive an insurance policy's proceeds.

- <u>Sources of Contract Law:</u> There are three sources of contract law. They are as follows:
    1. Common law of contracts – This law was developed from early court decisions that eventually became precedent for subsequent decisions. Many of the principles developed under the common law are still the same today.
    2. Uniform Commercial Code (U.C.C.) – The purpose of this law is to establish a uniform system of commercial law in the United States. It is important to note that the U.C.C. takes precedence over common law.
    3. Restatement (Second) of Contracts – Though this compilation of contract law principles is law, it is used more often as a guide due to its statutory nature as opposed to law.

- <u>Types of Contracts:</u> There are a variety of contracts, each of which have differences that you must be aware of.
    1. *Bilateral contract* – This type of contract involves a promise for a promise. For example, "I promise to wash your car if you promise to take me to the movies." Acceptance is in the form of a promise.
    2. *Unilateral contract* – This type of contract involves a promise for performance. For example, "If you mow the lawn, I will pay you $10.00." There is no contract until the offeree performs the requested act of mowing the lawn. Acceptance is in the form of performance.

3. ***Express contract*** – Simply stated, these are either oral or written agreements between two parties. An example would be an oral agreement to buy someone's radio and a written agreement to buy someone's home.

4. ***Implied-in-fact contracts*** – This type of contract is implied on the conduct of the parties. There are certain requirements that must be met before a court will find that this type of contract exists. These requirements are:
   - The plaintiff gave services or property to the defendant.
   - The plaintiff expected compensation for the property or services. In other words the property or services were not gifts.
   - Even though the defendant could have refused to accept the property or services given by the plaintiff, he or she did not.

5. ***Objective Theory of Contracts*** applies to both express and implied-in-fact contracts - It does not matter whether or not the contract is express or implied-in-fact; the court will still apply the reasonable person standard. This means, would a reasonable person conclude that the words and conduct of the parties as well a surrounding circumstances were enough to demonstrate that the parties intended to create a contract? Subjective intent is irrelevant as it is the objective intent based on the reasonable person standard that will be examined.

6. ***Quasi-contracts*** - The term quasi-contract is an equitable one and is also known as implied-in-law contract. The Court will create a contract even though there is not an actual contract between the parties, if the plaintiff provided goods or services to the defendant without compensation. Further reinforcement for the creation of a quasi-contract exists when it is shown that it would be unjust not to require the defendant to pay for the benefit received.

7. ***Formal contracts*** - A formal contract is one requiring a special method or form to create it. Some examples of formal contracts are contracts under a state's wax seal, a recognizance for example in the form of a bond, negotiable instruments as per the Uniform Commercial Code, and letters of credit which are also governed by the Uniform Commercial Code.

8. ***Informal contracts*** - All contracts that do not require a special form or method to create are considered informal contracts.

9. ***Valid contract*** - A valid contract is one that meets all of the required elements to establish a contract.

10. ***Void contract*** - A void contract is one that does not have any legal affect.

11. ***Voidable contract*** - A voidable contract is one that enables one party to avoid his or her contractual obligations. Examples of where this situation may exist absent certain exceptions are contracts entered into by minors, insane individuals, intoxicated persons, those acting under undue influence, duress, or fraud and where there is a mutual mistake.

12. Unenforceable contract - If there is a legal defense to the enforcement of the contract, the contract is unenforceable. An example of this would by if a writing such as the case with the purchase of real estate is required to be in writing as per the Statute of Frauds.

13. Executed contract - If both parties have performed their required obligations under the contract, the contract is said to be executed.

14. Executory contract - If only one side has fully performed his or her obligations of the contract, the contract is said to be executory.

- Equity Court and Contracts - The equity courts of England developed a set of rules whose foundation was premised on fairness, moral rights, and equality. Equity principles were applied when the remedy at law was not adequate or in the interest of fairness, equitable principle had to be applied.

- Importance of the Uniform Computer Information Transactions Act (UCITA) - This act targets a majority of the legal issues that are faced when conducting e-commerce over the Internet. Since a majority of the states have adopted some or all of the act, it is anticipated to become the foundation for the creation and enforcement of cyberspace licenses and contracts.

- Importance of The United Nations Convention on Contracts for the International Sale of Goods - The CISG is important because it incorporates rules from all of the prominent legal systems. It is substantially similar to the Uniform Commercial Code. This is another reason that Americans conducting overseas business should be familiar with its provisions.

Refresh Your Memory

The following exercise will enable you to refresh your memory on the rules and principles presented to you in this chapter. Read each question twice and place your answer in the blanks provided. Review the chapter material for any question you miss or are unable to remember.

1. What is a contract? _____
    _____

2. What are the two parties to a contract often referred to as? The _____ and the _____.

3. What are the four basic elements of a contract? (1) _____, (2) _____, (3) _____ _____, and a (4) _____ _____.

4. What are two defenses to the enforcement of a contract? (1) _____ of _____ and (2) _____ and _____.

5. List three sources of contract law. (1) _____, (2) _____, and (3) _____.

6. If an offeror's promise is answered with the offeree's promise of acceptance, the contract is _____.

7. If the offeror's offer can be accepted only by the performance of an act, the contract is _____.

8. An actual contract may be either _____ or _____.

9. Contracts that are stated in oral or written words are known as _____ contracts.

10. The intent to enter into an implied-in-fact or express contract is judged by the _____ _____ standard.

11. A contract that requires a special form or method of creation is known as a _____ _____.

12. If a contract does not equate to a formal contract, it is called an _____ contract.

13. Equity courts based their decisions on _____.

14. The purpose of the Uniform Commercial Code was to _____
_____.

15. The equitable doctrine of _____, allows a court to award monetary damages to a plaintiff for providing services or work to a defendant even though the parties did not have an actual contract between them.

Critical Thought Exercise

Ricky Boggs, a 27-year-old country singer was severely injured in an automobile accident. Boggs was airlifted by Bishop County Air Ambulance to Bishop Trauma Center for surgery and treatment. Boggs slipped into a coma and after seven weeks was transported to Bishop County Extended Care Hospital. Boggs remained in the hospital for fourteen months before he died without ever having regained consciousness. The total charges assessed by Bishop County for the care of Boggs exceeded $370,000.00. After he died, Bishop County sued the Boggs estate to recover the expenses of the air ambulance, trauma treatment, surgery, hospital stay, and extended care.

Was there a contract between Bishop County and Boggs? If so, how much can Bishop County recover from the estate?

Answer. _____

_____

_____

_____

_____

_____

_____

_____

_____

_____

_____

_____

_____

_____

_____

_____

_____

_____

Practice Quiz

True/False:

1. ___ The Restatement (Second) of Contract is law that takes precedence over the common law of contracts. [p 193]

2. ___ Under the objective theory of contracts, the subjective intent of either party who enters into a contract plays an important role in determining the true intentions of the parties. [p 196]

3. ___ Every contract involves at least two parties. [p 191]

4. ___ Consideration is defined as bargained-for exchange that is legally sufficient. [p 191]

5. ___ The contract is bilateral if the offeror's offer can be accepted only by the performance of an act by the offeree. [p 194]

6. ___ If there is an ambiguity as to whether a contract is bilateral or unilateral, it will be presumed to be a bilateral contract. [p 194]

7. ___ The theory of quasi-contract applies to actual contracts between two parties. [p 197]

8. ___ The Uniform Commercial Code usually takes precedence over the common law of contracts. [p 193]

9. ___ If a contract is required to be in writing under the Statute of Frauds but it is not, the contract is unenforceable because of the legal defense to enforcement of the contract. [p 199]

10. ___ A contract is voidable where at least one party has the option to avoid his or her contractual obligations. [p 198]

11. ___ A void contract is one that meets all of the essential elements to establish a contract. [p 198]

12. ___ An executed contract is one that has been fully performed on both sides. [p 199]

13. ___ A contract will not be implied by law regardless of the unjust enrichment of one of the parties. [p 200]

14. ___ A contract that is inferred from the conduct of the parties is known as an implied-in-fact contract. [p 200]

15. ___ A formal contract does not require a special form or method of creation. [p 198]

16. ___ The purpose of a nondisclosure agreement is to assure that the person receiving the information will not steal or reveal the information to anyone else. [p 195]

17. ___ If consent to a contract is gained by duress, undue influence or fraud, the court will find there has been no genuineness of assent. [p 192]

18. ___ A contract may still be created if the offer is not accepted. [p 191]

19. ___ The parties to a contract may voluntarily perform a contract that is unenforceable. [p 199]

20. ___ In an equitable action, there is no right to a jury trial. [p 200]

Multiple Choice:

21. The four basic requirements to have an enforceable contract are [p 191]
     a. duty, breach, causation, and damages.
     b. bilateral, unilateral, executed and executory.
     c. agreement, consideration, capacity, and lawful object.
     d. offeror, offeree, offer and acceptance.

22. A bilateral contract is [p 200]
     a. a promise for performance.
     b. a promise for money.
     c. a promise for a promise.
     d. a promise for an offer.

23. Two types of defenses that may be raised to the enforcement of a contract are [p 192]
     a. writing and form and genuineness of assent.
     b. uniform commercial code and common law of contracts.
     c. contributory negligence and assumption of the risk.
     d. unilateral and bilateral promise.

24. A contract to commit a crime is [p 198]
     a. valid.
     b. void.
     c. voidable.
     d. informal.

25. The Uniform Computer Information Transaction Act will be useful in acting as [p 194]
     a. a quasi-contract.
     b. the reasonable person standard.
     c. the basis for establishing legally sufficient consideration.
     d. the basis for the creation and enforcement of cyberspace contracts and licenses.

26. An oral agreement to purchase a neighbor's gardening tools is an example of [p 195]
     a. an implied-in-fact contract.
     b. an express contract.
     c. an executory contract.
     d. a void contract.

27. If Cathy and Central Properties prepare their own lease agreement for an apartment that Cathy is renting, this contract would be considered [p 198]
     a. a voidable contract.
     b. an informal contract.
     c. a formal contract.
     d. an obligatory contract.

28. In the situation where Judy Smith angrily offers to sell her neighbor Roger Jones a piece of land located in the next town for $150,000., the type of contract that has been formed is [p 196]
     a. a valid contract as all essential elements have been met.
     b. a subject contract as Judy intended to sell Roger the land for a set price.
     c. no contract as the offer was made in anger.
     d. an objective contract as both Judy and Roger were willing to enter into a contract.

29. If Joe's Car Dealership sells Jim a car and Jim pays Joe's Car Dealership for the car, the type of contract the parties entered into would be [p 200]
    a. an executed contract.
    b. an executory contract.
    c. an informal contract.
    d. implied-in-fact contract.

30. An offer to create a unilateral contract can be revoked by the offeror except [p 194]
    a. when the uniform commercial code applies.
    b. when the offeror's intent is based on the reasonable person standard.
    c. when there is a nondisclosure agreement.
    d. when the offeree has begun or has substantially completed performance.

Short Answer:

31. What does the equitable doctrine of quasi-contract allow a court to do? [p 197]
    _____
    _____

32. Formal contracts require _____. [p 198]

33. What is the difference between a void and a voidable contract? [p200] _____
    _____

34. A contract implied by law to prevent unjust enrichment is a _____. [p 200]

35. The United Nations Convention on Contracts for the International Sales of Goods (CISG) applies to contracts for _____. [p 201]

36. If Cassie tells her son Rex that she will give him everything she owns if he loves her the rest of her life, would a valid contract exist between the two? [p 191] _____
    _____

37. Jan Ruiz, a business owner says to Mary Munoz, a decorator, "If you promise to wallpaper my waiting room by December 1, I will pay you $600.00." Mary promises to do so. What type of contract has been created? [p 194] _____

38. Dr. Kurt Crandall says to Collin Jones, a contractor, "If you promise to have the extra rooms to my office built and ready to see patients by May 5, I will pay you $25,000." What type of contract may have been created? [p 194] _____
    _____

39. Which act is expected to become the basis for the creation and enforcement of cyberspace contracts and licenses? [p 194] _____

40. What type of contract is formed where Anthony says to Paul, "I will give you $10,000 if you help my friend Joe rob A & B liquor?" [p 198] _____
    _____

41. Why is the Uniform Commercial Code important to the law of contracts? [p 193] _____
    _____

42. Why was the Uniform Computer Information Transactions Act developed? [p 194] _____
    _____

43. What is the reasoning behind requiring someone to sign a nondisclosure agreement?
    [p 195] _____
    _____
    _____

44. Give at least two examples where there would not be a genuineness of assent in the creation of a
    contract. [p 192] (1) _____ and (2) _____

45. If Alan has painted George's entire house except for the front door, may George revoke his offer to
    pay Alan for painting his house? [p 195] _____

46. What elements must be established to create an implied-in-fact contract? [p 195] _____
    _____
    _____
    _____

47. What does the objective theory of contracts hold? [p 196] _____
    _____
    _____

48. Give four examples of formal contracts. [p 198] _____
    _____
    _____

49. When is a quasi-contract imposed? [p 197] _____
    _____
    _____

50. What is the result if both parties to a contract avoid their contractual obligations? [p 198]
    _____
    _____

Answers to Refresh Your Memory

1. A contract is an agreement between two parties that is enforceable by a court of equity or law.
2. offeror and the offeree
3. agreement, consideration, contractual capacity , and a lawful object
4. genuineness of assent and writing and form
5. common law, Uniform Commercial Code, and the Restatement (Second) of Contracts
6. bilateral
7. unilateral
8. express or implied-in-fact
9. express
10. reasonable person
11. formal contract

12. informal
13. fairness
14. create a uniform system of law among the 50 states.
15. quasi-contract

Critical Thought Exercise Model Answer

For parties to have an express contract, the terms of the agreement must be fully and explicitly stated in words, either oral or written. If there is no express agreement, an implied-in-fact contract may be created in whole or in part from the conduct of the parties, rather than their words. In this case, Boggs was unconscious, so he never manifested an assent to any agreement to pay for services, either by his words or conduct. In this type of situation, a plaintiff may have to rely upon a theory of quasi contract. A Quasi contract is a fictional contract imposed on parties by a court in the interests of fairness and justice. Quasi contracts are usually imposed to avoid unjust enrichment of one party at the expense of another. Society wants medical personnel to come to the aid of injured persons without regard to the existence of a contract before services are rendered. This is especially true in an emergency situation where life may be in jeopardy. Though Boggs never consented to an agreement, it would be unfair for Bishop County to render medical treatment to Boggs to save his life and then receive no compensation. Boggs would then be unjustly enriched at the expense of Bishop County. The amount of recovery, however, is not dependent upon the charges assessed by the county. Because Boggs was never able to bargain for the amount or extent of services, the court will only allow Bishop County to recover the reasonable value of the medical services rendered. The $370,000.00 in bills will be scrutinized by the court and reduced if they exceed a reasonable cost for Boggs' treatment.

Answers to Practice Quiz

True/False:

1. False   The Restatement of the Law of Contracts is not law, but instead acts as a guide. The Uniform Commercial Code takes precedence over the common law of contracts.
2. False   The subjective intent of a party to enter into a contract is immaterial. Under the objective theory of contracts, intent is judged by whether a reasonable person would conclude that the parties intended to make a contract.
3. True   There are at least two parties, the offeror and the offeree, to every contract.
4. True   Consideration is bargained-for exchange that is legally sufficient.
5. False   A bilateral contract involves a promise for a promise. The example given states the definition for a unilateral contract.
6. True   Though the offeror's promise must be carefully examined, the courts usually hold that ambiguities as to whether a contract is bilateral or unilateral will usually result in a finding of the contract to be bilateral.
7. False   Quasi-contracts are also called implied-in-law contracts and are created because there is no actual contract.
8. True   The Uniform Commercial Code usually does take precedence over the common law of contracts.
9. True   An unenforceable contract is one where some legal defense to the enforcement of the contract exists.
10. True   Where at least one party has the option to avoid his or her contract obligations, the court will find that the contract is voidable.

11 False A void contract is one that has no legal effect. A valid contract on the other hand is one that meets the essential elements to establish a contract.

12. True If both parties have performed each of their obligations to the contract, the contract is said to be executed.

13. False Under the theory of quasi-contract, a contract will be implied by laws in order to prevent unjust enrichment.

14. True The parties conduct can result in a contract.

15. False A formal contract does in fact require a special form or method of creation.

16. True The nondisclosure agreement helps protect a person with a great idea so that the idea is not stolen or given to anyone else.

17. True The consent of the parties to form a contract must be genuine. If there is undue influence, duress or fraud, then the genuineness of assent is negated.

18. False No contract is formed if the offer is not accepted.

19. True Even though an unenforceable contract exists where there is a legal defense to its enforcement, the parties may still voluntarily perform the unenforceable contract.

20. True In an equitable action, a judge decides the issue, not a jury.

Multiple Choice:

21. C Answer C correctly states the requirements to have an enforceable contract. Answer A is incorrect as these are the necessary requirements for a negligence cause of action. Answer B is incorrect as these are four types of contracts as opposed to requirements. Answer D is incorrect, as it states the two parties to a contract and only part of what is required to form a contract.

22. C Answer C correctly defines a bilateral contract as it is a promise for a promise. Answer A is incorrect as this is the definition of a unilateral contract. Answer B is incorrect as the way it is phrased could imply either a bilateral or a unilateral contract. Answer D is incorrect as a promise for an offer could imply a unilateral contract.

23. A Answer A correctly states the two types of defenses that may be raised to the enforcement of a contract. Answer B is incorrect as the Uniform Commercial Code and the common law of contracts are both sources of contract law not defenses. Answer C is incorrect as these are defenses to a negligence cause of action. Answer D is incorrect as unilateral and bilateral refer to the types of contracts verses defenses to the enforcement of a contract.

24. B Answer B is correct as a contract to commit a crime has no legal effect and is therefore void, as though no contract had ever been created. Answer A is incorrect as contracting to commit a crime is not a lawful object, which would make the contract void. Answer C is incorrect, as a contract is only voidable when one party has the option of performing or not performing. In the situation where the main object of the contract is to commit a crime, this option is not available. Answer D is incorrect as an informal contract is one that does not qualify as a formal contract. A contract to commit a crime is not a contract at all and as such would not fall under either the formal or informal categorization of contracts.

25. D Answer D is correct as it succinctly states the purpose of the Uniform Computer Information Transaction Act. Answer A is incorrect as a quasi-contract is an equitable remedy that is enforced to prevent unjust enrichment. Further, the UCITA does not need to be present in order to enforce a quasi-contract. Answer B is incorrect as the UCITA was not designed to define the reasonable person standard. Answer C is incorrect as even though the act will help address issues such as consideration in the formation of cyberspace contracts, that is not the sole purpose or issue to be addressed by the act.

26. B Answer B is correct as this is a primary example of an oral, express contract. Answer A is incorrect as implied-in-fact contracts are implied from the conduct of the parties. The facts are silent as to any conduct, but instead state that there was an oral agreement. Answer C is incorrect

as an executory contract is one that is not fully performed by one or both of the parties. There is nothing in the facts that would indicate nonperformance by either or both parties. Answer D is incorrect as a void contract is one that has no legal effect and is against public policy. In the example given, purchasing a neighbor's gardening tools is not a crime nor is it against public policy.

27. B   Answer B is correct as the facts state that Cathy and Central Properties prepared their own lease agreement, which indicates that no special form or method of creation was necessary in order to make the agreement. Answer A is incorrect as the facts do not indicate a potentially voidable contract situation as would possibly be the case if a minor, intoxicated or insane person was involved. Answer C is incorrect as simple contracts such as leases, service contracts and sales contracts usually do not qualify as formal contracts, whereas contracts under seal, negotiable instruments, recognizances and letters of credit are examples of formal contracts.

28. C   Answer C is correct, as contracts made in anger negate the intent to create a contract when the reasonable person standard is applied. Answer A is incorrect because even though all of the elements to form a valid contract appear to be present, a reasonable person would conclude that because Judy Smith was angry when she offered to sell her land to Roger, she did not intend to enter into a contract with him. Answer B is incorrect as this answer makes no sense, since there is no such thing as a subject contract. Answer D is incorrect as Judy's anger makes her intent to enter into the contract with Roger questionable.

29. A   Answer A is correct as Joe's Car Dealership and Jim have both fully performed their obligations under the contract. Answer B is incorrect as an executory contract exists where the contract is not fully performed by one or both parties. Answer C is incorrect as an informal contract refers to the fact that no special form or method of creation is necessary. Answer D is incorrect as the facts are not indicative of a contract that is inferred from conduct, but instead give details of the parties agreement.

30. D   Answer D is correct as generally an offer to create a unilateral contract may be revoked at anytime prior to the offeree's performance of the requested act, unless the offeree has begun or substantially completed performance. Answer A is incorrect as application of the Uniform Commercial Code has no significance regarding when a unilateral contract may be revoked. Answer B is incorrect as the reasonable person standard is irrelevant in terms of when revocation may take place. Answer C is incorrect as nondisclosure agreements are entered into for the purpose of protecting an invention or trade secret or things of that nature that one of the parties does not want disclosed. Nondisclosure agreements have no relevance in terms of the period of time for revocation.

Short Answer:

31.   It allows a court to award monetary damages to a plaintiff for providing work or services to a defendant even though no actual contract existed between the parties.

32.   a special form or method of creation.

33.   No contract exists if the contract is void. Compare this to a voidable contract where a party has the option of voiding or enforcing the contract.

34.   quasi-contract.

35.   the international sale of goods.

36.   Probably not as moral obligations such as loving one's mother would not be construed as bargained-for consideration that is legally sufficient.

37.   A bilateral contract was created the moment that Mary promised to wallpaper the waiting room.

38.   Dr. Crandall's offer created a unilateral contract whereby the offer can be accepted only by the contractor's performance of the requested act.

39.   The Uniform Computer Information Transactions Act (UTICA)

40.   A void contract as entering into a contract to commit a crime has no legal effect.

41.   It helps to establish a uniform system of commercial law among the 50 states.

42. It was developed to establish uniform legal rules for the formation and enforcement of electronic contracts and licenses.

43. A nondisclosure agreement acts as protection for a person who has a good idea and want to share it but also wants the assurance that the person who learns of the idea will not steal or tell what he or she has just found out to anyone else.

44. duress and fraud or undue influence

45. No, George may not revoke his offer as Alan has substantially completed the entire house with the exception of the front door.

46. These elements must be shown in order to create an implied-in-fact contract: 1) The plaintiff provided property or services to the defendant. 2) The plaintiff expected to be paid by the defendant for the property or services and did not provide the services or property gratuitously. 3) The defendant was given an opportunity to reject the property or services provided by the plaintiff but did not.

47. This theory hold that the intent to enter into an implied-in-fact contract or an express contract is judged by the reasonable person standard.

48. Letters of credit, negotiable instruments such as checks, notes, certificates of deposits, recognizances, and contracts under seal are examples of formal contracts.

49. It is imposed where one party confers a benefit on another who keeps the benefit and it would be unjust not to require that person to pay for the benefit received.

50. Both parties are released from their contractual obligations.

Chapter 10

AGREEMENT

Chapter Overview

As you will recall in Chapter 9, you learned about the different types of contracts as well as the requirements for contract formation. This chapter expands upon the requirement of agreement. You will learn what constitutes a valid offer as well as the various ways that an offer can be terminated. Offers such as rewards, advertisements, auctions and counteroffers are also discussed. Additionally, you will learn many ways that an acceptance can be effectuated with special attention being paid to the mailbox rule. Finally, the author gives a clear explanation of the enforceability of computer shrink-wrap licenses.

Objectives

Upon completion of the exercises in this chapter, you should be able to:
1. Give the definition of an offer and acceptance.
2. List the requirements of an offer.
3. List the terms that can be implied in a contract.
4. Discuss the requirements of special offers such as rewards, advertisements and auctions.
5. Discuss what a counteroffer is as well as its impact.
6. Discuss the various ways an offer may be terminated.
7. Discuss what an option contract is.
8. Describe what the mailbox rule is and how it is applied.
9. Discuss the enforceability behind computer shrink-wrap licenses.

Practical Application

You should be able to recognize whether or not a valid offer has been made and whether or not the essential terms are included within it. You should also be able to know if an offer has been properly terminated or if the mailbox rule applies. Finally, with your basic knowledge, you should be able to draft a simple offer by utilizing the information contained in this chapter.

Helpful Hints

Each chapter, especially in the area of contracts builds on one another. As such, it is vital that you understand the information given in each chapter and know how to apply it to given fact situations. Your initial analysis of a potential contract should begin with the offer. You should use a mental checklist of what is required to establish a valid offer. If one of the elements is missing, then ask yourself whether there is a rule of law that may apply to satisfy that missing element. Next, you should determine whether or not you are examining a special offer such as a reward, an advertisement, auction or counteroffer. Once again, quickly review your mental checklist on any special rules that may apply to these types of offers. Before you proceed any further, look at the facts and determine whether or not the offer has been terminated. Next, has there been an acceptance to the offer you have analyzed? If so, you need to address the issue of whether the acceptance was proper. Examine whether the offer specified a means of acceptance, the time for acceptance, method of communication and the mailbox rule. The Study Tips section that follows gives easy to remember lists of what is required for the aspects of this chapter.

Study Tips

Offer

Definition as per Section 24 of Restatement (Second) of Contracts: "The manifestation of willingness to enter into a bargain, so made as to justify another person in understanding that his assent to that bargain is invited and will conclude it."

Requirements
- The offeror must objectively intend to be held to the offer. Remember objective intent is gauged against a reasonable person in the same or similar circumstances.
  a. Were mere preliminary negotiations going on between the parties? If the offeror is asking a question as opposed to making a statement of intent to bargain, it is probably an invitation to make an offer and not indicative of the offeror's present intent to contract.
  b. Was the offer made in anger, jest or undue excitement? If any of these exist, the objective intent is missing and the offer cannot result in a valid contract.
  c. Offers made as an expression of opinion are not enforceable promises.
- The offer's terms must be definite or reasonably certain.
  a. Were the terms clear so that the offeree was able to accept or reject the terms of the offer?
  b. Did the offer contain an identification of the parties, identification of the subject matter, the consideration to be paid and the time for performance? If the answer is yes, then the offer will probably be considered definite and certain.
  c. Were there any implied terms?
     Common Law: If any of the terms were missing, the offer would fail.
     Modern Law: There is more leniency, as the court will supply a missing term if a reasonable term can be implied, such as for price and time or performance.
- The offer has to be communicated to the offeree. Without communication, there can be no acceptance.

Special Types of Offers

Advertisements
- These are treated as invitations to make an offer.
- The exception to it being an invitation is if the offer is definite or specific that it is obvious that the advertiser had the present intend to be bound by the advertisement, then it will be considered to be an offer.

Rewards
- An offer to pay a reward is an offer to form a unilateral contract.
- The two requirements to accept a reward are that the offeree had knowledge of the reward before completing the requested act and he or she performed the requested act.

Auctions
- Usually a seller uses an auctioneer to offer to sell his or her goods.
- Auctions are with reserve as they are usually considered an invitation to make an offer. The seller can withdraw his or her goods from the sale and refuse the highest bid.

- Note, that if the auction is without reserve, the seller must accept the highest bid and cannot take his or her goods back.

Termination of an Offer By the Parties

An offer may be terminated by the parties by revoking the offer, rejecting the offer or by a counteroffer made by the offeree. These three means of terminating an offer are discussed below.

Revocation of an offer by the offeror

- At common law, the offeror could revoke his or her offer any time before the offeree accepted.
- The revocation may be express or implied by the offeror or a third party.
- The majority of states rule that the revocation is not effective until it is received.
- Revocation of an offer made to the public may be revoked by communicating in the same way that the offer was made for the same length of time.
- Prevention of revocation by the offeror is accomplished through an option contract. The offeree usually pays the offeror money to keep the offer open for an agreed-upon period of time. During this period of time the offeror agrees not to sell the subject matter of the offer to anyone else. Keep in mind that death or incompetency does not terminate the option contract unless it was a personal service contract.

Rejection of an offer by the offeree

- The rejection may be express or implied by the offeree's conduct.
- The rejection is not effective until it is received.
- An acceptance by the offeree after the offeree has rejected the offer is construed as a counteroffer.

Counteroffer by the offeree

- It terminates the original offer.
- It creates a new offer that the original offeror is now free to accept or reject.

Termination of the Offer by Operation of Law

An offer may be terminated by operation of law in several situations. It can be terminated by destruction of the subject matter or by death or incompetency of the offeror or offeree, by a supervening illegality or by lapse of time.

Destruction of the Subject Matter

- The offer is terminated if the subject matter of the offer is destroyed through no fault of either party before the offer is accepted.
- An example of this would be if a boat that was listed for sale sank and was unable to be recovered, the offer would automatically terminate

Death or Incompetency of the Offeror or Offeree

- Death of either the offeror or offeree terminates the offer.
- Incompetency of the offeror or offeree terminates the offer.
- Notice of the death or incompetency is not a requirement.
- Death or incompetency will not terminate an option contract unless it was a personal service contract.

Supervening Illegality

- If the object of the offer is made illegal before the offer is accepted, the offer terminates. For example, if a bog frog becomes an endangered species after an offer is made for its sale to pet stores, but before the pet stores accept, the offer is terminated.
- Many times statutes are enacted that make the object of the offer illegal.

Lapse of Time

- The offer sometimes limits the time in which it can be accepted.
- The time begins to run from the time it is actually received by the offeree and extends until the stated time period ends.
- If no time is stated in the offer, then the offer terminates within a "reasonable time" and on a case-by-case basis.
- If an offer is made over the telephone or face to face, then the offer usually terminates after the conversation.

Acceptance

Defined: Simply stated, an acceptance is an outward manifestation of assent to be bound by the terms of the offer as assessed by the reasonable person standard.

Basic Facts about Acceptance

- Only the offeree can accept the offer to create a contract.
- If an offer is made to more than one person, each person has the power to accept the offer.
- If an acceptance is made by one party, it terminates the offer as to the other individuals to whom the offer was made.
- If a joint offer has been made, the offer must be accepted jointly.

Mirror Image Rule

- This rule states that the offeree must accept the offeror's terms. The acceptance must be unequivocal.
- Grumbling acceptances do form contracts.
- Acceptances however that add conditions to them are not unequivocal and thus fail.

Silence as Acceptance

- The general rule is that silence is not held to be an acceptance despite the offeror stating it is.
- There are several exceptions to the general rule.
    a. Where the offeree by his words intended his silence to mean acceptance.
    b. A signed agreement by the offeree allowing continued delivery until notice was given. For example, if Sid continued to buy crafts from a monthly craft club then his silence would indicate acceptance until he notifies the craft club that he wants to discontinue his membership.
    c. Prior course of dealings by the parties where silence is construed as an acceptance.
    d. The offeree accepts the benefit of goods or services given by the offeror even though the offeree had the opportunity to reject the services or goods.

Time and Method of Acceptance

Mailbox Rule

- This rule is also known as the acceptance-upon-dispatch rule.

- Acceptance is effective when it is placed in the mailbox, or dispatched, even if it gets lost along the way.
- The rule does not apply if a rejection is sent first and then an acceptance is mailed.
- The acceptance has to be properly dispatched. In other words, it has to be properly addressed, packaged and have proper postage applied. Under common law, if the acceptance wasn't properly dispatched, it wasn't effective unless received by the offeror.

Mode of Acceptance
- The usual rule is that the offeree must accept by an authorized mode of communication.
- The offer can state how it is to be accepted. This is called express authorization.
  Note: If the offeree uses a different means to communicate his or her acceptance instead of the means stipulated to be the parties, then the acceptance is ineffective.
- Implied authorization may apply where it is customary in similar transactions between the parties, or prior dealings or usage of trade. Implied authorization will be allowed "by any medium reasonable in the circumstances." Section 30 of the Restatement Second.

Importance of the Comity Principle
This ethical rule states that each nation will respect the other nations' laws. It is usually applied in cases of concurrent jurisdiction and where the foreign law is different from the country where the case is being brought. Its purpose is to develop respect for the laws of other nations.

Enforceability of Computer Shrinkwrap Licenses
A recent issue before the courts involved whether licenses and contracts that are shrinkwrapped inside software boxes and computer equipment boxes are enforceable against purchasers. The courts have held that they are enforceable as the "accept-or-return" portion of the agreements inside of the shrinkwrap sufficiently protected the consumers or potential licensees against goods they did not want to accept as they were still allowed to return the goods under the contract.

Refresh Your Memory

The following exercise will enable you to refresh your memory on the rules and principles presented to you in this chapter. Read each question twice and place your answer in the blanks provided. Review the chapter material for any question you miss or are unable to remember.

1. An _____ is the manifestation by two or more individuals of the substance of a contract. [p 205]

2. If June says to Monica, "I will give you ten dollars to wash my car." Who is the offeree in this example? [p 205] _____

3. The offeror must _____ intend to be bound by the terms of the offer. [p 205]

4. The terms of the offer must be definite or _____ _____. [p 205]

5. Which theory is used in determining whether the parties intended to enter into a contract? The _____ _____ of contracts. [p 205]

6. If Homer asked Ernie, "Would you be interested in selling your car to me?" Would this be a valid offer? [p 206] _____

7. Under the modern law of contracts, which two terms of an offer may be implied? [p 207]
_____ and _____ _____ _____

8. _____ are usually viewed as invitations to make an offer. [p 208]

9. What type of auction provides that the seller must accept the highest bid and cannot withdraw the goods from sale? An _____ [p 209]

10. An offer is terminated if the offeree _____ it. [p 210]

11. A _____ by the offeree terminates the offeror's offer and creates a new offer at the same time. [p 211]

12. The offer terminates by operation of law if the _____ _____ of the offer is destroyed through no fault of either party before its acceptance. [p 212]

13. The offeree's acceptance must be _____. [p 213]

14. Under the mailbox rule, acceptance is effective upon _____. [p 215]

15. Usually an offeree must accept an offer by an _____ means of communication. [p 215]

16. Implied authorization may be inferred from _____
_____. [p 216]

17. Why is an opinion not an enforceable promise? [p 206] _____
_____

18. Only the _____ has the power to accept an offer and create a contract. [p 213]

Critical Thought Exercise

Gus Vincent sent invitations to a number of potential buyers to submit bids for the mineral rights to his 2,000-acre parcel in upstate New York on the outskirts of the City of Hudson. Seven bids were received, including the highest bid from International Mining and Cement Company, LTD. (IMC). Vincent then decided to hold onto the land for a few more years and never responded to any of the bidders. IMC claimed that a contract had been formed by submission of its winning bid and sued Vincent for breach of contract.

Did a contract exist?

Answer. _____
_____
_____
_____
_____
_____

_____
_____
_____
_____
_____
_____
_____
_____
_____
_____
_____
_____

Practice Quiz

True/False:

1. ____ The objective theory of contracts is used to determine whether there was an intent to enter a contract. [p 205]

2. ____ A valid contract may result from preliminary negotiations. [p 205]

3. ____ The owner of the Z store shouts in frustration, "For even $50,000, I'd sell the whole business along with its company cars!" This statement will not be considered a valid offer. [p 206]

4. ____ Under modern law, the court will not imply terms in a contract. [p 207]

5. ____ An offer may be accepted even though it has not been communicated. [p 207]

6. ____ Generally speaking, price and time of performance can be implied even if these terms are not present. [p 207]

7. ____ An advertisement is considered an offer if it is so definite or specific that it is obvious that the advertiser has the present intent to be bound by the terms of the ad. [p 205]

8. ____ An auction with reserve is not considered an invitation to make an offer. [p 209]

9. ____ A majority of states do not require receipt of an offeror's revocation in order to be effective. [p 210]

10. ____ Rejection of an offer is effective upon receipt. [p 210]

11. ____ A counteroffer by the offeree doesn't terminate the original offer, as it is considered to be a mere inquiry. [p 211]

12. ____ If a snowmobile being purchased by Sam is destroyed after Jan makes the offer but before Sid accepts the offer is terminated. [p 212]

13. ___ The offeror may accept his or her own offer. [p 213]

14. ___ Generally speaking, a grumbling acceptance is a valid, legal acceptance. [p 213]

15. ___ Silence may also be considered an acceptance if the offeree has demonstrated that silence means assent. [p 214]

16. ___ Under the mailbox rule, acceptance is effective upon receipt. [p 215]

17. ___ An offeree must accept an offer by an authorized means of communication. [p 216]

18. ___ Unilateral contracts may only be accepted by the offeree's performance. [p 213]

19. ___ Implied authorization cannot be implied from prior transactions between the parties. [p 216]

20. ___ The comity principle is a rule that states nations will respect the laws of other nations. [p 216]

Multiple Choice:

21. Sam Brown stated to Mary Powers, "I will buy your house for $350,000." His statement was [p 206]
    a. a valid offer.
    b. a preliminary question.
    c. an opinion.
    d. a bilateral contract.

22. A car dealer tells his customer that he feels the car she is interested in buying is the best car on his lot and will probably give her a lifetime of happiness. If the customer buys the car and immediately has problems, the customer may [p 206]
    a. enforce the car dealer's promise.
    b. return the car for her money back.
    c. not enforce the promise.
    d. none of the above

23. To be considered a valid offer, the communication must contain [p 207]
    a. an offer, acceptance and consideration.
    b. protection against potential breach.
    c. the parties, consideration, time for performance and identification of the subject matter.
    d. a provision against communications made in jest or anger.

24. In order to be entitled to collect on an offer to pay a reward, the offeree must [p 209]
    a. return the lost property or capture the criminal.
    b. offer the goods for sale through an auctioneer.
    c. let the offeror know that he or she is there to collect the reward.
    d. have knowledge of the reward before completing the requested act and perform the requested act.

25. Under common law, an offeror could revoke his or her offer [p 210]
    a. any time prior to its acceptance by the offeree.
    b. once a counteroffer has been made by the offeree.
    c. upon dispatch into a U.S. mailbox.
    d. by an authorized means of communication.

26. Two ways to terminate an offer by operation of law are [p 212]
    a. by rejection and revocation.
    b. death or incompetency of the offeror or offeree.
    c. rewards and auctions.
    d. intoxication and incapacity.

27. The ABC Corporation mailed an offer of employment to Ernest. The offer stated that acceptance of the job was to be by certified mail. Ernest was so elated about the idea of working for the ABC Corporation, that he flew to the city ABC was locate in and hand delivered his acceptance within the time stated in the offer. Has a contract been formed between ABC and Ernest? [p 216]
    a. No, because Ernest used an unauthorized means of communication to give his acceptance.
    b. Yes, as an offeree may accept an offer by an unauthorized means of communication.
    c. No, because the Restatement (Second) of Contracts permits implied authorization by "any medium reasonable in the circumstances."
    d. Yes, because adherence to the comity principle requires that ABC respect the law that Ernest is applying

28. In order for an offer to be effective, which elements must be established? [p 205]
    a. The offeror must objectively intend to be bound by the offer.
    b. The terms of the offer must be definite and reasonably certain.
    c. The offer must be communicated to the offeree.
    d. All of the above.

29. Implied authorization for acceptance of an offer may be [p 216]
    a. inferred by properly addressing and packaging and dispatching the acceptance.
    b. expressly stating that acceptance is not effective until received.
    c. inferred from prior dealings, trade usage, or what is customary from similar transactions.
    d. by stipulation that acceptance must be by specified means.

30. Mrs. Sweet, the President of Sweetest Things Corporation, puts an offer to sell the packaging division in writing to Mr. Baker but does not send it. Thereafter, Mrs. Baker stops in to visit Mrs. Sweet and notices the written offer on Mrs. Sweet's desk. She then goes home and tells Mr. Baker about the offer. Can Mr. Baker accept the offer to buy the packaging division of the Sweetest Things Corporation? [p 207]
    a. Yes, as Mrs. Baker was acting as a proxy for Mr. Baker.
    b. No, as Mrs. Baker did not tell Mr. Baker all of the particulars of the offer.
    c. Yes, as a wife, Mrs. Baker steps into the shoes of her husband and may convey the message to Mr. Baker.
    d. No, because Mrs. Sweet never communicated the offer to Mr. Baker and therefore there is no offer to be accepted.

Short Answer:

31. The statement, "I will purchase your mountain bike for $350.00" is a valid offer because it
_____. [p 206]

32. Hilda and Mildred are having a fun dinner together complete with wine and laughter. Hilda in a hysterical fit of laughter tells Mildred, "Since you are my funniest friend, I'll sell you my California farm for $30,000." Has Hilda made a valid offer to Mildred? [p 206]

_____

_____

33. If Tom, a tractor salesperson places an advertisement in a local circular that reads, "like new, 2002, Edwards Co. tractor, serial no. 3478942, $6,200." Is this an offer? [p 208]

_____

34. Sean accidentally leaves his grandfather's top hat in a fancy restaurant he was dining at. He places an ad in the Bradley News Gazette stating, "$500.00 reward for the return of an old, black top hat left in Patrano's Italian Restaurant on March 15, 2003, at approximately 8 p.m. Call 911-555-1212. Dawn, who has not seen the offer, finds Sean's top hat and also notes that there is a phone number on a tag inside of it. She telephone's Sean and determines that she has found his top hat. Dawn's friend Sally thereafter tells Dawn that there is a reward for finding the hat as she had seen the ad in the paper and recognized that the number in the newspaper is the same as the number inside of the hat. Is Dawn entitled to the reward money? [p 209]

_____

_____

35. What type of auction is considered to be an invitation to make an offer? [p 209] _____

_____

36. If Marcia places an ad in the Sunset News Press offering a reward for her lost cat Barney and she lets the ad run for five weeks, what must she do to revoke the ad? [p 210]

_____

_____

_____

37. If Sue says to Julius, "I think $3,500. is too high for your old truck. I will pay you $2,500 instead." What is the effect of Sue's statement? [p 211] _____

_____

38. What is the result if a flood from a broken pipe destroys the bolts of silk fabric Martha was intending to buy? [p 212] _____

_____

39. If Omar decides to sell Jane his motor home for $60,000, provided she decides by May 1, and Omar is adjudged insane before Jane makes her decision, what is the effect of Omar's insanity? [p 212]

_____

_____

40. Acceptance is defined as [p 213] _____

_____

41. A bilateral contract may be accepted by [p 213] _____

42. What does the mirror image rule require? [p 213] _____

_____

43. What is an option contract? [p 213] _____

_____
_____

44. What happens if a person waits too long to accept an offer? [p 213] _____

_____

45. Why is silence usually not considered an acceptance even if the offeror states that it is? [p 214]

_____

46. Under the common law, what was the effect of an acceptance that was not properly dispatched? [p 215] _____

47. What is another name for an offer that stipulates that acceptance must be by a specified means of communication? [p 216] _____

48. The statement, "I will buy your dining room set for $5,000" is a valid offer because [p 206]

_____

49. If the price term is missing from an offer, when can it be implied? [p 207] _____

_____

50. What is the effect of a supervening illegality on an offer? [p 212] _____

_____

Answers to Refresh Your Memory

1. agreement [p 205]
2. Monica, as she is the one to whom the offer is being made. [p 205]
3. objectively [p 205]
4. reasonably certain [p 205]
5. objective theory [p 205]
6. No, it is not a valid offer as it is a preliminary negotiation. [p 206]
7. price and time for performance [p 206]
8. Advertisements [p 208]
9. auction without reserve [p 209]
10. rejects [p 210]
11. counteroffer [p 211]
12. subject matter [p 212]
13. unequivocal [p 213]
14. dispatch [p 215]
15. authorized [p 215]
16. what is customary in similar transactions, usage of trade, or prior dealings between the parties. [p 216]
17. Because an opinion leaves room for uncertainty and an opinion does not manifest an intent to be bound by the representation. [p 206]
18. offeree [p 213]

Critical Thought Exercise Model Answer

To have an offer that is capable of acceptance, three elements must be present: (1) There must be a serious, objective intention by the offeror; (2) The terms of the offer must be reasonably certain, or definite, so that the parties and the court can ascertain the terms of the contract; and, (3) The offer must be communicated to the offeree. There appears to be sufficient information in the bid to find definite terms. Sending the request for a bid to IMC fulfilled the communication requirement. The issue centers on whether the request for a bid was accompanied by a serious intent to be bound by the offeror. Intent is not determined by the subjective intentions, beliefs, or assumptions of the offeror. What meaning Vincent attached to his invitation to bid is not relevant. Intent is determined by what a reasonable person in the offeree's position would conclude the offeror's words and actions meant. A request or invitation to negotiate is not an offer. It only expresses a willingness to discuss the matter and possibly enter into a contract after further negotiations. A reasonable person in the position of IMC would not conclude that the invitation evidenced an intention to enter into a binding agreement. As in construction contracts, an invitation to submit a bid is not an offer, and the bidding party does not bind the party who requests bids merely by submitting a bid. The party requesting the bids is free to reject all the bids or not act at all. Vincent was not bound by the bid of IMC merely because it was the highest submitted. Vincent never manifested an intent to be bound by the invitation to bid and he remained free to reject the bid of IMC or simply change his mind and take no action at all.

Answers to Practice Quiz

True/False:

1. True   The basis of the objective theory of contracts is whether a reasonable person viewing the situation would conclude that the parties intended to be legally bound.
2. False   A valid offer may not result from preliminary negotiations, as they do not evince the offeror's intent to contract.
3. True   Offers made in jest, anger, or undue excitement cannot result in a valid contract as a reasonable person would conclude that in light of the circumstances, the parties did not intend to be bound.
4. False   Modernly courts are more lenient and will imply terms such as price and time for performance. Price will be implied if there is a market or source to determine the price of the item or service. The time for performance will be implied based on what is reasonable under the circumstances.
5. False   An offer cannot be accepted if it is not communicated to the offeree by the offeror or an agent or representative of the offeror.
6. True   Price will be implied if there is a market or source to determine the price of the item or service. The time for performance will be implied based on what is reasonable under the circumstances.
7. True   Generally advertisements are treated as invitations to make an offer. However, if the offer is so definite and specific that it is obvious that the advertiser has the present intent to bind himself or herself to the terms of the advertisement, it will be considered an offer.
8. False   An auction with reserve is an invitation to make an offer. In this situation, the seller keeps the right to refuse the highest bid and may withdraw the goods from sale.
9. False   Most states provide that in order for the revocation to be effective, it must be received by the offeree or the offeree's agent.
10. True   A rejection is not effective until it is actually received by the offeror.
11. False The effect of a counteroffer is that it terminates the offeror's offer and creates a new offer.

12. True   The offer terminates if the subject matter, in this case the snowmobile, of the offer is destroyed through no fault of either party prior to its acceptance.

13. False   The offeree is the only one who has the legal power to accept an offer and create a contract.

14. True   The offeree may feel discontented; a grumbling acceptance is a legal acceptance, as he or she is not adding any conditions to the offer before accepting.

15. True   This is an exception to the general rule that silence usually is not considered acceptance even if the offeror states that it is. If the offeree has indicated that silence means assent, then it will be construed as an acceptance. A classic example is when someone indicates that if you haven't heard from them by a date certain, then go ahead and send the order.

16. False   Under the mailbox rule, acceptance is effective upon dispatch, not receipt.

17. True   This is the general rule that an offeree must accept an offer by an authorized means of communication.

18. True   Unilateral contracts may only be accepted by the offeree's performance of the required act. Compare this to a bilateral contract where it can only be accepted by an offeree who promises to perform the requested act.

19. False   Implied authorization may be implied from what is customary in similar transactions.

20. True   The ethical based rule provides for each nation to respect other nations' laws.

Multiple Choice:

21. A   Answer A is correct as Sam's statement indicates his present intent to enter into a binding contract with Mary. Answer B is incorrect as there is not any question involved, but rather a statement. Answer C is incorrect as there is nothing in the statement that states what Sam believes in order to classify it as an opinion. Answer D is incorrect as this is a one-sided statement that is impossible to determine if a return promise is forthcoming to create a bilateral contract.

22. C   Answer C is correct as the car dealer expressed his opinion that he felt the car was the best car on his lot and would probably give her a lifetime of happiness. Traditionally expressions of opinions are not actionable as promises as they do not satisfy the intent requirement of the formation of a contract. Answer A is incorrect for the reason stated above. Answer B is incorrect as her grounds for rescission only appear to be based on the car dealer's opinion, which would not substantiate granting her money back. Answer D is incorrect for the reasons stated above.

23. C   Answer C is correct as it states what is needed in order to establish a valid offer. Answer A is incorrect as these elements are part of what composes a valid contract. Answer B is incorrect as it makes no sense and it is not an element to establish a valid offer. Answer D is incorrect for the same reasons that answer B is incorrect.

24. D   Answer D correctly states what is required of an offeree in order to collect a reward that is being offered. Answer A is incorrect, because even though the return of lost property or the capturing of a criminal may be the requested act to be performed, these do not address the two basic elements of knowledge of the reward and performance of the act that is required. Answer B is comical at best as it also does not address the requirements of an offeree in order to collect a reward. Answer C is incorrect as there is nothing to indicate that the individual had knowledge of the reward or performed a requested act before notifying the offeror that he or she is there to collect the reward.

25. A   Answer A is correct as revocation at common law could be accomplished any time prior to the offeree's acceptance. Answer B is incorrect as a counteroffer terminates a prior offer and creates a new offer therefore disposing of the need for revocation of the original offer. Answer C is incorrect as this states the mailbox rule, which applies to acceptance. Hence acceptance is effective upon dispatch. Answer D is incorrect as not all offers may be revoked by any

authorized means of communication. For example, an offer to the public must be revoked by the same means and for the same length of time as the offer itself.

26. B Answer B is correct as death or incompetency of the offeree or offeror are two ways by operation of law that an offer may be terminated. Answer A is incorrect as rejection and revocation are ways that the parties may terminate an offer. Answer C is incorrect, as it does not make any sense. Answer D is incorrect as intoxication and incapacity are defenses to the enforcement of a contract not ways to terminate an offer.

27. A Answer A is correct as an offer may stipulate that acceptance must be by a specified means of communication, such as registered mail. Further, since Ernest used an unauthorized means of communication by hand delivering his acceptance, the acceptance of employment is not effective even if it is received by the ABC Corporation in a timely manner because the means of communication was a condition of acceptance. Ernest should have accepted by certified mail as stated in the offer from the ABC Corporation. Answer B is incorrect as the general rule states that an offeree must accept an offer by an authorized means of communication, not an unauthorized means of communication. Answer C is incorrect as implied authorization usually applies in circumstances of prior dealings between the parties, or it is implied from what is customary in similar transactions or usage of trade. Accepting employment does not appear to fit within any of the categories given for an implied authorization situation. Answer D is incorrect as the comity principle is an ethical rule that states that nations will respect other nations laws. This principle does not apply in this particular case.

28. D Answer D is correct as answers A, B, and C all correctly state the necessary elements to establish a valid offer.

29. C Answer C is correct as implied authorization may be inferred from prior dealings between the parties, usage of trade and from what is customary in similar transactions. Answer A is incorrect as this states the proper dispatch rule. Answer B is incorrect as it not only is contradictory in that authorization cannot be implied and expressed at the same time. Further, the general rule regarding acceptance is that it is effective upon dispatch unless there was a stipulation by the parties that acceptance was effective upon receipt. Answer D is incorrect as once again the answer is phrased in contradictory terms to the question. Authorization may not be implied and stipulated to at the same time.

30. D Answer D is correct, as an offer may not be accepted if it is not communicated to the offeree by the offeror or a representative or agent of the offeror. Since Mrs. Sweet did not communicate the offer to Mr. Baker, he cannot accept the offer to buy the packaging division of the Sweetest Things Corporation. Answer A is incorrect, as the rule does not apply to representatives or agents of the offeree, but rather representatives or agents of the offeror. Answer B is incorrect as the fact that Mrs. Baker did not tell Mr. Baker all of the offer's particulars is irrelevant as she cannot communicate the offer to her husband. Answer C is incorrect, as even though she as a manner of speaking may wear the shoes in their family, she may not make the offer to her husband. Mrs. Sweet as the offeror must make the offer to Mr. Baker, the offeree.

Short Answer:

31. indicates the offeror's present intent to enter into a contract.
32. No, as offers made in jest do not satisfy the element of intent to be bound by the terms of the offer as judged by a reasonable person under the same circumstances.
33. Yes, as the advertisement was definite and specific enough to demonstrate that Tom intended to bind himself to the terms of the advertisement.
34. No, because Dawn did not have prior knowledge of the reward before she found Sean's missing top hat.
35. an auction with reserve

36. Marcia must communicate the revocation in the Sunset News Press for five weeks as the general rule is that revocation of offers made to the public must be by the same means and for the same length of time as the original offer.
37. Sue has made a counteroffer that in effect terminated the original offer from Julius and created a new offer.
38. The offer is automatically terminated by operation of law as the subject matter, here the bolts of silk fabric was destroyed through no fault of either party (flooding from a broken pipe) prior to the offer being accepted.
39. The offer automatically terminates since there is no contract prior to Omar being adjudged insane.
40. a manifestation of assent by the offeree to the terms of the offer in a manner invited or required by the offer as measured by the objective theory of contracts.
41. an offeree who promises to perform.
42. The mirror image rule requires the offeree to accept the offeror's terms. Acceptance must be unequivocal.
43. An option contract is one in which an offeror is prevented from revoking his or her offer by receiving compensation from the offeree to keep the offer open for an agreed-upon period of time.
44. An offer terminates when a stated time period ends. If no time is stated, an offer terminates after a reasonable time.
45. Because this rule is intended to protect offerees from being legally held to offers because they did not respond.
46. Under common law, if an acceptance was not properly dispatched, it was not effective until it was actually received by the offeror.
47. express authorization
48. it indicates the offeror's present intent to contract.
49. A price term can be implied if there is a market or source from which to determine the price of the service or item.
50. It terminates the offer.

Chapter 11

CONSIDERATION

Chapter Overview

This chapter explores the element of consideration, which as you know is important in determining whether or not a contract has been formed. Upon reviewing this chapter, you will have an in depth understanding of what is meant by consideration as it pertains to the law of contracts. Additionally, the material provided in this chapter will enable you to analyze promises that are not supported by consideration, as well as enforceable promises that are lacking consideration.

Objectives

Upon completion of the exercises contained in this chapter, you should be able to:
1.   Define consideration.
2.   Explain the meaning of legal value.
3.   Define and identify bargained-for-exchange.
4.   Explain output and requirements contracts.
5.   Explain when a best efforts contract provision is used.
6.   Define what an illusory promise is and its impact.
7.   Describe when promises lacking consideration are enforceable.
8.   Define an accord and satisfaction and the effect it has on the original contract.
9.   Discuss the doctrine of promissory estoppel.

Practical Application

You should be able to recognize whether there is sufficient consideration in a contractual situation to become part of the basis of the bargain between the parties. You should also be able to recognize what type of consideration is being given. Further, if consideration is lacking, you should be able to determine whether it will or will not be enforceable.

Helpful Hints

It will be very beneficial to you to break down the definition of consideration into several parts as well as give an example for each. Additionally, it would be especially helpful to analyze the cases given at the end of the chapter in your text and attempt to apply the contract principles you have learned up to this point.

As you begin to analyze the cases at the end of the chapter, it is important to make a notation of the issues you spot on the case itself. You will do a more thorough job if you analyze the cases line by line. This will enable you to address the legal concerns that may be present in each fact situation. Each contract question should be read twice before being answered. Also, you will find that making an outline of your answer before actually writing it is very useful as it provides a means to organize and prepare a make shift rough draft before your final response to each question is written.

Study Tips

Consideration

- Defined: "Something of legal value."
  Examples: money, property, forbearance of a right, the provision of services or anything else of legal value
- Presumption: A written contract is presumed to be supported by consideration.
- Two requirements for consideration
  1. Something of legal value must be given, and
  2. There must be a bargained-for exchange.

  Elaboration of the two requirements:
  - **Legal Value** is established if the promisee suffers a legal detriment or the promisor receives a legal benefit.
  - **Bargained-for exchange** refers to the exchange that parties engage in that leads to an enforceable contract. Gift promises and gratuitous promises by themselves are not enforceable, however if the promissee offers to do something in exchange for either of these two types of promises, then consideration is established.

Output Contracts
The seller agrees to sell all of its production to one buyer.

Requirements Contracts
The buyer contracts to purchase all of the requirements for an item from a single seller.

Nominal Consideration
This type of consideration is minimal in light of the subject matter of the contract. As such it is not considered legally sufficient in states that recognize the "shock the conscience of the court" standard for determining the adequacy of the consideration.
Example: "I will give you $1.00 for your ocean front home." One dollar is hardly adequate for an oceanfront home and in most states would "shock the conscience of the court."

Best Efforts Clause
This clause usually states that one or both of the parties will use their best efforts to achieve the objective of the contract. It's important to remember that the courts have held that imposition of the duty to use best efforts is sufficient consideration to make a contract enforceable.

Contracts that Lack Consideration

- **Illegal Consideration**
  A contract based on illegal consideration is void. A promise to refrain from doing an illegal act will not be enforceable as illegal consideration is part of the bargained-for exchange.
  Example: "If you pay me $5,000, I will not damage your brand new car!"

- **Illusory Promises**
  If the parties enter into a contract, but one or both of them choose not to perform, then consideration will be lacking.

Example: Fred says to Jim, "I will paint your garage if I feel like it."

- **Moral Obligations**
  The general rule regarding moral obligations is that they lack consideration.
  The minority rule however allows for the enforcement of moral obligations.
  Example: Deathbed promises or contracts based on affection and love are promises based upon moral obligations.

- **Preexisting Duty**
  If a person promises to perform an act or do something he or she is already under an bligation to do, then the promise is unenforceable because no new consideration has been given. In other words, the individual had a preexisting duty.
  Exception: If a party encounters substantial unforeseen difficulties while performing his or her contractual duties and the parties modify their contract to accommodate these difficulties, no new consideration is necessary.

- **Past Consideration**
  When a party to a contract promises to compensate another for work that has been performed in the past, then the situation involving past consideration exists. A contract must be supported by new consideration in order to be binding.

Settlement of Claims Involving Accord and Satisfaction

- **Accord**
  An accord is an agreement where both parties agree to accept something different in satisfaction of the original contract
- **Satisfaction**
  Simply stated, this is the performance of the accord.

Promissory Estoppel

The purpose of promissory estoppel is to give a remedy to a person who has justifiably relied upon another's promise, but that person takes back his or her promise. Further, because there is no agreement or consideration, the recipient of the promise cannot sue based on breach of contract. This doctrine estops the promisor from revoking his or her promise and thereby prevents unjust enrichment by the promisor. An injustice would occur if the promise were not enforced.

Refresh Your Memory

The following exercise will enable you to refresh your memory on the rules and principles presented to you in this chapter. Read each question twice and place your answer in the blanks provided. Review the chapter material for any question you miss or are unable to remember.

1. To be enforceable, a contract must arise from a _____.

2. Give two types of promises that are unenforceable because they lack consideration.
   _____ and _____ _____

3.   Define an output contract _____

4.   Define a requirements contract _____

5.   Why is nominal consideration considered inadequate and legally insufficient in some states?
      _____

6.   A contract supported by a promise to refrain from doing an illegal act is considered to be
      _____   _____.

7.   A contract that provides that one of the parties only has to perform if he or she chooses to is an example of an _____   _____.

8.   A majority of jurisdictions hold that promises made out of a sense of moral obligation are
      _____.

9.   If a person promises to perform an act or do something he or she is already required to do, this is called a _____   _____.

10.   An agreement made by the parties to a contract whereby the parties agree to accept something different in satisfaction of the original contract is known as an _____.

11.   Performance of an accord is known as _____.

Critical Thought Exercise

David Johnson was a well-known businessman in Connecticut and was considering a political career. Johnson desired to enter the race for his local Congressional seat. Johnson had a 21-year old daughter, Stacey, who had studied theater at an Ivy League School and was ready to seek her fame and fortune in movies. When no roles in movies were forthcoming, Stacey was offered a lucrative contract to perform in adult films. David Johnson was afraid that his daughter's pornographic film career would cause great embarrassment to his family and ruin his political career. Stacey would not listen to her father and was anxious to make the adult films. Mr. Johnson offered his daughter $750,000 if Stacey refrained from making any adult films of any other film that involved nudity for a period of ten years. The offer by Mr. Johnson was conveyed to Stacey in a letter. Stacey agreed to her father's offer and stated in a return letter that she would use his promise to motivate her to lead a more moral life. Stacey rejected the offers to make adult films and refrained from making any film wherein she appeared nude for a period of ten years. At the end of ten years, Stacey requested that her father pay the $750,000 as promised. Mr. Johnson refused to pay the money, stating that Stacey had given him nothing in return for his promise except a promise to be a good person. Mr. Johnson took the position that their agreement lacked legally sufficient consideration.

Was a contract formed that was supported by consideration?

Answer. _____
_____
_____
_____
_____
_____

_____

_____

_____

_____

_____

_____

_____

_____

_____

_____

Practice Quiz

True/False:

1. ___ Legal value is where the promisee suffers a legal detriment or the promissory receives a legal benefit. [p 222]

2. ___ Written contracts are presumed to be supported by consideration. [p 222]

3. ___ Forbearance of a legal right and refraining from drinking or smoking for a period of time are not forms of consideration. [p 222]

4. ___ To change a gift promise into an enforceable promise, the offer must be supported by consideration. [p 223]

5. ___ Parties in requirements and output contracts have an obligation to act in good faith. [p 224]

6. ___ If Bob promises to sell Marie his condominium in San Francisco for $1.00, this will be an enforceable promise despite the small consideration involved. [p 224]

7. ___ A contract that imposes a duty to use one's best efforts in achieving the contract's objective is enforceable. [p 225]

8. ___ Contracts supported by illegal consideration are valid. [p 225]

9. ___ Lucy's statement to Winnie that she may buy Winnie's house if she feels like it is enforceable. [p 225]

10. ___ Contracts based on deathbed promises are not enforceable. [p 225]

11. ___ A police officer may accept a reward for arresting a criminal. [p 225]

12. ___ If a party encounters unforeseen difficulties while performing duties under the contract, any modification that is made to the contract must be supported by new consideration. [p 226]

13. ___ Satisfaction of a new agreement refers to the performance of an accord. [p 227]

14. ___ Jay promises to pay Kelly an extra $1,000 for the concert she performed in last month. If Jay fails to pay Kelly, then Kelly may enforce the promise. [p 226]

15. ___ A compromise agreement is another name for an accord. [p 227]

16. ___ A minority of states will not examine sufficiency of the consideration in a contract between two parties. [p 228]

17. ___ A promise where one or both parties chooses to perform or not perform is a preexisting duty promise. [p 227]

18. ___ If John promises to perform an act that he is already under an obligation to do, the promise is unenforceable. [p 225]

19. ___ The doctrine of promissory estoppel allows the promissor to revoke his or her promise if necessary. [p 229]

20. ___ Mike's threat to graffiti Jeff's house if Jeff doesn't give him money is unenforceable. [p 225]

Multiple Choice:

21. Which of the following would not be viewed as sufficient consideration? [p 225]
    a. Money
    b. Property
    c. Receiving additional money for a house that was painted two months ago
    d. Refraining from drinking for six months.

22. If Melvin says to Bryan, "I will make sure you will never walk again unless you agree to pay me $25,000," this type of contract will be [p 225]
    a. void and unenforceable.
    b. valid and enforceable.
    c. voidable.
    d. valid as to part of the contract and invalid as to the other part of the contract.

23. Contracts that are primarily focused on love and affection are [p 225]
    a. unenforceable as individuals have a preexisting duty to love those they contract with.
    b. unenforceable as the contract lacks consideration.
    c. enforceable as otherwise the property would escheat to the state.
    d. unenforceable as it would be difficult for the court to determine how much love was bargained for in the contract.

24. The doctrine of promissory estoppel prevents the promissor from [p 229]
    a. accepting his or her own promise.
    b. revoking his or her promise.
    c. inducing the promisee to rely on his or her promise.
    d. enforcing his or her promise.

25. What type of contract exists where the seller agrees to sell of its production to a single buyer? [p 224]
    a. A requirements contract
    b. An output contract
    c. A moral obligation contract
    d. An illusory contract

26. What type of contract exists where a buyer contracts to purchase all of what is needed for an item from one seller? [p 224]
    a. A requirements contract
    b. An output contract
    c. An adhesion contract
    d. An unenforceable contract as the terms are vague and uncertain

27. If Karissa and Monica disagree about what Monica owes Karissa under a contract between the two of them, they may attempt to reach a compromise agreement that is called
    a. an arbitration.
    b. a legal value agreement.
    c. quasi contract.
    d. an accord.

28. If Monica pays Karissa the settlement that they agree to under the contract, her performance of rendering the newly agreed upon amount is called [p 227]
    a. satisfaction.
    b. welching on an agreement.
    c. a breach of contract as the contract could not be altered or modified.
    d. a best efforts contract.

29. A contract that provides that Waldo only has to clean Margie's swimming pool if he chooses to do so is an [p 225]
    a. example of best efforts.
    b. example of good faith and fair dealing.
    c. example of past consideration.
    d. example of an illusory promise.

30. A contract is considered supported by legal value if [p 222]
    a. it is based on a moral obligation.
    b. if the promisor suffers a legal detriment or the promisee receives a legal benefit.
    c. if there is a market or standard to which the court can set a value should it be missing.
    d. the promisee suffers a legal detriment or the promisor receives a legal benefit.

Short Answer:

31. A thing of legal value given in exchange for a promise is _____. [p 222]

32. If Mr. Smith promised to give his nephew Frank $20,000 and then rescinded the promise, it would be unenforceable. Rewrite this example to make it an unenforceable promise. [p 223]

33. Kathleen performed at a local vaudeville theatre two months ago. Laura, the owner tells Kathleen, "Since you made the crowds laugh and brought in such good tips to the theatre, I'm going to give you an extra $100. Kathleen attempts to collect on Laura's promise, but Laura refuses. Support your answer and tell whether or not the promise is enforceable. [p 226]

    _____

    _____

34. An _____ is one way to compromise a dispute over what is owing under a contract. [p 227]

35. Why are gratuitous promises unenforceable? [p 223] _____

    _____

36. The naming of a low dollar amount to satisfy the potential problem of there being a lack of consideration is known as _____ _____. [p 224]

37. A _____ _____ clause is one in many business contracts that requires one or both parties to do the finest job that can be cone to achieve the objective of the contract. [p 225]

38. What type of situation allows the parties to modify their contract even though it not supported by new consideration? [p 225] ___ _____

    _____

39. What is past consideration? [p 226] _____

    _____

40. If Maria says to Eva, "I will purchase all of the red paint that you have," what kind of contract has she possibly entered into? [p 224] _____

41. Contracts based on illegal consideration are _____. [p 225]

42. In terms of the settlement of claims, what does the term satisfaction mean? [p 227] _____

    _____

43. When is the doctrine of promissory estoppel used? [p 229] _____

    _____

    _____

44. If Hank agrees to sell all of his canned tuna to Patricia, what type of contract may apply to this situation? [p 224] _____

45. "I will give you $600," is an example of a _____ _____. [p.11-13]

46. What type of obligation does the law impose on the performance of the parties to requirements and output contracts? [p 224] _____ _____

47. Why won't refraining from doing an illegal act serve as a basis for an enforceable contract? [p 225]

    _____

    _____

48. If Mrs. French says to Brandon, "If you come to class every day this semester as you are supposed to, I will take you to lunch at the restaurant of your choice," would this be an enforceable promise?

[p 225] Support your answer. _____

_____ _____

49. What is an illusory promise? [p 225] _____

_____

50. A contract must arise from a _____ in order to be enforceable. [p 223]

Answers to Refresh Your Memory

1. bargained-for exchange [p 223]
2. gift promises and gratuitous promises [p 223]
3. The seller agrees to sell all of its production to a single buyer. [p 224]
4. Where a buyer contracts to purchase all of the requirements for an item from one seller. [p 224]
5. Because it "shocks the conscience of the court" standard for determining adequacy of consideration. [p 224]
6. illegal consideration [p 225]
7. illusory promise [p 225]
8. unenforceable [p 225]
9. preexisting duty [p 225]
10. accord [p 227]

Critical Thought Exercise Model Answer

The fact that a party has made a promise does not mean that the promise is enforceable. In contract law, a basis for the enforcement of promises is consideration. Consideration is the value given in return for a promise. It is usually broken into two parts: (1) something of legally sufficient value must be given in exchange for the promise, and (2) there must be a bargained-for exchange. Something of legally sufficient value may consist of (1) a promise to do something that one has no prior legal duty to do, (2) the performance of an action that one is otherwise not obligated to perform, or (3) the refraining from an action that one has a legal right to undertake. Stacey has the legal right to enter into a contract to perform in adult movies. She has suffered a detriment by forfeiting income that she was legally entitled to obtain. The second element of consideration is that it must provide the basis for the bargain that was struck between the parties to the agreement. The consideration given by the promisor must induce the promisee to incur a legal detriment and the detriment incurred must induce the promisor to make the promise. This keeps the promise from being a gift. Stacey was induced to refrain from making adult films by the promise of her father to pay her $750,000. She was anxious to make the films and did not sign the contract offered to her because of Mr. Johnson's promise. Keeping his daughter out of adult films is what induced Mr. Johnson to make his promise to pay her money. Therefore, the agreement between Mr. Johnson and Stacey was supported by legally sufficient consideration. Because Stacey fulfilled the requested act and suffered the detriment requested by Mr. Johnson, he is now legally obligated to pay her $750,000.00.

Answers to Practice Quiz

True/False:

1. True   When the promisee suffers a legal detriment or the promissory receives a legal benefit, there is consideration.
2. True   If a contract is in writing, the court will presume that it is supported by consideration.
3. False Forbearance of a legal right and refraining from drinking or smoking for a period of time are special forms of consideration.
4. True   In order for a promise of a gift to be enforceable, it must be supported by consideration such as another promise or the performance of an act.
5. True   The law imposes an obligation of good faith on the performance of the parties to requirements and output contracts.
6. False The low consideration of $1.00 is akin to consideration associated with a gift promise. This minimal consideration for the San Francisco condominium is known as nominal consideration, which is legally insufficient as it, would "shock the conscience of the court" when determining the value of the condominium. The promise would not be enforceable.
7. True   A requirement that one or both of the parties use their best efforts in achieving the objective of the contract is sufficient consideration to make the contract enforceable.
8. False Contracts based on illegal consideration are void.
9. False Lucy's statement would be viewed by a court as being illusory in that it does not indicate a present intent to enter into the contract. Illusory contracts are not enforceable.
10. True   Deathbed promises are those made out of a sense of moral obligation or honor. These types of contracts are generally unenforceable as they lack consideration.
11. False Many statutes prohibit police officers from accepting rewards for arresting criminals as they are already under a preexisting duty to apprehend the criminals as part of their job. Because of this preexisting duty, there is no new consideration being given and any reward that is offered may not be enforced by the police office.
12. False If a party runs into substantial unforeseen difficulties while performing his or her duties under the contract, the parties may modify their contract to accommodate these unforeseen difficulties even if the modification is not supported by new consideration.
13. True   The performance of an accord is called satisfaction.
14. False Jay's offer to pay Kelly additional compensation for the concert she performed last month is viewed as being past consideration and would therefore be unenforceable.
15. True   An accord is an agreement whereby the parties agree to accept something different in satisfaction of the original contract and in essence is a compromise.
16. False The majority of states usually do not inquire into the sufficiency of the consideration. However, the minority of jurisdictions will look at the adequacy of the consideration and if It "shocks the conscience of the court," a party will be relieved from his or her duties under the contract.
17. False A promise where one or both parties choose to perform or not perform is an illusory promise.
18. True   If a John promises to perform an act or do something he is already under an obligation to do, the promise lacks consideration and is unenforceable. This is known as a preexisting duty.
19. False The doctrine of promissory estoppel prevents the promisor from revoking his or her promise.
20. True   Mike's threat would be considered illegal consideration and therefore the contract is void and unenforceable.

Multiple Choice:

21. C   Answer C is correct as receiving additional money for a house that was painted two months ago would be viewed as past consideration, which is unenforceable. Answers A, B, and D are considered sufficient consideration.

22. A   Answer A is correct as contracts based on illegal consideration such as threatening to inflict serious bodily harm on another are void and unenforceable. Answers B, C, and D are incorrect based on the reasoning given for answer A.

23. B   Answer B is correct as promises made out of a sense of moral obligation or honor such as love and affection are generally unenforceable due to the lack of consideration. Answer A is incorrect as it is a misstatement of the law. Answer C may be a reality in some cases, however, a majority of states hold that contracts based on moral obligations are unenforceable. Answer D is incorrect, as moral consideration such as love and affection are not treated like legal consideration.

24. B   Answer B is correct the doctrine of promissory estopel estops the promissor from revoking his or her promise. Answer A is incorrect, as a promissory cannot accept his or her own promise. Answer C is incorrect, as it is the inducement by the promisor that helps to establish a cause of action based on promissory estoppel. Answer D is incorrect as promissory estoppel provides a remedy to a person who relied on another person's promise, which may include enforcing the promissor's promise.

25. B   Answer B is correct, as an output contract is where the seller agrees to sell all of its production to a single buyer. Answer A is incorrect as a requirements contract refers to a buyer who contracts to purchase all of the requirements for an item from one seller. Answer C is incorrect as contracts based on moral obligations usually involve promises of love or deathbed promises. Answer D is incorrect as an illusory contract involves one or both parties choosing whether they want to perform or not under the contract.

26. A   Answer A is correct as when a buyer contracts to purchase all of what is needed for an item from a seller, this is called a requirements contract. Answer B is incorrect as output contracts involve the seller agreeing to sell all of its production to a single buyer. Answer C is incorrect as an adhesion contract is an unconscionable one whereby one of the parties is induced by undue influence or duress or fraud to enter into the contract. Answer D is incorrect as despite the appearance of being vague and not definite, courts have recognized these types of requirements contracts with the understanding that the parties have a duty to act in good faith.

27. D   Answer D is correct, as an accord is an agreement whereby the parties agree to accept something different in satisfaction of the original contract, and hence compromise. Answer A is incorrect as arbitration is a means in which to settle a dispute by way of a neutral third party. The facts are silent as to whether the contract permits arbitration and if there is another individual involved in resolving the dispute. Answer B is incorrect as there is no such thing as a legal value agreement. Answer C is incorrect as a quasi contract is an equitable remedy that is sometimes imposed by the court when there isn't a contract. The facts clearly state that there is a contract between Monica and Karissa.

28. A   Answer A is correct as the performance of an accord or the new agreement is called the satisfaction. Answer B is incorrect as it is contradictory to the facts as Monica is paying Karissa what they have agreed to and hence could not be welching on their agreement. Answer C is incorrect as there is nothing in the facts that indicates that the contract could not be altered or modified. Answer D is incorrect as the term best efforts usually refers to a clause, not an entire contract. Further, a best efforts clause is one where the court imposes a duty to act in good faith in the performance of the objective of the contract.

29. D   Answer D is correct as Waldo's option of cleaning or not cleaning Margie's swimming pool is too indefinite to be enforced and is an example of an illusory contract. Answer A is incorrect as the term best efforts refers to the parties' duty to act in good faith in the performance of the objective of the contract. As such, Waldo's option to clean or not to clean would not be an example of one acting in good faith to get Margie's pool cleaned. Answer B is incorrect for the

reasons that answer A is incorrect. Answer C is incorrect as there is nothing in the facts to indicate that additional compensation is being given to Waldo for a job that he has already performed.

30. B   Answer B is correct as the modern law of contract provides that a contract is supported by legal value if the promisee suffers a legal detriment or the promissory receives a legal benefit. Answer A is incorrect, as moral obligations have been found to have no legal value. Answer C is correct if the price is missing in a contract, however, answer B provides a broader in assisting the court in determining legal value. Answer D incorrectly states who suffers the legal detriment and who receives the legal benefit. The answer as stated has the roles reversed.

Short Answer

31.   consideration
32.   Mr. Smith promises to give his nephew Frank $20,000 if Frank refrains from drinking for one year. If Frank refrains from drinking for the time stated, Mr. Smith's promise will be enforceable. Note that answers will vary.
33.   The promise is not enforceable as it is based on past consideration, which is not considered to be of legal value.
34.   accord
35.   Because they are not supported by consideration.
36.   nominal consideration.
37.   best efforts
38.   Where a party encounters substantial unforeseen difficulties while performing his or her contractual duties and a modification to the contract is made to accommodate those difficulties, the modification will be enforced even though there is no new consideration.
39.   Past consideration is when a part to a contract promises to pay additional compensation for work done in the past.
40.   She has possibly entered into a requirements contract.
41.   void
42.   The performance of an accord.
43.   It is used to provide a remedy to a person who has relied on another person's promise, but the other individual takes back his or her promise and is not subject to a breach of contract cause of action because either the agreement or consideration is missing.
44.   An output contract may apply to this situation.
45.   a gift promise.
46.   good faith
47.   Because refraining from an illegal act is viewed as illegal consideration, any promise attempting to support a contract based on not performing an illegal act will not be enforced.
48.   No, because Brandon is under a preexisting duty to come to class every day as he is expected to do that as a student.
49.   An illusory promise is one in which one or both parties have the option of performing or not performing an act.
50.   bargained-for exchange

Chapter 12

CAPACITY AND LEGALITY

Chapter Overview

This chapter's main focus concerns the capacity to enter into contracts as well as the lawfulness of certain contracts. You will learn about the obligations minors, intoxicated and insane individuals have under contracts that they enter into. Additionally, contracts that are contrary to statutes or those that are unconscionable are also explored in this chapter/

Objectives

Upon completion of the exercises contained in this chapter, you should be able to:
1. Describe and recognize situations where the infancy doctrine applies.
2. Explain when minors, intoxicated individuals and insane individuals are responsible for what they contract for.
3. Describe legal insanity and explain its impact on contractual capacity.
4. Describe intoxication and explain its impact on contractual capacity.
5. Recognize and explain illegal contracts that are contrary to statutes.
6. Recognize and explain illegal contracts that are contrary to public policy
7. Explain what a covenant not to compete is and recognize when they are lawful.
8. Explain the use for exculpatory clauses and explain when they are lawful.
9. Describe what an unconscionable contract is and when it is unlawful.

Practical Application

You should be able to determine whether an incapacitated individual will be responsible for what they contract for. Further, you should be able to determine whether the rules of law regarding the infancy doctrine, legal insanity and intoxication will have an impact on any contracts that you may enter into. Additionally you should be able to determine whether covenants not to compete as well as any exculpatory clauses are lawful based on the knowledge you should have obtained. Finally, your knowledge should enable you to determine whether or not a contract may be unconscionable, void or voidable.

Helpful Hints

This chapter lends itself toward simple organization based on who may be involved in a contractual situation as well as what type of clause the parties are concerned with. The rules are very straightforward in this chapter and simple to learn. It is very beneficial to explore the critical legal thinking cases at the end of the chapter in your text as well as answer the critical thought exercise contained herein. The more exposure you have to situations involving capacity and legality, the easier and more recognizable these issues will become for you.

Study Tips

You should start your studying of this chapter by learning that the general presumption is that the law presumes that parties that enter into a contract have the capacity to do the same.

Next, you should examine the contractual situation for any potential capacity issues. These usually involve minors, intoxicated or insane individuals.

Minors

- Who is considered to be a minor?
  <u>Common law</u>: Females under 18 years of age and Males under 21 years of age
  Most states have statutes specifying the age of majority
  Most prevalent age of majority is 18 years old for males and females.
  Any age below the statutory age of majority is called the period of minority.

- Infancy Doctrine - This gives minors the right to disaffirm most contracts they have entered into with adults. It serves as a minor's protection against unscrupulous adults who may want to take advantage of a minor. It is an objective standard.
  - A minor may choose whether or not to enforce the contract. If both parties are minors, both parties have the right to cancel the contract.
  - A minor cannot disaffirm as to part of the contract and affirm as to another part of the contract.

- Disaffirmance
  - A minor in may disaffirm a contract in writing, orally or by conduct.
  - No formalities are needed.
  - It must be done prior to reaching the age of majority or a reasonable time thereafter. Reasonable is assessed on a case-by-case basis.

Restoration and Restitution

If either party has not performed the contract, the minor only needs to disaffirm the contract.
If the minor has given consideration to the competent party before disaffirming, the competent party must place the minor in the status quo. In other words, he or she must give the minor back his or her money to make him or her whole again. This is also known as the *competent party's duty of restitution.*

Minor's duty of restoration

Upon disaffirmance of the contract, the minor must return the goods to the adult, even if the goods are lost, destroyed, consumed or have depreciated in value.

Minor's duty of restitution

In a majority of states, the minor will be required to put the adult in status quo upon disaffirming the contract if the minor was intentionally or grossly negligent in his or her conduct thereby causing the adult's property to lose value. Some states require the minor to make restitution of the reasonable value of the item when disaffirming any contract.

Minor's misrepresentation of age

- At common law the minor would still be able to disaffirm the contract despite the misrepresentation.
- Modernly most states hold the minor must place the adult in the status quo if he or she disaffirms the contract and hence would owe the duties of restoration and restitution to the adult.

Ratification

- Simply define: To accept.
- How is ratification accomplished? Ratification may be expressed, impliedly or by conduct.
- Rule of law: A minor may ratify a contract before reaching the age of majority or a reasonable time thereafter. If disaffirmance does not occur in this time frame, it is considered accepted.

Contracts that are Enforceable Against Minors

- Minors are required to pay for the necessaries of life that they contract for.
- Examples of necessaries: food, clothing, tools of the trade, medical services, education.
- Note that the minor is required to pay the reasonable value of the services or goods.
- Also, statutes exist that make minors liable for certain contracts. Examples of some of these special types of contracts as per the statutes include, child support, education, medical, surgical and pregnancy cares to name a few.

Parents' Liability for Their Children's Contracts

- If the parents have not sufficiently provided for their children's necessaries of life, then they are liable for their children's contracts.
- Exception: If a minor becomes emancipated by voluntarily leaving home and living apart from his or her parents and can support him or herself, then the parents have no duty to support their child. This is looked at on a case-by-case basis.

Mentally Incompetent Persons

- In order for a person to be relieved of his or her duties under a contract, the law mandates that the person have been legally insane at the time he or she entered into the contract.

- Legal insanity defined: Legal insanity is determined by using the *objective cognitive understanding test* which involves determining whether the person was incapable of understanding or comprehending the nature of the transaction.

- The following do not qualify as insanity: delusions, light psychological or emotional problems or weakness of intellect.

- Impact of being found insane: If an individual is adjudged insane, the contract is void.

- <u>Impact of being insane, but not adjudged insane:</u> The contract is voidable by the insane person. The other party does not have the option to avoid the contract unless that party doesn't have the contractual capacity either.

- The other party must put the insane party back to the status quo. The sane party must also be placed back to the status quo if he or she was unaware of the other party's insane condition.

- <u>Liability of insane people:</u> Under a quasi-contract, insane individuals are liable for the reasonable value for the necessaries of life that they receive.

Intoxicated Individuals

- <u>General rule</u>: Contracts entered into be intoxicated individuals are voidable by that person. Intoxication may be by alcohol or drugs.

- The contract is voidable only if the person was so intoxicated that he or she was incapable of understanding or comprehending the nature of the transaction. Note, that some states will only allow the person to disaffirm the contract if he or she was forced to become intoxicated.

- <u>Impact of disaffirming the contract based on intoxication:</u> The intoxicated one must be returned to the status quo. Also, the intoxicated person must return the consideration under the contract thereby making restitution to the other party and returning him or her to the staus quo.

- <u>Liability of intoxicated individuals:</u> These individuals are liable in quasi-contract to pay the reasonable value for the necessaries that they receive.

Illegality

- The object of a contract must be lawful. If the object is illegal, then the contract is void and unenforceable.

- <u>Illegal contracts</u>

    - **Usury laws-** These laws set an upper limit on the annual rate that can be charged on certain loans. They are enacted to protect borrowers from loan sharks. Consequences for violating these laws include criminal and civil penalties.

    - **Gambling Statutes-** All states have some sort of regulation or prohibition concerning gambling,
    - **Lotteries, wagering and games of chance**. Consequences for violating these laws also include criminal and civil penalties.

    - **Sabbath Laws-** These are also known as blue laws or Sunday laws. They prohibit or limit the carrying on of certain secular activities on Sundays. Only certain states enact these laws.

    - **Contracts to commit a crime-** These are void. However, if the object of the contract became illegal after the contract was entered into because of a governmental statute, both parties no longer have to perform under the contract.

- **Licensing Statutes** – All states require that certain occupations and professions be licensed in order to practice. There are two types of statutes to be aware of, regulatory and revenue-raising statutes. The regulatory statutes concern those that protect the public. For example, an unlicensed doctor may not collect payment for services that a regulatory statute requires a licensed person to provide. The revenue-raising statutes are made to raise money for the government. Their purpose is to gather revenue. Protecting the public is not a consideration with this type of statute.

Contracts contrary to Public Policy

- If the contract has a negative impact on society or impacts public safety or welfare, it is void.

- Example: Immoral contracts may be against public policy, such as a contract that requests sexual favors. Societal beliefs and practices are used as a guide in determining what immoral conduct is.

- Exculpatory Clauses - An exculpatory clause relieves one or both parties from tort liability under a contract. This type of clause can relieve a party from ordinary negligence but not be used in cases of gross negligence, intentional torts, fraud, or willful conduct. Courts do not condone exculpatory clauses unless the parties have equal bargaining power.

- Covenants Not to Compete - These types of ancillary contracts are lawful if reasonableness can be demonstrated based on the line of business protected, the duration of the restriction and the geographical area that is being protected. The court can refuse to enforce it or alter it to make it reasonable if there is a need.

- Effect of Illegality - Generally speaking one cannot enforce an illegal contract. However, there are exceptions to every rule, including this one. Those that may enforce an illegal contract include innocent persons who justifiably relied on the law or fact making the contract illegal or, persons who were induced to enter into a contract to name just a few.

- Unconscionable Contracts - Some contracts are so unfair that they are unjust. The public policy based doctrine of unconscionablility allows the courts to refuse to enforce the contract, refuse to enforce the unconscionable clause but enforce the rest of the contract or limit the application of any unconscionable clause in order to avoid an unconscionable result.

- Requirements to Demonstrate a Contract is Unconscionable
  - The parties possessed severely unequal bargaining power.
  - The dominant party unreasonably used its unequal bargaining power to obtain unfair contract terms.
  - The subservient party had no reasonable alternative

Refresh Your Memory

The following exercise will enable you to refresh your memory on the rules and principles presented to you in this chapter. Read each question twice and place your answer in the blanks provided. Review the chapter material for any question you miss or are unable to remember.

1. The law presumes that the parties to a contract have the requisite contractual _____ to enter into the contract.

2. Any age below the statutory age is called the _____ of _____.

3. The infancy doctrine is an _____ standard whereby the court will not inquire into an individual's knowledge, sophistication or experience.

4. Under the infancy doctrine, the contract is _____ by the minor.

5. If both parties to the contract are minors, both parties have the right to _____ the contract.

6. A minor can expressly disaffirm a contract _____, in _____, or by the minor's _____.

7. Minors who misrepresent their age must place the adult in _____ if they disaffirm the contract.

8. To ratify means to _____.

9. Why are licensing statutes enacted? _____
_____

10. Contracts that have a negative impact on society or interfere with public safety and welfare are _____.

11. An exculpatory clause is _____

12. What are some of the factors that the court will consider before they will strike down an exculpatory clause? _____
_____

13. What are the three aspects that the courts will consider in determining whether or not to enforce a covenant not to compete? _____
_____

14. What is meant by the term in pari delicto? _____

15. An unconscionable contract is also known as a contract of _____

Critical Thought Exercise

You manage a small bicycle shop and sell a very good product, with some bikes costing $2,000. A young man comes into your store and wants to buy a mountain bike for $1,200. He has the cash. You are very happy to sell it to him. He tells you that he is an ambitious high school student who is taking classes at the local university and needs a bicycle that is capable of handling the large hills between the high school and college so that he can make it to class.

Two years later, the young man comes into the shop and tells you that yesterday was his 18th birthday and after drinking a great deal of alcohol, he rode his bike down the Cuesta Grade and crashed into a Ford Expedition. He hands you a piece of bent frame and states that this is all that was left of the bicycle when he went back to the accident scene this morning. He asks for his $1,200 back as he now "desires to undue the contract."

Will you agree to the full refund? Why or why not?

Answer. _____

_____

_____

_____

_____

_____

_____

_____

_____

_____

_____

_____

_____

_____

_____

_____

_____

_____

Practice Quiz

True/False:

1. ___ Unconscionable contracts are unenforceable. [p 234]

2. ___ Minors always have the maturity and experience they need to enter into contracts with adults. [p 234]

3. ___ The law does not recognize the infancy doctrine. [p 234]

4. ___ Contracts for the necessities of life are exempt from the infancy doctrine. [p 234]

5. ___ If both parties are minors when entering into a contract, only one party may disaffirm the contract. [p 234]

6. ___ The infancy doctrine is a subjective standard in most states. [p 234]

7. ___ A minor may affirm one part of the contract and disaffirm another part. [p 234]

8. ___ A minor may disaffirm a contract if neither party has performed and the minor's contract is executory. [p 235]

9. ___ The competent party to a contract must return the minor to status quo if the minor transferred consideration, money, property or other valuables to the competent party before disaffirming the contract. [p 235]

10. ___ A minor is not required to put the adult in status quo upon disaffirmance of the contract if the minor's intentional or grossly negligent conduct caused the loss of value to the adult's property. [p 235]

11. ___ To ratify is another term for disaffirm. [p 235]

12. ___ A minor's ratification may be accomplished by express, oral or written words or implied from the minor's conduct. [p 235]

13. ___ Minors are obligated to pay for the necessaries of life that they contract for. [p 236]

14. ___ Minors are not responsible for such things as shelter, clothing, food, or medical services. [p 236]

15. ___ The court will not consider the minor's lifestyle, age and status in life in determining what is necessary. [p 236]

16. ___ When a minor voluntarily leaves home and lives apart from his or her parents, this is known as emancipation. [p 237]

17. ___ The subject cognitive understanding test is used to determine legal insanity in most jurisdictions. [p 237]

18. ___ If a person is insane, but not adjudged insane, the contract he or she has entered into is void. [p 237]

19. ___ Contracts made while an individual was not legally sane can be disaffirmed. [p 237]

20. ___ Insane individuals are liable in quasi-contract to pay the reasonable value for the necessaries of life they receive. [p 237]

Multiple Choice:

21. Parents owe a legal duty to their children to provide [p 237]
    a. a good post secondary education so that they can get a good job.
    b. a place to live until they get married.
    c. food, clothing, shelter and other necessaries of life.
    d. tools of the trade for the occupation they are interested in.

22. People who are suffering from substantial mental incapacity will be protected from having contracts enforced against them because [p 237]
    a. they may have emotional problems rendering them legally insane.
    b. they may have been intoxicated.
    c. they may be delusional when entering into the contracts.
    d. they may not understand the consequences of their actions in entering into a contract.

23. Any contract entered into by a person who has been adjudged insane is [p 237]
    a. valid.
    b. void.
    c. voidable.
    d. enforceable.

24. A person who has contracted with an insane person must place that insane person [p 237]
    a. in status quo if the contract is void or voided by the insane person.
    b. in pari delicto with the competent party to the contract.
    c. in counseling to help him or her out.
    d. in status quo if the contract is void or voided by the sane person.

25. Most states hold with regard to intoxication that a contract is voidable only if the person [p 238]
    a. was so intoxicated when he or she entered into the contract that he or she was aware of how many drinks he or she had consumed.
    b. was so intoxicated that a subjective individual would be able to validate the nature of his or her transaction.
    c. was so intoxicated that he or she could not remember where he or she was.
    d. was so intoxicated that he or she was incapable of understanding or comprehending the nature of the transaction.

26. The amount of drugs or alcohol that is necessary to be consumed for an individual to be considered legally intoxicated to disaffirm contracts [p 238]
    a. is usually two or more alcoholic beverages.
    b. is a reasonable amount.
    c. varies from case to case.
    d. none of the above.

27. An individual who disaffirms a contract using intoxication as his or her basis must [p 238]
    a. be awarded punitive damages against the server of alcohol or drugs.
    b. be returned to status quo.
    c. understand or comprehend the nature of the transaction.
    d. pass a breathalyzer test.

28. Intoxicated individuals are liable in quasi-contract to pay for [p 238]
    a. the alcohol or drugs that may be consumed.
    b. the reasonable value for necessaries they receive.
    c. damages and attorneys fees if they lose.
    d. all of the above.

29. Which of the following would not be considered to be an illegal contract? [p 239]
    a. a higher interest rate than what is allowed by state usury laws
    b. medical services provided by an unlicensed physician
    c. state operated lottery
    d. insurance that you purchased on your neighbor's car

30. Usury laws were created to [p 239]
    a. make certain forms of gambling illegal.
    b. protect the public.
    c. raise revenue.

   d. to protect unsophisticated borrowers from loan sharks and others who charge outlandish rates
       of interest.

31. Bob and Francis entered into a contract whereby Bob was to sell Francis green and brown
     striped tree frogs to sell in Francis' pet store. Thereafter the green and brown striped tree frog
     became protected under a state statute, which added it to its endangered species list. What impact
     does the statute have on the contract between Bob and Francis? [p 239]
     a. It has no impact whatsoever as the parties entered into the contract before the statute was
         enacted.
     b. It has no impact on the frogs sold after the statute becomes law.
     c. Bob and Francis must adhere to the statute as it was designed to protect the public from
         unlicensed sellers of tree frogs.
     d. Bob and Francis are discharged from the contract.

32. A statute that states that medical services can only be provided by physicians who have graduated
     from medical school and passed appropriate board exams would be categorized as a [p 240]
     a. revenue-raising statute.
     b. Sabbath law.
     c. licensing statute.
     d. contrary to public policy.

33. Which of the following applies to revenue-raising statutes? [p 241]
     a. They are enacted to raise money for the government.
     b. They are enacted to protect the public.
     c. They prohibit or limit the carrying on of certain secular activities on Sundays.
     d. They have a negative impact on society and interfere with the public's safety and welfare.

34. Contracts are contrary to public policy if [p 241]
     a. they have a negative impact on society.
     b. they interfere with the public's welfare.
     c. they interfere with the public's safety.
     d. all of the above.

35. If Lee remarks to Hanna that her employment will be based upon granting him sexual favors, this
     type of contract would be considered [p 241]
     a. voidable as Hanna may assert that Lee is suffering from substantial mental incapacity.
     b. necessary in order for Hanna to obtain her job.
     c. void as it is an immoral contract that is against public policy.
     d. a covenant not to compete for other job opportunities.

Short Answer:

36. What is a covenant not to compete? [p 245] _____
     _____
     _____
     _____

37. A contract that is so oppressive or manifestly unfair that it would be unjust to enforce it is known as
     an _____ _____. [p 246]

38. A doctrine that gives minors the right to affirm or disaffirm a contract entered into with an adult is
     _____ _____. [p 234]

39. The act of a minor to rescind a contract under the infancy doctrine is known as
    _____. [p 236]

40. The minor's _____, _____ and status in life are what are looked at in determining what are necessaries as they pertain to contracts the minor has entered into. [p 236]

41. What is emancipation? [p 237] _____
    _____

42. Under most state laws, contracts entered into by certain intoxicated individuals are
    _____. [p 238]

43. An immoral contract is _____
    _____. [p 241]

44. What are the two standards that have been developed under the law regarding contracts of mentally incompetent persons? [p 237] _____
    _____

45. If Anita Brown sells her croissant shop in Phoenix, Arizona to Margo Jones and at the time of sale has signed a covenant not to compete. In the covenant, Anita has agreed not to open another croissant shop in Arizona for a 20-year period. Will the covenant be enforced by the courts as written? Be sure to provide justification and support for your answer.
    [p 245] _____
    _____

46. What elements must be shown in order to prove that a contract or clause in a contract is unconscionable? [p 246] _____
    _____

47. Wanda has entered into a contract with Wilma to purchase Wilma's car. On the day that the parties are about to exchange the keys and title to the car for the purchase price, Wanda tells Wilma that she thought she was buying a tractor and does not want the car after all. What will be the probable result if Wilma sues Wanda and Wanda claims that she was insane at the time she entered into the contract with Wanda? [p 237] _____
    _____

48. Ronald, a seventeen year old purchases several different types of wrenches from Ace Tools. He has purchased these tools on credit with the store as he has just started as an apprentice plumber with his uncle Joe. Ronald's first bill from Ace Tools arrives and he finds that he cannot pay it. He immediately notifies Ace Tools of the situation. Ace Tools wants to enforce the credit agreement against Ronald and they indicate this to him. His response is that he is a minor and does not have to pay for the tools. If Ace Tools attempts to enforce the agreement against Ronald, what is the probable outcome? [p 236] _____
    _____

49. Peter and Mike were in a bar one day after a long day at work when Peter commented to Mike on how lucky he was to live out of the hustle and bustle of the city. Mike agreed that living on the farm was quite nice, however, he claimed he missed the nightlife of the city. The two co-workers continued to talk, have dinner and partake in a couple of alcoholic beverages. After a few beers,

Mike said to Peter, "You want the country life and I want the city life, I'll sell you my California farm from for $50,000." Peter immediately jumped at the offer and accepted. The next day when Peter came up to Mike with proof that he had obtained the necessary financing for Mike's farm, Mike laughed at him and said, "You've got to be kidding, I'm not selling my farm! My wife would have my head! I was too drunk last night to know what I was doing!" If Peter tries to enforce the agreement between the two of him, what factors will be considered in determining whether Mike was intoxicated? Also, what is the majority rule regarding contracts entered into while intoxicated? [p 238] _____

_____
_____
_____

50.   Charlie is interested in buying Sue's high performance speedboat for $10,000. Sue begins to ask a few questions regarding Charlie's previous experience with this type of watercraft, his means of financing and finally his age. He indicates to her that he has grown up with speedboats, he has the money from a trust fund and that he is eighteen years old. Sue, a very trusting individual lets Charlie purchase the speedboat for the asking price. Charlie immediately takes the boat for a ride on the nearby lake and loses control of the boat due to large branches under the water that could not be seen. The boat crashes into a dock and sustains $5,000 in damages. What must Charlie who is really only sixteen years old do if he wants to disaffirm the contract? [p 235] _____

_____
_____

Answers to Refresh Your Memory

1.   capacity [p 234]
2.   period of minority [p 234]
3.   objective [p 234]
4.   voidable [p 234]
5.   disaffirm [p 234]
6.   orally writing conduct [p 235]
7.   status quo [p 235]
8.   accept [p 235]
9.   They are enacted to protect the public from those who may not have met the state standard for a particular profession. [p 240]
10.   illegal [p 241]
11.   It is a clause that relieves one or both parties from the contract. [p 242]
12.   The court will consider the type of activity involved, the relative bargaining power of the parties, knowledge, experience, and sophistication of each of the parties. [p 243]
13.   The court will consider the type of business being protected, the geographical area being protected and the length of time the restriction will be in place. [p 245]
14.   It refers to when both parties are equally at fault in an illegal contract. [p 246]
15.   adhesion [p 246]

Critical Thought Exercise Model Answer

In almost all states, the age of majority for contractual purposes is eighteen years old. With some exceptions, the contracts entered into by a minor are voidable at the option of the minor. For a minor to exercise their option to disaffirm a contract, he or she only needs to manifest an intent not to be bound by the contract. The contract can normally be disaffirmed at any time during minority or for a reasonable time after attaining the age of majority. When a minor disaffirms a contract, all property that he or she has given to the adult as consideration must be returned to the minor. Upon disaffirmance, most states require that the minor need only return the goods or money that were the subject of the contract, provided that the minor still has the goods or money. The minor may disaffirm the contract even if the goods are lost, stolen, damaged, or destroyed. A minor may disaffirm a contract for necessaries, such as food, clothing, shelter, and medical services. However, the minor remains liable for the reasonable value of the goods used when the goods are deemed a necessary. Transportation is normally not considered a necessary. The young man who purchased the bike told me that he was only in high school. This should have put me, as the agent for the store, on notice that I was dealing with a minor. It is irrelevant that the minor drank alcohol before he crashed the bicycle. I will be obligated to return the total purchase price unless my store is in one of the few states that require the minor to put me in the same position as before the contract. In that state, the minor would only be entitled to a refund of the purchase price minus the cost of the damage to the bicycle. Since the bicycle was destroyed, no refund would be warranted.

Answers to Practice Quiz

True/False:

1. True   A contract that is so oppressive or manifestly unfair that it would be unjust to enforce it is unconscionable and hence unenforceable.
2. False   Minors do not always have the maturity, experience or sophistication they need to enter into contracts.
3. False   The law does recognize the infancy doctrine so that minors are protected and allowed to disaffirm most contracts that they have entered into.
4. True   Minors are obligated to pay for the necessaries of life that they contract for.
5. False   Both parties have the right to disaffirm the contract.
6. False   The infancy doctrine is an objective standard.
7. False   A minor may not affirm one part of the contract and disaffirm another part.
8. True   If the minor has not yet performed and neither party has performed, the minor may disaffirm the contract.
9. True   If the minor has transferred consideration to the competent party before disaffirming the contract, that party must place the minor in status quo.
10. False   A majority of jurisdictions hold that the minor must put the adult in status quo upon disaffirmance of the contract, even if the minor's intentional or grossly negligent conduct cause the loss of value to the adult's property.
11. False   Ratify means to accept not disaffirm.
12. True   Ratification may be accomplished by express, oral or written words or implied by the minor's conduct.
13. True   Minors are obligated for contracts they enter into involving the necessaries of life.
14. False   Though necessary of life has not been defined by the court, items such as shelter, clothing, food or medical services are found to be necessaries of life.
15. False   The court will examine the minor's age, status in life influence and lifestyle in determining what is necessary.
16. True   Emancipation involves the termination of the parental duty of support, which is judged by a minor's voluntary departure from the home and proof of his or her ability to be self-supporting.
17. False   It is the objective cognitive understanding test that most states utilize in determining legal insanity.

18. False   If no formal ruling has been made to adjudge an individual insane, then the court will find that the contract entered into by one who suffers a mental impairment is voidable.
19. True   A person may disaffirm a contract that he or she entered into while he or she was not legally sane.
20. True   Despite the individual being insane, he or she is still responsible for the necessaries of life that he or she contracts for under a theory of quasi-contract.

Multiple Choice:

21. C   Answer C is correct as parents do owe a legal duty to provide clothing, food, shelter and other necessaries of life for their minor children. Answer A is incorrect as parents are not responsible for their children's post-secondary education. Answer B is incorrect as parents are not obligated to their children for a place to live once they marry. Answer D is incorrect as parents are not responsible for tools of the trade their children are interested in.

22. D   Answer D is correct as those suffering from substantial mental incapacity may be legally insane and may be incapable of understanding or comprehending the nature of the contracts they are a part of. Answer A is incorrect as emotional problems do not constitute legal insanity under the law. Answer B is incorrect as the question is directed toward insanity and not intoxication. Answer C is incorrect, as delusions do not constitute insanity under the law.

23. B   Answer B is correct as a person who is adjudged insane becomes a ward of the court and any contract entered into by the insane individual is void. Answer A is incorrect because a contract entered into by an individual who has been adjudicated as insane cannot be valid. Answer C is incorrect as a contract is voidable if the individual is insane but not adjudged Insane. Answer D is incorrect for the reason that answer A is incorrect.

24. A   Answer A is correct as a majority of states hold that a party who was unaware that he or she was dealing with an insane individual must return the insane individual to status quo if the contract is either void or voided by the insane person. Answer B is incorrect, as it makes no sense since in pari delicto means that both parties are equally at fault in an illegal contract. There is no such situation in the present fact situation concerning contracting with insane individuals. Answer C is incorrect as though this is an admirable thing to do, under contract law, an individual is not responsible for placing the insane person in counseling to help him or her out. Answer D is incorrect as the contract must be void or voided by the insane individual not the sane person.

25. D   Answer D is the correct answer as this states the majority rule of law with regard to whether a contract will be enforceable or not in situations involving intoxication. Answer A is incorrect because if the person was so intoxicated, how could he or she be aware of how man drinks that he or she consumed? Therefore, this answer does not make sense. Answer B is incorrect as the factors that are considered in determining whether a person is legally intoxicated include the user's physical characteristics and his or her ability to tolerate or hold intoxicants, not someone else's validation of the nature of the transaction that had been entered into. Answer C is incorrect as it is not whether the intoxicated individual could remember where he or she was at, but rather was he or she so intoxicated that he or she was incapable of understanding or comprehending the nature of the transaction?

26. C   Answer C is correct as the amount of alcohol or drugs to be considered legally intoxicated varies from case to case taking the user's physical characteristics and ability to hold intoxicants into consideration. Answer A is incorrect as not every individual becomes intoxicated on two or more alcoholic beverages, as it is determined on a case-by-case basis. Answers B and D are incorrect based on the reasoning given in Answer C.

27. B   Answer B is correct as the disaffirming party claiming intoxication as a reason for not accepting the terms of the contract must be returned to the status quo. Answer A is incorrect, as generally an individual may not receive punitive damages in a cause of action based on contract law. Answer C is incorrect because if the individual understood or comprehended the nature of the

transaction, he or she would not be able to disaffirm the contract based on intoxication. Answer D is incorrect as there is nothing in contract law that would require an individual utilizing intoxication as a reason for disaffirming a contract to pass a breathalyzer test.

28. B   Answer B is correct, as intoxication does not relieve an individual from paying the reasonable value for the necessaries that they contract for. Answer A is incorrect, as alcohol is not considered a necessity. Answer C is incorrect as this is a vague statement that does not indicate exactly what the intoxicated individual may lose. Answer D is incorrect for the reasons given above.

29. C   Answer C is correct as state-operated lotteries are permitted in many states under their gambling statutes. Answers A, B, and D are all forms of illegal contracts, and are therefore the incorrect answers.

30. D   Answer D is correct as usury laws set an upper limit on the annual interest rate that can be charged on certain types of loans. By doing this, it helps to protect unsophisticated borrowers from being taken advantage of by loan sharks and others who charge astronomical rates of interest. Answer A is incorrect as gambling statutes make certain types of gambling illegal not usury statues. Answer B is incorrect as even though this is a true statement, it is does not elaborate on what the public is being protected from and therefore it is not the best answer. Answer C is incorrect, as usury laws have no bearing on whether or not revenue is raised. Revenue-raising statutes are separate statutes from usury statutes.

31. D   Answer D is correct, as contracts to commit criminal acts are void. However, since the object of Bob and Francis' contract, became unlawful under the state statute after their contract was entered into, the parties are discharged from their contract. The contract is not illegal unless Bob and Francis agree to go forward and complete it. Answer A is not correct, as it does not matter that they entered into the contract before the object of their contract became illegal. Answer B is incorrect as frogs that are sold after the statute becomes law would be in direct violation of the statute thereby making the contract between the parties an illegal one. Answer C is incorrect as the statute is designed to protect the tree frogs that have been placed on the endangered species list, not to protect the public from unlicensed sellers of tree frogs.

32. C   Answer C is correct as licensing statutes require members of certain professions and occupations to be licensed by the state in which they practice by showing they have the proper schooling, experience, and moral character required by the applicable statute. Answer A is incorrect as revenue-raising statutes are designed to gather revenue not protect the public. Answer B is incorrect as Sabbath laws prohibit or limit the carrying on of certain secular activities on Sundays of which graduating from medical school and passing appropriate board exams are not included. Answer D is incorrect as graduating from medical school and passing appropriate board exams would have a positive impact on society whereas contracts contrary to public policy would have a negative impact on society or interfere with the public's safety and welfare.

33. A   Answer A is correct, as the main purpose of a revenue-raising statute is to raise revenue. Answer B is incorrect as protection of the public is not a consideration of revenue-raising statutes. Answer C is incorrect as Sabbath laws, not revenue raising statutes prohibit or limit the carrying on of certain secular activities on Sundays. Answer D is incorrect as this refers to contracts that are contrary to public policy.

34. D   Answer D is correct as answers A, B, and C all describe aspects that describe contracts that are contrary to public policy.

35. C   Answer C is correct, as a contract that is based on sexual favors has been held as immoral and against public policy. Answer A is incorrect as there is nothing in the facts that would indicate that Lee might have some sort of mental incapacity to make the contract voidable. Answer B is incorrect as it should never be necessary to grant sexual favors in exchange for obtaining a job. Answer D is incorrect as a covenant not to compete is usually an ancillary agreement between the parties and not the crux of the contract itself. Additionally, there is nothing in the facts that

indicates a restriction of the type of business, geographic location or duration of the restriction to qualify it as a covenant not to compete.

Short Answer:

36. A covenant not to compete is an ancillary agreement between parties to the sale of a business or employment contract whereby the seller agrees with the buyer not to engage in a similar business or occupation within a specified geographical area for a specified period of time upon sale of the business or departing the employment situation. All aspects must be reasonable to be enforceable.
37. unconscionable contract.
38. infancy doctrine.
39. disaffirmance
40. age, lifestyle
41. Emancipation is when a minor voluntarily leaves home and lives apart from his or her parents. The courts will view a minor's ability to be self-supportive in determining emancipation.
42. voidable
43. one whose objective is the commission of an act that is considered immoral by society.
44. adjudged insane and insane, but not adjudged insane
45. The covenant probably will not be enforced as written as it is unreasonable in geographic restriction (the entire state of Arizona) as well as in duration (twenty years).
46. In order to show that a clause or contract is unconscionable, it must be shown that: 1) The parties possessed severely unequal bargaining power. 2) The dominant party unreasonably used its unequal bargaining power to obtain oppressive or manifestly unfair contract terms. 3) The adhering party had no reasonable alternative.
47. Wilma's insanity defense may fail as mere weakness of intellect or delusions do not constitute legal insanity. If in a state that utilizes the objective cognitive understanding test, they will apply it and determine if Wilma was incapable of understanding the nature of the transaction. This would be her best argument if indeed she was incapable, otherwise, she may be held to the contract with Wanda.
48. Tools of the trade have been found to be a necessary of life in some situations. Arguably Ronald is an apprentice plumber learning the vocation with his uncle, and as such the tools may be a necessity for his livelihood. So, despite the fact that he is a minor and under different circumstances may have been able to disaffirm the contract based on the infancy doctrine, because they are tools necessary for life, the court would probably hold Ronald to the contract.
49. Since the amount of alcohol that needs to be consumed for a person to become legally intoxicated is viewed on a case-by-case basis, the courts will consider Mike's physical characteristics and his ability to hold alcohol. If Mike is in a jurisdiction that provides that contracts entered into by intoxicated individuals are voidable by that person, the contract may not be enforced against him. However, the contract is voidable only if Mike was so intoxicated when the contract between he and Peter was entered into that he was incapable of comprehending that he was selling his California farm for $50,000. Further, if Mike and Peter are in a jurisdiction that only allows Mike to disaffirm the contract if he was forced to become intoxicated or did so unknowingly, he is out of luck. Mike will then have to sell his farm to Peter as agreed in the bar, especially because there is nothing to indicate that Mike was forced to drink the alcohol.
50. Minors who misrepresent their age must place the adult in status quo if they disaffirm the contract. Since Charlie told Sue that he was eighteen years old when in reality he was only sixteen years old when he entered into the contract, he owes the duties of restoration and restitution. Charlie must return the damaged speedboat plus $5,000 to Sue.

Chapter 13
GENUINENESS OF ASSENT

Chapter Overview

The preceding chapters have discussed the requirements for creation of a contract as well as agreement, capacity and consideration. Even though an individual may consent to a contract, if his or her assent is not genuine, it may make the contract unenforceable. The issues that this chapter focuses on are in the areas of mistake, misrepresentation, duress and undue influence.

Objectives

Upon completion of the exercises in this chapter, you should be able to:
1. Give an explanation of genuineness of assent.
2. Explain assent as it applies to software "click-wrap" licenses.
3. Give an explanation on how mutual mistake of fact excuses performance.
4. Describe and apply the requirements to prove intentional misrepresentation (fraud)
5. Understand and explain the difference between fraud in the inception and fraud in the inducement.
6. Understand and explain by example fraud by concealment or silence.
7. Describe innocent misrepresentation
8. Differentiate between physical and economic duress.
9. Explain undue influence and its applicability to contracts

Practical Application

You should be able to recognize whether a mistake as it applies to a contractual situation is a unilateral or a mutual mistake along with the particulars for each. Additionally, you should be able to decide whether or not a fraudulent misrepresentation or the more difficult types of fraud exist and the remedies that are available for the same. Finally you should be able to understand the impact of both physical and economic duress as well as undue influence upon a contractual situation. The information in this chapter will be particularly useful to you in developing a sense of what is genuine assent.

Helpful Hints

The five main areas you should be familiar with are broken down into easy to remember sections in the Study Tips section. Since differentiating between the different types of fraud can be confusing, it is important that you gain exposure to as many cases and examples as possible. The exercises provided for this chapter will help to enhance the exercises given at the end of the chapter in your text.

Study Tips

Genuineness in General

Keep in mind you are studying the areas of mistake, misrepresentation, duress and undue influence. These areas impact whether or not a party's assent to a contract is genuine or whether other factors influenced his or her consent to enter into the contract in the first place.

Assent

The facts you should know are:
- It must be present to have an enforceable contract.
- It may be accomplished by express words or conduct.
- A special situation exists with click-wrap licenses.
    a. The Uniform Commercial Code provides that "a contract for the sale of goods may be made in any manner sufficient to show agreement, including conduct by both parties that recognizes the contract's existence."
    b. Under the new Uniform Information Transaction Act, "a licensee is bound by the terms of the license if the licensee manifests assent before or during the party's initial use of or access to the licensor's software."

Mistake

Mistakes occur when one or both of the parties have an incorrect belief about the subject matter, value or some other area of the contract.

Two types of mistake

- Unilateral mistake – This is where one party is mistaken about a material fact concerning the subject matter of the contract.

    1. <u>General rule regarding unilateral mistakes</u>: The mistaken party usually will not be allowed to rescind the contract.

    2. <u>Exceptions to the general rule include:</u>
        - If one party is mistaken and the other party knew or should have known about the mistake, then the mistake is treated like a mutual mistake and rescission is allowed.
        - If a unilateral mistake is made because of a clerical or mathematical error and is not because of gross negligence.
        - The gravity of the mistake makes enforcing the contract unconscionable.

- Mutual mistakes – A mistake made by both parties concerning a material fact that is important to the subject matter of the contract.

    1. <u>General rule regarding mutual mistakes</u>: Either party may rescind the contract if there has been a mutual mistake of a past or existing material fact.

What is considered to be a material fact?

There are several explanations for this question.

First, anything that is significant to the subject matter of the contract.

An ambiguity may also qualify as a mutual mistake of material fact.

An ambiguity is where there is confusion as to the meaning of a word or term in the contract.

Two types of mutual mistakes:

- Mutual mistake of fact – The contract may be rescinded because there has bee no meeting of the minds between the parties as the subject matter is in dispute.

- Mutual mistake of value – The contract remains enforceable because the subject matter is not in dispute and the parties are only mistaken at to the value.

Fraudulent Misrepresentation

The mnemonic you utilized in chapter 4 is also applicable here. The mnemonic is MISJD

<u>M</u> - Misrepresentation of a material fact that was false in nature
<u>I</u> - Intentionally made to the innocent party
<u>S</u> - Scienter (knowledge) of the statement's falsity by the wrongdoer
<u>J</u> - Justifiable reliance on the false statement by the innocent party
<u>D</u> - Damages were suffered by the injured party

Fraudulent misrepresentation as an inducement to enter into a contract – The innocent party's assent is not genuine and the contract is voidable. The remedies that are available are rescission and restitution or enforce the contract and sue for damages.

There are *five types of fraud* you need to become familiar with.

1) **Fraud in the Inception** (also known as fraud in the factum) - The person is deceived on what he or she is signing. The contract is void.
2) **Fraud in the Inducement** – The person knows what he or she is signing, but has been fraudulently induced to enter into the contract. The contract is voidable by the innocent party.
3) **Fraud by Concealment** – Where one party specifically conceals a material fact from the other party.
4) **Silence as Misrepresentation** – One need not divulge all facts to the other party, however, if the nondisclosure would cause death or bodily injury or there is a fiduciary relationship or federal or state statutes require that a fact be disclosed, then fraud may be implied. ·
5) **Misrepresentation of Law** – The general rule is that this is not actionable as fraud. However, if one party to the contract is a professional who should know what the law is and still intentionally misrepresents the law to a less knowledgeable party, this will be enough to allow rescission of the contract.

Innocent Misrepresentation

This occurs when a party makes a statement of fact that he or she honestly believes is true even though it is not. The injured party may rescind the contract but may not seek damages. This type of misrepresentation is sometimes treated like a mutual mistake.

Duress

There are two types, both of which involve threatening to do a wrongful act unless the other party enters into a contract.

1. Duress via physical harm or extortion or to bring or not drop a criminal lawsuit is the first type. Note, the threat to bring or not drop a civil lawsuit is not duress, unless it's a frivolous suit.
2. Economic duress is the second type, which occurs when one party refuses to continue performing his or her duties unless the other party pays more money and enters into a second contract. The innocent party must show that her or she had no choice but to pay the extra money and succumb to the threat. Economic duress is also known as business compulsion.

Undue Influence

Rescission based on undue influence is allowed if it can be shown that a fiduciary or confidential relationship existed between the parties and the dominant party unduly used his or her influence to persuade the servient party to enter into a contract. This contract is voidable.

Refresh Your Memory

The following exercise will enable you to refresh your memory on the rules and principles presented to you in this chapter. Read each question twice and place your answer in the blanks provided. Review the chapter material for any question you miss or are unable to remember.

1. Assent may be shown by express _____ or _____ of the parties.

2. What is the proposed model act for transacting e-commerce? The _____
_____.

3. What are the two types of mistake? _____ and _____

4. What is meant by the term rescission? _____

5. When only one party is mistaken about a material fact regarding the subject matter of the contract, this is known as a _____ mistake.

6. What is a mutual mistake of fact? _____

7. If Ken telephones the manager of Your Home Town Electronics store and asks how much the smallest high density television he sells is and the manager replies, "Fourteen twenty." Thereafter Ken says, "Put my name on one as I can't pass up a bargain like that!" Ken arrives at the store ready to pay fourteen dollars and twenty cents for the small high-density television set at which point the manager laughs hysterically and says, "Buddy you must be joking! The smallest set we have costs one thousand four hundred twenty dollars!" If Ken tries to enforce the contract he claims has been formed against Your Home Town Electronics store, what would Home Town's best defense be? _____

8. What does a party need to prove in order to establish a cause of action for false misrepresentation? _____
   _____
   _____
   _____

9. Fraud in the inception is known as _____.

10. If Sheila buys a car from Howard on the representation that it has never had anything major repaired on it and thereafter takes the vehicle to the dealer for a routine check only to discover that it has had three transmissions, what cause of action may Sheila bring against Howard? _____

11. An _____ _____ happens when an individual makes a statement of fact that he or she honestly and reasonably believes to be true, even though it is not.

12. When one party threatens to do a wrongful act unless the other party enters into a contract, this is known as _____.

13. If Bart Brown, a contractor tells Mary Morris a homeowner that he will not finish her room addition on her home unless she agrees to pay him an additional $10,000 and Mary feels pressured to give him the additional compensation, this may be construed as _____
   _____.

14. A threat to bring or drop a civil lawsuit will not be considered duress unless _____
   _____.

15. Undue influence happens when one person takes advantage of another person's _____,
   _____, or _____ weakness and unduly persuades that person to enter into a contract.

Critical Thought Exercise

At Rip-Off Motors, an exotic used car dealership, you are the general manager and Slick is your dishonest salesman. Slick told a potential customer, Dupe, that the Porsche he was interested in purchasing had been driven only 25,000 in four years and had never been in an accident. Dupe hired Grease, a mechanic, to appraise the condition of the car. Grease said that the car probably had at least 75,000 miles on it and probably had been in an accident. In spite of this information, Dupe still thought the car would be a good buy for the price, which was still lower than a Porsche with 75,000 miles. Dupe bought the car and it immediately developed numerous mechanical problems which would cost over $10,000 to repair. Dupe has now come back to Rip-Off Motors and is seeking to have you rescind the contract on the basis of Slick's fraudulent misrepresentations of the car's condition. If you rescind the contract, it will cause the dealership to lose over $13,000.
   Write a letter to either:
   A) Dupe, if you are refusing to rescind the contract, or
   B) Mr. Big, the owner of Rip-Off Motors, if you intend to rescind the contract and suffer the loss.
   Explain the reasons for your decision, citing authority for your action.

Answer. _____

_____

_____

_____

_____

_____

_____

_____

_____

_____

_____

_____

_____

Practice Quiz

True/False:

1. ___ A unilateral mistake occurs when only one party is mistaken regarding a material fact about the subject matter of the contract. [p 253]

2. ___ If each party has a different subject matter in mind, the court will probably find that the contract does not exist. [p 254]

3. ___ The courts make no distinction between a mutual mistake of value and a mutual mistake of fact. [p 254]

4. ___ Only one party may rescind a contract if there has been a mutual mistake of past or existing mistake of fact. [p 254]

5. ___ If Brandon asks his mother to take him to the store to buy a new mouse and she takes him to the pet store when he wanted to go to the electronics store for a computer mouse, any contract between the two of them may be rescinded based on mutual mistake of fact. [p 254]

6. ___ Fraud in the inception is also known as fraud in the inducement. [p 256]

7. ___ If Chris fails to tell William about the wobbly frame on a bike he just bought from him and William loses control of the steering on his first ride resulting in a broken leg and collar bone, William may not bring suit under the theory of silence as misrepresentation. [p 256]

8. ___ John calls Funco Inc. to inquire about one of their arcade games and is told that it costs thirty- two fifty. Thereafter John tells the representative of Funco, "That's a great price. Put my name on it and I'll be right there to pick it up. Upon arrival he is told that the game costs three thousand two hundred and fifty dollars. Despite this fact, John will be able to purchase the arcade game for thirty-two dollars and fifty cents. [p 255]

9. ___ A misrepresentation of law will not be allowed as a ground for rescission of a contract even if one of the parties to a contract is a professional who should know what the law is and intentionally misrepresents the law to a less knowledgeable contracting party. [p 257]

10. ___ The innocent party to a contract may rescind the contract based on fraud and obtain restitution or enforce the contract and sue for damages. [p 255]

11. ___ Justifiable reliance will be found in a cause of action for fraud even if the innocent party knew the misrepresentation was false. [p 256]

12. ___ An intentional misrepresentation occurs when someone negligently induces another to rely and act on a misrepresentation. [p 255]

13. ___ Fraudulent misrepresentation is the same as fraud. [p 255]

14. ___ A party's assent to a contract need not be genuine. [p 255]

15. ___ Intent in a cause of action based on fraud may never be inferred from the circumstances. [p 256]

16. ___ To recover damages for fraud, the innocent party must show economic injury occurred. [p 255]

17. ___ A mutual mistake of value exists if both parties know the value of the contract but are mistaken as to the subject matter. [p 254]

18. ___ Predictions or opinions about the future usually do not qualify as a material misrepresentation of fact. [p 256]

19. ___ Click-wrap licenses are not enforceable contracts. [p 252]

20. ___ Nondisclosure is a misrepresentation if it constitutes a failure to act in good faith. [p 257]

21. ___ A misrepresentation is not actionable unless the innocent party to whom the misrepresentation was made acted upon it. [p 256]

22. ___ Justifiable reliance may be found in the situation where Ned offers to sell Betty his brand new sport utility vehicle for $1,500 even though it is worth $32,000. [p 256]

23. ___ The measure of damages for fraudulent misrepresentation is the difference between the value of the property when purchased and the resale value. [p 256]

24. ___ If George talks Ben into signing what Ben thinks is a receipt for handyman work that has been performed at George's country home, but he really has transferred all of his property to George, Ben would be able to void the contract based on fraud in the inception. [p 256]

25. ___ Innocent misrepresentation is looked upon as a mutual mistake. [p 258]

Multiple Choice:

26. If a party's assent to a contract is not genuine, the courts will permit the innocent party to [p 252]
    a. enforce the contract.
    b. accept part and reject part of the contract.
    c. avoid the contract.
    d. restore the dominant party to status quo.

27. Assent is determined by [p 252]
    a. relevant facts surrounding the negotiation and formation of the contract.
    b. the bargaining power of the less sophisticated party.
    c. the gravity of the mistakes made when creating the contract.
    d. the intent to deceive an innocent party in negotiating the contract.

28. If an innocent misrepresentation has been made, what type of action may the innocent party bring? [p 258]
    a. An action for fraudulent misrepresentation.
    b. An action for specific performance.
    c. An action based on undue influence.
    d. An action for rescission of the contract without damages.

29. If Walter threatens to bring a criminal lawsuit against Joshua if Joshua doesn't sign a fencing contract giving Walter the job, this would constitute [p 258]
    a. a misunderstanding between the parties.
    b. duress.
    c. undue influence over Joshua.
    d. mutual mistake of fact.

30. Economic duress is also known as [p 259]
    a. economic hardship.
    b. economic losses.
    c. business compulsion.
    d. covenant not to compete.

31. If a unilateral mistake happens because of a mathematical or clerical error that is not the result of gross negligence, a contract between the parties will [p 253]
    a. be enforced.
    b. be deemed unconscionable.
    c. not be enforced.
    d. rewritten to reflect the correct mathematical amount.

32. An innocent party's assent to a contract is not genuine when [p 255]
    a. the innocent party has made a unilateral mistake.
    b. a fraudulent misrepresentation is used to induce the innocent party to enter into the contract.
    c. the innocent party knew that the misrepresentation was false or so extravagant to be obviously false.
    d. the innocent party has participated in the fraudulent misrepresentation.

33. In a fraudulent misrepresentation cause of action, the element of scienter means [p 256]
    a. knowledge that the representation was false.
    b. that the representation was made without sufficient knowledge of the truth.
    c. "guilty mind."
    d. all of the above.

34. A misrepresentation is not actionable unless [p 256]
    a. the innocent party to whom the misrepresentation was made acted upon it.
    b. the measure of damages gives the innocent party the benefit of the bargain.
    c. the innocent party knew the misrepresentation was false or obviously false.
    d. none of the above.

35. Dan, a real estate agent tells Cindy that the house she will be buying has a roof that has special shingles that swell and shrink with the weather. Cindy believes Dan and signs the purchase agreement. Thereafter escrow closes and the first rain of the season causes substantial damage to Cindy's furniture in her new home as the roof leaks. What would be the best cause of action Cindy should bring against Dan in order to recoup the damages to her furniture? [p 256]
    a. Fraud in the inception
    b. Fraud by concealment
    c. Misrepresentation of law
    d. Fraud in the inducement

Short Answer:

36. What are the three situations when a unilateral contract will not be enforced? [p 253]

    _____
    _____
    _____

37. What are the elements necessary for proving fraudulent misrepresentation? [p 256]

    _____
    _____
    _____

38. What is the measure of damages in a cause of action for fraud? [p 256] _____

    _____

39. What is meant by the term undue influence? [p 259] _____

    _____

40. An action to undue a contract is known as _____. [p 252]

41. What is an ambiguity? [p 254] _____

    _____

42. When one party takes specific action to hide a material fact from another party, this is known as _____. [p 256]

43. Kendra visited a garage sale and offered to buy an ugly gray and black quilt with red stitching for $10.00. The owner accepted and was glad to get the quilt out of house. It is later determined that it is a quilt of morning from the Civil War and worth $50,000. Neither party was aware of this fact at the time of contracting. If the original owner wants to recover the quilt, will she be able to? Be sure to support your reason. [p 254] _____

44. Henry and Kevin are at a restaurant where both men run tabs on their purchases. Henry tells Kevin that the slip of paper he has is Kevin's tab and to go ahead and sign it so that Henry can get their bill taken care of in a quicker fashion. Kevin does not read what he is signing and quickly jots his signature on the slip of paper pushed before him. Later Kevin finds out that he has signed over the title to his corvette automobile. What cause of action should Kevin bring against Henry? Be sure to support your answer. [p 256]

45. If Ralph threatens to punch Albert in the face if Albert does not enter into a contract with Ralph to buy Albert's boat, this is known as _____. [p 258]

46. What is a mutual mistake of value? [p 254] _____

47. Jenna visits the Fine Furniture Store in her town every day. With each visit she sits on a dark blue leather sofa located in the front window of the store. The same sales representative sees her each day and finally asks her if she would like to purchase the sofa. She answers in the affirmative and says she wants that couch as she points between the dark blue leather couch and a silver leather couch next to it. The paperwork is signed and delivery is set for the following day. When the couch arrives, it is the silver leather one that is set up in her living room. She wants to rescind the contract based on a unilateral mistake. Will she succeed in her cause of action? Support your answer. [p 253] _____

48. What types of issues might affect an individual's assent to a contract? [p 252] _____

49. What act provides that a licensee who has the opportunity to review the terms of the license is bound by those terms if the licensee "manifests assent" before or during the party's initial use of or access to the licensor's software? [p 252] _____

50. A contract is _____ by the innocent party when a fraudulent misrepresentation is used to induce another to enter into a contract. [p 255]

Answers to Refresh Your Memory

1. words, conduct [p 252]
2. The Uniform Computer Information Transaction Act [p 252]
3. unilateral and mutual [p 252]
4. Rescission is an action to undo an act. [p 252]
5. unilateral [p 253]
6. A mutual mistake of fact is one both parties are mistaken about as it pertains to the subject matter of the contract. [p 254]
7. Home Town's best defense would probably be that there was a material term (price) that was expressed in an ambiguous way to which Home Town should be allowed to rescind the contract. [p 254]
8. A party needs to show the following: 1) There was a misrepresentation of material fact. 2) There was an intent to deceive. 3) There was knowledge of the falsity of the statement made to the innocent party. 4) The innocent party justifiably relied on the representation. 5) The innocent party suffered economic injury as a result of the misrepresentation. [p 256]
9. fraud in the factum [p 256]
10. fraud by concealment [p 256]
11. innocent misrepresentation [p 258]
12. duress [p 258]
13. economic duress [p 259]
14. such a suit is frivolous or brought in bad faith [p 258]
15. mental, physical, or emotional [p 259]

Critical thought Exercise Model Answer

Dear Mr. Dupe:

    I agree with you that my salesman, Slick, made a misrepresentation to you concerning the mileage and condition of the Porsche you purchased. In order for you to recover damages for the tort of fraud, you must show: (1) a misrepresentation of a material fact; (2) an intent on the part of Slick to deceive you; and, (3) you, the innocent party, must have justifiably relied on the misrepresentation. In our situation, you took the car to an independent mechanic, Grease, who informed you that the car had greater mileage than represented by Slick and had probably been in an accident. You decided that the car was still a good value despite this additional information. You did not rely upon the misrepresentations of my salesman when you purchased the car. As a result, you are not entitled to damages for fraud, nor are you entitled to rescind the agreement.

Yours truly,
General Manager

Answers to Practice Quiz

True/False:

1. True   When only one party is mistaken about a material fact regarding the subject matter of the contract, this is known as a unilateral mistake.

2. True   When each party has a different subject matter in mind, there may have been a mutual mistake of a past or existing material fact that is susceptible to more than one logical interpretation. This is known as a mutual mistake of fact of which the court will probably find that no contract has been formed, as there has been no meeting of the minds between the parties.

3. False   The courts have to distinguish between mutual mistakes of value and mutual mistakes of fact, as with the former the contract will remain in tact. The rationale for this is because if it did not anyone wanting a better deal under the contract would have an uncontrolled right to rescind all contracts entered into.

4. False   Both parties may rescind the contract on the ground that no contract has been formed because there is no meeting of the minds between the parties.

5. True   Because Brandon and his mother were each referring to a different type of mouse, there can be no binding contract and rescission would be an option since there was no meeting of the minds between the parties.

6. False   Fraud in the Inception is known as fraud in the factum as the innocent person is deceived as to the nature of his or her transaction. Compare this to fraud in the inducement whereby the innocent party knows what he or she is signing but was fraudulently induced to do so.

7. False   William may bring a cause of action under the theory of silence as misrepresentation since Chris's failure to tell William of the wobbly frame resulted in bodily injury, here a broken leg and collarbone.

8. False   Two meanings were obviously applied to the term thirty-two fifty whereby the difference between what each party meant was significant. To quote the language utilized in *Konic International Corp v. Spokane Computer Services, Inc. 708P.2d932 (1985),* "The mutual understanding of the parties was so basic and so material that any agreement the parties thought they had reached was merely an illusion." John will not be able to enforce the agreement.

9. False   The basic rule regarding misrepresentation of law is that it is not actionable as fraud. However, the exception to the rule is that if one of the parties to the contract is a professional who should know what the law is and intentionally misrepresents the law to a less knowledgeable individual, then the misrepresentation will be grounds for rescission.

10. True   The remedy when a fraudulent misrepresentation is used to induce another to enter into a contract is to either rescind the contract and obtain restitution or enforce the contract and sue for damages.

11. False   Justifiable reliance is usually found unless the innocent party was aware of the misrepresentation's falsity or the misrepresentation was so outlandish as to be obviously false.

12. False   An intentional misrepresentation occurs consciously when an individual is attempting to induce another to rely and act upon a misrepresentation, not negligently.

13. True   Fraudulent misrepresentation is also known as fraud.

14. False   There can be no contract if the assent is not genuine.

15. False   If a party's assent to a contract is not genuine, the courts will permit the innocent party to avoid the contract. If a party's assent is not genuine, other individuals make get away with claiming mistake, committing fraud, utilizing duress and undue influence to get what they want.

16. True   The innocent party must prove that the fraud caused economic injury. The measure of damages is the difference between the value of the property as represented and the actual value of the property.

17. False   A mutual mistake of value exists if both parties know the subject matter of the contract but are mistaken as to the value of the contract.

18. True   To be actionable as fraud, the misrepresentation must be of a past or existing material fact. Statements of predictions or opinions are usually not a basis for a fraud cause of action.

19. False   Under the Uniform Computer Information Transaction Act, the modern e-commerce view of contracts is that click wrap licenses are enforceable contracts between software licensors and user licensees.

20. True   Silence as misrepresentation has several exceptions to the general rule that neither party owes a duty to the other to disclose all of the facts of the transaction. However, nondisclosure is a misrepresentation if it equates to a failure to act in "good faith."

21. True   An innocent party to whom a misrepresentation was made must act upon it in order for it to be actionable.

22. False   Betty should know that the statement concerning the price of the brand new sport utility vehicle is false and so way out of line to be true. As such the court probably will not find that Betty justifiably relied upon Ned's statement.

23. False   The measure of damages is the difference between the value of the property as represented and the actual value of the property.

24. True   Since George deceived Ben as to the nature of what he was signing, there is fraud in the inception of which Ben is entitled to void the contract.

25. True   Since the individual making the statement believes it to be true even thought it is not and the individual relying on the mistaken statement believes it to be true, both are mistaken based on the innocent misrepresentation. Therefore, it is often viewed as a mutual mistake.

Multiple Choice

26. C   Answer C is correct, as the court will permit the innocent party to avoid the contract if a party's assent is not genuine. Answer A is incorrect, as a contract may not be enforced where genuine assent is lacking. Answer B is incorrect as accepting part and rejecting part of the contract is not an option when there is no assent. Answer D is incorrect as restoring the dominant party to status quo is an incorrect statement of law, as it does not pertain to assent.

27. A   Answer A is correct as all of the relevant facts surrounding negotiation and formation are examined in order to show that there has been an agreement. Answer B is incorrect as even though the bargaining power of the less sophisticated party may be one of the facts that are examined in determining assent, it is not the sole factor to decide this aspect of a contract. Answer C is incorrect, as the gravity of the mistakes would not have as much of a bearing on assent as would the type of mistake. Answer D is incorrect as once again, the intent to deceive an innocent party may be one factor that is examined in determining assent, but certainly not the sole basis for every contract transaction.

28. D   Answer D is correct as an action based on innocent misrepresentation warrants rescission without relief for damages. Answer A is incorrect as an innocent misrepresentation does not warrant a cause of action for fraudulent misrepresentation as the person making a statement of fact in the former situation honestly and reasonably believes the statement he or she has made is true. Compare this to a fraudulent misrepresentation whereby the person making the statement intends to deceive the innocent party. Therefore, one type of statement does not warrant a cause of action based on a theory that is completely opposite. Answer B is incorrect as the equitable remedy of specific performance is utilized when the remedy at law is not adequate which in the case of an innocent misrepresentation rescission would be sufficient. Answer C is incorrect as an action based on undue influence has no relation to an action based on innocent misrepresentation.

29. B   Answer B is correct as Walter is threatening to do the wrongful act of bringing a criminal lawsuit against Joshua unless Joshua gives him the fencing contract. This constitutes duress. Answer A is incorrect as there is nothing in the facts that indicates there is a misunderstanding between the parties. Answer C is incorrect as even though the facts indicate that Walter was threatening Joshua, there is nothing to indicate that Walter took advantage of Joshua's mental, emotional or physical weakness nor that the parties had a fiduciary or confidential relationship. Answer D is incorrect as a mutual mistake of fact exists where both parties are mistaken as to the subject matter of the contract of which this theory is not supported by the facts given.

30. C   Answer C is correct, as business compulsion is another term for economic duress. Answer A is incorrect as event though economic duress may cause a hardship, it is not referred to as such. Answer B is incorrect as it is a false statement. Answer D is incorrect as a covenant not to compete is an ancillary agreement to a contract not a situation where one individual uses threats to accomplish a contract.

31. C   Answer C is correct, as it is one of the exceptions to the general rule that a contract based on a unilateral mistake will not be enforced. Answer A is incorrect as this is one of the exceptions where a contract based on a unilateral mistake will not be enforced. Answer B is incorrect as there is nothing in the facts that would "shock the conscience" of the courts to deem it unconscionable. Answer D is incorrect because as an exception to the general rule of enforcing contracts based on unilateral mistakes, rewriting the contract would be antagonistic to not enforcing the contract based upon the exception.

32. B   Answer B is correct, as the use of a fraudulent misrepresentation to induce another to enter into a contract is unenforceable. Answer A is incorrect as the making of a unilateral mistake does not have a bearing on assent unless of course the mistake was based on one of the exceptions to the general rule regarding the enforcement of contracts based on unilateral mistakes. The facts are silent on this point. Answer C is incorrect as acquiescence to false representation is an acceptance that qualifies as an assent since the innocent party knew of the misrepresentation thereby giving the innocent party a chance to make an informed decision. Answer D is incorrect as once again participating in the fraudulent misrepresentation would probably constitute acceptance of the terms being represented and hence genuine assent.

33. D   Answer D is correct as the term scienter means all of the statements given in answers A, B, and C.

34. A   Answer A is correct, as an innocent party must act upon a misrepresentation in order for it to be actionable. Answer B is incorrect as the pertinence of the measure of damages is with regard to the requirement that the innocent party must suffer economic injury. It has nothing to do with how damages are measured. Answer C is incorrect, as the innocent party's knowledge of the statement's falsity would negate the element of justifiable reliance, which is necessary element in a cause of action for fraudulent misrepresentation. Answer D is incorrect for the reasons given above.

35. D   Answer D is correct, as Cindy knows that she is signing a purchase agreement but was fraudulently induced to do so by Dan's representation about the special shingles that swell and shrink with the weather. Answer A is incorrect as fraud in the inception occurs when a person is deceived as to the nature of his or her transaction, which was not the case with this set of facts. Answer B is incorrect as fraud by concealment occurs when one party takes specific action to conceal a fact from another. Answer C is incorrect, as the facts do not indicate that there has been a misrepresentation of law, which generally is not actionable as fraud.

Short Answer:

36. Where one party makes a unilateral mistake of fact and the other party knew (or should have known that a mistake was made. Also, a unilateral mistake occurs because of a clerical or mathematical error that is not the result of gross negligence. Finally, the mistake is so serious that enforcing the contract would be unconscionable.

37. The elements for proving fraudulent misrepresentation are: 1) The wrongdoer made a false misrepresentation of material fact. 2) The wrongdoer intended to deceive the innocent party 3) The innocent party justifiably relied on the misrepresentation. 4) The innocent party was injured.

38. The measure of damages is the difference between the value of the property as represented and the actual value of the property.

39. Undue influence is when one individual takes advantage of another person's mental, emotional or physical weakness and unduly persuades that person to enter into a contract.

40. rescission.

41. An ambiguity is when a word or term in the contract is susceptible to more than one logical interpretation.

42. fraud by concealment.

43. Since it was a mistake of value, the owner may not recover the quilt as the subject matter is not at issue.

44. Kevin should bring a cause of action against Henry based on Fraud in the Inception as Kevin was deceived by Henry as the nature of his transaction by being told he was signing a restaurant tab.

45. duress

46. A mutual mistake of value happens if both parties know the object of the contract, but are mistaken as to its value.

47. Yes, as the Fine Furniture Store should have known that a mistake was made as Jenna visited the store daily and sat on the blue leather sofa in front of the window every day. Also, the same representative was at the store when she did this. Jenna should not be obligated under the contract as her circumstances satisfy an exception to the general rule that unilateral contracts are enforceable.

48. Mistake, misrepresentation, undue influence and duress might affect the genuineness of assent in a contract.

49. The Uniform Computer Information Transaction Act

50. voidable

Chapter 14
WRITTEN AND E-COMMERCE SIGNATURE LAW

Chapter Overview

Even if an individual can establish that a contract has been created, issues concerning whether or not the contract was required to be in writing or was in a proper form can be present. This chapter explores the Statute of Frauds and which contracts are required to be in writing. Additionally, it discusses if and when prior oral or written agreements between the parties on the same subject matter can be utilized to explain what the parties intended. Explanations of how the court may interpret the parties contract language as well as whether several documents or references may constitute a contract are also discussed. It also examines international as well as electronic agreements and issues concerning the writing and signature requirements of each.

Objectives

Upon completion of the exercises in this chapter, you should be able to:
1. Describe the contracts that must satisfy the Statute of Frauds.
2. Discuss the impact of the failure to adhere to the Statute of Frauds.
3. Discuss how part performance satisfies the Statute of Frauds writing requirement for purchases of land.
4. Explain the application of the Statute of Frauds in situations involving contracts that cannot be performed within one year.
5. Explain what a guaranty contract is.
6. Explain the need for an agent's contract to be in writing.
7. Discuss the sale of goods and the need to satisfy the statute of frauds.
8. Discuss and apply the doctrine of promissory estoppel.
9. Explain parol evidence and its exceptions.
10. Discuss the writing requirements for international contracts.

Practical Application

You will be able to determine which documents comprise a contract based on the expressions used by the parties as well as the location of the documents. Further, you should be able to recognize contractual situations that require the application of the Statute of Frauds and whether or not the writing requirement can be satisfied in the absence of a writing. Also, you should be able to determine whether there are any issues concerning parol evidence and if any exceptions exist.

Helpful Hints

Since most of this chapter concentrates on the Statute of Frauds, it is beneficial to thoroughly understand this concept. A mnemonic has been provided for you to accomplish this objective.

Once this primary goal has been fulfilled, the remaining information will be more manageable for you to apply and learn.

Study Tips

Statute of Frauds

<u>General Information</u>
Certain kinds of contracts must be in writing in order to memorialize the significant terms and prevent misunderstanding or fabrications, otherwise known as fraud. The mnemonic given below will help give you an easy way to remember which contracts are required to be in writing. The information that follows the mnemonic is organized in the same order as the mnemonic to provide you with an organized learning method.

<u>M</u>r. <u>D</u>ibbles <u>P</u>laces <u>M</u>any <u>F</u>ancy <u>R</u>eal <u>E</u>state <u>A</u>ds.

Mr.	–	Contracts in consideration of **M**arriage
Dibbles	–	**D**ebt of another
Places	–	**P**art Performance
Many	–	**M**ust be performed within one year
Fancy	–	**F**or goods $500 or more
Real **E**state	–	Transfers of ownership interests in **R**eal **E**state such as mortgages, leases
Ads	–	**A**gency contracts

Contracts in Consideration of Marriage

These types of contracts must be in writing for the most obvious reason, to determine ownership of property and assist in determining benefits and property distribution upon death or dissolution of the same. Also it is important for income tax purposes to know exactly who is a dependent if filing jointly.

Debt of Another

A collateral or guaranty contract occurs where one person agrees to answer for the debts or duties of another individual.

Part Performance

This involves the situation where there is an oral contract for the sale of land or other transfer of interest in real property and there is some sort of partial performance. In order for the partial performance to act as an exception to the Statute of Frauds, many courts require that the purchaser either take possession of the property and pay part of the purchase price or make valuable improvements on the land. If part performance can be shown, the oral contract will be ordered to be specifically performed in order to prevent an injustice.

Must be Performed Within One Year

If a contract cannot be performed by its own terms within one year, it must be in writing. If it can be performed within one year, the contract can be oral.

For Goods $500 or More

The Uniform Commercial Code requires contracts for the sale of goods that cost $500 or more to be in writing in order to be enforceable. Modifications that cause the goods to escalate in price to $500 or more will also need to be in writing.

Real Estate

Contracts that transfer an ownership interest in land must be in writing. This includes mortgages, leases, life estates, and most easements.

Real property includes the land, its buildings, trees, soil, minerals, timber, plants, crops, and permanently affixed things to the buildings (fixtures).

Agency Contracts

Agent's contracts to sell real estate must be in writing under the *equal dignity rule*.

Electronic Contracts and the Writing Requirement of the Statute of Frauds

- The Electronic Signature in Global and National Commerce Act put electronic contracts on the same level as paper contracts.
- Electronic agreements meet the Statute of Frauds writing requirement.
- The act provides for record retention requirements.

Promissory Estoppel

- Promissory estoppel is also known as equitable estoppel.
- It is an exception to the Statute of Frauds
- It involves an oral promise that is enforceable if three conditions are met.
    1. The promise induces action or forbearance of action by another.
    2. The reliance on the oral promise was foreseeable, and
    3. Injustice can be avoided only by enforcing the oral promise.
- The effect of this doctrine is to estop the promisor from raising the Statute of Frauds as a defense.

Sufficiency of the Writing

Things you should know:
- A contract does not have to be drafted by a lawyer.
- A contract does not have to be formally typed to be binding.
- A contract can be a letter, telegram, invoice, sales receipts, checks and even handwritings on scraps of paper.
- The contract must be signed by the party to be charged.
- A signature can be a nickname, initial, a symbol, and even the letter 'X'. Also, modernly, a
- Fax may also constitute a signature even though it's a document by electronic means, if the party trying to enforce the contract can demonstrate that the obligation was intentionally incurred.

Japan's Use of a Signature in a Writing

- In Japan, they use a stamp with a set of characters on the end of it. This is called hanko.
- In China it is called chop.
- Hankos and chops are registered with the government.
- The signatures can be made of gold, wood, plastic, ivory, jade or agate.
- The use of hankos and chops are debated. Some say they promote fraud. Others value the rich tradition and feel it will remain in tact.

Integration of Several Writings

An entire writing does not have to be in one single document in order to be enforceable. Several writings can be combined or *integrated* to form a single written contract. Integration may be accomplished by expressly referring to it in one document that refers to and incorporates another document in it. This is known as *incorporation by reference*.

Interpreting Contract Words and Terms

- The parties may explain the words and terms used in the contract.
- Some contracts contain a glossary that defines the terms and used in a contract.
- If the words and terms are not defined, the courts will interpret using the following standard.
- Ordinary words- given the meaning as stated in the dictionary.
- Technical words – given their technical meaning.
- Specific terms qualify general terms.
- Typed words prevail over preprinted words.
- Handwritten words prevail over preprinted and typed.
- If an ambiguity exists, it will be resolved against the party who drafted the contract.
- If both parties are in the same sort of trade, then the words used in the trade will be given their meaning as per trade usage.
- Interpretation will be to advance the object of the contract.

Parol Evidence Rule

- Parol means word.
- Any words outside of the four corners of the contract are called parol evidence.
- The parol evidence rule states that if a written contract is a complete and final expression of the parties' agreement, any prior oral or written statements that alter, contradict, or are in addition to the terms of the written contract Are inadmissible in any court proceeding concerning the contract.

Refresh Your Memory

The following exercise will enable you to refresh your memory on the rules and principles presented to you in this chapter. Read each question twice and place your answer in the blanks provided. Review the chapter material for any question you miss or are unable to remember.

1. All states have enacted a _____ of _____that requires certain types of contracts to be in writing.

2. An executory contract is _____ _____ by either party under the Statute of Frauds.

3. Any contract that transfers an _____ _____ in land must be in writing under Statute of Frauds.

4. Give three examples of real property as it pertains to the Statute of Frauds.
   _____, _____, _____

5. Give four examples of real estate interests that must be in writing under the Statute of Frauds. _____, _____,
   _____, _____

6. What is the purpose of the one-year rule? _____
   _____

7. What must a purchaser of land under an oral contract do in order for the doctrine of promissory estoppel apply? _____
   _____

8. When will contracts for the sale of goods have to be in writing? _____
   _____

9. A written contract does not have to be drafted by a _____ or formerly typed in order to be _____.

10. Give three examples of writings that can be enforced as a contract. _____,
    _____, _____

11. Under the U.C.C., what is acceptable as a signature? _____
    _____
    _____

12. What needs to be shown for a fax to be a signature? _____
_____

13. What method does the Japanese use for their signature? _____
_____
_____

14. Define the term integration. _____
_____

15. What is meant by the term incorporation by reference? _____
_____

Critical Thought Exercise

On February 1, Professor Herbert was hired by your company's vice-president as the company historian at a rate of $1,400 per month for as long as Herbert lived, with $700 to be paid on the first and fifteenth of each month. Herbert was paid regularly for eight months and then the president decided that he didn't like Herbert digging into company history. No further payments were made to Herbert. Herbert claimed that the company had breached the oral contract and brought suit, seeking damages of $1,400 per month for the rest of his life. The company president asserts that the contract is not enforceable because contracts that cannot be performed within one year must be in writing under the Statute of Frauds.

Draft a memorandum to the president advising him as to the applicable law and whether you believe that the company will be able to defend against Herbert's claim based upon the one-year rule.

Answer. _____
_____
_____
_____
_____
_____
_____
_____
_____
_____
_____
_____
_____
_____
_____
_____

Practice Quiz

True/False:

1. ____ The signature of the person enforcing the contract is necessary when enforcing a contract. [p 274]

2. ____ The doctrine of promissory estoppel is an equitable doctrine that prohibits enforcement of oral contracts that should have been in writing. [p 272]

3. ____ The placing of several documents in a tube may indicate integration. [p 275]

4. ____ A contract must be in writing, contain the essential terms, and be drafted by a lawyer in order to be binding. [p 274]

5. ____ International contracts may be proved by witnesses. [p 277]

6. ____ Attaching several documents together by a staple is not integration. [p 275]

7. ____ Words in a contract will be interpreted to promote the principle object of the contract. [p 276]

8. ____ The Uniform Commercial Code does not allow several writings to be integrated to form a single written contract. [p 276]

9. ____ The term parol means that one may be released from prison for good behavior. [p 276]

10. ____ In Japan individuals do not use their hand written signatures to sign legal documents. [p 275]

11. ____ An express easement need not be in writing in order to be enforceable. [p 268]

12. ____ A lease term that is over one year must be in writing under the Statute of Frauds. [p 268]

13. ____ Merger clauses prevent parol evidence from being introduced to prove fraud, duress, misrepresentation, mistake or undue influence. [p 277]

14. ____ The law will not accept a telegram as a writing to constitute a contract. [p 274]

15. ____ Parol evidence may be allowed to explain an ambiguity. [p 276]

16. ____ One of the main features of federal law is that it recognizes an e-signature. [p 275]

17. ____ Contracts for the sale of goods for $400 or more need to be in writing. [p 271]

18. ____ If there is a typographical error in a contract, the court will reform it and allow parol evidence to prove this. [p 277]

19. ___ A fax may not constitute a signature. [p 274]

20. ___ A clause that stipulates the contract is a complete integration and the exclusive expression of their agreement is a merger clause. [p 277]

21. ___ Handwritten words do not prevail over preprinted and typed words in a contract. [p 276]

22. ___ Incorporation by reference may be accomplished by express reference in one document that refers to and incorporates another document within it. [p 275]

23. ___ Parol evidence may not be used to fill in a missing price in the contract, as that is the job of the court. [p 276]

24. ___ A detailed, definitional section in a contract is called a glossary. [p 276]

25. ___ The doctrine of part performance is a legal doctrine allowing monetary damages on an oral contract. [p 268]

Multiple Choice:

26. Evan and Gloria, both non-merchants enter into an oral contract whereby Gloria agrees to purchase Evan's piano as he has developed severe arthritis and cannot play anymore. He sends her a sloppily written letter with an illegible "e" as his signature setting for the terms of their agreement including the $1,200. sales price. Will Evan's signature be sufficient to satisfy the Statute of Frauds and the Uniform Commercial Code if Evan decides to keep the piano and give it to his granddaughter? [p 274]
    a. Yes, as Evan's signature need not be his full legal name. As long as the "e" indicates Evan's intent to enter into the contract, it will be sufficient to be binding.
    b. Yes, as long as Gloria's signature appears on the letter as well.
    c. No, because Evan did not sign his full legal name.
    d. No, because Evan really did not intend to sell the piano to Gloria as he wanted to give it to his granddaughter.

27. A clause in a contract that stipulates that it is the complete integration and the exclusive expression of the parties agreement is known as a [p 277]
    a. promissory estoppel clause.
    b. marital clause.
    c. incorporation by reference clause.
    d. merger clause.

28. Real property as it pertains to the Statute of Frauds includes [p 267]
    a. timber, crops, fixtures, soil and buildings.
    b. stocks, bonds, money, and certificates.
    c. timber, inoperable automobiles, plants and minerals.
    d. fixtures, crops, and farm equipment.

29. James Albertson says to his son Henry and daughter-in-law Grace, "If you quit your jobs in Florida and come take care of me in Texas for six months, I will give you my mansion." Thereafter both Henry and Grace quit their well paying jobs and move from Florida to Texas to take care of James. They pay off a second mortgage on James' property, move In with James and add a room addition so that James can look out onto the ocean. Six months elapse and Henry and Grace ask James to sign over the deed to the Texas mansion. Henry laughs and indicates that they do not have any grounds to enforce what they are claiming. What would be Henry and Grace's best theory in order to succeed in a cause of action against James? [p 268]
    a. An injunction to prevent James from moving from his Texas home.
    b. The equitable doctrine of part performance.
    c. The integration theory.
    d. Incorporation of all oral statements by referencing when Henry and Grace moved to Texas.

30. Which aspect of the Statute of Frauds is intended to prevent disputes about contract terms that may otherwise occur toward the end of a long-term contract? [p 269]
    a. The part performance exception.
    b. The guaranty contract rule.
    c. The one year rule.
    d. Goods for $500 or more.

31. A collateral or guaranty contract happens where [p 270]
    a. contracts for the sale of goods $500 or more are present.
    b. one person agrees to answer for the debts or duties of another person.
    c. electronic commerce agreements are a secondary means of enforcement to formal contracts.
    d. the most recent agreement of the parties is integrated with the former contract thereby guaranteeing its enforcement.

32. Jane and John enter into a contract for the purchase of Jane's computer, with delivery set for December 15. Upon signing the contract John discovers that a price has not been set. Which rule would best assist the parties for enforcing the contract? [p 277]
    a. The Kelly Blue Book rule
    b. The promissory estoppel rule
    c. The parole evidence rule
    d. The equal dignity rule

33. Cameron expressly grants to Jennifer the right to use his land to get from her land to the boat dock that is adjacent to the end of his property. If Cameron decides that Jennifer cannot use his land to get to the boat dock, what must Jennifer show in order to enforce the right to use Cameron's land? [p 268]
    a. That an easement was created.
    b. That she was given a right to use Cameron's land.
    c. That the right to use Cameron's land was in writing.
    d. All of the above.

34. Isabel has brought a cause of action against Murphy for a contract that was induced by fraud. What would Isabel's best argument be in order to void the contract? [p 276]
    a. An exception to the parol evidence should be validated as it can be utilized for showing that a contract is void or voidable.
    b. That Murphy was a scoundrel for tricking her into a fraudulent contract.
    c. That the doctrine of promissory estoppel should apply in order to prevent an injustice.
    d. None of the above.

35. Herbert and Albert enter into an electronic contract for the purchase of Herbert's set of encyclopedias. Thereafter Herbert's niece tells Herbert that she would like to have the set of encyclopedias to do her homework. Herbert tries to rescind the agreement, however, Albert cites law that is favorable to the enforcement of the parties' agreement. What law Could have Albert cited that would promote the enforcement of an electronic agreement? [p 272]
    a. The Electronic Signature in Global and National Commerce Act
    b. The Digital Millennium Copyright Act
    c. An exception to the Statute of Frauds
    d. The Merger of Documents Act

Short Answer:

36. Give two exceptions to the parol evidence rule. [p 276] _____
    _____

37. What is a merger clause? [p 277] _____

38. If the Statute of Frauds requires a contract to be in writing, however, despite this requirement the parties have already executed an oral agreement, neither party may seek _____ based on noncompliance with the Statute of Frauds. [p 266]

39. The doctrine of promissory estoppel prevents the _____ from raising the Statute of Frauds as a defense to the enforcement of an oral contract. [p 272]

40. Only the signature of the party _____ needs to be on the contract. [p 274]

41. Briefly define the meaning of fixtures as they pertain to real estate. [p 267] _____
    _____

42. Give an example of a contract that should be in writing because it will often last longer than a year. [p 269] _____

43. What is a guaranty contract? [p 270] _____

44. A _____ is one who agrees to pay the debt if the primary debtor does not. [p 271]

45. What type of contract has been formed if Stephanie agrees to pay Sally's debt to Visa? [p 270] A _____ contract

46. If Bert decides to sell his golf cart to Kurt for $800.00, what will be required? [p271]

_____

47. What is the rule that says that agent's contracts to sell property covered by the Statute of Frauds must be in writing to be enforceable? [p 272] _____

48. With regard to the Electronic Signature in Global and National Commerce Act, what are the three requirements for record retention? [p 272] _____

_____

_____

49. Explain why faxes that are not signed may still be enforceable. [p 274] _____

_____

50. What ways may a digital signature be verified? [p 275] _____

_____

_____

Answers to Refresh Your Memory

1. Statute of Frauds [p 266]
2. not enforceable [p 266]
3. ownership interest [p 267]
4. trees, timber, minerals, plants, crops and fixtures [p 267] (answers will vary)
5. mortgages, leases, life estates and easements [p 268]
6. The purpose of the one-year rule is to prevent disputes about contract terms that might occur toward the end of a long-term contract. [p 269]
7. The purchaser must either pay part of the purchase price as well as take possession of the property or make valuable improvements on the land. [p 268]
8. The Uniform Commercial Code requires that contracts for the sale of goods costing $500 or more must be in writing in order to be enforceable. [p 271]
9. lawyer, binding [p 274]
10. letters, telegrams, checks and sales receipts [p 274] (answers will vary)
11. A signature may be a person's full legal name, the person's nickname, initials, seal, stamp, a symbol or mark as long as it indicates the person's intent to be bound by the terms of the contract. [p 274]
12. In order for a fax to be considered signed, it must be shown that the obligation was intentionally incurred. [p 274]
13. The Japanese use a stamp as their signature, which is composed of a character or a set of characters carved onto the end of a round cylindrical shaped piece held in a person's hand. The Japanese call this a hanko. [p 275]
14. Integration is the combination of several writings to form a single contract. [p 275]
15. When integration is made by express reference in one document that refers to and incorporates another document within it, this is known as incorporation by reference. [p 275]

Critical Thought Exercise Model Answer

Each state has a Statute of Frauds under which certain types of contracts must be in writing to be enforceable. The primary purpose of the statute is to ensure that there is reliable evidence of the existence and terms of certain types of contracts that are deemed important. These types of contracts include those involving interests in land, contracts that cannot by their terms be performed within one year from the date of formation, those that create collateral promised for one person to answer for the debt or duty of another, and contracts for the sale of goods priced at $500 or more. Contracts that cannot, by their own terms, be performed within one year from the day after the contract is formed must be in writing to be enforceable. The test for determining whether an oral contract is enforceable under the one-year rule of the statute is not whether the agreement is likely to be performed within one year from the date the contract was formed but whether performance within a year is possible. When performance within one year is impossible, the contract is unenforceable if it was not in writing. An exception to this "possibility of performance within one year" standard is raised by a lifetime employment contract. Some states rely upon the traditional view that the contract can be performed within one year because a person may die within the first year. The modern view is that a lifetime employment contract anticipates a relationship of long duration, well in excess of one year. These states hold the view that to allow an oral contract for lifetime employment would eviscerate the policy underlying the statute of frauds and would invite confusion, uncertainty and outright fraud. The determination of the enforceability of this oral contract for lifetime employment for Professor Herbert will depend upon whether the jurisdiction adopts the traditional or modern view of the one-year rule.

Answers to Practice Quiz

True/False:

1. True   The U.C.C. requires the written contract to be signed by the party against whom enforcement is sought.
2. False   The doctrine of promissory estoppel is an equitable doctrine that enforces oral contracts and estops the promisor from raising the Statute of Frauds as a defense to the enforcement of the oral contract.
3. True   The placing of several documents together in a container may be implied integration thereby forming a single written contract.
4. False   As long as all of the essential terms are contained in a contract, it need not be drafted by a lawyer to be binding.
5. True   Article 11 of the United Nations Convention on Contract for the International Sale of Goods provides that "a contract of sale need not be concluded in or evidenced by writing and is not subject to any other requirement concerning form. Further, it may be proved by any means, including witnesses.
6. False   The physical attachment of several documents, including by stapling may indicate integration that will imply that the documents form a single contract.
7. True   Words will be analyzed to promote the principal object of a contract.
8. False   The Uniform Commercial Code does allow several writings to be integrated to form a single written contract.
9. False   The term parol means word.
10. True   The Japanese use a stamp called a *hanko*.

11. False   Express easements must be in writing to be enforceable.
12. True   The Statute of Frauds requires leases for a term over one year to be in writing.
13. False   Merger clauses do not prevent the introduction of parol evidence to prove duress, misrepresentation, mistake or undue influence.
14. False   Any writing including telegrams can be an enforceable written contract.
15. True   The use of parol evidence to explain an ambiguity is an exception to the general rule that excludes parol evidence.
16. True   The federal law known as the Electronic Signature in Global and National Commerce Act gives an e-signature the same force and effect as a signature written on paper.
17. False   The Uniform Commercial Code requires that contracts for the sale of goods costing $500 or more must be in writing to be enforceable.
18. True   The court will allow parol evidence to correct an obvious clerical or typographical error and the court can reform the contract to show the correction.
19. False   A fax can compose an enforceable guarantee if the name of the party to be charged is printed upon it.
20. True   This is the explanation for a merger clause, which expressly restates the parol evidence rule.
21. False   Handwritten words do prevail over preprinted and typed words.
22. True   Expressly referring to one document and incorporating it into another document is incorporation by reference.
23. False   Parol evidence may be used to fill in the gaps in a contract if a price term or time for performance term is missing from a written contract.
24. True   A glossary defines many of the terms and words in a contract.
25. False   The doctrine of part performance is an equitable doctrine, which allows the court to order specific performance on an oral contract so that an injustice may be prevented.

Multiple Choice:

26. A   Answer A is correct because as long as the illegible "e" indicates Evan's intent to sell Gloria the piano, it can be binding. The signature does not have to be Evan's full legal name. Answer B is incorrect, as the Uniform Commercial Code requires the written contract to be signed by the party to be charged. In this case, the party to be charged would be Evan. Gloria's signature is not necessary. Answer C is incorrect based on the reasoning given for Answer A. Answer D is incorrect as the facts do not indicate that he had mixed feelings on who the piano was to go to, but, instead reflect that he intended for Gloria to buy the piano as is evinced by the messy letter that he sent to her.
27. D   Answer D is correct as the question explains what a merger clause is which expressly restates the parol evidence rule. Answers A and B are incorrect as there is no such thing as a promissory estoppel clause or a marital clause. Answer C is incorrect as an incorporation by reference clause refers in one document to another document and incorporates the outside document into the original one.
28. A   Answer A is correct and timber, crops, fixtures, soil and buildings are considered real property for purposes of the Statute of Frauds. Answer B is incorrect and these are not real property and are considered intangible property under some legal circumstances. Answer C is incorrect as inoperable automobiles are not considered real property. Answer D is incorrect as farm equipment is personal property and not real property.
29. B   Answer B reflects the best theory that Henry and Grace should utilize against James as the parties agreement appears to be oral in nature and both Henry and Grace paid off the second mortgage, moved in with James, and added a room onto the property for James to see the ocean. As such, the court will allow the oral contract to be specifically performed in order to prevent an injustice to Henry and Grace. Answer A is incorrect as an

injunction is not the remedy that is used in a potential breach of contract cause of action. Answer C makes no sense, as there is nothing in the facts to suggest that there were any documents that were kept together that would imply one contract. Answer D is incorrect as it incorrectly utilizes the term incorporation by reference by associating it with oral statements.

30. C   Answer C is correct as an executory contract that cannot be performed by its own terms within one year of formation must be in writing so as to avoid disputes that may occur toward the end of a long-term contract. Answer A is incorrect as the part performance exception is primarily used in situations involving oral contracts and land. Answer B is incorrect as this refers to answering the debt of another. Answer D is incorrect, as the statement does not reflect a measure to prevent disputes but rather states part of a type of contract that needs to be in writing according to the Statute of Frauds.

31. B   Answer B is correct as it correctly states what a collateral or guaranty contract is. Answer A is incorrect as though the goods may in fact cost over $500, there is no dollar amount requirement when it comes to answering for another's debts. Answer C is incorrect as it does not make any sense. Answer D is incorrect as integrating one agreement with another agreement does not necessarily guarantee its enforcement nor does it correctly explain what a collateral or guaranty agreement is.

32. C   Answer C expresses the rule that would help the parties the most as an exception to the parol evidence rule is that if there is a gap such as price in the contract, the court may fill in that price. Answer A is incorrect as there is no such thing as the Kelly Blue Book Rule. Answer B is incorrect as the doctrine of promissory estoppel is utilized in oral contract situations where enforcement is necessary to prevent an injustice. The facts indicate that there is a written contract that was signed, and as such promissory estoppel would not be applicable. Answer D is incorrect as the equal dignity rule concerns the requirement that an agents' contract to sell property must be in writing in order to be enforceable.

33. D   Answer D is correct as answers A, B, and C all state what Jennifer must show in order to enforce the right to use Cameron's land.

34. A   Answer A is correct as it provides the best argument for Isabell since an exception to the parol evidence rule is that parol evidence can be admitted to show that a contract was induced by fraud. Answer B is incorrect because even though this might be how Isabel feels, it is a mere accusation verses a legal basis for her cause of action. Answer C is incorrect as the facts are silent as to whether the contract was oral or in writing as well as what the subject matter of the contract is. As such it is nearly impossible to make a determination of the applicability of the doctrine of promissory estoppel.

35. A   Answer A is correct, as electronically signed contracts cannot be denied effect because they are in electronic form or because they are electronically delivered. Answer B is incorrect as this pertains to intellectual property law. Answer C is incorrect as there is not an electronic agreement exception to the Statute of Frauds as of yet. Answer D is incorrect as there is no such thing as the Merger of Documents Act.

Short Answer:

36.   Two exceptions to the parole evidence rule are to fill in the gaps when price or time for performance is missing and to explain ambiguous language. (Note, answers will vary.)

37.   A merger clause stipulates that it is a complete integration and exclusive expression of the parties' agreement.

38.   rescission

39.   promissor

40. against whom enforcement is sought
41. Fixtures are personal property that is permanently adhered to the real property such as the lights on the ceiling in a house.
42. an employment contract
43. A contract between the guarantor, which is the person who agrees to pay the debt if the primary debtor does not, and the creditor.
44. guarantor
45. guaranty
46. It will be required to be in writing under the Statute of Frauds as the golf cart costs more than $500.
47. Equal Dignity
48. The consumers must consent to receiving electronic records and contracts. Next, consumers must be able to show that they have access to electronic records. Finally businesses must tell consumers that they have the right to receive hardcopy documents.
49. Because the name of the parties printed on the fax itself may be sufficient to constitute a signature in light of the heavy use of electronic transmissions in conducting business in today's technologically advanced world.
50. It can be verified by something the signatory knows, such as a password, a pet's name, etc. or by something a person has such as a smart card that stores information. Finally, the digital signature may be verified by biometrics that digitally recognizes fingerprints or the iris or retina of the eye.

Chapter 15
THIRD-PARTY RIGHTS
AND DISCHARGE

Chapter Overview

This chapter examines third party rights under other individual's contracts, more specifically assignees and intended third-party beneficiaries. Additionally it explores conditions to performance and the various ways of discharging the duty of performance. The delegation of contractual duties by mutual agreement, impossibility of performance and operation of law are also discussed.

Objectives

Upon completion of the exercises contained in this chapter, you should be able to:
1. Define the meaning of assignment as it pertains to contracts.
2. Discuss what contracts are assignable.
3. Define the meaning of delegation of duties and discuss the parties' liability in a delegation.
4. Define an intended beneficiary and discuss his or her rights under a contract.
5. Differentiate between a creditor, donee and incidental beneficiary.
6. Define a covenant.
7. Define and differentiate between conditions precedent, conditions subsequent and concurrent conditions.
8. Discuss the impact of objective impossibility on a contract.
9. Discuss the meaning of commercial impracticability and when it applies.
10. Discuss the various ways that contracts are discharged by operation of law.

Practical Application

Upon mastering the concepts in this chapter, you should be able to recognize whether or not a contract may be assigned or delegated and any liabilities that may have been incurred as a result of the delegation. Further, you will be able to determine if a third party to a contract has any rights as a beneficiary to the contract. Finally, you should be able to analyze questions and real life situations concerning the various ways a contract may be discharged by law.

Helpful Hints

Since it is often difficult keeping the parties straight in contracts involving more than two parties, it is helpful to diagram the transaction either in box form as is displayed within your text, or by use of a triangle or any other means that may be useful to you. It is also especially helpful to imagine yourself as the person being given an assignment or right, delegation or duty. If you substitute yourself into the question or hypothetical, the concepts begin to become clear.

Do not get burdened by the titles assignee, assignor, delagatee, delegator, or obligor and obligee. It is much easier to learn the concept behind the titles first and then the titles and who is doing what and its impact will become second nature to you.

Study Tips

It is very important that you become familiar with the terminology expressed in this chapter as it can become confusing.

Vocabulary

Privity of Contract – The state of two specified parties being in contract.

Obligor –The party who owes the duty of performance.
Obligee – The party owed a right under a contract.
Assignor – This is the obligee in disguise as he or she is transferring his or her right under a contract.
Assignee – The party to whom the right has been transferred.
Anti-delegation clause – A clause that prohibits the delegation of duties under the contract. The courts will enforce this clause.
An assignment and a delegation – Where both the rights and duties are transferred under the contract.

Assignment

The transfer of contractual rights by the obligee to another party. No formalities are necessary, however, words to express the intent of the assignor are carefully examined. Words such as transfer, give and convey have been used to express intent in an assignment.

Rights that may not be assigned include:

*   Personal service contracts are not assignable.
    Exception: A professional athletics contract with a clause that permits the contract to be assigned.

*   Assignment of Future Rights- The general rule is that a person may not assign a currently non- existing right that he or she is expecting in the future.

*   Contracts Where Assignment Would Materially Alter the Risk of the Obligor – A classic example would be assigning your homeowner's insurance to a friend of yours who cannot afford it.

*   Assignment of Legal Actions – An individual may not assign the right to sue, however, he or she may assign the right to the judgment once it is procured.

Effect of an Assignment

The assignee stands in the shoes of the assignor. The assignor is entitled to performance by the obligor. The assignment extinguishes all rights of the assignor against the obligor.

The assignee must notify the obligor about the assignment and the performance by the obligor must be given to the assignee. If there is no notice given to the obligor, he or she can continue performing under the contract to the assignor. The assignees only recourse is to sue the assignor for damages.

Rules used for Successive Assignments

- The American Rule (New York Rule) – The majority of states use this rule, which states that the first assignment in time prevails regardless of notice.

- The English rule – This rule states that the first to give notice prevails.

- The Possession of Tangible Token Rule - Under either the American or English rule, if the assignor makes a successive assignment of a contract right that is represented by a tangible token, such as a savings passbook, stock certificate etc, the first assignee who receives delivery of the tangible token prevails over subsequent assignees.

If the obligor knows of the assignment but continues to perform to the assignor, the assignee can due the obligor for payment. He or she will also have to pay to the assignor and to the assignee. Further he or she may sue the assignor for damages.

Anti-assignment and Approval Clauses

- The anti-assignment clause prohibits the assignment of rights under the contract.
- An approval clause is one in which the obligor must approve any assignment.

Delegation of Duties

- A transfer of contractual duties by the obligor to another party for performance.
- Delegator – The obligor who transferred his or her duty.
- Delagatee – The party to whom the duty has been transferred.

Duties that May Not be Delegated Include:

- Personal service contracts that require the discretion, expertise and the exercise of personal skills.
- Contract whose performance would materially vary if the obligor's duties were delegated.

Effect of Delegation of Duties:

- The delegator remains legally liable for the performance of the contract, thereby being subjected to a lawsuit if the delegatee does not perform properly.

- The delegate's liability depends on if there has been a declaration of duties or an assumption of duties. If the word assumption or a similar term is contained in the delegation, then there has been an assumption of duties.

- Compare though, if a delegatee has not assumed the duties under the contract, then this is called a declaration of duties. In the case of a declaration of duties, the delegatee is not obligated to the obligee for nonperformance, and the obligee can only sue the delegator.

Third-Party Beneficiaries

- Third parties who claim rights under contracts are either intended or incidental. The intended beneficiaries are either donee or creditor beneficiaries.

- Intended:
  Donee beneficiary contract – A contract, which confers a benefit, or gift on an intended third party.
  Donee- The third party to whom the benefit is conferred.
  Creditor beneficiary contract – A contract where a debtor has borrowed money from a creditor to buy an item. The debtor enters into an agreement to pay the creditor back with interest. The debtor thereafter sells the item to another individual before the loan is paid off. The new buy then promises the debtor that he or she will pay the balance of the loan amount to the creditor.
  Creditor- The party that becomes a beneficiary under the new debtor's contract with another party.

- Incidental beneficiary:
  An incidental beneficiary is one who is incidentally benefited by other people's contracts

Covenants and Conditions

- Covenant – An unconditional promise to perform.
- Nonperformance of a covenant equals a breach of contract giving the other party the right to sue.

- Condition – A conditional promise is not as definite as a covenant.

- Types of conditions:

  1. Condition precedent – The occurrence or nonoccurrence of an event before a party is obligated to perform under the contract.

<u>Example</u>: Condition precedent based on satisfaction. There are two tests to determine whether this unique form of condition precedent has been met. They are:

The personal satisfaction test – This is a subjective test whereby the person is to act in good faith in matters involving personal taste and comfort.

The reasonable person test – This is an objective test that is used to judge contracts involving mechanical fitness and most commercial transactions. This is used when a third person is involved who is used to judge another's work.

Time of performance as a condition precedent:
If a party is not jeopardized by a delay, this will be considered a minor breach. If *"time is of the essence,"* performance by the stated time is an express condition. This will be considered a breach of contract if performance is not rendered by the start date.

2. Condition Subsequent
    This condition exists when a contract provides that the occurrence or nonoccurrence of a certain event automatically excuses the performance of an existing duty to perform.
    In the Restatement (Second) of Contracts, there is no distinction between a condition precedent and a condition subsequent.

3. Concurrent Conditions
    This condition occurs when both parties render performance at the same time.

4. Implied Conditions
    Any of the above conditions may be considered to be express or implied in nature. A condition is implied from the situation surrounding the contract and the parties' conduct.

Discharge of Performance

- There are three ways to discharge a party's duty under a contract. They are by mutual agreement of the parties, by impossibility of performance, or by operation of law.

- **Discharge by agreement** is accomplished by:

1. Mutual rescission – The parties to a contract can mutually agree to discharge or end their contractual duties.
2. Substituted contract – The parties can enter into a new contract that revokes and discharges a prior contract.
3. Novation – This agreement substitutes a new party for one of the original contracting parties. All three must be in unison regarding the substitution.

4. Accord and Satisfaction – The settlement of a contract dispute where the parties accept something different than originally agreed upon and performance of the same. If an accord is not satisfied when it is due, the injured party may enforce either the accord or the original agreement.

- **Discharge by Impossibility**
  - Discharge by impossibility occurs under the following circumstances:

  - Impossibility of Performance
    This excuse of nonperformance is excused if the contract becomes objectively impossible to perform.
  - Examples:
    Death of a promissory in a personal service contract.
    Destruction of the subject matter prior to performance.
    A supervening illegality makes performance of the contract illegal.

  - Commercial Impracticability
    This excuse of nonperformance indicates that if an extreme or unexpected development or expense makes it impractical for the promissory to perform, then this excuse may be recognized.

  - Frustration of Purpose
    If the object or benefit of the contract is made worthless to the promisor and both parties knew what the purpose was, and the act that frustrated the purpose was reasonably unforeseeable, then
    This doctrine will excuse the performance of commercial obligations.

  - Force Majeure Clauses
    These type of clauses are where the parties agree in their contract as to the events that will excuse nonperformance of the contract. These typical force majeure clause excuses nonperformance
    caused by natural disasters. Modernly labor strikes, and shortages of materials excuse performance by way of a force majeure clause.

Discharge by Operation of Law

The legal rules that discharge parties from performing their duties under their contracts are as follows:

- Statute of Limitations – The statutory frame in which to bring a lawsuit. The U.C.C. indicates that four years is the time frame to bring a cause of action based on breach of contract.

- Bankruptcy- If the debtor's assets are inadequate to pay all of the creditors' claims, then the debtor receives a discharge of the unpaid debts and is relieved of liability to pay the discharged debts.

- Alteration of Contract –This occurs when a party to the contract intentionally alters the contract 's material terms such as price or quantity. The innocent party may discharge the contract or enforce it on its original or modified terms.

Refresh Your Memory

The following exercise will enable you to refresh your memory on the rules and principles presented to you in this chapter. Read each question twice and place your answer in the blanks provided. Review the chapter material for any question you miss or are unable to remember.

1. The state of two specified parties being in contract is known as _____ of _____.

2. What is an assignment? _____.

3. The party owed a right under the contract is known as the _____.

4. The party who owes the duty of performance is known as the _____.

5. When an assignee assigns the right to another person, this new assignee is sometimes called a _____.

6. Joseph cannot assign his expected right to receive inheritance from his living grandmother because _____.

7. Edna assigns her homeowner's insurance to Betty, as Betty cannot get insurance. What is the effect of this assignment? _____

8. If an obligor does not want to deal with or render performance to an unknown third party, what type of clause may he or she use? _____

9. What is an approval clause? _____

10. A transfer of contractual duties by the obligor to another party for performance is a _____.

11. A third party who is not in privity of contract but who has rights under the contract against the obligor is an _____ _____.

12. The original creditor who becomes a beneficiary under the debtor's new contract with another party is a _____ _____.

13. An agreement that substitutes a new party for one of the original contracting parties and relieves the existing party of liability on the contract is known as a _____.

14. In order for Ralph to be relieved of his contractual duties under the excuse of impossibility of performance, he must show that the impossibility was _____ in nature.

15. A force majeure clause is one in which the parties may agree _____.

Critical Thought Exercise

The Rocky Mountain Plumbing Company (RMP), which you manage, is very successful and has an excellent reputation. Your business is known for its fairness, prompt performance and superior work. After a severe earthquake that measured 7.4 on the Richter scale, billions of dollars worth of pipe damage occurred to hundreds of structures within the area serviced by your company. RMP has signed several huge contracts to repair or replace plumbing for government buildings, hospitals, and three hotels owned by Alexis. Each of these contracts will be for $800,000 or more.

You are uncertain if RMP will be able to meet the deadlines set in the contracts as the urgency of the work needing to be done to so many buildings might call for more time.

You have the option of assigning some of the work to Bob's Plumbing, a far less reputable company, or making other arrangements with the county, the hospital district, and Alexis. You are afraid that if you inform people that RMP is unable to perform the contracts on time, it may lose the contracts along with the huge profits they will bring.

Your partners share your skepticism about meeting the deadlines and want to hire Bob's Plumbing immediately without mentioning it to any of the parties involved.

RMP's partners request that you draft a memorandum advising them of the options and risks involved with each option.

Answer. _____

_____
_____
_____
_____
_____
_____
_____
_____
_____
_____
_____
_____
_____
_____
_____
_____
_____
_____
_____
_____
_____

Practice Quiz

True/False:

1. ___ The unconditional assignment of a contract right extinguishes all the assignor's rights, including right to sue the obligor directly for nonperformance. [p 284]

2. ___ The assignee has no duty to notify the obligor of the assignment nor about to whom performance must be rendered. [p 285]

3. ___ If an obligor is notified of an assignment but still continues to give the assignor performance, the assignee can sue the obligor and recover payment. [p 285]

4. ___ Mandy hires Dr. Saran, a plastic surgeon to give her a new nose. Thereafter Dr. Saran delegates his contract with Mandy to Dr. Foiler, another plastic surgeon. This is an acceptable delegation of duties. [p 286]

5. ___ If a delegatee does not perform his or her duties under a delegation, then the obligee can only sue the delegatee. [p 286]

6. ___ A declaration of duties is present when the delegatee has not yet assumed the duties under a contract. [p 287]

7. ___ When there has been a transfer of both rights and duties under a contract, an assignment as well as delegation has occurred under the contract. [p 287]

8. ___ When a person enters into a contract with the intent to confer a benefit or a gift on an intended third party, the contract is called a creditor beneficiary contract. [p 287]

9. ___ In a creditor beneficiary situation, the creditor is the new intended creditor beneficiary to a second contract. [p 288]

10. ___ When the parties to a contract unintentionally benefit a third party, this third party is referred to as a donee beneficiary. [p 289]

11. ___ A covenant is a conditional promise to perform. [p 290]

12. ___ Nonperformance of a convenat is a breach of contract that allows the other party the right to sue. [p 290]

13. ___ A conditional promise is more definite than a covenant. [p 290]

14. ___ The personal satisfaction test is an objective test that requires the use of a third person to determine satisfaction. [p 291]

15. ___ The reasonable person test is an objective test used in situations involving mechanical fitness and commercial contracts. [p 291]

16. ___ If there has been a minor delay causing a contract to not be performed within the time frame stated, then the court will treat it as a minor breach and give the breaching party more time to complete the contract. [p 292]

17. ___ A clause that permits the ABC Corporation to terminate a contract if Sharon Smith does not pass a drug test is an example of a condition subsequent. [p 292]

18. ___ When each party's absolute duty to perform is conditioned on the other party's absolute duty to perform, this is known as a concurrent condition. [p 292]

19. ___ An implied-in-fact condition is one that is stated in the parties' contract. [p 292]

20. ___ Unilateral rescission of a contract does not result in breach as long as notice is given to the other party. [p 293]

21. ___ If Rod Cool, a famous singer dies before his New Year's Eve concert, the contract will be discharged based on impossibility of performance. [p 294]

22. ___ A force majeure clause is one that that parties have agreed to that states which events will excuse nonperformance of the contract. [p 295]

23. ___ Commercial impracticability excuses performance under a contract if an unforeseeable event make impractical for the promisor to perform. [p 295]

24. ___ The Uniform Commercial Code provides that the statute of limitations for a breach of a sales or lease contract is one year after the cause of action accrues. [p 296]

25. ___ If George purposefully changes his hourly rate from $18 per hour to $28 per hour when he walks his paperwork over to Human Resources of the ABC Corporation, this alteration may discharge the contract. [p 296]

Multiple Choice:

26. Which two exceptions allow third parties to acquire rights under other parties' contracts? [p 283]
    a. A majeure clause and an approval clause
    b. An assignment and a discharge of duties
    c. An assignment and a third-party beneficiary contract
    d. An assignment and a conveyance of personal or real property

27. An obligee who transfers the right to receive performance is called [p 283]
    a. a delegator.
    b. an assignor.
    c. a delegatee.
    d. a lessor.

28. An assignee is [p 283]
    a. the party who transfers the right to receive performance.
    b. the party who transfers the right to suspend performance.
    c. the party to whom the right has been transferred.
    d. the party to whom the right has been delegated.

29. Which of the following is an exception, which would allow the assignment of personal service contracts? [p 284]
    a. A professional football player's contract that contains a clause that permits the contract to be assigned.
    b. A poisonous snake handler at a world famous zoo
    c. An auto insurance policyholder wanting to give his or her son the insurance policy
    d. All of the above.

30. In order to protect an individual's rights under an assignment, an assignee should [p 285]
    a. just notify the obligor that an assignment has been made.
    b. notify the assignor that an assignment has been made and that he or she will accept performance from the obligor.
    c. notify the obligor of the assignment and notify the assignor that he or she will not accept performance from the obligor.
    d. notify the obligor that an assignment has been made and indicate to the obligor that performance must be rendered to the assignee.

31. A transfer of contractual duties by the obligor to another party for performance is known as [p 286]
    a. an assignment of rights
    b. a delegation of duties
    c. a declaration of duties
    d. an assignment and a delegation

32. If a person hires an experienced horse trainer for the circus, and the horse trainer decides to go on vacation and substitutes in a teenage rider who has had some horse training, will this be an effective delegation of duties? [p 286]
    a. Yes, because most individuals regardless of age have experience with horses.
    b. No, because the teenager may not want to do the job.
    c. No because the performance of the teenage rider verses the experienced horse trainer would be so different that the delegation of the duty would defeat the purpose of the contract.
    d. Yes because the teenage rider may get experience once he or she gets the job to train the circus horses.

33. Tom's Tourist Shop is located on the beach next to where a new high-rise hotel is going in. There is supposed to be sixteen floors to the hotel, however, Charter Construction Company decides to stop building at the thirteenth floor. Since the beginning of the project, the owner of Tom's has noticed a definite increase in business. He knows that once the hotel is complete, his profits will escalate due to the patrons staying at the hotel. Tom decides to bring a cause of action against the Charter Construction Company for breach of contract as he is claiming that his tourist shop was a beneficiary of the hotel and Charter Construction Company contract. What will be the probable result? [p 289]
    a. Tom will win because his shop is a donee beneficiary under the hotel and Charter Construction Company.
    b. Tom will lose, as his shop is merely an incidental beneficiary as his business unintentionally benefited from the contract just by being located next to the new hotel.
    c. Tom will win because if it were not for Tom, the area surrounding the hotel would be unappealing to tourists.
    d. Tom will lose because he did not give notice of the benefit to Charter Construction.

34. Nonperformance of a covenant entitles the other party to [p 290]
    a. sue for punitive damages.
    b. sue for breach of contract.
    c. sue for an injunction.
    d. sue for breach of condition.

35. If there has been an extreme or unexpected development expense that makes it impractical for the promisor to perform, this is known as [p 290]
    a. subjective impossibility.
    b. accord and satisfaction.
    c. commercial impracticability.
    d. frustration of purpose.

Short Answer:

36. The transfer of contractual rights is called an [p 283] _____.

37. Can Julie transfer her sailboat insurance to her roommate Liz? Be sure to include why or why not. [p 284] _____

38. Who is an assignee entitled to receive performance from? [p 285] _____

39. Which rule states that the first assignment in time prevails? [p 285] _____

40. What are the three ways that a party's duty of performance may be discharged? [p 293]
    _____
    _____

41. Give examples of terms or words that may indicate that the assignor intends to transfer a contract right. [p 283] _____

42. Alice is suing Roger for injuries she sustained when his tractor plowed into the back of her small sports car she was driving. She is tired of all of the delays in getting the case to trial and assigns her legal action to her best friend Stephanie. What is the effect of Alice's assignment? [p 284] _____

43. What is the effect of an unconditional assignment of a contract right? [p 285] _____
    _____

44. Which rule regarding assignments provides that the first assignee to give notice to the obligor prevails? [p 285] _____

45. If Sid assigns his savings passbook to Marla and then assigns the same savings passbook to Claude but delivers the actual passbook to Claude, who is entitled to the savings account and why? [p 285] _____
    _____

46. What type of contract language is necessary for there to be an assumption of duties? [p 286] _____

47. Sarah assigns Abbot the right to collect her lottery proceeds and then Sarah proceeds to assign Morgan the same right followed by assigning Greg that same right, but Morgan is the first to give notice to the lottery commission, who will get the lottery proceeds and why? [p 285] _____

48. What type of condition is distinguished by the phrase, "time is of the essence?" [p 292] _____

49. What type of condition can be inferred from the circumstances surrounding a contract and the parties conduct? [p 293] _____

50. What is the name of the test that applies to contracts involving personal taste and comfort called? [p 291] _____

Answers to Refresh Your Memory

1. privity of contract [p 283]
2. An assignment is the transfer of contractual rights by the obligee to another party. [p 283]
3. obligee [p 283]
4. obligor [p 283]
5. subsequent assignee or subassignee [p 283]
6. It's an assignment of a future right not yet in existence. [p 284]
7. The assignment will not have any effect, as it would materially alter the risk and duties of the insurance company. [p 284]
8. an anti-assignment clause [p 285]
9. An approval clause is one that permits the assignment of the contract only upon receipt of an obligor's approval. [p 285]
10. delegation of duties [p 286]
11. intended beneficiary [p 287]
12. creditor beneficiary [p 288]
13. novation [p 293]
14. objective [p 294]
15. that certain events will excuse the performance under the contract [p 295]

Critical Thought Exercise Model Answer

To: RMP Partners
From: Your Partner
RE: Options for performing the contracts

The obligor in a contract must be careful to refrain from informing the obligee that he or she is unable to perform. This may cause the obligee to treat the statement as an anticipatory repudiation and a breach. Therefore, RMP should pursue an option that does not create a breach. It is lawful to transfer the duties under a contract to another party. This delegation of duties does not relieve the party making the delegation of the obligation to perform in the event that the party to whom the duty has been delegated. No special form is required to create a valid delegation of duties. Some duties cannot be delegated, such as when performance depends upon the special skills of the obligor, when the contract expressly prohibits delegation, when special trust has been placed in the obligor, or when performance by a third party will vary materially from that expected by the obligee. These contracts were awarded to us because we are capable of handling the work. This does not mean that Bob's Plumbing is incapable of performing the same duties. RMP would be within its rights to delegate the duties under one or more of the contracts to Bob's Plumbing. RMP would remain liable for any breach of the contract by Bob's Plumbing. Because Bob's Plumbing is a far less reputable company than RMP, we may not want to expose ourselves to greater liability. Another safer option is to enter into a novation with one or more of the obliges and Bob's Plumbing which will allow a new contract to be formed between Bob's Plumbing and an obligee and then extinguish our contract. This will relieve us of any liability under that particular contract, but it will also cause us to lose the profit from the contract and hurt our reputation. Our reputation will be hurt worse if we become embroiled in a contract dispute with the schools and hospital, not to mention a very influential businessperson, Alexis. We should calculate how much of the business we can handle and then approach the parties involved in the smaller contracts and suggest a novation. If the novation is refused, we will then have no choice but to delegate some of the work to Bob's Plumbing.

Answers to Practice Quiz

True/False:

1. True   Where there has been a valid assignment of rights, the assignee "stands in the shoes of the assignor." Thus the unconditional assignment of a contract right extinguishes all the assignor's rights, including the right to sue the obligor directly for nonperformance.
2. False   The assignee is under a duty to notify the obligor of the assignment and that performance is to be rendered to the assignee.
3. True   In situations where the obligor continues to give the assignor performance regardless of having been notified of an assignment, the assignee can sue the obligor and recover payment.
4. False   Obligations under personal service contracts calling for the exercise of personal skills, discretion, or expertise such as in this case with a plastic surgeon are not delegable.
5. False   The obligee can sue the obligor-delegator for damages.
6. True   If the delegatee has not assumed the duties under a contract, this delegation of duties is a mere declaration of duties wherein the delegatee is not legally liable to the obligee for nonperformance.
7. True   An assignment and a delegation occurs where there is a transfer of duties and rights under a contract.
8. False   A contract with the intent to confer a benefit or gift on an intended third party is called a donee beneficiary contract, not a creditor beneficiary contract.
9. True   In a creditor beneficiary contract, the orginal creditor becomes a beneficiary under the debtor's new contract with another party.
10. False   A party who is unintentionally benefited by other individual's contracts is an incidental beneficiary.
11. False   A covenant is an unconditional promise to perform.
12. True   A covenant that is not performed gives the other party the right to sue for breach of contract.

13 False A conditional promise is not as definite as a covenant.

14. False The personal satisfaction test is a subjective test that is used if the performance involves personal taste and comfort.

15. True Contracts involving mechanical fitness and most commercial transactions use the reasonable person test which is an objective standard as judged by a third person's satisfaction.

16. True If the other party is not jeopardized by the delay, the court will allow extra time to perform in cases where a time delay has caused a minor breach of the parties' contract.

17. True A condition subsequent exists when a contract states that the occurrence or nonoccurrence of a specific event automatically excuses the performance of an existing duty to perform. Hence, if Sharon Smith does not pass the drug test, the ABC Corporation does not have to employ her.

18. True Concurrent conditions occur when the parties to a contract must give their performance simultaneously.

19. False An implied in-fact condition is one that can be implied from the circumstances surrounding a contract and the parties' conduct. It is not a condition that is stated in the contract.

20. False Unilateral rescission of a contract is equivalent to a breach of that contract. Notice does not have any significance concerning unilateral rescission.

21. True Impossibility of performance is an objective standard, which indicates, "it cannot be done" under the contract. The death of the promisor, here Rod Cool, before the New Year's Eve performance of his contract would be discharge under this rule as this personal service contract, the singing concert cannot be done.

22. True The parties may agree by way of a force majeure clause that certain events will excuse nonperformance of the contract.

23. True Nonperformance that is excuse if an unexpected or extreme circumstances or expense makes it impractical for the promisor to perform is known as commercial impracticability.

24. False The Uniform Commercial Code provides that a breach of sales or lease contract must be brought within four years after the cause of action accrues.

25. True Since George intentionally altered a material part of his contract, his hourly pay, the ABC Corporation may choose to either discharge or enforce the contract.

Multiple Choice:

26. C Answer C is correct as assignments and third-party beneficiary contracts allow third parties to acquire rights under other parties' contracts. Answer A is incorrect as a majeure clause involves an agreement between the parties regarding events that will excuse non-performance under a contract. Further an approval clause permits the assignment of a contract only upon the receipt of the obligor's approval. Answer B is incorrect as it is only partially correct in stating an assignment. The discharge of duties however is incorrect as this would discharge performance as opposed to acquire a right under another's contract. Answer D is incorrect as once again it is only partially correct with respect to the assignment. However, the conveyance of personal or real property is incorrect in terms of acquiring rights under other parties' contracts.

27. B Answer B is correct, as an assignor is also an obligee that transfers the right to performance. Answer A is incorrect as a delegator is one who transfers duties under a contract. Answer C is incorrect as a delegatee is one who receives duties under a

contract. Answer D is incorrect as a lessor is inapplicable in terms of transferring the right to receive performance.

28. C   Answer C is correct as the party to whom a right has been transferred is referred to as the assignee. Answer A is incorrect as the party who transfers the right to receive performance is the assignor. Answer B is incorrect as there is not a name for a party who attempts to suspend performance nor is this a legally recognized right. Answer D is incorrect as the party to whom the right has been delegated is confusing terminology as it mixes terms associated with assignments and delegations.

29. A   Answer A is correct as the parties may agree that a personal service contract may be assigned which is customary in many professional athletic contracts. Answer B is incorrect, as there is nothing to indicate that the parties have agreed by way of a clause in their contract. Answer C is incorrect as the assignment of an automobile insurance policy would materially alter the risks and duties of the insurance company and is therefore invalid. Answer D is incorrect based on the reasons given above.

30. D   Answer D is correct as the assignee should provide notification to the obligor of the assignment as well as inform the obligor that performance should be made to the assignee. Answer A is incorrect as it is only partially correct, as the obligor would not know whom performance is to be rendered to. Answer B is incorrect as once again notification is only part of what the assignee must do to be protected. Further, acceptance of the performance by the obligor is implied and need not be stated. Answer C is incorrect as even though the notification of the assignment to the obligor will partially protect the assignee, informing the obligor that the assignee will not accept performance from him or her defeats the purpose of the assignment.

31. B   Answer B is correct, as a delegation of duties is a transfer by the parties of the performance of their duties under the contract to other parties. Answer A is incorrect as an assignment involves the transfer of rights, not duties under a contract. Answer C is incorrect as a declaration of duties arises when the delegatee has not assumed the duties under the contract. Answer D is incorrect as there is nothing in the facts that indicate that rights have also been transferred, only duties. Thus, only a delegation has occurred.

32. C   Answer C is correct as the performance of the horses and the teenage trainer would be so varied if the duty to train the horses for the circus took effect, that it would be an invalid delegation. The circus has a substantial interest in having the experienced horse trainer perform the training of its horses under the contract. Answer A is incorrect as this may not necessarily be a true statement since not everybody does in fact have experience with horses. Answer B is incorrect, as the teenager's desire to do the job has no bearing on the circus' interest in having an experienced horse trainer perform the training of its horses. Answer D is incorrect as getting the experience after the   fact defeats the purpose of being interested in having an experienced horse trainer perform the training required by the contract.

33. B   Answer B is correct as Tom's Tourist Shop was unintentionally benefited by the hotel and Charter Construction Company Contract since there is nothing to indicate at the inception of their contract or thereafter that the parties intended to benefit the shop. Answer A is incorrect as the hotel and the Charter Construction Company did not intend to confer a benefit or gift on Tom's Tourist Shop. Therefore, the shop is not a donee beneficiary. Answer C is incorrect, as the appeal of the surrounding area has no bearing on whether Tom should win. Answer D is incorrect as giving notice is not a requirement to receiving benefits especially in a situation involving an incidental beneficiary.

34. B   Answer B is correct as a breach of an unconditional promise to perform, hence a covenant entitles the innocent party to sue. Answer A is incorrect as punitive damages are usually not available in causes of action involving contracts. Answer C is incorrect as

the equitable remedy of injunction is more appropriately applied in situations involving tortuous actions verses those concerned with breach of contract. Answer D is incorrect as a covenant is more definite than a condition and the breach of a covenant does not necessarily entitle one to sue for breach of a condition.

35. C Answer C is correct as commercial impracticability excuses performance if an unforeseeable event makes it impractical for the promisor to perform. Answer A is incorrect as subjective impossibility is not applicable to unforeseeable events. Answer B is incorrect as accord and satisfaction concern a dispute over a contract that is resolved by a new agreement and performance of the same. Accord and satisfaction do not apply to situations involving commercial impracticability. Answer D is incorrect as the doctrine of frustration of purpose excuses the performance of contractual obligations if the object or benefit of the contract is made worthless to a promisor, and both parties knew what the purpose was and the act that frustrated the purpose was reasonably foreseeable.

Short Answer:

36. assignment of rights.
37. No, because an assignment of the right to sailboat insurance would materially alter the risk and duties of the insurance company.
38. the obligor
39. The American Rule
40. A party's duty of performance may be discharged by agreement of the parties, excuse of performance, or by operation of law.
41. give, sell, transfer, convey
42. Legal actions involving personal rights cannot be assigned.
43. It extinguishes all of the assignor's rights including the right to sue the obligor directly for nonperformance.
44. The English Rule
45. Claude is entitled to the savings account under the possession of tangible token rule.
46. The word assumption or other similar language is used in a delegation.
47. Morgan will get the lottery proceeds under the English Rule, which provides that the first to give notice will prevail when there are successive assignments.
48. "Time is of the essence" is an express condition.
49. An implied-in-fact condition can be inferred from the circumstances surrounding a contract and the parties conduct.
50. The personal satisfaction test.

Chapter 16
REMEDIES FOR
BREACH of TRADITIONAL
AND ONLINE CONTRACTS

Chapter Overview

This chapter differentiates between the types of performance in a contract as well as the consequences for the same. Additionally, it clearly explains the various types of legal damages as well as equitable remedies that are available for breach of contract. The torts associated with contracts along with the consequences of punitive damages are also explored. Finally, with technology becoming so much a part of our daily lives, Internet contracts and the breach of the same are also discussed.

Objectives

Upon completion of the exercises in this chapter, you should be able to:
1.   Discuss complete performance in relation to discharging contractual duties.
2.   Explain inferior performance as well as material breach of contract.
3.   Explain and differentiate between compensatory, consequential and nominal damages.
4.   Define what liquidated damages are and explain when they are a penalty.
5.   Discuss the duty of mitigation of damages.
6.   Discuss the remedy of rescission of a contract.
7.   Discuss the equitable remedies of injunction, quasi-contract and specific performance.
8.   Explain the torts that are associated with contracts.
9.   Define punitive damages
10. Explain breach as it applies to Internet contracts.

Practical Application

Upon learning the objectives in this chapter, you should be able to determine whether a minor or material breach has occurred in a contract as well as what remedies, legal or equitable may be available for the breach. Further, you will have a better understanding of what is necessary in order to seek the equitable remedies of specific performance, injunction and quasi-contract. Additionally, you will be able to recognize the torts that sometimes accompany contracts and whether punitive damages may be an option. Finally, you will have a better understanding of breach as it applies to Internet contracts.

Helpful Hints

It is important that you learn the terminology associated with this chapter in order to know which types of remedies apply to certain situations. Some mnemonics for the equitable remedies of injunction as well as specific performance have been provided for you to assist you in committing what is required for these equitable remedies to memory. The material will be easier to grasp if you list and learn the legal remedies separately from the equitable remedies.

Study Tips

You should begin your study of remedies recognizing that there are three levels of performance of a contract. Each level of performance as well as what is meant by it is given below.

Level 1 – Complete Performance

Complete performance happens when a party to a contract gives performance exactly as outlined in the parties contract. If the contract is fully formed, it is said to be executed. Also, be aware
that a contracting party's unconditional and absolute offer to perform will also discharge a party's obligations under the contract.

Level 2- Substantial Performance

Substantial performance happens when a party to a contract gives performance that only has a Little bit left to do before it will be considered completely performed. The non-breaching party has several options available to him or her. He or she can convince the breaching party to lift his or her performance to completion of the contract. Or, he or she may deduct whatever it costs to repair the defect from the contract price and give the remaining amount under the contract to the breaching party. Finally, if the breaching party has been paid, the innocent party may sue the breaching party to recover the cost of repair.

Level 3 - Inferior Performance: Material Breach

A material breach happens when a party gives inferior performance of his or her contractual obligations so much so that it destroys or impairs the purpose of the contract. The courts will examine each case individually to determine whether the breach is a minor or material breach. The non-breaching party may rescind the contract and seek restitution of any monies paid under the contract is there has been a material breach. A material breach allows the non-breaching party from further performance. Another option for the non-breaching party is to sue for breach of contract and ask for damages.

What About Anticipatory Repudiation?

Anticipatory repudiation happens when one party lets the other party know in advance that either he or she will not perform or may not perform the contractual duties when they come due. The repudiator may expressly state this or his or her conduct may show it. The non-breaching party's obligations are discharged immediately and he or she may sue for breach of contract immediately without waiting for performance to become due.

Damages

The next section categorizes the legal remedies for you, otherwise known as damages. You should be familiar with the differences between compensatory, consequential, liquidated and nominal damages as well as the requirement for mitigation of the same.

- **Compensatory Damages**
    Purpose- to compensate a non-breaching party for the loss of the bargain.

These were designed to "make the person whole again."
The court determines how much will be awarded based upon the type of contract involved.

- **Types of contracts and the compensatory damages for the same**:
  <u>Sale of Goods</u> - The measure of compensatory damages for a breach of sales contract is the difference between the contract price and the market price at the time and place of delivery of the goods.

  <u>Construction Contracts</u>- The amount of compensatory damages available for breach depends upon the status of the construction project itself. In other words, it depends on the stage of completion that the project is in when the breach happens. The contractor may recover the profits that he or she might have made on the contract if the owner breaches before the construction begins.

  <u>Employment Contracts</u> –Recovery based on an employer breaching equals lost wages or salary as compensatory damages. If however the employee breaches, the employer can recover the costs of hiring a new employee plus any salary increase to pay the replacement.

- **Consequential Damages**
  These types of damages are foreseeable damages that happen because of circumstances not related to the contract itself. In order to recover consequential damages, the breaching party must be aware or have reason to know that the breach will cause special damages to the other party.

- **Liquidated Damages**
  Sometimes the parties to a contract agree in advance as to the amount of damages that will be payable in the event of a breach. This is known as liquidated damages. In order for this type of damages to be enforced, it must be shown that the actual damages are difficult or impracticable to determine and the liquidated amount must be reasonable in the circumstances. This is an exclusive remedy regardless of what the actual damages later are assessed as being.

  CAVEAT – A liquidated damages clause is looked upon as a penalty if the actual damages are clearly able to be determined in advance and if the liquidated damages are unconscionable or excessive. When a liquidated damages clause is viewed as a penalty, it is unenforceable.

- **Nominal Damages**
  These damages are awarded based on principle and are usually a very small amount. No real financial loss is suffered when a party brings a suit based upon principle.

Mitigation of Damages

The law places a duty on the non-breaching party to avoid and reduce the resulting damages. This is referred to as mitigating the damages. A party's duty of mitigation will be based on the type of contract involved.

Enforcement of Remedies

Once a judgment has been rendered, an attempt to collect it is made. If the breaching party fails to satisfy the judgment, then the court may issue a Writ of Attachment or Issue a Writ of Garnishment.

- Writ of Attachment – The writ orders the sheriff to seize the breaching party's property that he or she has in his or her possession and to sell the property to satisfy the judgment. Not all property can be sold depending on the applicable state exemptions.

- Writ of Garnishment- Wages, bank account and other property owned by the breaching party that Is being handled by a third party, such as a bank must be paid to the non-breaching party. There are limitations on the amount of wages or salary that can be garnished as per federal and state laws,

Rescission and Restitution as Remedies

- Rescission – This is an action to undo a contract where there has been a material breach of contract due to fraud, duress, undue influence or mistake. The parties must make restitution of the consideration they received under the contract if they are going to rescind it. In other words, they must return the goods, property, money or other consideration that was received from the other property. Notice of the rescission is a requirement.

Equitable Remedies

If the remedy at law is not adequate, then the equitable remedies of specific performance, quasi-contract and injunction and reformation may be available so that an injustice may be prevented.

- Specific Performance - This is a discretionary remedy the courts may award if the subject matter is unique and a service contract is not involved. The following mnemonic is a practical application memory device you may use when analyzing whether specific performance applies.

  <u>C</u>athy <u>A</u>lways <u>E</u>ats <u>M</u>uch <u>C</u>andy <u>D</u>uring <u>E</u>aster

  <u>C</u> - Was there a **contract** for unique goods or land between the parties?
  <u>A</u> - The remedy at law was not **adequate.**
  <u>E</u> - The contract may only be **enforced** by this remedy.
  <u>M</u> - The remedy is **mutual**; both the buyer and seller may ask for it.
  <u>C</u> - All **conditions** have been satisfied by the party asking for the remedy.
  <u>D</u> - A discussion of any **defenses** is also brought to light.
  <u>E</u> - A reminder that this is an **equitable** remedy.

- Reformation - This is an equitable remedy that allows the court to rewrite the parties' contract to reflect their true intentions.

- Quasi Contract - This equitable remedy is an implied-in-law contract often referred to as quasi-meruit. Under this remedy, a party may receive compensation even though there is not an actual enforceable contract due to a failure of the Statute of Frauds or lack of consideration, etc. The reasonable value of materials or service is the recovery that is available in order to prevent unjust enrichment.

- Injunction - An injunction is an equitable remedy that prohibits a person from doing a certain act. The following mnemonic is a practical application memory device that you may use in determining whether an injunction may be sought.

  Ted Always Enjoys Potatoes and Ham at Dinner

  T - Usually a **tort** is involved which must first be proven.
  A - The remedy at law was not **adequate**.
  E - The tortuous conduct may only be **enforced** by this remedy.
  P - There is a **property** right involved.
  H - A **hardship** will be suffered if this remedy is not enforced.
  D - A discussion of **defenses** is shown if they apply.

Torts Associated With Contracts

If a party demonstrates that a contract-related tort has occurred, tort damages will also be available to a party. These include compensation for pain and suffering, emotional damages, possible punitive damages and personal injury. The torts in this area include interference with contractual relations and breach of implied covenant of good faith and fair dealing.

- Intentional Interference with Contractual Relations - This occurs when a third party induces a contracting party to breach the contract with another party. Note that a third party will not be held to have induced a breach if the breach already existed between the original parties.

- Breach of Implied Covenant of Good Faith and Fair Dealing - This is implied in certain types of contracts whereby the parties are held to act in "good faith" and deal fairly in also aspects in obtaining the contract's objective. This tort is sometimes called the tort of bad faith.

Punitive Damages

These are usually not recoverable for breach of contract. Nonetheless, if certain tortuous conduct such as fraud, or intentional conduct is associated with the nonperformance of a contract, punitive damages in addition to actual damages may be awarded to punish the defendant. Other purposes of punitive damages are to prevent similar conduct from happening in the future and to set an example for other individuals.

Refresh Your Memory

The following exercise will enable you to refresh your memory on the rules and principles presented to you in this chapter. Read each question twice and place your answer in the blanks provided. Review the chapter material for any question you miss or are unable to remember.

1.   What are the three levels of performance of a contract? _____
_____

2.   What are the equitable remedies available for breach of contract? _____
_____

3.   What duty does a contracting party owe if a contractual duty has not been discharged or excused? _____

4.   A fully performed contract is called an _____ contract.

5.   _____ performance happens when there has been a minor breach.

6.   A _____ breach occurs when inferior performance has been rendered under a contract.

7.   When there has been a material breach, the non-breaching party may _____ the contract.

8.   _____ damages help to compensate a non-breaching party for the loss of the bargain.

9.   The compensatory damages for a breach of contract involving the sale of goods is _____
_____

10.   What can an employee whose employer has breached an employment contract recover in damages? _____

11.   When parties agree in advance to the amount of damages payable upon a breach of contract, this is known as a _____ _____ clause.

12.   Cases involving nominal damages are brought based on _____.

13.   To mitigate means to _____ or _____.

14.   What is the term that means to undo a contract called? _____

15.   The term restitution means _____.

Critical Thought Exercise

The Cheersville Fire Department (CFD) entered into a written contract on 2-17-02 with American Emergency Truck Co. (AET) for the purchase of a $290,000.00 ladder/pump truck. The contract set forth a delivery date of September 1, 2002 as insisted upon by CFD. According to CFD Chief Sam Miller, their 1932 pumper truck was not going to last beyond that date and time was of the essence. On August 1, 2002, the CFD truck died and was not able to be repaired. The Cheersville Town Council voted to wait until the new truck arrived on September 1, 2002 instead or renting another old truck from Friendsville Fire District. On August 15, 2002, AET notified CFD that the truck would not be ready for delivery until October 1, 2002. The Town Council again decided to wait without renting another truck. Cheersville notified AET that its truck was out of service and the new truck was desperately needed by September 1, 2002. On September 15, 2002, a major fire damaged the Cheersville School. The fire started in the kitchen and could have easily been controlled with normal fire fighting equipment. The damage to the school was estimated to be approximately $2,800,000.

AET denies any liability. The truck was delivered by AET on October 5, 2002. You are on the Cheersville Town Council and have been assigned the task of drafting a memorandum for the council detailing the following:

1. Whether Cheersville has grounds to sue American Emergency Truck.
2. What damages would be recoverable from AET.
3. What defenses AET may assert.

Answer. _____

_____

_____

_____

_____

_____

_____

_____

_____

_____

_____

_____

_____

_____

_____

_____

_____

_____

_____

_____

_____

_____

_____

Practice Quiz

True/False:

1. ___ Monetary damages are the most common remedy for breach of contract. [p 302]

2. ___ Equitable remedies are premised on the idea of fairness. [p 302]

3. ___ A material breach of contract occurs when performance deviates only slightly from complete performance. [p 303]

4. ___ Though compensatory damages help defer costs associated with a breach of contract, they do not compensate a non-breaching party for the loss of the bargain. [p 304]

5. ___ The standard measure of damages for a breach of sales contract involving goods is the difference between the contract price and the market price. [p 305]

6. ___ If an employee breaches an employment contract, the employer can recover the costs to hire a new employee including an increase in salary paid to the replacement. [p 305]

7. ___ A liquidated damages clause may not act as a penalty if there were actual damages that could have been assessed in advance. [p 307]

8. ___ Nominal damages are usually awarded in small amounts. [p 308]

9. ___ To mitigate means to divide evenly among those awarded damages. [p 309]

10. ___ The court may issue a Writ of Attachment in order to assist in the collection of a judgment. [p 310]

11. ___ The remedy of rescission is available if there has been fraud, undue influence or mistake involved with regard to the parties' contract. [p 310]

12. ___ A party may seek the remedy of specific performance for any contract he or she is having difficulty enforcing. [p 311]

13. ___ Specific performance of personal service contracts is usually not granted due to the difficulty in monitoring performance. [p 311]

14. ___ An equitable doctrine that allows the court to rewrite the parties contract to reflect their true intentions is known as reformation. [p 312]

15. ___ A quasi contract is a written contract that is imposed to prevent unjust enrichment. [p 312]

16. ___ A party may seek damages for a breach of the covenant of good faith and fair dealing. [p 314]

17. ___ Punitive damages are recoverable in a cause of action for breach of contract. [p 314]

18. ___ Tender of performance discharges a party's contractual obligations. [p 302]

19. ___ Anticipatory breach refers to the excitement of waiting for a breach to occur. [p 304]

20. ___ The amount of damages recoverable for a breach of a construction contract depends on how much of the contract has been completed. [p 305]

21. ___ Forseeable damages that arise from circumstances outside the contract are consequential damages. [p 306]

22. ___ In order to mitigate damages where the employer has breached the contract, the employee must take any employment offered or he or she will also have damages assessed against him or her. [p 309]

23. ___ In an action for rescission, the rescinding party must give sufficient notice to the breaching party. [p 310]

24. ___ Consequential damages are an example of an equitable remedy. [p 311]

25. ___ If Morton and Nathan sign a contract that has a clerical error, and neither one notices it till after the fact, the court will be unable to offer a remedy as it was reasonable that they should have been more careful in reading what they were signing. [p 312]

Multiple Choice

26. Complete performance of a contract occurs when [p 302]
    a. a party to a contract gives almost complete performance.
    b. a party to a contract renders performance exactly as required by the contract.
    c. a party to a contract renders inferior performance that destroys the essence of the contract.
    d. a party to the contract is not sure whether he or she can perform the contract or not.

27. Perfecto Home Construction Inc. contracts with Delia Bloom to build her dream home. Perfecto has constructed the home exactly to plan however it has forgot to put little ceramic knobs on the laundry room cupboards. What type of performance has Perfecto rendered to Delia? [p 303]
    a. Inferior performance
    b. Complete performance
    c. Substantial performance
    d. No performance

28. Which of the following permits the court to rewrite a contract to express the parties' true intentions? [p 312]
    a. Rescission
    b. Restitution
    c. Reformation
    d. Reconstruction

29. Patsy asked her daughter Ellie to leave her job and move from Wisconsin to come and take care of her in Arizona for two years when Patsy would be moving into an assisted living facility. In exchange for Ellie doing this, Patsy orally told Ellie that she would sign

the deed over to the lovely 3,000 square foot home. Ellie quit her well paying job, loaded a moving van and moved in with Patsy into her Arizona home. Ellie had a lot of spare time on her hands, so she painted all of the interior walls of the house and hired a contractor to add on a large family room as well as add a built-in swimming pool. Two years passed very quickly and Patsy has decided to stay in her new and improved home. She refuses to sign the deed to the home over to Ellie. If Ellie sues Patsy, which theory would give her the greatest chance at getting the Arizona home? [p 312]
   a. One based on quasi contract
   b. One based on rescission
   c. One based on injunction
   d. One based on reformation

30. A court order that prohibits a person from doing a certain act is [p 312]
   a. a no trespass order.
   b. prohibitum orderis.
   c. an order for specific performance.
   d. an injunction.

31. The Lemoore Contracting Company agrees to build a racquetball court for Maxine Mills and the parties sign the $50,000 contract, but, before Lemoore begins, Maxine decides she does not want to ruin her grass with the racquetball court addition. Thereafter she calls and tells Lemoore Contracting that she is canceling the job. If Lemoore brings a suit against Maxine, what might they try to recover? [p 305]
   a. The difference between the contract price and the market price of the racquetball court at the time and place where the contract was signed.
   b. The profits that Lemoore Contracting would have made on the contract .
   c. Lost wages as compensatory damages.
   d. None of the above.

32. The Random Engineering Corporation has hired Lisa Sharpe as a robotics engineer to design housekeeper robots. Lisa contracted with Random to give her an initial annual income of $132,000 plus benefits. Additionally, if she can design a microchip to place in the robot which will enable it to garden as well, Random will give Lisa a percentage of the profits and a twelve percent salary increase. Lisa works for Random for two months and Random decides to downsize and use engineers who have been employed with them for twenty or more years to design the housekeeper/gardener robots. Lisa is told she will need to find another place to work. If Lisa brings a lawsuit against Random based on breach of her employment contract, what does she need to do in order to mitigate her damages? [p 309]
   a. She will need to gather as much information about Random as possible.
   b. She will need to try to find comparable, substitute employment.
   c. She will need to beg to be given a second chance, as she is the best person for the job.
   d. She will need to ask for specific performance based upon her skills and experience.

33. If the liquidated damages are excessive or unconscionable and the actual damages are clearly able to be determined in advance, the liquidated damages clause will be considered to be [p 307]
   a. an adhesion clause.
   b. enforceable.
   c. a penalty.
   d. compensation for a breach of contract.

34. In order to obtain an injunction, the requesting party must show that he or she [p 312]
    a. will suffer irreparable harm unless the injunction is issued.
    b. deserves the injunction more than the other party.
    c. requires recovery of compensation even though no enforceable contract exists.
    d. needs the contract to be rewritten to reflect the true intentions of the parties.

35. In order to recover for the tort of intentional interference with contract relations, what must be shown? [p 313]
    a. The third party had knowledge of a valid enforceable contract between contracting parties.
    b. A valid, enforceable contract between the contracting parties existed.
    c. The third party induced one of the parties to breach the contract.
    d. All of the above.

Short Answer:

36. A quasi contract is also known as _____ _____ or an _____ _____ contract. [p 313]

37. Give one reason why punitive damages are awarded. [p 314] _____

38. Internet contracts are given the same _____ as a regular paper contract. [p 313]

39. Compensatory damages place the non-breaching party in the same position as if the contract had been fully performed by restoring the _____ of the _____. [p 304]

40. Give examples of what restitution consists of. [p 310] _____

41. What may the court do if a judgment is entered against a breaching party and the breaching party refuses to pay it? [p 310] _____

42. What is a Writ of Garnishment? [p 310] _____

43. Give a purpose for an equitable remedy. [p 311] _____

44. Why won't the court grant specific performance of service contracts? [p 311] _____

45. A breach that occurs when a party renders substantial performance of his or her contractual duties is called a _____ _____. [p 303]

46. If Dr. Goodings stops to give medical assistance to an injured pedestrian of an automobile accident, what theory may he attempt to recover the reasonable value of his services under if he sues the pedestrian? [p 312] _____

47. What types of damages are recoverable under tort law? [p 313] _____
_____

48. If an individual has not acted in good faith nor has he or she dealt fairly in all respects in obtaining the objective of the contract, he or she may have breached the _____
_____. [p 314]

49. Silvia tells Horatio that he must give her $10,000 to invest in the stock market so that it will triple overnight. Horatio does so trusting what Silvia has said is true. Upon receiving the $10,000 Silva takes a vacation to Hawaii. What type of damages should Horatio seek against Silvia? [p 314] _____
_____

50. Define monetary damages. [p 304] _____

Answers to Refresh Your Memory

1. complete, substantial and inferior [p 302]
2. specific performance, reformation, quasi contract and injunction [p 302]
3. An absolute duty to perform the duty. [p 302]
4. executed [p 302]
5. Substantial [p 303]
6. material [p 303]
7. rescind [p 303]
8. Compensatory [p 304]
9. the difference between the contract price and the market price. [p 305]
10. lost wages or salary as compensatory damages. [p 305]
11. liquidated damages [p 307]
12. principle [p 308]
13. avoid or reduce [p 309]
14. rescission [p 310]
15. to return goods or compensation [p 310]

Critical Thought Exercise Model Answer

Before either party to a contract has a duty to perform, one of the parties may make an assertion or do an act that indicates they will not perform their obligations under the contract at a future time. This called an anticipatory repudiation of the contract and is treated as a material breach. The non-breaching party may immediately bring an action for damages, wait to see if the breaching party changes their name, or may seek specific performance by the breaching party. When AET notifies CFD that it will not be able to deliver the truck as promised, CFD must decide what course of action it will take. The damages that may be sought would be any increase in cost that CFD as to pay to obtain the truck from another seller plus any consequential or incidental damages. In this situation, CFD needs the truck more than it needs money damages.

The CFD had a duty to protect the citizens of Cheersville and another truck is not readily obtainable. The truck that was being built for CFD by AET was somewhat unique and failure to perform the contract would create great hardship for CFD. However, CFD had to make an election at the time of the breach, which took place on August 15, 2002. Because CFD failed to elect to pursue specific performance, they will be left with an action for damages. Specific performance is not available at this late point in time because the truck was actually delivered on October 5, 2002. CFD will seek consequential damages for the damage caused to the Cheersville School. AET will be liable for those damages if they were reasonably foreseeable at the time of the breach or fire occurred. CFD had previously notified AET that their truck was old and would not last in service beyond September 1, 2002. CFD again told AET of the urgency when the truck was taken out of service on August 1, 2002. Knowing the need for the truck and the fact that CFD was without a truck after August 1, 2002, AET continued to promise to perform the contract. The damages to the school were probably foreseeable because they are the exact type of damages that would occur if the CFD was without a truck.

AET will have two possible defenses to the contract. The most obvious is that Cheersville failed to fulfill its duty of mitigation of damages. This rule requires the plaintiff to have done whatever was reasonable to minimize the damages caused by the defendant. CFD failed to take any action to mitigate their damages. The city council decided to not rent a replacement truck even after their only truck was taken out of service. Because they failed to mitigate their damages, Cheersville will have their damages reduced by those amounts they could have prevented. In this case, the facts state that the damages to the school could have been minimized if a temporary replacement truck had been obtained. A rental was available from Friendsville and Cheersville failed to mitigate their damages by renting the truck. The second defense that AET may assert is that Cheersville agree to a modification of the contract when they did not pursue any action when notified of the delay in the delivery date. This defense is weak because Cheersville notified AET that it desperately needed the truck by the original contract date of September 1, 2002. Cheersville did nothing that could be deemed as acquiescence in the request by AET to extend the delivery date. Therefore, no modification of the original agreement was ever accomplished. Cheersville will prevail in their breach of contract suit, but the amount of damages will be relatively small due to Cheersville's failure to mitigate damages.

Answers to Practice Quiz

True/False:

1. True   Monetary damages, which are often termed the "law remedy", are the most common remedy for a breach of contract cause of action.
2. True   Legal remedies are based on monetary awards and equitable remedies are based on fairness.
3. False   A material breach occurs when there has been inferior performance under the contract.
4. False   Compensatory damages do compensate a non-breaching party for the loss of the bargain.
5. True   In contracts involving the sales of goods, the difference between the contract price and the market price is the standard measure of damages in a breach of contract cause of action.
6. True   The costs to hire a new employee as well as an increase in salary paid to that new employee are recoverable by an employer if an employee has breached an employment contract.

7. False   A liquidated damages clause may act as a penalty if there were actual damages that could have been assessed in advance.

8. True   Nominal damages are based on principle and therefore awarded in small amounts.

9. False   To mitigate means to avoid or reduce.

10. True   The Writ of Attachment is a court order directing the sheriff to seize property in the possession of the breaching party that he or she owns. Then the sheriff is to sell the property at the auction in order to satisfy the judgment.

11. True   Rescission is an available remedy for a material breach of contract where fraud, undue influence, duress or mistake is involved.

12. False   Courts have been prone to enforcing the remedy of specific performance in situations involving unique goods or land. Thus, it is not an available remedy for any contract that the parties are having difficulty in enforcing.

13. True   The courts would find it very difficult or impracticable to supervise or monitor the performance of a personal service contract.

14. True   Reformation permits the court to rewrite a contract to express the parties' true intentions.

15. False   A quasi contract is an implied-in-law contract that permits recovery of compensation even though no enforceable contract exists between the parties.

16. True   The tort of the implied covenant of good faith and fair dealing allows for the recovery of damages.

17. False   Punitive damages usually are not recoverable for breach of contract.

18. True   A party's contractual obligations are discharged by a tender of performance.

19. False   Anticipatory breach occurs when the contracting party informs the other party in advance that he or she will not perform his or her contractual duties when due.

20. True   The damages recoverable for a breach of a construction contract vary depending on the stage of completion the project is in at the time of the breach.

21. True   Consequential damages are foreseeable damages that arise from circumstances outside of the contract.

22. False   Though the employee owes a duty to mitigate damages by finding substitute employment, the employee is only required to accept comparable employment in relation to such factors as rank, status, job description, geographical location, etc.

23. True   The rescinding party is required to give sufficient notice to the breaching party in an action for rescission.

24. False   Consequential damages are foreseeable damages that arise from circumstances outside of the contract and are not an equitable remedy.

25. False   The court can offer the remedy of reformation and rewrite the contract to correct the clerical error to read what the parties originally intended.

Multiple Choice:

26. B   Answer B is the correct answer as when a party to a contract renders performance exactly as required by the contract, performance is said to be complete. Answer A is incorrect as rendering performance that is slightly less than perfect is not complete performance. Answer C is incorrect, as rendering inferior performance constitutes a material breach of contract, which is not complete performance. Answer D is incorrect as this answer is more reflective of a situation involving anticipatory repudiation where a party indicates that he or she cannot perform a contract verses complete performance where a party has fully performed his or her obligations under the contract.

27. C   Answer C is the correct answer as substantial performance is slightly less than complete performance of which the facts would fit within this description. The lack of ceramic knobs on the laundry room cupboards would qualify as a minor breach as the rest of the house is complete thereby indicating that Perfecto Home Construction Inc. has substantially performed under its contract with Delia Bloom. Answer A is incorrect as inferior performance would indicate that a material breach has taken place which is not the case since most of Delia Bloom's house has been completed with the exception of the ceramic knobs on her laundry room cupboards. Answer B is incorrect as Perfecto Home did not reflect a tender of complete performance as the knobs on the laundry room cupboard still needed to be installed. Answer D is incorrect as Perfecto Home completed almost all of what it was required to do under its contract with Perfecto Home Construction Inc.

28. C   Answer C is correct as the equitable remedy of reformation permits the court to rewrite the parties' contract to reflect the true intentions of the parties. Answer A is incorrect as the remedy of rescission is used when a party wants to undo a contract not rewrite it. Answer B is incorrect as the remedy of restitution involves giving goods or compensation back to a party when a contract has been rescinded. Answer D is incorrect as there is no such remedy as reconstruction.

29. A   Answer A is correct, as the court will create a quasi contract to prevent unjust enrichment in cases where there is no enforceable contract between the parties. The example given is one that may be a promissory estoppel situation in that Ellie detrimentally relied upon Patsy's promise by quitting her job and moving all of her belongings from Wisconsin to Arizona. Further, Ellie made substantial improvements to Patsy's home and moved in with her as well. Answer B is incorrect as Ellie does not want to undo the contract which is what a cause of action based on rescission would do. Answer C is incorrect as an injunction is a remedy that is sought when a party wants another to stop doing something. This is inapplicable to the facts. Instead Ellie wants Patty to sign over the deed to the Arizona home as promised. Answer D is incorrect as reformation is a remedy whereby the parties ask the court to rewrite the contract to reflect the true intentions of the parties. There is no written contract to rewrite and as such this remedy does not apply.

30. D   Answer D is correct, as an injunction is a court order that prohibits a person from doing a certain act. Answers A and B are incorrect as there are no such things as a trespass order or a prohibitum orderis. Answer C is incorrect as an order for specific performance implies that you want a party to perform and continue with the obligations under the contract not prohibit him or her from doing something.

31. B   Answer B is correct as a contractor may recover the profits he or she would have made on the contract if the owner breaches the construction contract before the construction begins. This is exactly what happened in the example. Maxine breached her contract with Lemoore Construction before the building of the racquetball court began. Answer A is incorrect as this answer incorporates the measure of damages for breach of contract for the sale of goods. Answer C is incorrect as the remedy for lost wages is usually applicable in situations involving the breach of employment contracts. Answer D is incorrect for the reasons stated above.

32. B   Answer B is correct, as an employee owes a duty to mitigate damages by trying to find substitute employment that is comparable to that which they had. Answer A is incorrect as gathering as much information about Random will not assist her in mitigating her damages though it may assist her in the discovery process should she decide to sue. Answer C is incorrect as begging for a second chance will not be a factor that the court will consider in determining whether Lisa has mitigated her damages. Answer D is incorrect as the courts usually do not grant specific performance where contracts of

personal service is involved. Arguably, this would be a personal service contract that would be nearly impossible for the court to monitor.

33. C Answer C is correct, as the liquidated damages clause will be considered to be a penalty if actual damages are clearly able to be determined in advance or if they are excessive or unconscionable. Answer A is incorrect as an adhesion clause speaks to only the aspect of unconscionablility and not to the ability to assess actual damages. Answer B is incorrect as the clause will not be enforceable if the damages are excessive or unconscionable or able to be determined in advance. Answer D is incorrect as under the facts as presented the clause would not be considered compensation for breach of contract since it would be a penalty.

34. A Answer A is correct as the court will grant the equitable remedy of injunction if the party can show that irreparable harm will come if it is not granted. Answer B is incorrect as demonstration of need over another is not a requisite in obtaining the enforcement of an injunction. Answer C is incorrect as this answer is mixing a legal remedy involving compensation with the equitable remedy of injunction as stated in the facts. Answer D is incorrect as it speaks to the equitable remedy of reformation and not injunction.

35. D Answer D is correct as answers A, B, and C are all things that must be shown in order to recover for the tort of intentional interference with contract relations.

Short Answer:

36. quantum meruit or implied-in-law contract.
37. to punish the defendant (note answers will vary)
38. protection
39. benefit *of the* bargain
40. returning goods, property, money or other consideration received from the other party
41. The court may issue a Write of Attachment or a Writ of Garnishment.
42. An order that garnishes wages, bank accounts or other property of the breaching party that is in a third parties hands to be paid over to the non-breaching party.
43. To prevent unjust enrichment.
44. Because they are too hard to monitor and enforce.
45. minor breach
46. He may bring a cause of action based on a quasi contract theory.
47. compensation for personal injury, emotional distress, pain and suffering and possible punitive damages.
48. implied covenant of good faith and fair dealing.
49. He should seek actual damages of $10,000 and punitive damages as the tort of fraud was involved with the contract between Silvia and Horatio, which may entitle him to this type of damages.
50. An award of money.

Chapter 17
INTELLECTUAL PROPERTY AND INFORMATION TECHNOLOGY

Chapter Overview

This chapter provides information about the various types of intellectual property. Intellectual property consists of trade secrets, patents, trademarks, copyrights, computer law and domain names. You will learn a wealth of information concerning this type of property including the remedies for infringement of the rights that are attached to them. Further, you will become familiar with the protection that is attached to technology based intellectual property.

Objectives

Upon completion of the exercises in this chapter, you should be able to:
1. Define what intellectual property consists of.
2. Explain the business tort of misappropriating a trade secret.
3. Discuss what criminal conduct violates the Economic Espionage Act.
4. Explain the process for obtaining a patent
5. Explain how cyber business plans are protected under patent law.
6. Discuss the types of writings afforded protection under copyright laws.
7. Discuss the remedies available for copyright, patent and trademark infringement.
8. Explain the rights held by computer software designers over their works.
9. Explain the NET Act and its effect on copyright infringement.
10. Explain what changes were made by enacting the Digital Millennium Copyright Act.
11. Differentiate between trademarks, service marks and certification marks.
12. Explain what international protection is given to intellectual property rights.

Practical Application

You should be able to differentiate between a copyright, trademark and patent and know whether or not an infringement has occurred. Further, you will be more familiar with the various intellectual property acts and what they apply to. This chapter provides a clearer understanding of what is involved in intellectual property and which acts and laws will afford the greatest protection to the creator.

Helpful Hints

Since there is a wealth of information with the various intellectual property acts, the easiest way to study the material is to categorize all of the information and acts in a methodical fashion that is consistent throughout the chapter. The Study Tips section that follows attempts to organize the information for you so that studying becomes more manageable.

Study Tips

Each intellectual topic area is organized in the same fashion so that it becomes habit for you to learn the information in a logical manner. When studying, it will help you to have someone ask you the questions under each heading to determine what you have learned.

Trade Secrets

<u>What is a trade secret?</u> A product, formula, pattern, design compilation of customer data or any other business secret. Note, the federal definition includes,

<u>What is considered a violation of a trade secret?</u> The defendant, usually an employee must have obtained the trade secret through unlawful means, such as theft, bribery, etc.

<u>Does an owner of a trade secret have any obligations under the law?</u> Yes, he or she must take all reasonable protections to protect his or her trade secret. If the owner does not protect his or her trade secret, then there is no protection under the law for it.

<u>What laws afford protection of a trade secret?</u>
State unfair competition laws, which may include the Uniform Trade Secrets Act.
The federal Economic Espionage Act of 1996 makes it a federal crime to steal another person's trade secrets.

<u>What may the owner recover if he or she is successful in a trade secret action?</u>
The owner may recover profits, damages and procure an injunction to stop the offender from using or revealing the trade secret.
Under the Economic Espionage Act, organizations may be fined up to $5 million dollars per criminal act and $10 million if the act benefited a foreign government. Also, individuals may get up to 15 years of prison time per violation increasing to 25 years if the act benefited a foreign government.

Patents

<u>What is required to get a patent?</u> An invention that is novel, useful and nonobvious.

<u>What types of things can be patented?</u> Processes, machines, improvements of existing machines, compositions of matter, asexually reproduced plants, designs for an article of manufacture, living material invented by a person

<u>How does an individual get a patent?</u> Briefly stated, an individual applies for a patent with the Patent and Trademark Office and is assigned a number. While waiting for approval, the individual may affix the terminology, "patent pending" on the thing to be protected.

<u>What other laws are available to help inventors?</u> Under the *American Inventors Protection Act* of 1999, an inventor may file a provisional application with the Patent and Trademark Office pending the final completion and filing of a patent application. The inventor has "provisional rights" for three months pending the filing of a final application.

<u>Federal Law and Patents</u> – The *Federal Patent Statue* protects patented inventions from infringement. There are no state patent laws.

<u>Changes in Patent Laws-</u> In 1994, the General Agreement on Tariffs and Trade extended patent protection from 17 to 20 years. Also, the patent term now begins to run from the date that the application is filed instead of when the patent is issued.

Cyber Business Plans and *financial models* that are used over the Internet are protected by patent law.

<u>Law to be aware of -</u> The <u>*Public Use Doctrine*</u> (also called the one-year "on sale" doctrine) states that a patent may not be granted if the invention was used by the public for more than one year prior to the filing of the patent application. This law encourages timely patent applications.

<u>What may the patent holder recover in a successful patent infringement action?</u> A patent holder may recover money equal to a reasonable royalty rate on the sale of infringed article, damages such as loss of customers, an injunction preventing future infringing action and an order requiring destruction of the infringing material. If the court finds that the infringement was intentional, then it may award treble the damages.

Copyrights

<u>What can be copyrighted?</u> Only tangible writings that can be physically seen may be copyrighted. This includes, books, sermons, greeting cards, jewelry, and glassware.

<u>What is required in order to get a copyright?</u> The work must be the original, tangible work of the author. Notice is not required, however it is recommended that notice be place on the work so as to prevent the claim of innocent infringement. Registration with the U.S. Copyright Office is needed as well.

<u>What laws afford protection of an individual's work?</u>
Copyright Term Extension Act of 1998 - This act added 20 years to existing copyrighted work and to future copyrighted works. For individual copyright holders, copyright protection is for the life of the author plus 70 years. For a Corporate copyright holder, protection is ninety-five years from the year of first publication or 120 years from the year of creation, whichever is the shorter of the two.

Computer Software Copyright Act – Computer programs were added to the list of tangible items protected by copyright law. It has been held that the creator of a copyrightable software program obtains automatic copyright protection. The *Judicial Improvement Act* allows for the acceptance and recordation of any document relating to computer software. Finally, the *Semiconductor Chip Protection Act of 1984* provides protection of a computer's hardware components, and masks that are used to create computer chips.

The Digital Millennium Copyright Act – This act " prohibits the unauthorized access to copyrighted digital works by circumventing the wrapper or encryption technology that protects the intellectual property." Civil and criminal penalties are imposed under this act. Actual damages, treble damages, attorney's fees, and injunction and statutory damages are some of the remedies available. Criminal penalties in the form of fines and prison time may also be ordered. The level of protection of digital copyrighted works has risen as a result of this act.

The World Intellectual Property Organization prompted the *Copyright Treaty* that "protects computer programs and their data and grants the copyright holders the exclusive right to make their works available on the Internet and other wireless means". The *Phonogram Treaty* gives "performers and producers the exclusive right to broadcast, reproduce, and distribute copies of their performances by any means, including video recording, digital sound, or encryption signal."

The *No Electronic Theft Act (NET act)* provides from criminalizing certain types of copyright infringement. It "prohibits any person from willfully infringing a copyright for either the purpose of commercial advantage or financial gain, or by reproduction or distribution even without commercial advantage or financial gain, including by electronic means where the retail value exceeds $1,000. Up to one year imprisonment and fines up to $100,000 are the penalties for violating this act.

Can work be used even if it is copyrighted? Under the *Fair Use Doctrine,* certain limited, unauthorized use of copyrighted materials is permitted without it being an infringement. Quotations from a review or criticism of a work, brief news report quotations, a small reproduction of a work by a teacher in order to teach a lesson and reproduction of a work in a judicial or legislative hearing are considered fair use.

What may an individual recover in a successful copyright infringement action? The plaintiff may recover any profit made by the infringer, damages suffered by the plaintiff, an order to impound or destroy the infringing work, an injunction to prohibit future infringement and statutory damages in lieu of actual damages may be awarded.

Trademarks

What can be trademarked? Marks such as distinctive marks, symbols, names, words, mottos or slogans can be trademarked. Color may even be trademarked when it is associated with a particular good.

Note the difference between a trademark and other marks, such as a service mark, certification mark or a collective mark

Service mark – Used to set apart the services of the holder from the competition. *Ex: Weight Watchers*
Certification mark – A mark used to certify that goods are of a certain quality or come from a certain geographical location. *Ex: Santa Maria Tri-Tip Sandwiches*
Collective mark –A mark used by associations or cooperatives, etc. *Ex: Big Brothers of America*

What is the purpose of a trademark? To protect the owner's investment and good will in a mark.

What is needed to qualify for protection of a mark? The mark must have acquired secondary meaning and be distinctive. Both of these aspects must be present or the mark will not be protected. A term that becomes descriptive loses its distinction and its protection.

How does an individual register a trademark? Trademarks are registered with the U.S. Patent and Trademark Office in Washington D.C. The original mark is valid for 10 years and renewable for an unlimited number of 10-year periods. The registered user ma y use the trademark symbol, however, it is not necessary. Registration is permitted if a mark was in used in commerce or the Individual verifies a good faith intention to use the mark within six months of registration.

What laws protect a trademark?

The *Federal Lanham Trademark Revision Act of 1998* which made it easier to register trademarks, but more difficult to maintain them.

The *Federal Dilution Act of 1995* protects famous marks from dilution. There are three requirements under this act that must be met. The mark must be famous and used for commercial purposes by the other party. Also, the use must cause dilution of the distinctive aspect of the mark. The purpose of this act is to stop those who try to benefit from others monetary and creative efforts in promoting their famous marks. Many situations that call for the use of this act's protection are domain name cases.

The *Agreement on Trade-Related Aspects of International Property Rights* requires that member nations of the WTO must comply with the "international treaties and conventions protecting copyrights in traditional works, computer programs, and digital works, and related intellectual property laws." If one country thinks that another country is not complying with this law, a nation can file a charge with the WTO.

State antidilution statutes allow companies and individuals to register service marks and trademarks in an effort to prevent infringement on and dilution of a mark that has been registered. Local businesses take advantage of registering under the state's protection.

Refresh Your Memory

The following exercise will enable you to refresh your memory on the rules and principles presented to you in this chapter. Read each question twice and place your answer in the blanks provided. Review the chapter material for any question you miss or are unable to remember.

1.   What types of writings are subject to copyright registration? _____

2.   Give examples of the term writing. _____

3.   What did the Copyright Term Extension Act of 1998 do? _____
     _____

4.   What is a trade secret? _____

5.   What was the main purpose of enacting the federal Espionage Act of 1996? _____
     _____

6.   What was the purpose of Congress enacting the Federal Patent Statute? _____
     _____

7.   What three aspects must be present for an invention to be patented? The invention must be
     _____, _____, and _____.

8.   Give an example of three things that may be patented. (1) _____
     (2) _____   (3) _____

9.   Under current patent law, when does the patent term begin to run? _____
     _____

10. What does the one-year "on sale" doctrine state? _____
     _____

11. The Semi-conductor Chip Protection Act protects _____ that are used to create
     computer chips.

12. When does copyright infringement occur? _____
     _____

13. A doctrine that permits certain limited use of a copyright by someone other than the
     copyright holder without permission is the _____ _____ doctrine.

14. How has the Digital Millennium Copyright Act changed the traditional fair use doctrine?
     _____
     _____

15. The No Electronic Theft Act _____ certain kinds of copyright infringement.

Critical Thought Exercise

Lindsey and Tony decide to establish an Internet business called Our Business is E-Business (OBE) in Greenport, while enrolled a Green Valley College. The business sells electronic equipment including computers, CD players, home theater systems, and PDA's. The merchandise is high quality, but sales have been in a slump due to competition. They need more sales to keep the business operating. Lindsey and Tony add you as a partner with a 1/3 interest for you investment of $20,000. Lindsey comments that if all the students who were listening to the latest hits from artists like Linkin Park, O-Town, and Sheryl Crow would buy apiece of equipment from them, OBE would be an overnight success. Lindsey purchased CDs from twelve popular music artists and establishes a link for listening to this music once an item is purchased from OBE. For every $100 spent on OBE merchandise, the customer can listen to an hour of music for free. Lindsey and Tony have not been making very mush profit on each individual sale, especially since many items sold by OBE are relatively inexpensive, such as remote controls, surge protectors, CD cases, and audio/video cables. As a partner, you are worried that there may be something wrong with using the artist's music to help sell OBE merchandise. You ask Tony and Lindsey to remove the link to the free music from the OBE Internet site. Mainly because sales have increased by 30% since the music link was added to the OBE site, they vote against you and insist that the music link remain part of the site unless you can prove to them that it is not in the best interest of OBE to continue with the "free music" offer.

Prepare a memorandum to your partners on the intellectual property rights that may be involved in your situation and the consequences of any infringement for OBE.

Answer. _____
_____
_____
_____

_____
_____
_____
_____
_____
_____
_____
_____
_____
_____
_____
_____
_____
_____
_____
_____
_____
_____
_____
_____
_____
_____

Practice Quiz

True/False:

1. ____ In order to bring a lawsuit for misappropriation, the defendant must have obtained the trade secret through unlawful means. [p 323]

2. ____ A trade secret owner need not do anything to prevent discovery of his or her trade secret. [p 324]

3. ____ There are no state patent laws. [p 324]

4. ____ Any party may challenge the issuance of a patent. [p 324]

5. ____ Improvements to existing machines cannot be patented. [p 325]

6. ____ An injunction is one remedy that is available for patent infringement. [p 327]

7. ____ An idea by itself is copyrightable. [p 332]

8. ___ One of the things the American Inventors Protection Act does is that it permits an inventor to file a provisional application with the Patents and Trademark Office. [p 331]

9. ___ The Digital Millennium Copyright Act imposes only civil penalties. [p 339]

10. ___ A brief quotation in a news report is not subject to fair use. [p 336]

11. ___ Cyber business plans and financial models are subject to patent protection. [p 330]

12. ___ Copyrightable software programs obtain automatic copyright protection. [p 336]

13. ___ The copyright holder may still recover for infringement where fair use is found. [p 337]

14. ___ It is illegal to access copyrighted material by breaking through the digital wrapper that protects the work. [p 339]

15. ___ If Sam Sly copies a very tiny part of the back of your business law text and places it in his text entitled, "Business Law for Numbskulls!," he will not be held liable as he did not copy the entire work. [p 334]

16. ___ A mark used to certify that goods and services are of a certain quality is an example of a collective mark. [p 342]

17. ___ A trademark can be a motto. [p 342]

18. ___ Color cannot be trademarked. [p 342]

19. ___ In order for a mark to qualify for federal protection, it must have acquired secondary meaning. [p 343]

20. ___ The Digital Millennium Copyright Act has raised the level of protection of digitally copyrighted works above that of nondigital copyrighted works. [p 339]

21. ___ A trademark that becomes a common term for the product line loses its protection under the federal trademark law. [p 345]

22. ___ A state law that allows persons and companies to register trademark and service marks are antidilution statutes. [p 347]

23. ___ Bonnie has invented a clothes-sorting machine but is not sure if it will be a big selling item. She places the product in various retail stores for a year and a half and is astounded by how well they have done. Thereafter she decides to seek a patent on her invention. Since she has come up with a novel idea, she will have no problem getting her patent. [p 324]

24. ___ A service mark is used to differentiate the services of the holder from its competitors. [p 342]

25. ___ In a cause of action for willful copyright infringement, the court can award damages up to one hundred thousand in lieu of actual damages. [p 329]

Multiple Choice:

26. In order for an invention to receive a patent, it must [p 324]
    a. be novel, useless, and non-obvious.
    b. be novel, useful and non-obvious.
    c. be novel, useful and obvious.
    d. be novel, functional and clandestine.

27. Examples of trade secrets include [p 323]
    a. patterns, designs, and slogans.
    b. formulas, patterns and designs.
    c. postcards, tapestries, and glass
    d. maps, books, and tangible writings.

28. A trademark is good for [p 341]
    a. 10 years and can be renewed for one more ten year period.
    b. 10 years.
    c. 10 years and can be renewed for an unlimited number of 10 year periods.
    d. 20 years plus the life of the creator.

29. What federal act specifically provides protection for trademarks, service marks and other marks? [p 341]
    a. The Lanham Trademark Act
    b. The Landon Act
    c. The Mask Work Act
    d. The Sony Bono Term Extension Act

30. What are the state trademark statutes called? [p 347]
    a. Distinct and secondary meaning statutes
    b. Public use doctrine statutes
    c. No electronic theft statutes
    d. Antidilution statutes

31. Which of the following would not be protected under copyright laws? [p 342]
    a. Photographs
    b. Poems
    c. Color
    d. Maps

32. The World Intellectual Property Organization extended copyright protection to [p 340]
    a. inventions used by the public for more than one year.
    b. computer programs and data compilations.
    c. the Sonny Bono Term Extension Act.
    d. tangible writings.

33. The Federal Dilution Act was designed to [p 347]
    a. stop cybersquatters who have appropriated famous marks on the Internet.
    b. sort through the frivolous trademark applications.
    c. allow persons and companies to register service marks.
    d. None of the above.

34. Shelly operates a small clothing boutique in a rural area. In order to bring in more business, she placed an ad in a neighboring town's newspaper indicating that with every purchase over $25.00, the purchaser would be allowed to read a chapter from the newest teen idol book by I. M. Cool for free. This marketing strategy worked for her as her business tripled. If I.M. Cool is informed of what Shelly is doing, what would be his best theory to pursue against her? [p 334]
    a. patent infringement
    b. trademark infringement
    c. violation of the Lanham Trademark Act
    d. copyright infringement

35. Which doctrine allows certain limited, unauthorized use of copyrighted materials? [p 336]
    a. The Fair Use Doctrine
    b. The public use doctrine
    c. The Federal Dilution Act
    d. The No Electronic Theft Act

Short Answer:

36. The _____ _____ _____ Act has been adopted by many states to give statutory protection to trade secrets. [p 323]

37. If Robby steals the secret recipe to Chandler's Chunky Cocoa Cookies and opens up his own cookie shop, what should Chandler's cause of action against Robby be based on? [p.17-7] _____

38. If Chandler finds out that Robby stole his recipe by hacking into his computer files, what federal act will give Chandler the best chance of recovering his economic damages from Robby? [p 324] The federal _____ _____ _____

39. Which act allows the federal government to criminally attack copyright infringement and help put an end to digital piracy? [p 339] _____

40. _____ qualifies for trademark registration when it is linked with a particular good and obtained a secondary meaning that signifies a particular brand and manufacturer as its source. [p 343]

41. Which agreement outlawed the unauthorized taping of sounds or images of live musical performances? [p 347] _____

42. What statute established the requirements for obtaining a patent and protects patent inventions from infringement? [p 325] _____

43. If Winston Watube sues Tom Teacher for copyright infringement based on Tom's use of Winston's poem to provide an example of iambic pentameter for his class, what is Tom's best defense to a lawsuit brought by Winston? [p 336] _____

44. The American Automobile Association's slogan "travel with someone you trust" is an example of a _____. [p 342]

45. "Girl Scouts of America" is an example of a _____ _____. [p 342]

46. Give two examples of marks that cannot be registered. [p 342] _____
_____

47. What remedies may Madison seek in a trademark infringement case against Ross? [p 343]
_____
_____
_____
_____

48. What is meant by the terminology, "secondary meaning?" [p 341] _____
_____

49. A trademark that becomes a common term for a product line or type of service is a
_____ _____. [p 345]

50. If Andrew Abbot, a new an upcoming author wants to write a book that can be read off of the Internet, but is afraid that it might be stolen, which treaty may give him added protection for his work? [p 340] The _____ treaty.

Answers to Refresh Your Memory

1. Only tangible writings are subject to copyright registration. [p 332]
2. books, newspapers, tapestries, postcards, maps, etc. [p 332]
3. It extended the term of existing copyrighted works and future copyrighted works 20 years. [p 333]
4. A product, formula, pattern, design, or other business secret. [p 323]
5. It makes it a federal crime to steal another person's trade secrets. [p 324]
6. To provide an incentive for inventors to invent, make their inventions public and protect against infringement. [p 324]
7. novel, useful and nonobvious [p 325]
8. machines, asexually reproduced plants, processes [p 325]
9. It begins to run from the date the application is filed. [p 327]
10. If an invention was used by the public for more than one year, a patent cannot be granted. [p 329]
11. masks [p 334]
12. When a party copies a substantial and material part of another's work without permission. [p 334]
13. fair use [p 336]
14. It has made it illegal to even access the copyrighted material by breaking through the digital wrapper or encryption technology that protects the work. [p 339]
15. criminalizes [p 339]

Critical Thought Exercise Model Answer

To: Tony and Lindsey
From: Your Partner
Re: Possible Copyright Infringement

Copyrights are designed to protect the rights or artists while preserving the public's right to benefit from the works of these artists. Use of copyrighted material is legal only if there is permission from the copyright holder or there is permissible use under the fair use doctrine. The fair use doctrine allows limited use of copyrighted material for a specific purpose, such as education, editorial comment, parody, criticism, news reporting, research, and scholarship. Fair use does not apply to situation where the use is for a commercial purpose. A court will also examine the effect the use will have upon the potential market for the value of the copyrighted material. Because we are using the music to enhance our sales, this is an impermissible commercial use. Though we are not copying the music, we may be liable for contributory infringement if a court finds that we, with knowledge of the infringing activity, induce, cause, or materially contribute to the infringing conduct of another. We are making it possible for customers to have access to a copy of the music. Contributory infringement includes a simple link to a website with infringing files on it. Liability extends to both the linking site and the site where the files are located. WE are not only linking to copyrighted material but we are knowingly and willingly hosting the files with the intent of distributing the music. The penalties for this activity are up to five years in prison and a fine of $250,000 for the first offense.

A solution to this problem is to obtain a license from the copyright holder that would allow us to use the music with their permission. The license fee will be negotiable and we may be able to obtain it for a very fair price when we explain the limited use and nature of our business. The artist may consider the limited use to be a form of free publicity, much like play time on a radio station. The failure to cease using copyrighted material subjects all three of us to civil and criminal penalties. Failure to cure this infringement violated your fiduciary duty to me as a partner. If you do not immediately get OBE in compliance with 17 U.S.C Section 101 et seq., I will be forced to terminate our partnership.

Answers to Practice Quiz

True/False:

1. True   The defendant must have procured the trade secret through unlawful means such as industrial espionage, bribery or theft.
2. False   An individual who owns a trade secret must take all reasonable precautions to prevent those secrets from being discovered by others, including locking the doors, hiring security, etc.
3. True   Federal patent law is exclusive.
4. True   The issuance of a patent may be challenged by any party.
5. False   Improvements to existing machines can be patented.
6. True   One remedy available for patent infringement is an injunction preventing the infringer from such action in the future.
7. False   An idea alone is not copyrightable, however the expression of an idea is.
8. True   This act does provide for a provisional application pending the preparation and filing of a final and complete patent application with the Patent and Trademark Office.
9. False   The Digital Millennium Copyright Act imposes both civil and criminal penalties.

10. False   A brief quotation in a news report is subject to the protection of the fair use doctrine.
11. True   Many cyber business plans and financial models have received patents and are protected.
12. True   Under the Computer Software Copyright Act, the creator of copyrightable software programs obtains automatic copyright protection.
13. False   When fair use is found, the copyright holder may not recover for infringement.
14. True   Under the Digital Millennium Copyright Act, it is illegal to access copyrighted material by breaking through the digital wrapper or encryption technology that protects the work.
15. False   The copying does not have to be either word for word or the whole work.
16. False   A certification mark is one that says that goods and services are of a certain quality.
17. True   Trademarks can be mottos, symbols, names, distinctive marks, etc.
18. False   Color can be trademarked.
19. True   A mark must have acquired secondary meaning and be distinctive to qualify for federal protection.
20. True   Protection is increased for digital copyrighted works.
21. True   Loss of federal trademark protection occurs when a mark becomes descriptive instead of distinctive and hence it is then a common term.
22. True   Antidilution statutes allow companies and persons to register service marks and trademarks.
23. False   Bonnie will not be able to get her patent under the one-year "on sale" doctrine as her clothes sorting machine was used by the public for over a year before filing her patent application.
24. True   Different names of the same types of services are differentiated by the types of service marks that they bear.
25. True   The court has discretionary power to award damages ranging from $200 for innocent copyright infringement up to $100,000 for willful infringement in lieu of actual damages.

Multiple Choice:

26. B   Answer B is the correct answer as an invention must be novel, useful and nonobvious to qualify for a patent. Answer A is incorrect, as the term useless is an incorrect element to qualify for a patent. Answer C is incorrect as the term obvious is an incorrect element to qualify for a patent. Answer D is incorrect as the term clandestine is an incorrect element to qualify for a patent.
27. B   Answer B is the correct answer as formulas, patterns and designs are all examples of trade secrets. Answer A is incorrect as slogans are afforded trademark not trade secret protection. Answer C is incorrect as these are examples of things that are afforded copyright protection. Answer D is incorrect as these are also examples of things that are afforded copyright protection.
28. C   Answer C is the correct answer that reflects how long trademark protection is good for. Answers A, B, and D are all incorrect as they do not reflect the correct time periods, and in the case of answer D give a misstatement of law.
29. A   Answer A is the correct answer as the Lanham Trademark Act gives trademarks, service marks, and other marks such as certification marks protection. Answer B is incorrect as there is no such act. Answer C is incorrect as the Mask Work Act pertains to computer chips. Answer D is incorrect as this act extended copyright protection.
30. D   Answer D is the correct answer as state trademark statutes are often called antidilution statutes. Answer A is not correct, as there is no such type of statute. Answer B is

incorrect as public use refers to the time frame in which an invention has been used by the public not the terminology for a state trademark statute. Answer C is incorrect, as the No Electronic Theft Act has no bearing on the name for the state trademark statutes.

31. C   Answer C is the correct answer as color is protected by trademark laws. Answers A, B and D are all incorrect as they reflect tangible writings that would be protected under copyright laws.

32. B   Answer B is correct as computer programs and data compilations have now been added to the types of tangible writings that are afforded copyright protection. Answer A is incorrect, as copyright protection does not protect inventions. Answer C is incorrect, as an act cannot be extended copyright protection. Answer D is incorrect as tangible writings were protected prior to the extension of including computer programs and data compilations.

33. A   Answer A is correct as this act was implemented to stop cybersquatters from appropriating famous marks on the Internet. Answer B is incorrect as it is an incorrect statement. Answer C is incorrect as trademark law has governance over persons and companies registering Service marks not the Federal Dilution Act. Answer D is incorrect for the reasons given above.

34. D   Answer D is correct as Shelly is making money indirectly from I.M. Cool's book, by offering a free reading with a clothing purchase. Since she did not ask I.M. Cool for permission to use his book, she may be found to have committed copyright infringement. Answer A is incorrect, as the facts do not involve an invention. Answers B and C are incorrect as the facts do not involve a motto, symbol, word, etc that would indicate that a trademark might be involved.

35. A   Answer A is correct as the Fair Use Doctrine allows certain limited, unauthorized use of copyrighted materials. Answer B is incorrect as the public use doctrine refers to the use of an invention by the public prior to the filing of a patent invention. Answer C is incorrect as the Federal Dilution Statute protects against cybersquatters on famous marks. Answer D is incorrect as the No Electronic Theft Act criminalizes willful copyright infringement for commercial advantage or financial gain.

Short Answer:

36.   Uniform Trade Secrets
37.   misappropriation
38.   Economic Espionage Act
39.   No Electronic Theft Act
40.   Color
41.   The international Agreement on Trade Related Aspects Property
42.   Federal Patent Statute of 1952
43.   fair use
44.   trademark
45.   collective mark
46.   the U.S. flag and geographical names standing alone (ex: "North") answers will vary
47.   Ross' profits, damages caused to Madison's business and reputation and an order destroying all goods containing the unauthorized mark and an injunction preventing Ross from infringing in the future.
48.   When an ordinary term has become a brand name.
49.   generic name
50.   WIPO Copyright Treaty

Chapter 18
DOMAIN NAMES, INTERNET
LAW AND E-COMMERCE

Chapter Overview

The evolution of the Internet as well as the vast amount of information available to users all over the world has given rise to several legal issues. This chapter discusses Web businesses and the operation of the same as well as registration of domain names. Further, it explores the roles of the Uniform Electronic Transactions Act as well as the Computer Information Transactions Act in e-commerce. Other additional laws concerning the creation, transfer and enforcement of e-commerce and informational licensing contracts are also discussed.

Objectives

Upon completion of the exercises in this chapter, you should be able to:
1. Explain how freedom of speech applies to the Internet using the rationale expressed in the case of *Reno v. American Civil Liberties Union.*
2. Explain the procedure for procuring Internet domain names.
3. Explain the provisions of the Federal Dilution Act that prohibit domain names from diluting or tarnishing famous trademarks.
4. Discuss what a license is and the parties to a licensing agreement.
5. Explain the provisions of the Federal Electronics Signature Act for e-commerce.
6. Discuss the importance of the Uniform Electronic Transactions Act (UETA)
7. Discuss the importance of the Uniform Computer Information Transactions Act (UCITA)
8. Explain what informational rights are protected by UCITA
9. Explain how UCITA provides comprehensive rules for the creation, performance and enforcement of licensing agreements.
10. Discuss the process of arbitration involving Internet domain name disputes.

Practical Application

You will have a clearer understanding of the various electronic and computer information acts that apply to the Internet as well as web businesses. Also, you will have a better understanding of e-commerce created licensing contracts as well as what necessary steps you may need to take if confronted with an Internet domain name dispute.

Helpful Hints

Since this chapter involves technology and the Internet, it would be very helpful for you to familiarize yourself with the technical terminology associated with the Information Age of today. Additionally, it is imperative that you learn the acts that protect as well as guide your conduct on the Internet in order to responsibly do business with the world. By learning the various acts, you will have a better understanding of what is expected of you as well as what you should expect of transactions on the Web.

Study Tips

There are two acts that were promulgated to provide a uniform and comprehensive set of rules involving for software and information licenses and contracts concerning computer information transactions. These acts are the Uniform Electronic Transaction Act and the Uniform Computer Information Transaction Act. However, prior to discussing these and other important acts associated with technology and business, you must get a firm grasp of the basic technological vocabulary.

Basic Vocabulary and Terminology

Internet – a collection of millions of computers that enable a network of electronic connections to exist between computers.

Electronic mail otherwise referred to as **e-mail** – Written communication between individuals whose computer is connected to the Internet.

Electronic communication – This involves any writing, images, sound, data, transfer of signals or any intelligence that is communicated electronically.

World Wide Web- The connection between millions of computers that enforces a standard set of rules for exchanging information referred to as Hypertext Transfer Protocol (HTTP).

Computer formatting – This refers to the use of common code languages such as Java and Hypertext Markup Language (HTML).

Web site- A combination of Web pages stored on various servers throughout the world.

Domain name – This identifies and differentiates one web site from another. Suffixes, or endings that are often used are *com* for commercial use, *org* for organizations, *edu* for educational institutions and *net* for networks.

Internet Corporation for Assigned Names and Numbers (ICANN) – This is an organization whose job is to regulate the issuance of domain names on the Internet.

Licensor- The party who owns the informational rights or the intellectual property and obligates Him or herself to transfer rights in the property or information to the licensee.

Licensee- The party who is given limited rights in or access to the informational rights or intellectual property.

License- This grants the contractual rights that are expressly stated in the license and the right to use any informational rights within the licensor's control that are necessary to exercise the expressly described rights. [UCITA Sec.307]

Exclusive License- This license gives the licensee exclusive rights in the information as described in the license for a specified period of time.

Licensing Agreement – A very detailed agreement between licensor and licensee that sets forth the terms of their agreement concerning the uses granted with respect to the intellectual property and informational rights.

Title to Copy – This is established by the license as the licensor may reserve title to the copy or the copy can transfer to the licensee.

Authenticate – This means executing an electronic symbol, sound or message linked to a record or signing the contract.

Uniform Dispute Resolution Policy – This policy mandates that all ICANN registered domain name users agree to utilize this dispute resolution policy as part of their accreditation.

Various Acts that Protect and Guide Internet Transactions

The Electronic Communications Privacy Act (ECPA)
- It is a crime to intercept "electronic communication" at any stage of its delivery.

- There are exceptions to the ECPA that allow access to the electronic communications without being in violation of the act. They are:

- The individual providing the service. An example would be your boss accessing information from your work computer.

- Government and law enforcement agencies that are investigating suspicious illegal activity are allowed if a valid search warrant is in place.

- Violation of the ECPA include criminal and civil penalties.

Anticybersquatting Consumer Protection Act
- The act was promulgated to oust cybersquatters who register Internet domain names of famous people and companies thereby holding them hostage for ransom payments from the famous individual or company.

- Two Requirements for this act:
  The name has to be famous. Trademarked names qualify, as do nontrademarked names of famous personalities.

  The domain name was registered in bad faith. Bad faith can be shown by considering the degree of resemblance between the holder's name and the famous individuals name, whether services and goods are being sold under the names, and the number of Internet domain names of famous individuals and companies that have been acquired by the holder.

Uniform Computer Information Transaction Act (UCITA)

- This act provides an exhaustive set of uniform rules that sets the standard for performance, and enforcement of computer information transactions. This act creates contract law for the licensing of information technology rights. For purposes of this act, a computer information transaction is an agreement to create, transfer, or license computer information or informational rights. [UCITA Sec.102 (a)(11)]. A state makes UCITA law by way of a state statute. Further, federal law preempts UCITA.

- Consumers are benefited by this act if they make an electronic error in contracting. UCITA provides that consumers are not bound if they learn of the error and tell the other party. Further, the consumer must not derive any benefit from the information. Also, the consumer must deliver all copies of the information to the third party or destroy the information as per the third party's instruction and the consumer must pay all shipping and processing costs of the other party.

- UCITA provides for the limitation of remedies for a breach of contract. They may be limited to return of copies and repayment of the licensing fee or to just the repair and replacement of the nonconforming copies. These limitations are enforceable unless they are found to be unconscionable.

The Uniform Electronic Transactions Act (UETA)

- This act was developed to create uniform laws for electronic signatures and electronic records. The purpose was to put electronic signatures and records on the same plane as written signatures and contracts. UETA only applies to electronic transactions between parties. Two main provisions are elaborated on within the act. First, UETA finds that an electronic record is sufficient for a contract as well as for purposes of the Statute of Frauds. Next, UETA acknowledges an electronic signature by giving it the same equivalence as a written signature. If the electronic signature requires notarization and witnessing; UETA finds this has been satisfied provided that all the necessary information regarding the notarization, acknowledgment, etc. are included.

- A state must adopt the act as its own statute in order for UETA to become law.

The Electronic Signature in Global and National Commerce Act

- This federal statute's purpose was to provide electronic commerce with the same credence as written contracts in the United States. As such, it recognizes an e-signature, or electronic signature as being validated in one of three ways. First, by something the signatory knows, such as the answer to a personal question. Second, by something the person has that stores personal information. Finally, by the use of a digitally calibrated device that recognizes fingerprints or parts of the eye. This technology is known as biometrics.

- This act also provides that electronic contracts satisfy the writing requirements of the Statute of Frauds. Further, record retention requirements are fulfilled by electronically stored records.

- This federal act preempts state law with the exception of state enacted e-signature provisions as per the UETA.

- There is a problem area with this act and that is that some countries have developed their own electronic commerce statutes that are different from those in the United States. Therefore, conflicts could arise without a global solution regarding contracts.

<u>How does an individual or business get a domain name?</u>

Step 1 - Determine whether anyone else owns the name.
You may search the databases of InterNIC or Network Solutions, which lists domain names that have been registered.
Step 2 - The registration form must be completed which by the way may be done online.
Step 3 - Submit the proper registration fee.

Formation of an Online Contract

- An online contract is much like that of a written one in that the same elements of offer, acceptance and consideration must be satisfied.
- If an electronic offer elicits an electronic acceptance, then an electronic contract is formed upon receipt of that acceptance. Changing the terms of the contract when accepting a conditional offer does not create a contract under UCITA.
- If the transaction involves merchants, any proposed terms become part of the contract unless they are objected to or if they are material alterations, then no contract is formed. If one party is a merchant and the other one is not, any proposed changes by way of the acceptance will be viewed as a counteroffer.
- The Statute of Frauds does not apply to contracts covered under the Uniform Computer Information Technology Act.
- Tender of Performance amounts to the offering of complete performance.

<u>Risk of loss of the copy</u> – Risk of loss passes to the licensee upon receipt of the copy if it is not delivered by carrier or delivered electronically.

<u>Risk of loss in a designated delivery contract</u> – The risk remains with the licensor until tendered to the designated destination. Otherwise, the risk of loss is placed with the carrier when the licenses are transferred to the carrier.

<u>Acceptance of a copy</u> – This occurs when the licensee through conduct signifies that there was conforming tender, keeps a copy despite the nonconformity or commingles the information with other information, receives a significant benefit from nonreturnable copy or uses the copy inconsistently with the licensor's ownership of the copy.

<u>Excuse of Performance</u> –A delay in performance under a license agreement due to impracticability will not constitute a breach if the requirements of UCITA are met. The party must reasonably notify the other party of the delay.

<u>What types of warranties attach to a license of informational rights?</u>
- Warranties of noninterference and noninfringement - A licensor warrant that no third person holds any claim or interest that would interfere with the licensor's use or enjoyment of the information.

- Express Warranty – Any affirmation of fact or promise made by the licensor about the software's quality or information. Statements of opinion do not constitute an express warranty.
- Implied Warranty of Merchantability of the Computer Program –_The computer program is fit for the ordinary purpose for which the program was going to be used.
- Implied Warranty of Informational Content – This warranty implies that there is no inaccuracy in the content of the information caused by the failure of the merchant to perform with reasonable care.
- Implied Warranty of Fitness for a Particular Purpose-When a licensee relies on the licensor's skill or judgment to select or furnish suitable information for which the computer information is required by the licensee, then the implied warranty of fitness for a particular purpose applies.

General Disclaimers of Warranties – UCITA permits disclaimers of all implied warranties with phrases like "as is." The language and disclaimers must be conspicuous.

Electronic Self-Help
If the licensee does not pay the license fee, the licensor can give at least a 15 day notice and activate a disabling bug that is embedded in the software or information that will prevent further access to the same. Proper notice to enable the licensee to make lawful adjustment must be made. Self-help is not available if it causes or results in public health or safety issues or personal injury.

Breach of License Agreements
- Licensee's refusal of defective tender_– The licensee may refuse the defective tender, accept the tender or accept any commercially reasonable units and refuse the rest.
- Licensee's revocation of acceptance- The licensee may revoke his or her acceptance if he or she could not have reasonably discovered the nonconformity at the time of acceptance or the nonconformity was discovered upon acceptance and the licensor agreed to cure the defect but it was not reasonably cured.

Adequate assurance of performance – This is akin to anticipatory repudiation whereby an aggrieved party may suspend performance if he or she has reasonable grounds to believe that the performance from the other party is not going to be forthcoming. The aggrieved party may demand adequate assurance of performance within a specified time frame.

Remedies

A party cannot recover more than once for the same loss, nor may it be more than the loss caused by the breach.

- Cancellation – The ending of a contract by a contracting party upon the material breach of contract by the other party.

- Licensor's damages – The licensor may sue a licensee who is in breach and seek monetary damages caused by the breach.

- Licensor's right to cure – Under UCITA, a licensor may cure a breach if the time for performance under the contract has not expired, or if it has expired, the licensor had reasonable grounds to feel that the performance would be acceptable and would cure within a reasonable time. Also, if the licensor making a conforming performance before cancellation by the licensee.

- Licensee's Damages – Damages depend on the facts of the situation. The licensee may cover or recover the value of the performance. Remember cover means engaging in a commercially reasonable substitute transaction.

- Licenssee can get Specific Performance – If this remedy was agreed to in the parties' contract, or if the performance that was agreed upon was unique, then it will be available to the parties.

- Limitation of Remedies –The parties may limit which remedies are available in the event of a breach. Limitation of remedies is enforceable unless they are unconscionable.

Refresh Your Memory

The following exercise will enable you to refresh your memory on the rules and principles presented to you in this chapter. Read each question twice and place your answer in the blanks provided. Review the chapter material for any question you miss or are unable to remember.

1. The _____ is a collection of millions of computers that enable a network of electronic _____ to exist between computers.

2. A combination of Web pages stored on various servers throughout the world is a _____.

3. Written communication between individuals whose computer is connected to the Internet is known as _____.

4. Which act makes it a crime to intercept an "electronic communication" at any stage of its delivery? _____

5. A _____ _____ is a unique name that signifies an individual's or a company's Web site.

6. What is the purpose of the Anticybersquatting Consumer Protection Act? The purpose is to _____.

7. Who is responsible for regulating the issuance of domain names on the Internet? _____

8. What is the arbitration procedure for challenging cybersquatting called? _____

9. What is a license? _____

10. Who are the parties to a license? The _____ and the _____

11. Which act establishes a uniform and exhaustive set of rules the rule the creation, performance and enforcement of computer information transactions? _____

12. What is an exclusive license? _____

13. What is meant by authenticating the record? _____

14. What is one of the main features of the federal Electronic Signature in Global and National Commerce Act? _____

15. Which act addresses unilateral electronic errors made by consumers? _____

Critical Thought Exercise

The James Co. of New York has been in the business of retail chocolate and confection sales since 1923. As the Internet has developed, James has commenced doing business by e-mail. Mrs. Dubyah communicates with James by numerous e-mails, negotiating the sale of 300 one-pound chocolate Easter eggs. They agree that the price will be $18 per egg and they will be shipped for arrival in Maryland 10 days before Easter. James produces the eggs and ships them in a timely manner. At the last minute, Mrs. Dubyah decides to order her Easter gifts from another company. When the shipment arrives in Maryland, Mrs. Dubyah wants to reject the shipment and order her eggs from her friend in Oklahoma. As the business secretary for Mrs. Dubyah, you are responsible for advising Mrs. Dubyah on business matters and executing her contracts as instructed.

Write a brief memorandum to Mrs. Dubyah, explaining to her your position on whether she can rely upon the Statute of Frauds as a defense to a damages claim by James Co. and whether the shipment should be accepted.

Answer. _____

_____

_____

_____

_____

_____

_____

_____

_____

_____

_____

_____

Practice Quiz

True/False:

1. ____ An exception to the Electronic Communications Privacy Act is an employer who accesses stored e-mail communications on an employee's personal computer. [p 357]

2. ____ Domain names can be registered. [p 358]

3. ____ Electronic contracts do not meet the Statute of Frauds requirements. [p 357]

4. ____ An agreement used to transfer limited rights in property and information for specified purposes and a stated time period is a license. [p 361]

5. ____ The license will govern a licensee's right to possess, control and use a copy of the licensed software. [p 364]

6. ____ The Internet Corporation for Assigned names is not responsible for regulating the issuance of domain names on the Internet. [p 359]

7. ____ Mary has entered into an electronic contract with Watson for the purchase of Watson's motorcycle. Mary authenticates the contract by using an electronic symbol. Mary's means of authentication will be insufficient to constitute a signing. [p 364]

8. ____ A contract can be formed by operation of electronic agents. [p 363]

9. ____ Electronic agents usually do not have the ability to evaluate and accept counteroffers or to make counteroffers. [p 363]

10. ____ The Uniform Electronic Transactions Act was promulgated to establish uniform laws for electronic signatures and electronic records. [p 364]

11. ____ The Uniform Dispute Resolution Policy makes arbitration of domain name disputes optional. [p 360]

12. ____ A transaction that is provided for by the UCITA is subject to the Statute of Frauds. [p 363]

13. ____ If an electronic offer brings about and electronic acceptance, then a contract is formed when the electronic acceptance is received. [p 363]

14. ____ One of the shortcomings of the Electronic Signature in Global and National Commerce Act is that the act does not provide for verification of digital signatures. [p 365]

15. ____ If a copy is delivered electronically or a common carrier is not used, the risk of loss of the copy passes to the licensee upon receipt of the copy. [p 366]

16. ____ The harsh rules of UCITA provide that a party's delay in performance or nonperformance of a license agreement is not excused even if there was impracticability involved. [p 366]

17. ___ The implied warranty of informational content warrants that there is inaccuracy in the informational content caused by the merchant's failure to perform with reasonable care. [p 368]

18. ___ The warranty that the computer program is fit for the ordinary purposes for which the computer program is used is called the implied warranty of merchantability of the computer program. [p 368]

19. ___ An express warranty is illustrated through statements of opinion. [p 368]

20. ___ Electronic self-help can be utilized by activating disabling bombs for those who fail to pay their license fee. [p 369]

21. ___ A licensor can recover lost profits as a result of the licensee's failure to accept or complete performance of the contract. [p 370]

22. ___ Regardless of any material breach of a contract, the aggrieved party may cancel the contract. [p 370]

23. ___ Electronic errors by non-consumers are handled by the Uniform Commercial Code and the common law of contracts. [p 367]

24. ___ If Ryan cancels a license that Victor gave to him, Victor has no right to have all copies of the licensed information returned by Ryan. [p 370]

25. ___ Under UCITA, if a licensing agreement is breached, the statute of limitations is open ended due to the electronic nature of the transaction. [p 370]

Multiple Choice:

26. Which of the following is one of the most widely used means of communication over the Internet? [p 356]
    a. Licensing agreements
    b. Electronic mail
    c. Chat rooms
    d. None of the above

27. In the case of *Reno v. American Civil Liberties Union,* what was the court's opinion with regard to the Communications Decency Act and the freedom of speech? [p 355]
    a. The act is effective in allowing freedom of speech.
    b. The act is vague and has a chilling effect on free speech.
    c. The act is specific and protects our children from sexually oriented speech.
    d. The act appropriately protects all that are concerned.

28. What are the two requirements necessary to show a violation under the Anticybersquatting Consumer Protection Act? [p 359]
    a. The Internet Domain name must be famous and the domain name must be registered within the statutory period.
    b. The Internet Domain name need not be famous, just registered and the registration must accompany the proper fee.
    c. The Internet Domain name must be famous and the domain name must be registered in bad faith.
    d. The Internet Domain name must be famous and the domain name must be registered in good faith.

29. Who is the owner of intellectual property or informational rights who transfers rights in the property or information to the license? [p 361]
    a. The licensee
    b. The licensor
    c. The obligor
    d. The obligee

30. A software license granting the licensee the right to obtain information in the possession of the licensor is called an [p 362]
    a. access agreement.
    b. acceptable license.
    c. computer transfer.
    d. limited confirmation contract.

31. This procedure is used to verify electronic authentication and to find errors or modifications in electronic authentication by using codes, algorithms, encryption and other means. [p 364]
    a. Arbitration
    b. Dispute resolution
    c. Attribution procedure
    d. Hypertext investigation

32. When a party offers to complete the performance of his or her duties under the contract, this is known as [p 365]
    a. nonconforming tender.
    b. tender of performance.
    c. good faith performance.
    d. all of the above.

33. Which act places an electronic signature on the same level as a pen-inscribed signature on paper? [p 365]
    a. The Pen and Paper Act of 2002
    b. The Electronic Paper Act
    c. The Electronic Signature in Global and National Commerce Act
    d. The Electronic Data Base Inscription Act

34. If a license agreement requires the licensor to deliver a copy to a particular destination, who bears the risk of loss? [p 366]
    a. The licensee
    b. The Internet Service Provider
    c. The state in which the agreement was enacted
    d. The licensor

35. A licensee who has tendered a copy of the license by the licensor is said to have accepted the copy if the licensee [p 366]
    a. signifies that the tender was conforming.
    b. that his or her acts signify that the tender was conforming
    c. keeps a copy despite its nonconformity
    d. all of the above.

Short Answer:

36. What is e-mail? [p 356] _____
    _____

37. What type of remedies are provided for by the Electronic Communications Privacy Act? [p 357] _____

38. When will a party's delay in performance or nonperformance under a license agreement be excused? [p 366] _____

39. What can a party do if he or she has been notified that there is a delay or nonperformance caused by impracticability? [p 366] _____
    _____

40. Jeremy licenses a product database from Productdata.com, Inc. for two years to use in his business. However, after only two months of using the database, he receives a court order stating that he must cease and desist use of the product database as it infringes on a copyright that Productsforyou.com holds. If Jeremy sues Productdata.com, Inc., what would be his best theory to sue under? [p 367] _____

41. Which warranty warrants that its software is fit for the ordinary purposes for which the computer program is used? [p 368] _____

42. What is the Implied Warranty of Informational Content? [p 368] _____

43. What is an express warranty? [p 368] _____
    _____

44. What is a licensor liable for if he or she uses electronic self-help improperly? [p 369]
    _____

45. Give examples of expressions of general disclaimers of all implied warranties that are permitted under the UCITA. [p 369] _____

46.   When may specific performance be obtained under UTICA? [p 371] _____

_____

47.   When may a licensor cure a breach of a license? [p 371] _____

_____

_____

48.   What does the term cover mean? [p 371] _____

_____

49.   What may an aggrieved party do if he or she thinks that prior to the performance date the other party might not deliver performance when do? [p 370] _____

_____

50.   What may a licensee to whom a defective tender of copy has been made do? [p 370]

_____

Answers to Refresh Your Memory

1.   Internet, connecting [p 354]
2.   Web site [p 357]
3.   electronic mail [p 356]
4.   Electronic Communications Privacy Act [p 357]
5.   domain name [p 358]
6.   Oust cybersquatters who register Internet domain names of famous people and companies by holding them hostage for ransom money. [p 359]
7.   Internet Corporation for Assigned Names and Numbers [p 359]
8.   Uniform Dispute Resolution Policy (UDRP) [p 360]
9.   A contract that transfers limited rights in informational and intellectual property. [p 361]
10.   licensor and licensee [p 361]
11.   Uniform Computer Information Transaction Act (UCITA) [p 362]
12.   A license granting exclusive rights in the information as described in the license for a specified period of time. [p 361]
13   This means either, executing a symbol, sound or message linked to a record or signing the contract. [p 364]
14.   One of the main features is its recognition of the electronic signature. [p 365]
15.   The Uniform Computer Information Transaction Act [p 367]

Critical Thought Exercise Model Answer

It is understood that e-mail is a convenient way to negotiate and agree on contract terms and to ultimately agree on a final contract. Assuming that all the elements to establish a valid contact are present, the fact that the contract is communicated by e-mail does not prevent the agreement from being valid and enforceable. In this instance, the subject matter, parties, price, and delivery terms have all been negotiated and agreed upon. While this is a contract for goods exceeding $500 that requires a written contract, there is no reason why the e-mails cannot be printed and used as the required writing. The e-mails will amply demonstrate the parties' intent and desire to enter into the agreement. The ordering of the eggs by Mrs. Dubyah by e-mail will have no less effect than a written letter. Thus, e-mail contracts meet the writing requirements for enforceable contracts.

Mrs. Dubyah is therefore advised to accept the shipment and pay for it as agreed. The Statute of Frauds will not supply a viable defense and it would be unethical for her to cancel the order based merely upon a whim.

Answers to Practice Quiz

True/False:

1. False   An exception to this act is an employer who accesses stored e-mail communications on the employer's service not on the employee's personal computer.
2. True   Domain names can be registered with a domain name registration service by paying the applicable fee.
3. False   Since parties to an e-mail contract can print a paper copy of the electronic contract, the writing requirement of the Statute of Frauds is met.
4. True   This is the correct definition of a license.
5. True   The license states the terms of the party's agreement.
6. False   It is responsible for regulating the issuance of domain names on the Internet.
7. False   Mary may authenticate her contract with Watson by using the electronic symbol that is attached to, included in, or linked with the record as provided for under the Uniform Computer Information Transactions Act.
8. True   A contract can be formed in any manner showing agreement including the operation of electronic agents.
9. True   Under the Uniform Computer Information Transactions Act, limitations of e-commerce are acknowledged thereby providing that a contract is formed if a person takes action resulting in the electronic agent causing performance or a promise of benefits to the individual.
10. True   This act was designed to provide uniform laws for electronic signatures and electronic records.
11. False The UDRP requires arbitration of domain name disputes.
12. False A transaction cover by the UCITA is not subject to the Statute of Frauds.
13. True   The electronic formation of a contract as described is provided for in the UCITA at section 201(f).
14. False The act does in fact provide three ways to verify a digital signature.
15. True   In order for the risk of loss to pass in an electronic delivery situation with no carrier, the licensee must receive the copy.
16. False The UCITA provides that delay or nonperformance where impracticability is involved will excuse performance.
17. False The Implied Warranty of Informational Content warrant that there is no inaccuracy of informational content caused by the merchant's failure to perform with reasonable care.
18. True   The law implies that a merchant licensor warrants that the computer program is fit for the ordinary purposes for which the computer program is used.
19. False A licensor's statements of opinion does not create an express warranty.
20. True   The activation of disabling bugs, and embedded time bombs can be utilized when a licensee fails to pay his or her license fee.
21. True   Lost profits is the measure of damages a licensor may recover for the licensee's failure to accept or complete performance of the contract.

22. False   There has to be a material breach that has not been cured before the aggrieved party may cancel the contract.

23. True   Note that UCITA applies only to consumers making electronic contracting errors and as such the Uniform Commercial Code and the common law handle electronic errors made by nonconsumers.

24. False   The licensor, Victor has the right to have all copies of the licensed information returned by Ryan upon cancellation of the license.

25. False   A cause of action must be brought within one year after the breach was or should have been discovered, but no more than five years after the breach occurred. [UTICA Sec.805]

Multiple Choice:

26. B   Answer B is the correct answer as electronic mail is the most widely used means of communication over the Internet. Answer A is incorrect as licensing agreements are not a typical means of communication that are widely used. Answer C is incorrect as even though chat rooms are popular, electronic mail is more widely used. Answer D is incorrect for the reasons given above.

27. B   Answer B is the correct answer as the court's opinion stated that the Computer Decency Act is a content-based regulation of speech which raised special First Amendment concerns due to its chilling effect on free speech. Also, the criminal nature of the act will stifle communication that might be entitled to protection. Answer A is an incorrect statement in light of the court's analysis in the case. Answer C is incorrect as the act is not specific nor does it appear to protect our children from sexually oriented speech. Answer D is blatantly incorrect in light of the rationale for the answers given above as well as the court's lengthy reasoning given in the case.

28. C   Answer C correctly states the two requirements in order to prove a violation of the Anticybersquatting Consumer Protection Act. Answers A, B, and D are incorrect as none of these answers state the two necessary requirements under the act.

29. B   Answer B is correct, as the owner of informational rights who transfers rights is the licensor. Answer A is incorrect as the licensee receives the rights. Answers C and D do not make sense in this question as even though duties and possible rights might be inferred from the terms obligor and obligee, there is nothing to indicate a license is involved with respect to an oligor and obligee.

30. A   Answer A is correct as an access contract/agreement allows the licensee to access the information for an agree-upon number of uses. Answers B, C, and D are nonexistent in terms of legal terminology and therefore erroneous.

31. C   Answer C is correct as an attribution procedure verifies electronic authentication and detects errors or changes in electronic authentication. Answer A is incorrect as arbitration refers to alternative dispute resolution, not the verification of electronic authentication, etc. Answer B is incorrect, as once again, dispute resolution does not apply to verification of electronic authentication. Answer D is incorrect as there is no such thing as hypertext investigation.

32. B   Answer B is correct as tender of performance occurs upon completion of performance of a party's duties under the contract. Answer A is incorrect as complete performance is the opposite of nonconforming tender. Answer C is incorrect as the offer of complete performance has good faith implied within it and is not known as good faith performance per se. Answer D is incorrect based on the reasons stated above.

33. C   Answer C is correct as the Electronic Signature in Global and National Commerce Act places an electronic signature on par with a pen-inscribed signature. Answers A, B, and D are incorrect as these acts do not exist.

34. D   Answer D is correct as the risk of loss remains with the licensor until the copy is tendered at the designated destination. Answers A, B, and C are incorrect, as they do not have applicability to the rules regarding risk of loss of the copy.
35. D   Answer D is correct as answers A, B, and C all indicate acceptance of a copy by the licensee.

Short Answer:

36. Electronic written communication between individuals using computers connected to the Internet.
37. civil and criminal penalties
38. It will be excused when performance has been made impracticable.
39. The party may terminate the contract and be discharged from the unperformed portion of the contract.
40. Jeremy's best theory would be one based on Breach of Warranty of Noninterference and Noninfringement.
41. The Implied Warranty of Merchantability of the Computer Program.
42. This is an implied warranty that there is no inaccuracy in the informational content caused by a merchant-licensor's failure to perform with reasonable care.
43. It is any affirmation of promise or fact by the licensor about the quality of its information or software.
44. A licensor is liable for damages.
45. "as is" or "with all faults"
46. If the parties agree to it or if the agreed upon performance is unique.
47. If the time of performance of the contract has not expired or if the licensor had reasonable grounds to believe the performance would be acceptable, then the licensor has a reasonable time to make conforming performance or before the licensee cancels the contract.
48. Cover means "engaging in a commercially reasonable substitute transaction."
49. The aggrieved party may make a demand for adequate assurance of due performance from the other party.
50. The licensee may refuse the tender, accept the tender, or accept any commercially reasonable units and refuse the rest. [UTICA Sec. 704]

Chapter 19
FORMATION OF
SALES AND LEASE CONTRACTS

Chapter Overview

This chapter focuses on the formation of sales and lease contracts and the requirements for the same. Also, the requirements and exceptions as they pertain to modification, the Statute of Frauds, and parol evidence are explored.

Objectives

Upon completion of the exercises in this chapter, you should be able to:
1. Explain what sales contracts are governed by Article 2 of the UCC.
2. Explain lease contracts as governed by Article 2A of the UCC.
3. Be able to apply the principles of good faith and reasonableness as per the UCC
4. Discuss how sales and lease contracts are formed.
5. Discuss the impact of the UCC's gap-filling rules.
6. Explain the UCC's firm offer rule.
7. Explain the UCC's additional terms rule and how to apply it to the "battle of the forms"
8. Discuss the UCC's written confirmation rule
9. Discuss the requirements for modification in sales and lease contracts.
10. Explain what is considered unconscionable in sales and lease contracts.

Practical Application

You should be able to determine what is necessary as well as acceptable to form a valid sales or lease contract. Further, your studies should provide you with the knowledge you need to modify, explain or validate either of these types of contracts should the need arise.

Helpful Hints

It is important to remember that basic contract principles also apply to sales and lease contracts, so, in essence, you are not learning all new material. By reviewing the elements of basic contract formation, and adding to it, you will have a better chance at retaining the information. As you study this chapter, keep the Uniform Commercial Code's leniency in forming sales and lease contracts. As a reminder, when you are analyzing a fact situation or a contract, it is advisable to read and analyze each line separately so that you do not miss any potential issues.

Study Tips

This chapter primarily focuses on Article 2 (Sales) and Article 2A (Leases) of the Uniform Commercial Code. It is easiest to study this chapter if you learn the basic scope of each of these articles. Article 2 involves transactions in goods whereas Article 2A involves consumer and finance leases.

Article 2 (Sales)

- You must learn what a sale is. A sale is the passing of title from a seller to a buyer for a price.

- <u>Next, what are goods?</u> Goods are tangible things that are movable at their identification. Be careful in this area, as there are some things that are not considered to be goods. These include money, intangible items, bonds, patents, stocks and land. Another caveat, things that are severable from the land can be goods.

Services are not covered under Article 2, however, when there is a mixed sale of both goods and services, if the goods dominate the transaction, then Article 2 does in fact apply. Each case involving a mixed sale is examined individually.

Article 2 applies to all sales regardless of a person's status of being or not being a merchant in the transaction. Note though that some sections of Article 2 apply only to merchants as well as expressed the special rules of duty placed upon merchants.

Article 2A (Leases)

- This article applies to personal property leases, which also involves the formation, performance and default of leases.

- <u>What is a lease?</u> A lease is the conveyance of the right to the possession and use of the named goods for a set time period in return for certain consideration.

- <u>What are the parties to a lease?</u> The lessor who is the person who transfers the right of possession and use of the goods under the lease and the lessee who obtains the right to possession and use of goods under a lease.

- <u>What is a finance lease?</u> This involves three parties, the lessor, the lessee, and the vendor (supplier). Here the lessor is not a manufacturer or supplier of goods, but still acquires title to the goods or the right to use and possess in connection with the lease terms.

Formation of Both Sales and Lease Contracts

As with other contracts, both sales and lease contracts require an offer, acceptance and consideration in order to be properly formed.

Offer

At common law, all necessary terms needed to be in place.
Modernly under the UCC, if a term is left open, the courts will apply the following rules:

Open Terms- The court will look at the parties' intent to make a contract and then determine if there is a reasonably certain basis for giving an appropriate remedy. When open terms are allowed to be read into the contract, this is referred to as gap-filling rules.

Open Price term
If a price in a contract is missing, the court will imply a "reasonable price" at the time of delivery.

Open Payment Term
In the absence of an agreement on payment terms, payment is due at the time and place where the buyer is to receive the goods.

Open Delivery Term
If there is no agreed upon place of delivery, then delivery is to take place at the seller's place of business.

Open Time Term
The contract must be performed within a reasonable time if there is no provision in the parties contract for a set specified time of performance.

Open Assortment Term
This occurs when the buyer is given the option of choosing the goods from an assortment of goods.

Acceptance

At common law and under the UCC, a contract is created when the buyer or lesee sends his or her acceptance to the offeror, not upon receipt.

Acceptance may be accomplished in any manner and by any reasonable medium of acceptance. If a buyer makes an offer, then the seller's acceptance is signified by either the seller's prompt promise to ship or his or her prompt shipment of conforming or nonconforming goods.

Acceptance of the goods by the buyer occurs if after the buyer has a reasonable opportunity to accept the goods, either indicates that the goods are conforming, or signifies that he or she will keep the goods regardless of their nonconformity or if he or she fails to reject the goods within a reasonable period of time after delivery of the goods.

Accommodation Shipment is Not an Acceptance- A shipment of nonconforming goods is not considered an acceptance if the seller seasonably notifies the buyer that the shipment is being offered as an accommodation to the buyer. An accommodation shipment is considered a counter offer from the seller to the buyer.

Importance of the Mirror Image Rule- At common law, an offeree's acceptance had to mirror the Image of the offer. If additional terms were included, it was considered a counteroffer. The UCC

However has given flexibility to this rule.

If one or both parties are *nonmerchants*, any additional terms become *proposed additions* to the contract. The proposed additions do not terminate the offer nor does it constitute a counteroffer. If the offeree's proposed additions are accepted by the offeror, they become part of the contract.

If both parties are *merchants,* the additional terms become part of the contract unless the acceptance is expressly conditional on assent to the terms of the offer or the additional terms materially alter the terms of the original contract or the offeror notifies the offeree that he or she is rejecting the additional terms.

Consideration

Consideration is also required in the formation of sales and lease contracts.
However, unlike common law, the UCC indicates that modification of sales and lease contracts do not require consideration, but, they do require the element of *good faith.*
Statute of Frauds

Goods costing $500 or more and lease payments of $1,000 or more must be in writing. The agreement must be signed by the party to be charged.

Exceptions to the Statute of Frauds – These sale and lease situations do not have to meet the writing requirement of the Statute of Frauds:

Specially Manufactured Goods
Admissions in Pleadings or Court
Part Acceptance

Important Note: If both parties are merchants and one of the parties to the oral contract sends written confirmation within a reasonable time after entering into the contract and the other merchant does not object to the contract within ten days of his or her receipt of the confirmation, then the Statute of Frauds is satisfied.

Modification Required to be in Writing
If the parties state that the modification must be in writing, then it has to be. However, in general, an oral modification is sufficient if it does not violate the Statute of Frauds.

Parol Evidence

A rule that states that a written contract is the complete and final expression of the party's agreement.

Any prior or contemporaneous oral or written statements to the contract may not be introduced to alter or contradict or add to the written contract.

Exceptions to the parol evidence rule:
When the contract's express terms are unclear, the court may consider the course of performance, course of dealing and usage of trade as outside sources to clarify the terms of the parties' agreement.

Refresh Your Memory

The following exercise will enable you to refresh your memory on the rules and principles presented to you in this chapter. Read each question twice and place your answer in the blanks provided. Review the chapter material for any question you miss or are unable to remember.

1. What is the name of the statutory based law that covers most facets of commercial transactions called? _____

2. Article 2 and Article 2A of the Uniform Commercial Code govern _____.

3. _____ are tangible things that are moveable at the time they are identified to the contract.

4. A sale that involves both goods and services is called a _____ _____.

5. Article _____ is primarily concerned with personal property leases.

6. A _____ is a transfer of the right to the possession and use of the named goods for a set term in return for a specified consideration.

7. How may an offer for a contract for the sale or lease of goods be formed? _____
   _____

8. What price will the Uniform Commercial Code affix to a good if none is stated? _____
   _____

9. If the parties to a sales contract do not agree to the place, time and manner of delivery of the goods, where will the place of delivery be? _____

10. What type of acceptance does the Uniform Commercial Code permit? _____
    _____

11. If one or both parties to a sales contract are both nonmerchants, any additional terms would be considered _____ _____ to the contract.

12. According to the Statute of Frauds, what types of sales and lease contracts need to be in writing? _____

13. Part of the _____ _____ rule states that "when a sales or lease contract is evidenced by a writing that is intended to be a final expression of the parties' agreement ... the terms of the writing may not be contradicted by evidence..."

14. What three situations involving a sales or lease contract will still warrant their enforcement despite the fact that they are not in writing as per the Statute of Frauds? _____
    _____

15. What act enables the prosecution of Fraud over the Internet? _____
    _____

Critical Thought Exercise

Apex Mattress Company, for whom you are the vice-president of material acquisition, entered into an oral agreement with Davis Wool Ranch (DWR), a wool supplier, in which DWR agreed to sell Apex 800 bundles of wool, each weighing 350 pounds. Shortly after your conversation with Dan Davis of DWR, you sent Davis an e-mail confirming the terms of the oral contract. Davis did not respond to the e-mail or offer any objection to the terms stated in the e-mail. When the delivery date arrived four months later, you contacted DWR to finalize the delivery terms. DWR stated that there was no agreement and DWR had sold the 800 bundles to Fluffy-Air Mattress because the price of wool had doubled on the open market since the date of the oral agreement. The board of directors of Apex requests that you inform them of your position in regards to bringing suit against DWR and the likelihood that Apex will prevail.

Write a memo to the board setting forth your position and authority for your conclusion.

Answer. _____

_____

_____

_____

_____

_____

_____

_____

_____

_____

_____

_____

_____

_____

_____

_____

_____

_____

_____

Practice Quiz

True/False:

1. ____ A lessor is the individual who transfers the right of use and possession of goods under a lease. [p 383]

2. ____ Goods are tangible things that are immobile at the time of their identification to the contract. [p 382]

3. ____ Stocks, bonds, patents and money are tangible goods. [p 382]

4. ____ A finance lease is a three party transaction. [p 384]

5. ____ Article 2 of the U.C.C. governs such things as equipment, and auto leases. [p 383]

6. ____ Under the UCC, an agreement sufficient to constitute a contract for the sale or lease of goods may not be found if the moment of its making is undetermined. [p 384]

7. ____ Under a finance lease, the lessor selects, manufactures or supplies the goods. [p 384]

8. ____ Sale and lease contracts require an offer, acceptance and consideration. [p 384]

9. ____ The UCC is very lenient with open contract terms. [p 384]

10. ____ Under the UCC rules, a court will not fill in gaps if terms are missing. [p 384]

11. ____ A seller or buyer who reserves the right to fix a price must do so in good faith. [p 385]

12. ____ If Jon, a seller and Nathan, a buyer do not agree on payment terms, payment is due when Nathan accepts the goods. [p 385]

13. ____ When goods are to be shipped but the shipper is not named, the buyer is obligated to make the shipping arrangements. [p 384]

14. ____ The firm offer rule states that a merchant who offers to buy, sell, or lease goods and gives a separate signed, written assurance that the offer will be held open cannot revoke the offer for the time state, or if no time is stated, for a reasonable time, not to exceed three months. [p 385]

15. ____ Common law and the UCC state that a contract is created when the offeree sends an acceptance to the offeror, not when the offeror receives the acceptance. [p 385]

16. ____ If an order or other offer to buy goods requires prompt or current shipment the offer is accepted if the seller holds the goods and waits for the buyer to pick them up. [p 386]

17. ____ An accommodation is a shipment that is offered to the buyer as a concession for the original shipment when the original shipment cannot be filled. [p 386]

18. ____ Consideration is required for the formation of lease and sales contracts. [p 387]

19. ____ A modification of a lease or sales contract requires consideration to be binding. [p 387]

20. ____ Generally speaking, contracts for specially manufactured goods do not need to be in writing. [p 388]

21. ____ As a rule, oral modifications to sales and lease contracts are binding if they do not violate the Statute of Frauds. [p 389]

22. ____ If an oral modification brings a contract within the Statute of Frauds, then it must be in writing in order to be enforceable. [p 389]

23. ___ The purpose of the parol evidence rule is to ensure certainty in written sales and lease contracts. [p 389]

24. ___ Shawndra and Janet entered into a written agreement for the purchase of Shawndra's boat. Janet may be allowed to introduce an oral conversation that took place at the same time as the written agreement whereby Janet claims Shawndra agreed to reupholster the boats vinyl seats. Janet will be allowed to introduce this oral conversation. [p 389]

25. ___ Karissa, a lessor, orally contracts to lease 60 video arcade games to Monique and Monique accepts the first 15 tendered by Karissa. Thereafter Monique refuses to take delivery of the remaining 45 arcade games. Monique must pay for the 15 games she originally received and accepted. [p 388]

Multiple Choice:

26. Goods for $500 or more must [p 387]
    a. be insured.
    b. be in writing.
    c. be inspected.
    d. all of the above.

27. Examples of things that are severable from real estate and are considered goods are [p 382]
    a. stocks, patents, bonds.
    b. money, coins.
    c. dental services and legal services.
    d. minerals, structures, and growing crops.

28. A merchant is [p 383]
    a. a person who deals in the good of the kind involved in the transaction.
    b. a person by his or her occupation holds him or herself out as having knowledge or skill peculiar to the good involved in the transaction.
    c. answer a only.
    d. answers a and b.

29. Article 2 applies to [p 383]
    a. merchants.
    b. nonmerchants.
    c. sales contracts.
    d. all of the above.

30. In a finance lease situation, the lessor [p 384]
    a. selects goods.
    b. acquires title to the goods or right to their possession and use in connection with the terms of the lease.
    c. manufactures goods.
    d. supplies the goods.

31. The term gap-filling rules refers to [p 384]
    a. layman supplied language to bridge the gap between legal terms and layman's terms.
    b. open terms that are permitted to be read into a sales or lease contract.
    c. acceptance by a lessor of the terms of the lease.
    d. delivery in an authorized way and made by way of document of title.

32. Contracts involving a mixed sale are [p 382]
    a. governed by the UCC if the goods are the predominant part of the transaction.
    b. are not given any guidance by the UCC on how to decide them.
    c. are decided by the courts on a case-by-case basis.
    d. all of the above.

33. An offer to make a sales or lease contract may be accepted [p 386]
    a. by a specified manner.
    b. by a specified method of communication.
    c. by any reasonable manner or method of communication.
    d. by both a specified manner and method of communication.

34. If Josephine has had a reasonable opportunity to inspect goods bought from Alma, Josephine may accept the goods by [p 386]
    a. signifying that the goods do not meet the standard she expected.
    b. signifying that she will not take the goods.
    c. signifying that the goods were perishable in a volatile market.
    d. signifying that the goods are conforming.

35. If both parties to a lease or sales contract are merchants, the Statute of Frauds requirement can be met if [p 388]
    a. one of the parties to the oral agreement sends a written confirmation within a reasonable time after contracting and the other party does not give written notice of an objection within 10 days of receiving the confirmation.
    b. one of the parties sends an oral confirmation.
    c. one of the parties to the oral agreement sends a written confirmation.
    d. one of the parties has his or her agent or broker send an oral confirmation.

Short Answer:

36. List three things that are not goods. [p 382] _____
    _____

37. Minerals, structures and growing crops are considered to be _____. [p 382]

38. Who is the person who acquires right to possession and use of goods under a lease?
    [p 384] _____

39. A three-party transaction consisting of the lessor, the lessee and the vendor (supplier) is a
    _____ _____. [p 384]

40. When open terms are read into a sales or lease contract, this is referred to as _____
    _____ rules. [p 384]

41. The maximum amount of time permitted under the firm offer rule is _____ _____. [p 385]

42. Modification of a sales or lease contract must be made in _____ _____. [p 388]

43. When express terms are not clear and need interpretation, what three things will the court look at? [p 389] _____, _____, _____

44. An _____ contract is where an offeree pays consideration to keep the offer open. [p 385]

45. Article 2A of the UCC governs _____. [p 383]

46. What is a mixed sale? [p 382] _____
_____

47. The _____ _____ _____ is a comprehensive statutory scheme that includes laws that cover most aspects of contract transactions. [p 381]

48. _____ are tangible things that are moveable at the time of identification to the contract. [p 381]

49. Under the _____ _____ rule, the offeree's acceptance must be the same as the offer. [p 387]

50. An accommodation contract is _____
_____. [p 386]

Answers to Refresh Your Memory

1. Uniform Commercial Code [p 381]
2. govern personal property leases [p 381]
3. goods [p 382]
4. mixed sale [p 382]
5. Article 2A of the UCC [p 383]
6. lease [p 384]
7. A contract for the lease or sale of goods may be made in any manner adequate to show agreement. [p 384]
8. a reasonable price [p 384]
9. seller's place of business [p 385]
10. any reasonable manner or method of communication [p 386]
11. proposed additions [p 387]
12. Contracts for the sale of goods $500 or more and lease contracts involving payments of $1,000 or more must be in writing. [p 387]
13. parol evidence [p 389]
14. specially manufactured goods, admissions in pleadings or court, part acceptance [p 388]
15. Federal Trade Commission Act [p 390]

Critical Thought Exercise Model Answer

If both parties to an oral sales contract are merchants, the Statute of Frauds requirement can be satisfied if one of the parties to the oral agreement sends a written confirmation of the sale within a reasonable time after making the agreement and the other merchant does not give written notice of an objection to the contract within 10 days after receiving the confirmation. If both merchants are within the United States, UCC section 2-201(2) will control. If one of the merchants is a foreign entity, then the 1980 United Nations Convention on Contracts for the International Sal of Goods (CISG) will apply. Under the CISG, Article 11, an international sales contract "need not be concluded in or even evidenced by writing and is not subject to any other requirements as to form."

When the confirming e-mail was sent to DWR, they did not respond within a ten-day period or voice any objections to the contents of our e-mail. Modernly, an e-mail can serve as a writing. Thus, Apex had a legally binding contract with DWR. The failure of DWR to tender delivery of the 800 bundles of wool on the delivery date put them in breach. The fact that DWR desired to sell the wool for a larger profit hurts their position and helps us because of the requirement that they deal with us in good faith.

Lastly, we will have to obtain the wool from another source and may be required to pay a premium for the wool because of the urgency that we face due to the actions of DWR. We should be able to recover damages in an amount equal to the difference between the contract price and market price at the time we enter into a new contract with a different wool supplier.

Answers to Practice Quiz

True/False:

1. True   An individual who transfers the right of possession and use of goods under a lease is called the lessor.
2. False   Goods are tangible things that are mobile (not immobile) at the time of their identification to the contract.
3. False   These are all examples of intangible things.
4. True   A finance lease consists of the lessor, lessee and the supplie thereby making it a three-party transaction.
5. False   Article 2 of the UCC governs sales of goods not leases.
6. False   The UCC provides that an agreement that is adequate to constitute a sale or lease of goods may still be found despite not knowing when it was made.
7. False   The lessor acquires title to the good or the right to their possession and use in connection with the terms of the lease.
8. True   Under the UCC, sales and lease contracts also require an offer, acceptance and consideration to be binding.
9. True   The UCC will utilize gap-filling rules when there are missing terms and is very lenient in this area.
10. False   As was stated in the previous answer, if there is a missing term, the court will read certain terms into a sales or lease contract if the parties intended to make a contract and there is a reasonably certain basis for giving an appropriate remedy.
11. True   UCC 2-305 (2) states that when a seller or buyer reserves the right to set a price, he or she must do so in good faith.

12. False   Payment is due at the time and place that Nathan is to receive the goods, not when he accepts the goods.
13. False   The seller is obligated to make the shipping arrangements where the goods are to be shipped, but the shipper is not named.
14. True   UCC 2-205, 2A-205 states the requirements and time limitations of the firm offer rule.
15. True   A contract is created with the offeree sends and acceptance to the offeror. This is true for both common law and the UCC.
16. False   The offer is accepted if the seller promptly promises to ship the goods or promptly ships either conforming or nonconforming goods. The shipment of conforming goods signals acceptance of the buyer's offer.
17. True   An accommodation is a shipment that is offered to the buyer as a replacement for the original shipment when the original shipment cannot be filled.
18. True   Consideration is a necessary requirement in order for a sales or lease contract to be formed.
19. False   UCC 2-209(1), 2A-208(1) state that an agreement modifying a sales or lease contract does not need consideration to be binding.
20. True   The case of specially manufactured goods is a situation in which a contract will be enforceable despite not being writing if the goods are not suitable for sale or lease to others in the ordinary course of the lessor's or seller's business and the seller or lessor has made commitments for their procurement or a substantial beginning of their manufacture.
21. True   In the absence of an agreement between the parties requiring modifications to be in writing, oral modifications to a sales or lease contract are binding if they do not violate the Statute of Frauds.
22. True   An oral modification must be in writing if the contract is brought within the Statute of Frauds.
23. True   The parol evidence rule was promulgated so that written contracts would evince the parties' final expression of their agreement, thereby leaving no room for doubt.
24. False   The parol evidence rule prevents Janet from introducing her oral conversation with Shawndra, as it would contradict the parties written agreement. There is nothing in the facts to indicate that the terms of the parties' agreement is not clear on its face. However, if that uncertainty were the case, then the court would look at the course of performance, course of dealing and usage of trade with respect to the agreement. Further, there is nothing that would indicate that Janet was using the oral agreement to demonstrate, fraud, duress or a mistake. The facts as they stand would not permit the use of parol evidence to be introduced.
25. True   Monique's acceptance of the first fifteen video arcade games from Karissa is a classic example of part acceptance. Even though their contract was not in writing, it is a contract that is enforceable to the extent to which Monique received and accepted the goods from Karissa.

Multiple Choice:

26. B   Answer B is correct, as the Statute of Frauds requires goods for $500 or more to be in writing. Answer A is incorrect, as though it might be a good idea to insure goods costing $500 or more it is not a requirement. Answer C is incorrect as there is no rule that correlates a dollar amount and an inspection. Answer D is incorrect for the reasons given above.

27. D Answer D is correct, as mineral, structures and growing crops are severable as per Article 2 of the UCC. Answer A is incorrect as stocks, patents and bonds are intangible items that do not fall within the UCC's definition of goods. Answer B is incorrect as money and coins also do not fall within the UCC's definition of goods. Answer C is incorrect, as contracts for the provision of services are not covered by Article 2 of the UCC.

28. D Answer D is the correct answer as both answer A and answer C correctly define what a merchant is. Answer B is incorrect as answer A is not the only definition of what a merchant is.

29. D Answer D is correct as Article 2 applies to merchants and nonmerchants and is primarily concerned with sales contracts thereby making Answers A, B, and C all correct choices.

30. B Answer B is correct as it correctly states the role of the lessor in a finance situation. Answers A, C and D are simply incorrect statements.

31. B Answer B is correct as the UCC attempts to prevent against the contract from failing for indefiniteness by allowing open terms to be read into a contract by way of gap-filling rules. Answer A is an incorrect statement of law. Answer C is incorrect as gap-filling rules and acceptance have nothing to do with one another. Answer D is incorrect as it makes no sense and does not properly address the meaning and function of gap-filling rules.

32. D Answer D is correct as all three statements in answers A, B, and C correctly state the law as well as facts concerning a mixed sale.

33. C Answer C is correct as any reasonable manner or method of communication is a proper way to accept an offer to make a sales or lease contract. Answer A is incorrect as a broad statement such as "specified manner" may not be reasonable. Answer B is incorrect as the statement "by a specified means of communication" may not be reasonable. Answer D is incorrect for the reasons given above.

34. D Answer D is correct as Josephine's acceptance of the goods after a reasonable inspection may be signified by indicating that the goods are conforming. Answer A is incorrect, as an acceptance would not necessarily include a statement of the goods not meeting the standard she expected. Answer B indicates rejection and not acceptance. Answer C is incorrect as signifying the perishability of goods in a volatile market is not a recognized means of acceptance.

35. A Answer A is correct as it properly states the law with regard to merchants and the Statute of Frauds. Answer B is incorrect as sending an oral confirmation will not satisfy the Statute of Frauds. Answer C is incorrect as sending a written confirmation is not enough to satisfy the Statute of Frauds. Answer D is incorrect as sending a party's agent or broker with an oral confirmation is also insufficient under the Statute of Frauds.

Short Answer:

36. stocks, bonds and money
37. goods
38. lessee
39. finance lease
40. gap-filling
41. three months
42. good faith
43. course of performance, course of dealing, usage of trade
44. option
45. leases
46. A sale that involves both the provision of a good and a sale is a mixed sale.

47. Uniform Commercial Code
48. goods
49. mirror image
50. a shipment that is offered to the buyer as a replacement for the original shipment when the original shipment cannot be filled.

Chapter 20

PERFORMANCE OF SALES AND LEASE CONTRACTS

Chapter Overview

This chapter provides a clear understanding of sales and destination contracts as well as risk of loss and the passage of title to goods. Additionally, it provides a good understanding of sales on approval and how it differs between a sale or return. Further emphasis is placed on insurable interest in goods, good faith purchasers for value and the rules that were created to prevent fraud in bulk transfers of goods.

Objectives

Upon completion of the exercises in this chapter, you should be able to:
1. Explain the difference between a shipment and destination contract and when title passes.
2. Explain the different shipment and delivery terms.
3. Identify who bears the risk of loss when goods are damaged or lost in shipment.
4. Differentiate between a sale on approval and a sale or return.
5. Discuss a sale on consignment.
6. Classify who has an insurable interest in goods.
7. Determine who bears the risk of loss when goods are stolen and resold.
8. Explain the meaning of a good faith purchaser for value.
9. Explain the meaning of a buyer in the ordinary course of business.
10. Discuss the rules designed to prevent fraud in bulk transfers of goods.

Practical Application

You should be able to determine what type of contract has been formed as you analyze the shipping terms. Additionally you should be able to determine who bears the risk of loss in situations involving damaged, lost or stolen and resold goods. You will have gained a better familiarity with the laws involving consignments, as well as laws that will assist you in protecting against fraud with bulk transfers of goods.

Helpful Hints

As you peruse the material in this chapter, it is helpful to keep in mind who is receiving the most benefit with regard to the type of contract the parties are entering into. If you remember that the seller begins with the letter "s" and usually will want a shipment (also begins with the letter "s") contract as the carrier that the goods are placed on will then bare the risk of loss. Further, that a buyer will want the contract to be a destination contract as the seller will bare the risk of loss up until the time that the buyer receives the goods.

The remaining rules in this chapter are fairly easy to learn and have been categorized in an order that will make sense as you apply each to any given fact situation. One of the easiest ways to analyze facts in this area is to ask the following questions in the following order.

1) Who are the parties?
2) Have the goods been identified to the contract?
3) Do the parties have a shipment or a destination contract?
4) Who bears the risk of loss in light of the type of contract that exists?
5) What if anything has happened to the goods?
6) Are there any third parties involved?
7) If so, what is their capacity or role in the facts?
8) Are there any special rules of law that apply?

Study Tips

Identification

This can occur at any time and in any manner.
If no time is specified, then the UCC will state when it occurs.
Already existing goods are identified at the contract's inception.
Goods that are part of a bulk shipment are identified when specific merchandise is separated or tagged.

Shipment contract

Creation is accomplished in one of two ways:
1) by using the term shipment contract or
2) using delivery terms such as F.O.B., F.A.S., C.I.F. or C.& F

This requires the seller to ship and deliver goods to the buyer via a common carrier.
Proper shipping arrangements are required.
Title passes to the buyer at the time and place of shipment.
Risk of loss passes to the buyer when conforming goods are delivered to the carrier.

Destination contract

Creation is accomplished in one of two ways:
1) by using the term destination contract or
2) using delivery terms such as: F.O.B. *place of destination*, ex-ship, or no-arrival, no-sale contract

This requires the seller to deliver the goods to buyers place of business or another specified destination.
The seller is also required to replace any goods lost in transit.
Title passes when the seller tenders delivery of the goods at the specified destination.
Risk of loss does not pass until the goods are tendered at the specified destination.

Special Situation Involving Goods That Are Not Moved

Where goods are not required to be moved by the seller, passage of title is dependent upon whether or not document of title is required to be given to the buyer.

If the Seller is a Merchant –Risk of loss does not pass until the goods are received.

If the Seller is a Nonmerchant – Risk of loss occurs when there is a *tender of delivery* of the goods.

Sale on Approval

A sale does not occur unless the buyer accepts the goods.
The situation presents itself when a merchant allows a buyer to take the goods home for a specified period of time to determine if it meets the customer's needs.

Acceptance is shown by:
1) expressly accepting the goods
2) failing to notify the seller of buyer's rejection
3) use of the goods inconsistently with the purpose of the trial

Risk of loss and title stay with the seller and do not pass until the buyer accepts the goods.
Goods are not subject to buyer's creditor's claims until buyer accepts them.

Sale or Return

The seller delivers the goods to the buyer letting the buyer know that he or she may return them if they are not used or resold within a stated period of time.

If the buyer doesn't return them within a reasonable time, the goods are considered sold.

Risk of loss and title pass when the buyer takes possession of the goods.
Buyer's creditors may make claims against the buyer while the goods are in the buyer's possession.

Risk of Loss Involving Breach of Contract Situations

Seller in Breach

Breach occurs when the seller tenders nonconforming goods to the buyer.
If the buyer has the right to reject the goods, the *risk of loss* stays with the seller until the nonconformity or defect is cured or the buyer accepts the non-conforming goods.

Buyer in Breach

Breach occurs where the buyer refuses to take delivery of conforming goods. Also, if the buyer repudiates the contract or otherwise breaches the contract.
The *risk of loss* rests on the buyer for a commercially reasonable time.
Buyer is liable for any loss in excess of insurance covered by the seller.

Risk of Loss in Lease Contracts

The parties may agree who will bear the risk of loss if the goods are lost or destroyed.

If there is no provision, the UCC states that in an ordinary lease, the *risk of loss* stays with the lessor. If it is a finance lease, then the *risk of loss* passes to the lessee. [UCC 2A-219]

If tender of delivery of goods fails to conform to the lease contract, the *risk of loss* stays with the lessor or supplier until acceptance or cure. [UCC 2A-220(1)(a)].

Sales by Nonowners

This category involves individuals who sell goods that they do not have good title to.

Void Title and Lease: Stolen Goods

Where the buyer purchases goods from a thief, title to the goods does not pass and the lessee does not require any leasehold interest in the goods.

The real owner of the goods may reclaim the goods from the buyer or lessee. Title is void.

Voidable Title: Sales or Lease of Goods to Good Faith Purchasers for Value

A seller has voidable title to goods if the goods were obtained by fraud, dishonored check, or impersonation of another person.

An individual with voidable title may transfer good title to goods to a good faith purchaser for value or a good faith subsequent lessee.

Note, a good faith purchaser for value is one who pays consideration or rent for the goods to one he or she honestly believes has good title to those goods. The real owner cannot reclaim the goods from this type of purchaser.

Entrustment Rule

If an owner entrusts the possession of his or her goods to a merchant who deals in the particular type of goods, the merchant may transfer all rights to *a buyer in the ordinary course of business.* The real owner cannot reclaim the goods from this type of buyer.

Article 6 of Bulk Sales

The rules under Article 6 of the UCC established rules that were made to prevent fraud when there is a bulk transfer of goods. This often happens when assets to a business are sold. The owner transfers a major part of the business's merchandise, inventory, equipment or material not in the ordinary course of business.

Requirements for a Bulk Transfer:
1) Seller is to give buyer a list of all of the business's creditors.
2) The buyer is to notify all of the listed creditors at least 10 days prior to taking possession of or paying for the goods. The buyer is not responsible or liable for creditors that are not listed.
If the requirements are met, then the buyer receives title to the goods free of all of seller's creditor's claims. If the requirements are not met, then the buyer takes possession subject to the seller's creditor's claims for six months after the date of possession.

Refresh Your Memory

The following exercise will enable you to refresh your memory on the rules and principles presented to you in this chapter. Read each question twice and place your answer in the blanks provided. Review the chapter material for any question you miss or are unable to remember.

1. The UCC has promulgated specific rules for determining the passage of _____ in sales contracts.

2. The common law places the _____ of _____ to goods on the party who had title to the goods.

3. Goods that are part of a larger mass of goods are identified when _____
    _____.

4. Future goods are those that are not _____.

5. Excluding crops and unborn children, future goods are identified when the goods are
    _____, _____, or otherwise designated by the seller or lessor as
    the goods referred to in the parties contract.

6. A _____ contract requires the seller to ship goods to the buyer via a
    common carrier.

7. A _____ contract requires the seller to deliver the goods either to the buyer's
    place of business or to another destination set forth in the sales contract.

8. A shipment contract requires the seller to ship goods _____ to the contract via a
    _____.

9. A destination contract requires the seller to _____ conforming goods to a specific
    destination.

10. What types of terms signify a destination contract? _____
    _____

11. Who bears the risk of loss if the goods are stolen or destroyed after the contract date and before the
    buyer picks up the goods from the seller who is a merchant? _____
    _____

12. When do nonmerchant sellers pass the risk of loss to the buyer? _____
    _____

13. Give the definition of a bailee. _____
    _____

14. A type of sale in which there is not an actual sale unless the buyer accepts the goods is a _____
    _____.

15. An arrangement where a seller delivers goods to the consignee for sale is a _____.

Critical Thought Exercise

Bristol Physical Therapy (BPT) contracted with Summit Pools, Inc. for the purchase of a "fully installed portable therapy whirlpool" for the sum of $14,000. The price included all labor and parts but the order form was not itemized. The freight carrier hired by the manufacturer delivered the pool to the parking lot just outside the building occupied by BPT. A receptionist for BPT signed the delivery invoice and immediately called Summit Pools. When the installation crew for Summit Pools arrived five days later to install the whirlpool, it was gone.

In this situation, had the risk of loss of the whirlpool passed from Summit Pools to BPT?

Answer: _____

_____

_____

_____

_____

_____

_____

_____

_____

_____

_____

_____

_____

Practice Quiz

True/False:

1. ____ The Uniform Commercial Code dictates when the identification of goods occurs. [p 395]

2. ____ The seller or lessor retains the risk of loss of the goods until the goods are identified to the contract. [p 395]

3. ____ Goods such as unborn young animals and crops to be harvested cannot be identified to a contract. [p 395]

4. ____ Once the goods exist and are identified, the seller may pass title to the buyer. [p 395]

5. ____ The time and place of passage of title will be the same regardless if a document of title is required. [p 395]

6. ____ The UCC places the risk of loss to goods on the party who has title to the goods. [p 397]

7. ____ The UCC is reluctant to allow the parties to a sales contract too much leniency in determining who will bear the risk of loss if the goods subject to the contract are lost or destroyed. [p 397]

8. ___ Sales contracts are recognized as being shipment contracts rather than destination contracts. [p 397]

9. ___ The delivery terms to a contract will dictate the risk of loss of goods while they are being transported. [p 397]

10. ___ Marla's Magnificent Creations, a large Oklahoma clothing manufacturer places the term, F.O.B. Atlanta when shipping an order of clothes to Tamara's Boutique in Atlanta, Georgia. Marla's will bear the expense and risk of loss until Tamara's Boutique has the goods tendered upon it. [p 398]

11. ___ Under a no-arrival, no-sale contract, the buyer must bear the expense and risk of loss of the goods during transportation. [p 398]

12. ___ A sale does not occur in a situation involving a sale on approval until the buyer accepts the goods. [p 399]

13. ___ In a sale on approval, the risk of loss and title to the goods remains with the buyer. [p 400]

14. ___ In a sale or return contract, the seller delivers goods to a buyer making it clear that the buyer may not return the goods if they are not used within a stated or reasonable period of time. [p 400]

15. ___ In a consignment situation, the consignee delivers goods to a consignor to sell. [p 400]

16. ___ A buyer may breach a sales contract if he or she refuses to take delivery of conforming goods. [p 401]

17. ___ Betty purchases goods from Slick, a thief who has stolen them. Betty does not acquire title to these goods and Slick does not acquire a leasehold interest in the goods. [p 403]

18. ___ A good faith purchaser or lessee for value is someone who pays insufficient consideration or rent for goods to the person he or she honestly believes has good title to those goods. [p 403]

19. ___ Article 6 of the UCC provides for efficient ways in transferring large lots of goods. [p 405]

20. ___ Ed buys a television from his friend Doug for fair market value. Doug originally had obtained the television with a dishonored check. The appliance store that sold the television may reclaim the television. [p 403]

21. ___ Cory is short on money and is referred to Pam for buying inexpensive gifts. Cory purchases a diamond bracelet for his girlfriend for pennies on the dollar. Upon further investigation, it is revealed that Pam obtained the diamond bracelet in a jewelry store robbery. The jewelry store may reclaim the diamond bracelet. [p 403]

22. ___ A buyer in the ordinary course of business is an individual who in good faith and without knowledge that the sale violates ownership or security interest of a third party buys the goods in the ordinary course of business from a person in the business selling goods of that kind. [p 403]

23. ___ Title to goods passes even if a person steals the goods. [p 403]

24. ___ Title to goods is voidable if the goods were procured through fraud. [p 403]

25. ___ The parties may provide in their contract that will bear the risk of loss if the goods are lost or destroyed. [p 402]

Multiple Choice

26. Future goods that are in existence are identified when [p 395]
    a. they are conceived or have yet to be harvested.
    b. they are shipped, marked or otherwise designated by the seller or lessor.
    c. they are part of a larger mass of goods.
    d. it is mandated that they be identified.

27. A shipment contract is [p 395]
    a. one requiring the seller to deliver the goods to the buyer's place of business.
    b. one requiring the seller to deliver the goods to a destination specified in the contract between the parties.
    c. one requiring the seller to ship the goods to the buyer via a common carrier.
    d. one requiring the seller to deliver the goods without moving them.

28. If a document of title is required, title passes [p 396]
    a. when and where the buyer delivers the document to the seller.
    b. when and where the buyer delivers the document to the carrier.
    c. when and where the seller delivers the document to the carrier.
    d. when and where the seller delivers the document to the buyer.

29. What option does a buyer have in a sale or return contract? [p 400]
    a. The buyer may deliver the goods to an agreed upon destination.
    b. The buyer has the option of returning all of the goods or any commercial unit of the goods.
    c. The buyer has no option available to him or her in this type of contract.
    d. None of the above.

30. A buyer orders 5,000 toy racecars that light up when pushed along a flat surface. The contract between the parties was a shipment contract. Further, the cars that were shipped were plain racecars that did not have the light up feature. The toy cars are smashed flat while in transit. Who will bear the risk of loss in this situation? [p 401]
    a. The buyer will as it is a shipment contract passing the risk of loss to the buyer.
    b. The buyer will as he or she did not purchase insurance to cover potential loss.
    c. The seller will as he or she did not ship conforming goods.
    d. Both the buyer and seller are responsible due to the nature of their transaction.

31. Jacob wants to purchase insurance to protect against financial loss in case the goods that he sells are damaged, destroyed, lost or stolen. He is told that he must have an insurable interest in the goods. What does this mean? [p 402]
    a. He must have a valid driver's license with no convictions against him.
    b. He must retain title or have a security interest in the goods.
    c. He must sell the goods to a good faith purchaser for value.
    d. He must not have an insurable interest at the same time as the buyer.

32. If Joe steals an entire shipment of computers that are owned by Computer City and resells them to Computer Land who does not know that they are stolen, Computer City may reclaim the goods from Computer Land because [p 403]
    a. it found out where the goods were located.
    b. Computer Land was a good faith purchaser for value.
    c. as a seller with an insurable interest in the computers, Computer City is protected.
    d. Joe had no title in the goods and title was not transferred to Computer Land.

33. A seller or lessor has voidable title to goods if the goods were obtained by [p 403]
    a. fraud.
    b. a dishonored check.
    c. impersonating another person.
    d. All of the above.

34. A person to whom good title can be transferred from a person with voidable title is [p 403]
    a. a thief.
    b. a lessor.
    c. a good faith purchaser for value.
    d. the real owner.

35. A person to whom a lease interest can be transferred from a person with voidable title is [p 403]
    a. a good faith purchaser for value.
    b. a lessee.
    c. an insured interested party.
    d. a good faith subsequent lessee.

Short Answer:

36. The irrevocable _____ of _____ was developed to manage international sales risks whereby the seller is afraid that he or she will not be paid after delivery of the goods and the buyer is afraid that he or she will not receive the goods after paying for them. [p 396]

37. Generally speaking, goods that are shipped by railroad, ship, or truck may be considered to be pursuant to a _____ contract if there is no indication of the destination stated along with the shipping term. [p 397]

38. In a shipment contract, the _____ bears the risk of loss during transportation. [p 397]

39. In a destination contract, the risk of loss does not pass until the goods are tendered to the buyer at a _____ _____. [p 397]

40. The shipping term C.I.F. stands for _____, _____, and _____, which are costs that the seller is responsible for. [p 398]

41. The shipping term F.A.S. requires the seller to deliver and tender the goods _____ _____. [p 397]

42. When does a sale on approval occur? [p 399] _____

43. A seller breaches a sales contract if he or she tenders _____ goods. [p 401]

44. In the case of an ordinary lease, the risk of loss is kept by the _____. [p 402]

45. If the goods are so nonconforming that the buyer has the right to reject them, the risk of loss remains on the seller until the defect or nonconformity is cured, or the buyer _____ _____. [p 401]

46. A buyer who breaches a sales contract before the risk of loss would normally pass to him or her bears the risk of loss as to which goods? [p 401] _____

47. A holder of goods who is not a seller or a buyer is a _____. [p 399]

48. In a sale on approval, the risk of loss remains with the _____. [p 399]

49. Give an example of a document of title. [p 396] _____

50. Legal, tangible evidence of ownership of goods is known as _____. [p 395]

Answers to Refresh Your Memory

1. title [p 395]
2. risk of loss [p 395]
3. the specific merchandise is designated [p 395]
4. yet in existence [p 395]
5. shipped, marked or otherwise designated by the lessor or seller. [p 395]
6. shipment [p 395]
7. destination [p 395]
8. conforming, carrier [p 397]
9. deliver [p 397]
10. F.O.B. place of destination, ex-ship, or no-arrival, no-sale contract [p 397]
11. A merchant-seller bears the risk of loss between the time of contracting and the time that the buyer picks up the goods. [p 399]
12. Non-merchant sellers pass the risk of loss to the buyer upon tender of delivery of the goods. [p 399]
13. A holder of goods who is not a seller or a buyer. [p 399]
14. sale on approval [p 399]
15. consignment [p 400]

Critical Thought Exercise Model Answer

The goods in this case, a whirlpool, had been delivered to the customer and a representative of BPT had signed for the shipment. The whirlpool had been placed on BPT's property by the common carrier. Normally, the risk of loss passes in a shipment contract when the goods are placed with the common carrier. In this case, however, the goods are being resold by Summit Pools to BPT. Thus, the risk of loss will not pass to BPT until they have been delivered to BPT as dictated by the agreement. In this agreement, the goods were to be fully installed as part of the contract and there was no separation of the goods from the installation services in the agreement.

In a mixed goods and services contract, a court will look to see whether the goods or services are the predominant item to be provided. The whirlpool being sold to BPT is considered a portable unit, so the installation services appear to be a secondary purpose in the sales contract. Risk of loss will therefore not pass to BPT until the whirlpool is fully installed as required by the agreement. The theft or loss of the whirlpool unit will fall upon Summit Pools.

Answers to Practice Quiz

True/False:

1. True In the absence of an agreement indicating the time and manner of the identification of goods, the UCC may mandate when identification occurs.
2. True The goods must be identified before risk of loss and title will pass from the seller to the buyer.
3. False Unborn young animals are identified at conception and crops to be harvested are identified when the crops are planted or otherwise become growing crops.
4. True Title to the goods may be transferred from the seller to the buyer once the goods have been identified.
5. False The time and passage of title does depend on whether the seller is to deliver a document of title.
6. False This was the law under common law not the UCC. The UCC mandates who will bear the risk of loss.
7. False Article 2 does allow the parties to a sales contract to agree among themselves who will bear the risk of loss if the goods subject to the contract are lost or destroyed.
8. True Sales contracts are presumed to be shipment contracts rather than destination contracts.
9. True The risk of loss of goods while they are being transported depends on the contract and the delivery terms contained therein.
10. True The shipping term F.O.B. Atlanta indicates that the Oklahoma seller intended to create a destination contract whereby Marla's will have to bear the expense and risk of loss until the goods are tendered at Tamara's Boutique in Atlanta, Georgia.
11. False The seller must bear the expense and risk of loss of the goods during transportation in a no-arrival, no-sale contract.
12. True In a sale on approval, there is no sales until and unless the buyer accepts the goods.
13. False The risk of loss to the title of the goods remains with the seller in a sale on approval.
14. False The seller delivers goods to a buyer with the understanding that the buyer may return the goods if they are not used or resold within a stated or reasonable period of time under a sale or return contract.
15. False The consignor delivers goods to the consignee to sell.
16. True A buyer's refusal to take delivery of conforming goods constitutes a breach of contract.
17. True Where a buyer buys goods or a lessee leases goods from a thief who has stolen them, the purchaser, in this case Betty, does not acquire title to the goods and the lessee, here Slick, does not acquire a leasehold interest in the goods.
18. False A good faith purchaser for value is someone who pays sufficient (not insufficient) consideration or rent for the goods to the person he or she honestly believes has good title to those goods.
19. False Article 6 of the UCC created rules that were made to prevent fraud when there is a bulk transfer of goods.
20. False The appliance store cannot reclaim the television because Ed, the second purchaser bought the television in good faith and for value.

21. True   The jewelry store may reclaim the diamond bracelet because the second purchaser was not a good faith purchaser for value. Pennies on the dollar would not constitute sufficient consideration for a diamond bracelet.
22. True   This correctly states the meaning of a buyer in the ordinary course of business.
23. False   A thief acquires no title to the goods that he or she steals.
24. True   Fraudulently acquired goods prevent title from passing and as such title is voidable.
25. True   The issue of who will bear the risk of loss may be agreed to in a contract between the parties.

Multiple Choice

26. B   Answer B is correct as future goods other than unborn young and harvested crops are identified when the goods are shipped, marked or otherwise designated by the seller or lessor. Answer A is incorrect based on the reasoning given for answer B. Answer C is incorrect as it is irrelevant whether the future existing goods are part of a larger mass of goods or not. Answer D is incorrect as it makes it appear that the only time they have to be identified is if it is mandated in an agreement.
27. C   Answer C is correct, as the seller must ship goods via a common carrier in a shipment contract. Answer A is incorrect as this implies a destination contract. Answer B is incorrect as it clearly gives the explanation for a destination contract. Answer D is incorrect as this is neither a shipment nor a destination contract.
28. D   Answer D is correct as it correctly states when title passes. Answer A is incorrect as the buyer is not the party who would deliver the document of title. Answer B is incorrect, as the buyer would not be delivering the document of title to the carrier. Answer C is incorrect, as the seller would not be delivering the document of title to the carrier either.
29. B   Answer B is correct as the buyer has the option of returning all the goods or any commercial unit of the goods in a sale or return contract. Answer A is incorrect, as it makes no sense in terms of a sale or return contract. Answer C is incorrect as the buyer does have an option of returning all of the goods or any commercial unit of the goods. Answer D is incorrect for the answers stated above.
30. C   Answer C is correct as the seller bears the risk of loss since he or she shipped nonconforming goods. Answer A is incorrect as despite the fact that a shipment contract would ordinarily shift the risk of loss once the seller placed the goods with a carrier, the fact that the seller shipped nonconforming goods is enough to have the risk of loss remain with the seller. Answer B is incorrect, as the fact that the buyer did not purchase insurance to cover the potential loss does not exonerate the seller from the fact that he or she shipped nonconforming goods. Answer D is incorrect as it is an untrue statement, as the buyer does not share in the risk of loss when a seller ships nonconforming goods.
31. B   Answer B is correct as it correctly explains what an insurable interest means. Answer A is incorrect as this answer is referring to insurance one might get for an automobile not with respect to goods being lost, destroyed or damaged. Answer C is incorrect as selling the goods to a good faith purchaser for value has no bearing on a seller's retention of title and security interest in goods. Answer D is incorrect as both the buyer, and seller or lessee and lessor can have an insurable interest in the goods at the same time.
32. D   Answer D is correct as the purchaser, Joe does not acquire title to goods and the lessee does not acquire any leasehold interest in goods thereby making the title void and the goods subject to reclamation by the real owner, Computer City. Answer A is incorrect, as this does not supply the proper reasoning as to why Computer City may reclaim the goods. Answer B is not correct as the rules applicable to stolen goods as is the case with this fact situation are different than that of a seller having voidable title whereby a good faith purchaser for value is involved which in turn precludes the original owner from reclaiming the goods. Answer C is incorrect, as the insurable

interest would provide reimbursement from the insurance company for the loss of the goods verses the right to reclaim the goods.

33. D   Answer D is correct as answers A, B, and C all correctly state when a seller has voidable title to goods.

34. C   Answer C is correct as a person with voidable title to goods can transfer good title to a good faith purchaser for value. Answer A is incorrect, as good title may not be transferred to a thief. Answer B is incorrect as the person accomplishing the transfer is usually the lessor. Answer D is incorrect as it makes no sense.

35. D   Answer D is correct as a good faith subsequent lessee can acquire a lease interest from a person with voidable title. Answer A is incorrect as the term good faith purchaser for value refers to one paying for goods versus the transferring of a lease interest from a person with voidable title. Answer B is incorrect as it is only partially correct by the terminology lessee. Answer C is incorrect, as it makes no sense that a lease interest could be transferred from an insured interested party with voidable title.

Short Answer:

36.   letter of credit
37.   shipping
38.   buyer
39.   specified destination
40.   cost, insurance and freight
41.   alongside the named vessel or on the dock designated and provided by the buyer
42.   When a merchant allows a customer to take the goods home for a specified period of time.
43.   nonconforming
44.   lessor
45.   accepts the nonconforming goods
46.   To any goods identified to the contract.
47.   bailee
48.   seller
49.   warehouse receipt or a bill of lading
50.   title

Chapter 21
REMEDIES FOR BREACH OF
SALES AND LEASE CONTRACTS

Chapter Overview

The Uniform Commercial Code provides several remedies to an injured party based on a breach of a sales or lease contract. This chapter explores the prelitigation as well as litigation remedies available to an injured party. Additionally, the performance of obligations and options of the remedies that are available for breach of sales and lease contracts are also examined.

Objectives

Upon completion of the exercises in this chapter, you should be able to:
1. Describe the seller's and lessor's obligations under a contract.
2. Differentiate between a shipment and destination contract and determine the risk of loss in each.
3. Discuss the "perfect tender rule."
4. Describe the buyer's and lessee's obligations under a contract.
5. Explain what is meant by assurance of performance
6. Explain anticipatory repudiation and the remedies that are available for the same.
7. Discuss what remedies are available to a seller and lessor if a buyer or lessee breaches the contract.
8. Discuss what remedies are available to a buyer or lessee if a seller or lessor breaches the contract.
9. Define the statute of limitations of any oral or written sales or lease contract.
10. Discuss agreements that could affect the remedies available to a buyer or seller under a contract.

Practical Application

This chapter should enable you to know what types of obligations are expected of you as a buyer or a seller. Additionally it will solidify the remedies that are available to you in the event of a breach of a sales or lease contract if you are a buyer and lessee or a seller and lessor.

Helpful Hints

As with many of the chapters involving the area of contracts, it is helpful to organize your studying around the parties as well as the concepts that pertain to those parties. In this chapter, you are studying the buyer and seller's obligations as well as the remedies available in the event of a breach by the buyer or seller. As such, the study tips section has been created to enable you to learn what each parties obligations are as well as what remedies are available to each of them in the event of a breach.

Study Tips

Seller and Lessor's Obligations

Basic obligation – The seller must tender delivery in accordance with his or her contract terms with the buyer.

Tender of Delivery – There are a few things to remember about this topic:
1) Tender of delivery refers to conforming goods.
2) Seller must give the buyer reasonable notice of the delivery and delivery must be at a reasonable hour and goods must be kept for a reasonable time.
3) Goods must be delivered in one single delivery unless the parties agree to another arrangement.

Place of Delivery –The contract may state where delivery is to take place.
1) The contract may state that the buyer will pick up the goods.
2) If nothing is stated in the contract, the UCC will dictate this term.
3) If no carrier is involved, then delivery is at the seller's or lessor's business.
4) If the parties know the goods are located in another location, then that is the place of delivery.
5) If a carrier is involved, it will depend on if the contract is a shipment or a destination contract.
   a. If it is a *shipment* contract, the seller must deliver the goods to the carrier, obtain proper contract documentation and give the buyer notice.
   b. If it is a *destination* contract, the seller is required to deliver the Goods to the buyer's place of business or wherever is designated in the parties' contract. Delivery must be at a reasonable time and in a reasonable manner accompanied with proper notice and documents of title.

Perfect Tender Rule – The seller is under a duty to deliver conforming goods to the buyer.
1) If tender is not perfect, the buyer may:
   a. reject the whole shipment
   b. accept the whole shipment
   c. reject part and accept part of the shipment
2) The parties may also agree to limit the application of the perfect tender rule by doing so in their written contract.
3) If a carrier is involved, the UCC mandates a commercially Reasonable substitute be used if the agreed upon manner of delivery fails or becomes unavailable.

4) If nonconforming goods are delivered, the UCC gives the
   Seller the chance to cure the defective delivery if the time
   For performance has not expired or the lessor gives the
   Buyer notice that he or she will make a conforming delivery
   within the time frame stated in the parties' contract.

Installment contract- One that requires or authorizes the good s to be accepted or
                        delivered in separate lots.
                           1) The UCC alters the perfect tender rule by allowing the buyer to
                              reject the entire shipment if the noncomformity substantially
                              impairs the entire contract.
                           2) The court will view installment contracts on a case-by-case basis.

Destruction of Goods – If the destruction of goods is not the fault of either party and the goods
                  have been identified to the contract, the contract will be void.
                  but, if the goods are partially destroyed, the buyer may then inspect
                  and partially accept the goods or treat it as void. If the buyer opts to
                  accept, compensation will be adjusted accordingly.

Good Faith and Reasonableness – These two principles rule the performance of lease and sales
                  contracts. These principles apply to both the buyer and the seller.

Seller's and Lessor's Remedies

The seller and lessors have several remedies available if the buyer or lessee breaches the contract. These remedies are as follows:

Right to Withhold Delivery – Delivery of the goods may be withheld if the seller is in possession of the goods when the buyer or lessee is in breach. If there has been a partial delivery of the goods when the breach occurs, then the seller or lessor may withhold delivery of the remaining part of the goods. A buyer or lessee's insolvency will also justify a seller or lessor's withholding of delivery of the goods under the contract.

Right To Stop Delivery of Goods in Transit –Goods are in transit when they are in the carrier's bailee's possession. If a buyer is discovered to be insolvent while the goods are in transit, the seller may stop the goods while in transit.
 If the buyer or lessee repudiates the contract, delivery can be withheld only if it is a carload, a planeload or a truckload. Notice to the carrier or bailee is required.

The seller must hold the goods for the buyer after the delivery has been stopped. If the seller resells the goods, the amount received must be credited against the judgment procured against the buyer.

Right to Recover Damages for Breach of Contract – A cause of action to recover damages caused by the breach of contract may be brought where the buyer or lessee repudiates a sales or lease contract or wrongfully rejects tendered goods.

The measure of damages is the difference between the contract price and the market price at the time and place where the goods were delivered plus incidental damages. If this does not place the seller in a position as though the contract was performed, the seller may recover lost profits that would have resulted from full performance plus an allowance for reasonable overhead and incidental damages.

<u>Right to Cancel the Contract</u> – The seller or lessor may cancel the contract if the buyer or lessee breaches the contract by revoking acceptance of the goods, rejects the contract or fails to pay for the goods or repudiates all or any part of the contract. The cancellation may apply to the entire contract or to only the affected goods.

Effect of the cancellation- The seller or lesser who notifies the buyer or lessee of the cancellation is discharged from any further obligations under the contract, and he or she may also seek damages against the buyer or lessee for the breach.

<u>Right to Reclaim Goods</u> – Reclamation refers to a seller or lessor's right to demand the return of goods from the buyer or lessee under certain situations.

Where the buyer is insolvent – Seller has 10 days to demand the return of the goods.

Where the buyer has misrepresented his or her solvency in writing three months before delivery or presents a check that is later dishonored, reclamation may occur at any time.

Requirements of reclamation include:
> Written notice to the buyer or lessee
> Refraining from self-help if the buyer refuses.
> Use of legal proceedings must be instituted.

<u>Right to Dispose of Goods</u> – If the buyer or lessee breaches or repudiates before the seller or lessor disposes of the goods, then the seller may release or resell goods and recover damages from the buyer or lessee.

Disposition of the goods must be in good faith and in a commercially reasonable manner. Disposition may be as a unit or in parcels and publicly or privately. Notice must also be given.

Damages incurred as a result of disposition are measured by the disposition price and the contract price. Incidental damages may also be recovered.

Unfinished Goods- If a sales or lease contract is breached or repudiated before the goods are finished the seller can:
1) stop manufacturing of the goods and resell them for scrap or salvage value or
2) complete the goods and resell, release or otherwise dispose of them.
3) recover damages from the buyer or lessee.

<u>Right to Recover the Purchase Price or Rent</u> – The UCC allows a seller to sue the buyer for the purchase price or rent as provided in the parties sale or lease contract. This remedy is available when:

1) The buyer or lessee accepts the goods but does not pay for them when the rent is due.
2) The buyer or lessee breaches the contract after the goods have been identified to the contract and the seller or lessor cannot dispose of or sell the goods.
3) The goods are damaged or lost after the risk of loss passes to the buyer or lessee.

Buyer and Lesee's Obligations

Basic obligation—If properr tender of delivery is made to the buyer (lessee), the buyer is then obligated to accept and pay for the goods as per the parties' contract or as mandated by the UCC in the event that there is no contract.

Right of Inspection – Buyer has the right to inspect goods that are tendered, delivered or identified to the contract.
1) If the goods are shipped, inspection will be at the time the goods arrive. If the goods are nonconforming, buyer may reject the goods and not pay for them.
2) Parties may agree as to time, place and manner of inspection. If there Is no agreement, then it must be at a reasonable time, place and manner. Reasonableness is determined by common usage of trade, prior course dealings, etc. If the goods conform to the contract, buyer pays for the inspection. If the goods are nonconforming, the seller pays for the inspection.
3) C.O.D. deliveries are not subject to buyer inspection until the buyer pays for the goods.

Payment of the Goods – Goods that are accepted must be paid for when the goods are delivered even if the delivery place is the same as the place where the goods are shipped.
1) Goods paid for on credit have a credit period that begins to run from the time that the goods are shipped.
2) Goods may be paid for using any acceptable method of payment unless The agreed upon terms involve cash only. If cash is all that a seller will accept from the buyer, then the buyer must be given extra time to procure the cash.
3) Payment by check is conditioned on the check being honored

Assurance of Performance – If one party has reasonable grounds to believe that the other party either will not or cannot perform his or her contractual obligations, The other party may demand assurance for performance in writing. Also, the aggrieved party may suspend his or her own performance if it is commercially practicable to do so until the assurance is forthcoming from the potential wrongdoer.

Anticipatory Repudiation – The repudiation of a lease or sales contract by one of the parties before the date set for performance.

    1) Simple wavering of performance does not equate to anticipatory Repudiation.

    2) The aggrieved party may:
        a. await performance for a commercially reasonable time or
        b. treat the contract as breached at the time of the anticipatory repudiation
        c. both remedies allow the aggrieved party to suspend performance.

    3) An anticipatory repudiation may be retracted before the aggrieved parties performance is due if the aggrieved party has not:
        a. cancelled the contract or
        b. materially changed his or her position or
        c. otherwise stated that the repudiation is viewed as final.
        Repudiation may be made by any method as long as the intent to perform the contract is clearly expressed.

Buyer and Lessee's Remedies

The buyer or lessee also has many remedies available to him or her upon the breach of a sales or lease contract by the seller or lessor. These remedies are as follows:

Right to Reject Nonconforming Goods or Improperly Tendered Goods – If tender of delivery fails, the buyer may

    1) reject the whole,
    2) accept the whole or
    3) accept any commercial unit and reject the rest.

Note, a buyer who rejects nonconforming goods must identify the defects that are able to be determined by a reasonable inspection. Rejection must be within a reasonable time after delivery and in a reasonable manner. The buyer must also hold the goods for a reasonable period of time.

Right to Recover Goods from an Insolvent Seller or Lessor – If the buyer makes a partial payment to the seller and the seller or lessor becomes insolvent within tend days of the first payment, the buyer or lessee may recover the goods from the seller or lessor. This is called capture.

Right to Obtain Specific Performance – When the remedy at law is inadequate and the goods are unique, the buyer or lessee may ask for specific performance of the sales or lease contract.

Right to Cover – The buyer or lessee may cover if the seller or lessor fails to make delivery of goods or repudiates the contract or the buyer or lessee rightfully rejects the goods or justifiably revokes their acceptance. Renting or purchasing substitute goods accomplish covering.

<u>Right to Replevy Goods</u> – A buyer or lessee may recover scarce goods wrongfully withheld by a seller or lessor by demonstrating that he or she was unable to cover or the attempts to cover will not come to fruition. This remedy is only available as to goods identified to the lease or sales contract.

<u>Right to Cancel the Contract</u> –Failure to deliver conforming goods , repudiation of the contract by the seller, rightful rejection of the goods, or justifiable revocation of goods that were accepted all may enable the buyer to cancel with respect to the affected goods or the whole contract if the breach is material in nature.

<u>Right to Recover Damages for No delivery or Repudiation</u> – The buyer or lessee may recover damages that equate to the difference between the contract price and the market price, along with incidental and consequential damages, less expenses saved if a seller or lessor fails to deliver the goods or repudiates the sales or lease contract.

<u>Right to Recover Damages for Accepted Nonconforming Goods</u> – A buyer may seek to recover damages from any loss as a result of the nonconforming goods accepted from the seller. Incidental damages as well as consequential damages may also be recovered. The buyer must give notice of the nonconformity to the seller within a reasonable time of when the breach should have been discovered.

<u>Statute of Limitations</u>- Under the UCC, an action for breach of any written or oral sales or lease contract must be within four years. The parties can agree to a one-year statute of limitations.

<u>Agreements Affecting Remedies</u>

<u>Preestablished damages -</u> These are called liquidated damages, which act as a substitute for actual damages.

<u>Consequential damages</u> for the breach of sales or lease contract may be excluded or limited unless it would be unconscionable to do so.

Refresh Your Memory

   The following exercise will enable you to refresh your memory on the rules and principles presented to you in this chapter. Read each question twice and place your answer in the blanks provided. Review the chapter material for any question you miss or are unable to remember.

1. Parties to a sales or lease contract owe a duty to perform the _____ as specified in their agreement.

2. The seller's or lessor's obligation is to transfer and _____ the _____ to the buyer or lessee.

3. When one party breaches the _____ or _____ contract, the UCC gives the aggrieved party a variety of remedies.

4. What are the remedies designed to do for the aggrieved party? _____
    _____

5. The failure of a party to perform an obligation in a sales or least contract is known as
_____.

6. The seller's or lessor's basic obligation is to _____
in accordance with the sales or lease contract.

7. If the parties have no agreement respecting the time, place and manner of delivery, tender
must be made at a _____ hour and the goods must _____
_____.

8. Payment of a sales contract is due _____ unless there has been an
extension of credit arrangement between the parties.

9. If the parties' agreement does not specify where delivery will take place, the _____
will stipulate the place of delivery depending on whether a carrier is involved.

10. In noncarrier cases, the place of delivery is the _____.

11 A sales contract that requires the seller to deliver the goods to the buyer's place of business
or other specified location is a _____ contract.

12. The UCC gives a seller or lessor who delivers nonconforming goods a chance to _____
the nonconformity.

13.. What is an installment contract? _____
_____

14. The UCC alters the perfect tender rule concerning _____ contracts.

15. If goods are shipped, the buyer's right to inspection may take place _____ their
arrival.

Critical Thought Exercise

Sanco Corporation agreed to sell two seven-ton diesel forklifts to Agro-Star, Inc., for $250,000, with an option to purchase four more at $500,000. The forklifts were to be installed in a produce cooling warehouse according to specific design and performance standards. Sanco did not deliver and Agro-Star covered by purchasing different forklifts from Power Arm Lifts for $200,000, plus an additional $300,000 for testing and development by Power Arm Lifts. Agro-Star also bought the four additional lifts that they needed from Power Arm Lifts for $350,000. At trial, Agro-Star is awarded $250,000, the difference between Sanco's price for the first two forklifts and the cost of the first two Power Arm forklifts.

As an officer in Sanco Corporation, you must decide whether to pay the judgment or pay an additional $20,000 in attorney's fees and appeal the judgment. Will you authorize the appeal? Why? Is it fair for Sanco to receive the benefit of a bargain struck by Agro-Star when they covered?

Answer. _____

_____

_____

_____

_____

_____

_____

_____

_____

_____

_____

_____

_____

_____

_____

_____

_____

_____

_____

Practice Quiz

True/False:

1. ___ The obligation of the seller or lessor to transfer and deliver goods to the buyer or lessee pursuant to a sales or lease contract is known as tender of delivery. [p 410]

2. ___ If Eb's Furniture Store calls Charlene Jones at 2:00a.m. to let her know the delivery truck will be at her home in 30 minutes, Charlene must allow Eb to tender delivery of the goods. [p 410]

3. ___ If goods are delivered in lots, payment is calculated for each lot. [p 410]

4. ___ If a seller or lessor does not have a place of business, then the place of delivery is the buyer's business. [p 410]

5. ___ Under a shipment contract, one thing that the seller must do is put the goods in the carrier's possession and contract for the safe and proper transportation of the goods. [p 410]

6. ___ In a destination contract, delivery of the goods is to be tendered at the buyer's place of business or other location designated in the sales contract. [p 411]

7. ___ The seller or lessor is under a duty to deliver nonconforming goods. [p 411]

8. ___ A cure may be attempted if the time for performance has expired and the seller or lessor has notified the buyer or lessee of his or her intention to deliver conforming goods within the time stated in the contract. [p 412]

9. ___ If an installment is impaired and the defect cannot be cured, the buyer or lessee may reject any nonconforming installment if the value of the installment is impaired and the defect cannot be cured. [p 413]

10. ___ A contract is void if identified goods to a lease or sales contract are totally destroyed through no fault of either party before the risk of loss passes to the buyer or lessee. [p 413]

11. ___ The parties' prior course of dealing, common usage of trade and the overall circumstances are factors the court looks at in determining reasonableness with respect to the buyer's right to inspection. [p 415]

12. ___ Buyers who agree to C.O.D. deliveries are entitled to inspect the goods before paying for them. [p 415]

13. ___ Payment is usually due from a buyer where and when the goods are delivered even if the place of delivery is the same place of shipment. [p 415]

14. ___ The repudiation of a sales or lease contract by one of the parties after the date set for performance is known as anticipatory repudiation. [p 417]

15. ___ A buyer contracts to purchase 2,500 tires from a tire manufacturer with delivery set for May 1 and partial payment due March 1. In February the buyer learns that automobile sales have decreased by 38% and assembly line workers have been laid off in the small plant that he would need the tires in. The tire manufacturer contacts the buyer and wants a written demand for adequate assurance on February 18. The buyer fails to give adequate assurance of performance. The tire manufacturer has no recourse and must now wait until March 1 when partial payment is due before it can do anything. [p 417]

16. ___ An anticipatory repudiation may be retracted by any method that clearly indicates the repudiating party's desire to perform the contract. [p 417]

17. ___ Delivery of goods may not be withheld if the seller or lesser is in possession of them when the buyer or lessee breaches the contract. [p 418]

18. ___ The right to withhold delivery of goods is available if the lessee or buyer wrongfully revokes or rejects acceptance of the goods. [p 418]

19. ___ A seller or lessor that learns of a lessee's or buyer's insolvency while the goods are in transit may not stop delivery of the goods regardless of the size of the shipment. [p 418]

20. ___ The principles of good faith and commercial reasonableness must be applied if the seller is exercising his or her right to dispose of the goods when a buyer or lessee breaches or repudiates the sales or lease contract before the seller has even delivered the goods. [p 419]

21. ___ The measure of damages incurred while disposing of goods are defined as the difference between the disposition price and the original contract price. [p 419]

22. ___ If a buyer or lessee repudiates a lease or sales contract or wrongfully rejects tendered goods, the lessor or seller may not sue to recover the damages caused by the lessee's or buyer's breach. [p 420]

23. ___ The amount of damages for a wrongful repudiation or rejection of goods is the difference between the contract price and the market price of the goods at the time and place the goods were to be delivered to the buyer plus incidental damages. [p 420]

24. ___ The seller or lessor may not cancel a sales or lease contract by the buyer or lessee's failure to pay for the goods. [p 420]

25. ___ A buyer or lessee has an option to reject the whole shipment of goods if the goods or the seller or lessor's tender of delivery fails to conform to the sales or lease contract in any way. [p 421]

Multiple Choice

26. The perfect tender rule is altered when [p 411]
    a. the parties to the sales or lease contract agree to limit the effect of the rule.
    b. the buyer or lessee rejects the whole shipment of goods.
    c. the buyer or lessee rejects part of the shipment of goods.
    d. the buyer or lessee accepts the entire shipment of goods.

27. Rachel contracted for a crystal chandelier from Phoebe, a crystal dealer. Phoebe agrees to deliver the chandelier to Rachel's home. The truck delivering the chandelier breaks down and the chandelier is stolen while the delivery driver has walked away trying to find help. What effect does the theft of the chandelier have on the parties' agreement? [p 413]
    a. The risk of loss had already passed to Rachel and she is responsible for payment.
    b. The risk of loss remains with Rachel, but, she can get her insurance to cover the damage.
    c. The risk of loss is shared between both parties as the situation involved a thief which requires both parties to share the cost of the damages.
    d. The risk of loss had not yet passed to Rachel and as such, the contract is voided and she does not have to pay for the chandelier.

28. Under the UCC, payment for goods may be by [p 415]
    a. check, credit card, or the like.
    b. cash if the seller demands payment in cash.
    c. a specific form as named in the parties' agreement.
    d. all of the above.

29. When an anticipatory repudiation occurs, the aggrieved party may [p 417]
    a. treat the contract as breached at the time of the anticipatory repudiation.
    b. await performance by the repudiating party for a reasonable time.
    c. suspend performance of his or her obligations under the contract.
    d. all of the above.

30. Which remedy is available to the seller or lessor if the buyer or lessee fails to make a payment when payment is due? [p 418]
    a. The seller or lessor has a right to withhold delivery of the goods. .
    b. The seller or lessor has the right to get angry and wait until the buyer finally renders payment to him or her.
    c. The seller or lessor has the right to repudiate his or her obligations.
    d. None of the above.

31. A seller or lessor who discovers that the buyer or lessee is insolvent before the goods are delivered may [p 418]
    a. refuse to deliver as promised unless the buyer or lessee pays cash for the goods.
    b. make a statement to help in the buyer's reorganization bankruptcy.
    c. make the delivery in good faith that the buyer will remit payment when able.
    d. all of the above.

32. If Jaclyn's Fine Vases begins manufacture of 50 vases all of which have a sculpted form of sea life on them and the buyer, a tourist shop on the ocean goes out of business before the goods are finished, Jaclyn, the seller may choose to [p 419]
    a. open up the buyer's business and try to sell the vases herself.
    b. stop manufacturing the goods and resell them for scrap or salvage value.
    c. use self-help in reclaiming what is due her under the parties' agreement.
    d. obtain an injunction against the buyer to prevent him or her from contracting with her again.

33. A buyer enters into a sales contract to purchase a rare pink diamond ring with a platinum band for $1.3 million. When the buyer tenders payment, the seller refuses to sell the rare ring to the buyer. What type of action may the buyer bring in order to get the ring? [p 422]
    a. The buyer may bring an action for damages.
    b. The buyer is out of luck and will have to find another jeweler.
    c. The buyer may bring an equity action to obtain a decree of specific performance from the court ordering the seller to sell the ring to the buyer.
    d. The buyer may bring an action in tort for embezzlement.

34. A buyer or lessor who rightfully covers may sue the seller or lessor to recover [p 422]
    a. the difference between the cost of cover and the contract price or rent.
    b. incidental damages.
    c. consequential damages less expenses saved.
    d. all of the above.

35. The measure of damages a buyer or lessor may recover for a seller or lessor's failure to deliver the goods is [p 424]
    a. an equitable decree of specific performance.
    b. the difference between the contract price and the market price at the time the buyer or lessee learned of the breach.
    c. the difference between the market price and the contract price at the time the buyer or lessee learned of the breach.
    d. a set amount that is preestablished by using a liquidated damages clause.

Short Answer

36. A warehouse is an example of a _____ as it is a holder of good who is not a seller or a buyer. [p 410]

37. The buyer may reject the goods if a _____ delay or the seller's causes loss failure to make a proper contract for the shipment of goods or properly _____ the buyer of the shipment. [p 411]

38. What must the seller provide the buyer with in order for the buyer to obtain goods from a carrier? [p 411] _____

39. A sales contract requires the seller to deliver 80 silk tablecloths to a buyer. When the buyer inspects the delivered goods, it is discovered that 79 tablecloths conform to the contract and one tablecloth does not conform. If the buyer accepts the nonconforming tablecloth, what if any recourse does the buyer have against the seller? [p 411] _____

   _____
   _____

40. Define the meaning of cure. [p 412] _____ _____
   _____

41. Give an example of an installment contract. [p 413] _____
   _____

42. What is a C.O.D. shipment? [p 415] _____
   _____

43. If a buyer pays for goods by check, payment is conditional upon _____
   _____ when it is presented to the bank for payment. [p 415]

44. What is a commercial unit? [p 415] _____

45. List at least two things must occur in order for a revocation by the buyer to be effective.
   [p 416] _____
   _____

46. When may an adequate assurance of due performance be demanded of one party by the other party? [p 417] _____

47. If the repudiation impairs the value of the contract to the aggrieved party, it is called
   _____ _____. [p417]

48. A seller or lessor who discovers that the buyer or lessee is insolvent before the goods are delivered may refuse to deliver as promised unless _____
   _____. [p 417]

49. What is the measure of damages a seller or lessor may recover when disposing of goods? [p 417] _____

50. What is reclamation? [p 418] _____

Answers to Refresh Your Memory

1. obligations [p 410]
2. deliver, goods [p 410]
3. sales, lease [p 410]

4. The remedies are designed to place the injured party in as good of a position as if the breaching party's contractual obligations were fully performed. [p 410]
5. breach [p 410]
6. transfer and deliver goods to the buyer or lessee [p 410]
7. reasonable, be kept available for a reasonable period of time [p 410]
8. upon tender of delivery [p 410]
9. UCC [p 410]
10. seller or lessor's place of business [p 410]
11. destination [p 411]
12. cure [p 412]
13. An installment contract is one that requires or authorizes the goods to be delivered in separate lots. [p 413]
14. installment [p 413]
15. after [p 415]

Critical Thought Exercise Model Answer

Yes, I will authorize the appeal. Under UCC 2-715, the remedy of cover allows the buyer, on the seller's breach, to purchase the goods, in good faith and within a reasonable time, from another seller and substitute them for the goods due under the contract. If the cost of cover exceeds the cost of the contract goods, the breaching seller will be liable to the buyer for the difference, plus incidental and consequential damages.

In our case, the cost of the contracted forklifts was to be $750,000. Agro-Star had to pay only $550,000 for the forklifts, plus the incidental damages of $300,000 for further testing and development. By exercising their right of cover, Agro-Star only suffered damages of $100,000. The cost of the appeal is only $20,000 and we will likely have the award reduced by $150,000.

It is both fair and ethical for us to take advantage of the cover rule. The purpose of contract damages is to put the non-breaching party in the same position they would have been if the breach had not occurred. Damages awarded after the non-breaching party has covered make the buyer whole while avoiding a punitive result to the seller.

Answers to Practice Quiz

True/False:

1. True   The transfer and delivery of goods otherwise known as the tender of delivery is the seller or lessee's basic obligation with the sales or lease contract.
2. False   Charlene does not have to allow Ed the opportunity to fulfill his obligation in that tender must be at a reasonable hour, of which 2:00a.m. would not be considered reasonable for a furniture delivery.
3. True   Goods that are rightfully delivered in lots may have the payment apportioned for each lot.
4. False   If a seller or lessor does not have a place of business, then the place of delivery is the seller or lessor's residence.
5. True   The safe and proper transportation of goods as well as putting the goods in the carrier's transportation is one of the obligations of a seller.
6. True   Tender of delivery in destination contracts is either the buyer's place of business or other place specified in the parties' contract.

7. False   The lessor or seller is under a duty to deliver conforming goods.
8. False   The UCC gives a lessor or seller an opportunity to cure nonconforming goods if the time for performance has not expired and the seller or lessor notifies the buyer or lessee of his or her intention to make a conforming delivery within the contract time.
9. True   If the value of an installment is impaired by a defect and the defect cannot be cured, the buyer or lesee may reject the nonconforming installment.
10. True   If goods that are identified to a lease or sales contract are totally destroyed without either party being at fault before the risk of loss passes to the buyer or lessee, the contract is void.
11. True   The court will consider common usage of trade, prior course of dealings between the parties, and other types of similar factors in determining reasonableness as it pertains to a buyer's right to inspection.
12. False   Buyers are not entitled to inspection of goods before paying for them when he or she has agreed to cash on delivery (C.O.D.) deliveries.
13. True   The place in which goods are delivered, even if it is the same as the place of shipment, is the place where payment is due from the buyer.
14. False   Repudiation of a lease or sales contract by one of the parties prior to the date set for performance is known as anticipatory repudiation.
15. False   The buyer does have recourse as he or she may suspend performance and treat the sales contract as repudiated.
16. True   If a party clearly indicates his or her intent to perform a contract after a situation involving anticipatory repudiation, then there may be an effective retraction of the anticipatory repudiation.
17. False   Delivery of the goods may be withheld if the lessor or seller is in possession of them when the lessee or buyer is in breach of the contract.
18. True   If the buyer or lessee wrongfully rejects or revokes acceptance of the goods, then the seller has the right to withhold delivery of the goods.
19. False   The delivery can only be stopped if it is a truckload, planeload, carload or larger express freight shipment.
20. True   If the seller or lessor is exercising his or her right to dispose of the goods when the lessee or buyer breaches or repudiates the lease contract before the seller has even delivered the goods, then the principles of good faith and reasonableness must be applied.
21. False   Damages incurred on disposition of goods are the difference between the disposition price and the contract price.
22. False   The seller or lessor may sue to recover the damages caused by the buyer's or lessee's breach if a lessee or buyer repudiates a sale or lease contract or wrongfully rejects tendered goods.
23. True   This is a proper statement of damages for a wrongful repudiation or rejection of goods.
24. False   If a buyer or lessee breaches a contract by failing to pay for goods, the seller or lessor may cancel a sales or lease contract.
25. True   One of the options a buyer or lesse has if the goods or the seller's or lessor's tender of delivery fails to conform is that he or she may reject the whole shipment.

Multiple Choice:

26. A   Answer A is the correct answer as the UCC alters the perfect tender rule when the parties agree to limit the effect of it or in cases involving a substitution of carriers. Answers B,

C, and D are all incorrect answers as they pertain to the buyer's remedies in certain situations.

27. D   Answer D is the correct answer as the risk of loss had not passed to Rachael. The contract is voided and she does not have to pay for the chandelier. Answer A is incorrect as the facts are indicative of a destination contract wherein a buyer does not assume the risk of loss until the goods are delivered. Here the goods were not delivered as the chandelier was stolen. Answer B is incorrect as once again, the risk of loss had not passed. Further, the fact that she has insurance, though a nice benefit, does not assist in the allegation of the risk of loss passing to her, as it did not. Answer C is incorrect as it is a misstatement of law.

28. D   Answer D is the correct answer as the UCC provides for payment of goods by all of the means given in answers A, B, and C.

29. D   Answer D is the correct answer as answers A, B, and C are all options for an aggrieved party involving situations of anticipatory repudiation.

30. A   Answer A is the correct answer as the delivery of goods may be withheld if the seller or lessor is in possession of them when the buyer or lessee breaches the contract by failing to make payment when payment is due. Answer B is incorrect as anger is not a right recognized by the law. Answer C is incorrect as even though the seller may suspend his or her performance as a result of the buyer's breach, answer A is a better answer as it pertains to the delivery of the goods itself.

31. A   Answer A is the correct answer as the UCC 2-702 (1), 2A-525 (1) provides for a seller's refusal to deliver goods upon receiving information that the buyer or lessee is insolvent. The UCC provides for this refusal unless the buyer or lessee pays cash for the goods. Answer B is incorrect as helping by way of a statement geared toward the buyer's reorganizational bankruptcy is not a recognized option under the law. Answer C is incorrect as this states a personal option that the seller may or may not want to do, not a legal option as stated under the law. Answer D is incorrect based on the reasoning given above.

32. B   Answer B is the correct answer as the UCC provides for cessation of the manufacturing of goods where the buyer or lessee has breached or repudiated the contract before the goods are finished. Answer A is incorrect as this is not an option under the UCC where unfinished goods are involved. Answer C is incorrect as self-help is also not an option that the seller or lessor has under the UCC. Answer D is incorrect as an injunction would not be a proper remedy for a sales contract situation.

33. C   Answer C is the correct answer as the good, here a rare pink diamond with a platinum band is unique and the remedy at law would be inadequate. Therefore, the buyer or lessee may obtain specific performance of the sales or lease contract. Answer A is incorrect as damages would not be an adequate remedy in light of the unique nature of the good Answer B is incorrect as it is an untrue statement. Answer D is incorrect as embezzlement is not a proper cause of action to bring in light of the facts, as the parties involved do not have an employer/employee relationship and the facts state that the parties have a contract to purchase a good (the ring) the fact of which would not establish any element necessary for the tort of embezzlement.

34. D   Answer D is the correct answer as answers A, B, and C all state the remedies available to a buyer or seller who rightfully covers.

35. B   Answer B is the correct answer as a buyer may recover the difference between the contract price and the market price at the time the buyer learns of the breach when a seller or lessor fails to deliver the goods. Answer A is incorrect, as the remedy of specific performance does not involve damages. Answer C is incorrect as it is worded backwards of the true remedy as stated in answer B. Answer D is incorrect as liquidated damages would need to be in the parties agreement and as such liquidated damages is not

a standard measure of damages that is available to buyers and lessors who want to bring a cause of action against sellers and lessees for a failure to deliver goods.

Short Answer:

36. bailee
37. material, notify
38. The seller must provide the buyer with appropriate documents of title.
39. remedies
40. Cure refers to the opportunity to repair or replace defective or nonconforming goods.
41. An example of an installment contract is one in which a buyer orders 200 mountain bikes, to be delivered in four equal installments of 50 items.
42. A C.O.D. shipment is one in which the buyer agrees to pay cash on delivery of the goods.
43. the check being honored
44. A commercial unit is a unit of goods that commercial usage deems is a single whole for purposes of sale.
45. It must be shown that the goods are nonconforming and the nonconformity substantially impairs the value of the goods to the buyer or lessee.
46. An adequate assurance of performance may be demanded of a party if one party to the contract has reasonable grounds to believe that the other party either will or cannot perform his or her contractual obligations.
47. anticipatory repudiation
48. the buyer or lessee pays cash for the goods.
49. A seller may recover the difference between the disposition price and the contract price.
50. Reclamation is the right of a seller or lessor to demand the return of goods from the buyer or lessee under certain situations.

Chapter 22
SALES AND LEASE
WARRANTIES

Chapter Overview

This chapter provides a thorough explanation of the different types of warranties as well as clear examples for each. Further, it provides a concise understanding of the remedies that are available for breach of the various warranties. Also disclaimers and their lawfulness are examined.

Objectives

Upon completion of the exercises in this chapter, you should be able to:
1. Discuss the warranties of good title and no infringements.
2. Define and discuss what an implied warranty is.
3. Discuss the implied warranty of merchantability.
4. Discuss the implied warranty of fit for human consumption.
5. Explain the implied warranty of fit for a particular purpose.
6. Recognize warranty disclaimers and determine their lawfulness.
·7. Discuss overlapping and inconsistent warranties and which take priority.
8. Explain the available damages for breach of warranty.
9. Discuss the importance of the Magnuson-Moss Warranty Act and its impact on consumer goods.
10. Explain the requirements of warranty disclaimers and the limitation of liability clauses in software licenses.

Practical Application

You will be able to recognize the various types of warranties as they exist within a transaction. Additionally, you will be able to assess whether or not a warranty has been breached. Further, you should be able to recognize disclaimers and determine whether or not they are lawful as well as the impact of limitation of liability clauses on software licenses.

Helpful Hints

It is helpful to understand that there are three categories of warranties. That is to say that there is an oral, express and implied warranty. Further, as you study warranties, it is helpful to not only keep them organized according to the type of warranty it is, but, to keep an example of each type in mind so that the material can be kept clear.

Study Tips

Consumers have often been taken advantage of in their daily transactions. Initially one of the only protections afforded a consumer was *Caveat Emptor,* which in Latin means, "Buyer Beware." However, various Uniform Commercial Code laws have been developed thereby establishing certain warranties as being applicable to the sales of goods and certain lease transactions. A warranty is like insurance to a consumer in that it is a way to make sure that goods meet certain standards.

Warranties of Title and No Infringements

- **Good Title**
  General Rule: Sellers of goods warrant that they have valid title to the goods
  Exception: If there is a disclaimer involved, good title is not warranted.

- **No Security Interests**
  General Rule: Sellers of goods automatically warrant that the goods they sell are delivered free of any encumbrances, liens or third-party security interests.

- **No Infringements**
  General Rule: A lessor or seller who is a merchant who regularly deals in goods of the kind leased or sold automatically warrants that the goods are delivered free of Any third-party patent, copyright or trademark claim. This is known as the Warranty against infringements.
  Exception: If the parties agree otherwise.

Warranties of Quality

- General Rule: The goods meet certain standards of quality and are warranted expressly or impliedly.

No Interference

- General Rule: In a lease transaction, the lessor warrants that no person holds a claim or interest in the goods that arose from an act or omission of the lessor that will interfere with the lessee's enjoyment of his or her leasehold interest.

Express Warranties

Creation: Express warranties are created when a seller or lessor affirms that the goods he or she is selling or leasing meet certain criteria of quality, performance, description or condition.
Usual Form: These warranties are found in brochures, ads, catalogs, diagrams, etc.
Basis of the Bargain: If the warranty was a contributing factor that induced the buyer to Buy the product or the lessee to lease the product, this is called the basis of the bargain.

Special Notations: Retailers are responsible for express warranties made by manufacturers of goods it sells.
But, manufacturers are not liable for express warranties made by

wholesalers and retailers unless the manufacturer ratifies or authorizes
the warranties.

Statements of Opinion: Puffing or statements of opinion do not create an express warranty.
In order to be an express warranty, it must qualify as an affirmation
of fact.

Affirmation of Value: An affirmation of value does not create an express warranty.

Implied Warranties

Implied Warranty of Merchantability
Requirements: The goods must be fit for the ordinary purpose for which they are used.
The goods must be adequately contained, packaged, and labeled.
The goods must be of a kind, quality and quantity with each unit.
The goods must conform to any promise or affirmation of fact made on
the container or label.
The quality of the goods must pass without objection in the trade.
Fungible goods must meet a fair average or middle range of quality.

Implied Warranty of Fitness for Human Consumption (a warranty within the implied warranty of
Merchantability)
Application: This warranty applies to food and drink consumed on or off the premises.
Foreign Substance Test: Used to determine whether food products are unmerchantable. A food
product is unmerchantable if a foreign object in a product causes injury
to an individual.
Consumer Expectation Test: Merchantability is tested based on what the average consumer
would expect to find in his or her food products.

Implied Warranty of Fitness for a Particular Purpose
Application: Applies to both merchant and nonmerchant sellers and lessors.
Explained: A warranty that comes about where a seller or lessor warrants that the goods will
Meet the buyer's or lessee's expressed needs.

Overlapping and Inconsistent Warranties
Express and implied warranties may exist within the same transaction
The intent of the parties determines which warranty dominates if the warranties that overlap are
inconsistent.

Warranty Disclaimers

- Defined: Statements that negate implied and express warranties.

- Disclaimer of Implied Warranties: This is accomplished by words such as *without fault,
as is, etc.* This is primarily good for used products.

- Disclaimer of Implied Warranty of Merchantability – this can be oral or written, but must use the term merchantability. Example: *"There are no warranties that extend beyond the description on the face hereof."*

- Disclaimer of Implied Warranty of Fitness for a Particular Purpose – Disclaimer can be accomplished by using general language without using the word fitness, but it must be in writing.

  - Special Notation: There are no implied warranties with regard to any defects that an examination of the goods would have revealed.
    Requirement: The disclaimer must be conspicuous to a reasonable person.

- Unconscionable disclaimers – The court has three options when the clause is unconscionable:
  1) refuse to enforce the unconscionable clause; 2) refuse to enforce the entire contract; or
  3) limit the application of the clause.

  Factors in deciding unconscionability: Bargaining power of the parties, sophistication, education, and whether the contract was offered on a "take it or leave it" basis.

General disclaimer of warranty provisions and limitation of liability clauses in software contracts
Include:
Limited warranty
Customer's remedies
No other warranty
No liability for consequential damages

Third Party Beneficiaries of Warranties

- Common Law: The parties had to be in privity of contract in order to have rights.

- Modern Law: The UCC limits the doctrine of privity thereby giving a third party the option of choosing three alternative provisions for liability to third parties.

Damages for Breach of Warranty
- The buyer or lessee may sue the seller or lessor for compensatory damages.

- Compensatory damages are equal to the difference between the value of the goods as warranted and the actual value of the goods accepted at the time and place of acceptance.

Statute of Limitations
- The UCC has a four year statute of limitations. The parties may agree to reduce the statute of limitations to not less than one year.
- The statute begins to run upon tendering the goods to the buyer or lessee.
- Exception: If the warranty extends to the future performance of the goods. An example of this would be an extended warranty on an automobile.

Magnuson Moss Warranty Act

General Information: This act involves written warranties as they pertain to consumer products. If the product exceeds ten dollars and an express warranty is made, then the Warranty must be labeled as "full" or "limited."

Full warranty- The warrantor must guarantee free repair or replacement of the defective product as well as the time limit of the warranty. Additionally, the warranty must be conspicuous and able to be understood.

Limited warranty – A limitation of the scope of the warranty is placed on the product. Also, the warranty must be conspicuous and able to be understood.

Damages- Under the act, a consumer may recover damages, attorney's fees, and costs. The consumer must go through the act's arbitration procedure first before taking legal action.

Limitation of Disclaiming Implied Warranties –The act modifies the state law of implied warranties by forbidding sellers or lessors who make express written warranties from disclaiming or modifying implied warranties of merchantability or fitness for a particular purpose. Time limits may be placed on implied warranties but the time limits must correspond to that of the written warranties.

Refresh Your Memory

The following exercise will enable you to refresh your memory on the rules and principles presented to you in this chapter. Read each question twice and place your answer in the blanks provided. Review the chapter material for any question you miss or are unable to remember.

1.   What does caveat emptor mean? _____

2.   What purpose do warranties have? _____
_____

3.   Generally speaking, sellers of goods warrant that they have _____ title to goods.

4.   What does the warranty of no security interests hold? _____
_____

5.   What is a warranty against infringement? _____
_____

6.   A warranty that the goods meet certain standards is called the _____.

7.   What is a warranty against interference? _____
_____

8. Express warranties may be made by mistake because _____

   _____

9. When may buyers and lessees recover for breach of an express warranty? _____

   _____

10. The statement, "This boat has barely been driven 500 miles" is an _____ warranty.

11. Give at least two standards that must be met under the implied warranty of merchantability.

    _____

    _____

12. Which warranty applies to food and drink consumed on or off premises? _____

    _____

13. If five-year old Bobby Brown cuts his mouth on a piece of metal found in pudding, which test will the court apply to determine if the pudding is unmerchantable? _____

    _____

14. With respect to the merchantability of food products, what is expected of those who prepare food? _____

    _____

15. What was the implied warranty of fitness for a particular purpose designed for? _____

    _____

Critical Thought Exercise

Bob French, an engineer with Worldwide Construction, travels to Accu-Steel Company in Pennsylvania for the purpose of buying steel cable made by Accu-Steel to help support the upper decks of a new football stadium the Worldwide is building in California. The representative of Accu-Steel reviews the plans for the stadium and sells its recommended cable to Worldwide. The stadium is built using the cable selected by Accu-Steel.

During an exciting football game, the upper deck collapses onto the lower deck due to the inability of the cable to support the weight load. Worldwide Construction now faces suit from thousands of plaintiffs injured or killed in the collapse. Assuming that the steel cable was not defective in either its design or manufacturing process, does Worldwide have a cause of action against Accu-Steel?

Answer. _____

_____

_____

_____

_____

_____

_____

_____

_____
_____
_____
_____
_____

Practice Quiz

True/False:

1. ____ Article 2 of the UCC applies to warranties and only the sale of goods. [p 431]

2. ____ Warranty of title means that the seller is warranting that he or she has good title and that the transfer of title is rightful. [p 431]

3. ____ Centralville Inc. owns a fleet of limousines. A thief steals one of them and sells it to Evan, an entrepreneur who just started his limousine business. Evan does not know that the limousine is stolen. Centralville Inc. has reclaimed the stolen limousine from Evan. Evan is out of luck and cannot recover against the thief for breach of warranty of title. [p 431]

4. ____ A warranty of no security interest is an implied warranty that the goods have third party security interests, liens, and encumbrances that automatically come with the goods when they are delivered. [p 431]

5. ____ Blake sells his efficient weed picking machine called the Weed-O-Rama to a national home and garden retailer. One day while purchasing plants for his garden, Christopher Mills discovers the machine for sale. Thereafter he claims as well as proves that he has a trademark and patent on it. Since the home and garden retailer paid valuable consideration for the tool, Christopher is out of luck. [p 432]

6. ____ When goods are leased, the lessor in effect warrants that a person holds an interest or a claim in the goods that arose from an act or omission of the lessor that will interfere with the lessee's enjoyment of his or her leasehold interest in the goods. [p 432]

7. ____ Express warranties may be written, oral or implied. [p 432]

8. ____ Unless there is a showing to the contrary, all statements by the seller or lessor before the time of contracting are presumed to be part of the basis of the bargain. [p 432]

9. ____ Statements of opinion such as, "This is the best house you will every buy," create an express warranty. [p 433]

10. ____ One of the standards for the implied warranty of merchantability is that they be adequately contained, packaged and labeled. [p 434]

11. ___ Grocery stores, restaurants, fast-food chains, and vending operators do not come within the purview of the warranty of fitness for human consumption. [p 435]

12. ___ The foreign substance test is used to find out whether food products are merchantable. [p 436]

13. ___ Most of the states have abandoned the consumer expectation test in determining the merchantability of food products. [p 436]

14. ___ The warranty of fitness for a particular purpose applies to both merchants and nonmerchants. [p 437]

15. ___ Under the UCC, warranties are cumulative if they are inconsistent with one another. [p 439]

16. ___ Warranties may be disclaimed as well as limited. [p 439]

17. ___ The courts construe conspicuous as noticeable to the unreasonable person. [p 441]

18. ___ One of the options a court may have if it finds an unconscionable clause is to enforce it. [p 441]

19. ___ Software licenses are reluctant to place warranty disclaimers and liability limiting clauses in their packaging. [p 441]

20. ___ Under common law, only those in privity of contract were given rights under the contract. [p 442]

21. ___ The UCC has limited the doctrine of privity by giving provisions for liability to third parties. [p 442]

22. ___ The Magnuson-Moss Warranty Act applies to all goods regardless of cost. [p 443]

23. ___ The Magnuson-Moss Warranty Act provides for the creation of implied warranties. [p 443]

24. ___ In order for a full warranty to have effect, the warrantor must limit the scope of its warranty in some way. [p 443]

25. ___ In a limited warranty, the warrantor must guarantee free repair or replacement of the defective product. [p 443]

Multiple Choice

26. Under which warranty do sellers of goods automatically warrant that the goods that they sell are delivered free from any third-party liens, or encumbrances that are unknown to the buyer? [p 431]
    a. Good title
    b. The doctrine of caveat emptor
    c. Warranty of no security interests
    d. Warranty against infringements

27. Warranties of quality include [p 432]
    a. implied warranty of fitness for human consumption .
    b. implied warranties of merchantability.
    c. express warranties.
    d. all of the above.

28. The warranty of quiet possession [p 432]
    a. is also known as the warranty against interference.
    b. holds that no person holds a claim or an interest in goods from an act or omission of the lessor.
    c. protects a lessee's enjoyment of his or her leasehold interest.
    d. all of the above.

29. Express warranties are created when [p 432]
    a. a seller or lessor affirms that the goods that are being sold or leased meet certain standards of quality, or condition.
    b. a seller or lessor affirms that the goods that are being sold or leased do not meet certain standards of quality or condition.
    c. it is expected by the parties conduct.
    d. none of the above.

30. Which of the following statements is true concerning the "basis of the bargain?" [p 433]
    a. The UCC does not define the term.
    b. All statements prior to the time of contracting become part of the basis of the bargain.
    c. All post sale statements that modify the contract are part of the basis of the bargain.
    d. All of the above.

31. The statement, "This gold necklace is worth more than money can pay" creates [p 433]
    a. an express warranty.
    b. an implied warranty.
    c. no warranty.
    d. a statement of warranty.

32. The statement, "This tractor has only been driven 1,500 miles " creates [p 433]
    a. statement of opinion.
    b. an express warranty.
    c. a puffing remark.
    d. an affirmation of mileage.

33. The implied warranty of merchantability does not apply to [p 434]
    a. sales by merchants.
    b. sales by nonmerchants.
    c. leases by merchants.
    d. a vacuum cleaner salesperson.

34. Which of the following has been incorporated into the implied warranty of merchantability? [p 435]
    a. The warranty of fitness for human consumption
    b. The warranty of good title
    c. The warranty of no security interests
    d. The warranty against infringement

35. When two or more warranties are inconsistent and in the same sales or lease transaction, the UCC will determine which is dominant by looking at [p 439]
    a. which is servient.
    b. which is more conspicuously written.
    c. the intention of the parties.
    d. which is more merchantable.

Short Answer

36. If a party wants to disclaim the implied warranty of merchantability, he or she must specifically mention the term _____. [p 440]

37. What language might Lydia use if she wants to disclaim the implied warranty of fitness for a particular purpose? [p 440] _____
    _____

38. Expressions like "as is" and "with all faults" may be used in _____ warranties of quality. [p 440]

39. If the court finds a disclaimer clause to be unconscionable, what might it do in order to avoid an unconscionable result? [p 441] _____
    ____ _____

40. Disclaimers and limitations of liability have no effect against _____
    _____. [p 442]

41. What is the statute of limitations that applies to obvious and hidden defects? [p 442] ____
    _____

42. If Edmonds, a lighting manufacturer warrants free repair or replacement of any defective lights, he has probably given a _____ warranty. [p 443]

43. Jan's Shoes has placed the following on the boxes of all of her shoes, "return of your purchase price if with a receipt within fourteen days." What type of warranty could this be? [p 443] _____

44. A warranty by the seller or lessor that goods meet certain criteria of quality is a _____
    _____ of _____. [p 432]

45. An affirmation that goods meet certain standards of quality, performance, description or condition creates an _____ warranty. [p 432]

46. A seller's statement of _____ does not create an express warranty. [p 433]

47. Tell why the implied warranty of merchantability would not apply when a neighbor sells a fish tank to another neighbor. [p 434] _____
    _____

48. Why would an apple pie with a seed in it still be considered merchantable? [p 436]
    _____

49. Which test have most states adopted in order to determine the merchantability of food products? [p 436] _____

50. Which test do some states use to determine whether food products are unmerchantable? [p 435] _____

Answers to Refresh Your Memory

1. Let the buyer beware. [p 431]
2. Warranties give the buyer or lessee assurances that goods meet certain standards. [p 431]
3. valid [p 431]
4. This warranty holds that goods are delivered free from any third-party security interests, liens, or encumbrances known to the buyer. [p 431]
5. It is a warranty that the goods are delivered free from any third-party patent, trademark or copyright claim. [p 432]
6. warranty of quality [p 432]
7. A warranty by the lessor that no person holds a claim or interest in the goods that came about from an act or omission of the lessor that will interfere with the lessee's enjoyment of his or her leasehold interest. [p 432]
8. the seller or lessor does not have to specifically intend to make the warranty. [p 432]
9. Buyers and lessors may recover for breach of an express warranty if the warranty was a contributing factor that induced the buyer to purchase the product or to lease the product to the lessee. [p 433]
10. express [p 433]
11. The goods must be fit for the ordinary purposes for which they are used. The goods must be adequately packaged, contained and labeled. [p 434] (answers will vary)
12. The implied warranty of fitness for human consumption. [p 435]
13. The foreign substance test. [p 436]
14. A consumer would expect that a food preparer would remove all foreign objects from the food. [p 436]
15. It was designed to meet the specific needs of the buyer or lessor. [p 437]

Critical Thought Exercise Model Answer

An implied warranty of fitness for a particular purpose arises under UCC 2-315 when the buyer's purpose or use for goods is expressly or impliedly known by the seller and the buyer purchases the goods in reliance on the seller's selection of the goods. Accu-Steel was informed of the express purpose for which the steel cable was being bought. Accu-Steel sold the cable to Worldwide that it recommended for the job. Accu-Steel may also liable to Worldwide and the injured plaintiffs based upon a theory of product liability founded upon Accu-Steel's negligence. Due care must be used by the manufacturer in designing the product, selecting materials, using the appropriate manufacturing process, assembling and testing the product, and placing adequate warnings on the label or product. Accu-Steel selected the size of the cable to be produced. By failing to select a thicker and stronger cable, Accu-Steel was negligent and is liable to those persons who were foreseeable victims of its failure to perform its duties in a reasonable manner. Accu-Steel knew that the cable was going to be used in a stadium where spectators would be the end consumer.

Answers to Practice Quiz

True/False:

1. True   Article 2 applies to warranties and only the sale of goods, whereas Article 2A was established to apply warranties to lease transactions.
2. True   When sellers of goods warrant that they are able to transfer rightful title and that they have valid title, this is referring to warranty of title.
3. False   Evan can recover against the thief for implied warranty of good title as the thief impliedly warranted that he or she had good title to the limousine and that the transfer of title to Evan was rightful.
4. False   The warranty of no security interest automatically warrants that they are delivered free from any third-party security interests, not that the goods have a third-party security interest.
5. False   Christopher may notify the home and garden retailer that they can no longer use the Weed-O-Rama without his permission except for a fee. The home and garden retailer may rescind its contract with Blake based on the no infringement warranty.
6. False   A lessor warrants that no person holds an interest or a claim in the goods not that a person does hold an interest in the goods.
7. True   A seller's writing, conduct or words may create or imply an express warranty.
8. True   All prior, concurrent and post sale statements are presumed to be part of the basis of the bargain unless there is something there is something contradictory in nature.
9. False   Puffing or commendations of goods does not create an express warranty.
10. True   The lessor or seller of goods is a merchant with respect to the goods of that kind, of which the goods must be adequately contained packaged and labeled accordingly.
11. False Restaurants, fast-food outlets and grocery stores as well as vending machine operators do come within the purview of the implied warranty of fitness for human consumption.
12. False The foreign food substance test is used to determine whether food is unmerchantable based on objects that are found in the food.
13. False A majority of the stated have adopted the consumer expectation test to determine whether food products are merchantable.
14. True   Merchants and nonmerchants come within the UCC's implied warranty of fitness for a particular purpose.
15. False Warranties are cumulative if they are consistent with one another not inconsistent with one another.
16. True   Warranties may be disclaimed or limited.
17. False Conspicuous is construed as noticeable to the reasonable person not the unreasonable person.
18. False A court may refuse to enforce an unconscionable clause, refuse to enforce the entire contract or limit application of the clause but it will not enforce an unconscionable clause.
19. False Most software licenses do contain warranty disclaimer and limitation on liability clauses in their packaging.
20. True   Common law provided rights only to those who were a party to the contract.
21. True   The UCC provides for a choice between three alternative provisions for liability to third parties.
22. False It applies if the cost of the good is more than $10 and the warrantor selects the option of making an express warranty.
23. False The Magnuson-Moss Warranty Act covers written warranties.

24. False To be considered a full warranty, the warrantor must guarantee free repair or replacement of the defective product.

25. False In a limited warranty, the scope of a full warranty is limited in some way.

Multiple Choice:

26. C Answer C is the correct answer as the warranty of no security interests provides that the goods that are sold are free from any third-party security interest, liens, or encumbrances that are unknown to the buyer. Under this warranty, this is automatically done by the seller. Answer A is incorrect as sellers of goods warrant that the title they possess is good and that the transfer of title is rightful. Answer B is incorrect as the doctrine of caveat emptor simply means, "Let the buyer beware." Answer D is incorrect as this warranty involves a lessor who is a merchant dealing in the goods of the kind that are being leased or sold automatically warrants that the goods are delivered free of any third-party trademark, copyright or patent claims.

27. D Answer D is the correct answer as answers A, B, and C all correctly state what the warranties of quality include.

28. D Answer D is the correct answer as answers A, B, and C are all correct statements with regard to the warranty of quiet possession.

29. A Answer A is the correct answer as express warranties can be made as an assurance of the fulfillment of a goods standards or quality by the seller or lessor to the buyer or lessee. Answer B is incorrect, as this would act more as a disclaimer if a seller or lessor affirmed that the goods do not meet certain criteria or quality.

30. D Answer D is the correct answer as answers A, B, and C are all correct statements regarding the basis of the bargain.

31. C Answer C is the correct answer as it is an affirmation of value, which does not create any warranty under UCC 2-313(2). Answer A is incorrect, as statements that involve affirmation of value do not create an express warranty. Answer B is incorrect based on the reasoning given for answer C. Answer D is also incorrect based on the reasoning given above.

32. B Answer B is the correct answer as the statement is an affirmation of fact, which creates an express warranty. Answer A is incorrect as it is not a statement of opinion as it is factual as opposed to puffing with regard to the quality of the product. Answer C is incorrect based on the reasoning given with regard to answer A. Answer D is incorrect as there is no legal basis known as an affirmation of mileage.

33. B Answer B is the correct answer as nonmerchants are not included in the provisions related to the implied warranty of merchantability. Answer A is incorrect as the implied warranty of merchantability does apply to merchants. Answer C is incorrect as the implied warranty of merchantability also applies to leases by merchants. Answer D is incorrect as a vacuum cleaner salesperson would be a merchant to whom the implied warranty of merchantability would apply based on his or her status of being a merchant.

34. A Answer A is the correct answer as the UCC incorporates the implied warranty of fitness for human consumption into the implied warranty of merchantability. Answer B is incorrect as the warranty of good title stands on its own merit without being incorporated into another warranty. Answer C is incorrect as this is an automatic warranty that also stands on its own merit. Answer D is incorrect as this is also an automatic warranty that is not incorporated as a subcategory of another warranty.

35. C Answer C is the correct answer, as the court will look at the parties' intent in determining which warranty is dominant in the case of inconsistent warranties. Answer A is incorrect as there is no basis from which to determine the status of dominant or servient. The

answer provided is vague and somewhat conclusive. Answer B is incorrect as the conspicuousness of a warranty does not necessarily indicate which warranty the parties wanted to be dominant in their transaction. Answer D is incorrect as comparison of merchantability is not possible in terms of warranties in general and more specifically with regard to determining the dominant warranty in an inconsistent warranty situation.

Short Answer:

36.   merchantability
37.   Lydia may want to use the terminology, "There are no warranties that extend beyond the description on the face hereof."
38.   implied
39.   It might refuse to enforce the clause or refuse to enforce the entire contract or limit the application of the clause.
40.   third parties.
41.   The UCC statute of limitations is four years.
42.   full
43.   It could be a limited warranty.
44.   warranty of quality
45.   express
46.   opinion
47.   The warranty of merchantability would not be applicable, as it does not apply to casual sales.
48.   It would still be considered merchantable because a reasonable consumer would expect to find an apple seed in an apple pie as that would not be a foreign substance to the product.
49.   The consumer expectation test.
50.   The foreign substance test.

Chapter 23
NEGOTIABLE INSTRUMENTS
AND BANKING

Chapter Overview

This chapter focuses on the different types of negotiable instruments as well as their creation and the transfer of the same. Additional attention is given to nonnegotiable contracts, transfer of negotiable instruments by assignment and negotiation, as well as the various types of indorsements.

Objectives

Upon completion of the exercises in this chapter, you should be able to:
1. Differentiate between a negotiable and a nonnegotiable instrument.
2. Discuss drafts and checks as well as name the parties to these instruments.
3. Explain promissory notes and certificates of deposit as well as name the parties to these
4. Give the formal requirement of a negotiable instrument.
5. Differentiate between promises to pay and orders to pay.
6. Explain the difference between instruments that are payable on a demand and those that are payable at a definite time.
7. Explain the difference between instruments payable to order and payable to bearer.
8. Discuss the process for indorsing and transferring negotiable instruments.
9. Differentiate between blank and special indorsements.
10. Discuss and apply the imposter rule and the fictitious payee rule.

Practical Application

This chapter will enable you to have a better understanding of negotiable instruments and their importance in conducting your personal as well as business affairs. Further, it will give you the tools that you need in the creation of a negotiable instrument. You will also obtain invaluable knowledge with regard to the different types of indorsements as well as requirements and restrictions for each.

Helpful Hints

Since this chapter involves one form or another of a negotiable instrument, the chance of you having used one or more of these instruments in your lifetime is great. If you keep in mind what you have used or are familiar with in terms of commercial paper, this chapter will be very understandable for you. The best approach is a simple approach. As with other chapters that have had confusing names for the parties involved, it is best to keep the parties separated on a sheet of paper to be able to view how they differ. The more you expose yourself to hypotheticals in this area, the easier the material becomes. Also, if you imagine yourself in one or more of the party's positions, it becomes easier.

Study Tips

Negotiable Instruments

Importance: Commercial paper aids in conducting personal and business affairs.

Three functions:
Negotiable instruments act as a substitute for money. An example is a check.
Negotiable instruments may also act as a credit device.
Negotiable instruments also may serve as a record-keeping device for preparing tax returns, etc.

Types of Negotiable Instruments

Draft – A three-party instrument that is an unconditional written order by one party that orders
a second party to pay money to the third party. The parties involved are the drawer,
the drawee and the payee. Note that the drawee is also known as the acceptor because
of his or her obligation to pay the payee instead of the drawer.

> Drawer – The customer who writes (draws) the check.
> Drawee – The financial institution upon which the check is written.
> Payee – The party to whom the check is written.

Promissory Note – An unconditional written promise by one party to pay money to another
party.

> Maker – This is the borrower who makes the promise to pay.
> Payee – This is the lender to whom the promise is made.

> Collateral – Sometimes the lender needs security known as collateral is needed when a
> promissory note is made.

> Examples of promissory notes: Mortgage notes which are notes that are secured by real
> estate.
> Collateral notes are notes that are secured by personal property.

Certificates of Deposit – A specially created note that is created upon a depositor depositing
Monies at a financial institution in exchange for the institution's promise to pay the deposited
amount back with an agreed upon amount of interest after a set period of time.

Creation of a Negotiable Instrument

In order to create a negotiable instrument in compliance with UCC 3-104(a), the following must
be present and must appear on the face of the instrument:

It must be in writing. – This involves permanency and the writing must be portable.

It must be signed by the maker or drawer. – The UCC is broad with this requirement. Symbols,
typed, printed, lithographed, rubber-stamped or other mechanical signatures are allowed.

It must be an unconditional promise or order to pay. – Mere debt acknowledgement is not sufficient for this requirement.

It must state a fixed amount of money. – The principal amount of the instrument has to be on the face of the instrument. Note, money is a "medium of exchange authorized or adopted by a foreign or domestic government as part of its currency." [UCC 1-201(24)]

It must not require any undertaking in addition to the payment of money.

It must be payable on demand or at a definite time. – Payable on demand instruments are created by language such as "payable on sight," or "payable on demand." Checks are an example of payable on demand instruments. Payable at a definite time are called time instruments.

It must be payable to order or to bearer.

Nonnegotiable Contracts

If a promise or order to pay does not meet the requirements discussed under negotiable instruments, then it is a nonnegotiable contract. A nonnegotiable contract is enforceable under contract law.

Transfer by Assignment or Negotiation

After issuance, negotiable instruments may be transferred to subsequent parties either by negotiation or assignment. The transferees rights will depend on how the transfer was effectuated. There are two main types:

Transfer by Assignment – It transfers contract rights of the assignor (transferor) to the assignee (transferee). An assignment results when there has been a transfer of a nonnegotiable instrument.

Transfer by Negotiation - Negotiation is defined as the transfer of a negotiable instrument by a person other than the issuer.

Indorsements

Defined – The signature of a signer (not the maker, drawer or acceptor) that is put on an instrument to negotiate it to another person. The signature may be by itself, state an individual to whom the instrument is to be paid or be with other words.

Indorser – The one who indorses the instrument.
Indorsee – The payee named in the instrument.

Types of Indorsements

Blank– No indorsee is given and it creates bearer paper.

Special indorsement – It contains the indorser's signature and it indicates the person to whom the indorser intends the instrument to be payable to. Special indorsements create order paper, which are preferred over bearer paper.

Unqualified indorsement – "An indorsement whereby the indorser promises to pay the holder or any subsequent indorser the amount of the instrument if the maker, drawer, or acceptor defaults on it."

Qualified indorsement – "Indorsements that disclaim or limit liability on the instrument." Note that there is no guarantee d payment of the instrument by the qualified indorser if the maker, drawer, or acceptor defaults on the instrument. These types of indorsements are often used by individuals signing instruments in the capacity as a representative.

Nonrestrictive indorsement- This is an indorsement without conditions or instructions attached to the payment of the funds.

Restrictive indorsement – An indorsement with an instruction from the indorser.
There are two restrictive indorsements you should be familiar with as provided for under UCC 3-206.

> Indorsement for Deposit or Collection – This is an indorsement that establishes the indorsee The indorser's collecting agent. For example: "for deposit only."

> Indorsement in Trust- An indorsement for the benefit or use of the indorser or another individual.

Misspelled or Wrong Name

If the payee or indorsee name is misspelled, the payee or indorsee in the negotiable instrument may indorse the instrument in the misspelled name, the correct name or both.

Multiple Payees or Indorsees

If more than one person are listed as indorsees or payees on a negotiable instrument and are listed jointly, both indorsements are needed to negotiate the instrument. Example: Payable to Joe and Jan Smith requires both Joe and Jan's signature.

If the instrument indicates that one or the other may negotiate the instrument, then each person's signature is sufficient to negotiate the instrument. Example: Payable to Ann or Mark Jones would allow either Ann or Mark signature.

If a *Virgule* (which is a slash mark) is used, then the negotiable instrument may be paid in the alternative. Example: Maile Price/Winnie Simms indicates that either person may individually negotiate the instrument.

Forged Instrument
The general rule is that unauthorized indorsements are inoperative as the indorsement of the person who signed it. The loss is born by the party accepting the forged instrument. There are two exceptions, the imposter rule and the fictitious payee rule.

Imposter rule -The drawer or maker is liable on the instrument to any person who in good faith pays the instrument or takes it for value or for collection.

The fictitious payee rule – A drawer or maker is liable on an unauthorized or forged indorsement of a fictitious payee rule.

Refresh Your Memory

The following exercise will enable you to refresh your memory on the rules and principles presented to you in this chapter. Read each question twice and place your answer in the blanks provided. Review the chapter material for any question you miss or are unable to remember.

1. A _____ is a special form of note that is created when a depositor deposits money at a financial institution in exchange for the institution's promise to pay back the amount of the deposit plus and agreed-upon rate of interest upon the expiration of a set time period agreed upon by the parties.

2. A person who issues a draft is a _____.

3. A person to whom the check is made payable is the _____.

4. The financial institution where the drawer's checking account is located is the _____.

5. The owner of the checking account at a financial institution and who issues the check is the _____.

6. The portability and permanency requirements of a writing as it pertains to a negotiable instrument are best accomplished by placing the written promise on _____.

7. To be negotiable, the promise or order must be _____.

8. To be negotiable, an instrument must have a promise or order to pay a fixed _____.

9. Under the UCC, money is defined as _____.

10. Instruments that are payable on demand are called _____.

11. An _____ clause allows the date of maturity of an instrument to be extended to some time later on.

12. If a promise or order to pay does not meet the UCC requirements of negotiability, it is a _____ _____.

13. An _____ is the transfer of rights under the contract.

14. _____ is the transfer of a negotiable instrument by an individual other than the issuer.

15. The signature of a signer that is placed on an instrument to negotiate it to another person is an _____.

Critical Thought Exercise

The Gold Coast Investment Group (IG) is building a large office building that it is financing itself through its banking arm, Gold Coast Bank (GCB). When payments for the final phase of the building come due, GC issues checks to the contractors with a condition on the front of the check that states:

"This instrument valid only after a permit to occupy the building is granted by all governmental agencies from which a permit is mandatory."

Ace Construction deposits the check with its bank, First City Bank. The occupancy permits are not issued by the city or county entities where the building is located. When presented with the checks by First City Bank, GCB refuses to honor them.

Ace Construction then brings suit against First City Bank, GCB, and IG.

Should GCB be compelled to pay the checks presented to it by First City Bank on behalf of Ace Construction? Was it ethical for IG to place a condition upon the negotiation of the instrument?

Answer. _____

_____

_____

_____

_____

_____

_____

_____

_____

_____

_____

_____

_____

_____

_____

_____

_____

_____

Practice Quiz

True/False:

1. ____ An example of a substitute for money is a check. [p.449]

2. ____ The drawee must be obligated to pay the drawer money before the drawer can order the drawee to pay this money to the payee. [p.450]

3. ___ The drawee of a check is the financial institution where the drawer has his or her account. [p. 451]

4. ___ The party who makes the promise to pay is the payee. [p.452]

5. ___ Examples of collateral that may be used as security against repayment of a note to a lender include cars, homes or other property. [p.453]

6. ___ A maker is the party to whom the promissory note is made payable which is usually the lender. [p.454]

7. ___ A payee is the financial institution that issues the certificate of deposit. [p.454]

8. ___ A writing on Kleenex does not meet the permanence aspect of the writing requirement of negotiable instruments. [p.454]

9. ___ A promise to pay that is indented in a steel girder would qualify as a negotiable instrument because the girder is freely transferable in commerce. [p.455]

10. ___ The drawer or maker is not liable on the instrument unless his or her signature appears on it. [p.455]

11. ___ The term signature is broadly defined under the UCC thereby allowing any symbol executed or adopted by a party with a present intent to authenticate the writing. [p.455]

12. ___ To be negotiable, the promise or order must be conditional. [p.456]

13. ___ A negotiable instrument does not have to contain a promise or order to pay a fixed amount of money. [p.456]

14. ___ The value of an instrument can be determined with certainty by having a fixed amount. [p.457]

15. ___ The term money as defined by the UCC is a medium of exchange authorized or adopted by a domestic or foreign government as part of its currency. [p.457]

16. ___ U.S. gold is negotiable. [p.457]

17. ___ A note requiring the maker to pay a stated amount of money and perform a service is not negotiable. [p.457]

18. ___ Instruments that are payable on demand are called time instruments. [p.458]

19. ___ The negotiability of an instrument is not affected by prepayment, acceleration or extension clauses in an instrument. [p.458]

20. ___ A prepayment clause does not allow the maker to pay the amount due prior to the due date of the instrument. [p.458]

21. ___ Examples of nonnegotiable instruments are implied or oral instruments. [p.459]

22. ___ The signature on an instrument may be by an authorized representative. [p.459]

23. ___ After issuance of a negotiable instrument, it may be transferred to a subsequent party. [p.460]

24. ___ An assignment happens when a nonnegotiable contract has not been transferred. [p.460]

25. ___ The transfer of a negotiable instrument by a person other than the issuer is known as negotiation. [p.460]

Multiple Choice:

26. Negotiable instruments serve which function [p.449]
    a. as a substitute for money.
    b. as a credit device.
    c. as a record keeping device.
    d. all of the above.

27. A drawer of a draft is the [p.454]
    a. person to whom the check is made payable.
    b. person who issues the draft.
    c. person to whom the draft is made payable.
    d. person who owes money to the drawer.

28. To qualify as a negotiable instrument under the UCC, the writing must [p.455]
    a. contain an unconditional promise to pay.
    b. contain an unconditional order to pay.
    c. contain an unconditional promise or order to pay.
    d. none of the above.

29. A draft or check's unconditional order for the drawee to pay must [p.456]
    a. be more than an authorization or request to pay.
    b. be precise.
    c. contain the word pay.
    d. All of the above.

30. A promise or order to pay may include [p.459]
    a. authorization or power to protect collateral.
    b. a vague amount.
    c. a conditional promise to perform.
    d. an immobile writing.

31. An allonge is [p.461]
    a. the person who indorses a negotiable instrument.
    b. the person to whom a negotiable instrument is indorsed.
    c. a separate piece of paper attached to the instrument on which the written indorsement appears.
    d. the signature written on behalf or by the holder somewhere on the instrument.

32. An indorsement is [p.461]
    a. a negotiable instrument.
    b. the signature written by or on behalf of the holder somewhere on the instrument.
    c. the indorser.
    d. the indorsee.

33. A blank indorsement is [p.462]
    a. a special indorsement.
    b. an unqualified indorsement.
    c. an indorsement for deposit or collection.
    d. an indorsement that does not specify a particular indorsee.

34. Stewart draws a check payable to the order of Kurt. Kurt indorses the check and negotiates it to Martha. When Martha presents the check for payment, there are insufficient funds in Stewart's account to pay the check. If Kurt is an unqualified indorser and is liable on the check, who may Kurt recover against? [p.463]
    a. Martha
    b. Henry
    c. Martha's daughter
    d. Stewart

35. A qualified indorsement is [p.464]
    a. one that is for the benefit or use by another individual.
    b. one that makes the indorsee a collecting agent.
    c. one that disclaims or limits liability on the instrument.
    d. all of the above.

Short Answer:

36. Examples of negotiable instruments include _____. [p.449]

37. The main benefit of a negotiable instrument is that it can be used as a substitute for _____. [p.449]

38. Ellen owes Grace $100. Grace writes out a draft ordering Ellen to pay the $100 to Bart. Ellen agrees to this change of obligation and accepts the draft. Grace is the drawer and Bart is the _____. [p.450]

39. A _____ is an unconditional written promise by one party to pay money to another party. [p.451]

40. A _____ note is one that is payable at a specific time. [p.452]

41. A note payable on demand is known as a _____ _____. [p.452]

42. The party who makes the promise to pay is known as the maker of the note or the _____. [p.452]

43. The party to whom the promise to pay is made is the payee of a note or the _____ _____. [p.452]

44. What two elements must be present in order to establish the writing requirement of a negotiable instrument? [p.454] _____

45. List three requirements that must be on the face of an instrument in order to be considered a negotiable instrument. [p.454] _____
_____

46. Why is an order or promise that is conditional on another promise or event nonnegotiable? [p.456] _____

47. What is meant by the term fixed amount? [p.457] _____
_____

48. What is an unqualified indorser? [p.463] _____
_____

49. Who may indorse and negotiate the instrument if the instrument is payable as follows: Lucy Lee/Brenda Barton? [p.465] _____
_____

50. If an instrument is payable jointly to two individuals, who must indorse the instrument in order to negotiate it? [p.465] _____

Answers to Refresh Your Memory

1. certificate of deposit [p.453]
2. drawer [p.454]
3. payee [p.454]
4. drawee [p.454]
5. drawer [p.454]
6. traditional paper [p.455]
7. unconditional [p.456]
8. amount of money [p.456]
9. a "medium of exchange authorized or adopted by a domestic or foreign government as part of its currency." [p.457]
10. demand instruments [p.458]
11. extension [p.458]
12. nonnegotiable contract [p.460]
13. assignment [p.460]
14. Negotiation [p.460]
15. indorsement [p.461]

Critical Thought Exercise Model Answer

The general rule is that the terms of the promise or order must be included in the writing on the face of a negotiable instrument. UCC 3-104(a) requires that the terms must also be unconditional. The terms cannot be conditioned on the occurrence or nonoccurrence of some other event or agreement.

By placing the condition on the face of the instrument, IG prevented the checks from being valid negotiable instruments. Both First City Bank and GCB would be within their rights to refuse to honor the checks. A promise to pay that is conditional on another event, such as the issuing of the occupancy permits, is not negotiable because the risk of the other event not occurring would fall on the person who held the instrument. A conditional promise like the one place on the check by IG is subject to normal contract law.

IG will not have made payment on the required contractual installments and may now be in breach of contract. Ace Construction will be able to recover against IG for failure to meet its contractual obligations unless the occupancy permits were a condition of payment contained in the parties' original contract.

The placing of the condition upon the face of the check by GC appears to be unethical. If the condition were not part of its contract with Ace, it would be unethical to attempt to unilaterally modify the terms of their agreement. If the purpose of placing the condition on the check were to cause the checks to be dishonored and thus delay payment, this would also be unethical. IG would be employing a trick to avoid lawful payment, which may damage Ace Construction when it is unable to meet its financial obligations.

Answers to Practice Quiz

True/False:

1. True   A check is an example of a substitute for money.
2. True   Before the drawer can order the drawee to pay money to a third party, the drawee must be obligated to pay the drawer money.
3. True   The financial institution where the drawer has his or her account is the drawee of the check.
4. False   The maker of the note is the party who makes the promise to pay.
5. True   Security against repayment of the note that lenders often require may include cars, homes or other security.
6. False   A maker is the party who issues the promissory note, which is usually the borrower.
7. False   The maker is the financial institution that issues the certificate of deposit.
8. True   Kleenex does not meet the permanence requirement.
9. False   A steel girder is not freely transferable in commerce.
10. True   Unless a drawer or maker's signature appears on an instrument, he or she is not liable.
11. True   The UCC is very liberal when defining the meaning of signature, which may include symbols, marks, etc.
12. False The promise or order must be unconditional.
13. False A negotiable instrument must contain a promise or order to pay a fixed amount of money.
14. True   The fixed amount requisite helps to guarantee that the value of the instrument may be assessed with certainty.
15. True   This is the proper definition of money as expressed by the UCC.
16. False US gold is not negotiable as it is not payable in a medium of exchange of the U.S. government.
17. True   A promise or order to pay cannot state another undertaking by the person ordering or promising payment to do any act in addition to the payment of money.
18. False Demand instruments are instruments that are payable on demand.

19. True   Acceleration, prepayment or extension clauses do not affect an instrument's negotiability.
20. False   A prepayment clause allows the maker to pay the amount due prior to the due date of the instrument.
21. True   Implied or oral instruments are examples of nonnegotiable instruments.
22. True   An authorized representative may sign a negotiable instrument.
23. True   Negotiable instruments can be transferred to subsequent parties after they have been issued.
24. False   When a nonnegotiable contract is transferred, an assignment results.
25. True   Negotiation happens when a transfer of a negotiable instrument by a person other than the issuer takes place.

Multiple Choice:

26. D   Answer D is the correct answer as answers A, B, and C all state the functions that negotiable instruments serve.
27. B   Answer B is the correct answer as a person who issues the draft is the drawer of the draft. Answer A is incorrect as this states the definition of a payee. Answer C is incorrect as this is also the definition of a payee. Answer D is incorrect as this states the definition of the drawee.
28. C   Answer C is the correct answer, as the writing must contain either an unconditional order or promise to pay. Answer A is incorrect as this is not the only requirement that the UCC allows in determining whether an instrument is negotiable. Answer B is incorrect for the same reasoning given with regard to answer A. Answer D is incorrect based on the reasoning given above.
29. D   Answer D is the correct answer as answers A, B, and C all correctly state what a draft or check's unconditional order must contain.
30. A   Answer A is the correct answer as it correctly states what is allowed under the UCC 3-104. Answer B is incorrect as vague amounts are not allowed; fixed amounts of money are. Answer C is incorrect as the instrument must contain an unconditional promise. Answer D is incorrect as it makes no sense.
31. C   Answer C is the correct answer as it correctly defines the meaning of allonge. Answer A, B, and D define the terms indorser, indorsee, and indorsement respectively and therefore are all incorrect.
32. B   Answer B is the correct answer as it properly defines the meaning of an indorsement. Answers A, C, and D are all incorrect as they do not define the term indorsement.
33. D   Answer D is the correct answer as an indorsement that does not specify a particular indorsee is a blank indorsement. Answers A, B, and C are all separate types of indorsements that are not blank indorsements.
34. D   Answer D is the correct answer as Kurt may recover against Stewart as the order and liability of the indorsers is presumed to be the order in which they indorse the instrument. Answer A is incorrect as Martha is not the one who defaulted on the instrument. Answer B is incorrect as Henry is not involved in the hypothetical. Answer C is incorrect as Martha's daughter isn't in the hypothetical either.
35. C   Answer C is the correct answer, as indorsements that disclaim or limit liability on the instrument are known as qualified indorsements. Answers A, B, and D all incorrectly state the meaning of a qualified indorsement.

Short Answer:

36. checks and promissory notes
37. money
38. payee
39. promissory note
40. time note
41. demand note
42. borrower
43. lender
44. writing and permanent and portable
45. Be in writing, be an unconditional promise or order to pay and be signed by the maker or drawer.
46. Because the risk of the other promise or event not occurring would fall on the person who held the instrument.
47. The term fixed amount is a requirement of a negotiable instrument that ensures that the value of the instrument can be determined with certainty.
48. An unqualified indorser is one who signs an unqualified indorsement to an instrument.
49. The *Virgule* (slash mark) allows the instrument to pay either party upon indorsement.
50. If the word and is used when the instrument is payable jointly, both person's indorsements are needed to indorse the instrument.

Chapter 24
HOLDER IN DUE COURSE
AND LIABILITY

Chapter Overview

In the previous chapter, you learned about the various types of negotiable instruments as well as their creation and the ability to transfer the same. This chapter expands on the concept of commercial paper being a substitute for money by exploring the liability of parties on negotiable instruments, as well as the requisites that must be satisfied in order to be deemed a holder in due course. Further, you will learn the defenses that can be raised against the imposition of liability as well as what is involved in discharging liability.

Objectives

Upon completion of the exercises in this chapter, you should be able to:
1.   Explain the meaning of a holder and a holder in due course.
2.   Discuss and apply the requisites for becoming a holder in due course.
3.   Differentiate between primary and secondary liability on negotiable instruments.
4.   Discuss the signature liability of makers, drawers, drawees, acceptors and accommodation parties.
5.   Discuss transfer warranties as well as the liability of parties for breaching them.
6.   Discuss the presentment warranties and describe the liabilities for breaching them.
7.   Recognize real defenses that can be asserted against a holder in due course.
8.   Recognize personal defenses that cannot be asserted against a holder in due course.
9.   Explain the Federal Trade Commission rule that prohibits the holder in due course rule in consumer transactions.
10.   Explain how liability on a negotiable instrument is discharged.

Practical Application

This chapter will provide you with the understanding that you need to determine if you are a holder in due course of negotiable instruments. Further, you will be aware of any defenses that you may be able to assert, as well as what is involved in discharging liability.

Helpful Hints

Since this chapter lays out a list of requirements that are necessary to be a holder in due course as well as requirements for each of the elements contained within the basic definition, it is especially helpful to make use of lists. To facilitate your studies in this area, the study tips section has been organized so that you will be able to easily refer to the lists when analyzing the case studies or hypotheticals presented to you.

Study Tips

<u>**Holder**</u> *versus* <u>**Holder in Due Course**</u>

<u>Defined</u>: A person in possession of
An instrument that is payable to bearer
or an identified person who is in
possession of an instrument payable
to person.

<u>Defined</u>: A holder who takes an instrument
for value, in good faith, and without notice
that is defective or is overdue.

Requisites for being a Holder in Due Course

The individual must be a holder of a negotiable instrument that was taken:

1. **for value** (as elaborated on in UCC 3-303)
   a. if the holder performs the agreed-upon promise.
   b. acquires a security interest or lien on the instrument.
   c. takes the instrument in payment of or as security for an antecedent claim.
   d. Gives a negotiable instrument as payment
   e. Gives an irrevocable obligation as payment.

2. **in good faith**
   a. means honesty in fact.
   b. Honesty is a subjective test as judged by the circumstances.
   c. Good faith only applies to the holder.

3. **without notice of defect**
   a. means that a person cannot be a holder in due course is he or she knows that the instrument is defective in any way.
   b. Defect can be construed as
      1. it being overdue.
      2. it has been dishonored.
      3. it contains an unauthorized signature or has been altered (the red light doctrine).
      4. there is a defense against it.

4. **Other important information**
   a. A holder may not be a holder in due course if at the time of negotiation to the holder, It was forged or altered casting doubt on its authentication.
   b. Payees usually are not considered to be holders in due course because of their knowledge of claims or defenses against the instrument.
   c. Signature liability involves identifying those who are obligated to pay on the negotiable instrument. The signature's location on the instrument gives a clue as to the signer's capacity. The general presumption is that the signature is that of the **indorser**.
      1. Defined- any word, symbol, mark in lieu of written signature that is handwritten, typed, stamped, etc. and adopted or executed by a party to authenticate the writing.
      2. Agent's signature – An individual may sign the negotiable instrument him or herself or authorize an agent to do so. The represented person is the principal. No formal appointment is needed.

3. Unauthorized Signature – This is a signature made by a purported agent without authority from the alleged principal. The purported agent is liable to any individual who in good faith pays the instrument or takes it for value. The alleged principal is liable if he or she ratifies the unauthorized signature.

5. **Primary Liability**
   a. Makers of certificates of deposits and promissory notes have what is known as primary liability. The maker unconditionally promises to render the amount stipulated in the note when it is due.
   b. No party is primarily liable when a draft or check is issued since these instruments are merely an order to pay.

6. **Secondary Liability**
   a. Secondary liability attaches to the drawers of checks and drafts and unqualified indorsers of negotiable instruments.
   b. This is easy to remember, as it's similar to a guarantor of a simple contract.
   c. The drawer is obligated to pay if it is an unaccepted draft or check that is dishonored by the drawee or acceptor.
   d. Requirements for Secondary Liability
      1. The instrument must be properly presented for payment.
      2. The instrument is dishonored.
      3. Notice of the dishonor is given in a timely manner to the person who is to be secondarily liable on the instrument.

7. **Accommodation Party**
   a. Defined- A party who signs an instrument and lends his or her credit (and name) to another party to the instrument.
   b. Special notations:
      1. Guarantee of Payment- The accommodation party who signs an instrument is basically guaranteeing payment and is primarily liable on the instrument.
      2. Guarantee of Collection – This arises where the accommodation party guarantees collection rather than payment. Requirement of payment arises only if:
         a. execution of judgment against the other party has been returned unsatisfied,
         b. the other party is in an insolvency proceeding or is insolvent,
         c. the other party is unable to be served with process, or
         d. it is otherwise obvious that payment cannot be received from the other party. [UCC3-419(d)]

Warranty Liability of Parties

Basic information – Warranty liability is placed upon a transferor irrespective of whether the Transferor signed the instrument or not.

Two types of implied warranties:
1. Transfer of warranties – As defined in your main text, "Any passage of an instrument other than its issuance and presentment for payment is consider a **transfer.**" There are five warranties that are made when a person transfers a negotiable instrument for consideration. They are:

a. The transfer of good title to the instrument or authorization to obtain acceptance or payment on behalf of one who does have good title.
b. All signatures are authentic or authorized.
c. The instrument has not been altered materially.
d. No defenses of any party are applicable against the transferor.
e. The transferor is unaware of any insolvency proceeding against the maker, the acceptor, or the drawer of an unaccepted instrument.
f. **Special notation** – Instruments other than checks may disclaim transfer warranties with the use of an indorsement such as "without recourse" [UCC3-416 (c)]

2. Presentment Warranties – As defined in your main text, "Any person who presents a draft or check for payment or acceptance makes the following warranties to a drawee or acceptor who pays or accepts the instrument in good faith [UCC 3-417(a)]:
a. The presenter has good title to the instrument or is authorized to obtain payment or acceptance of the person who has good title.
b. The material has not been materially altered.
c. The presenter has no knowledge that the signature of the maker or drawer is unauthorized.

Defenses

There are real and personal defenses that arise from the underlying transaction concerning the creation of negotiable instruments.

Real defenses	**versus**	**Personal defenses**
These can be raised against both holders and holders in due course If one of these defenses is proven, neither holder nor holder in due course can recover on the instrument.		These can be raised against enforcement of a negotiable instrument by an ordinary holder.
Minority Extreme duress Mental incapacity Illegality Discharge in bankruptcy Fraud in the Inception Forgery Material alteration		Breach of Contract Fraud in the Inducement Other Personal Defenses - mental illness - illegality of a contract - ordinary duress or undue influence UCC3-305(a)(ii) -discharge of an instrument by payment or cancellation [UCC 3-602 and 3-604]

FTC Elimination of Holder in Due Course Status
Concerning Consumer Credit Transactions

The rule puts the holder of due course of a consumer credit contract on the same level as an assignee of a simple contract. The result is the holder of due course of a consumer credit instrument is subject to all of the defenses and claims of the consumer.

This rule applies to consumer credit transactions that includes a promissory note, the buyer signs an installment sales contract that contains a waiver of defenses clause, and the seller arranges consumer financing with a third-party lender.

Discharge

There are several rules that are specified by the UCC on when and how certain parties are discharged from liability on negotiable instruments. The three main ways that will relieve the Parties from liability are:

- By payment of the instrument
- By cancellation
  - by any manner or
  - by destroying or mutilating a negotiable instrument with the intent of getting rid of the obligation.
- By impairment of the right of recourse which is accomplished by
  - releasing an obligor from liability or
  - surrendering collateral without the consent of the parties who would benefit by it.

Refresh Your Memory

The following exercise will enable you to refresh your memory on the rules and principles presented to you in this chapter. Read each question twice and place your answer in the blanks provided. Review the chapter material for any question you miss or are unable to remember.

1. A _____ is a person in possession of an instrument that is payable to an identified person or a bearer in possession of an instrument payable to that person.

2. A _____ in _____ _____ is a holder who takes an instrument for value, in good faith, and without notice that is defective or is overdue.

3. Suppose Monica draws a check "payable to the order of Greg Wallace" and delivers the check to Greg. Greg indorses the check and gives it as a gift to his son. Can Greg's son qualify as a holder in due course? _____
_____

4. Good faith as it applies to holder means _____ in fact in the conduct or transaction concerned.

5. Steve, a thief steals a negotiable instrument and transfers it to Cindy. Cindy is unaware that the instrument is stolen. Since Cindy meets the good faith test, she will qualify as a _____ _____ _____ _____.

6. A person cannot qualify as a holder in due course if he or she has _____ that the instrument is defective in certain ways.

7. An instrument that specifies a definite date for payment of the instrument is known as a _____.

8. An instrument that is payable on demand is known as a _____ _____.

9. When an instrument has been presented for payment and payment has been refused, it is _____.

10. Which doctrine says a holder cannot qualify as a holder in due course if he or she has notice of an unauthorized signature or an alteration of the instrument or any adverse claim or defense to its payment? The _____ _____ doctrine

11. A person cannot be held contractually liable on a negotiable instrument unless his or her signature appears on the instrument. This is known as _____ liability.

12. A person who has been authorized to sign a negotiable instrument on behalf of another person is an _____.

13. A person who authorizes an agent to sign a negotiable instrument on his or her behalf is known as a _____.

14. A signature that is made by a purported agent without authority from the purported principal is an _____ signature.

15. Liability on a negotiable instrument that is imposed on a party only when the party primarily liable on the instrument defaults and fails to pay the instrument when due is known as _____ _____.

Critical Thought Exercise

Betty Smith made out a check to George Bell of Bell Plumbing for $1,500 as a partial payment for plumbing renovation of her kitchen. When it was time for Bell to begin his work, he did not appear, nor could Ms. Smith locate him. Smith immediately ordered her bank to stop payment on the check. Bell had already cashed the check at Redi-Cash. When the check was returned to Redi-Cash marked "payment stopped by account holder," Redi-Cash was contacted by an attorney for Smith who informed Redi-Cash that the plumber did not have a license and that engaging in a contracting trade without a license was a crime. Therefore the contract was void and his client would not honor the check.

As manager of Redi-Cash, will you commence suit against Smith to collect the amount of the check?

Answer. _____

_____

_____

_____

_____

_____

_____

_____

_____

_____

_____

_____

_____

_____

_____

Practice Quiz

True/False:

1. ____ If Samantha is in possession of a negotiable instrument that is drawn, issued or indorsed to her, or to bearer, or in blank, she may be a holder. [p 473]

2. ____ Under the UCC, value has been given if the holder gives an irrevocable obligation as payment. [p.474]

3. ____ Good faith applies to both the transferor of the instrument as well as the holder. [p 475]

4. ____ An instrument is dishonored when it is presented for payment and the payment is accepted. [p 475]

5. ____ A holder cannot qualify as a holder in due course if he or she has notice that the instrument contains an unauthorized signature. [p 475]

6. ____ Payees do not meet the requirements for being a holder in due course. [p 476]

7. ____ Signature liability refers to an individual's contractual liability on a negotiable instrument and whether or not his or her signature appears on it. [p 476]

8. ____ The location of a signature on the instrument usually determines the signer's capacity. [p 477]

9. ____ The signature on a negotiable instrument can only be by name. [p 477]

10. ____ When a person authorizes a representative to sign an instrument on his or her behalf, the representative is the principal. [p 477]

11. ____ A signature made by a purported agent without authority from a purported principal is an authorized signature. [p 478]

12. ____ The makers of promissory notes and certificates of deposit have primary liability for the instrument. [p 478]

13. ____ Drawers on unaccepted drafts and checks and unqualified indorsers are primarily liable on negotiable instruments. [p 479]

14. ____ One of the requirements for imposing secondary liability on a negotiable instrument is if the instrument is dishonored. [p 480]

15. ____ An accommodation party is one who signs an instrument guaranteeing payment and is secondarily liable on the instrument. [p 481]

16. ____ An accommodation party may sign an instrument guaranteeing collection rather than payment on an instrument. [p 481]

17. ____ The two types of implied warranties are transfer warranties and presentment warranties. [p 482]

18. ____ Transfer warranties may be disclaimed with regard to checks. [p 483]

19. ____ A holder in due course takes instrument free from real defenses. [p 483]

20. ____ The defense of forgery is a personal defense. [p 484]

21. ____ An instrument that has been materially and fraudulently altered cannot be enforced by an ordinary holder. [p 485]

22. ____ Personal defenses may be raised against a holder of due course. [p 485]

23. ____ Fraud in the inducement happens when a wrongdoer makes a misrepresentation to another person to lead that person to enter into a contract with the wrongdoer. [p 485]

24. ____ A holder of a negotiable instrument may discharge the liability of any party to the transaction by cancellation. [p 488]

25. ____ A holder does not owe any duties to others when seeking recourse against the liable parties or the collateral. [p 488]

Multiple Choice:

26. A holder is [p 473]
    a. a person who takes an instrument for value and in good faith.
    b. a person who takes without notice that it is defective or overdue.
    c. a person in possession of an instrument that is payable to bearer or an identified person who is in possession of an instrument payable to that person.
    d. a person who takes a negotiable instrument free of all claims and most defenses.

27. To be classified as a holder in due course, the transferee must [p 474]
    a. be the holder of a negotiable instrument taken for value.
    b. be the holder of a negotiable instrument in good faith.

    c. be the holder of a negotiable instrument that bears no apparent evidence of forgery.

    d. all of the above.

28. If Megan promises to perform but has not done so yet and there has been no value given, Megan is not a [p 474]

    a. holder in due course.

    b. third-party beneficiary.

    c. holder without value.

    d. None of the above.

29. If a time instrument is not paid on its expressed date, then it [p 475]

    a. becomes effective.

    b. becomes overdue and is defective as to its payment.

    c. is payable on demand.

    d. can be made payable according to business practices.

30. Signers of instruments include [p 477]

    a. drawers of drafts.

    b. drawees who certify checks.

    c. agents who sign on behalf of others.

    d. all of the above.

31. An agent has no personal liability on an instrument he or she signs on behalf of a principal if the signature shows [p 477]

    a. a symbol.

    b. a mark.

    c. unambiguously that it is made on behalf of a principal who is identified in the instrument.

    d. ambiguously that it is made on behalf of a principal who is identified in the instrument.

32. Absolute liability to pay a negotiable instrument, subject to certain real defenses is known as [p 478]

    a. secondary liability.

    b. primary liability.

    c. personal liability.

    d. real liability.

33. Liability on a negotiable instrument that is imposed on a party only when the party primarily liable on the instrument defaults and fails to pay the instrument when due is referred to as [p 479]

    a. indorser's liability.

    b. secondary liability.

    c. primary liability.

    d. None of the above.

34. Hugo draws a check on Coast Bank "payable to the order of Lamar Huff." When Lamar presents the check for payment, Coast Bank refuses to pay it. Lamar can collect the amount of the check from Hugo because Hugo is [p 479]
    a. the maker.
    b. the drawee.
    c. the person who ratified the check.
    d. the drawer.

35. A demand for acceptance or payment of an instrument made upon the maker, acceptor, drawee, or other payor by or on behalf of the holder is referred to as [p 480]
    a. a notice of dishonor.
    b. an unqualified indorser.
    c. the red light doctrine.
    d. presentment.

Short Answer:

36. A holder is a person who is in possession of a _____ _____ that is drawn, issued, or indorsed to him or his order, or to bearer, or in blank. [p 473]

37. _____ defenses may be asserted against a holder in due course. [p 473]

38. The holder must be given _____ for the negotiable instrument to qualify as a holder in due course. [p 474]

39. A demand instrument is one that is _____ [p 475]

40. A time instrument is one that specifies _____ [p 475]

41. What is the red light doctrine? _____
_____ [p 475]

42. A person who forges a signature on a check may be held liable to a _____
_____. [p 477]

43. Unqualified indorsers are _____ liable on negotiable instruments they indorse. [p 479]

44. Indorsers who indorse instruments "without recourse" or similar language that disclaims liability are referred to as _____ indorsers. [p 480]

45. Brittany, a high school senior wants to buy a car on credit from Townsend Motors. She baby sits every other weekend, but does not have a sufficient income or credit history to enable her to receive credit by herself. Brittany asks her father to co-sign the note to Townsend Motors, which he does. The father is an _____
_____ and is _____ liable on the note. [p 481]

46. A transfer is _____
_____. [p 482]

47. Mental incompetency is a _____ defense that can be raised against holders in due course. [p 484]

48. Breach of contract is a _____ defense that can be raised against enforcement of a negotiable instrument by an ordinary holder. [p 485]

49. When is an instrument dishonored? [p.475] _____

_____

50. An accommodation party is a party who signs _____

_____. [p 481]

Answers to Refresh Your Memory

1. holder [p 473]
2. holder in due course [p 473]
3. Greg's son may not qualify as a holder in due course because he has not given value for it. [p 474]
4. honesty [p 475]
5. holder in due course [p 475]
6. notice [p 475]
7. time instrument [p 475]
8. demand instrument [p 475]
9. dishonored [p 475]
10. red light [p 475]
11. signature [p 476]
12. agent [p 477]
13. principal [p 477]
14. unauthorized [p 478]
15. secondary liability [p 479]

Critical Thought Exercise Model Answer

A holder of a negotiable instrument is a holder in due course (HDC) pursuant to UCC 3-302 if he or she takes the instrument (1) for value; (2) in good faith; and (3) without notice that it is overdue, that it has been dishonored, that any person has a defense against it or claim to it, or that the instrument contains unauthorized signatures, alterations, or is so irregular or incomplete as to call into question its authenticity. Redi-Cash gave value for the instrument when they cashed it for Bell. The UCC defines good faith as "honesty in fact and the observance of reasonable commercial standards of fair dealing." UCC 3-103(4). It is immaterial whether the transferor acted in good faith. There is nothing in the facts to show that Redi-Cash did anything but act in good faith. There appears to have been nothing that would have put Redi-Cash on notice that Smith had a defense against the instrument. The fraud, deceit, or illegality of Bell's actions do not keep Redi-Cash from being a HDC.

Unless the instrument arising from a contract or transaction is, itself, made void by statute, the illegality defense under UCC 3-305 is not available to bar the claim of a holder in due course.

Therefore, Redi-Cash should be viewed as a HDC and actually has rights greater than Bell in regards to this negotiable instrument. Smith should be ordered to pay Redi-Cash the $2,500 that Redi-Cash paid for the instrument. Smith will have to seek recourse against Bell.

Answers to Practice Quiz

True/False:

1. True   A holder is an individual in possession of a negotiable instrument that is drawn, issued, or indorsed to him or his order, or to bearer, or in blank.
2. True   A holder giving an irrevocable obligation as payment is one of the things that qualify as value being given under UCC 3-303.
3. False   Good faith only applies to the holder.
4. False   An instrument is dishonored when it is refused upon presentment for payment.
5. True   The red light doctrine provides that if a holder has notice that the instrument contains an unauthorized signature or has been altered or has an adverse claim against or defense to its payment, a holder cannot qualify as a holder in due course.
6. True   Payees know about any claims or defenses against the instrument and therefore do not meet the requirements of being a holder in due course.
7. True   Signature liability is known as contract liability.
8. True   A signer's capacity is often determined by the location of his or her signature.
9. False   A signature on a negotiable instrument may be by word, name, mark or any symbol that is handwritten, stamped, typed or otherwise affixed.
10. False   One who authorizes another to do an act on his or her behalf is the principal.
11. False   One whose signature is made by one without authority from a purported principal is an unauthorized signature.
12. True   Makers of certificates of deposit and promissory notes have absolute liability to pay the negotiable instrument, subject to liability known as primary liability.
13. False   Unqualified indorsers are secondarily liable on negotiable instruments that they indorse.
14. True   A party is secondarily liable on a negotiable instrument if the instrument is dishonored.
15. False   A party who signs an instrument guaranteeing payment is an accommodation and is primarily liable on the instrument.
16. True   An accommodation party may agree to sign an instrument guaranteeing collection rather than payment of an instrument.
17. True   Transfer and presentment warranties are the two implied warranties when negotiating instruments.
18. False   Transfer warranties cannot be disclaimed regarding checks however, they can be disclaimed with regard to other instruments.
19. False   A holder in due course takes the instrument free from personal defenses.
20. False   Forgery is a real defense.
21. True   The fraudulent and material alteration of an instrument prevents an ordinary holder from enforcing the same.
22. False   Personal defenses can be raised against the enforcement of a negotiable instrument by an ordinary holder.

23. True   When a wrongdoer makes a false statement to lead another person to enter into a contract with him or her, this is known as fraud in the inducement.

24. True   The liability of any party to an instrument may be discharged by cancellation of the instrument by the holder.

25. False   A holder owes a duty not to impair the rights of others when seeking recourse against the liable parties or the collateral.

Multiple Choice:

26. C   Answer C is correct as a holder is an identified person who is in possession of an instrument payable to that person or a person in possession of an instrument that is payable to bearer. Answers A and B are incorrect as they each partially state the definition for a holder in due course. Answer D is incorrect as this states a fact with regard to an individual who is a holder in due course.

27. D   Answer D is the correct as answers A, B, and C all state what the transferee must be in order to be classified as a holder in due course.

28. A   Answer A is the correct answer as Megan does not meet the requirements of taking for value and performing the agree-upon promise as is required in order to be a holder in due course. Answer B is incorrect, as it makes no sense since third-party beneficiaries need not perform nor give value per se. Answer C is incorrect, as it makes no sense. Answer D is incorrect based on the reasoning given above.

29. B   Answer B is the correct answer as time instruments that are not paid on their expressed due dates become overdue the next day and are indicative of some type of defect in payment. Answer A is incorrect because this is not a true statement. Answer C is incorrect as an instrument that is payable on demand is somewhat opposite of one where a due date is expressed as in the time instrument. Answer D is incorrect as making an instrument payable according to business practices refers to what may be used to determine a reasonable time for payment of other demand instruments as per UU 3-304.

30. D   Answer D is the correct answer as answers A, B, and C state all who may be signers of instruments.

31. C   Answer C is the correct answer as it correctly states when an agent will not be held liable for signing on behalf of a principal. Answers A, and B are incorrect as these merely state the types of signatures that are acceptable. Answer D is incorrect as the term ambiguous may infer liability of an agent who signs on behalf of a principal as it may cast doubt on the agent's capacity.

32. B   Answer B is the correct answer as primary liability is defined as absolute liability to pay a negotiable instrument, subject to certain real defenses. Answer A is incorrect as secondary liability occurs on a negotiable instrument when the party primarily liable on the instrument defaults and fails to pay with the instrument is due. Answer C is incorrect as there is no principal known as personal liability with respect to payment of negotiable instruments. Answer D is incorrect based on the reasoning given for answer C.

33. B   Answer B is the correct answer as secondary liability refers to liability on a negotiable instrument that is imposed on a party only when the party primarily liable on the instrument defaults and fails to pay the instrument when due. Answer A is incorrect as indorser's are secondarily liable on negotiable instruments that they indorse. Answer C is incorrect as primary liability is absolute liability to pay a negotiable instrument, subject to certain real defenses. Answer D is incorrect for the reasons stated above.

34. D   Answer D is the correct answer as Hugo as the drawer is secondarily liable on the dishonored check. Answer A is incorrect as makers are usually the borrowers who make the promise to pay, which is not the case in this, hypothetical. Answer B is incorrect, as

Coast Bank would be considered the drawee, as they are the financial institution upon which the check is written. Answer C makes no sense as Hugo cannot accept his own check if he has given it to Lamar Huff.

35. D   Answer D is the correct answer as a presentment is a demand for acceptance or payment of an instrument made upon the maker, acceptor, drawee, or other behalf of the holder. Answer A is incorrect as a notice of dishonor refers to the formal act of letting the party with secondary liability to pay a negotiable instrument know that the instrument has been dishonored. Answer B is incorrect as an unqualified indorser is someone who is secondarily liable on negotiable instruments that they indorse. Answer C is incorrect as the red light doctrine refers to a holder having notice of an unauthorized signature or an alteration of an instrument or any adverse claim against or defense to its payment.

Short Answer:

36.   negotiable instrument
37.   real
38.   value
39.   payable on demand
40.   a definite date for payment of the instrument
41.   The red light doctrine asserts that a holder cannot qualify as a holder in due course if he or she has notice of an unauthorized signature or an alteration of the instrument or an alteration of the instrument or any adverse claim against or defense to its payment.
42.   holder in due course
43.   secondarily
44.   qualified
45.   accommodation maker, primarily
46   any passage of an instrument other than its issuance and presentment for payment.
47.   real
48.   personal
49.   An instrument is dishonored when it has been presented for payment and has been refused.
50.   an instrument and lends his or her name and credit to another party in the instrument

Chapter 25
CHECKS AND DIGITAL BANKING

Chapter Overview

This chapter is primarily concerned with checks, the most common form of negotiable instrument. In this chapter you will learn about several different kinds of checks as well as the process involved regarding payment and collection of checks through the banking system. Additionally, this chapter explores the duties as well as liabilities of banks and other parties in the collection process along with electronic fund transfers.

Objectives

Upon completion of the exercises in this chapter, you should be able to:
1. Differentiate between a cashier's check, certified and traveler's checks.
2. Explain the system of processing and collecting checks through the banking system.
3. Discuss postdated and stale checks.
4. Recognize when a bank participates in a wrongful dishonor of a check.
5. Explain the liability of parties when a signature or indorsement on a check is forged.
6. Explain the liability of parties when a check has been altered.
7. Discuss a bank's midnight deadline for deciding whether or not to dishonor a check.
8. Discuss the requisites of the Expedited Funds Availability Act.
9. Explain the electronic fund transfer system.
10. Explain the term wire transfer and discuss the main provisions of Article 4A of the Uniform Commercial Code.

Practical Application

Since almost everyone will have the opportunity to either have a checking account or purchase one of the various types of checks, this chapter will prove to be an invaluable resource to those who study it. It will provide insight into the banking procedures involving payment and collection of checks as well as assist you in knowing what the banks' duties and other parties' duties and liabilities are in the collection process. Further, you will gain useful information concerning electronic fund transfers.

Helpful Hints

This chapter will be relatively easy for most individuals to learn, since much of what is presented has already been experienced in most individuals' everyday personal and business affairs. There may be a few terms that you recognize by definition but not by term that you will want to review a little more carefully. Examples of these types of terms include but are not limited to such words as stale checks, incomplete checks, deferred posting, provisional posting, etc. This chapter's high applicability makes it a very interesting learning experience.

Study Tips

Checks

Explained: A substitute for money and also a record-keeping device.
Special Notation: They do not serve a credit function.

The Banking Relationship:

The customer is the creditor.
The bank is the debtor.
A principal-agent relationship may also be formed whereby the customer is the principal ordering the bank to collect or pay on the check. The bank in turn is the agent that is obligated to follow the customer as principal's order.

The Basics of Banking:

Ordinary checks   When a customer goes to a bank, fills out the proper forms along with a signature card, followed by a deposit, the bank issues checks to him or her. Thereafter, the customer uses the checks for his or her purchases. The checks are presented to the bank and paid provided the drawer's signature matches the signature card.

Parties to a check   Drawer – This is the customer with a checking account.
     Drawee - This is the bank (or payor) at which the check is drawn.
     Payee – The one to whom the check is written.

Indorsement   This refers to the holder or payee signing the back of the check. The payee is the indorser and the person to whom the check is indorsed is the indorsee.

Point-of-Sale
Terminals   The customer's account is immediately debited for the amount of the purchase by using a bank issued debit card to make a purchase.

Direct Deposits
And Withdrawals   The customer's bank and the payee's bank must belong to the same clearinghouse in order to provide the service of paying recurring payments and recurring deposits.

Pay-by-Internet   Customers may pay bills from their account using their PIN number and account number, the amount of the bill to be paid, and the account number of the payee.

Special Checks: Bank checks are special checks. There are certified checks, cashier's checks, and traveler's checks.

     Certified checks – With this type of check, the bank agrees in advance to accept the check when it is presented for payment and pay the check out of funds set aside from the customer's account. These types of checks are payable at any time from when they are issued. The bank writes or stamps the word *certified* across the face of an ordinary check thereby certifying it. The date, amount being certified and the individual certifying the check also are placed on the check. Payment may not be stopped on a certified check.

Cashier's check – This is a bank-issued check where the customer has paid the bank the amount of the check and a fee. The bank guarantees the payment of the check. The bank acts as the drawer and the drawee with the holder as payee. The bank debits its own account when the check is presented.

Traveler's checks – This type of check is a two-party instrument where the bank who issues it is both the drawer and the drawee. An interesting notation about this type of check is that it has two signature lines, one for the purchaser to sign when he or she purchases the checks and the other for the purchaser to sign when he or she uses the check for purchases. This type of check is especially popular among travelers as it serves as a safe substitute for cash, as it is not negotiable until it is signed a second time.

Honoring Checks	The customer of a bank agrees to keep sufficient funds in the account to cover any checks written. If the customer keeps his or her end of this implied agreement, the bank is under a duty to honor the check and charge the customer (or drawer's) account for whatever amount(s) the check(s) were written for.
Stale Checks	A stale check is one that has been outstanding for more than six months. Under UCC 4-404, the bank is not obligated to pay on a stale check. If the bank does pay it, it may also in good faith charge the drawer's account.
Incomplete Checks	If a drawer fails to provide information on a check, the holder may complete the information and the bank may charge the customer's account the amount of the completed amount. The exception to this is if the bank receives notice that the completion was improper.
Death or Incompetence of A Drawer	Checks may be paid against the accounts of deceased customers on or prior to the date of death for 10 days after the date of death. With regard to incompetent customers, the checks may be paid against their accounts until the bank has actual knowledge of the condition and has had a reasonable chance to act on the information given.
Stop Payment Order	This is an order by a drawer of a check to the payor bank not to pay or certify a check. It may be accomplished orally or in writing, however, if it is oral, the order is good for only fourteen days. If it is in writing, the order is good for six months, and may be renewed in writing for additional six months periods.
Overdrafts	If a customer does not have sufficient funds in his or her account to cover the amount, the payor bank may either dishonor the check or honor the check and create an overdraft in the drawer's account. In the event of a dishonor, the payor bank notifies the drawer of the dishonor and returns the check to the holder marked insufficient funds. If the holder resubmits the check and there still are insufficient funds in the customer's account, then the holder may seek

recourse against the drawer.

Wrongful dishonor   When the bank fails to honor a check where there are sufficient funds in the drawer's account to pay a properly payable check, it is liable for wrongful dishonor. The bank is liable to the drawer for damages that were proximately caused by the dishonor along with consequential damages and damages that may have resulted from criminal prosecution.

Forged and Altered Checks:

Forged signature of the drawer:

The bank is under a duty to verify the drawer's signature by matching the signature on the check with that of the signature card on file at the bank.

Impact of a forged signature – The instrument is inoperative. The bank cannot charge the customer's account if it pays a check over a forged signature. The bank's recourse is against the party who presented the check provided he or she was not aware of the unauthorized signature. The forger is liable on the check if he or she can be found.

Altered checks:

An unauthorized change in the check that modifies a legal obligation of a party is an altered check. The check may be dishonored by the bank if it discovers the alteration. If an altered check is paid by the bank, the bank may charge the drawer's account for the original tenor (amount) of the check, but not the altered amount.

The warranty of presentment applies here especially if there has been an alteration in a chain of collection. Each party in the chain may collect from the preceding transferor based on a breach of this warranty.

The Collection Process:

The collection process is ruled by Article 4 of the UCC. When an individual receives a check, he or she may go to the drawer's bank or to his or her own bank (known as the **depository bank**). The depository bank must present the check to the payor bank for collection. Banks not classified as a payor or depository bank are **intermediary banks.**

The Federal Reserve System

The Federal Reserve System helps banks to collect on checks. Member banks may submit paid checks to the Federal Reserve Bank for payment. Member banks pay the federal reserve to debit and credit their accounts and to show collection and payment of checks.

362

Deferred Posting

Deferred posting applies to all banks. This refers to a daily cutoff for posting checks or deposits. Weekends and holidays do not count as business days unless all of the banks functions are carried on as usual on those days.

Provisional Credits

"When a collecting bank gives credit to a check in the collection process prior to its final settlement. Provisional credits may be reversed if the check does not "clear.""

Final Settlement

A check is deemed finally settled if the payor bank pays the check in cash, settles for the check without having the right to revoke the settlement or fails to dishonor the check within certain time periods. UCC 4-215(a)

If the drawer and holder have accounts at the same bank, then the check is called an **"on us"** item. The check is considered paid if the bank fails to dishonor the check by business on the second banking day following the receipt of the check.

If the drawer and holder have accounts at different banks, the check is an **"on them"** item. Each bank must take action prior to its **midnight deadline** following the banking day it received an "on them" check for collection. UCC 4-104(a)(10)

A deposit of money becomes available for withdrawal at the opening of the next banking day following the deposit. UCC 4-215 (a)

Four Legals that Prevent Payment of a Check

1. Receipt of notice of customer's death, bankruptcy and adjudication of incompentcy.

2. Receipt of court order freezing the customer's account.

3. Receipt of a stop payment order from the drawer.

4. The payor bank's exercise of its right of setoff against the customer's account.

Failure to Examine Bank Statements in A Timely Manner

Generally banks send monthly statements to their customers. If this does not occur, banks must provide adequate information to allow the customer to be aware of which checks were paid and when and for what amount. If the checks are not given back to the customer, then the bank must keep the checks or copies for seven years.

Customer's duty - To examine the statements promptly and with reasonable care. If an error or forgery is present, the customer must promptly notify the bank.

Liability of Collecting Banks for Their Own negligence

The collecting bank owes a duty to use ordinary care in presenting and sending a check for collection. A bank is liable only for losses caused by its own negligence. UCC 4-202

Commercial Wire Transfers

A commercial wire transfer involves the transferring of money over one or both of the two main wire systems, the Federal Reserve wire transfer network and the New York Clearing House Interbank Payments System.

Article 4A of the UCC governs wholesale wire transfers. It only applies to commercial electronic fund transfers.

Security procedures that are commercially reasonable should be established.

Refresh Your Memory

The following exercise will enable you to refresh your memory on the rules and principles presented to you in this chapter. Read each question twice and place your answer in the blanks provided. Review the chapter material for any question you miss or are unable to remember.

1. _____ are the most common form of negotiable instrument.

2. Upon making a deposit into a bank, a _____ relationship is formed.

3. Give one way a principal-agent relationship is created. _____
_____

4. What types of rules and principles does Article 4 of the UCC regulate? _____
_____

5. Which article of the UCC establishes rules that regulate the creation and collection of and liability for wire transfers? _____

6. What is a check? _____

7. The customer who maintains the checking account and writes checks against the account is known as the _____.

8. The payee is the _____ and the person to whom the check is indorsed is the _____.

9. The bank on which the check is drawn is the _____.

10. Give three examples of bank checks. _____, _____, and _____.

11. When is a check considered to be certified? _____

12. Individuals usually purchase these types of checks to use as a safe substitute for cash while on vacation or other trips. _____ _____

13. Which act regulates consumer electronic fund transfers? The _____ _____ _____ Act

14. List at least two things that are protected under Regulation E. _____

15. What duty does the bank have if it receives a properly drawn and payable check? _____

Critical Thought Exercise

Dave Austin of Austin Imports is an antique dealer who often makes purchases without sufficient funds in his account because he must often act quickly to purchase a one-of-a-kind item before another dealer can take advantage of a very profitable sale price. Austin often postdates checks for the purchases of furniture, art, rugs and other items that he resells. Austin has a very good relationship with Everglades Bank in Miami, where his main studio is located. The operations officer of Everglades Bank knows that Austin uses postdated checks for purchases approximately 50-75 times per year out of a total of 1,200 checks written on his account.

When the operations officer at Everglades Bank took a position with another bank, four postdated checks totaling $58,000 were negotiated before the written date, causing 47 other checks to be dishonored.

If Austin sues Everglades Bank to recover incidental and consequential damages for wrongful dishonor, will he prevail?

Answer. _____

_____

_____

_____

Practice Quiz

True/False:

1. ____ Checks act as a substitute for money and serve a credit function too. [p 494]

2. ____ A payee is the customer who maintains the checking account and draws checks against the account. [p 495]

3. ____ Traveler's checks are issued without a named payee. [p 497]

4. ____ It is not necessary that a traveler's check be signed a second time. [p 497]

5. ____ The bank must pay on a stale check if it has been outstanding for more than six months. [p 499]

6. ____ Kami owes Kathy $250, and draws a check payable to Kathy on Main Bank. Kami signs the check but omits to fill in the amount of the check. Kathy fraudulently fills in "$2,500" and presents the check to Main Bank, which pays it. Main Bank may charge Kami's account $2,500. [p 499]

7. ____ Checks may not be paid against the accounts of deceased customers. [p 499]

8. ____ A stop-payment order on a check may be done orally or in writing. [p 500]

9. ____ If Joanne does not have enough money in her account when a properly presented check is presented for payment, the bank may honor the check and create an overdraft in Joanne's account. [p 500]

10. ____ If Greenville bank does not honor a check when there is sufficient funds in Ed Koski's account to pay a properly payable check, the Greenville bank will be liable for wrongful dishonor. [p 500]

11. ____ Under the Forged Signature Act, a bank is exempt from verification of signatures involving customers who have banked with them for more than ten years. [p 501]

12. ____ If a payor bank pays on an altered check, it can charge the drawer's account of the original tenor as well as the altered amount. [p 501]

13. ____ A depository bank is the bank where the payee or holder has an account. [p 502]

14. ____ An intermediary bank is the depository bank and other banks in the collection process. [p 502]

15. ___ Under the deferred posting rule, banks are not allowed to fix an afternoon hour as a cutoff for the purpose of processing items. [p 503]

16. ___ An "on us" item refers to the fact that both the drawer and the payee or holder have accounts at the same bank. [p 503]

17. ___ An "on them" item refers to the fact that a drawer and the payee or holder have accounts at different banks. [p 504]

18. ___ A deposit of money to an account becomes available for withdrawal immediately following the deposit. [p 504]

19. ___ The bank's receipt of notice that a customer has died will prevent payment of a check. [p 504]

20. ___ There is no set period for which a bank must retain a customer's checks if the checks are not returned to the customer. [p 505]

21. ___ One of the benefits of using wire transfers is speed. [p 506]

22. ___ Article 4A applies only to commercial electronic fund transfers. [p 506]

23. ___ Debit cards may be used regardless if the merchant has a point-of-sale terminal. [p 496]

24. ___ Purchasers of traveler's checks must have an account at the issuing bank. [p 498]

25. ___ If a bank fails to pay electronic fund transfer when there are sufficient funds in the customer's account to do so, the bank will be liable for wrongful dishonor. [p 498]

Multiple Choice:

26. Which of the following is not true with regard to checks? [p 494]
    a. Checks act as a substitute for money.
    b. Checks are a good record-keeping device.
    c. Checks serve a credit function.
    d. Checks are the most common form of negotiable instrument.

27. In order for a bank to provide the service of paying recurring payments and crediting recurring deposits, which of the following is necessary? [p 496]
    a. The customer's bank and the payee's bank must belong to the same clearinghouse.
    b. The customer must have a computer to pay his or her bills on the Internet.
    c. The customer must qualify for a debit card at the bank that holds his or her money.
    d. None of the above.

28. Which of the following is a type of check where a bank agrees in advance to accept the check when it is presented for payment? [p 496]
    a. A point-of-sale terminal check
    b. A traveler's check
    c. An automatic withdrawal check
    d. A certified check

29. A stale check is one that [p 499]
    a. has been left on the counter for a week.
    b. has been presented for payment of a drawer's properly drawn check by the drawee bank.
    c. has the risk of loss of an incomplete item on the drawer.
    d. has been outstanding for more than six months.

30. An oral stop-payment order is binding for [p 500]
    a. ten days.
    b. fourteen calendar days.
    c. an indefinite period of time.
    d. for six months and renewable for additional six-month periods.

31. The term original tenor refers to [p 501]
    a. the original amount for which the drawer wrote the check.
    b. the original amount that the parties initially spoke of.
    c. the first singer in a choir.
    d. none of the above.

32. What is the effect of a drawer's failure to report a forged or altered check to the bank within the prescribed time frame? [p 502]
    a. It has no effect on the bank's liability.
    b. Both the drawer and the bank are liable.
    c. It relieves the bank of any liability for paying on the instrument.
    d. The drawer may go to the payor's bank and seek recourse.

33. The midnight deadline refers to [p 504]
    a. proper action being taken on a check before midnight of the next banking day.
    b. monies becoming available for withdrawal at the opening of the next banking day.
    c. depositing an "on them" check for collection.
    d. a depositor's loss of his or her account at midnight.

34. What type of duty does a bank owe in presenting and sending a check for collection? [p 505]
    a. It owes a duty to inspect.
    b. It owes a special duty of care
    c. It owes a duty to use ordinary care.
    d. It owes a higher duty of care.

35. What type of duty does a customer owe when determining if any payment was unauthorized due to alteration of a check or forged signature? [p 505]
    a. The customer does not owe any duty whatsoever.
    b. The customer owes a duty to change banks.
    c. The customer owes a duty to promptly examine the statements and determine if payment was unauthorized.
    d. The customer owes a duty to apprise the bank of its duty.

Short Answer:

36. Which article establishes the requisites for finding a negotiable instrument? [p 494]
_____.

37. Who is the drawer of a check? [p 495] _____

38. What does the bank process of certification involve? [p 496] _____
_____

39. What will the bank who is obligated on a cashier's check be held liable for? [p 497]
_____

40. If a check is dishonored because of insufficient funds, it is said to have _____.
[p 500]

41. A check with a forged drawer's signature is called a _____ _____.
[p.501]

42. A check that has been altered without authorization that modifies the legal obligation of the
party is an _____ _____. [p 501]

43. In terms of banking, what is meant by provisional credit? [p 503] _____
_____
_____

44. What is meant by presentment across the counter? [p 504] _____
_____

45. When is the process of posting considered to be complete? [p 504] _____
_____

46. If Kurt wants to write a post-dated check to Mona, what must he do to accomplish this
under the rules of UCC 4-401(c)? [p 499] _____
_____

47. Wanda, a customer of Mississippi Bank and Trust passes away on January 1. What is the
rule regarding the length of time that her bank may pay or certify checks drawn on her
account? [p 499] _____

48. The amount of money a drawer owes a bank after it has paid a check despite insufficient
funds in the drawer's account is known as an _____. [p.500]

49. Bank One receives a $25,000 deposit from Walter Dole. If Bank One fails to file a
Currency Transaction Report (CTR) in order to avoid the reporting requirements, what
repercussions might it face for its negligence? [p 501] _____
_____

50. An order by a drawer of a check to the payor bank to not pay or certify a check is a
_____. [p 500]

Answers to Refresh Your Memory

1. Checks [p 494]
2. creditor-debtor [p 494]
3. If a deposit is a check that the bank must collect for the customer, a principal-agent relationship is created. [p 494]
4. It regulates bank deposits and collection procedures for checking accounts offered by commercial banks. [p 494]
5. Article 4A (Funds Transfer) [p 494]
6. The UCC 3-104(f) defines a check as " an order by the drawer bank to pay a specified sum of money from the drawer's checking account to the named payee (or holder)." [p 495]
7. drawer [p 495]
8. indorser, indorsee [p 495]
9. drawee [p 495]
10. certified, cashiers, and travelers [p 496]
11. When the bank stamps or writes the word certified across an ordinary check's face. [p 496]
12. traveler's checks [p 497]
13. Electronic Fund Transfer [p 498]
14. lost or stolen debit cards and evidence of transactions (answers will vary) [p 498]
15. The bank has a duty to honor the check and charge the drawer's account the amount of the check. [p 499]

Critical Thought Exercise Model Answer

A bank may charge a postdated check against a customer's account as a demand instrument, unless the customer notifies the bank of the postdating in time to allow the bank to act on the notice before the bank commits itself to pay on the check. If the bank receives timely notice from the customer and nonetheless charges the customer's account before the date on the postdated check, the bank may be liable for any damages incurred by the customer as a result.

Austin had discussed the use of postdated checks with Austin and permitted his practice of postdating a significant number of checks each year. Everglades Bank will have a difficult time convincing a court that it was not on notice that postdated checks were being written by Austin. However, the UCC makes it clear that the customer must not only give notice that a postdated check has been issued, but must also describe the postdated check with reasonable certainty. Austin never contacted the bank to describe the checks with any certainty. He just relied upon the practice of a prior employee of the bank who examined his checks carefully before charging them to his account. Under the UCC, Everglades Bank has not received notice concerning the specific checks. Therefore, Austin should not prevail in a suit to recover damages caused by having the other 47 checks dishonored.

Answers to Practice Quiz

True/False:

1. False   Even though checks are a substitute for money, they do not serve a credit function.
2. False   A payee is the party to whom the check is written. The drawer is the customer who maintains the checking account.

3. True   Traveler's checks are issued without a named payee so that their holder may fill in the payee as he or she makes purchases.

4. False   The purchaser initially signs the traveler's check upon purchases of the same and then must sign the second blank when he or she uses the checks to purchase goods or services.

5. False   The bank is under no obligation to pay on a check that has been outstanding for more than six months.

6. True   Main Bank may in good faith make payment on a completed check and can charge Kami's account the $2,500 unless it has notice that the completion was improper.

7. False   The bank may pay or certify checks drawn on the deceased customer's account on or prior to the date of death for 10 days after the date of the death.

8. True   An order to stop payment on a check may be accomplished in writing or orally.

9. True   UCC 4-401(a) allows for the payor bank to honor a check and create an overdraft in the drawer's account if the drawer does not have enough money in his or her account when a properly payable check is presented for payment.

10. True   Wrongful dishonor happens when there are sufficient funds in a drawer's account to pay a properly payable check, but the bank does not do so. As such the Greenville Bank will be liable for wrongful dishonor.

11. False A bank is under a duty to verify the drawer's signature when the drawer presents a check to the drawer bank for payment.

12. False The payor bank may charge the drawer's account for the original tenor of the check, but not the altered amount.

13. True   The bank where the payee or holder has an account is the depository bank.

14. False An intermediary bank is a bank in the collection process that is not the depository or payor bank.

15. False The deferred posting rule allows banks to fix an afternoon hour of 2:00P.M. or later as a cutoff hour for the purpose of processing items.

16. True   A check that is presented for payment where the depository bank is also the payor bank is an "on us" item.

17. True   When the drawer and payee or holder have accounts at different banks, this is referred to as an "on them" check.

18. False A deposit of money to an account becomes available for withdrawal the next banking day following the deposit.

19. True   This is one of the "four legals" that effectively prevent payment of the check.

20. False The bank must keep either the original checks or legible copies for seven years.

21. True   Most transfers are completed in the same day thereby being a great benefit when conducting business.

22. True   Article 4A governs wholesale wire transfers and applies only to commercial electronic fund transfers.

23. False Debit cards may only be used if the merchant has a point-of-sale terminal.

24. False Purchasers of traveler's checks do not necessarily have to have an account at the issuing bank.

25. True   If a customer has sufficient funds in his or her account and the bank fails to pay an electronic fund transfer, it will be liable for wrongful dishonor.

Multiple Choice:

26. C   Answer C is the correct answer, as checks do not serve a credit function. Answers A, B and D are incorrect as they all true statements with regard to checks.

27. A   Answer A is the correct answer as it is necessary that the customer's bank and the payee's bank must belong to the same clearinghouse in order to provide the service of paying recurring payments and crediting recurring deposits. Answer B is incorrect as having a computer to pay bills by the Internet may be convenient, however, it would not accomplish or assist the bank in its role of paying recurring payments and crediting recurring deposits. Answer C is incorrect as qualifying for a debt card would has no impact on the banks service of paying recurring payments and crediting recurring deposits. Answer D is incorrect based on the reasoning given above.

28. D   Answer D is the correct answer as a certified check is one in which the bank agrees in advance to accept the check when it is presented for payment and pay the check out of funds set aside from the customer's account and either placed in a special certified check account or held in the customer's account. Answer A is incorrect as there is no such thing as a point-of-sale terminal check. Point-of-sale terminal refers to terminals used in conjunction with bank issued debit cards for use in making purchases that are directly debited from the customer's account. Answer B is incorrect as traveler's checks are used instead of cash when people are on vacation or on other trips. Answer C is incorrect as once again, there is no such thing as an automatic withdrawal check.

29. D   Answer D is the correct answer as a stale check is one that has been outstanding for six months or more. Answer A is incorrect as this definition is not the correct definition used in the banking industry. Answer B is incorrect as it indicates that the check has been presented whereas a stale check has not been presented. Answer C is incorrect it makes no sense whatsoever.

30. B   Answer B is the correct answer as UCC Article 4 states that an oral order is binding on the bank for 14 calendar days, unless confirmed in writing during this time. Answer A is incorrect as ten days is not the correct time period that an oral order is binding for. Answer C is incorrect as this is an untrue statement. Answer D is incorrect as written not oral orders Are effective for six months and can be renewed in writing for an additional six months under UCC 4-403.

31. A   Answer A is the correct answer as original tenor translates to the original amount for which the drawer wrote the check. Answer B is incorrect as oral conversation concerning an amount is not the same as the actual written amount of a check. Answer C is incorrect as this is a reference to a different meaning of tenor and does not apply to banking transactions. Answer D is incorrect for the reasons stated above.

32. C   Answer C is the correct answer as a bank is relieved of any liability for paying on a forged or altered check if the drawer of the check failed to make a timely report that it was either forged or altered. Answer A is incorrect as it is an untrue statement. Answers B and D are both incorrect as they are untrue statements.

33. A   Answer A is the correct answer as this succinctly states what the midnight deadline means. Answer B is an untrue statement as applied to the midnight deadline. Answer C is incorrect as an "on them" check is a check presented for payment by the payee or holder where the depository bank and the payor bank are not the same bank. Answer D is incorrect as customers would not make deposits if they lost their accounts at midnight.

34. C   Answer C is the correct answer as the collecting bank owes a duty to use ordinary care in presenting and sending a check for collection as well as other banking actions in the collection process. Answer A is incorrect, as the bank has no such duty with regard to its banking actions. Answer B is incorrect, as the bank does not owe a special of duty of care with regard to its banking actions in the collection process. Answer D is incorrect based on the reasoning given above.

35. C   Answer C is the correct answer as bank customers are under a duty to promptly examine their bank statements to determine if any payment was unauthorized due to alteration of a check or forged signature. Answer A is incorrect as this is an untrue statement. Answer B is incorrect as the duty to change banks is not a legally recognized duty. Answer D is incorrect as not only is it untrue, but customers normally do not let the bank know of its duty as the bank already knows that it has a duty of ordinary care.

Short Answer:

36.   Article 3
37.   The checking account holder and writer of the check.
38.   The bank process of certification involves the accepting bank writing or stamping the word certified on the ordinary check of an account holder and sets aside funds from the account to pay the check.
39.   The bank can be held liable for the amount of the check, expenses, and loss of interest resulting from nonpayment.
40.   bounced.
41.   forged instrument.
42.   altered check.
43.   Provisional credit is when a collecting bank gives credit to a check in the collection process prior to its final settlement. These types of credits may be reversed if the check fails to clear.
44.   Presentment across the counter refers to a depository physically presenting the check for payment at the payor bank instead of depositing an "on them" check for collection.
45.   It is considered to be complete when the responsible bank officer has made a decision to pay the check and the proper book entry has been made to charge the drawer's account the amount of the check.
46.   Kurt must postdate the check to Mona to some date in the future. Also, Kurt must give separate written notice to the bank describing the check with reasonable certainty and notifying the bank not to pay the check until the date on the check.
47.   Mississippi Bank and Trust may pay or certify checks drawn on Wanda's account on or prior to the date of death for 10 days after the date of Wanda's death.
48.   overdraft
49.   Bank One may be fined for negligent violations of the currency reporting requirements. Also, willful failure to file reports may subject Bank One to civil monetary penalties, charges of aiding and abetting the criminal activity, and prosecution for violating the money-laundering statutes.
50.   stop-payment order

Chapter 26
CREDIT AND SURETYSHIP

Chapter Overview

This chapter examines the rights of creditors and debtors under federal and state consumer protection laws. In this chapter, you will explore the repercussions of noncompliance with the recording statutes, as well as the foreclosure process in real estate. Further, you will learn about deficiency judgments, lender liability and the difference between a surety and a guaranty arrangement. Finally, this chapter gives a good explanation of attachment, garnishment and execution as well as the difference between a composition agreement and an assignment for the benefit of creditors.

Objectives

Upon completion of the exercises in this chapter, you should be able to:
1. Explain unsecured credit verses secured credit.
2. Discuss mortgages and deeds of trust.
3. Explain the repercussions of noncompliance with recording statutes.
4. Explain how foreclosure comes about and how it is accomplished.
5. Explain what a deficiency judgment is and discuss the effects of an antidifficiency statute.
6. Discuss lender liability.
7. Explain material person's liens.
8. Discuss the difference between a surety and guaranty arrangement.
9. Discuss attachment, garnishment and execution as they pertain to judgments.

Practical Application

This chapter will provide you with greater insight about the various types of credit along with security interests in real and personal property. Further, you will gain a better understanding of the available remedies associated with personal property transactions. Also, you will have a broader base of knowledge concerning surety and guaranty arrangements as well as remedies associated with the collection of debts.

Helpful Hints

Many items are purchased on credit. The best way to approach this chapter is by differentiating between the main terms such as secured verses unsecured credit, real verses personal property, and surety arrangement verses a guaranty arrangement. Once you have a grasp of these main terms, the remedies that are available become easier to understand and learn. The exercises that follow, as well as the critical thinking exercises located at the end of the chapter in your main text, are very helpful in solidifying the concepts you should be familiar with.

Study Tips

Basic vocabulary

Debtor – The borrower in a credit transaction.
Creditor – The lender in a credit transaction.

Types of credit:
Unsecured – Credit that does not need any collateral to protect the debt.
Secured – Credit that does need collateral to secure the payment of the loan.

Deficiency judgment – When a debtor has insufficient collateral to cover the debt, the court will issue an order allowing the creditor to recover other property or income from the defaulting debtor.

Personal property – This involves tangible property such as furniture, automobiles, and jewelry, and intangible property such as intellectual property, and securities.

Vocabulary relating to Real Property

Mortgage – A property owner borrows money from a creditor who thereafter uses a deed as a means of security (collateral) to secure the repayment of the loan.

Mortgagor – This is the owner-debtor in a mortgage transaction.

Mortgagee – This is the creditor in a transaction involving a mortgage.

Note- A legal instrument that is proof of the borrower's debt to the lender.
Deed of Trust – A legal instrument that evinces the creditor's security interest in the debtor's property that is pledged as collateral.

Land Sales Contract – The transfer and sale of real property in accordance with a land sales contract whereby the owner of the real property agrees to sell the property to a buyer, who assents to pay the asking price to the owner-seller over a stated, agreed period of time. The loan is termed as *"carrying the paper."* If the purchaser defaults, the seller may claim a forfeiture and retake possession of the property. The right of redemption is allowed in many states.

Recording Statute – Law that requires the mortgage or deed of trust to be recorded in the county recorder's office of the county where the real property is located.

Material Person's Lien – When an individual provides contracting or a service toward improvement of real property, their investments are protected by statutory law that allow them to file a material person's lien (also referred to as a mechanic's lien) against the improved real property.

Vocabulary relating to Third Person Liability on a Debt

Surety arrangement – A situation where a third party promises to be primarily liable with the borrower for the payment of the borrower's debt.

Surety- This is the third person who agrees to be liable in a surety arrangement and in essence acts as a co-debtor and is often called an accommodation party or a co-signer.

Guaranty arrangement – A situation where a third party promises to be secondarily liable for the payment of another's debt.

Guarantor – This is the third person who agrees to be liable in a guaranty arrangement.

Defenses of a Surety or Guarantor

A surety or guarantor may utilize the same defenses as the principal debtor against the creditor. Possible defenses include fraudulent inducement to enter into the guaranty agreement or surety, duress and the guarantor's or surety's own bankruptcy or incapacity.

Remedies

Foreclosure – A legal procedure whereby the mortgagee can declare the entire debt due and payable if a debtor defaults on his or her loan.

Deficiency judgments – As stated above, some states allow a mortgagee to bring a separate legal action to recover a deficiency from the mortgagor.

Antideficiency statute – Many states prohibit deficiency judgments on mortgages, especially those involving residential property.

Right of Redemption – Many state laws follow the common law, which gives the mortgagor the right to redeem his or her real property after default and before foreclosure. The mortgagor must pay the entire debt including principal, interest, and other costs bore by the mortgagee as a result of the mortgagor's default. The mortgagor will obtain title free and clear upon redeeming the property. *Note,* a majority of states allow any party holding an interest in the property may redeem the property during the redemption period.

Collection Remedies

Attachment – This remedy involves a prejudgment order allowing the seizure of the debtor's property while the lawsuit is pending.

Execution – This remedy concerns a postjudgment court order allowing seizure of the debtor's property that is in possession of the debtor.

Garnishment – This is also a postjudgment court order. However it allows the seizure of the debtor's property that is in the possession of third parties.

Title III of the Consumer Credit Protection Act - This law protects debtors who are subject to a writ of garnishment to keep the greater of seventy-five percent of their weekly disposable earnings (after taxes) or an amount equivalent to thirty hours of work paid at federal minimum wage.

Refresh Your Memory

The following exercise will enable you to refresh your memory on the rules and principles presented to you in this chapter. Read each question twice and place your answer in the blanks provided. Review the chapter material for any question you miss or are unable to remember.

1. If Janet uses her credit card to purchase a stereo from the Music City Stereo store, she is the _____ and Music City Stereo store is the _____.

2. There are two basis from which credit may be extended. They are on either an _____ or _____ basis.

3. If Bob is not required to have any security to protect the payment of a debt to Fine Lamps, Inc., then it may be said that Bob has _____ credit.

4. If a debtor has little or no property or income for a creditor to garnish, the debtor is said to be _____ _____.

5. _____ is a security interest in the debtor's property that secures payment of a loan.

6. _____ interests in property may be taken in real, personal or even intangible property.

7. When a creditor brings a lawsuit against a debtor to recover on a loan what the collateral cannot satisfy, the lawsuit is for recovery of a _____ _____.

8. Give at least four examples of personal property, two of which are tangible and two that are intangible. _____, _____, _____, and _____.

9. What is an artisan's or mechanic's lien? _____
    _____

10. What is a mortgage? _____
    _____

11. Carrie signs a piece of paper that indicates her debt to United Bank. What is this piece of paper called? It is called a _____.

12. What is a legal instrument that gives a creditor a security interest in the debtor's property that is pledged as collateral called? It is called a _____ of _____.

13. What requires the mortgage or deed of trust to be documented in a county office where real property is located? _____ _____.

14. Edna fails to pay her monthly mortgage payment on the ranch she is purchasing from California Savings and Loan. What legal procedure may California Savings and Loan bring against Edna? _____

15.   A law prohibiting a mortgagee from recovering the amount that is lacking from the mortgagor's residential property is an _____ _____.

Critical Thought Exercise

Steve and Bonnie West purchased an old Victorian home outside St. Louis and planned on renovating it and selling it for a profit before moving onto another renovation project. Bonnie's brother, Doug Nixon did most of the major work on the house and hired trades people to assist in areas that are beyond his expertise. Nixon hired Summit Roofing to replace the old shake roof with a fire resistant composite product that matched the house in color and style. The cost of the new roof is $17,400, including all labor and materials. Steve and Bonnie pay Doug $86,500 for the entire project. Doug failed to pay Summit Roofing and absconded with all the funds.

Steve and Bonnie West entered into a real estate purchase agreement with Lucy Rogers to purchase the home for $515,000. The contract between West and Rogers states that the property is free of all encumbrances and escrow will close in 30 days.

Summit Roofing filed a mechanics lean against the property. The West's demanded that Summit Roofing seek payment from Doug Nixon. Summit Roofing gave notice that it was going to foreclose against the property to recover the $17,400 owed to it.

What action should Steve and Bonnie West take to ensure that the sale to Rogers will not be thwarted?

Answer. _____

_____

_____

_____

_____

_____

_____

_____

_____

_____

_____

_____

_____

_____

_____

_____

_____

_____

Practice Quiz

True/False:

1. ___ Artisan's liens are called super-priority liens. [p 514]

2. ___ If Mark defaults on his mortgage, First Bank who hold the note may declare the entire debt due and payable immediately. [p 518]

3. ___ States that allow deficiency judgments regarding certain types of mortgages have enacted antideficiency statutes. [p 518]

4. ___ The right of redemption mandates that the mortgagor pay the full amount of the debt which includes principle, interest and other costs. [p 518]

5. ___ A majority of the states prohibit the sale of real property by way of land sale contracts. [p 518]

6. ___ Under a land sale contract, the seller in good faith gives the purchaser the title to the property while the seller continues to pay the purchase price plus interest. [p 519]

7. ___ A surety arrangement involves a third person who agrees to be liable in a guaranty arrangement. [p 521]

8. ___ A surety is a third person who agrees to be liable in a surety arrangement. [p 520]

9. ___ In a guaranty arrangement, the debtor is secondarily liable for the debt of the debtor. [p 521]

10. ___ Samson purchases a riding lawnmower on credit and Gloria acts as the surety for the debt. Thereafter, both Samson and Gloria discover that the gearshift is defective. Both Samson and Gloria may assert the defect as a defense to liability. [p 521]

11. ___ An attachment is a postjudgment order permitting seizure of the debtor's property. [p 522]

12. ___ Automobiles, furniture and jewelry are examples of personal property. [p 514]

13. ___ Real estate owners cannot create security interests in their property. [p 515]

14. ___ In some states a deed of trust may be used in place of a mortgage. [p 515]

15. ___ Under a power of sale, the procedure need not be contained in the mortgage or deed of trust. [p 518]

16. ___ Only a few states provide a statutory procedure that must be adhered to foreclose on a land sales contract. [p 519]

17. ____ Felix, a contractor files a mechanics' lien against Virginia for laying brick around Virginia's home. Felix may not use the improvements as security for payment on the services and materials. [p 520]

18. ____ The general time frame to foreclose on a lien is anywhere from six months to two years from the date that the lien is filed. [p 520]

19. ____ Hank , a painter places a lien on Chelsea's house for his services. Thereafter she pays the amount due and owing to him. Chelsea may now obtain a lien release that attests to Hank's receipt of the payment. [p 520]

20. ____ If Johnson, a contractor places a lien on Sheldon's property, Johnson need not give any notice of the lien to Sheldon, as the lien speaks for itself. [p 520]

21. ____ The International Bank for Reconstruction and Development is a United Nations agency that helps businesses finance international operations. [p 522]

22. ____ The Export-Import Bank has a useful role in that it provides loan guarantees as well as insurance to foreign buyers of U.S. products. [p 523]

23. ____ Credit that requires collateral to protect the payment of a debt is known as unsecured credit. [p 513]

24. ____ The mortgagee is the owner-debtor in a mortgage situation. [p 515]

25. ____ Although legal title is with the trustee, the trustor has all of the legal rights to possession of the real property. [p 515]

Multiple Choice:

26. A person's ownership interest in real property is usually detailed in writing in [p 515]
    a. a foreclosure.
    b. a deed.
    c. a lien.
    d. a letter.

27. An improperly recorded mortgage or deed of trust is not effective against [p 516]
    a. debtors.
    b. subsequent purchasers of real property.
    c. mortgagor.
    d. the original mortgagee.

28. The Right of redemption requires [p 518]
    a. an antideficiency statute.
    b. the mortgagee to state that the entire debt is due and payable.
    c. the mortgagor to pay the principal, interest and other costs.
    d. none of the above.

29. The benefits of a statutory procedure of foreclosing on a land sale contract include [p 519]
    a. the fact that it is a simpler way to foreclose.
    b. the fact that it is less time consuming.
    c. the fact that it is less expensive than foreclosure on a mortgage or deed of trust.
    d. all of the above.

30. In a surety situation, the co-debtor promises [p 520]
    a. to file a notice of a mechanic's lien with the county recorder's office.
    b. to seek assistance from the World Bank.
    c. to be secondarily liable for the payment of another's debt.
    d. to be liable for the payment of another's debt.

31. Which of the following is not true with respect to a surety or guarantor's defenses to liability? [p 521]
    a. The defense of fraudulent inducement may be asserted as a defense to liability.
    b. The surety or debtor can assert the debtor's incapacity as a defense against liability.
    c. The defense of duress may be asserted as a defense to liability.
    d. The surety or guarantor's own incapacity or bankruptcy may be asserted as a defense to liability.

32. A garnishment is defined as [p 522]
    a. a post judgment order that allows the seizure of the debtor's property that is in possession of a third party.
    b. a postjudgment order permitting seizure of the debtor's property in possession of the debtor.
    c. a prejudgment court order that allows seizure of the debtor's property while litigation is pending.
    d. none of the above.

33. A writ of execution is [p 522]
    a. a court order that allows for the seizure of the debtor's property in the possession of third parties.
    b. a court order that allows the seizure of the debtor's property that is in the debtor's possession.
    c. a court order that permits seizure of the debtor's property while the litigation is pending.
    d. a court order stating that the debtor is primarily as well as secondarily liable on the debt.

34. A writ of attachment is [p 522]
    a. a court order that states that the debtor must pay the creditor an amount equal to 30 hours of work paid at federal minimum wage.
    b. a court order that directs the sheriff to seize the debtor's property and authorizes a judicial sale of the property.
    c. a prejudgment order allowing seizure of the debtor's property while litigation is pending.
    d. a court order stating that property such as tools of the trade, homestead exemption and clothing are exempt from being levied upon.

35. The Consumer Credit Protection Act provides that debtors may [p 522]
    a. have their wages garnished up to 75 percent of their weekly disposable earnings after taxes.
    b. have their wages garnished up to 30 hours of work paid at federal minimum wage.
    c. retain up to 75 percent of their weekly disposable earnings or an amount equal to 30 hours of work paid at federal minimum wage, which ever is greater of the two.
    d. protect debtors from the garnishment of any wages whatsoever.

Short Answer:

36. What is meant by the terminology unsecured credit? [p 513] _____

37. What purpose does collateral have? [p 513] _____

38. Shelby contracts with Eloise to paint different rural scenes in each room of Eloise's home. Upon completion of the last room, Eloise refuses to pay for Shelby's services. If Shelby decides to place an artisan's lien on Eloise's home, what must she do? [p 514] _____

39. Give at least one difference between a mortgage and a deed of trust. [p 515] _____

40. What legal option is available to a mortgagor who has defaulted on a loan but has not yet been foreclosed upon? [p 518] _____

41. What types of real property interests are sold using a land sale contract? [p 519] _____

42. What must a creditor do in order to obtain a writ of attachment? [p 522] _____

43. In a writ of execution, who are the proceeds from the debtor's property used for? [p 522]

44. What is meant by the terminology "super-priority liens?" [p 514] _____

45. Where is legal title placed under a deed of trust? [p 515] _____

46. What is involved with a foreclosure by power of sale? [p 518] _____

47. A surety is called an accommodation party or a _____. [p 520]

48. Explain what role a guarantor plays with regard to a debtor's debt. [p 521] _____

_____

49. Explain a deficiency judgment. [p 518] _____

_____

50. The defenses that the principal debtor has against the creditor may also be asserted by a _____. [p 521]

Answers to Refresh Your Memory

1. debtor, creditor [p 513]
2. unsecured, secured [p 513]
3. unsecured [p 513]
4. judgment-proof [p 513]
5. collateral [p 513]
6. security [p 513]
7. deficiency judgment for the difference [p 513]
8. furniture, jewelry, copyrights, and automobiles [p 514]
9. An artisan or mechanic's lien is one in which a worker in the ordinary course of business works on or provides materials to another person and by statute are allowed to place on lien on the goods until the work or materials are paid for. [p 514]
10. A mortgage is a collateral situation where a property owner borrows money from a creditor who uses a deed as collateral for repayment of the loan. [p 515]
11. note [p 515]
12. deed of trust [p 515]
13. A recording statute requires that the mortgage or deed of trust be recorded in the county recorder's office of the county in which the real property is located. [p 516]
14. California Savings and Loan may bring a foreclosure procedure against Edna. [p 518]
15. antideficiency statute [p 518]

Critical Thought Exercise Model Answer

Contractors and laborers who expend time and money for materials that are used for improvements upon real property may protect themselves by filing a mechanic's lien against the real property upon which the improvement was made by the contractor or laborer. In order to obtain a mechanic's lien, the contractor will usually have to meet the following requirements to perfect their lien: (1) File a notice of lien with the county recorder's office in the county where the real property is located; (2) The notice must state the amount of the claim, a description of the real property, the name of the property owner, and the name of the claimant; (3) The notice must be filed within the statutory time as set forth in the statute (usually 30-120 days), and; (4) Notice of the lien must be transmitted to the owner of the real property.

Summit Roofing performed actual work upon the West's house and is entitled to file a mechanic's lien if they are not paid. When Nixon absconded with the funds, the West's may have been defrauded by Nixon, but this does nothing to prevent a proper fining of the lien. The lien will prevent the West's from conveying clear title and is an encumbrance upon the property. The West's will be in breach when the date for closing arrives and they are unable to convey clear title to Rogers. The only recourse that the Wests have in this case is to pay Summit Roofing and obtain a release of lien before the escrow closing date. The West's should be careful to have all the contractors, laborers, and material persons who have worked on their home or supplied materials sign the lien release. The West's can then proceed against Nixon to recover their $17,400.

Answers to Practice Quiz

True/False:

1. **True**   Mechanics as well as artisan liens are termed super-priority liens because they are given priority over any existing lien on the goods.
2. **True**   First Bank's right to declare the entire debt due and payable immediately can be enforced through foreclosure proceedings.
3. **False**   If a state allows deficiency judgments, it certainly would not enact an antideficiency statute that prohibits deficiency judgments.
4. **True**   A mortgagor is given the right to redeem his or her property but cannot do so in part. As such, he or she must pay the full amount owing on the debt, plus interest and costs.
5. **False**   Most states allow the sale and transfer of real property by using land sale contracts.
6. **False**   Under a land sales contract, the seller keeps the title to the property until the purchaser pays the purchase price along with the interest.
7. **False**   A surety arrangement involves a third party who promises to be primarily liable with borrower for the payment of the borrower's debt whereas a guaranty arrangement occurs when a third party promises to be secondarily liable for the payment of another's debt. The third party may be one or the other, but, not both at the same time.
8. **True**   A surety arrangement involves a surety who is a third person agreeing to be liable for the borrower's debt.
9. **False**   The debtor may not be secondarily liable for his or her own debt. A third party usually acts as a guarantor who agrees to be secondarily liable for payment of the debtor's debt.
10. **True**   The defenses that Samson the debtor has against whom he purchased the lawnmower from may also be asserted by Gloria, the surety.
11. **False**   An attachment is a prejudgment order that permits seizure of the property while litigation is pending.
12. **True**   Since automobiles, furniture and jewelry are tangible property, they are considered to be personal property.
13. **False**   Security interests in real estate can be created by the owners of real property.
14. **True**   The deed of trust is the legal instrument that gives the creditor a security interest in the property of the debtor that is pledged as collateral. The deed of trust acts in place of a mortgage in some states.
15. **False**   The power of sale must be expressly conferred in the mortgage or deed of trust.
16. **False**   Several states set forth a statutory procedure that must be adhered to when foreclosing on a land sale contract.
17. **False**   The brick around Virginia's home would be considered an improvement that Felix may use as security for the payment of his services and materials.
18. **True**   The statutory period to foreclose on a lien is from six month to two years depending on the jurisdiction the parties are in.

19. True   A lien release is an affidavit attesting to receipt of the payment to contractors, laborers, material persons, etc. One of the purposes of a lien release is to defeat a lien holder's attempt to obtain payment once it has already been paid.
20. False   In general, notice of the lien must be given to the owner of the real property that the lien is being placed on.
21. True   Since international business ventures are viewed as riskier than domestic ventures, the International Bank for Reconstruction and Development help engage in direct investment through loans as well as equity investments thereby assisting in international operations.
22. True   The Export-Import bank helps to arrange for credit to foreign buyers of U.S. credit and also helps provide insurance too.
23. False   Credit that requires security to secure payment of the loan is known as collateral.
24. False   The mortgagor is the owner-debtor in a mortgage situation whereas the mortgagee is the creditor.
25. True   The trustor has full legal rights to possession of the real property while the legal title to the property is placed with the trustee.

Multiple Choice:

26. B   Answer B is correct, as a deed is a written instrument that describes a person's ownership interest in real property. Answer A is incorrect as a foreclosure involves the sale of a debtor's property in order to satisfy the debt. Answer C is incorrect as a lien is usually present when there has been some sort of service or goods that have been rendered and that improve the property. The lien acts as security in receiving payment for those goods and services verses a way of describing an ownership interest in the real property itself. Answer D is incorrect, as letters do not usually detail a person's ownership interest in real property.
27. B   Answer B is the correct answer as an improperly recorded document is not effective against subsequent purchasers of real property or other lienholders or mortgages who do not have any notice of the prior mortgages. Answer A is incorrect, as a debtor who is the mortgagor is still obligated to pay the amount of the mortgage according to its terms even if the mortgage is improperly recorded or not recorded at all. Answer C is incorrect as this is a false statement. Answer D is incorrect as there are not enough facts to determine who was or is the original mortgagee.
28. C   Answer C is the correct answer as common law as several state statutes require that the full amount of the debt, plus interest and costs be satisfied before a property may be redeemed under the right of redemption. Answer A is incorrect, as the right of redemption and the underlying concept of an antideficiency statute have nothing to do with one another. Answer B is incorrect as the right of redemption is governed by statute of which the statement in this answer is not a requirement therein. Answer D is incorrect based on the reasoning given above.
29. D   Answer D is correct as all of the statements given in answers A-C state a benefit of utilizing a statutory procedure for foreclosing on a land sale contract.
30. D   Answer D is correct as the surety otherwise known as a co-debtor promises to be liable for the debt of another in a strict surety arrangement. Answer A is incorrect as the filing of a mechanic's lien is irrelevant to a surety arrangement. Answer B is incorrect as the World Bank assists in helping finance international operations not in agreeing to be liable in a surety arrangement. Answer C is incorrect as this describes a guarantor's role in a guaranty arrangement.

31. B   Answer B is correct as it states the statement that is false with regard to the defenses that may be asserted concerning a surety or guarantor's liability, as the surety or debtor may not assert the debtor's incapacity as a defense against liability. Answers A, C, and D are all incorrect as they are all viable defenses that may be asserted against liability.

32. A   Answer A is correct as this correctly states the definition of a garnishment. Answer B is incorrect as this states the definition of an execution not a garnishment. Answer C is incorrect as this states the definition of an attachment. Answer D is incorrect for the reasons stated above.

33. B   Answer B is correct as it correctly states the formal explanation of a writ of execution. Answer A is incorrect as this sets forth the definition of a garnishment. Answer C is incorrect as this states the definition of an attachment. Answer D is incorrect as the debtor may not be both primarily as well as secondarily liable on the debt.

34. C   Answer C is correct, as a writ of attachment is a prejudgment order allowing seizure of the debtor's property while litigation is pending. Answer A is incorrect as it is an untrue statement. Answer B is incorrect as this states the explanation for a writ of execution. Answer D is incorrect as exemptions such as those listed are usually with respect to a writ of execution.

35. C   Answer C is correct as it states what the debtors may keep without having their wages abusively garnished. Answer A is incorrect, as the Consumer Credit Protection Act does not allow for the debtor's wages to be garnished up to 75 percent of their weekly disposable earnings after taxes. Answer B is incorrect as this is also an untrue statement under the act since the act allows a debtor to keep up to 30 hours of work paid at federal minimum wage if it is greater than 75 percent of his or her weekly disposable earnings after taxes. Answer D is incorrect as the act does protect the debtor from abusive garnishment actions by creditors but does not shield the debtor completely from garnishment.

Short Answer:

36.   It means that the creditor relies on the debtor's promise to pay the principal plus interest when due and the credit does not require any security or collateral for the debt.

37.   Collateral secures payment of the loan.

38.   Shelby must give the required notices pursuant to the relevant state statute.

39.   A mortgage is a two-party instrument having a collateral arrangement. A deed of trust is a three-party instrument with legal title being placed with the trustee.

40.   A mortgagor has the option of exercising his or her right to redemption of the property by paying the full amount of the purchase price, plus interest and other costs.

41.   Undeveloped property, farms and similar types of property are sold using land sale contracts.

42.   A creditor must follow the procedures set forth by state law, give the appropriate notice to the debtor and post a bond with the court.

43.   The proceeds are utilized to pay the creditor the amount of the final judgment with any surplus being paid to the debtor.

44.   Super-priority liens refer to the fact that artisan's and mechanic's liens are given priority over any existing lien on the goods.

45.   Legal title is placed with a trustee under a deed of trust.

46.   The procedure for the sale must be contained in the mortgage or deed of trust itself.

47.   co-signer

48.   A guarantor agrees to pay the debt of the main debtor should he or she default and not pay on the debt when it is due.

49. A court judgment allowing a secured lender to recover other income or property from a defaulting debtor if the collateral is insufficient to repay the unpaid loan.

50. a surety or guarantor

Chapter 27
SECURED TRANSACTIONS

Chapter Overview

This chapter elaborates on the concept of security interests as they pertain to the items that are purchased or some other personal property of the debtor. The security interest that is taken by a creditor is known as a secured transaction. You will learn about the creation of security interests as well the ways to perfect the same by studying these and other rules as presented by Article 9 of the Uniform Commercial Code.

Objectives

Upon completion of the exercises in this chapter, you should be able to:
1. Discuss the concepts in Article 9 of the U.C.C.
2. Explain how a security interest is created in personal property.
3. Explain how filing a financing statement creates a perfected security interest.
4. Explain how taking possession of collateral perfects a security interest.
5. Discuss the meaning of purchase money security interest.
6. Explain the meaning of floating lien.
7. Discuss priority of claims regarding competing security interests.
8. Discuss the buyer's rights in the ordinary course of business.
9. Explain the remedies that are available to secured creditors when a debtor defaults.
10. Discuss the effect that the revised Article 9 has on electronic commerce.

Practical Application

You will be able to apply the Uniform Commercial Code rules of Article 9 when creating as well as enforcing security interests you may have in personal property. Further, you will become more familiar with the terminology associated with secured transactions. You should also be able to determine the priority among conflicting claims of creditors and whether or not an exception to the perfection-priority rule applies. Additionally, if you are a secured party, you will be more aware of the remedies that are available to you should a debtor default on a security agreement.

Helpful Hints

If you have been in a situation involving a secured transaction, this chapter will be like second nature to you. However, for the individual who is studying this material for the first time, it is advisable to understand the basic vocabulary first and then look upon the remaining materials like building blocks from which to gather and expand the information obtained from Article 9 of the UCC. The first building block that you should familiarize yourself with is that of creation of a security interest in personal property, followed by the floating lien concept. The third building block involves perfecting a secured interest, and then termination followed by the last two building blocks of priority of claims and remedies for the creditor. The following Study Tips section utilizes the building block approach to make your learning easier.

Study Tips

Basic Information and Vocabulary

Article 9 of the Uniform Commercial Code governs secured transactions. When a creditor loans money to a debtor in exchange for the debtor's pledge of personal property as security (collateral), then a secured transaction is created.

Debtor – The party owing payment or some other performance of the secured obligation.

Secured Party – The individual, albeit seller, lender or other person who holds the security interest.

Security Interest – A personal property interest that secures payment or performance of an obligation.

Security Agreement – The agreement created by the secured party and the debtor that allows for a security interest in personal property.

Collateral – Property, including chattel paper and accounts that is subject to a security interest.

Secured Transaction
 -Two-party secured transaction – Where a seller sells goods to a buyer on credit and keeps a security interest in the goods.
 -Three-party secured transaction –Where a seller sells goods to a buyer who has financed the goods.

Building Block #1

Creation of a Security Interest in Personal Property

Writing Requirement – In general, security interests must be in writing unless the creditor is in possession of the collateral. The following lists what the writing must contain.
 1) The collateral must be clearly described so that it may be easily identified.
 2) The writing must state the debtor's promise to pay the creditor as well as the terms of Repayment.
 3) The writing must state what the creditor's rights are in the event of a debtor's default.
 4) The debtor must sign the writing.

Value Requirement – The secured party must give any adequate consideration that will support a simple contract. The debtor must owe a debt to the creditor.

Debtor has Rights in the Collateral – The debtor must have a present or future right in or the right to possession of the collateral in order to give a security interest in that property.

Attachment – If the writing, value and debtor's rights in the collateral are met, then the rights of the secured party attach to the collateral and the creditor can satisfy the debt out of the collateral if need be.

Building Block # 2 – The Floating-Lien Concept

This concept has been placed in a category by itself because it deals with security agreements that refer to either property that is acquired after the security agreement is executed or future advances.

After-Acquired Property – This refers to property that the debtor obtains after the execution of the security agreement.

Future Advances- As defined in your main text, this is "personal property of the debtor that is designated as collateral for future loans from a line of credit."

Building Block #3 – Perfecting a Security Interest

Perfection is a legal process that is accomplished by three main methods to establish a secured creditor's rights against the claims of other creditors.

Filing a Financing Statement – This method is the most common way to perfect a creditor's interest. The financing statement must contain the debtor's name and address, as well as the creditor's name and address and a statement that reveals the types of collateral or a description of the items. Further, the secured party may file the security agreement as a financing statement. [UCC 9-402(1)]. The financing statement must be filed with the appropriate state or county office.

Perfection by Possession of Collateral – This method does not require the secured party to file a financing statement if the creditor has possession of the collateral. However, the secured creditor is required to use reasonable care in the collateral's custody and preservation if he or she holds the debtor's property.

Perfection by a Purchase Money Security Interest in Consumer Goods – This method is an **interest that a creditor gets automatically when it gives credit to a consumer to purchase consumer** goods. Examples of consumer goods include television sets, home appliances, furniture and the like that are mainly used for family, personal or household use. Since the creditor does not have to file a financing statement or take possession of the goods, this interest is termed **perfection by attachment** or the **automatic perfection rule.**

Exceptions to the Perfection-Priority Rule

The UCC recognizes several exceptions to the perfection-priority rule.

Purchase Money Security Interest: Inventory as Collateral
"If the collateral is inventory, the perfected purchase money security interest prevails if the purchase money secured party gives written notice of the perfection to the perfected nonpurchase money secured party before the debtor receives possession of the inventory." [UCC 9-312(3)]

Purchase Money Security Interest: Noninventory as Collateral
UCC 9-312 (4) provides that "if the collateral is something other than inventory, the perfected purchase money security interest would prevail over a perfected nonpurchase money security interest in after-acquired property if it was perfected before or within 10 days after the debtor receives possession of the collateral."

Buyers in the Ordinary Course of Business
UCC 9-307(1) provides that "a buyer in the ordinary curse of business who purchases goods from a merchant takes the goods free of any perfected or unperfected security interest in the merchant's inventory even if the buyer knows of the existence of the security interest."

Secondhand Consumer Goods
UCC 9-307(2) provides that "buyers of secondhand consumer goods take free of security interest if they do not have actual or constructive knowledge about the security interest, give value, and buy the goods for personal, family, or household purposes. The filing of a financing statement by a creditor provides constructive notice of the security interest."

Building Block #4

This should really be termed tumbling block #4, as once a secured consumer debt has been satisfied, a termination statement must be filed with the same state or county office that the financing statement was filed with. The termination statement must be filed within a month of the debt's satisfaction or within ten days from receipt of the debtor's demand to do so. If the termination statement is not filed, the creditor is liable to the debtor for $100 along with any other losses suffered by the debtor.

Building Block #5 – Priority of Claims

In order to determine which creditor's claim on the same collateral or property takes priority over another, the UCC decides based on whether the claim is secured or unsecured and the time at which secured claims were perfected or attached.
Secured vs. Unsecured Claims – Secured creditors take priority over unsecured creditors.

Competing Unperfected Secured Claims – If there are two or more secured yet unperfected claims to the same collateral exist, then the first to attach takes priority.

Perfected vs. Unperfected – If two or more have a claim or interest in the same collateral, where one is perfected and the other is unperfected, the perfected claim will take priority.

Competing Perfected Secured Claims – When two or more secured parties have perfected security interests in the same collateral, the first to perfect either by filing a financing statement or taking possession of the collateral has priority over the other.

Perfected Secured Claims in Fungible, Commingled Goods- If goods that have a perfected security status associated with them become commingled with other goods that also have perfected security interests to the point where the goods have lost their identity, then security interests will be determined according to the ratio that cost of goods "to which each interest originally attached bears to the cost of the total product or mass."

Building Block #6 – Default and Remedies

Article 9 sets forth the rights, duties and remedies of the secured party if the debtor defaults. You should know that the parties might define the term default in their security agreement. There are several remedies that a secured party may pursue upon default by the debtor.

Taking Possession of the Collateral
Many secured creditors repossess the goods from the defaulting debtor and then either keep the collateral or sell it and dispose of it to satisfy the debtor's debt. "The secured party must act in good faith and with commercial reasonableness, and with reasonable care to preserve the collateral in his or her possession." [UCC 9-503]

Retention of Collateral
Notice of a secured creditors intention to repossess and keep the debtor's collateral must be sent to the debtor unless there is a signed written statement renouncing this right. Beware, a secured creditor cannot keep the collateral and must dispose of it if he or she receives a written objection from a person entitled to receive notice within 21 days of the notice being sent or if the debt concerns consumer goods and the debtor has paid 60 percent of the cash price or loan. Here, the secured creditor must dispose of the goods within 90 days after taking possession of them. A consumer may renounce his or her rights under this section. [UCC 9-505(1)]

Disposition of Collateral
A secured creditor in possession of a debtor's collateral may sell, lease or otherwise dispose of the collateral in a commercially reasonable manner if the debtor is in default. However, the proceeds from the sale must be applied in the order prescribed by UCC 9-504(1) and (2).

Deficiency Judgment
If the proceeds from the disposition of the collateral are insufficient to satisfy the debt, then the secured party may bring a cause of action to recover a deficiency judgment against the debtor. UCC 9-504(2)

Redemption Rights
The debtor may redeem the collateral by paying all obligations secured by the collateral as well as expenses reasonably incurred by the secured party in retaking and holding the collateral along with any attorney's fees and legal expenses provided for in the security agreement and not prohibited by law. [UCC 9-506]

Relinquishment of the Security Interest and Proceeding to Judgment on the Underlying Debt
The secured creditor may proceed to judgment against the debtor to recover on the underlying debt instead of repossessing the collateral.

Security Agreements Covering Real and Personal Property
When a security agreement involves both real and personal property, the secured party may proceed against the personal property as per the provisions in Article 9, or as to both with the rights and remedies provided for by state law. If state law is opted for, Article 9 of the UCC is not applicable.

Revised Article 9 Recognizes E-Commerce

Article 9 in its revised state indicates the awareness and the need for upgrading commercial law to reflect the increased use of digital information and e-commerce. Some of the important aspects include being able to file financing statements, perfecting security interests and prioritizing conflicting security interests involving purchase money security interests in software verses security interests in computer hardware, all of which can be done electronically.

Refresh Your Memory

The following exercise will enable you to refresh your memory on the rules and principles presented to you in this chapter. Read each question twice and place your answer in the blanks provided. Review the chapter material for any question you miss or are unable to remember.

1.   The party who owes payment or other performance of the secured obligation is the
      _____.

2.   What article of the UCC governs secured transactions? Article _____.

3.   When a creditor extends credit to a debtor and takes a security interest in some property of
      the debtor, this is called a _____ _____.

4.   A seller, lender, or other party in whose favor there is a security interest is called a
      _____.

5.   _____ is the property subject to a security interest.

6.   A situation whereby a seller sells goods to a buyer who has obtained financing from a third-
      party lender who takes a security interest in the goods sold is referred to as a _____-
      _____ _____.

7.   The type of agreement between the debtor and the secured party that creates or provides for
      a security interest is a _____ agreement.

8.   When the creditor has an enforceable security interest against the debtor and can satisfy the
      debt out of the designated collateral, this is known as _____.

9.   A security interest that attaches to property that was not originally in the possession of the
      debtor when the agreement was executed is referred to as a _____ _____.

10.   Property that the debtor acquires after the security agreement is executed is called _____-
      _____ property.

11.   An interest a creditor automatically obtains when it extends credit to a consumer to
      purchase consumer goods is a _____ _____ _____ _____.

12.   What is the name of the document that the secured party files that ends a secured interest
      because the debt has been paid? _____ _____

13. Since default is not specifically defined by Article 9 of the UCC, what may the parties do to provide for this aspect of security agreements? _____

_____

14. _____ is a right granted to a secured creditor to take possession of the collateral upon default by the debtor.

15. Which two types of liens are called super-priority liens? _____ _____, or the _____ _____.

Critical Thought Exercise

Carl Rice and Carpet City, Inc., signed a security agreement with Pacific Ocean Bank for $86,400, plus interest. The collateral for the loan was a commercial truck used for the business run by Rice. The truck had a large hydraulic lift attached to the truck that allowed Rice to load and offload heavy rolls of carpet. Rice and Carpet City defaulted, and the bank took possession of the truck. The bank solicited bids for the truck by word of mouth from other financial institutions, two local furniture stores and some bank customers. Pacific Ocean Bank sold the truck to a local business for $69,000. The buyer did not need a truck equipped for transporting carpet so they did modifications and repairs totaling $17,000 and sold it two years later for $62,000. Pacific Ocean Bank sued Rice and Carpet City for the difference between the amount due on the loan and the proceeds from the sale. Pacific Ocean Bank did not advertise the truck nor did it contact any carpet stores that might desire to purchase a truck equipped with an integrated hydraulic lift. Rice does not contend that the sale price was wholly unreasonable, only that Pacific Ocean did not use all reasonable means to get the best price.

Should Pacific Ocean Bank be allowed to recover the deficiency from the sale or did it fail to sell the truck in a commercially unreasonable manner, which would preclude recovery by the bank?

Answer. _____

_____

_____

_____

_____

_____

_____

_____

_____

_____

_____

_____

_____

_____

Practice Quiz

True/False:

1. ___ A debtor must have possessory or ownership rights to property in order to give a security interest in that property. [p 528]

2. ___ A debtor may obtain a security interest in after acquired property. [p 529]

3. ___ The purpose of perfecting a security agreement is to establish the right of a secured creditor against other creditors who claim an interest in the collateral. [p 530]

4. ___ The filing of a financing statement in the proper government office is the least common method of perfecting a creditor's security interest in the debtor's collateral. [p 530]

5. ___ If a creditor has physical possession of the collateral, then he or she does not have to file a financing statement. [p 531]

6. ___ Penelope borrows $10,000 from Bradley and tells him that he may come and pick up her boat on Saturday as collateral for the loan. Bradley forgets. Meanwhile, another creditor obtains a lien against Penelope. Despite the fact that Bradley did not file a financing statement, his interest in the boat is still perfected thereby preventing the other creditor from recovering the boat from him. [p 531]

7. ___ Phillip, the owner of Phil's Electronics must file a financing statement if he extends credit to Mike, a consumer in his store. Once Phil does this he will have a purchase money security interest. [p 532]

8. ___ If the collateral in a purchase money security interest is something other than inventory, then the purchase money security interest prevails over a perfected nonpurchase money security interest. [p 535]

9. ___ A buyer in the ordinary course of business who purchases goods from a merchant takes the goods subject to any perfected or unperfected security interest in the merchant's inventory. [p 535]

10. ___ Buyers of secondhand consumer goods take free of security interest if they have actual or constructive knowledge about the security interest or give value, and buy the goods for personal, household or family purposes. [p 535]

11. ___ If the proceeds from the disposition of the collateral are not adequate to satisfy the debt to the secured party, the debtor is personally liable to the secured party for the deficiency. [p 537]

12. ___ A debtor may not redeem the collateral before the priority lienholder has disposed of it. [p 537]

13. ___ A secured creditor may give up his or her security interest in the collateral and proceed to judgment against the debtor to recover the underlying debt. [p 538]

14. ___ Collateral is not subject to a security interest. [p 527]

15. ___ The term debtor means a seller, lender or other party in whose favor there is a security interest. [p 527]

16. ___ If Winston borrows $8,000 from Nigel and gives Nigel his brand new car as security for the loan, this agreement does not have to be in writing because Nigel has possession of Winston's car. [p 528]

17. ___ There is not a security agreement if the debtor is not indebted to the creditor. [p 528]

18. ___ After-acquired property is property that the debtor obtains before the security agreement is executed. [p 529]

19. ___ Article 9 of the UCC also applies to transactions involving real estate mortgages, artisan's or mechanic's liens, liens on wages, and judicial liens. [p 529]

20. ___ The terminology, protection of a security interest refers to the establishment of a right of a secured creditor against other creditors who claim an interest in the collateral. [p 530]

21. ___ In order for a creditor to perfect his or her security interest, he or she must file a financing statement or take possession of the goods. [p 532]

22. ___ In order to perfect a security interest in fixtures and motor vehicles, the creditor must file a financing statement. [p 532]

23. ___ The interest that a creditor automatically obtains when it extends credit to a consumer to purchase consumer goods is called a purchase money security interest. [p 532]

24. ___ A termination statement is a document filed by the secured party that ends a secured interest because the debt has been paid. [p 533]

25. ___ If two or more secured parties have perfected security interests in the same collateral, the last one to perfect has priority. [p 534]

Multiple Choice:

26. A valid written security agreement must [p 528]
    a. clearly depict the collateral so that it can be readily identified.
    b. describe the creditor's rights upon the debtor's default.
    c. contain the debtor's promise to repay the creditor, along with terms of repayment and the debtor's signature.
    d. all of the above.

27. The term value as it refers to what the secured party must give the debtor is defined as [p 528]
    a. any consideration sufficient to support a simple contract.
    b. an amount that must exceed $500.
    c. a minimum amount of $1,000 of worth not to exceed $25,000.
    d. none of the above.

28. Putt Putt Inc. is a tractor dealer. To finance its inventory of new automatic tractors, Putt Putt borrows money from Small Bank and gives the bank a security interest in the inventory. Putt Putt sells a tractor subject to the security interest to Fred Farmington, who signs a sales contract whereby he agrees to pay Putt Putt for the tractor in 36 equal monthly installments. If Putt Putt defaults on its payment to Small bank, the bank is entitled to [p 529]
    a. receive the remaining payments from Putt Putt.
    b. receive the remaining payments from Putt Putt and Fred Farmington.
    c. receive the remaining payments from one of Putt Putt's other creditors.
    d. receive the remaining payments from Fred Farmington.

29. A future advance is [p 529]
    a. the resulting assets from the sale, exchange, or disposal of collateral subject to a security agreement.
    b. personal property of the debtor that is designed as collateral for future loans from a line of credit.
    c. property that the debtor acquires after the security agreement is executed.
    d. a security interest in property that was not in the possession of the debtor when the security agreement was executed.

30. When two or more creditors claim an interest in the same collateral or property, the priority of claims is partially determined by [p 534]
    a. the order in which conflicting claims of creditors in the same collateral are solved.
    b. whether a secured creditor took possession of the collateral upon the default of the debtor.
    c. whether the claim is unsecured or secured.
    d. whether the UCC recognizes an exception to the perfection-priority rule.

31. Ed purchases a mountain bike on credit from Bike World, a retailer, to be used for personal purposes. Bike World obtains an automatically perfected purchase money security interest in the mountain bike. Bike World fails to file a financing statement and Ed sells his bike to his friend, Larry, for cash. Thereafter Ed defaults on his loan payments to Bike World. What may Bike World do? [p 535]
    a. Bike World may recover the mountain bike from Larry.
    b. Bike World may recover the mountain bike from Ed.
    c. Bike World cannot recover the mountain bike from Larry.
    d. None of the above.

32. After repossessing goods from a defaulting debtor, a secured party may [p 536]
    a. retain the collateral or sell or otherwise dispose of it to satisfy the debt from the proceeds of the sale or disposition.
    b. not do anything to the collateral unless the debtor consents.
    c. give the goods back to the debtor upon sufficient showing of remorse from being in default.
    d. dispose of the goods, including their destruction.

33.   One who purchases goods from a merchant and takes goods free of any perfected or unperfected security interest in the merchant's inventory even if he or she is aware of the existence of the security interest is known as a [p 535]
        a.   buyer of secondhand consumer goods.
        b.   debtor.
        c.   secured party.
        d.   buyer in the ordinary course of business.

34.   Which of the following is not true with regard to financing statements? [p 530]
        a.   The most common method of perfecting a creditor's security interest in collateral is by filing a financing statement with the appropriate government office.
        b.   Financing statements do not cover fixtures.
        c.   Financing statements serve as constructive notice to the world that the creditor claims an interest in the property.
        d.   Financing statements are effective for five years from the date of filing.

35.   College Clothing Inc., a retailer borrows money from Our Town Bank for working capital. In exchange, Our Town Bank gets a security interest in all College Clothing's current and after-acquired inventory. Our Town files a financing statement thereby perfecting its security interest. Subsequently College Clothing purchases new inventory on credit from Korean Clothing Works, a clothing manufacturer. Korean Clothing Works perfects its interest by filing a financing statement and notifies Our Town Bank of this fact prior to delivery of the new inventory. College Clothing Inc. defaults on its loans. Whose lien has priority? [p 535]
        a.   College Clothing Inc.
        b.   Korean Clothing Works
        c.   Our Town Bank
        d.   All of the above

Short Answer:

36.   A debtor is the party who _____
        _____. [p 527]

37.   What is a security agreement? [p.527] _____
        _____

38.   _____ means that the creditor has an enforceable security interest against the debtor and can satisfy the debt out of designated collateral. [p 528]

39.   Personal property of the debtor that is identified as collateral for future loans from a line of credit is known as a _____ _____. [p 529]

40.   When a creditor _____ a security interest, this establishes the right of a secured creditor against other creditors who claim an interest in the collateral. [p 530]

41.   What is a financing statement? [p.530] _____
        _____

42.   If two or more secured parties claim an interest in the same collateral, but neither has perfected a claim, who has priority? [p 534] _____

43.   If two or more secured parties have perfected security interests in the same collateral, what might the court look at to determine who has priority? [p 534] _____

_____

44.   A secured creditor who repossesses collateral may suggest to _____ the collateral in satisfaction of the debtor's obligation. [p 536]

45.   If a secured party decides to publicly or privately dispose of the debtor's collateral, what must the secured party do? [p.537] _____

_____

_____

46.   What type of situation would give rise to a creditor's relinquishment of his or her security interest in the debtor's collateral and an intent to proceed to judgment to recover the underlying debt? [p 538] _____

_____

47.   Collateral includes accounts and _____

_____. [p 527]

48.   If a debtor sells, disposes or exchanges collateral that is subject to a security agreement, the secured party automatically has the right to receive the _____ of the disposition, exchange or sale. [p 529]

49.   If the creditor has _____, then he or she does not have to file a financing statement. [p 531]

50.   Give examples of things that are often defined in the debtor and creditor's security agreement as default. [p 536] _____

_____

Answers to Refresh Your Memory

1.   debtor [p 527]
2.   9 [p 527]
3.   secured transaction [p 527]
4.   secured party [p 527]
5.   collateral [p 527]
6.   three-party [p 527]
7.   security [p 528]
8.   attachment [p 528]
9.   floating lien [p 529]
10. after-acquired [p 529]
11. purchase money security interest [p 532]
12. termination statement [p 533]
13. The parties may define it in their security agreement. [p 532]
14. repossession [p 536]
15. artisan's lien or mechanic's lien [p 536]

Critical Thought Exercise Model Answer

It is the secured party's duty to the debtor to use all fair and reasonable means to obtain the best price under the circumstances, but the creditor need not use extraordinary means. Under the circumstances of this particular case, the sale may be commercially reasonable even with a lack of advertising. One of the factors to be considered in determining whether the sale was commercially reasonable is the adequacy or insufficiency of the sale price after default. In this case, the truck was sold for far less than the purchaser had invested in its purchase and repair. Though Pacific Ocean may have been able to get a better price for the truck had it advertised the sale to carpet stores, there is no evidence that the sale was conducted in a commercially unreasonable manner. Therefore, Pacific Ocean should recover the full amount of the deficiency.

Answers to Practice Quiz

True/False:

1. True   A debtor who does not have possessory or ownership rights to property cannot give a security interest in that property.
2. False   The secured party may obtain a security interest in after-acquired property.
3. True   Perfection of a security interest is a legal process that creates the right of a   secured creditor against other creditors who claim an interest in the collateral.
4. False   The filing of a financing statement in the correct government office is the most common method of perfecting a creditor's security interest in collateral.
5. True   If someone who is not the debtor has possession of the property used as collateral, a potential creditor is put on notice that another may have an interest in the debtor's property, thereby eliminating the need to file a financing statement.
6. False   Bradley's interest is not perfected because he did not have possession of the boat.
7. False   Phil automatically obtains a security interest as a creditor when it extended credit to Mike to purchase goods in his store.
8. True   The purchase money security interest prevails over a perfected nonpurchase money security interest if the collateral in a purchase money security interest is something other than inventory.
9. False   A buyer who purchases goods from a merchant takes the goods free of any perfected or unperfected security interesat in the merchant's inventory.
10. False Buyers of secondhand consumer goods take free of security interest if they do not have constructive or actual knowledge about the security interest, give value and buy the goods for family, personal or household purposes.
11. True   The debtor is personally liable to the secured party for the deficiency if the disposition of collateral is insufficient to satisfy the debt to the secured party.
12. False A debtor or another secured party may redeem the collateral before the priority lienholder has disposed of it.
13. True   A secured creditor has the option of proceeding to judgment against the debtor to recover on the underlying debt instead of repossessing the collateral. If this option is chosen, the creditor may relinquish his or her security interest in the collateral.
14. False Collateral such as accounts and chattel paper that have been sold are examples   of property that are subject to security interests.
15. False This is a definition for a secured party, whereas the term debtor refers to the party who owes payment or other performance of the secured obligation.
16. True   The oral security agreement is enforceable as Nigel is in possession of the collateral.

17. True   A security agreement does not exist unless the debtor owes a debt to the creditor.
18. False Property that the debtor acquires after the security agreement is executed is referred to as after-acquired property.
19. False Article 9 is inapplicable to real estate mortgage transactions, landlord's liens, liens on wages, artisan's or mechanic's liens, liens on wages, etc.
20. True   The right of a secured creditor is established by perfection of a security interest against other creditors who claim an interest in the collateral.
21. False Under the perfection by attachment or automatic perfection rule, a creditor who extends credit to a consumer to purchase a consumer good under a written security agreement obtains a purchase money security interest in the good thereby automatically perfecting the creditor's interest at the time of the sale.
22. True   Under UCC 9-302(1)(d), financing statements must be filed in order to perfect a security interest in fixtures and motor vehicles.
23. True   A creditor's extension of credit to a consumer to purchase a consumer good as per a written security agreement automatically gives the creditor what is known as a purchase money security interest.
24. True   Once a secured consumer debt has been paid, the creditor the secured party must file a termination statement.
25. False If two or more secured parties have perfected security interest in the same collateral the first to perfect has priority.

Multiple Choice:

26. D   Answer D is correct as answers A, B, and C are all correct statements of what must be contained in a valid written security agreement.
27. A   Answer A is correct as UCC 1-201(44) states that value is explained as any consideration sufficient to support a simple contract. Answers B and C are incorrect as UCC 1-201 does not place a limit on what the secured party must give to the debtor. Answer D is incorrect for the reasons stated above.
28. D   Answer D is correct as UCC 9-203 provides that if a debtor sells, exchanges, or disposes of collateral subject to a security agreement, the secured party automatically has the right to receive the proceeds of the sale or exchange, or disposition. Here Putt Putt Inc. sold a tractor on an installment basis to Fred Farmington. Since Putt Putt defaulted on its loan with Small Bank, the bank is entitled to collect the proceeds from Putt Putt's tractor sale to Fred Farmington in order to satisfy the debt. Answer A is incorrect, since Putt Putt defaulted he probably does not have the money to pay what is remaining due and payable to Small Bank. Answer B is incorrect for the reasoning stated in answer A, and the bank may collect from Fred Farmington as explained in more detail as per answer D. Answer C is incorrect, as Small Bank may not collect what Putt Putt owes it from one of Putt Putt's other creditors, as they are not party to the security agreement.
29. B   Answer B is correct as collateral for future loans from a line of credit is personal property that may be used as a future advance. Answer A is incorrect as this gives an explanation of what sale proceeds are. Answer C is incorrect as this states the definition of after-acquired property. Answer D is incorrect as this describes what a floating lien is.
30. C   Answer C is correct as the priority of claims involving the same property or collateral is established by viewing whether the claim is secured or unsecured and the time at which the secured claims were perfected or attached. Answer A is incorrect, as it makes no sense. Answer B is incorrect, as possession has no impact on priority especially if perfection of a creditor's security interest may be accomplished automatically at the time of the sale of goods. Answer D is incorrect as priority of claims may be established without the need for relying on a recognized exception to the perfection-priority rule.

31. C   Answer C is correct as Bike World's failure to file a financing statement, which would have given notice to Larry of its interest in the mountain bike. Answer A is incorrect, as Larry did not have notice of Bike World's interest. Answer B is incorrect, as Ed no longer has the mountain bike, since he sold it to Larry. Answer D is incorrect for the reasons given above.

32. A   Answer A is correct as the majority of secured parties seek to cure a default by taking possession of the collateral in the manner set forth in answer A. Answer B is incorrect as the defaulting debtor's consent is irrelevant in terms of the creditor's right to repossession of the goods. Answer C is incorrect as there is no legal requirement on the part of the debtor to show that he or she is remorseful for being in default, nor is there a requirement that the creditor give the goods back to the debtor even if he or she is remorseful for the default. Answer D is incorrect as there is no UCC provision that indicates the creditor must dispose of and destruct goods that have been repossessed.

33. D   Answer D is correct as this gives the definition of a buyer in the ordinary course of business. Answer A is incorrect as buyers of secondhand consumer goods take free of security interest if they do not have constructive or actual knowledge about the security interest, give value, and buy the goods for household, family or personal purposes. Answer B is incorrect as a debtor is a party who owes payment or other performance of the secured obligation. Answer C is incorrect as a secured party is a lender, seller, or other party in whose favor there is a security interest.

34. B   Answer B is correct, as it is the only false statement among the answer choices. Financing statements do cover fixtures and this type of statement is called a fixture filing. Answers A, C, and D are incorrect as they are all true statements regarding financing statements.

35. B   Answer B is correct as the perfected purchase money security interest prevails if the purchase money secured party gives written notice of the perfection to the perfected nonpurchase money secured party before the debtor receives possession of the inventory. UCC 9-312(3). Here Korean Clothing Works notified Our Town Bank before delivery of the inventory and as such its lien has priority. Based on this reasoning, answers A, C and D are incorrect.

Short Answer:

36. owes payment or other performance of the secured obligation.
37. A security agreement is the agreement between the debtor and the secured party that creates or provides for a security interest. UCC 1-201 (37)
38. Attachment
39. future advance
40. perfects
41. A financing statement is a document that is filed by a secured creditor with the correct government office that constructively notifies the world of his or her security interest in personal property.
42. The first party to attach has priority.
43. The court will examine which party has perfected his or her interest by either filing a financing statement or taking possession of the collateral in determining who has priority.
44. retain
45. The secured party must notify the debtor in writing about the place and time of any private or public sale or any other intended disposition of collateral.
46. If the value of the collateral is reduced below the amount of the secured interest and the debtor has other assets from which to satisfy the debt, the secured creditor may give up his or her security interest in the collateral and proceed to judgment against the debtor.

47. chattel paper that have been sold.
48. proceeds
49. physical possession of the collateral
50. Bankruptcy of the debtor, failure to make regular payments when due, breach of the warranty of ownership as to the collateral, and other occurrences are often referred to as default.

Chapter 28
BANKRUPTCY AND REORGANIZATION

Chapter Overview

This chapter explores Chapter 7 liquidation bankruptcy as well as Chapter 13 consumer debt adjustment bankruptcy and Chapter 11 business reorganization bankruptcy. Individual debtors as well as businesses often find that they are unable to be responsible for the debts that they have incurred, and as such must rely on the federal bankruptcy laws to free them from their obligations for past debts. You will become more familiar with the procedure involved in filing for bankruptcy as well as creditors' rights, the order of priority for paying creditors, the meaning of an automatic stay in bankruptcy, and voidable transfers and preferential payments.

Objectives

Upon completion of the exercises contained in this chapter, you should be able to:
1. Define the primary purpose of federal bankruptcy law.
2. Discuss the procedure for filing for bankruptcy.
3. Explain what is involved in a Chapter 7 liquidation bankruptcy.
4. Explain the meaning of an automatic stay in bankruptcy.
5. Discuss voidable transfers and preferential payments.
6. Be familiar with the order of priority for paying creditors in a Chapter 7 bankruptcy.
7. Be aware of examples of nondischargeable debts in bankruptcy.
8. Explain secured and unsecured rights in bankruptcy.
9. Explain business reorganization as it pertains to a Chapter 11 bankruptcy.
10. Discuss a Chapter 13 consumer debt adjustment bankruptcy.
11. Explore the bankruptcy of Dot-Com companies.

Practical Application

You should be able to better understand the main purpose of bankruptcy law as well as be familiar with the different types of bankruptcies. Additionally, you will have a clearer understanding of the impact of bankruptcy as well as which creditors take priority with regard to payment of the same.

Helpful Hints

The concepts in this chapter are easier to learn if you keep it simple by learning each of the three types of bankruptcies separately. The study tips section that follows gives you background information, procedures and little nuances that may be important to know for each kind of bankruptcy. As you will notice, under each type of bankruptcy has main points that you should become familiar. The most important terms are boldly printed.

Study Tips

Two Important Facets of Bankruptcy Law:

There are two preliminary aspects of bankruptcy that you should keep in mind. The first is that the law of bankruptcy is federally governed. Secondly, the main purpose of bankruptcy is to free the debtor from cumbersome debts.

Chapter 7 Liquidation Bankruptcy

This is the most common type of bankruptcy and is also referred to as a ***straight bankruptcy***. The debtor's nonexempt property is sold to obtain case and then the money is distributed to the debtor's creditors. Debts that are not paid are then discharged.

The procedure to file and maintain a Chapter 7 bankruptcy includes the ***filing of a petition*** by either the debtor (a voluntary petition) or by one or more creditors (an involuntary petition). When a voluntary or involuntary petition is filed, this is known as an ***order for relief***. After the order for relief, the court must call a ***meeting of the creditors*** wherein the debtor is questioned by his or her creditors without a judge being present. At this meeting, a ***permanent trustee*** is elected to be the legal representative of the debtor's estate. The trustee has many duties which include but are not limited to setting aside exempt property, looking into the debtor's finances, investigating the proof of claims and making reports to the debtor, his or her creditor's and the court concerning the estate's administration.

An ***automatic stay*** goes into effect upon the filing of an involuntary or voluntary petition. The effect of an automatic stay is that it suspends creditors' actions against the debtor or the debtor's property. It should also be noted that a debtor may have an injunction issued against its creditors for activity that is not covered in the automatic stay. However, a creditor does have some recourse against a bankrupt debtor. The secured creditor may seek a ***relief from stay*** in cases where the property is depreciating.

The bankruptcy ***estate*** involves all of the debtor's legal and equitable interests in all types of property, including community property from the onset of a Chapter 7 bankruptcy proceeding. If the debtor obtains property after he or she files his or her petition, this property usually is not considered to be part of the estate. However, there are certain exceptions, which include but are not limited to inheritance, divorce settlements, and the like if obtained within 180 days of the filing of the petition.

Exempt property may be kept by the debtor. The Federal exemptions are given on p.549 of your main text. Some state laws also provide for exemptions which are broad in scope. Some states require that the debtor choose between federal or state exemptions or adhere to the state laws.

Distribution of nonexempt property has to be distributed to the debtor's unsecured and secured creditors. The secured creditors take priority over the unsecured creditors. After the property has been distributed to satisfy the claims that are allowed, then the debtor is no longer responsible for the remaining unpaid claims. Only individuals may be given a ***discharge.***

Nondischargeable debts are those that are not dischargeable in bankruptcy. Some examples are alimony, child support and certain fines payable to federal, local and state authorities. Other examples may be found on page 554 of your main text.

Chapter 11 Reorganization Bankruptcy

Under this type of bankruptcy, the court assists the debtor in reorganizing his or her financial affairs. Individuals, corporations, nonincorporated associations, railroads and partnerships are able to utilize this type of bankruptcy. Corporations use Chapter 11 bankruptcies the most.

A unique feature about this type of bankruptcy is that the debtor is left to run his or her business while the reorganization proceeding is taking place. The debtor is referred to as a *debtor-in-possession.* The debtor-in-possession has the authority to enter into contracts and operate the business accordingly.

The debtor has a right to file a *plan of reorganization* within 120 days of the *order for relief.* The reorganization plan describes the debtor's proposed new capital structure that indicates the different classes of claims and interests. The creditors and equity holders must be given a court approved *disclosure statement.*

The court must *confirm* the debtor's plan for reorganization in order for it to become effective. Confirmation may be accomplished by giving the different classes of creditors the chance to accept or reject the plan. The court looks at whether the plan is in the best interests of each class of claims, if the plan is feasible, if at least one class has accepted the plan and whether or not each class of claims and interests is nonimpaired. Confirmation may also be achieved using the *cram down method.* Under this method, the plan has to be fair and equitable to the impaired class. Remember, the impaired class can be forced to take part in the plan of reorganization.

The debtor is given a *discharge* of all claims that were not a part of the plan of reorganization.

Chapter 13 Consumer Debt Adjustment

Under this plan, the court may oversee the debtor's plan for installment payments of his or her unpaid debts. Chapter 13 is beneficial to both the debtor as well as creditor. The debtor's costs are less under this type of proceeding as well as the fact that he or she may keep more property than is exempt under Chapter 7. The creditors are able to elicit a greater amount of the debts that are owing to them.

The debtor must file a *petition* claiming that he or she is insolvent or not able to pay his or her debts when they are due. A debtor may ask for more time (an *extension*) to pay his or her debts or ask for a *composition* which reduces his or her debts. Subsequent to the filing of the petition, the debtor has to give the court a *list* of his or her creditors, liabilities and assets. Then there is a *meeting of creditors* where the debtor must be present. A *trustee* is then *appointed* to confirm the plan.

As with a Chapter 7 filing, once a debtor files a petition under Chapter 13, an *automatic stay* is in place regarding liquidation bankruptcy proceedings, creditors' judicial and nonjudicial actions and creditors' collection activities. The automatic stay is not applicable concerning business debts.

The debtor must file a ***plan of payment*** within 15 days of filing his or her petition. The plan may not go beyond three years, however, the court may grant a five-year period plan. The debtor must make payments within 30 days of filing his or her plan. If a debtor's circumstances change, then his or her plan may be ***modified.***

As with a Chapter 11 bankruptcy, the plan must also be ***confirmed*** under a Chapter 13 bankruptcy.

When the debtor has made all payments under the plan, the court will ***discharge*** the debtor from all unpaid debts. Most debts are dischargeable except for such things as child support, alimony and trustee fees. The court will grant a ***hardship discharge*** if there are unforeseeable circumstances, or the unsecured creditors have been given an amount equal to what they would have received under a Chapter 7 liquidation proceeding or it is not feasible to modify the plan.

Refresh Your Memory

The following exercise will enable you to refresh your memory on the rules and principles presented to you in this chapter. Read each question twice and place your answer in the blanks provided. Review the chapter material for any question you miss or are unable to remember.

1. Give two examples of core proceedings that bankruptcy judges decide. _____
    _____

2. Decisions on personal injury, civil proceedings and divorce are examples of _____
    _____

3. Since federal bankruptcy law discharges the debtor from cumbersome debts, it is in essence
    giving the debtor a _____ _____ by relieving them from legal
    responsibility for past debts.

4. Chapter 7 liquidation bankruptcy is also known as a _____ _____.

5. Once a debtor's nonexempt property is sold for cash, the money is given to the creditors,
    and any unpaid debts are _____.

6. The debtor begins a Chapter 7 bankruptcy by filing a _____.

7. Under Chapter 7, a petition filed by the debtor is said to be _____.

8. An involuntary petition is one filed by the debtor's creditors that states _____
    _____.

9. What does the filing of a voluntary petition or an unchallenged involuntary petition
    designate? _____

10. After an order for relief is granted, then the court calls a _____ _____ .

11. Who is elected at the first meeting of creditors? _____

12. What must unsecured creditors file that states the amount of their claims against the debtor? _____

13. What automatically stays certain action by creditors against the debtor's property or the debtor? _____ _____

14. When is the bankruptcy estate created in a Chapter 7 proceeding? _____ _____

15. There is some property that is _____ from being part of a bankruptcy estate.

Critical Thought Exercise

Nancy Mills attended two different institutions of higher learning. She received educational loans totaling $22, 480. After graduation, Mills was employed, but her monthly take-home pay was less than 1200. The monthly expenses for herself and her four children were approximately $1650. Mill's husband had abandoned the family and provided no financial support. Mills received no public assistance and had no possibility to increase her income. A neighbor paid her telephone, water, and gas bills for the two months prior to filing a petition in bankruptcy. Mills also had substantial medical bills and had not been well for months. In her bankruptcy petition, Mills sought to discharge her educational loans.

Are the educational loans owed by Mills dischargeable in bankruptcy? Why was the Bankruptcy Code amended to generally prohibit the discharge of student loans?

Answer. _____
_____
_____
_____
_____
_____
_____
_____
_____
_____
_____
_____
_____
_____
_____
_____

Practice Quiz

True/False:

1. ___ Federal bankruptcy law serves the main purpose of discharging the debtor from his or her onerous debts. [p 544]

2. ___ Banks, savings and loan associations, insurance companies, and credit unions are examples of businesses that are allowed to file a bankruptcy under Chapter 7. [p 545]

3. ___ There is no set time frame for filing a proof of claim in a Chapter 7 bankruptcy. [p 547]

4. ___ The court may issue an injunction to stop creditor activity that is not included in the automatic stay provision. [p 547]

5. ___ If secured property is not sufficiently protected during the bankruptcy proceeding, a secured creditor may file a petition for a relief from stay. [p 547]

6. ___ There is no bankruptcy estate in a Chapter 7 proceeding. [p 548]

7. ___ Property obtained after filing a Chapter 7 petition also becomes part of the bankruptcy estate. [p 548]

8. ___ Dividends, rents and interest payments are also considered property of the bankruptcy estate. [p 548]

9. ___ States that have Homestead Declarations as an exemption require that the debtor file this document before the bankruptcy. [p 549]

10. ___ A debtor's use of a preferential lien is a way of demonstrating a debtor's favoritism toward certain unsecured creditors. [p 551]

11. ___ The court may void preferential liens that are made to relatives, partners, partnerships, officers and directors of corporations or anyone else with a relationship to the debtor. [p 551]

12. ___ The Bankruptcy Code prevents the court from voiding fraudulent transfers of property if the transfers occurred within one year of the filing of the petition in bankruptcy. [p 551]

13. ___ Chapter 7 does not require the distribution of nonexempt property to the debtor's secured and unsecured creditors. [p 552]

14. ___ Once the property is distributed to satisfy any allowed claims, any existing unpaid claims will not be discharged and the debtor is still responsible for them. [p 553]

15. ___ Wilson files for a Chapter 7 bankruptcy and has several unsecured creditors, with the Handy Dandy Tool Co. being one of them. Wilson owes Handy Dandy $1,500, but his Bankruptcy estate has only enough to pay all of his unsecured creditors .05 on the

dollar. Handy Dandy will receive $75.00 from Wilson's estate and may thereafter collect the unpaid balance from Wilson in a separate lawsuit. [p 553]

16. ___ A creditor such as one who is owed alimony may participate in the distribution of the bankruptcy estate. [p 554]

17. ___ A party of interest may not file an objection to the discharge of a debt. [p 555]

18. ___ A bankruptcy may not be revoked if the discharge is obtained through the fraud of the debtor. [p 555]

19. ___ Chapter 11 is a means of reorganizing the debtor's financial affairs. [p 556]

20. ___ Banks, savings and loan associations, insurance companies and credit unions are a few of the types of businesses that may utilize Chapter 11 proceedings. [p 556]

21. ___ Creditors may involuntarily file a Chapter 11 petition or the debtor may voluntarily file the petition him/herself. [p 556]

22. ___ A debtor-in-possession has the authority to operate the debtor's business during the bankruptcy proceeding. [p 556]

23. ___ Under the Bankruptcy Code, a post petition unsecured creditor lien is not allowed on the debtor-in-possession's property. [p 556]

24. ___ The debtor has a right to file a plan of reorganization within the first 120 days after the date of the order for relief. [p 557]

25. ___ The debtors' creditors and equity holders must be given a disclosure statement concerning the suggested plan of reorganization. [p 557]

Multiple Choice:

26. A voluntary petition for bankruptcy must include which of the following? [p 545]
    a. A list of secured and unsecured creditors
    b. A list of the property owned by the debtor, including exempt property
    c. A statement of the debtor's financial affairs as well as the debtor's income and expenses
    d. All of the above.

27. An appointed trustee must not [p 547]
    a. set aside exempt property.
    b. separate secured and unsecured property.
    c. take immediate possession of the debtor's property.
    d. employ interested professionals to assist in the estate's administration.

28. If a debtor's equity in property exceeds the exemption limits, a trustee may [p 549]
    a. liquidate the property to realize the excess value for the bankruptcy estate.
    b. sell the home and not distribute the excess to the debtor's creditors.
    c. require the debtor to file a declaration of Homestead after the bankruptcy.
    d. none of the above.

29. A transfer that unfairly benefits the debtor or some creditors at the expense of others is evident when [p 551]
    a. a debtor transfers property to a creditor within 90 days before filing a petition in bankruptcy.
    b. the transfer is made for a preexisting debt.
    c. the creditor would receive more from the transfer than in a Chapter 7 proceeding.
    d. all of the above.

30. Since a secured creditor's claim takes priority over unsecured creditor's claims, what may the secured creditor do with regard to the debt that is owed? [p 552]
    a. Foreclose on the collateral and use the proceeds to satisfy the debt.
    b. Allow the trustee to keep the collateral, dispose of it at a sale and give the proceeds to him or her.
    c. Accept the collateral in full satisfaction of the debt.
    d. All of the above.

31. Which of the following is not a test that the court uses to confirm a plan of reorganization? [p 559]
    a. Each class must be impaired.
    b. The plan must be in the best interests of each class.
    c. The plan must be feasible.
    d. At least one class of claims must vote to accept the plan.

32. Once a plan of reorganization is confirmed, the debtor is [p 561]
    a. granted a discharge of all claims not included in the plan.
    b. not granted a discharge of all claims not included in the plan.
    c. not considered bankrupt.
    d. free to incur more debt using his or her same creditors.

33. The advantages of filing under a Chapter 13 bankruptcy include [p 562]
    a. the ability to keep more property than is exempt under Chapter 7.
    b. the fact that it is cheaper and there is less compilation involved.
    c. avoidance of having the tag of liquidation attached to the debtor and his or her credit history.
    d. all of the above.

34. Who may file a Chapter 13 petition for bankruptcy? [p 562]
    a. corporations
    b. banks
    c. only individuals with regular income with unsecured debts of less than $250,000 and secured debts of less than $750,000
    d. sole proprietors without debt

35. What type of bankruptcy is Chapter 13 a form of? [p 562]
    a. It is a form of reorganization bankruptcy.
    b. It is a form of family farmer bankruptcy.
    c. It is a form of liquidation bankruptcy.
    d. It is a form of state court bankruptcy.

Short Answer:

36. Allowing creditor claims and confirming plans of reorganization are examples of _____
   _____ that bankruptcy judges decide. [p 544]

37. Personal injury, divorce and other civil proceedings that are resolved in federal or state
   court are considered to be _____. [p 544]

38. What is meant by the term, "a fresh start?" [p.544] _____
   _____

39. What is the most familiar type of bankruptcy? [p 545] _____

40. What does Chapter 7 Bankruptcy involve? [p 545] _____
   _____

41. In terms of bankruptcy, what is a petition? [p 545] _____
   _____

42. What are the signing requirements for an involuntary petition if the debtor has more than 12
   creditors? [p 545] _____

43. What is the name of the bankruptcy meeting whereby the judge is not allowed to attend?
   [p 545] _____

44. What may a secured creditor whose claims exceed the value of the debtor's collateral do?
   [p 547] _____

45. Give three examples of property that is exempt from bankruptcy. [p 549] _____
   _____

46. What is a reaffirmation agreement? [p 553] _____
   _____

47. A claim resulting from fraud by the debtor while acting in a fiduciary capacity is an
   example of a _____ debt. [p 554]

48. What is a debtor-in-possession? [p.556] _____
   _____

49. What does the debtor's plan of reorganization usually contain? [p 557] _____
   _____
   _____

50. A plan of reorganization must be _____ by the court before it becomes
   effective. [p 559]

Answers to Refresh Your Memory

1. deciding claim preferences and creditor claims [p 544]
2. noncore proceedings concerning the debtor [p 544]
3. fresh start [p 544]
4. straight bankruptcy [p 545]
5. discharged [p 545]
6. petition [p 545]
7. voluntary [p 545]
8. the debtor is not paying his or her debts as they become due [p 545]
9. It constitutes an order for relief. [p 545]
10. first meeting of creditors [p 546]
11. A permanent trustee is elected at the first meeting of creditors. [p 546]
12. Unsecured creditors must file a proof of claim. [p 547]
13. The filing of a voluntary or involuntary petition suspends certain actions by creditors against the debtor or his or her property. [p 547]
14. The bankruptcy estate is created upon the start of a Chapter 7 proceeding. [p 548]
15. exempt [p 549]

Critical Thought Exercise Model Answer

The restriction against discharge of student loans was designed to remedy an abuse by students, who, immediately upon graduation, would file bankruptcy to secure a discharge of educational loans. These students often had no other indebtedness and could pay their debts out of future wages.

In this case, Mills has truly fallen on hard times. Her monthly income does not meet her usual expenses. The combination of no support from her husband, four in-home dependents, and no prospects for increased income, give rise to a situation where a court could easily find that repayment of the educations loans would create and undue hardship. The restriction against discharge of educational loans was passed by Congress to stop an abuse. The restriction was never intended to prevent a deserving petitioner from getting protection and a fresh start from the bankruptcy court. Mills should be allowed to have all of her debts discharged in bankruptcy to avoid undue hardship.

Answers to Practice Quiz

True/False:

1. True The main goal of federal bankruptcy law is to discharge the debtor from burdensome debts.
2. False These are examples of businesses that are prohibited from filing bankruptcy under Chapter 7.
3. False The proof of claim must be filed in a timely manner which is usually interpreted to mean within six months of the first meeting of creditors.
4. True The court has the power to issue injunctions that will prevent creditor activity that is not covered under the automatic stay provision.

5. True   A petition for relief from stay is usually brought by a secured creditor in situations involving depreciating assets where the property is not sufficiently protected during the bankruptcy proceeding.

6. False   A bankruptcy estate is created upon the commencement of a Chapter 7 proceeding.

7. False   Property that is obtained after the petition does not become part of the bankruptcy estate.

8. True   Earnings from the property estate such as the examples given are property of the estate.

9. True   The Declaration of Homestead must be filed by the debtor prior to bankruptcy.

10. True   Debtors who favor certain unsecured creditors often given them a secured interest in property by giving them a preferential lien.

11. True   Preferential liens may be voided by the court.

12. False   The Bankruptcy Code at Section 548 gives the court the authority to avoid fraudulent transfers of property that happen within one year of the filing of the petition in Bankruptcy.

13. False   Chapter 7 states that the nonexempt property of the bankruptcy estate must be distributed to the debtors' secured and unsecured creditors.

14. False   The debtor is no longer legally responsible for remaining unpaid claims once property has been distributed to satisfy the allowed claims.

15. False   The Handy Dandy Tool Co. cannot collect the remaining balance and must write it off as a bad debt as per the provisions stated in Chapter 7.

16. True   Creditors who have non-dischargeable debts such as alimony against the debtor may participate in the distribution of the bankruptcy estate.

17. False   Any party of interest is allowed to file an objection to the discharge of a debt.

18. False   If the discharge is procured through the fraud of the debtor, a party of interest is allowed to bring a motion for revocation of the bankruptcy.

19. True   The main goal of Chapter 11 is to reorganize the debtor with a new capital organization so that it will be able to come through the bankruptcy as a viable option.

20. False   These are examples of those businesses that may not utilize Chapter 11 proceedings.

21. True   A petition under Chapter 11 may be filed voluntarily by the debtor or creditors may involuntarily file a petition.

22. True   The debtor-in-possession has the power to operate the debtor's business while the bankruptcy proceeding is taking place.

23. False   The court is able to create a secured interest by affirming a post petition unsecured creditor lien on the debtor-in-possession's property.

24. True.   The debtor's right to file a plan of reorganization with the Bankruptcy is an exclusive right that must be accomplished within the first 120 days after the date of the order for relief.

25. True   The debtor's proposed plan of reorganization must be contained in the debtor's disclosure statement that the debtor gives to his/her creditors and equity holders.

Multiple Choice:

26. D   Answer D is the correct answer as answers A, B, and C all state what must be contained in a voluntary petition for bankruptcy.

27. D   Answer D is the correct answer as an appointed trustee may only employ disinterested professionals not interested professionals in the estate's administration. Answers A, B, and C are all incorrect as these state the things that an appointed trustee must do.

28. A   Answer A is the correct answer as it properly states what the trustee may do in the situation where the debtor's equity in property exceeds the exemption limits. Answer B is incorrect as the trustee may be able to sell a debtor's home, pay off the mortgage and

use the remaining proceeds to pay off the debtor's creditors. Answer C is incorrect as Declaration of Homesteads are usually filed prior to bankruptcy under most state laws. Answer D is incorrect for the reasons given above.

29. D   Answer D is the correct answer as the answers given in choices A, B, and C are all indicative of a transfer that unfairly benefits either the debtor or creditor at the expense of others.

30. D   Answer D is the correct answer as answers A, B, and C all state options that a secured creditor has with respect to the claims that may be made on a debtor's property.

31. A   Answer A is the correct answer as the requirement that each class must be impaired is incorrect and is not a test. Instead the test is that each class of claims and interest is non-impaired. Answers B, C, and D are incorrect as each state a test that the court uses to confirm a plan of reorganization.

32. A   Answer A is the correct answer as the debtor is granted a discharge of all claims not included in the confirmed plan of reorganization. Answer B is incorrect as it is not a true statement. Answer C is incorrect by virtue of the fact that the debtor is bankrupt if he or she has filed a plan of reorganization. Answer D is incorrect based on its absurdity.

33. D   Answer D is the correct answer as answers A, B, and C all state the advantages of filing under a Chapter 13 bankruptcy.

34. C   Answer C is the correct answer as it states specifically who may file a Chapter 13 petition for bankruptcy. Answers A, and B are incorrect as they may not utilize this type of bankruptcy proceeding. Answer D is incorrect, as a sole proprietor without debt would not have a need to file for bankruptcy in the first place.

35. A   Answer A is the correct answer as Chapter 13 is a form of reorganization bankruptcy. Answer B is incorrect as Family Farmer Bankruptcy is provided for in Chapter 12 of the Bankruptcy Code. Answer C is incorrect as liquidation bankruptcy refers to Chapter 7 of the Bankruptcy Code. Answer D is incorrect as there is no state court bankruptcy.

Short Answer:

36. core proceedings
37. non-core proceedings
38. The term fresh start refers to giving a debtor a relief from legal responsibility for past debts.
39. Chapter 7 liquidation bankruptcy is the most familiar type of bankruptcy.
40. The debtor's nonexempt property is sold for cash and then the cash is distributed to the debtor's creditors. Thereafter any unpaid debts are discharged.
41. A petition is a document that begins the bankruptcy proceeding. The petition is filed with the bankruptcy court.
42. The petition must be signed by at least three of them if the debtor has more than 12 creditors.
43. The name of the meeting is the first meeting of creditors.
44. The secured creditor may submit a proof of claim and become an unsecured claimant as to the difference.
45. Interest up to $2,400 in one motor vehicle, interest in jewelry up to $1,000 that is held for personal use, interest up to $1,500 in value in implements, tools, or professional books used in the debtor's trade. Note that answers will vary.
46. A reaffirmation agreement is a formal agreement that states the terms of repayment of an unsatisfied debt that is dischargeable in bankruptcy.
47. nondischargeable
48. A debtor-in-possession is one who is left in place to conduct the business during the reorganization proceeding.

49. The plan contains the debtor's proposed new capital structure wherein he or she designates the different classes of claims and interests.

50. confirmed

Chapter 29
AGENCY FORMATION
AND TERMINATION

Chapter Overview

This chapter will provide you with a thorough understanding of agency including the important role that it plays in the business world, as well as the creation and termination of the same. Additionally you will become familiar with the three most common types of employment relationships and how to differentiate between them.

Objectives

Upon completion of the exercises contained in this chapter, you should be able to:
1.   Discuss what an agency is.
2.   Recognize and define a principal-independent contractor relationship.
3.   Discuss a principal's liability for the actions of independent contractors.
4.   Discuss the creation of an express agency verses and implied agency.
5.   Discuss the definition of an apparent agency.
6.   Discuss the various ways an agency may be terminated by the acts of the parties.
7.   Discuss how an agency is terminated by operation of law.
8.   Discuss who should be notified upon the termination of an agency.
9.   Discuss wrongful termination of an agency contract.
10.   Discuss when an agency becomes irrevocable.

Practical Application

You will learn how the different types of agencies are created as well as terminated. You will also be able to recognize an irrevocable agency and whether or not there has been a wrongful termination of an agency contract. Further, you will know the difference between the three main types of employment relationships and the liabilities associated with each. This chapter will be especially useful to anyone in business, because agencies are an essential part of any successful business.

Helpful Hints

Since most of us have been or will be in some sort of employment relationship in our lifetime, this chapter is very easy to apply to either our past employment experiences or our future endeavors. Many of us have been agents and have not realized that fact. You will find this chapter easier to learn if you place yourself in the shoes of the situation you are trying to learn about. Additionally, if you familiarize yourself with the basic terminology given in the Study Tips section that follows, the concepts will become easier and clearer for you to understand.

Study Tips

Basic Terminology

Agency: Section 1(1) of the Restatement Second of Agency defines agency as "a fiduciary relationship which results from the manifestation of consent by one person to another that the other shall act in his behalf and subject to his control, and consent by the other so to act."

Principal – A party who employs another individual to act on his or her behalf.

Agent – A party who agrees to act on behalf of another.

Employer-employee relationship – An association that results when an employer hires an employee to perform some type of physical service.

Principal-agent relationship – A relationship whereby an employee is hired and given the authority to act and enter into contracts on the employer's behalf.

Independent contractor – A person or business who is not an employee but who is hired by a principal to perform a certain task on his behalf. This person is not controlled by the principal with regard to the performance of the task that he or she is employed to do.

At-will employee – An employee without an employment contract.

Express Agency – An express agreement between a principal and agent thereby agreeing to enter into an agency agreement with one another.

Exclusive agency contract – A distinct contract between the principal and agent whereby the principal agrees not to employ any agent other than the exclusive agent.

Power of Attorney – An agency agreement that expressly gives an agent the authority to sign legal documents on the principal's behalf. The agent in this situation is referred to as an Attorney-in-fact.

Implied Agency- An agency that is inferred from the parties' conduct and where there has not been an express creation of an agency between the principal and the agent.

Apparent Agency – An agency that the principal creates that appears to exist but really does not exist.

Agency by Ratification – An agency that is created by a principal ratifying an agency that is created by an unauthorized act such as the misrepresentation of oneself as another's agent when in fact he or she is not an agent at all.

Wrongful Termination – A violation of the terms of the agency contract thereby resulting in the termination of the agency contract.
Revocation of Authority – The termination of an agency contract by a principal.

Renunciation of Authority – The termination of an agency contract by an agent.

418

Strategic Alliance – An agreement between two or more businesses from different countries to accomplish a certain purpose or function.

Agency Basics

Capacity – If an individual has the capacity to enter into a contract, then he or she can appoint an agent to act on his or her behalf.

Purpose – The agency must be formed for a lawful purpose.

Three types of employment relationships:

- Employer-Employee Relationship – Where an employer hires an employee to perform some sort of physical service.

- Principal-Agent Relationship– Where an employer hires an employee and gives the employee power to act and enter into contracts on his or her behalf.

- Principal-Independent Contractor Relationship– Persons and businesses who are hired to perform certain tasks on behalf of the principal. The *degree of control* that an employer has over an agent is the determining factor on whether one is an employee or an independent contractor. Other considerations include but are not limited to: *The duration of the agent's employment by the principal, the degree of skill required to complete the task, whether the principal provides the equipment and tools needed in the work, etc.*

Agency Formation

There are four ways that an agency may be formed. They are expressly, impliedly, apparently and by ratification.

- **Express Agency** – This is the most common type of agency wherein an agent and a principal expressly agree to enter into an agency agreement with one another. It may be oral or in writing. An example of an express agency is a *power of attorney*. The power of attorney may be *general* thereby giving broad powers to the agent to act in any matters on the principal's behalf or it may be *special* giving limited powers as provided for in the parties' agreement. *Incidental authority* is implied authority to act in emergency situations and other contingent circumstances in order to protect the principal's property and rights.

- **Implied Agency** – An agency that is created by the parties' conduct. The implied authority of the agent may be given by custom in the industry, the agent's position or the prior dealing between the parties. There cannot be a conflict between the express and implied authority.

- **Apparent Agency** – An agency by estoppel (or apparent agency) is created when a principal gives the appearance of an agency that in reality does not exist. Upon creation of this type of agency, the principal is bound to contract entered into by the apparent agent while acting within the parameters of the apparent agency.

- **Agency by Ratification** – An agency that is a result of a principal ratifying an unauthorized act by another who represents him or herself as another's agent when the reality is that he or she is not the principal's agent.

Termination of an Agency and Employment Contract

An agency contract may be terminated by an act of the parties or by operation of law. There are four ways to terminate an agency relationship by the actions of the parties.

- **Mutual Agreement** – The parties may mutually agree to terminate their agreement.
- **Lapse of Time** – The agency agreement will end after a certain period of time passes.
- **Purpose Achieved** – The agency ends when the purpose of the agreement is accomplished.
- **Occurrence of a Specified Event** – The agency ends when a specified event in the parties' agreement happens.

There are six ways to terminate an agency relationship by operation of law.

- **Death** – The death of either the agent or principal ends the agency relationship.
- **Insanity** – Insanity of either party ends the agency relationship.
- **Bankruptcy** – If the principal is found bankrupt, the agency is terminated. However, an agent's bankruptcy usually does not end the agency.
- **Impossibility** – The agency ends if circumstances make the agency impossible. The following have been recognized under this method of termination:
    - **Loss or destruction of the subject matter of the agency**
    - **Loss of a required qualification** – For example, a private physician loses his or her license.
    - **A change in the law** – If the agency contains a provision that becomes illegal, the agency contract will end.
- **Changed circumstances** – If there are changed circumstances that lead the agent to determine that the original instructions he or she received from the principal no longer apply, then the agency will be terminated.
- **War** – War between the agent and principal's country terminates the agency.

Irrevocable Agencies – These are referred to as agencies coupled with an interest. This type of agency is not ended by death or incapacity of either party and only terminates upon performance of the agent's obligations. It is irrevocable and created for the agent's benefit.

Wrongful Termination of an Agency or Employment Contract – If the principal's or agent's termination of an agency contract breaches the agency contract, then the termination may be considered to be wrongful.

Revocation of Authority – When a principal ends an agency agreement, he or she is terminating the agency agreement by revocation of authority.

Renunciation of Authority – When an agent ends an agency agreement, it is called a renunciation of authority.

Refresh Your Memory

The following exercise will give you the opportunity to refresh your memory of the principles given to you in this chapter. Read the question twice and place your answer in the blanks provided. If you do not remember, go to the next question, and come back to the one you did not answer.

1. A party who employs another individual to act on his or her behalf is called a _____.

2. An individual who agrees to act on behalf of another is called an _____.

3. Individuals who lack _____ _____ cannot appoint an agent.

4. What are the three types of employment relationships? _____
_____

5. An employee is an agent if he or she is given specific powers to _____
_____ on the principal's or employer's behalf.

6. What is an independent contractor? _____
_____

7. What are some of the characteristics of an independent contractor? _____
_____

8. An _____ agency is the most common type of agency.

9. A _____ of _____ is a formal type of agency agreement that is used to empower an agent to sign legal documents.

10. What is an apparent agency? _____
_____

11. If no termination date is stated, when does an agency terminate? _____
_____

12. Give three ways to terminate an agency by operation of law. _____
_____

13. The agency relationship is ended if the _____ is declared bankrupt.

14. An agent that is coupled with an interest is a unique agency relationship that is formed for the _____ benefit.

15. A revocation of authority refers to when a _____ terminates an agency contract.

Critical Thought Exercise

Dave Polk was a self-employed handyman, doing business under the name Polk Speedy-Fix. From 1994-2001, Polk performed maintenance and repair work for numerous people in Sun City West, Arizona, including Frank and Martha Hamilton. Polk did landscape maintenance, cactus trimming, painting, plumbing, and carpentry. Polk completed a job in May 2001 for the Hamilton's wherein he replaced a toilet and vanity. Polk was then hired to trim a 30-foot tall palm tree in the Hamilton's side yard. Polk was paid $20 per hour for his previous jobs by the Hamiltons. Polk was to receive the same rate of pay for trimming the palm tree.

When Polk arrived to trim the palm tree, Mr. Hamilton told him he wanted it trimmed to a height that was approximately the same as the house, along with trimming back the fronds so that they were at least five feet from the homes of both the Hamiltons and their neighbors. Polk took out several saws and two ladders from his repair van. Polk also borrowed a tree trimming saw and a rope from the Hamiltons. When his ladder was unable to reach the top areas of the tree, Polk climbed the tree. Polk fell from the palm tree when the rope broke and he received severe injuries to his back, pelvis, and internal organs. At age 32, he was totally unable to work.

Polk sued the Hamiltons to recover for his injuries, claiming that he was working as an employee at the time of his injuries and was therefore entitled to workers' compensation protection from the Hamiltons. The Hamiltons argued that Polk was an independent contractor.

Was Polk an employee of the Hamiltons or an independent contractor?

Answer. _____

_____

_____

_____

_____

_____

_____

_____

_____

_____

_____

_____

_____

_____

_____

_____

_____

_____

_____

_____

_____

Practice Quiz

True/False:

1. ___ The principal is the party who hires another person to act on his or her behalf. [p 571]

2. ___ Insane persons and minors may appoint agents regardless of capacity. [p 571]

3. ___ An employer-employee relationship exists when an employer hires an employee to perform some form of mental service. [p 572]

4. ___ A beanie baby assembly person is an employee of the Ty corporation because he or she performs a physical task. [p 572]

5. ___ A principal can give an independent contractor the authority to enter into contracts. [p 572]

6. ___ A wrongfully discharged employee can sue his or her employer for punitive damages if the employer has engaged in fraud or other intentional conduct. [p 575]

7. ___ Express agency contracts can only be in writing. [p 575]

8. ___ Another name for an apparent agency is an agency by estoppel. [p 577]

9. ___ A principal is estopped from denying the agency relationship exist when the apparent agency is established.

10. ___ Parties to an agency contract may not agree to terminate their agreement. [p 579]

11. ___ Changed circumstances are not enough to terminate an agency. [p 580]

12. ___ The death of either the agent or the principal will end the agency relationship. [p 580]

13. ___ The agency relationship is terminated if the principal is found to be bankrupt. [p 580]

14. ___ When an agent terminates an agency, it is called a revocation of authority. [p 581]

15. ___ An independent contract is a person or business who is an employee and who is employed by a principal to perform a certain task on his or her behalf. [p 572]

16. ___ An agreement between two or more businesses from different countries to accomplish a specific purpose or function is a strategic alliance. [p 582]

17. ___ An agency can only be formed to accomplish a lawful purpose. [p 571]

18. ___ The relationship whereby an employer employs an employee and gives that employee the authority to act and enter into contracts on his or her behalf is a principal-agent relationship. [p 572]

19. ___ If a principal asserts a great deal of control over a hired individual, then the person is an independent contractor. [p 573]

20. ___ The conduct of the parties can develop into implied-in-fact contracts. [p 575]

21. ___ One of the factors in determining whether an agency by ratification has occurred is if the purported principal accepts the authorized act. [p 578]

22. ___ An agency will terminate after a reasonable amount of time has passed if there is no specific termination date stated in the agency contract. [p 579]

23. ___ The loss or destruction of the subject matter of the agency will not terminate the agency. [p 580]

24. ___ The agent's bankruptcy usually will not terminate an agency. [p 580]

25. ___ If a hired professional's license has been revoked, the agency will terminate at the moment that the license is revoked. [p 580]

Multiple Choice:

26. A party who employs another individual to act on his or her behalf is called a(n) [p 571]
    a. agent.
    b. independent contractor.
    c. principal.
    d. vice-principal.

27. The three types of employment relationships are [p 572]
    a. employer-employee, principal-agent, and employer-principal.
    b. employer-employee, principal, employee-agent.
    c. employer-employee, principal-agent, principal-independent contractor.
    d. none of the above.

28. A principal-agent relationship is formed when [p 572]
    a. a person or business who is not an employee is hired to perform a certain task on the principal's behalf.
    b. an employer hires an employee and grants that employee authority to act and enter into contracts on his or her behalf.
    c. a principal authorizes an independent contractor to enter into contracts.
    d. the principal exerts a large degree of control over the employee.

29. Which of the following would be considered to be an independent contractor? [p 572]
    a. A stockbroker
    b. A dentist
    c. A certified public accountant
    d. All of the above

30. What is the most significant factor in determining whether someone is an employee or an independent contractor? [p 573]
    a. Whether the employee can act and enter into contracts on behalf of the principal.
    b. Whether the president of a corporation has the authority to enter into major contracts on the corporation's behalf.
    c. Whether the principal and agent expressly agree to enter into an agency agreement with one another.
    d. The degree of control that the employer has over the agent.

31. What is the most used common law exception to the employment at-will doctrine? [p 575]
    a. The public policy exception which states that an employee cannot be discharged if such discharge violates public policy.
    b. The implied-in-fact contract which is developed by the conduct of the parties.
    c. Title VII and other federal and state antidiscrimination laws that prohibit employers from engaging in discrimination.
    d. The environmental protection laws.

32. Which of the following would be an example of a statutory exception to the employment at-will doctrine? [p 575]
    a. An express agency
    b. Title VII and other state antidiscrimination laws
    c. A general power of attorney
    d. A wrongfully discharged employee

33. What type of authority can an agent exercise in the event of an emergency? [p 577]
    a. Apparent authority
    b. Incidental authority
    c. Express authority
    d. Implied authority

34. Authority that is derived from the conduct of the parties, custom and usage of trade, or act that is incidental to carrying out the agent's duties is [p 577]
    a. express authority.
    b. retroactive authority.
    c. obvious authority.
    d. implied authority.

35. If a principal hires a licensed real estate broker to sell his house and the house is sold, when does the agency terminate? [p 579]
    a. Upon finding another real estate broker.
    b. Upon rejection of the offer to sell the principal's home.
    c. On December 31st of the year the house is for sale.
    d. Upon the sale of the home and payment to the broker of the agreed-upon compensation.

Short Answer:

36. Agency agreements that are formed for illegal purposes are void and against _____ _____. [p 571]

37. When does the employer-employee relationship exist? [p 572] _____

38. A great deal of control over and individual may indicate that what type of relationship exists? [p 573] _____

39. What are the four ways that an agency and the resulting authority of an agent can arise? [p 575] _____
_____ _____

40. Whose actions create an apparent agency? [p 577] _____

41. Give three ways that the parties may terminate an agency relationship. [p 579] _____
_____

42. Give at least two ways that an agency relationship may terminate where a situation presents itself and thereby makes its fulfillment impossible. [p 580] _____
_____

43. When an agent terminates an agency, it is referred to as a [p 581] _____
_____

44. What determines whether or not an employee is an agent? [p 572] _____
_____

45. What is an independent contractor who is a professional called? [p .572] _____
_____

46. If a principal hires multiple agents to attempt to accomplish a given purpose, when do the agencies terminate? [p 575] _____
_____

47. When a principal creates the appearance of an agency that in actuality does not exist, this is known as an [p 577] _____

48. When an agency terminates by operation of law, what type of duty does the principal owe to third parties? [p 579] _____

49. What effect does the agent's actions after the principal dies have on the principal's estate? [p 580] _____

50. What does constructive notice of the termination of an agency usually consist of? [p 580]
_____

Answers to Refresh Your Memory

1. principal [p 571]
2. agent [p 571]
3. contractual capacity [p 571]
4. employer-employee, principal-agent, and principal-independent contractor relationship [p 572]

5. enter into contracts [p 572]
6. An independent contractor is an individual or business who is not an employee, but who are hired to perform certain tasks on behalf of a principal. [p.572]
7. Some of the characteristics include but are not limited to whether the principal supplies the tools and equipment used in the work, the method of payment, whether it is by time or by the job, and the degree of skill necessary to complete the task. [p 573]
8. express [p 575]
9. power of attorney [p 575]
10. An apparent agency is one that arises when a principal creates the appearance of an agency that in actuality does not exist. [p 577]
11. Where no termination date has been stated, the agency terminates after a reasonable time has passed. [p 579]
12. Death, insanity and bankruptcy are three ways an agency contract may be terminated by operation of law. [p 580]
13. principal [p 512]
14. agent's [p 581]
15. principal [p 581]

Critical Thought Exercise Model Answer

A court would have to determine Polk's status as to employee versus independent contractor based upon answering several questions.

Did the Hamiltons exercise control over the details of Polk's work? Polk was instructed to trim the tree to an approximate size. The Hamiltons gave no other instructions concerning how the task was to be accomplished.

Was Polk engaged in an occupation or business distinct from that of the Hamiltons? Polk had an ongoing handyman business and accepted work from numerous people. The Hamiltons were not in the home repair or landscape maintenance business.

Is the type of work usually done under the employer's direction or by a specialist without supervision? Tree trimming is a job that requires skill and training. It is not the type of job a homeowner would supervise. The Hamiltons did not supervise Polk.

Does the employer supply the tools at the place of work? Polk had his own van with tools for his jobs. In this case, Polk did borrow a saw and a piece of rope, but this does not appear to be the usual way that Polk accomplishes his tasks.

For how long was Polk employed? Polk was only hired for a limited time until a specific job was completed. He was hired separately for the bathroom work and the tree trimming.

What was the method of payment—periodic or upon completion of the job? Polk was paid an hourly wage, but he was paid by the job instead of receiving a paycheck every week or month.

What degree of skill is required of the worker? Each of the jobs performed by Polk required skill and specialized knowledge. The average homeowner does not have the skill or ability to trim large tree. A tree trimming service usually performs the cutting back of a large tree.

Polk's status as an independent contractor is borne out by the above analysis. Polk had his own handyman business with his own tools and possessed special skills for accomplishing tasks that are often handled by trades people and specialists. The fact that he was hired for more than one job does not change the fact that he acted as an independent contractor on each job. Therefore, the Hamiltons were under no obligation to purchase workers' compensation insurance for Polk.

Answers to Practice Quiz

True/False:

1. True   The party who hires another individual to act on his or her behalf is called the principal.
2. False   Individuals such as insane persons and minors lack contractual capacity and therefore may not appoint an agent.
3. False   An employer-employee relationship exists when an employer hires and employee to perform some sort of physical service not mental service.
4. True   An employer-employee relationship would be present in the beanie baby example as assembly of the beanie babies is a physical task.
5. True   Independent contractors may receive authorization from a principal to enter into contracts.
6. True   Remedies such as reinstatement, back pay and punitive damages are available to an employee who has been wrongfully discharged.
7. False   Express agency contracts can be either written or oral.
8. True   An apparent agency is also known as an agency by estoppel as the principal is estopped from denying the agency relationship and is bound to contracts entered into by the apparent agent while acting within the scope of the apparent agency.
9. True   When an apparent agent is acting with in the scope of the apparent agency, the principal is estopped from denying the agency relationship and is bound to contracts entered into by the agent.
10. False   The parties to an agency contract may mutually agree to end their agreement.
11. False   An unusual change in circumstances that would cause an agent to believe that the principal's original instructions are no longer valid is sufficient to terminate the agency.
12. True   The death of either party in an agency relationship will terminate the agency relationship.
13. True   The bankruptcy of the principal will terminate the agency. Note however that the bankruptcy of the agent in most cases will not terminate the agency.
14. False   An agent's termination of the agency is called a renunciation of authority whereas a principal's termination of the agency is called a revocation of authority.
15. False   An independent contractor is a person or business who is not an employee but who is employed by a principal to perform a certain task on his or her behalf.
16. True   A strategic alliance is a contract between two or more businesses from different countries to accomplish a specific purpose or function.
17. True   Agency contracts may not violate public policy and must be created to attain a lawful purpose.
18. True   When an employer hires and employee and grants that employee the power to act and enter into contracts on his or her behalf, a principal-agent relationship exists.
19. False   If upon examination of various factors it is shown that the principal exercises little control over a person, then that individual is an independent contractor.
20. True   Implied-in-fact contracts can be formed from the conduct of the parties.
21. False   One of the factors in determining whether an agency by ratification has occurred is if the purported principal has accepted the unauthorized act, not the authorized act.
22. True   The agency will terminate after a reasonable amount of time where no time is stated in the agency agreement.
23. False   The agency relationship ends upon the loss or destruction of the subject matter of the agency.

24. True   Unless the agent's credit standing is important to the agency relationship, the bankruptcy of the agent usually does not terminate the agency.

25. True   The loss of a required qualification such as a professional's license will terminate an agency relationship upon revocation of that license.

Multiple Choice:

26. C   Answer C is correct, as a principal is an individual who hires another party to act on his her behalf. Answer A is incorrect as an agent is the party who agrees to act on behalf of another not one who hires another to act on his or her behalf. Answer B is incorrect as an independent contractor is a party who is hired by a principal to perform a certain task on his or her behalf. Answer D is incorrect as there is no such terminology with regard to agency law.

27. C   Answer C is correct as it properly states the three types of employment relationships. Answers A, B, and D are all incorrect, as they do not adequately state the three types of relationships as asked.

28. B   Answer B is the correct answer as it states when a principal-agent relationship is formed. Answer A is incorrect as this states the definition of an independent contractor. Answer C is incorrect because even though a principal may authorize an independent contractor to enter into contracts on his or her behalf, the independent contractor is not an employee as is the requirement for a true principal-agent relationship to exist. Answer D is incorrect, as the mere exertion of a large degree of control over the employee would only substantiate an argument that an individual is an employee verses and independent contractor. Further, there would also need to be an assertion that the employee had the authority to enter into contracts on the employer's behalf thereby elevating his or her status to that of an agent.

29. D   Answer D is the correct answer as answers A, B, and C all correctly state individuals who would be considered to be independent contractors since they are persons who are not employees but who are hired to perform certain tasks on behalf of a principal.

30. D   Answer D is the correct answer as the degree of control that an employer has over the individual in determining whether someone is an employee or independent contractor. Answer A is incorrect as determining whether an individual could enter into contracts on another's behalf would be helpful in demonstrating whether or not someone was an agent, not an employee or independent contractor. Answer B is incorrect as once again, the answer lends itself toward determining whether the president is an agent or an employee. Answer C is incorrect as an agreement between principal and agent would not necessarily determine whether someone was an employee or an independent contractor as both an employee and independent contractor may be agents.

31. A   Answer A is the correct answer as the public policy exception is the most used common law exception to the employment at-will doctrine. Answer B is incorrect as the implied-in-fact contract is not an exception to the employment at-will doctrine. Answer C is incorrect as even though this is a statutory exception to the employment at-will doctrine, it is not the most used common law exception. Answer D is incorrect as the environmental protection laws are not included in the exceptions to the employment at-will doctrine.

32. B   Answer B is the correct answer as Title VII and other state antidiscrimination laws are examples of the statutory exception to the employment at-will doctrine. Answer A is incorrect as an express agency is not a statutory exception. Answers C and D are also incorrect, as they are not exceptions to the employment at-will doctrine.

33. B   Answer B is the correct answer as contingencies such as an emergency that may occur in the future regarding the fulfillment of the agency may require implied authority also

known as incidental authority to act. Answers A, C and D are not the types of authority that are incidental to authority originally granted.

34. D   Answer D is the correct answer as implied authority can be inferred from the parties' conduct, custom and usage of the trade. Answer A is incorrect as express authority is given to the agent by the principal without having to draw inferences from the parties' conduct. Answer B is incorrect as there is no legal basis entitled retroactive authority. Answer C is incorrect as there is also no legal basis entitled obvious authority.

35. D   Answer D is the correct answer as it indicates that the purpose of selling the house has been achieved thereby terminating the agency. Answers A, B, and C do not qualify as examples of acts by the parties that may terminate an agency agreement.

Short Answer:

36.   public policy
37.   It exists when an employer employs an employee to perform some form of physical service.
38.   It may indicate that an employee-employer relationship exists.
39.   The four ways are: an express agency, implied agency, apparent agency and an agency by ratification.
40.   The principal's actions create an apparent agency.
41.   Lapse of time, mutual agreement and purpose achieved are three ways that the parties may terminate an agency relationship.
42.   The loss or destruction of the subject matter of the agency and loss of a required qualification are two ways that an agency relationship may terminate if a situation presents itself that makes the agency purpose impossible to fulfill.
43.   renunciation of authority
44.   If an employee is given the authority to enter into contracts on behalf of the principal-employer, then the employee is an agent.
45.   a professional agent
46.   The agencies with all of the agents ends when any one of the agents fulfills the stated purpose.
47.   apparent agency
48.   There is no duty of notification to third parties when an agency terminates by operation of law.
49.   The agent's actions after the principal's death do not bind the principal's estate.
50.   Constructive notice involves placing a notice of the termination of the agency in a newspaper that is distributed throughout the community.

Chapter 30
LIABILITY OF PRINCIPALS
AND AGENTS

Chapter Overview

The previous chapter gave you an overview of the creation and termination of an agency as well as the various types of agencies. This chapter expands on what you have learned about agency by discussing the principal's and agent's duties as well as their liability for the breach of the same.

Objectives

Upon completion of the exercises in this chapter, you should be able to:
1. List and discuss the agent's duties to the principal.
2. Discuss the agent's breaches of loyalty to the principal.
3. List and discuss the principal's duties to the agent.
4. Discuss the principal's and agent's liability when there is a third party contract involved.
5. Discuss the agent's liability for his own torts.
6. Discuss the principal's liability for the agent's misrepresentations.
7. Discuss the meaning of the doctrine of respondeat superior.
8. Explain the principal's liability for the agent's negligent conduct.
9. Explain the principal's liability for intentional torts committed by the agent.
10. Explain the principal's liability for an independent contractor's torts.

Practical Application

You will be aware of the duties of both the agent as well as the principal as once day you may be in a position of fulfilling either of the roles. Additionally you will be more cognizant of the liabilities that both the agent and principal face for breach of their respective duties thereby giving you more insight into what is expected of an agent and a principal.

Helpful Hints

Many of the concepts that you will learn in this chapter are filled with common sense. However, in order to remember the duties of the principal and agent as well as the liabilities for breach of the same, it is much easier to not only list them separately, but, to commit them to memory by using the suggested mnemonics given in the Study Tips section that follows. Since this chapter is an expansion of the previous chapter, the concepts are easily learned.

Study Tips

The Agent's Duties

The agent's duties are presented in the parties' agency agreement or implied by law.
An easy mnemonic to remember the agent's duties is: <u>L</u>oyal <u>P</u>ercy's <u>A</u>ccounting is <u>N</u>oteworthy.

<u>L</u>oyalty –   The agent owes a duty to be faithful to the principal. The following are examples of breaches of loyalty:
  - An agent is prohibited from **undisclosed self-dealing** with the principal.
  - An agent may not **usurp an opportunity** that belongs to the principal unless upon consideration the principal has rejected it.
  - An agent may **not compete** with the principal during the agency relationship.
  - An agent may not **misuse confidential information** regarding the principal' affairs.
  - An agent may not act for two or more different principals in the same transaction as this is a **dual agency**. The parties may agree to it though.

<u>P</u>erformance – The agent owes a **duty to perform** the lawful duties stated in the parties' contract. Additionally the agent must meet the standard of reasonable care, skill and diligence that is implied in all contracts.

Beware, an agent that presents himself or herself as having higher than average skills will be held to a higher standard of performance. For example, a physician who contends that he or she is a plastic surgeon specialist will be held to a reasonable specialist in plastic surgery standard.

<u>A</u>ccountability – The agent owes a **duty to keep an accurate accounting** of all transactions performed on behalf of the principal. This means that the agent must keep records of all money that has been spent and all money that has been received during the duration of the agency.

The principal's separate account must be maintained by the agent and the principal's property must be used in an authorized manner.

<u>N</u>otification – The agent owes a **duty of notification** to the principal if the agent learns information that is important to the principal. It is assumed that the principal knows most information that the agent knows. This is called **imputed knowledge.**

The Principal's Duties

The principal's duties may also be stated in the parties' contract or implied by law.
An easy mnemonic to remember the principal's duties is: <u>C</u>onnie <u>R</u>emembers the <u>In</u>dian <u>C</u>oin.

<u>C</u>ompensation – The principal owes a **duty to compensate** an agent for the services he or she has provided. If the compensation is not stated in the parties' agreement, then compensation will be based on custom or what is the reasonable value for the agent's services.

<u>R</u>eimbursement – The principal owes a **duty to reimburse** the agent for all expenses the agent has expended from his or her own money if the expenses were authorized and within the scope of the agency and necessary to discharge the agent's duties in carrying out the agency.

<u>I</u>ndemnification – The principal owes a **duty to indemnify** the agent for any losses that the agent may suffer due to the principal's misconduct.

<u>C</u>ooperation – The principal owes a **duty to cooperate** with and help the agent in the performance of the agent's duties and the goal of the agency.

Contract Liability to Third Parties

Basic Information: If an agent is authorized by the principal to enter into a contract with a third party, then the principal is liable on the contract. In order to determine liability, the classification of the agency must be examined.

Agency Classifications: There are three types of agency classifications. They are the fully disclosed agency, the partially disclosed agency and the undisclosed agency.

- **Fully Disclosed** – The third party knows who the agent is acting on behalf of. The principal is liable in a fully disclosed agency situation. However, the agent will also be held liable if he or she guarantees that the principal will perform the contract.

- **Partially Disclosed** – The agent's status is disclosed but the principal's identity is undisclosed. Both the principal and agent are liable on a third-party contract. If the agent is made to pay, he or she may seek indemnification from the principal.

- **Undisclosed** – If a third party does not know about the agency or the principal's identity, then an undisclosed agency exists. The principal as well as the agent are liable on a contract with a third party as the agent's nondisclosure makes him a principal to the contract. However, the agent may seek indemnification from the principal if he or she is made to pay on the contract.

Agent Exceeding the Scope of Authority
- An agent who enters into a contract with a third party has in essence warranted that he or she has the authority to do so. However, the principal will not be liable on the contract where the agent has exceeded his or her authority on the contract unless the principal **ratifies** the contract.

Tort Liability to Third Parties

The principal and agent are personally responsible for their own tortious conduct. However, the principal is liable for the agent's conduct if he or she was acting within the scope of his or her authority. The agent though is only liable for the torts of the principal if he or she directly or indirectly participates in or abets and aids the conduct of the principal. The factors that are examined in determining whether an agent's conduct was within the scope of his or her employment include:
- Did the principal request or authorize the agent's act?

- Was the principal's purpose being advanced by the agent when the act occurred?
- Was the agent employed to perform the act that he or she completed?
- Was the act accomplished during the time that the time of employment authorized by the principal.

Misrepresentation
- As you may recall, this tort is also referred to as **fraud** or **deceit**.
- The principal is liable for the misrepresentation of the agent if it is made during the scope of his or her employment.
- The third party may rescind the contract with the principal and recover any consideration paid or affirm the contract and recover damages.

Negligence
Liability for negligence is based on the doctrine of **respondeat superior** which assesses liability based on the employment relationship between the princiapal and agent not on any fault of the principal. However there are some situations where liability is not clear.

- **Frolic and Detour** – This refers to the situation where an agent performs a personal errand while performing a job for the principal. Negligent acts in this situation are viewed on a case-by-case basis. The court will examine if the detour is minor or substantial.

- **The Coming and Going Rule** – Under common law, a principal is not held liable for injuries caused by employees and agents who are on their way to or from work. This rule holds true regardless if the principal provided the transportation.

- **Dual-Purpose Mission** – This situation refers to when the agent is doing something for him or herself and for the principal. The majority rule holds that both the principal and agent are liable if an injury occurs while the agent is on this sort of mission.

Intentional Torts
If the intentional tort occurs outside of the principal's scope of business, the principal is not liable. The doctrine of vicarious liability applies though in the situation where the agent or employee commits an intentional tort in the scope of his or her employment. The **Motivation Test** and the **Work-Related Test** are applied to determine if the torts were committed within the scope of the agent's employment.

- **The Motivation Test** – If the agent's motivation in performing the intentional tort was the principal's business, then the principal is liable for any injury caused by the tort.

- **The Work-Related Test** – If the intentional tort was performed during a work-related time or space, the principle is liable for any injuries caused by the intentional torts. The motivation of the agent is not considered in the use of this test.

Independent Contractor

As you may recall from the previous chapter, the degree of control that an employer has over an agent is the most important factor in determining whether someone is an employee or an independent contractor. Additional factors include but are not limited to:

- The amount of skill needed to finish the task.
- Whether the principal provides the equipment and tools used in the job.
- Whether payment is by time or by the job.
- Whether the employer controls the means and manner of completing the job.

Liability for Independent Contractor Torts

The general rule is that a principal is not liable for the torts of its independent contractors. However, there are some **exceptions**. They are:

- **Non-delegable duties** – A principal may not avoid liability by delegating non-delegable duties.
- **Special risks** – Principals may not avoid strict liability for dangerous activities by assigning them to independent contractors.
- **Negligence in the Selection of an Independent Contractor** – The hiring of an unqualified or knowingly dangerous person who injures someone while on the job will cause the principal to be held liable for such negligent selection of this type of independent contractor.

Refresh Your Memory

The following exercise will enable you to refresh your memory on the rules and principles presented to you in this chapter. Read each question twice and place your answer in the blanks provided. Review the chapter material for any question you miss or are unable to remember.

1. What four duties does the agent owe the principal? _____
_____

2. What are the two obligations that the agent owes the principal? _____
_____

3. What is an agent who does not perform his or her express duties or fails to use the standard degree of care, skill, or diligence liable to the principal for? _____

4. The majority of the information that the agent learns in the course of the agency is _____
_____ to the principal.

5. An agent's duty of loyalty is _____ in nature in that he or she is not to act against the principal's interest.

6. An agent may not usurp an opportunity for himself or herself unless _____
_____

7. What is a dual agency? _____

8. What does the duty of accountability encompass? _____
_____

9.   The principal owes a duty to _____ an agent for the services he or she provides.

10. If an agent spends some of his or her own money on behalf of the principal, then the principal has a duty to _____ the agent for these expense if they were _____ by the principal, within the _____ of the agency and necessary to discharge the agent's duties in carrying out the agency.

11. If an agent suffers losses because of the principal, the principal has a duty to _____ _____ the agent.

12. The principal owes a duty to _____ with and help the agent in the performance of the agent's duties and the fulfillment of the agency.

13. What type of agency occurs if the agent reveals his or her agency status, but does not disclose the principal's identity and the third party is unaware of the principal's identity from a different source? _____

14. What is an undisclosed agency? _____

15. When an individual enters into a contract on behalf of another party, he or she _____ _____ that he or she has the authority to do so.

Critical Thought Exercise

Earl West works for Dubyah International, an Illinois corporation that sells commercial fixtures and lighting to cities, developers, mall owners, and the government. West is mostly responsible for making sales calls for light poles, light standards, and lighting towers.

West is on the road 40 or more weeks per year and often does not come back to his home or office for three or more months at a time. Over the course of his 17 years of employment with Dubyah, West has had several stretches on the road that last six months or more.

When West is traveling for Dubyah, he often has to shop for food, toiletries, clothing, gifts, and business related items, such as computer accessories for his laptop computer.

During a sales trip to Indianapolis, Indiana in March 2001, West found it necessary to wash his laundry and buy an anniversary present for his wife. West went to the mall and then to Suds Town Laundromat to wash his clothes. While wrapping the present on a laundry-folding table, another patron of the Suds Town, Mike, spilled fabric softener on the wrapping paper. West then overloaded a dryer with flammable items, in direct violation of the warnings and rules posted directly above the dryer. This caused a dryer fire. When Mike verbally attacked West for starting the dryer fire, West punched Mike in the eye, causing severe eye damage. Suds Town then burned to the ground due to the dryer fire started by West.

Mike and Suds Town sue Dubyah for the damage caused by West. Dubyah argues that when the events at Suds Town occurred, West was not acting within the scope of his employment, relieving it of all liability.

If you were the judge in this case, what law would you apply and which party would prevail?

Answer. _____

_____

_____

_____

_____

_____

_____

_____

_____

_____

_____

_____

_____

_____

_____

_____

_____

_____

_____

_____

_____

_____

_____

_____

_____

_____

_____

_____

Practice Quiz

True/False:

1. ____ An ophthalmologist who holds him or herself out to be an expert in laser surgery will be held to a reasonable specialist in laser surgery standard. [p 587]
2. ____ The agent's duty of notification includes information he or she learns from a third party or other source that is not important to the principal. [p 587]

3. ___ An agent may complete with the principal upon the termination of the agency if the agent has not signed a valid covenant not-to-compete with the principal. [p 588]

4. ___ Property, money or other benefit obtained by the agent in the course of the agency belongs to the agent. [p 588]

5. ___ The amount of compensation an agent is to receive from the principal must be succinctly stated or the agency agreement will be null and void. [p 588]

6. ___ If Samantha Sanders is authorized to sign a contract for George Jentry, a fully disclosed principal but fails to properly sign by not indicating her status as an agent, then she can be held personally liable on the contract. [p 592]

7. ___ When a principal accepts an agent's authorized contract, this is known as ratification. [p 592]

8. ___ Misrepresentation, negligence and intentional torts are the three main areas of tort liability for principals and agents. [p 593]

9. ___ An innocent misrepresentation occurs when an agent intentionally makes a misrepresentation to a third party. [p 594]

10. ___ A principal is not liable for injuries caused by its agents while they are on their way to or from work. This is referred to as frolic and detour. [p 594]

11. ___ An agent that acts partly for himself or herself and partly for the principal is said to be an agent on a dual-purpose mission. [p 594]

12. ___ A principal is liable for the intentional torts of agents and employees that happen outside the principal's scope of business. [p 595]

13. ___ The agent's motivation in committing an intentional tort is irrelevant in using the motivation test to determine liability. [p 595]

14. ___ If an agent commits an intentional tort within a work-related time or space, the principal is liable for any injuries caused by the agent's intentional torts. [p 595]

15. ___ An independent contractor is one in which the employer has a substantial degree of control over. [p 596]

16. ___ The fact that the worker supplies his own tools and equipment used in the work for the principal is irrelevant in determining whether an individual is an employee or an independent contractor. [p 596]

17. ___ Principals may avoid strict liability for dangerous activities assigned to independent contractors as they probably are not supplying any tools for these activities. [p 597]

18. ___ A principal may be liable for injuries to another person caused by an unqualified or knowingly dangerous person as an independent contractor. [p 597]

19. ___ Edna sells real estate for Best Real Estate Inc. and is employed to purchase real estate for a principal. Meanwhile she decides to secretly sell her own property in the transaction without disclosing that she owns the property. Edna has done nothing wrong since she may do whatever she wants with her own property. [p 587]

20. ___ Lydia works for the Clean Air Equipment Company and is privy to the companies client list. One of Clean Air's competitors offers Lydia a company car and a job for $20,000 more per year if she'll disclose Clean Air's client list to them. It is okay for Lydia to sell Clean Air's list to one of its competitors. [p 588]

21. ___ A principal has a right to demand an accounting from the agent at any given time. [p 588]

22. ___ The principal does not have to assist the agent in the performance of the agent's duties and the accomplishment of the agency as the agent is presumed to know how to do his or her job. [p 589]

23. ___ A principal does not have a duty to compensate a gratuitous agent. [p 589]

24. ___ An individual may not accept a contingency fee if he or she is a professional agent. [p 589]

25. ___ A principal is liable for the tortuous conduct of agents that exceeds their scope of employment. [p 592]

Multiple Choice:

26. Information that is learned by the agent that is attributed to the principal is known as [p 587]
    a. reputable knowledge.
    b. performing knowledge.
    c. imputed knowledge.
    d. independent contractor information.

27. If an agent receives secret profits during the course and scope of the agency, what may the principal ask the court to do? [p 588]
    a. The principal may ask the court to call the agent and ask for the profits the agent has obtained.
    b. The principal may not ask the court for anything as there is no recourse for him or her.
    c. The principal may ask the court for specific performance.
    d. The principal may ask the court to impose a constructive trust on any secret profits on property purchased with the secret profits for the benefit of the principal.

28. Which of the following would be a viable option for a company that wishes to distribute its technology-oriented products without selling the technology? [p 589]
    a. Indemnification
    b. Reimbursement
    c. A contingency fee for the products' use
    d. A license

29. Which of the following would be considered a proper agent's signature in a fully disclosed agency? [p 592]
    a. Terry Adams, by George Clawson, agent
    b. George Clawson
    c. George Clawson, agent
    d. None of the above

30. Which properly states the available tort remedies to an injured third party as a result of the agent's torts? [p 593]
    a. Lost wages
    b. Emotional distress
    c. Medical expenses
    d. All of the above

31. The law that states that a principal generally is not liable by its agents and employees while they are on their way to or from work is the [p 594]
    a. frolic and detour rule.
    b. dual-purpose mission rule.
    c. coming and going rule.
    d. intentional tort rule.

32. Jane, a principal asks Joshua an employee to drop off some documents at one of his client's home on Joshua's way home. Joshua negligently injures a Pete, a pedestrian while on his way to deliver the documents. Who will be liable to the pedestrian? [p 595]
    a. Joshua, the agent is liable to the pedestrian.
    b. The pedestrian is liable for his or her own injuries.
    c. Joshua and the pedestrian are equally liable for the pedestrian's injuries.
    d. Jane, the principle is liable to the pedestrian.

33. Henry, a bouncer at Harry's Bar politely asked Fred to leave the premises as Fred was getting a bit too rowdy and had one two many alcoholic drinks. Fred became irate and punched Henry in the stomach. Henry doubled up his fist and responded with a punch to Fred's chin, which resulted in a bruised jaw and a broken tooth. Who is liable to Fred for his injuries caused by Henry's actions? [p 595]
    a. Henry is liable to Fred for the injuries he caused.
    b. Harry's Bar is liable to Fred for the injuries that Henry caused.
    c. Fred deserved the injuries he incurred and is responsible for his own injuries.
    d. None of the above.

34. Suppose Henry the bouncer in the previous question saw Fred, a man whom he cannot tolerate due to personal reasons in Harry's Bar. Henry is working the night that Fred comes into the bar and decides to punch him just because he is in the establishment. Fred suffers a broken jaw and arm. Who is liable to Fred for his injuries caused by Henry's actions? [p 595]
    a. Harry's Bar is vicariously liable for Henry's actions toward Fred.
    b. Fred is responsible for his own injuries as he should not have been in the bar.
    c. Henry is responsible for Fred's injuries.
    d. Harry's Bar as a business is responsible for Fred's injuries.

35. What is one of the most important factors in determining whether someone is an independent contractor or an employee? [p 596]
   a. One of the most important factors is whether the doctrine of respondeat superior applies.
   b. One of the most critical factors is the degree of control the employer has over the agent.
   c. One of the key factors is whether the agent committed any intentional torts within a work-related time and space.
   d. All of the above.

Short Answer:

36. What duties of the agent when combined together are known as the agent's duty of performance? [p 587] _____

_____

37. An agent who either intentionally or negligently fails to properly perform is liable in _____. [p 587]

38. Give at least two examples of what is considered an agent's breach of loyalty. [p 588]

_____

39. If an agent exceeds the scope of his or her authority, the principal is not liable on the contract unless _____. [p 592]

40. What remedies are available to a third party when an agent makes an innocent misrepresentation to him or her? [p 594] _____

_____

41. Under the doctrine of respondeat superior, what is the basis of the employer's liability? [p 594] _____

_____

42. If an agent deviates from an assignment to be accomplished for the principal and in turn causes injuries to another, who is liable for those injuries caused by the agent's tortuous conduct if the deviation is minor? [p 594] _____

_____

43. What is the rationale used in applying the "coming and going rule?" [p 594] _____

_____

44. A principal is _____ under the doctrine of vicarious liability for intentional torts of employees and agents that occur during the agent's scope of employment. [p 595]

45. If Bart's Crop Dusting Service hires Mike to dust crops and children playing near by develop a respiratory illness, Bart's Crop Dusting Service cannot avoid _____ _____ for the dangerous activities assigned to Mike in dusting the crops. [p 597]

46. What is involved with the duty of notification? [p 587] _____

_____

47. If Jenny a realtor, is hired by Bob to find a home at a reasonable price in light of the current housing boom and she in turn finds a great buy but does not tell Bob and puts a down payment on the home for her daughter, what duty has Jenny breached? [p 588] _____

_____

48. Give at least two factors that a court will examine in interpreting the scope of authority in the area of employment. [p 592] _____

_____

49. Under the _____ test, the agent's motivation is immaterial. [p 595]

50. If a principal exerts substantial control over an individual, the relationship is most likely that of an _____. [p 596]

Answers to Refresh Your Memory

1. The duties of performance, loyalty, notification and accountability. [p 587]
2. The two obligations an agent owes a principal are to perform the lawful duties that are expressed in the parties' contract and to meet the standards of reasonable care, skill and diligence which is implied in all contracts. [p 587]
3. The agent is liable to the principal for breach of contract. [p 587]
4. imputed [p 587]
5. fiduciary [p 587]
6. the principal rejects it after due consideration. [p 588]
7. An agent who acts for two or more principals in the same transaction is a dual agency. [p 588]
8. It includes the keeping of records of all monies expended and received during the duration of the agency. [p 588]
9. compensate [p 588]
10. reimburse, authorized, scope [p 589]
11. indemnify [p 589]
12. cooperate [p 589]
13. partially disclosed agency [p 590]
14. When a third party has no knowledge of the existence of an agency or the principal's identity, then the agency is an undisclosed one. [p 590]
15. impliedly warrants [p 591]

Critical Thought Exercise Model Answer

An employer may be liable for the torts of its employee under the doctrine or respondeat superior. This doctrine imposes vicarious, or indirect, liability on the employer without regard to the fault of the employer for torts committed by an employee in the course or scope of employment. There are several factors that a court will usually consider in deciding whether or not a particular act occurred within the course or scope of employment.

Whether the act was authorized by the employer. West was expected to be on the road making sales calls for long periods of time. Dubyah knew that West had to conduct personal business during sales trips for his employer.

The time, place, and purpose of the act. West was on a sales trip to a city where he was conducting Dubyah's business. The purpose of the act was to clean his laundry so that he could remain on the sales trip for a prolonged period. The overall purpose still favors the employer and would be within the scope of employment, especially when the past employment history and prior lengthy trips are taken into account.

Whether the act was one commonly performed by employees on behalf of their employers. Doing laundry and buying a gift may seem to be very personal tasks unless they are viewed from the broader perspective of the traveling salesperson. It is more economical for Dubyah and allows more sales calls to be made if West says on the road and performs his personal tasks on the road. The overall task or act is that of a sales trip and is clearly within the normal scope of West's duties that he usually performs for Dubyah.

The extent to which the employer's interest was advanced. The reasoning for this factor is the same. Dubyah benefits by having its sales representatives remain on prolonged trips. It is therefore expected that personal business will have to be conducted, allowing the employer to benefit from numerous sales calls to sell its products.

There was no instrumentality (such as an automobile) used for the act in this case, so the fact that an employer did or did not supply the instrumentality that caused an injury is not relevant to this analysis.

Whether the employer had reason to know that the employee would do the act in question and whether the employee had ever done it before. This factor is the most import one for deciding the liability issue. The act of conducting personal business while on the employers sales trip was obviously an act that had been repeated innumerable times by West over 17 years of employment with Dubyah. Dubyah knew about the long sales trips and apparently was active in creating the situation where personal business had to be conducted while on company trips.

Whether the act involved a serious crime. This factor is the one that draws a distinction between the negligent act of overloading the dryer and causing a fire and the act of striking Mike and severely injuring Mike's eye. The employer is not liable for the intentional torts of employees committed outside the employer's scope of business. However, an employer is liable under the doctrine of vicarious liability for intentional torts of employees committed within the employee's scope of employment. The court will apply either the **motivation test** or the **work-related test**. Under the motivation test, if the employee's motivation in committing the intentional tort is to promote the employer's business, the employer is liable. However, if the employee's motivation in committing the tort was personal, the employer is not liable. Under this rule, Dubyah would not be liable to Mike because West was motivated to conduct personal business, not company business. Under the work-related test, however, the result would be different. If the tort is committed within a work-related time or space, the employer is liable. Since West is working around the clock while on a sales trip, some states would hold the employer, Dubyah, liable for both the damage to Suds Town and the damage to Mike's eye.

Answers to Practice Quiz

True/False:

1. True   An agent who holds himself or herself as having higher-than-customary skills will be held to this higher standard of performance, which in this case would be that of a laser surgery specialist.
2. False   The agent's duty to notify the principal includes information that the agent learns from a third party or other source that is important to the principal.

3. True   Generally agents are prohibited from competing with the principal during the duration of the agency unless the principal agrees. However, if the agent and principal have not entered into a valid covenant-not-to-compete, the agent may compete with the principal once the agency is ended.

4. False   Property, money or other benefit obtained by the agent in the course of the agency belongs to the principal.

5. False   If the agency agreement does not specify the amount of compensation the agent is to be paid, the law will imply a promise that the principal will pay the agent whatever fee is customary in the industry. If a customary fee is unable to be created, then the principal owes a duty to pay the agent the reasonable value of his or her services.

6. True   Samantha Sanders may be held personally liable on a contract that she fails to properly sign as an agent for George Jentry.

7. False   Ratification refers to when a principal accepts an agent's unauthorized contract.

8. True   The three primary areas of tort liability for principals and agents are misrepresentation, negligence and intentional torts.

9. False   When an agent negligently makes a misrepresentation to a third party, innocent misrepresentation occurs.

10. False   This states the coming and going rule. Frolic and detour refers to when agents do things that further their own interest rather than the principal's.

11. True   A dual-purpose mission is one where the agent is acting partly from himself or herself and partly for the principal.

12. False   The principal is not liable for employees and agents tort that are committed outside of the principal's scope of business.

13. False   The agent's motivation is important if the agent committed an intentional tort to promote the principal's business.

14. True   The principal is liable for any injuries caused by an agent's intentional torts if they were committed within a work-related time or space.

15. False   The degree of control that an employer has over his or her agent is a crucial factor in determining whether an individual is an employee or an independent contractor. If an employer has a substantial degree of control over an individual, he or she is probably an employee, whereas if the control is minimal or nonexistent, he or she would probably be classified as an independent contractor.

16. False   If the worker supplies his or her own tool and equipment used in the work for the principal, it is very relevant in that it could indicate the individual is an independent contractor.

17. False   Principals are unable to avoid strict liability for dangerous activities that its independent contractors are assigned to regardless of the independent contractor supplying his or her own tools.

18. True   A principal may be liable for injuries to another person caused by an unqualified or knowingly dangerous independent contractor if the principal was negligent in the selection of the independent contractor.

19. False   Edna may not self-deal as she owes a duty of loyalty to Best Real Estate Inc. She is prohibited from undisclosed self-dealing with the principal.

20. False   Lydia may not sell Clean Air's list to one of its competitor as she is under a legal duty not to disclose or misuse confidential information during or after the course of the agency.

21. True   An accounting may be demanded by the principal at any time and as such, the agent owes a legal duty to do so.

22. False   The principal has a duty to cooperate with and assist the agent in the performance of the agent's duties and attaining the goal of the agency.

23. True   A principal is under no obligation to compensate a gratuitous agent.

24. False   Professional agents such as lawyers and salespersons often perform their services for a contingency fee.

25. False   A principal is only liable for the torts of agents that are committed within the scope of their employment.

Multiple Choice:

26. C   Answer C is correct as the majority of information learned by an agency during the duration of the agency is imputed to the principal. Answer A is incorrect as not all information obtained by an agent is reputable. Answer B is incorrect as there is no such thing as performing knowledge. Answer D is incorrect as not all agents are independent contractors nor is all information that an agent obtains about independent contractors.

27. D   Answer D is correct as the equitable remedy known as a constructive trust is imposed so that the profits may be preserved for the benefit of the principal. Answer A is incorrect as merely calling the agent would not necessarily insure that the profits made would be given to the principal. Answer B is incorrect, as it is a false statement since the principal may sue for damages caused by the breach as well as ask the court to impose a constructive trust on the secret profits on property purchased with the secret profits. Answer C is incorrect as specific performance would not be an appropriate remedy in light of the agent's misuse of profits that are rightfully the principals.

28. D   Answer D is the correct answer as licensing enables the licensor the ability to sell the right to use its technology in another country or to another company without selling it. Answer A is incorrect as indemnification involves one party protecting another from losses suffered during a business relationship such as an agency. Answer B is incorrect as reimbursement refers to the repayment of money to one who has spent his or her own money on the other person's behalf and in furtherance of an objective such as an agency. Answer C is incorrect as there is no such thing as a contingency fee for a product's use.

29. A   Answer A is the correct answer as George Clawson's signature clearly indicates that he is acting as an agent for Terry Adams, a specifically identified principal. Answer B is incorrect as it indicates only the agent's name. Answer C is incorrect as this signature is indicative of a partially disclosed agency since it only indicates the agent's name. Answer D is incorrect for the reasons stated above.

30. D   Answer D is the correct answer as answers A, B, and C all properly state tort remedies available to an injured party where liability is found.

31. C   Answer C is the correct answer as the question properly states the "coming and going" rule. Answer A is incorrect as the frolic and detour rule refers to a principal's liability based on an agent's detour to run a personal errand that results in injury to another while on assignment for the principal. Answer B is incorrect as the dual-purpose mission rule refers to an agent that is acting partly for himself and partly for the principal. Answer D is incorrect as there is no such thing as the intentional tort rule.

32. D   Answer D is the correct answer as the principal is liable to the pedestrian under the dual-purpose mission rule as Joshua was acting partly for himself and partly for his employer. Note that the majority of jurisdictions hold both the principal and agent liable for injuries caused while on this type of mission, however, in light of the choices of answers, answer D is the best answer. Answer A is incorrect as Joshua alone would not be liable to the pedestrian in light of the majority rule and the minority rule of holding the principal liable. Answer B is incorrect as there are not enough facts to indicate any type of negligence on the pedestrian's part, nor is there any information to base a contributory or comparative negligence analysis to assess whether the pedestrian may be found liable for his or her own injuries. Answer C is incorrect for the reasoning given to choices A and B above.

33. B   Answer B is the correct answer as Henry committed an intentional tort within a work-related time or space, hence when he was doing his job as a bouncer at a bar. As such, Harry's Bar would be responsible for any injury, including those incurred by Fred as a result of Henry's actions. Answer A is incorrect as Henry was merely doing his job of keeping the peace, which was work-related as a bouncer. Hence Henry will not be individually liable for the injuries caused to Fred. Answer C is incorrect as whether or not Fred deserved the injuries is not the issue, but rather who is liable for the injuries he incurred. Further, there are an insufficient amount of facts to determine whether a contributory or comparative negligence analysis would be applicable here. Answer D is incorrect for the reasons given above.

34. C   Answer C is the correct answer as Henry's motivation in committing the tort against Fred was personal, not in an effort to promote Harry's Bar. As such Harry's Bar is not liable even if the tort took place during business hours or on business premises. Answer A is incorrect based on the reasoning given for answer C above. Answer B is incorrect as whether or not Fred should have been in the bar is immaterial. The issue hinges on who is liable for the injuries Fred sustained while in another's business establishment. Answer D is incorrect as the injuries were not as a result of the agent's promotion of the principal's business, but instead were personally motivated. Hence, Harry's Bar is not responsible.

35. B   Answer B is the correct answer as the degree of control is one of the most crucial factors in determining whether someone is an independent contractor or an employee. The less control an employer has over an individual, the more likely he or she is an independent contractor. Answer A is incorrect as the doctrine of respondeat superior refers to vicarious liability during the course and scope of employment, not determining whether someone is an employee or an independent contractor. Answer C is incorrect as an agent's commission of torts during a work-related time or space would only be relevant in assessing liability for injuries caused by those torts, not in determining the status of the individual. Answer D is incorrect based on the reasons given above.

Short Answer:

36.   The agent must perform the lawful duties expressed in the contract and meet the reasonable care, skill and diligence that is implied in all contracts. Together these duties are referred to as the agent's duty of performance.

37.   tort

38.   Usurping an opportunity that belongs to the principal and the misuse of confidential information about the principal's affairs are two examples of an agent's breach of loyalty.

39.   the principal ratifies it.

40.   The third party may either rescind the contract with the principal and recover any consideration paid or affirm the contract and recover damages.

41.   The doctrine of respondeat superior is based on the legal premise of vicarious liability, meaning the principal is liable because of his or her employment contract with the agent not due to any fault on his or her part.

42.   Under the frolic and detour rule, if the deviation is minor, the principal is liable for injuries caused by the agent's torts.

43.   Since principals do not control where their employees and agents live, the y should not be held liable for tortuous conduct of agents on their way to and from work.

44.   liable

45.   strict liability

46.   The agent has a duty to notify the principal of information that he or she learns from third parties or other sources that is important to the principal.

47. Jenny has breached her duty of loyalty to the principal by competing with him in purchasing a house.
48. Among the various factors that the court will examine, it will ask, "Was the act specifically requested or authorized by the principal?" and "Was it the kind of act that the agent was employed to perform?"
49. work-related
50. employer-employee relationship

Chapter 31
ENTREPRENEURS AND SOLE PROPRIETORSHIPS

Chapter Overview

This chapter is primarily focused on the role of the entrepreneur and sole proprietorships in business. You will learn the advantages as well as disadvantages for operating a business as a sole proprietorship. Additionally you will become aware of the liabilities that a sole proprietor may face. This chapter will also give you insight on the international aspect of conducting business by the use of direct export or import sale as well as through the use of a branch office of a subsidiary corporation.

Objectives

Upon completion of the exercises in this chapter, you should be able to:
1. Discuss the role of entrepreneurs in beginning and operating businesses.
2. State the different entrepreneurial forms of conducting business.
3. Discuss the formation of Amazon.com
4. Explain the meaning of sole proprietorship.
5. Discuss formation of the sole proprietorship.
6. Explain the meaning of d.b.a.
7. Compare and explain the advantages and disadvantages of operating a business as a sole proprietorship.
8. Discuss the liability of the sole proprietor.
9. Discuss how business is conducted using agent, representatives, and distributors.
10. Explain how to conduct international business using direct export and import sales.

Practical Application

This chapter will enable you to be more aware of the positive and concerning aspects of operating a business as a sole proprietorship. You will have a greater understanding of the magnitude of the liability associated with conducting business in this manner as well. Further, you will have a hint of the ways in which you may consider conducting international business should the opportunities arise.

Helpful Hints

Since the information contained in this chapter primarily focuses on the single topic of entrepreneurs and sole proprietorship, the principles are quickly committed to memory.
The Study Tips section has been organized in much the same way as the chapter in your text has been presented. Since the information is so concisely written, the concepts will be easy to grasp.

Study Tips

When studying this chapter, it is best to commit the definition of an entrepreneur to memory as well as be familiar with the fact that there are various choices in which to operate an entrepreneur's business organization. As you know, the primary emphasis of this chapter is on the sole proprietorship, however, you will learn about the other forms that are mentioned in the chapters that follow.

Entrepreneur
An individual who creates and operates a new business.

Ways in which to operate a business organization include:
- sole proprietorship
- general partnership
- limited partnership
- corporation
- limited liability company
- franchise
- joint venture

Basic Information

Sole proprietorships are the simplest form of business organization as well as most common form in the United States. A sole proprietorship is not a distinct legal entity.

Advantages

1. Easy to form and relatively inexpensive.
2. The owner can make all management decisions, including hiring and firing.
3. The owner has the right to all profits of the business.
4. It is easily transferred or sold without anyone else's approval.

Disadvantages

1. Access to capital is limited to personal funds plus any loans the proprietor can obtain.
2. The sole proprietor is held responsible for the business's contracts and torts he/she or any of his or her employees employees commit in the course of employment.

Creation

No state or federal formalities are required.
Some local governments may require that a sole proprietor obtain a license to do business within the city.

Operation of a Sole Proprietorship

A sole proprietorship may conduct itself under the name of the sole proprietor or a trade name.

If a trade name is chosen, it is commonly referred to as **d.b.a.** (*doing business as*). Also, if a d.b.a. is used, most states necessitate the filing of a **fictitious business name statement**. This statement gives the name and address of the applicant, address of the business and the trade name. Publication of the notice of the trade name is often required.

Personal Liability of Sole Proprietors

- If the sole proprietorship fails, the owner will lose his or her entire contribution of capital.
- The sole proprietor has unlimited personal liability, thereby subjecting his or her personal assets to creditors claims.

The Use of Agents, Representatives and Distributors in Conducting International Business

- There are many ways of conducting business in a foreign country.

- **Direct selling, use of sales agents, representatives or distributors** are some of the ways. Sales people may solicit and take orders for the foreign employer.

- **Sales agents may enter into contracts** on behalf of the foreign employer. Sales agents and representatives do not take title to the goods.

- Both **representatives and agents are paid commissions** for the business that they bring in.

- **Distributors take title to the goods** and realize a profit on the resale of goods in the foreign country. A company wanting a more influential presence in a foreign market will make use of distributors.

- Simplest and most inexpensive way to do international business is by **direct export** or **import sale.**

Operating International Business using a Branch Office or a Subsidiary Corporation

- A **foreign branch** of a business may be established so as to gain access to a foreign market. This is a viable option if a business wants to keep sole control over the business. The disadvantages of establishing a foreign branch office include great expense as well as potential tort and contract liability and being subjected to foreign laws.

- If a business enters a foreign market by setting up a separate corporation, this is known as a **subsidiary corporation**. The parent corporation usually has a substantial ownership interest in the subsidiary corporation. If a business opts to establish a subsidiary corporation, the newly formed corporation will shield the parent corporation from tort and contract liability. The use of a subsidiary corporation enables the parent corporation to have a **substantial presence** in the foreign country.

Refresh Your Memory

The following exercise will enable you to refresh your memory on the rules and principles presented to you in this chapter. Read each question twice and place your answer in the blanks provided. Review the chapter material for any question you miss or are unable to remember.

1. What is an entrepreneur? _____
    _____

2. Give three examples of major forms of business organizations. _____
    _____

3. A _____ is the most basic form of business organization.

4. Give at least two advantages of operating a business as a sole proprietorship. _____
    _____

5. Give one disadvantage of operating a sole proprietorship. _____
    _____

6. What type of formalities are required to create a sole proprietorship? _____
    _____

7. What do the initials d.b.a. stand for? _____

8. What must a business file if it is operating under a fictitious business name? _____
    _____

9. Who bears the risk of loss in a sole proprietorship? _____

10. Where can creditors satisfy the claims they have against a sole proprietor? _____
    _____

11. What is the simplest form of conducting international business? _____
    _____

12. What is a sales representative of a foreign country able to do? _____
    _____

13. What can a sales agent do on behalf of his/her foreign employer? _____
    _____

14. A _____ _____ is used if a company wants a
    greater presence in a foreign market.

15. Sales _____ and _____ are paid commissions for the
    business that they bring in.

Critical Thought Exercise

Larry and Diane Ortiz own and operate Maria's Restaurant in Houston, Texas. As husband and wife, they operate the restaurant as a sole proprietorship. As part of the advertising plan for Maria's, they participate in several 2-for-1 dinner coupon books and school fundraiser sticker books. An average of 15 2-for-1 coupons are redeemed each week. After Larry Ortiz is struck with a serious illness, the restaurant is sold to Bob Nelson. Nelson files the proper fictitious business name statement with the county and city clerk. The sale of the restaurant did not include the assignment of any contracts entered into prior to the sale by Larry and Diane Ortiz.

After Nelson remodels the restaurant, he reopens it with a Grand Reopening advertising campaign. Signs stating, "New Owners" are posted at the restaurant and the same notice is in each advertisement. When Nelson refuses to honor the 2-for-1 coupons, 24 plaintiffs file suit against Maria's Restaurant and Bob Nelson for breach of contract and fraud.

Is Bob Nelson liable because he failed to honor coupons for Maria's Restaurant?

Answer. _____

_____

_____

_____

_____

_____

_____

_____

_____

_____

_____

_____

_____

Practice Quiz

True/False

1. ____ An entrepreneur may operate a new business by himself or herself or operate the business with others. [p 605]

2. ____ One of the major forms of business organization is a limited liability company. [p 605]

3. ____ The extent of an individual's personal liability should not be a factor in determining which form of business organization is best. [p 605]

4. ____ In a sole proprietorship, the owner is the business. [p 607]

5. ____ One of the advantages to operating a business as a sole proprietorship is the legal responsibility for the contracts and torts of the business. [p 607]

6. ___ The sole proprietor is not responsible for the business's contracts and torts that he or she or any of his or her employees commit during the course of employment. [p 607]

7. ___ The federal formalities for creating a sole proprietorship can be burdensome. [p 607]

8. ___ The most common form of business organization in the United States is the sole proprietorship. [p 607]

9. ___ The initials d.b.a. stand for debt burdened account. [p 607]

10. ___ Some local governments mandate the procurement of a license to operate a sole proprietorship with the city. [p 607]

11. ___ If a form of business organization has not been chosen, then it will operate by default as a sole proprietorship. [p 607]

12. ___ A sole proprietorship may operate under a trade name or under the name of the sole proprietor. [p 607]

13. ___ A fictitious business name statement need not contain the name of the applicant, as the trade name is sufficient for identification of the business. [p 607]

14. ___ A bank who lends money to a sole proprietor bears the risk of loss of the business if the business fails. [p 608]

15. ___ One of the advantages of being a sole proprietor is the amount of limited personal liability that is part of operating a business in this form. [p 608]

16. ___ Creditors may recover claims against the business from the sole proprietor's bank accounts. [p 608]

17. ___ The operation of a business under a different name does not create an entity distinct from the person operating the business. [p 609]

18. ___ Participating in direct export or import sales is one of the easiest ways to conduct international business. [p 610]

19. ___ Operating an export or import business is relatively inexpensive. [p 611]

20. ___ Export and import businesses usually only require the execution of contracts. [p 611]

21. ___ A distributor does not take title to the goods. [p 611]

22. ___ A sales representative does not have the authority to bind the company he or she works for contractually in a foreign sales transaction. [p 611]

23. ___ A sales agent may enter into sales contracts on behalf of his or her foreign employer. [p 611]

24. ___ It is best to enter a foreign market as a subsidiary corporation if a business wants to enter that market in a substantial way and keep exclusive control over the operation at the same time. [p 611]

25. ___ The advantage of using a branch over a subsidiary corporation is that it isolates the parent corporation from the tort and contract liability of the subsidiary corporation. [p 611]

Multiple Choice:

26. An entrepreneur is [p 605]
    a. an employee of another's business.
    b. an independent contractor.
    c. a person who forms and operates a new business.
    d. all of the above.

27. Which of the following is not a true statement regarding sole proprietorships? [p 607]
    a. Forming a sole proprietorship is easy and relatively inexpensive.
    b. The sole proprietor is not legally responsible for the business's contracts and torts his or her employees commit in the course of employment.
    c. The sole proprietorship form of doing business does not require any federal or state approval.
    d. The sole proprietor has the right to receive all of the business's profits.

28. Wilma owns and is doing business as Wilma's House of Beauty. Pricilla, one of Wilma's regular customers has Wilma try a new hair color, high sierra brown on her. Wilma applies the hair color and sets the timer for fifteen minutes as per the instructions that came with the color. Meanwhile, Wilma's mother Francine calls from Europe and Wilma fails to hear the timer go off. One hour passes, and when Wilma begins to wash Pricilla's hair, large sections begin to fall out leaving her with what looks more like a burned brownie color. If Pricilla brings a lawsuit against Wilma, which of the following may she seek to satisfy her claim of negligence against Wilma and her House of Beauty? [p 608]
    a. Pricilla may recover a claim against Wilma's home.
    b. Pricilla may recover a claim against Wilma's automobile.
    c. Pricilla may recover a claim against Wilma's bank accounts.
    d. All of the above.

29. Which of the following is a viable option for a company wishing to do business in a foreign country? [p 611]
    a. The company may appoint a local sales agent to represent them in a foreign country.
    b. The company may appoint a sales representative to represent them in a foreign country.
    c. The company may utilize a distributor that is separate and independent from the exporter to engage in international sales.
    d. All of the above.

30. Which of the following describes a benefit of operating as a sole proprietor? [p 607]
    a. A sole proprietorship has unlimited liability.
    b. A sole proprietor's access to capital is limited to personal funds and any loans that he or she can obtain.
    c. A sole proprietor has the right to make all management decisions concerning the business.
    d. A sole proprietor is responsible for the torts that his or her employee commits.

31. What is the easiest way for Sarah to be able to conduct her clothing business internationally? [p 610]
    a. Telephone
    b. Direct export or import sale
    c. A branch office
    d. A sales agent

32. What is one of the disadvantages to forming a branch office in a foreign country? [p 611]
    a. It subjects the owner to tort and contract liability in the foreign country and to foreign Laws.
    b. It helps a corporation enter a foreign market in a substantial way.
    c. It assists in helping a corporation's retention of exclusive control over the operation.
    d. None of the above.

33. What is one of the disadvantages of operating as a subsidiary corporation in a foreign country? [p 611]
    a. It isolates the parent corporation from the tort and contract liability of the subsidiary corporation.
    b. It is expensive and complicated to operate a subsidiary corporation in a foreign country.
    c. It assists in establishing a presence in a foreign country.
    d. It relieves the subsidiary corporation from abiding by the laws of the foreign country.

34. A business that enters a foreign market by establishing a separate corporation to conduct business in a foreign country is called a [p 611]
    a. risk taker.
    b. partnership.
    c. branch office.
    d. subsidiary.

35. Which of the following is not true with respect to distributors? [p 611]
    a. A foreign distributor is usually used when a company wants a reasonable presence in a foreign market.
    b. The distributor is often a local firm that is distinct and independent from the exporter.
    c. A distributor takes title to the goods and makes a profit on the resale of those goods in the foreign country.
    d. Distributors are usually given a country or a portion of a country as their territory.

Short Answer:

36. Give an example of a business that started with one individual as a sole proprietor and thereafter grew into a giant company. [p 605] _____

37. An individual's choice of the type of business organization that he or she wants to operate as depends on several factors. Give at least two of these factors. [p 605] _____
_____

38. Sandy Simpkins wants to open her own craft store. She asks for your input regarding the formalities in forming a sole proprietorship. What will you tell her? [p 607] _____
_____

39. If Ben Barnes conducts a business called Barnes Bikes, which of these two names is the trade name? [p 607] _____

40. What is another name for a fictitious business name statement? [p 607] _____
_____

41. The sole proprietor has _____ personal liability. [p 608]

42. A sole proprietorship is not a separate legal _____ from that of the person who owns it. [p 609]

43. If the Shiny Collectible Corporation desires to conduct business in other countries, the form that it chooses will depend on several factors. Give at least two of these factors. [p 610]
_____

44. Give three examples of the most common forms that the Shiny Collectible Corporation may consider in conducting its business in a foreign country. [p 610] _____
_____

45. If the Hilarious Hat Company wants to sell its hats to China, who is the exporter and who would be the importer in this transaction? [p 610] _____
_____

46. The Bratty Baby Doll Company wants to enter a foreign market and yet retain exclusive control over the operation. In light of this information, what would be the best choice for the Bratty Baby Doll Company to conduct its business in a foreign market? [p 611] _____
_____

47. A branch is an _____ of the corporate owner and is entirely owned by the home corporation. [p 611]

48. Why is operating a foreign branch of a corporation expensive? [p 611] _____
_____

49. The parent corporation and the subsidiary corporation are separate legal _____ that are separately funded. [p 611]

50. Sales _____ and _____ do not take title to the goods when conducting business with a foreign country. [p 611]

Answers to Refresh Your Memory

1. An individual who forms and operates a new business. [p 605]
2. sole proprietorship, general partnership, corporation (answers will vary) [p 605]
3. sole proprietorship [p 607]
4. The owner has the right to make all management decisions with regard to the business. The owner has the right to receive all of the profits made by the business. [p 607]
5. The sole proprietor's access to capital is limited to personal funds in addition to any loans that he or she may obtain. [p 607]
6. There are no formalities that are required to create a sole proprietorship. [p 607]
7. doing business as [p 607]
8. A business must file a fictitious business name statement. [p 607]
9. The sole proprietor bears the risk of loss. [p 608]
10. Creditors may satisfy their claims against the business from the personal assets of a sole proprietor. [p 608]
11. The simplest form of conducting international business is to take part in direct export or the import sale of goods. [p 610]
12. A sales representative may solicit and take orders for his or her foreign employer. [p 611]
13. A sales agent may enter into contracts on behalf of his or her foreign employer. [p 611]
14. subsidiary corporation [p 611]
15. agents and representatives

Critical Thought Exercise Model Answer

A sole proprietorship has no legal identity separate from that of the individual who owns it. In this case, the 2-for-1 offers were made by Larry and Diane Ortiz. Only Larry and Diane Ortiz can be held liable for not honoring the coupons and fundraiser stickers unless Nelson assumes the liability as part of an assignment and delegation. Bob Nelson did not assume any of the liabilities or assume any of the contracts that had been made with Maria's Restaurant when it was owned by Larry and Diane Ortiz. Bob Nelson did not assume liability for the coupons simply because he chose to use the same name for his restaurant. The sole proprietor who does business under one or several names remains one person. There is no continuity of existence for Maria's Restaurant because upon the sale of the restaurant, the sole proprietorship of Larry and Diane Ortiz ended.

In this case, "Maria's Restaurant" has no legal existence. Bob Nelson did not continue the previous sole proprietorship. He began a new sole proprietorship, that of Bob Nelson, doing business as Maria's Restaurant.

Answers to Practice Quiz

True/False:

1. True An entrepreneur may conduct a business alone or with others.
2. True A limited liability company is one of the many different forms of business organizations.
3. False The extent of an individual's personal liability is one of many factors that will be part of the decision making process with regard to the type of business organization that would be best suited to the individual.

4. True   The owner is the business in a sole proprietorship.
5. False   Liability for the torts and contracts of the business is a disadvantage of operating as a sole proprietorship.
6. False   The sole proprietor is responsible for the business's contracts and torts that he or she or any of his or her employees commit during the course of employment.
7. False   There are no federal formalities in creating a sole proprietorship.
8. True   In the United States, the most common form of business organization is the sole proprietorship.
9. False   The initials d.b.a. stand for doing business as.
10. True   In order to do business within the city, many local governments require the business to obtain a license for the same. This includes sole proprietorships.
11. True   A business will operate as a sole proprietorship where no form of business organization has been chosen.
12. True   Since a sole proprietor and a sole proprietorship are one and the same, a business may operate under the name of the sole proprietor or under a trade name.
13. False The fictitious business name statement must contain the name of the applicant, the applicant's address, trade name and business address.
14. False The sole proprietor bears the risk of loss if the business fails.
15. False The sole proprietor has unlimited personal liability which makes it a major disadvantage of operating a business in this form.
16. True   Creditors may recover claims against the business from the personal assets of the sole proprietor.
17. True   Conducting business under a different name does not form an entity different from the person operating the business.
18. True   Engaging in direct export or import sales is one of the simplest forms of conducting international business.
19. True   Since operating an export or import business usually concerns the entering of contracts, it is fairly inexpensive to do so.
20. True   Usually the execution of contracts is all that is needed when conducting an import or export business.
21. False A distributor does take title to the goods. It is the sales agent and sales representative that do not take title to the goods.
22. True   A sales representative may take orders or solicit for a foreign employer, however, he or she may not contractually bind the foreign employer.
23. True   A sales agent is able to enter into contracts on behalf of his or her foreign employer.
24. False Though entry into a foreign market as a subsidiary corporation will help to establish a substantial presence in a foreign country, it is the establishment of a branch that will assist a corporation in keeping exclusive control over the operation while entering the foreign market in a substantial way.
25. False A subsidiary corporation isolates the parent corporation from tort and contract liability, not a branch operation.

Multiple Choice:

26. C   Answer C is the correct answer as a person who forms and operates a new business is an entrepreneur. Answer A is incorrect as an employee of another business would not own and operate that business. Answer B is incorrect as an independent contractor is an individual who has been hired to perform a specific task, not one who forms and operates a new business. Answer D is incorrect for the reasons given above.
27. B   Answer B is correct as the statement as it currently reads is false. A sole proprietor is legally responsible for the business's contracts and torts his or her employees commit in

the course of employment. Answers A, C, and D are all true statements regarding proprietorships and are therefore the incorrect.

28. D   Answer D is the correct answer as Pricilla may recover against the business from Wilma's personal assets including her home, automobile and bank accounts.

29. D   Answer D is the correct answer as anyone of the options given in answers A, B, and C are viable options for a company wishing to do business in a foreign country.

30. C   Answer C is the correct answer as holding the exclusive right to make all management decisions, including the hiring and firing of employees is one of the benefits of operating as a sole proprietor. Answers A, B, and D are all incorrect as they state some of the disadvantages of operating as a sole proprietorship.

31. B   Answer B is the correct answer as the easiest way for Sarah to be able to conduct her clothing business internationally is to engage in direct export or import sale of her goods. Answer A is incorrect as the use of the telephone is helpful, but, certainly not an efficient nor practical way to operate a clothing business, especially on an international level. Answer C is incorrect as though a branch office may be an option for entering a foreign market, the Question asked, "What is the easiest way to conduct a clothing business internationally." Operating a branch is expensive and would be time consuming waiting for the business to get a lease or to build a facility. Answer D is incorrect as a sales agent would be a facet of doing business internationally but, a foundation of export and import sales would need to be in place first.

32. A   Answer A is the correct answer as being subject to tort and contract liability in a foreign country as well as to the foreign laws would be a disadvantage to forming a branch office internationally. Answers B, C, and D are all incorrect as they state advantages of forming a branch office in a foreign country.

33. B   Answer B is the correct answer as operating as a subsidiary corporation in a foreign country can be very costly and complex. Answers A, C, and D are all incorrect as these choices all state advantages to operating as a subsidiary corporation in a foreign country.

34. D   Answer D is the correct answer as a subsidiary is a separate corporation that is established to operate a business in a foreign country. Answer A is incorrect as though it may be risky to enter into business in a foreign country, this is not the proper terminology for a business that is doing business in a foreign country. Answer B is incorrect as the there is nothing to indicate any form of partnership. Answer C is incorrect as a branch is not a separate entity or corporation.

35. A   Answer A is the correct answer as it is not a true statement in that a distributor is usually utilized when a company wants to make a greater presence in a foreign market, verses a reasonable presence. Answers B, C, and D are all incorrect as they are true statements with regard to distributors.

Short Answer:

36. Bill Gates and the Microsoft Corporation started small and grew into a leader in the software and Internet company.

37. Two factors that may influence an individual's choice of business organization are the ease and cost of formation and the extent of personal liability. (Answers will vary.)

38. Sandy Simpkins should be told that there are no formalities in forming a sole proprietorship.

39. Barnes Bikes is the trade name as that is the name of the business that Ben Barnes, the individual is operating his business as.

40. Another name for a fictitious business name statement is a certificate of trade name.

41. unlimited

42. entity

43. Two factors that will influence the form of business the Shiny Collectible Corporation will choose is the amount of capital to be invested as well as legal and cultural restrictions. (Answers will vary.)

44. Three of the most common forms of conducting business that the Shiny Collectible Corporation may use are by direct selling, the use of sales agents, representatives or distributors.

45. The Hilarious Hat Company would be the exporter as it would be sending its hats to a foreign market for sale and China would be the importer.

46. The best choice for the Bratty Baby Doll Company would be a branch office, as it would enable it to enter into a foreign market and yet retain exclusive control over the operation.

47. extension

48. Operating a foreign branch of a corporation is expensive because the owner must build or lease plant or office premises. Additionally, the exposure to tort and contract liability in a foreign country may be costly as well.

49. entities

50. agents, representatives

Chapter 32
GENERAL PARTNERSHIPS

CHAPTER OVERVIEW

In this chapter, you will learn about general partnerships, their formation, and the rights as well as duties among the partners. You will learn that the right to participate in the partnership's management is as important as the right to share in the partnership's profits and losses. Further, you will gain familiarity with the duty of loyalty among partners and violation of the same. The duty of care along with the liabilities in contract and tort in addition to the incoming and outgoing partners are also discussed. Finally, you will become aware of how a partnership is terminated and how partners may continue a dissolved corporation.

Objectives

Upon completion of the exercises in this chapter, you should be able to:
1. Explain what a general partnership is as well as the formation of the same.
2. Discuss the rights and duties among partners.
3. Explain the partner's right to take part in the management of the partnership.
4. Explain the right a partner has is sharing the partnership's profits and losses.
5. Discuss the duty of care owed by a partner.
6. Explain the duty of loyalty as well as the violations and consequences for the same.
7. Discuss the contract and tort liability of partners.
8. Explain the liability of incoming and outgoing partners.
9. Explain the dissolution and termination of a partnership.
10. Explain the continued operation of a partnership after dissolution of the same.

Practical Application

This chapter will provide you with valuable knowledge that will enable you to make informed decisions regarding the possibility of conducting a business as a partnership. It will also give you insight on the legal duties and ramifications for failing to adhere to the duties expected of a partner under the law.

Helpful Hints

Since this chapter will be utilized by many wishing to operate a business with one or more partners, it is especially helpful to review as many of the exercises given within the study guide as well as at the end of the chapter in the main text. Though there are many benefits to operating a business as a partnership, as well as many situations that will subject a partner to liability. As such, it is especially important that you pay particular attention to the duties, what constitutes a breach and the liabilities that the partners may face.

Study Tips

This chapter is nicely organized beginning with formation and general partnership requirements followed by the rights and duties of the partners and their liabilities. The inevitable topic of dissolution is also explored. This chapter should be approached like the building of a house, one room at a time, beginning with the duties of the partners. Just as a contractor must adhere to the specifications of a home's blueprints, so must a partner comply with the provisions, express and implied in the partnership agreement. Failure to do so could subject the partners to liability. The topics of termination and dissolution due to an act of law or its owners are easily learned concepts especially if comparing them to the selling or destruction of a house.

Formation

Forming a partnership is akin to laying the foundation of a house and having a blueprint to build the house from. A partnership agreement is like a blueprint, in that it sets forth the terms of the parties' agreement, which includes but is not limited to the following:

- the name of the firm and names of the partners.
- the main partnership office as well as nature and scope of the business.
- the monetary contributions each partner is to be making.
- the distribution of profits and losses among the partners.
- the partners management duties.
- limitations on the partners' authority to bind the partnership.

Partnerships may be **expressly** formed or **impliedly** formed. There is no necessity to file a partnership's agreement in most states. However, a select few require a general partnership to file **certificates of partnership** with the proper government agency. Partnerships are viewed as **separate legal entities** that can hold title to real and personal property.

General Partnership Requirements

There are four requirements in order to be considered a general partnership. They are:
1. It must be an association of two or more persons.
    a. All partners must be in agreement of each participating co-partner.
    b. Person includes natural persons, partnerships, associations and corporations.
2. These persons must be carrying on a business.
    a. Co-ownership such as joint tenancy, tenancy by the entireties, and tenancy in common qualify.
    b. A series of transactions conducted over a period of time.
3. These individuals must be operating as co-owners.
    a. Essential to form a partnership.
    b. Co-ownership is evaluated based on the sharing of business profits and management responsibility.
4. The business must be for profit or have a profit motive.

General partners are personally liable for the obligations as well as debts incurred by the partnership.

Uniform Partnership Act (UPA)

The Uniform Partnership Act requirements is like the building code requirements of a house in that it is codified partnership law that has been adopted by 48 states. The Uniform Partnership Act details laws concerning formation, operation and dissolution of basic partnerships.

Property Rights of the Partnership and the Partners

Property rights of the partnership are like fixtures in a home in that all property brought into the partnership on account of the partnership is considered partnership property. A written record of all partnership property should be kept. If a partner dies, the partnership property passes to the remaining partners. However, the value of the deceased partner's share in the partnership passes to his or her heirs. A partner's interest in a partnership is his or her share of the profits and surplus of the partnership.

Assignment of a Partnership Interest

A partner may assign all or part of his or her interest. The assignee may receive the profits which the assigning partner is entitled to. This includes entitlement to rights on liquidation to which the assigning partner is entitled.

Judgment Creditors

A judgment by a creditor against an individual partner entitles the judgment creditor to be paid from the partner's partnership profits by way of a **charging order**. A charging order is similar to having a lien against one's home. It is important to note that judgment creditors do not become partners and is not able to take part in the partnership's management.

Partner's Rights

Like roommates or family members in a home, all partners have equal rights in the management of the partnership business. Each partner has a vote. The partners' unanimous consent is required for assignment of the partnership property for creditors' benefit as well as the disposal of the goodwill of the business. There are other issues that require a unanimous vote, which can be found on p. 621 of your text.

Right to an Accounting

Instead of being allowed to sue one another, partners may bring an **action for an accounting** against the other partners.

Other Important Rights

Partners have the following important rights under the Uniform Partnership Act:
- right to compensation
- right of indemnification
- right to return of advances
- right to return of capital
- right to information

Duties of Partners

The duties that partners owe one another and the partnership are:

The Duty of Loyalty includes:
- The duty not to self-deal.
- The duty not to usurp a partnership opportunity.
- The duty not to compete with the partnership.
- The duty not to make a secret profit from the partnership.
- The duty to keep partnership information confidential.
- The duty not to use partnership property for personal use.

The Duty of Obedience
- This refers to the partners duties to act in accordance with the partnership agreement.

The Duty of Care
- The duty of care encompasses the duty to use the same level of care and skill a reasonable businessperson would use in the same circumstances.
- Breach of the duty of care is equivalent to negligence.

The Duty to Inform
- Partners must inform their co-partners of all information they possess that concerns the partnership affairs.

Liability to Third Parties
- "General partners are personally liable for contracts entered into on the partnership's behalf."

Tort Liability of Partnerships and Partners
- The liability of the partnership for the torts of its partners, employees or agents depends on whether or not the person was acting within the ordinary course of the partnership business or with the authority of his or her co-partners. UPA Sections 13 and 14.

- **Joint and Several Liability of Partners** - Partners are jointly and severally liable for torts and breaches of trust regardless of a partner's participation in the act.

- **Liability of Incoming Partners** - A new partner is liable for existing debts and obligations only to the extent of his or her capital contributions. Further, he or she is liable for obligations and debts obtained by the partnership after becoming a partner.

Termination of Partnerships

Termination refers to the dissolution of a partnership. The Uniform Partnership Act at Section 29 defines dissolution as "The change in the relation of the partners caused by any partner ceasing to be associated in the carrying on of the business."

Dissolution may be accomplished by **an act of the parties**, which includes, termination of a stated time or purpose, the withdrawal of a partner, the expulsion of a partner, the admission of a partner or by mutual agreement of the partners.

Additionally, dissolution may be as a result of **an operation of law** such as the death of any partner, the bankruptcy of any partner or the partnership or an illegality. Further a **judicial decree of dissolution** may dissolve a partnership. This form of dissolution may be appropriate in situations such as the legal insanity of a partner and in extreme medical circumstances of a partner.

Finally, a partner may **wrongfully** attempt to **dissolve** the partnership by withdrawing before the expiration of the stated term. If a partner's actions constitute wrongful dissolution of the partnership, he or she is liable for damages caused by the wrongful dissolution.

Requirements for Dissolution of Partnership

Notice

All partners must be given notice of the dissolution. If a partner has not been given notice and he or she enters into a contract on behalf of the partnership, the contract will remain binding on all partners based on the premise of **apparent authority.**

The Uniform Partnership Act at Section 35 requires that third parties be given **notice** if the partnership is dissolved in a manner other than by operation of law. The relationship to the third party is very important.

- If the third party has had actual dealing with the partnership, then *actual notice*, oral or in writing must be given, or the third party must have obtained notice of the dissolution from another source.

- If the third party has **not** dealt with the partnership, but **has knowledge** of it, **constructive *or* actual notice** must be given. Publication of the notice in a local newspaper where the partnership business was normally conducted is sufficient to satisfy the constructive notice requirements.

- Third parties **without knowledge** of the partnership or who have **not dealt** with the partnership do not need to be given any notice of the dissolution.

Winding Up

Winding up is the process of selling the partnership's assets and distributing the proceeds to fulfill the claims against the partnership. The partners or the court may wind up the partnership. The Uniform Partnership Act at Section 40(b) provides that the debts of a partnership are satisfied in the following order:
- creditors (except partners who are creditors)
- creditor-partners
- capital contributions
- profits

Partners may agree to alter the order of distribution of the assets. If the partnership does not have sufficient means to satisfy the creditors' claims, the partners are personally liable for the obligations and debts of the partnership.

Termination – The End
Upon distribution of the proceeds, the partnership is automatically terminated.

Refresh Your Memory

The following exercise will enable you to refresh your memory on the rules and principles presented to you in this chapter. Read each question twice and place your answer in the blanks provided. Review the chapter material for any question you miss or are unable to remember.

1. The creation of a partnership creates _____ and _____ among partners and with third parties.

2. The _____ theory of partnerships view partnerships as separate legal bodies.

3. _____ partners are personally liable for the debts and obligations incurred by the partnership.

4. _____ are voluntary associations of two or more persons.

5. What are the two most significant factors in determining co-ownership? _____
    _____

6. Even though a business does not make a profit, it must have a _____ _____ in order to qualify as a partnership.

7. A general partnership may be created _____ or in _____.

8. Explain the meaning of a partnership for a term. _____
    _____

9. What is considered to be partnership property? _____
    _____

10. What is a partner's interest in a partnership? _____
    _____

11. What may a judgment creditor ask the court to issue against the debtor-partner's partnership interest in order to satisfy a debt? _____

12. All partners have equal rights in the _____ and conduct of the partnership business.

13. Since a partner may not sue the partnership or his or her partners, what is a partner allowed to do? _____

14. A partner is entitled to _____ for personal travel, business and other expenses on behalf of the partnership if they are reasonably made in the ordinary and proper conduct of partnership business.

15. Partners have a _____ relationship with one another and owe each other a duty of loyalty.

Critical Thought Exercise

The Commercial Bank of Anchorage (CBA) agreed to lend Coastal Medical Associates, a partnership, 3.2 million dollars to construct a medical office complex. The agreement, which was executed on August 23, 1992, provided that the money would be distributed in installments. A portion of the funds, totaling over $1.7 million, had been distributed before Richard Benson and Greg Mills joined the partnership. When Coastal failed to pay the loan, CBA sold the building and obtained a deficiency judgment for $1.85 million. CBA then filed suit against Coastal and the partners to recover that amount. Benson and Mills admitted that they had joined Coastal before all the funds were distributed, but they argued that because they had joined the partnership after the loan had been executed, they were not liable for any loan amount greater than the amount of their interests in the partnership assets.

Are Benson and Mills liable for $1.5 million in loan installments received by Coastal after they joined the partnership?

Answer. _____

_____

_____

_____

_____

_____

_____

_____

_____

_____

_____

_____

_____

Practice Quiz

True/False:

1. ____ General partners are personally liable for the debts and obligations of the partnership. [p 615]

2. ____ The Uniform Partnership Act deals with many of the problems that can occur in the formation, operation and dissolution of ordinary partnerships. [p 615]

3. ____ It is not necessary to have all partners agreeing to the participation of each co-partner. [p 616]

4. ____ The UPA definition of a partnership includes natural persons, partnerships and corporations. [p 616]

5. ____ The co-ownership of property by itself establishes a partnership. [p 616]

6. ___ In a partnership, a business, trade, profession or occupation must be conducted. [p 616]

7. ___ Co-ownership of a business is not necessary to create a partnership. [p 616]

8. ___ Proof of a share of business profits is prima facie evidence of a partnership. [p 616]

9. ___ Nonpartners generally are not given the right to share in the business profits. [p 616]

10. ___ The right to participate in the management of a business is conclusive evidence for determining the existence of a partnership. [p 616]

11. ___ The majority of states do not require general partnerships to file a partnership agreement. [p 618]

12. ___ Nonprofit organizations, which include charitable or fraternal organizations, can be organized as partnerships. [p 617]

13. ___ A written partnership agreement is sometimes referred to as articles of partnership. [p 618]

14. ___ It is all right if the partnership selects a name that indicates it is a corporation. [p 618]

15. ___ The UPA is prohibited from filling in the gaps in a partners' agreement. [p 619]

16. ___ Only designated partners may execute the conveyance of title in the partnership name. [p 619]

17. ___ Upon dissolution of a partnership, an assignee is not entitled to receive any of the rights of liquidation to which the assigning partner would be entitled. [p 620]

18. ___ If a vote in a partnership matter is tied, the action being voted on is viewed as defeated. [p 620]

19. ___ If a partnership agreement provides for profit sharing but does not indicate how losses are to be shared, the losses will be shared in the same ratio as the profits. [p 621]

20. ___ There is not any implication that the partners will devote full time and service to the partnership that they are involved in. [p 621]

21. ___ A partner who is offered an opportunity on behalf of the partnership may take the opportunity for himself before offering it to the partnership. [p 622]

22. ___ Permission of all partners is required before a partner may compete with the partnership. [p 622]

23. ___ Partners must follow the provisions of the partnership by complying with their duty of obedience. [p 623]

24. ___ A partner is not liable to the partnership for any damages caused by his or her negligence. [p 623]

25. ___ If a partner obtains information relative to the partnership's affairs, he or she has a duty to inform his or her co-partners. [p 623]

Multiple Choice:

26. Which of the following is not a requirement for qualifying as a general partnership? [p 616]
    a. An association of two of more persons
    b. The carrying on of a business
    c. A profit motive
    d. It must be for nonprofit purposes

27. Which of the following is not a true statement with respect to general partnerships? [p 618]
    a. General partnerships may be created orally or in writing.
    b. A partnership may not be for a fixed term.
    c. Partners may make loans of money or property to partnerships.
    d. Partners may agree to almost any terms in their partnership agreement.

28. A partnership by estoppel occurs when [p 619]
    a. a person who is not a partner consents to a partner's representation that he or she is a partner or makes a representation that he or she is a partner.
    b. a person withdraws from being part of a corporation and forms a business with another individual.
    c. an individual makes a material misrepresentation of fact to another who thereafter suffers damages.
    d. all of the above.

29. Bart made a $50,000 loan to B& B, a partnership that he is a partner in. B & B has three main creditors, First Bank who holds the mortgage to their building, and two Visa companies. The partnership has decided to dissolve and Bart wants his money back with interest and demands that he be paid first. Which of the following will be the probably outcome of his request? [p 622]
    a. Bart will be entitled to repayment of his loan before the other creditors.
    b. Bart will be entitled to the loan if he sues the partnership.
    c. Bart will lose all money loaned as the partnership is dissolving.
    d. Bart will be entitled to repayment of the loan but his right is subordinated to the claims of creditors who are not partners.

30. Which of the following would be considered a breach of the duty of loyalty by a partner? [p 622]
    a. Omar owns a piece of property that would be desirable for the partnership he is in to build an office on. Omar decides to sell the partnership his property but does not tell the partnership that he owns the property.
    b. Sally is a partner in a cookie baking business and decides to open a competing cookie business without her partner's permission.
    c. Ronald has been experiencing car problems lately and must be at a family reunion that is a two hour drive from where he lives. He decides to borrow the partnership's vehicle to go to the reunion. He uses the vehicle, washes it upon his return and fills it up with a full tank of gas.
    d. All of the above.

31. Velma has become a partner in The Incredible Dessert Shoppe. She is so excited about being privy to the award winning recipe for "Fun Festival Cookie Drops" that she brags and shares the recipe with a competitor, Doreen's Delectable Dessert Shoppe. What duty has Velma breached, if any to her partners? [p 623]
    a. Velma has breached the duty not to misuse partnership property for personal use.
    b. Velma has breached the duty of obedience.
    c. Velma has breached the duty of confidentiality, as she did not keep the partnership information a secret.
    d. Velma has not breached any duty as Doreen has not made any profit off of the "Fun Festival Cookie Drops" recipe.

32. Richard is contemplating becoming a partner in a famous shoe company but is uncertain about what his duties will entail if he enters the partnership. Which of the following is not a duty that Richard will need to be concerned about? [p 623]
    a. Duty of care
    b. Duty to withdrawal from the partnership
    c. Duty to inform
    d. Duty of obedience

33. If Whitney and Monica want to terminate their partnership, which of the following acts would accomplish that purpose? [p 627]
    a. Either partner may rightfully withdraw and dissolve the partnership at any time.
    b. Whitney and Monica could admit a new partner to their already existing business.
    c. Whitney and Monica could mutually agree to dissolve their partnership.
    d. All of the above.

34. If Whitney and Monica decide to admit Tara into their partnership, what debts and obligations would Tara be responsible for? [p 627]
    a. Tara would be liable for the existing debts and obligations of the partnership only to the extent of her capital contribution, as well as debts and obligations that the partnership incurs after she becomes a partner.
    b. Tara would only be liable for the debts and obligations that the partnership incurs after she becomes a partner.
    c. Tara would be liable for the debts and obligations to the extent of her contribution and would be able to seek indemnification for debts incurred after becoming a partner.
    d. Tara would not be liable for any of the debts or obligations of the partnership unless she personally incurred them.

35. If a partnership between Robert, Marie and Jonathan dissolves, which of the following is not true with respect to liquidation of the partnership assets? [p 630]
    a. The surviving or remaining partners have the right to wind up the partnership.
    b. If Robert, Marie or Jonathan is bankrupt, they can still participate in the winding up of the partnership.
    c. Winding up follows the dissolution of the partnership.
    d. None of the above.

Short Answer:

36. What do the initials UPA stand for? [p 615] _____

37. What was the goal of the UPA? [p 615] _____
_____

38. Why won't nonprofit organizations qualify as partnerships? [p 617] _____
_____

39. What is a partnership that does not have a fixed term called? [p 618] _____
_____

40. List three pieces of information that a partnership agreement should contain. [p 618] ____
_____

41. If Darwin travels across the United States to promote the coffee mugs that his partnership is famous for, what may he ask for if he pays for all of his travel expenses? [p 622]
_____

42. If John offers Barkley, a partner in the XYZ company the opportunity to purchase a business that makes component parts that would help the XYZ company, what must Barkley do? [p 622] _____
_____

43. Give a brief explanation of what the duty of loyalty encompasses. [p 622] _____
_____

44. What are the three stages of dissolution and termination of a general partnership? [p 627]
_____

45. If a partner's action results in the wrongful dissolution of the partnership, what is the partner liable for? [p 627] _____
_____

46. Give one instance in which a partnership may be dissolved by a judicial decree of dissolution. [p 628] _____
_____

47. What is the effect of the termination of a partnership? [p 630] _____
_____

48. Janice is a physician as well as partner in a medical facility. She is accustomed to meeting with the pharmaceutical representatives when they come into the practice. On one of Jared Jones, a pharmaceutical representative's visits to the practice, he remarks to Janice, "If your Practice promotes the Cold Zapper drug that we manufacturer, I'll guarantee you a kickback of ten percent of every sale we make from your patients. She quickly calculates the potential profit she may be able to make and agrees to prescribe Cold Zapper to her patients that may benefit from it. What duty if any has Janice breached and why? [p 623]
_____
_____

49. What happens if a partner does not comply with the provisions of the partnership agreement? [p 623] _____

50. All partners are _____ _____ for the debts and contracts of the partnership. [p 624]

Answers to Refresh Your Memory

1. rights and duties [p 615]
2. entity [p 615]
3. General [p 615]
4. Partnerships [p 616]
5. The two most significant factors are whether the parties share the business's profits and share management responsibility. [p 616]
6. profit motive [p 617]
7. orally writing [p 618]
8. A partnership with a fixed duration or time period is a partnership for a term. [p 618]
9. All property originally brought into the partnership on account of the partnership is considered to be partnership property. [p 619]
10. A partner's interest is his or her share of the profits and surplus of the partnership. [p 620]
11. a charging order [p 620]
12. management [p 620]
13. A partner is allowed to bring an action for an accounting against the other partners. [p 621]
14. indemnification (reimbursement) [p 621]
15. fiduciary [p 622]

Critical Thought Exercise Model Answer

Section 17 of the Uniform Partnership Act provides that a partner who joins an ongoing partnership is liable for all the obligations of the partnership arising before his admission, but also states that this liability shall be satisfied only out of partnership property. A partnership obligation arises, within the meaning of Section 17 of the UPA when the creditor extends the credit to the partnership. In this case, the obligation of Coastal to repay the loan arose on August 23, 1992 and not on the occasions when the bank disbursed funds to the partnership.

The loan documents had been executed by Coastal and CBA before Benson and Mills joined Coastal, and they had become obligations for both CBA and Coastal immediately upon their execution. This fact was not changed by the additions of partners or the fact that the proceeds of the loan were disbursed in installments. Therefore, the obligation arising under the loan existed before Benson and Mills joined Coastal, making them liable only up to the amounts of their interests in the partnership assets.

Answers to Practice Quiz

True/False:

1. True   The partnership's debts and obligations are the responsibility of the general partners who remain personally liable.
2. True   Problems that arise in the formation, operation and dissolution of ordinary partnerships are covered under the Uniform Partnership Act.
3. False   All partners are required to agree to the participation of each co-partner.
4. True   Natural persons, partnerships and corporations are included in the UPA definition of a partnership.
5. False   Co-ownership alone does not establish a partnership. Other factors such as whether the parties share the business's profits and share management responsibility are also considered.
6. True   The UPA at section 2 requires that a business, trade, occupation or profession must be conducted.
7. False   Co-ownership is vital to create a partnership.
8. True   Profits are not usually shared by nonpartners.
9. True   Business profits are not generally shared by nonpartners.
10. False   The right to participate in the management of a business is important, however, it is not conclusive evidence of determining the existence of a partnership as employees and creditors as well as others are sometimes given the right to participate in management.
11. True   General partnerships do not have to file partnership agreements in most states.
12. False   Nonprofit organizations may not be organized as partnerships as they do not meet the requirement of having a profit motive to qualify as a partnership.
13. True   The written partnership agreement is sometimes referred to as articles of partnership.
14. False   The partnership name may not indicate that it is a corporation.
15. False   The UPA is used to fill in the gaps of the partners' agreement.
16. False   Any partner may convey the title in the partnership name.
17. False   The assignee is entitled to receive the rights in liquidation to which the assigning partner is entitled.
18. True   The action being voted on is considered to be defeated if the vote is tied.
19. True   Losses are shared in the same proportion as profits if the partnership agreement is not indicative of how the losses are to be shared.
20. False   It is implied under the UPA that partners will devote full time and service to the partnership.
21. False   A partner may not usurp a partnership opportunity before offering it to the partnership.
22. False   Permission of the partners must be forthcoming before a partner may compete with the partnership.
23. True   The duty of obedience mandates the partner's compliance with the provisions of the partnership agreement.
24. False   A partner is in deed liable to the partnership for any damages caused by his or her negligence.
25. True   All information possessed by the partners that is relevant to the operation of the partnership must be given to the other co-partners under the duty to inform.

Multiple Choice:

26. D   Answer D is the correct answer as the statement is false in that a general partnership must have a profit motive and nonprofit purposes would not satisfy this requirement. Answers A, B, and C are incorrect as they are all requirements for qualifying as a general partnership.

27. B   Answer B is the correct answer as a partnership may be for a fixed term and thus the statement given in answer B is false. Answers A, C and D are all true statements with respect to general partnerships.

28. A   Answer A is the correct answer as it properly states the meaning of a partnership by estoppel. Answer B is incorrect, as the withdrawal of one business form to create another business form does not reflect a partnership by estoppel. Answer C is incorrect as this answer is partially hinting at the definition of fraud, which is not associated with a partnership by estoppel. Answer D is incorrect for the reasons given above.

29. D   Answer D is the correct answer as a partner who makes a loan to the partnership becomes a creditor of the partnership who is entitled to repayment, however, his or her right is subordinated to the claims of the creditors who are not partners such as First Bank and the two visa companies given in the example. Answer A is incorrect as the statement is an incorrect statement of law. Answer B is incorrect as it is also an incorrect statement of law. Answer C is incorrect, as the dissolution of a partnership does not automatically mean that A partner who makes a loan to the partnership will lose all of the money that has been lent.

30. D   Answer D is the correct answer as answer A gives an example of self-dealing which is considered a breach of loyalty. Answer B gives an example of competing with the partnership which is also considered a breach of loyalty. Answer C gives an example of misuse of partnership property which is a breach of loyalty as well. Therefore, all of the choices given exemplify a breach of loyalty thereby making choice D the correct answer.

31. C   Answer C is the correct answer as Velma's disclosure of The Incredible Dessert Shoppe's recipe for "Fun Festival Cookie Drops" was a secret of the partnership that should not have been disclosed to a competitor, and as such she has breached the duty of confidentiality. Answers A and B are incorrect as they do not apply to the facts that are given. Answer D is incorrect, as it is irrelevant that Doreen has not made a profit. The fact is that confidential information concerning the partnership was revealed by Velma thereby making her action a breach of the duty of loyalty.

32. B   Answer B is the correct answer as the UPA does not provide for a duty to withdraw from a partnership. Answers A, C, and D are incorrect answers as they all express duties that Richard should be concerned about if he is contemplating becoming a partner in a famous shoe company or any other company for that matter.

33. D   Answer D is the correct answer as all of the answers given in choices A, B, and C correctly state acts that both Whitney and Monica could do that would accomplish the termination of a partnership with one another.

34. A   Answer A is the correct answer as it succinctly states what Tara's debts and obligations would be. Answers B, C and D are all incorrect as they are all misstatements of law.

35. B   Answer B is the correct answer, as a bankrupt partner may not participate in the winding up of the partnership. Answers A and C are incorrect as they both are true statements with respect to the liquidation of the partnership assets. Answer D is incorrect for the reasons given above.

Short Answer:

36. Uniform Partnership Act
37. The goal was to establish consistent partnership law that was consistent throughout the United States.
38. Because they do not meet the requirement that the business venture must have a profit motive.
39. partnership at will
40. It should contain the firm name, the nature and scope of the partnership business and the duration of the partnership. (Answers will vary.)
41. Darwin may ask for indemnification (reimbursement) for his travel expenses.
42. Barkley must offer the opportunity to the XYZ company and if the XYZ partnership rejects it, then Barkley is free to consider it providing it is does not violate any other duties.
43. The partner owes a duty not to act adversely to the interest of the partnership.
44. The three stages are dissolution, winding-up and termination.
45. The partner is liable for damages.
46. If the partnership can be conducted only at a loss, the partnership may be dissolved by a judicial decree of dissolution.
47. The effect of termination of a partnership is that it ends the legal existence of a partnership.
48. Janice may have breached the duty of loyalty if it can be shown that she as a partner received a kickback from the pharmaceutical representative for the Cold Zapper drug and thereby made secret profits from her connection with the representative.
49. A partner who does not comply with the provisions of the partnership agreement may have breached the duty of obedience and is therefore liable to the partnership for any damages caused by the breach.
50. jointly liable

Chapter 33
LIMITED PARTNERSHIPS AND
LIMITED LIABILITY PARTNERSHIPS

Chapter Overview

This chapter provides a further exploration of partnerships, with an emphasis on limited partnerships and their formation as well as the differentiation between limited and general partners. Additionally, this chapter discusses the limited liability partnership and the partners' liability if involved in the same. The process of dissolution as well as winding-up of limited partnerships is also explained.

Objectives

Upon completion of the exercises in this chapter, you should be able to:
1. Discuss what is meant by a limited partnership.
2. Explain the difference between a limited and a general partner.
3. Explain the requirements for forming a limited partnership.
4. Discuss the defective formation of a limited partnership.
5. Explain the meaning of a foreign limited partnership.
6. Discuss the meaning of a master limited partnership.
7. Differentiate and explain the liability of general and limited partners.
8. Explain limited liability partnership (LLP).
9. Discuss the limited liability of partners of an LLP.
10. Explain the requirements of dissolution and winding-up of limited partnerships.

Practical Application

This chapter will provide you with a wealth of information that will enable you to differentiate between the various types of limited partnerships as well as give you the necessary knowledge of the liability involved in the partnerships discussed herein. For the student who wants to operate a business, the basic partnership explanations will be an invaluable tool in determining the type of business operation that would be best in light of an individual's circumstances.

Helpful Hints

Before beginning this chapter, it is helpful to review the previous study guide chapter on general partnerships, as it provides a solid foundation for this chapter to build upon. It is best to study this material in a methodical fashion in order for the information that is given to be of maximum benefit.

Study Tips

It is important that you learn the difference between a limited partnership and a limited liability partners.

Limited Partnership

A limited partnership involves general partners who conduct the business and limited partners who invest in the partnership but who do not participate in the management. A corporation may act as a general partner, but is liable only to the extent of its assets.

Formation of a Limited Partnership

- Creation is informal
- No public disclosure is required
- Two or more persons must execute and sign a **certificate of limited partnership** and thereafter file it with the secretary of state if required by state law.
- Items that must be contained in the certificate of limited partnership are on page 637 of your main text.
- The limited partnership is formed upon the filing of the certificate of limited partnership.

Amendments to the Certificate of Limited Partnership

- A limited partnership must be kept current by way of certificates of amendment, which must be filed within 30 days of the happening of certain events.
- A partner's capital contribution changes.
- A new partner's admission.
- A partner's withdrawal.
- A business's continuation after a judicial dissolution to dissolve the partnership.

Name of the Limited Partnership

- A limited partnership may not include the surname of a limited partner unless it is also The surname of the general partner or the business was carried on under that name before the limited partner was admitted to the firm.
- The name may not be deceptively similar to other corporations' names or other limited partnerships' names.

Limited Partnership Agreement

This agreement drafted by the partners describes the rights and duties of the general and limited partners and the conditions concerning operation, termination and dissolution. If the agreement does not state how the profits and losses are to be shared, then they will e shared based on the value of the partner's capital contribution.

Each limited partner has a right to information regarding the financial condition of the limited partnership.

Defective Formation

A limited partnership is defectively formed if the certificate of limited partnership is not properly filed or some other requirement is not met. However, if there has been **"substantial compliance in good faith"** with the statutory requisites, then it is deemed properly formed.

Admission of a new partner

The addition of a partner to an existing limited partnership can only be accomplished by the written consent of all partners. An amendment of the certificate of limited partnership effectuates the admission of the new partner. Withdrawal of a partner can be accomplished as per the certificate of limited partnership, upon the happening of an event or upon six months' prior notice to each general partner.

Dissolution and Winding Up

The affairs of a limited partnership may be dissolved and wound up just like an ordinary partnership. However a certificate of cancellation must be filed with the secretary of state that the limited partnership is organized. The **end of the limited partnership's life, the written consent of limited and genera partners, the withdrawal of a general partner and the entry of a decree of judicial dissolution** are the events that can cause dissolution of a limited partnership.

Winding Up

A limited partnership's general partners must wind up its affairs once it dissolves itself. RULPA established the order of distribution of partnership assets, beginning with creditors, followed by partners with regard to unpaid distributions, capital contributions and finally by the remainder of the proceeds.

Limited Liability Partnership (also called special partnerships)

All partners are given limited liability. Professionals commonly use this type of partnership. A limited partnership must have a minimum of one general partner and one limited partners. Any person may be a limited partner. There is no tax paid at the partnership level.

Revised Uniform Limited Partnership Act (RULPA)

A modern, comprehensive law for the formation, operation and dissolution of limited partnerships.

Capital Contributions

General and limited partners' capital contributions may be made in cash, property, services rendered or a promissory note.

Registration of Foreign Limited Partnerships

A foreign limited partnership must file an application for registration with the secretary of state before it conducts business with a foreign country. If the application is all in order, a certificate of registration will be issued so that it may transact business with a foreign country. Note that unregistered foreign limited partnership may not initiate litigation in a foreign jurisdiction.

Master Limited Partnership (MLP)

A limited partnership whose limited partnership interests are traded on organized securities exchanges. The tax benefits in owning a limited partnership. In an MLP are that MLP's do not pay any income tax, and partnership income and losses go directly onto the individual partner's income tax return. Double taxation is also avoided with an MLP.

Liability of General and Limited Partners

General partners have unlimited personal liability for the debts as well as obligations of the limited partnership. Limited partners however are only liable for the obligations and debts up to their capital contributions to the limited partnership. Limited partners may be liable on personal guarantees.

Participation in Management by Limited Partners

Limited partners forfeit their right to participate in the management control of the limited partnership. The limited partner is liable only to persons who reasonably believe him or her to be a general partner. RULPA Section 303 (a).

The allowable activities that a limited partner m engage in without losing his or her liability are listed on page 643 of your text.

Limited partners are not solely liable for the obligations or actions of the partnership beyond what is contributed as capital. The exceptions are when there has been a defective formation, participation in management or if there has been a personal guarantee.

Refresh Your Memory

The following exercise will enable you to refresh your memory on the rules and principles presented to you in this chapter. Read each question twice and place your answer in the blanks provided. Review the chapter material for any question you miss or are unable to remember.

1.   A new form of partnership entity that provides limited liability to all of its partners is a
     _____.

2.   What two types of partners do limited partnerships have? _____
     and_____.

3.   What are limited partnerships called in Louisiana? _____

4.   What has the Revised Uniform Limited Partnership Act done to improve Limited
     Partnerships? _____

5.   Name at least three things that must be contained in a certificate of limited partnership.
     _____

6.   When is a limited partnership formed? _____
     _____

7.   What form of capital contribution may the general limited partner make? _____
     _____

8.   When may a limited partnership include the surname of a limited partner in the firm name?
     _____

9.   What is a domestic limited partnership? _____
     _____

10. What is a master limited partnership (MLP)? _____
     _____

11. What are some of the tax benefits to owning a limited partnership interest in an MLP? ____
_____

12. What is the trade off for operating/participating in a limited partnership? _____
_____

13. Name two activities a limited partner may participate in without losing his or limited liability? _____
_____

14. What do banks often require of small businesses wishing to borrow money or obtain an extension of credit? _____
_____

15. The _____ partners of a limited partnership have the same rights, duties, and powers as partners in a _____ partnership.

Critical Thought Exercise

Harris, Nix, and Lewis for a limited partnership for the purpose of hiring and booking motivational speakers for corporate and government training seminars. Harris was a former boxing promoter and will act as the general partner. Nix and Harris contribute $35,000 each and Harris contributes all the furniture and supplies from his current office. A certificate of limited partnership is prepared in a proper and complete manner and filed with the secretary of state. The partnership begins to hire and book motivational speakers and is very successful. Fifteen months later, Harris has a heart attack and is unable to work for several months. Instead of hiring a temporary manager to run the business, Nix completely takes over the day-to-day running of the business. Nix wants to build the business and hire famous speakers. He signs a contract with a famous football coach to give two speeches at a rate of $200,000 each. Harris then returns to work and takes over management duties. Due to poor decisions made by Nix, the partnership is unable to pay the coach after he makes the two speeches. In his suit, the coach alleges that both Harris and Nix are personally liable for the damages caused by the partnerships breach of contract if the damages cannot be satisfied out of partnership assets.

Is Nix personally liable for damages to the coach even though he is only a limited partner?

Answer. _____
_____
_____
_____
_____
_____
_____
_____
_____
_____
_____

_____
_____
_____
_____
_____

Practice Quiz

True/False:

1. ____ A limited partnership must have a minimum of one general partner and one limited partner. [p 635]

2. ____ There are restriction as to the number of limited or general partners allowed in a limited partnership. [p 635]

3. ____ Only natural persons may be a limited partner. [p 635]

4. ____ A person may not be both a limited and a general partner in the same limited partnership. [p 635]

5. ____ A corporation may be the only general partner of a limited partnership. [p 635]

6. ____ The creation of a limited partnership is informal and does not require public disclosure of the same. [p 637]

7. ____ Where no limited partnership agreement exists, the certificate of limited partnership will act as the articles of limited partnership. [p 638]

8. ____ Where there has been "substantial compliance in good faith" with the statutory requirements, a limited partnership is deemed to have been properly formed. [p 638]

9. ____ There is no need to file an application for registration with the secretary of state before a foreign limited partnership may transact business in a foreign state. [p 642]

10. ____ The failure to register a foreign limited partnership will impair the validity of any act or contract of the unregistered foreign limited partnership and will prevent it from defending itself in any proceeding in the courts of the foreign state. [p 642]

11. ____ Unregistered foreign limited partnerships may initiate litigation in foreign jurisdictions. [p 642]

12. ____ General partners of a limited partnership have unlimited personal liability for the debts and obligations of the limited partnership. [p 642]

13. ____ Limited partners are usually only liable for the debts and obligations of the limited partnership up to their capital contribution. [p 642]

14. ___ A limited partner may engage in any activities on behalf of the limited partnership. [p 643]

15. ___ A limited partner who is properly employed by the partnership as a manager or executive is individually liable for the debts, obligations and tortuous acts of the partnership. [p 644]

16. ___ If a limited partner signed an enforceable personal guarantee that guarantees the performance of the limited partnership, he or she is individually liable. [p 644]

17. ___ Where there is no agreement specifying how profits and losses are to be allocated, the court will issue a judicial decision rendering the limited partnership terminated. [p 644]

18. ___ The limited partnership agreement may stipulate which transactions must be approved by which partners. [p 645]

19. ___ Under the RULPA, a limited partner may not withdraw from a limited partnership. [p 645]

20. ___ A limited partnership may be dissolved along with its affairs wound up much like an ordinary partnership. [p 645]

21. ___ In a limited liability partnership, there must be a general partner who is personally liable for the debts and obligations of the partnership. [p 646]

22. ___ In a limited liability partnership, all partners are limited partners who are at risk for loss of their capital contribution should the partnership fail. [p 646]

23. ___ A limited liability partnership need not register as a foreign limited liability partnership in order to do business in other states. [p 647]

24. ___ Limited liability partnerships have several tax benefits, including the fact that there is no tax paid at the partnership level. [p 647]

25. ___ The limited liability partnership must file articles of partnership with the secretary of state in which it is organized. [p 647]

Multiple Choice:

26. Which of the following must be contained in the certificate of limited partnership? [p 637]
    a. Proof of any improper certificate of partnership filings
    b. The latest date upon which the limited partnership is to dissolve
    c. Proof of incorporation
    d. None of the above

27. A defective formation of a limited partnership happens when [p 638]
    a. there are defects in a certificate that is filed.
    b. a certificate of limited partnership is not properly filed.

c. a statutory requirement for the creation of the limited partnership is not met.

d. all of the above.

28. Before a foreign limited partnership may begin conducting business in a foreign state, it must do which of the following? [p 642]

    a. It must cause injury to someone in the foreign state so that the court may have jurisdiction over it.

    b. It must initiate litigation in the foreign jurisdiction.

    c. It must file an application for registration with the secretary of state.

    d. It's ownership interest must be traded on organized securities exchanges.

29. A Master Limited Partnership is [p 642]

    a. a domestic limited partnership in the state in which it is organized.

    b. a foreign limited partnership in all of the states.

    c. a limited partnership whose limited partnership interests are traded on organized securities exchanges.

    d. an unregistered foreign partnership.

30. What do limited partners give up in exchange for limited liability? [p 643]

    a. They give up their capital investment into the partnership.

    b. They give up their right to participate in the control and management of the limited partnership.

    c. They give up liability only to persons who reasonably believe him or her to be a general partner.

    d. They give up acting as a surety for the limited partnership.

31. If the Bright Balloon Company wants to add Lily as a partner, which of the following is true with respect to the admission of a new partner? [p 645]

    a. A limited partner can withdraw from a limited partnership only at a time stated in the certificate of limited partnership.

    b. Lily can be added only upon the written consent of all partners of the Bright Balloon Company unless the limited partnership agreement provides otherwise.

    c. Lily cannot be added as the limited partnership agreement has the effect of waiving the right of partners to approve the admission of new general partners.

    d. Lily can be added as a partner upon proof of unequal voting rights.

32. Which of the following correctly expresses the order in which a limited partnership's assets are distributed once the assets have been liquidated? [p 646]

    a. Capital contributions, unpaid distributions, creditors, remainder of the proceeds

    b. Creditors of the limited partnership, the remainder of the proceeds, unpaid distributions, capital contributions

    c. Creditors of the limited partnership, partners with regard to unpaid distributions first, then capital contributions, with the remainder of the proceeds last

    d. None of the above

33. If Irene and Nicole are attempting to name the partnership that the two want to enter into together, which of the following would be good advice to help them? [p 638]

    a. Irene and Nicole may use a surname of a general partner.

b. It is not necessary that the name that they choose contain the actual words, limited partnership.

c. The name that they choose cannot be the same as or deceptively similar to the names of other limited partnerships and corporations.

d. The defect of noncompliance with regard to the name will not affect their rights as partners.

34. John is a limited partner in the Healthy For You Food Store. Which activity may John participate in without losing his limited liability? [p 643]

a. John may be a consultant or advisor to a general partner regarding the limited partnership.

b. John may bind the partnership to contracts.

c. John may participate in the management of the limited partnership.

d. John may participate in the control of the limited partnership.

35. What type of event would cause a certificate of amendment to be filed? [p 638]

a. The admission of a new partner would cause a certificate of amendment to be filed.

b. A change in a partner's capital contribution would cause a certificate of amendment to be filed.

c. The withdrawal of a partner would cause a certificate of amendment to be filed.

d. All of the above.

Short Answer:

36. What does the limited partnership agreement set out to do? [p 638] _____
_____

37. How far does a general partner's liability extend in a limited partnership? [p 642] _____
_____

38. What is one of the largest disadvantage for investors who are limited partners in a limited partnership? [p 642] _____
_____

39. Where would a partner find information regarding his or her rights, powers, duties and responsibilities? [p 644] _____
_____

40. What type of information may Alma, a limited partner in the Zippo Company obtain from Verne, a general partner in Zippo? [p 645] _____
_____

41. When is a decree of judicial dissolution of a limited partnership granted? [p 646] _____
_____

42. Give examples of who may be a general or limited partner. [p 635] _____
_____

43. Explain what a certificate of limited partnership is. [p 637] _____
_____

44. The Hastings Group, a Limited Partnership is in existence in Anytown, U.S.A. George wants to file a certificate of limited partnership for a new partnership he and a couple of other individuals are forming. He wants to file his certificate with the name of the Limited Partnership as The Hasting Group. What problem might he have if the name his partnership has chosen is filed? [p 638] _____

45. Which law governs a limited partnership's organization, internal affairs and the liability of its limited partners? [p 642] _____

46. If the Presto Company, a limited partnership is organized in Idaho, but, files an application for registration of its limited partnership in Montana, which state's courts may decide contracts disputes that arise in Montana? [p 642] _____

47. Once the dissolution and the initiation of the winding-up of a limited partnership have begun, what must be filed by the limited partnership? [p 645] _____

48. What right allows Judy Jones, a limited partner of the Smooth as Silk Company to view copies of federal, state, and local income tax returns? [p 645] _____

49. What type of partner may petition the court to wind up the affairs of a limited partnership? [p 646] _____

50. Why was the limited liability partnership created? [p 648] _____

Answers to Refresh Your Memory

1. limited liability partnership [p 635]
2. general and limited partners [p 635]
3. partnerships in commendam [p 635]
4. It has provided a more modern and comprehensive law for the formation, operation and dissolution of partnerships. [p 636]
5. The name of the partnership, general character of the business, and amount of cash, property, or services contributed by each partner and any contributes of cash, services or property promised to be made in the future. [p 637]
6. When the certificate of limited partnership is filed, the limited partnership is formed. [p 637]
7. The form of contribution may be in cash, property or services rendered, or a promissory note or other obligation to contribute cash, property or perform services. [p 638]
8. A limited partnership may include the surname of a limited partner in the firm name when it is also the surname of a general partner or the business was conducted under that name before the admission of the limited partner. [p 638]
9. A domestic limited partnership is a limited partnership in the state in which it was organized. [p 642]

10. A master limited partnership is one whose limited partnership interests are traded on organized securities exchanges such as the New York Stock Exchange. [p 642]
11. Master limited partnerships do not pay any income tax. The partnership's income as well as losses flow directly onto the individual partner's income tax return. This type of partnership also avoids double taxation of corporate dividends. [p 642]
12. The limited partners give up their right to take part in the control and management of the limited partnership. [p 643]
13. A partner may be an agent, an employee or a contractor of the limited partnership or a general partner. A partner may act as a surety for the limited partnership. [p 643]
14. Banks will sometime require owners of small businesses to personally guarantee the loan of the business. [p 643]
15. general, general [p 644]

Critical Thought Exercise Model Answer

General partners are personally liable to the partnership's creditors. The liability of a limited partner is limited to the capital that he or she contributes to the partnership. A limited partner gains this protection if the requirements for signing and filing the limited partnership certificate are met. In this case the certificate was properly filed. When the partnership began business, both Nix and Lewis had the protection afforded a limited partner.

However, under the Revised Uniform Limited Partnership Act (RULPA), section 303, limited partners only enjoy limited liability as long as they do not participate in management. A limited partner who undertakes management of the partnership's business will be just as liable as a general partner to any creditor who transacts business with the limited partnership and believes, based upon the acts of the limited partner, that the limited partner is a general partner [RULPA, section 303]. In this case, Nix took over complete management and was running the daily affairs of the partnership. With Harris not working at all during the time the contract was signed with the coach, Nix would have appeared to be the general manager and thus, a general partner. Therefore, Nix should be personally liable to the coach for damages for breach of contract. Harris, even though he was not working at the time, will also be personally liable because he is listed as the general partner on the partnership certificate. Lewis is the only partner who's liability to the coach will be limited to his investment in the partnership

Answers to Practice Quiz

True/False:

1. True   One limited partner and at least one general partner are required in a limited partnership.
2. False There are not any restrictions on the number of general or limited partners   allowed in a limited partnership.
3. False Any person, including natural persons, partnerships, limited partnerships, trusts, estates, associations and corporations may be a general or limited partner.
4. False A person may in fact be both a general and limited partner in the same limited partnership.
5. True   A corporation is permitted to be the only general partner of a limited partnership.
6. False The creation is formal and does require public disclosure.

7. True   The certificate of limited partnership act as the articles of limited partnership when there is no limited partnership agreement.

8. True   A limited partnership is said to have been properly formed if there has been substantial compliance in good faith with the statutory requirements. [RULPA Section 201 (b)]

9. False A foreign limited partnership is required to file an application for registration with the secretary of state prior to transacting business in that foreign state.

10. False The failure to register does not impair the validity of any act or contract of the foreign limited partnership that is not register nor does it stop it from defending itself in any proceeding in the court of the foreign state.

11. False Foreign limited partnerships that are not registered may not initiate litigation in a foreign jurisdiction.

12. True   A limited partnership's general partners have unlimited personal liability for the debts and obligations of the limited partnership.

13. True   The liability of limited partners for the debts and obligations of the limited partnership is usually only up to the amount of their capital contributions.

14. False A limited partner may not participate in the control and management of the limited partnership.

15. False A limited partner who participated in the management and control of the partnership is individually liable for the debts and obligations and tortuous acts of the partnership. The limited partner who is properly employed by the partnership as a manager or executive is the exception to the general rule.

16. True   An enforceable personal guarantee that guarantees the performance of a limited partnership subject the limited partner to liability if he or she signed the guarantee.

17. False If there is no agreement specifying the distribution of profits and losses, the profits and losses will then be shared according to the partner's capital contribution.

18. True   A stipulation concerning which transactions must be approved by which partners may be provided for in the limited partnership agreement.

19. False A limited partner can withdraw from a limited partnership subject to the provisions set forth in RULPA Section 603.

20. True   A limited partnership is like an ordinary partnership in terms of the dissolution and winding up of its affairs.

21. False There does not have to be a general partner who is personally liable for the debts and obligations of the limited liability partnership.

22. True   All partners are limited partners who are at risk of losing only their capital contribution should the partnership fail.

23. False The limited liability partnership must register as a foreign limited liability partnership in any foreign state that it wants to conduct business in.

24. True   The limited liability partnership has many tax benefits including the lack of tax to be paid at the partnership level.

25. True   The articles of partnership of a limited liability partnership must be filed with the secretary of state in which it is organized.

Multiple Choice:

26. B Answer B is the correct answer as under RULPA Sections 201 and 206, one of the pieces of information that must be included in the certificate of limited partnership is the

latest date upon which the limited partnership is to dissolve. Answers A, C and D are incorrect as answer A is presumptive that the partnership would file an improper certificate, answer C is ridiculous as proof of incorporation is not a necessary item that must be in the certificate, and answer D is incorrect based on the reasons given.

27. D   Answer D is the correct answer as answers A, B, and C all state situations in which a defective formation would be the end result of the actions stated.

28. C   Answer C is the correct answer as an application for registration with the secretary of state in the foreign state that the foreign limited partnership wishes to conduct business in must be filed. Answer A is incorrect as it is absurd to think a partnership must cause injury and harm to another in a state before being allowed to conduct business in that state. Answer B is incorrect as initiating litigation in a foreign state in order to transact business not only does not make sense, but also would be a costly and perhaps frivolous endeavor. Answer D is incorrect as there is no requirement of a foreign limited partnership to trade on an organized securities exchange prior to transacting business in a foreign state.

29. C   Answer C is the correct answer as it gives the proper explanation for a master limited partnership. Answer A is incorrect as there is nothing to indicate that this type of partnership could not be foreign as well. Answer B is incorrect as once again, there is nothing to indicate that this type of partnership is a foreign limited one in all states. Answer D is incorrect, as like other partnerships, it too must go through a registration process.

30. B   Answer B is the correct answer as limited partners do forfeit their right to participate in the control and management of the limited partnership in exchange for limited liability. Answer A is incorrect, as a limited partner does not give up his or her capital investment. If that were the case, no one would invest and become a limited partner. Additionally, liability of limited partners would be difficult to assess without something such as the capital investment to measure it by. Answer C is incorrect as it is a false and absurd statement. Answer D is incorrect as there is nothing that automatically implies that a limited partner automatically will act as a surety in exchange for limited liability.

31. B   Answer B is the correct answer as written consent of all partners is required under RULPA at Section 401 in order for Lily to be added as a partner to the Bright Balloon Company. Answer A is incorrect as it addresses the issue of withdrawal of a partner and not admission, which is what the question is concerned with. Answer C is incorrect as it is untrue. Answer D is incorrect, as the proof of unequal voting rights has nothing to do with the requirement of written consent to admit a new partner.

32. C   Answer C is the correct answer as it properly categorizes the order of distribution of a limited partnership's assets upon liquidation. Answers A, B, and D are all incorrect based on the incorrect order and reasoning given as to why answer C is correct.

33. C   Answer C is the correct answer as RULPA Section 102 provides in part that the name of a limited partnership cannot be the same or as deceptively similar to the names of corporations or other limited partnerships. Answer A is not correct in its entirety, as there are restrictions as per RULPA Section 102 that provide for the use of a surname thereby making this answer an incomplete choice. Answer B is incorrect as this is a false statement since the name must contain without abbreviation the words limited partnership. Answer D is incorrect as a defect in the name to be used may affect Irene and Nicole's rights and liabilities.

34. A   Answer A is correct as RULPA Sections 303 (b) and (c) provide for the activity stated in this answer as being one that a limited partner may engage in without losing his or her liability. Answers B, C, and D however are incorrect answers as they all state activities that would affect John's liability thereby making him liable as a general partner.

35. D   Answer D is correct as answers A, B, and C all state events that would cause a certificate of amendment to be filed.

Short Answer:

36.   It describes the rights and duties of the general and limited partners along with the conditions and terms regarding the operation, termination and dissolution of the partnership.
37.   General partners have unlimited personal liability in a limited partnership.
38.   Their investment is not liquid as there is no market for the purchase and sale of limited partnership interests.
39.   A partner could find information in the articles of limited partnership or the certificate of limited partnership.
40.   Alma has the right to obtain full information concerning the state of the business, as well as the financial condition of the business from Vern.
41.   A decree of judicial dissolution is granted when it is not reasonably practical to conduct the business in accordance with the limited partnership agreement.
42.   Any person including natural persons, partnerships, limited partnerships, estates, trusts, associations and corporations may be a general or limited partner.
43.   A certificate of limited partnership is a document that two or more persons must create and sign that makes the limited partnership legal and binding.
44.   The problem that may exist is that the name may be viewed as deceptively similar to an already existing name that bears substantial likeness but for the last letter thereby elevating the potential for confusion regarding general and liability matters.
45.   The law of the state in which the entity is organized governs a limited partnership's organization, internal affairs and the liability of its limited partners.
46.   Montana's state courts may decide contract disputes that arise in Montana as a foreign limited partnership may use the court of a foreign state to enforce contracts and other rights once the limited partnership is registered there.
47.   A certificate of cancellation must be filed.
48.   The right to information as provided for in RULPA Section 305 gives Judy Jones this right.
49.   Any partner may petition the court.
50.   It was created especially for professional such as accountants and lawyers so that they could offer their services under a shield of liability.

Chapter 34
LIMITED LIABILITY COMPANIES

Chapter Overview

The main focus of this chapter is the formation, operation and thorough explanation of the business entity called a limited liability company (LLC). A limited liability company is a hybrid company of sorts in that it has some of the desirable characteristics of general partnerships, corporations and limited corporations. The interesting fact about the LLC is that the owners are allowed to manage the business and yet have limited liability. Further, it is allowed to be taxed as a partnership. Since it does offer so many advantages, it is a very favorable way for new business entrepreneurs to begin their ventures.

Objectives

Upon completion of the exercises in this chapter, you should be able to:
1. Explain what comprises a limited liability company.
2. Explain the procedure for organizing a limited liability company.
3. Differentiate between and S corporation and a limited liability company.
4. Explain what is meant by the limited liability shield as it pertains to the limited liability company.
5. Explain why a limited liability company can be taxed as a partnership.
6. Explain what a foreign limited liability is.
7. Discuss what is contained in the limited liability company's operating agreement.
8. Differentiate between a member-managed limited liability company and a manager-managed limited liability company.
9. Decide and discuss when members and managers owe fiduciary duties of loyalty and care to the limited liability company.
10. Compare the equivalent forms of business to the limited liability company that are used in foreign countries.

Practical Application

You should be able to recognize the benefits from conducting a newly organized business in the form of a limited liability company. Your previous studies of partnerships will aide you in reaching a decision as to the form your own business may want to take. If you are not planning on operating a business, not only is this chapter useful for general information but, it will give you insight on the choices available as well as why a company may choose to function in this manner from a tax, liability and management perspective.

491

Helpful Hints

It is important to keep in mind that the Uniform Limited Liability Company Act is responsible for codifying the limited liability company law. Further, its primary goal is to establish a comprehensive limited liability company law that is uniform throughout the United States. Since it is vital to this type of business, it is crucial to realize that it is your foundation toward learning this area of the law.

A limited liability company is much like a work of unique art that begins much like an ordinary piece of work, but develops into a creation that others would like to have too. As you go through the study tips section, keep in mind that as with all forms of business, a limited liability company will need to be organized with articles of organization, time limits set, capital contributions noted, its management set in place and of course the duties of those operating under the company umbrella. Using your imagination to compare the characteristics of the limited liability company to an artistic endeavor will help to make the material enjoyable as well as manageable to learn.

Study Tips

General Information For You to Remember

- It's important to remember that limited liability companies are created by **state law.**
- A large number of states have adopted the **Uniform Limited Liability Company Act** which sets forth the laws concerning formation, operation and termination of the LCC.
- A limited liability company is referred to as a LLC and is a **separate legal entity** separate from its members.
- Limited liability companies can sue or be sued, enter into or enforce contracts, transfer and hold title to property and be civilly as well as criminally liable under the law.
- Owners are called **members** and members usually are not personally liable to third parties for debts obligations and liabilities of an LLC beyond their capital contribution.
- Debts and obligations of the LLC are entirely those of the LLC.

Why do business as a LLC?

- If you were to **compare an LLC to and S Corporation**, you would learn that the S Corporations have several undesirable restrictions concerning who can be shareholders, how many shareholders and the percentage of stock that may be owned, whereas the LLC has none of these limitations.

- In **comparing an LLC to a general partnership**, members of the LLC have limited liability instead of personal liability for the obligations of the general partnership.

- Finally, in **viewing a LLC against a limited partnership**, the LLC allows all members to take part in management of the business with limited liability to its members. The limited partnership however requires at least one general partner who is personally liable for the partnership's obligations. Further, limited partners may not take part in the management of the business.

Lawful Purpose

A limited liability company may be organized for any lawful purpose. An example would be a real estate development company. Beware, an LLC cannot operate the practice of certain professions, such as doctors or lawyers. However, these professionals can conduct business as a limited liability partnership.

Organization

A LLC can conduct business in all states, but may only be registered in one. A LLC is usually organized in the state that it will be transacting most of its business in.

Choosing a Name for the LLC

- The name must have the words **"limited liability company"** or limited company or the abbreviations L.L.C. or LLC or LC.
- Trademark issues must be explored so as to not violate federal law.
- The issue of similar names must be explored to determine if use of the name chosen is even a viable option for the new LLC.
- If the name is available, it may be reserved for 120 days while the organization process of the LLC is being completed.

Filing the Articles of Organization

Articles of organization must be delivered to the secretary of state's office for filing. If the articles are in **proper form**, the articles will be filed. The articles must contain the name and address of the initial LLC office, the name and address of the initial agent for service of process, the name and address of each organizer and whether the LLC is a term LLC and if yes, then the specifics of the term must be stated. Additionally, the article s must state whether the LLC is to be manager-managed and the identity and address(es) of the manager(s). Finally, the articles must indicate whether the members will be personally liable for the debts and obligations of the LLC.

Duration

An LLC is either an at-will LLC or a term LLC. The term LLC states how long the LLC will exist. An at-will LLC does not state a term of duration.

Capital Contribution

A member's capital may consist of money, real property, personal property, intangible property, services performed, and so on. A member's death will not excuse a member's obligation to contribute, nor will disability or the inability to perform.

Agent for Service of Process

An agent for service of process of notices, demands, litigation or administrative proceedings is required by the ULLCA. Usually a lawyer fills this capacity, however, other individuals may do so as well.

Certificate of Interest

This act like a stock certificate as it indicates a member's ownership interest in the LLC.

Conversion of an Existing Business to an LLC

Many businesses convert to operate as a limited liability company. They do so to obtain tax benefits as well as utilize the limited liability benefit. In order to convert, ULLCA at section 902 requires that there be a statement of terms contained in an agreement of conversion, that the agreement be approved by all parties and owners concerned, and that the articles of organization be filed with the secretary of state indicating the prior business name and form of operation.

Foreign Limited Liability Company

An LLC that is organized in one state may transact business in a different state. An LLC is termed a domestic limited liability company in the state where it is organized and a foreign limited liability company in all other states it is transacting business in. A certificate of authority is required to conduct business in states that it is not organized in. An alien liability company is an LLC organized in a foreign country, but conducting business in the United States.

Operating a Limited Liability Company

There are a variety of rights, duties and rules that you need to be aware of as they pertain to the transacting of business by an LLC

- **Powers of an LLC** – An LLC has the same powers as an individual that are needed to conduct business or affairs of the LLC.

- **Operating Agreement** – Members of an LLC may enter into an operating agreement to regulate the affairs of the company and the conduct of its business.

- **Liability of the LLC** – Liability for loss or injury caused by a wrongful act or omission by a member, agent, etc within the ordinary course of business of the LLC will attach to the LLC.

- **Member-Managed and Manager Managed LLCs** – An LLC is considered member-managed unless it is deemed manager-managed in the articles of organization. In a member-managed LLC, all of the LLC member have agency authority to enter into contracts and bind the LLC. In a manger-managed LLC however, only designated managers have agency authority to enter into contracts and bind the LLC and they also have equal rights in the management of the LLC business. Note, that the contracts must be in the ordinary course of business or ones in which the LLC has authorized.

- **Dissolution and Winding Up** – A member may disassociate him or herself from the LLC by withdrawing from both a term and an at-will LLC. Wrongful disassociation from an at-will LLC occurs if the power to withdraw is absent from the operating agreement. Once a member is disassociated, he or she may not participate in the management of the LLC. Also, the member's duties of loyalty and care to the LLC end upon disassociation. Rightful disassociation requires the LLC's purchase of the disassociated member's distributional interest.

- **Notice of Disassociation** – An LLC may give constructive notice of a disassociating member by filing a statement of disassociation with the secretary of state.

- **Restrictions on Contracting Authority** – The LLC's articles of organization or the operating agreement may contain provisions to restrict the members' and managers' authority to bind the LLC to contracts.

- **Division of LLC's Profits and Losses** – Generally speaking, a member has the right to an equal share in the LLC's profits. The members of the LLC may agree otherwise though.

- **Compensation and Reimbursement** – An LLC is required to reimburse members and manager for payments made on behalf of the LLC and to indemnify managers and members for liabilities incurred.

- **Members' Distributional Interest** – The ownership share of a member is called the distributional interest. A member's interest may be transferred.

- **Fiduciary Duties of Loyalty and Care Owed to LLC** – Regardless if a person is a member or a manager of a LLC, the duties of loyalty and care are fiduciary duties owed to the LLC. The duty of loyalty means that the parties must act honestly which means no usurping of LLC opportunities, no self-dealing, no competition with the LLC, and no making of secret profits. There is a limited duty of care owed to the LLC which means that a manger or member must not engage in a known violation of the law, grossly negligent conduct, reckless conduct, a known violation of the law, etc. Liability for ordinary negligence will be assessed against a member or manager of a LLC.

- **Duty of Good Faith and Fair Dealing** – A member of a LLC who is not a manger does **not** owe a duty of loyalty or care or duty of good faith and fair dealing.

- **Continuation of an LLC** –An LLC may be continued in two instances. The first situation is where the **members unanimously vote** prior to the expiration of the current LLC. The second situation is where there is **a simple majority vote** of the at-will LLC members.

- **Winding Up and LLC's Business** – Winding up is "the process of preserving and selling the assets of the LLC and distributing the money and property to creditors and members." Assets of the LLC must be used to pay the **creditors first**, followed by any surplus left over to be distributed to the members in equal shares unless the operating agreement provides otherwise. After dissolution and winding up, articles of termination may be filed with the secretary of state.

Refresh Your Memory

The following exercise will enable you to refresh your memory on the rules and principles presented to you in this chapter. Read each question twice and place your answer in the blanks provided. Review the chapter material for any question you miss or are unable to remember.

1. _____ law creates limited liability companies.

2. A limited liability company is a separate legal _____.

3. Owners of the LLC are usually called _____.

4. What is the main objective of the Uniform Limited Liability Act? _____

_____

5. What type of purpose may an LLC be organized for? _____

6. Where do most LLC's organize themselves? _____
_____

7. When selecting a name for a new LLC, what words must be contained in the name? _____
_____

8. Why is a LLC more favorable to use than and S Corporation? _____
_____

9. What is the main benefit of opting for an LLC instead of a general partnership for conducting business? _____

10. What is the primary advantage of an LLC as opposed to a limited partnership? _____
_____

11. What is an at-will Limited Liability Company? _____
_____

12. What form may a member's capital contribution be to an LLC? _____
_____

13. What document provides a member's ownership interest in an LLC? _____
_____

14. What is an alien liability company? _____

15. What is a statement of disassociation? _____

Critical Thought Exercise

Hal, Mike, Sue, and Gail are college friends and have talents in the areas of e-commerce, marketing, product development, and business management. The four meet with a fifth friend, Karl, who is a second–year law student. They explain to Karl their idea for an Internet business that sends local cuisine from participating restaurants and caterers to students and military personnel who are away from home and miss their favorite food. Karl draws up the articles of organization as his contribution to being brought in as a member of the new limited liability company, "GoodGrub.com, LLC." Karl then decides that he does not have the time or energy to devote to the business. Karl declines the offer to join the LLC. Sue files the articles of organization with the secretary of state, but there is no mention of whether GoodGrub.com will be a manager-managed or member managed LLC. It was originally anticipated that Hal would be the manager of the LLC but all four members begin to manage Good Grub.com and it is very successful. To keep up with demand and to expand their business into new markets, Hal and Gail secure a $200,000 loan from Jefferson Bank. When Hal is dividing up yearly profits, he gives each member 15% of the profits and invests the other 40% in the expansion efforts.

The resulting dispute over profits and quick expansion of the business leads to turmoil. GoodGrub.com is unable to meet its financial obligations. Mike, Sue, and Gail sue Hal for a full distribution of profits. Jefferson bank sues GoodGrub.com, Hal, Mike, Sue, and Gail to recover the $200,000 loan.

Did Hal have the authority to withhold distribution of profits? Who is liable to Jefferson Bank?

Answer. _____

_____

_____

_____

_____

_____

_____

_____

_____

_____

_____

_____

_____

_____

_____

_____

_____

_____

_____

Practice Quiz

True/False:

1. ___ Owners of an LLC are called members. [p 652]

2. ___ If a member agrees in the LLC's articles of organization to be personally liable for the debts of the LLC, this is sufficient to be binding. [p 653]

3. ___ LLC's are often utilized to conduct the business of accountants, doctors and lawyers. [p 655]

4. ___ The state of organization of the LLC is usually the one in which the LLC will be conducting most of its business. [p 655]

5. ___ The name chosen for a new LLC may be reserved with the secretary of state for a nonrenewable period. [p 656]

6. ___ The mere filing of the articles of organization by the secretary of state is not conclusive proof that the organizers have fulfilled all conditions required to create an LLC. [p 656]

7. ___ An LLC without a specified term of duration is called an at-will LLC. [p 657]

8. ___ A term LLC is another name for an at-will LLC. [p 657]

9. ___ A member's obligation to contribute capital is excused by a member's disability in performing. [p 658]

10. ___ An agent for service of process must be designated in the state of the LLC's organization. [p 658]

11. ___ A general partner who becomes a member of an LLC as a result of a conversion remains personally liable for the debts and obligations incurred by the partnership before the conversion is applicable. [p 659]

12. ___ Operating as an LLC provides an unlimited amount of liability. [p 659]

13. ___ An LLC may not own and transfer personal property. [p 660]

14. ___ The operating agreement of an LLC may be oral or written. [p 660]

15. ___ An LLC's managers are not personally liable for the debts, obligations, and liabilities of the LLC that they manage. [p 662]

16. ___ An LLC is a manager-managed LLC unless it is designated as a member-managed LLC in the articles of organization. [p 662]

17. ___ If Henrietta as a member of an LLC disassociates herself from a term LLC before the expiration of a specified term, her action will be considered wrongful. [p 667]

18. ___ One way for the Tiny Toy Company to give notice of a member's disassociation is by filing a statement of disassociation with the secretary of state. [p 667]

19. ___ A member does not have the right to an equal share in the LLC's profits. [p 663]

20. ___ A member's distributional interest may not be transferred in whole or in part. [p 664]

21. ___ A member of a member-managed LLC owes the duty of loyalty to the LLC. [p 664]

22. ___ Member-managed and a manager of a manager-managed LLC will not be liable to the LLC for committing acts deemed as ordinary negligence. [p 666]

23. ___ A non-manager member of a member-managed LLC owes a fiduciary duty of loyalty or care to the LLC or its other members. [p 666]

24. ___ Winding-up refers to the process of preserving and selling the assets of the LLC and then allocating the money and property to creditors and members. [p 668]

25. ___ All members, including those who have wrongfully disassociated from the LLC may participate in the winding-up of the LLC's business. [p 668]

Multiple Choice:

26. Which of the following are true with respect to limited liability companies? [p 652]
    a. Limited liability companies can sue and be sued.
    b. Limited liability companies may enter into as well as enforce contracts.
    c. Limited liability companies may be held civilly and criminally liable for violations of the law.
    d. All of the above.

27. Which of the following does not need to be placed in the articles of organization of an LLC? [p 656]
    a. The name and address of the initial agent for service of process
    b. The name and address of each organizer
    c. The name and address where the limited partnership will be primarily operating
    d. Whether the LLC is a term LLC and if so, the term specified

28. If an LLC is organized in Maine and conducts business in Vermont, what type of LLC is it in each of these states? [p 659]
    a. It is an alien liability company in Maine and a foreign limited liability company in Vermont.
    b. It is a foreign limited liability company in Maine and an alien liability company in Vermont.
    c. It is a domestic limited liability company in Maine and a foreign limited liability company in Vermont.
    d. It is a foreign limited liability company in Maine and a domestic limited liability company in Vermont.

29. Before Edward decides upon the way he wants to operate a business, he comes to you and asks about the powers that an LLC has. Which of the following best describes these powers? [p 660]
    a. An LLC has the power to waive the distribution of assets upon winding-up the LLC.
    b. An LLC has the power to own and transfer personal property.
    c. An LLC has the power to refuse reimbursement to members and managers for payments made on behalf of the LLC for business expenses.
    d. All of the above.

30. What does the duty of good faith and fair dealing impose upon a member of the member-managed LLC in discharging his or her duties to the LLC and its other members? [p 666]
    a. The members of a member-managed LLC are held to the express terms of the articles of organization and operating agreement and are required to act in "good faith" and deal fairly in all regards in achieving the objectives of the LLC.
    b. The members of a member-managed LLC are held to the express terms of the articles of organization, however, a member is not held to achieving the objectives of the LLC when discharging his or her duties to the LLC and its other members.
    c. The members must not usurp an LLC business opportunity.
    d. None of the above.

31. If a motorcycle dealer is operating as a term LLC and wants to continue the LLC, which of the following applies to the continuation of the motorcycle dealer's LLC at the expiration of its term? [p 668]
    a. The members of the motorcycle dealer's LLC may vote before the expiration date of the LLC for an additional specified term.
    b. The members must unanimously vote and file an amendment to the articles of organization with the secretary of state stating this fact.
    c. The LLC may continue as an at-will LLC utilizing a simple majority vote by the LLC members.
    d. All of the above.

32. If Brenda wants to operate an LLC under the name of Brenda's Beautiful Babes, which of the following must she be aware of? [p 656]
    a. She must be aware that LLC's have no restrictions on shareholders.
    b. She must be aware that the name she has chosen must contain the words limited liability company or an acceptable abbreviation as per the ULLCA code.
    c. She must be aware that the name she has chosen may not make a profit for her.
    d. She must be aware that trademark issues are not applicable to her.

33. Which of the following may Harry use as his capital contribution to the LLC that he is a member of? [p 658]
    a. Patents or other intangible property
    b. Promissory notes
    c. Services performed
    d. All of the above

34. If a general partnership wants to convert to operate as an LLC, which of the following requirements must be met? [p 659]
    a. There must be an agreement of conversion.
    b. The conversion must be approved by the parties or by a percentage of the owners.
    c. The articles of organization must be filed and state the prior form of business and its name before the conversion.
    d. All of the above.

35. Which of the following are similar to an LLC? [p 660]
    a. A limitada
    b. The sociedad de responsibilidades limitada
    c. A stock company
    d. All of the above

Short Answer:

36. How many persons may organize an LLC? [p 656] _____

37. What can a person who suffers loss due to any false statement made in the articles of organization or amendments recover? [p 657] _____

38. Why does an LLC need to designate an agent for service of process? [p 658] _____
    _____

39. The _____ is similar to a stock certificate issued by a corporation as it identifies a member's ownership interest in an LLC. [p 658]

40. What is a domestic LLC? [p 659] _____

41. What is a foreign limited liability company? [p 659] _____
_____

42. In a member-managed LLC, who has the authority to bind the LLC to contracts? [p 662]
_____

43. In a manager-managed LLC, who has the authority to bind the LLC to contracts? [p 662]
_____

44. When is an LLC bound to contracts? [p 662] _____
_____

45. What effect does a member's disassociation from an LLC have on the member with respect to the LLC? [p 667] _____
_____

46. How may an LLC terminate its existence after it has dissolved or wound-up its operations? [p 668]
_____

47. When does the existence of an LLC begin? [p 656] _____

48. How may the articles of organization be amended in an LLC? [p 657] _____
_____

49. What is an agreement of conversion? [p 659] _____
_____

50. A formal document that must be issued by the secretary of state of a state before a foreign LLC may conduct business in that state is a _____. [p 659]

Answers to Refresh Your Memory

1. State [p 652]
2. entity [p 652]
3. members [p 652]
4. The main objective is to establish a uniform comprehensive LLC law throughout the United States. [p 653]
5. An LLC may be organized for any lawful purpose according to ULLCA section 112(a). [p 655]
6. Most LLCs organize themselves in the state where the LLC will be conducting most of its business. [p 655]
7. The words "limited liability company" or "limited company" or an acceptable abbreviation under ULLCA Section 105(a) must be contained in the name. [p 656]

8. Because S Corporations have restrictions on who can be a stockholder and how many as well as the type of stock that can be held, whereas an LLC does not. [p 656]
9. Members of an LLC have limited liability as compared to a general partnership where the partners are personally liable for the obligations of the partnership. [p 656]
10. An LLC gives limited liability to all members regardless of their participation in the management of the business whereas a limited partnership requires that at least one general partner must be personally liable for the obligations of the partnership. [p 656]
11. An at-will LLC is one that has no specified term of duration. [p 657]
12. A member's capital contribution may take the form of personal or real property, money, tangible or intangible property, etc. (Answers will vary.) [p 658]
13. a certificate of interest [p 658]
14. It is an LLC that is organized in another country. [p 659]
15. It is a document that is filed with the secretary of state that gives constructive notice that a member has disassociated from an LLC. [p 667]

Critical Thought Exercise Model Answer

GoodGrub.com could be either a member-managed or manager-managed LLC depending upon the wishes of its members. An LLC is a member-manages LLC unless it is designated as a manager-manages LLC in its articles of organization. The articles of organization do no specify whether the members named any member as a manager. Therefore, GoodGrub.com will be deemed a member-managed LLC. As a member-managed LLC, all members have agency authority to bind the LLC to contractual obligations. An LLC is only bound to contracts that are in the ordinary course of business or that have been authorized. As members, Hal and Gail have full authority to enter into the loan agreement with Jefferson Bank. Their action will legally obligate GoodGrub.com to repay the loan from GoodGrub.com assets.

The failure of GoodGrub.com to observe company formalities does not create personal liability for the members for the debts of the LLC. There is not mention of how the four members were running the company, but nothing in the facts would allow Jefferson Bank to seek repayment of the loan from the individual members.

Though an LLC will usually have a written operating agreement that regulates the affairs of the company and how the members will run the company, the agreement may be oral. Though Hal was the anticipated manager of GoodGrub.com, the facts state that all four members assumed a management role and the articles of organization did not specify a manager-managed LLC. All four members have the right to determine how the profits will be divided or reinvested. Any matter relating to the business of the LLC is decided by a majority vote of the members. Hal is obligated to acquiesce in the desires of the other three members as to how the profits should be divided.

Answers to Practice Quiz

True/False:

1. True   Members are what the owners of the LLC are generally called.
2. True   Only if a member agrees to be in the articles of organization or other writing or if he or she personally guarantees repayment of the LLC's debts will the member be personally liable.
3. False   LLCs cannot conduct the practices of accountants, doctors and lawyers.

4. True   The state that an LLC conducts most of its business is usually its state of organization.

5. True   A nonrenewable period of usually 120 days is given for an LLC name reservation.

6. False   According to ULLCA Section 202, the filing of the articles of organization by the secretary of state is conclusive proof that the organizers have satisfied all conditions required to create an LLC.

7. True   An at-will LCC is one in which there is no specified term or duration.

8. False   These are two different terms with different meanings. An at-will LCC has no specified term or duration whereas a term LLC has a specified term or duration.

9. False   ULLCA Section 402 provides that a member's obligation to contribute capital is not excused by a member's disability in performing.

10. True   In order to receive service of process notice and demands in the event of litigation, etc., an agent for service of process must be designated.

11. True   ULLCA Section 902(g) provides for personal liability of a general partner who becomes a member of an LLC as a result of a conversion. He or she will remain personally liable for the obligations incurred by the partnership prior to the conversion.

12. False Operating as an LLC provides a limited liability shield.

13. False An LLC may own and transfer personal property.

14. True   Oral or written operating agreements and amendments are acceptable.

15. True   ULLCA Section 303(a) provides that the managers of LLCs are not personally liable for the debts, obligations and liabilities of the LLC that they manage.

16. False An LLC is a member managed LLC unless it is designated as a manger-managed LLC.

17. True   Disassociation from an LLC by a member prior to the expiration of the specified term is considered wrongful.

18. True   Constructive notice of a member's disassociation from an LLC is accomplished by filing a statement of disassociation with the secretary of state.

19. False A member does have the right to an equal share in the LLC's profits.

20. False A member's distributional interest may be transferred in whole or in part.

21. True   A duty of loyalty is owed by a member of a member-managed LLC. This duty refers to the fact that the member must act honestly in his or her dealings with the LLC.

22. True   Acts deemed to be ordinarily negligent in nature that are committed by member or managers will not subject them to liability to the LLC.

23. False A non-manager member does not owe a duty of loyalty or care to the LLC, and as such is treated equally to a shareholder in a corporation.

24. True   Winding-up is the method of preserving and selling the LLC's assets and then distributing the money and property to creditors and members.

25. False Members who have not wrongfully disassociated themselves from the LLC may take part in the winding-up of the LLC.

Multiple Choice:

26. D   Answer D is the correct answer as answers A, B, and C all are correct statements regarding limited liability companies.

27. C   Answer C is the correct answer as the name and address of where a limited partnership will be operating is not relevant to the information that must be contained in the articles of organization of an LLC. Answers A, B, and D all provide information that does need to be placed in the articles of organization and therefore are all incorrect answers as per the question.

28. D Answer D is the correct answer as the company is termed a domestic LLC in the state in which it is organized (here Maine) and is termed a foreign LLC in any state other than the one it was organized (here Vermont). Answers A, B, and C are all incorrect as none of them properly identify the type of LLC each is within any given answer.

29. B Answer B is the correct answer as it properly states one of the powers that Edward's LLC would have should he choose that form of business to operate under. Answer A is incorrect as it is a false statement. Answer C is incorrect as an LLC does not have the power to refuse reimbursement for expenses on behalf of the LLC. Answer D is incorrect based on the reasoning given above.

30. A Answer A is the correct answer as it correctly states ULLCA Section 409 (d)'s requirement of good faith and fair dealing and what it encompasses. Answer B is incorrect as members are held to achieve the objectives of the LLC as per the duty of good faith and fair dealing. Answer C is incorrect as the duty not to usurp an LLC opportunity would come under the duty of loyalty. Answer D is incorrect based on the reasoning given above.

31. D Answer D is the correct answer as answers A, B, and C all apply to the continuation of the motorcycle dealer's business upon expiration of its LLC term.

32. B Answer B is the correct answer as under ULLCA Section 105 (a), Brenda must make sure that the proper words or abbreviations are included in the name that she has chosen. Answer A is inapplicable to Brenda's operation and concern for the name she has chosen. Answer C is incorrect as it is not relevant in terms of the name she has chosen for her LLC. Answer D is incorrect as trademark issues are applicable and important to her, especially when choosing a name for an LLC.

33. D Answer D is the correct answer as answers A, B, and C all state acceptable forms of capital contributions that Harry utilize.

34. D Answer D is the correct answer as answers A, B, and C all state requirements that must be met in order for a general partnership to be able to convert to an LLC.

35. D Answer D is the correct answer as answer A, a limitada is a similar form of business in Latin America. Answer B, the sociedad de responsibilidades limitada is similar to an LLC in Spain and Answer C is similar to an LLC in England.

Short Answer:

36. One or more persons may organize an LLC.
37. damages
38. In order to receive service of process, notices and demands, an LLC must designate an agent for service of process.
39. certificate of interest
40. A domestic LLC is an LLC in the state in which it is organized.
41. A foreign limited liability company is an LLC in any state other than the one in which it is organized.
42. All members have agency authority to bind the LLC to contracts in a member-managed LLC.
43. Only the designated managers have authority to bind the LLC to contracts in a manger-managed LLC.
44. An LLC is bound to contract that are in the ordinary course of business or that the LLC has authorized.
45. A member's disassociation terminates that member's right to take part in the management of the LLC or act as an agent of the LLC, or conduct any of the LLC's business.
46. It may terminate its existence by filing articles of termination with the secretary of state.
47. It begins when the articles of organization are filed.

48. The articles may be amended by filing articles of amendment with the secretary of state.
49. It is a document that states the terms of converting an existing business to an LLC.
50. certificate of authority

Chapter 35
FORMATION AND OPERATION
OF CORPORATIONS

Chapter Overview

This chapter explores the formation as well as financing of corporations. Additionally, it explains the difference between publicly held and closely held corporations. Further it examines the various types of stock issues as well as the preferences associated with preferred stock. Other topics that are covered include promoters' liability, S Corporations, various issuances of stock as well as preferences that accompany preferred stock, rights of debenture and bondholders and the organization and operation of multinational corporations. Though a corporation is an unnatural being, it is one of the strongest as well as most important forms of business organization forms in business today.

Objectives

Upon completion of the exercises in this chapter, you should be able to:
1. Discuss the meaning and major characteristics of a corporation.
2. Discuss how a corporation is formed.
3. Differentiate between a publicly held corporation and a closely held corporation.
4. Discuss when promoters are liable on preincorporation contracts.
5. Explain what an S Corporation is and discuss its tax benefits.
6. Explain the meaning of common stock and differentiate between authorized, issued, treasury and outstanding shares.
7. Discuss the preferences that are connected with preferred stock.
8. Discuss debenture holder and bondholder rights.
9. Explain the organization and operation of multinational corporations.
10. Discuss the topic of Internet corporate alliances in China

Practical Application

You will have a better understanding of how a corporation is formed and operates. You will also be better aware of the benefits as well as concerns with operating a business as a corporation. Finally, you will have a better appreciation of the impact corporations have on business, the world and our every day lives.

Helpful Hints

Since there is a vast amount of information to learn in this chapter, organization is key to learning the various topics. A corporation is similar to raising a child, in that it starts out small without a name and eventually grows with the help of its family members into a fully functioning being. If you keep in mind that the different aspects of operating a business as a corporation all depend on one another, you will begin to see how the entire picture fits together. The most important key terms and concepts have been typed in bold in the Study Tips section that follows.

Study Tips

General Information

It is important to realize that corporations are **created according to the state laws** where it is incorporated. These laws are vital to a corporation's success as they regulate formation, operation and the dissolution of corporations. It is beneficial to learn the characteristics associated with a corporation as given below.

A corporation is considered to be **a legal person or legal entity** that is separate and distinct which include the following many interesting characteristics:

- A corporation is an artificial person that is state created.
- A corporation may bring a lawsuit or be sued.
- A corporation may enter into and enforce contracts, hold title to and transfer property.
- A corporation may be found civilly and criminally liable and may have fines assessed or its license revoked.

Other fascinating characteristics that may be attributed to corporations include:

- The shareholders have limited liability to the extent of their contributions.
- Corporate shares are freely transferable by the shareholder.
- Corporations have a perpetual existence if there is no duration stated in the corporation's articles of incorporation.
- Shareholders may voluntarily terminate the corporation's existence.
- Death, insanity or bankruptcy of a shareholder has no affect on a corporation's existence.
- The shareholders elect the directors who in turn appoint corporate officers to conduct the corporation's daily business.

Classifications of Corporations

Corporations are classified based on **location, purpose** or **owners**. Private corporations may be for **profit** or **non-profit**. Non-profit are created for charitable, educational, scientific or religious reasons. Note that non-profit corporations may not distribute any profit to their members, directors, or officers. **The Model Nonprofit Corporation Act** governs nonprofit corporations. **Government-owned** (or public) corporations are formed with a governmental or political reason in mind. **Private corporations** are created to carry on a privately owned business.

Publicly Held verses Closely Held Corporations

Publicly Held Corporations

These are generally large corporations with hundreds and even thousands of shareholders whose shares are **traded on organized securities markets**. Coca Cola and Bristol Myers are examples of publicly held corporations. An **important fact to know** about publicly held corporations is that the **shareholders seldom participate in** this type of corporation's **management**.

Closely Held Corporations

These are **relatively small** corporations whose **shares** are **held by** a few shareholders, mostly comprised of **family, friends and relatives**. An **important fact to know** and compare to publicly held corporations is that the **shareholders do participate in** a closely held corporation's **management**. Sometimes the shareholders attempt to prevent outsiders from becoming shareholders.

Professional Corporations

These are **formed by professionals**, such as dentists, doctors, lawyers, and accountants. The initials give a clue that it is a professional corporation. You may see the initials **P.C.** for Professional Corporation or **S.C.** for service corporation. This type of corporation is formed like other corporations and have many of the same traits. Its **professional members** are generally **not liable for** the **torts** committed **by** its **agents or employees**.

Domestic, Foreign and Alien Corporations

These terms should be somewhat familiar to you in light of the previous chapters, if you have had to study them.

Domestic corporation – A corporation in the state in which it was formed.

Foreign corporation – A corporation in any state or jurisdiction other than the one in which it was formed.

Alien corporation – A corporation that is incorporated in another country.

A corporation begins with promoter's activities

Now that you are familiar with the different types of corporations, let us study how a corporation begins. It begins with a promoter. **A promoter is an individual or individuals who organizes and starts the corporations**. Additionally he/she or they enter into contracts before the corporation is formed, find investors and sometimes subject themselves to liability as a result of all that is done.

Promoter's Liability

Promoters enter into contracts such as leases, sales contracts, property contracts, etc. Liability depends on the corporation keeping the following instances in mind.

- If the **corporation never** comes **into existence**, then the promoter is solely liable on the contract unless the third party exempts the promoter.
- If the **corporation is formed**, it is liable on the promoter's contract if it agrees to be bound to the contract as per a board of director's resolution.

- The promoter remains liable on the contract unless a **novation** is entered into. A novation is a three-party agreement wherein the corporation assumes the promoter's contract liability with the third party's consent. A novation has the effect of leaving the corporation solely liable on the promoter's contract.

Issues concerning incorporation procedures

An **incorporator** is the person or persons, partnerships or corporations that are responsible for the incorporation of the corporation.

The **articles of incorporation** also known as the corporate charter are the basic documents that must be file with and approved by the state in order to be officially incorporated. The **articles must contain:**
- the name of the corporation
- number of shares the corporation is authorized to issue
- address of the corporation's registered office
- agent for the corporation
- name and address of each incorporator
- duration, regulation of powers and corporate affairs
- the corporate purpose

Amendments to the articles of incorporation must be filed with the secretary of state after the shareholders approve them.

The organizers must:
- choose a name for the corporation
- the name must contain the words corporation, company, incorporated, limited or an abbreviation of any one of these
- the name cannot contain a word or phrase that states or implies that the corporation is organized for a purpose different than that in the articles of incorporation
- a trademark search should be conducted to make sure that the name is available for use
- a domain name search for purposes of Internet use should also be performed

A general purpose clause should be in a corporation's articles. Some corporations insert a limited purpose clause.

A registered agent must be identified along with a registered office. The purpose of the agent is to have someone be able to accept service of process on behalf of the corporation.

Corporate bylaws are a more exacting set of rules adopted by the board of directors. It contains provisions for managing the business and the affairs of the corporation. The bylaws may also be amended.

An organizational meeting of the first corporate directors must be held upon the filing of the articles of incorporation. The bylaws are adopted, officers elected and other business transacted at this initial meeting. Additional matters such as ratification of promoter's contracts, approving the form of stock certificates, etc are also discussed.

A corporate seal is a design affixed by a metal stamp containing the name and date of incorporation.

Corporate status begins when the articles of incorporation are filed. Upon the secretary of state's filing of the articles of incorporation, it is conclusive proof that the incorporators have satisfied all conditions of the incorporation. Note, failure to file the articles of incorporation is conclusive proof that the corporation does not exists.

S Corporation has been defined as those which elect to be taxed under Chapter S thereby avoiding double taxation. Note C corporations are all other corporations.

Financing the corporation – The sale of equity and debt securities is the most simple way to finance the operation of a corporation. **Equity securities** are stock which represent the ownership rights in the corporation in the form of **common stock** or **preferred stock**.

- **Common stock** - A kind of equity security that represents the residual value of the corporation. The creditors and preferred shareholders receive their interest first. There is no fixed maturity date. Common stockholders may vote on mergers, elect directors and receive dividends.
- **Par and no par value** – This refers to a value assigned to common shares. Par value is the lowest price that the shares may be issued. Most shares are no-par shares where no value is assigned to them.
- **Preferred stock** – This is a kind of equity security that is given preferences and rights over common stock. Holders of this type of stock are issued **preferred stock certificates**. The general rule with regard to voting is that this class of stock may not do so, unless there has been a merger or there has been a failure to pay a dividend.
- **Preferences of preferred stock include** dividend preference, liquidation preference, cumulative dividend right, cumulative preferred stock, the right to participate in profits participating preferred stock and convertible preferred stock.
- **Redeemable preferred stock (also termed callable preferred stock)** allows the corporation to buy back the preferred stock at a future date.

Authorized, Issued and Outstanding Shares

- **Authorized shares** are the number of shares that are provided for in the articles of incorporation.
- Authorized shares that have been sold are called **issued shares**.
- Repurchased shares are called **treasury shares**.
- Shares of stock that are in the shareholder hands are called **outstanding shares**.

Purchase of Stock and Corporate Debt

- **Consideration to be paid for shares** may include any property or benefit to the corporation as determined by the board of directors.
- **Stock Options and stock warrants** may be offered for sale. A **stock option** is generally given to **top-level managers**. It is the nontransferable right to purchase corporate stock at a set price during an option period. A **stock warrant** is an option that

is demonstrated by a **certificate** whereby the holder can exercise the warrant and buy the common stock at a state price during the warrant period. Warrants are both transferable and nontransferable.

- **Debt Securities** are securities that establish a debtor-creditor relationship in which the corporation borrows money from the investor to whom the debt security is issued.

- **Debenture** – A long-term unsecured debt instrument that is based on the corporation's general credit standing.

- **Bond** – A long-term debt security that is secured by some form of collateral.

- **Note** – A debt security with a maturity of five years or less.

- **Indenture agreement** – A contract between the corporation and the holder that contains the terms of the debt security.

Corporate Powers

A corporation has **express** and **implied powers**. Express powers may be found in the U.S. Constitution, state constitutions, federal statutes, articles of incorporations, bylaws and resolutions by the board of directors. Corporations may purchase, own, and lease real as well as personal property. They also may borrow money, incur liability, make donations and perform various other financial functions.

The **implied powers** of a corporation are those that **go beyond** the **express powers** and that allow a corporation to accomplish its corporate purpose.

Ultra Vires Act – This refers to a corporate act that goes beyond its express and implied powers. An injunction as well as damages and an action to enjoin the act or dissolve the corporation are the remedies available for the commission of an ultra vires act.

Dissolution and termination of corporations

There are three main ways to dissolve and terminate a corporation. One way is by **voluntary dissolution** which occurs upon recommendation of the board of directors and a majority vote of the shares entitled to vote. Another is by **administrative dissolution** which is an **involuntary dissolution** of a corporation that is order by the secretary of state to comply with certain procedures required by law. The third way is by **judicial dissolution** which occurs when a corporation is dissolved by a court proceeding initiated by the state.

Winding-Up, Liquidation and Termination

Winding-up and liquidation refers to the method which a dissolved corporation's assets are gathered, liquidated and then distributed to creditors, shareholders and other claimants.

Termination is the ending of the corporation that happens only after the winding-up of the corporate affairs, the liquidation of its assets and the distribution of the proceeds to the claimants.

Refresh Your Memory

The following exercise will enable you to refresh your memory on the rules and principles presented to you in this chapter. Read each question twice and place your answer in the blanks provided. Review the chapter material for any question you miss or are unable to remember.

1.   What is the only way that corporations may be created? _____
_____

2.   Define what a corporation is by elaborating on what it can or cannot do based upon its status as an artificial person. List at least two things. _____
_____

3.   Give three characteristics of a corporation. _____
_____

4.   What are the classifications of corporations based upon? _____
_____

5.   How are private corporations classified? _____
_____

6.   What are local government corporations called? _____

7.   What type of individuals form professional corporations? _____

8.   What do the initials P.C. stand for when identifying a corporation? _____
_____

9.   What do the initials S.C. stand for when identifying a corporation? _____
_____

10. What is a domestic corporation? _____
_____

11. What is a foreign corporation? _____
_____

12. What is an alien corporation? _____

13. What function does a novation have with respect to a corporate promoter? _____
_____

14. What are the articles of incorporation? _____
_____

15. What function do the corporate bylaws serve? _____
_____

Critical Thought Exercise

Gus Hill runs a successful sole proprietorship under the name "Custom Rides." Hill makes custom motorcycles that often sell for over $40,000 each. Hill decides to expand the business and make motorcycles that are more of a standard production. In order to do this, Hill decides to form a corporation and solicit investors through the sale of company stock. Hill contacts an attorney and requests that all of the paperwork necessary for the incorporation be prepared. To prepare for the expanded business that will be done by the corporation, Hill leases a large manufacturing building from LandCo for one year at $12,000 per month. Hill also signs a $175,000 contract with VanTolker Tool Co. for the purchase of equipment and an employment contract with Dirk Dodds, who was hired to serve as plant manager and chief financial officer. Dodds' contract stated that he understood that his $130,000 yearly salary would come from corporate income and that Hill had no ability to pay his salary.

The corporation is formed and all legal filings are complete. Custom Rides immediately begins making payments on all three contracts. Custom Rides, Inc. operates for eight months before poor sales make it unable to meet its financial obligations. Landco, Dodds, and VanTolker all file suit against Custom Rides, Inc. and Gus Hill personally to recover their contract damages.

Is Gus Hill personally liable for the contracts he signed on behalf of Custom Rides, Inc.?

Answer. _____

_____
_____
_____
_____
_____
_____
_____
_____
_____
_____
_____
_____
_____
_____
_____
_____
_____
_____
_____
_____
_____

Practice Quiz

True/False:

1. ___ There is a general federal corporation law governing the formation and operation of private corporations. [p 677]

2. ___ Government corporations are formed in order to meet a specific political or governmental purpose. [p 677]

3. ___ Members of professional corporations are liable for the torts committed by its employees or agents. [p 678]

4. ___ Most corporations are privately owned. [p 678]

5. ___ A domestic corporation is in the state in which it is incorporated. [p 679]

6. ___ An alien corporation is a corporation that is in all other states. [p 679]

7. ___ The articles of incorporation must be prepared and filed as well as approved by the state before the corporation can be officially incorporated. [p 681]

8. ___ If a domain name is already owned by another business, the new corporation may still use the name to conduct e-business over the Internet as there is not any protection for domain names. [p 683]

9. ___ A corporation may be formed for any unlawful purpose. [p 683]

10. ___ Corporations are governed by their bylaws and their articles of incorporation. [p 684]

11. ___ An organizational meeting of the initial corporate directors is optional. [p 686]

12. ___ One of the major disadvantages of doing business as an S corporation is that there is double taxation. [p 686]

13. ___ The secretary of state's filing of the articles of incorporation is conclusive proof of the nonexistence of the corporation. [p 686]

14. ___ Common stock is a type of equity security that is given certain preferences and rights over preferred stock. [p 687]

15. ___ One class of preferred stock may be given preferences over another class of preferred stock. [p 687]

16. ___ Redeemable preferred stock allows the corporation to buy back the preferred stock at some future date. [p 689]

17. ___ Treasury shares are the number of shares provided for in the articles of incorporation. [p 689]

18. ___ Stock options are nontransferable. [p 690]

19. ___ A debenture is a long-term debt security that is secured by some form of collateral. [p 690]

20. ___ Implied powers are those that are beyond express powers which allow a corporation to accomplish its corporate purpose. [p 691]

21. ___ In a voluntary dissolution, the liquidation is generally conducted by the board of directors. [p 693]

22. ___ Criminal penalties may be assessed against corporations. [p 675]

23. ___ The Revised Model Corporation Act helped to provide more consistent and substantial changes in carrying out the initial act of providing a uniform law for the regulation of corporations. [p 677]

24. ___ Nonprofit corporations may distribute their profit to their members, directors or officers. [p 677]

25. ___ Most shares that are issued by corporations are no par shares. [p 687]

Multiple Choice:

26. Which type of corporation is formed for educational, scientific, charitable or religious purposes? [p 677]
    a. An S Corporation
    b. A public corporation
    c. A nonprofit corporation
    d. A publicly held corporation

27. Which of the following is true with respect to professional corporations? [p 678]
    a. The abbreviation P.C. stands for professional corporation.
    b. Shareholders of professional corporations are called members.
    c. All states permit the incorporation of professional corporations.
    d. All of the above.

28. Which of the following is true with respect to the term par value? [p 687]
    a. Par share is a value given to common shares by the corporation.
    b. Par share is usually stated in the articles of corporation.
    c. Par is usually the lowest price at which shares may be issued by the corporation.
    d. All of the above.

29. Shares that are referred to as being authorized are [p 689]
    a. shares of stock that are in shareholder hands.
    b. the number of shares provided for in the articles of incorporation.
    c. shares of stock repurchased by the company itself.
    d. stock that permits the corporation to redeem the preferred stock at some future date.

30. An indenture agreement is [p 690]
    a. a contract between the corporation and the holder that contains the terms of a debt security.
    b. a debt security with a maturity of five years or less.

  c. a long term-debt security that is secured by some form of collateral.

  d. none of the above.

31. The term ultra vires refers to [p 692]

  a. powers beyond express powers that allow a corporation to accomplish its purpose.

  b. an act that is beyond a corporation's express or implied powers.

  c. powers given to the corporation by the U.S. Constitution.

  d. basic rights to perform acts and enter into contract as a physical person.

32. An administrative dissolution of a corporation is [p 692]

  a. a dissolution recommended by the board of directors.

  b. an involuntary dissolution by a judicial proceeding.

  c. an involuntary dissolution that is ordered by the secretary of state.

  d. all of the above.

33. The ending of a corporation that happens after the winding-up of the corporation's affairs is known as [p 693]

  a. winding-up.

  b. judicial dissolution.

  c. voluntary dissolution.

  d. termination.

34. A corporation in the state in which it is formed is a(n) [p 679]

  a. domestic corporation.

  b. alien corporation.

  c. foreign corporation.

  d. promoter's corporation.

35. Which of the following preferences might preferred stock have? [p 688]

  a. Cumulative dividend rights

  b. Liquidation preference

  c. A dividend preference

  d. All of the above

Short Answer:

36. A _____ is the person or persons who organize and start the corporation. [p 679]

37. Give three examples of promoters' contracts. [p 680] _____

38. List three things that the articles of incorporation must include. [p 681] _____

39. What must be filed upon approval of an amendment of the articles of incorporation by the shareholders? [p 681] _____

40. What is a registered agent? [p 683] _____

41. The internal management structure of the corporation is governed by the_____.
    [p 684]

42. The failure to file articles of incorporation is conclusive proof of _____
    _____. [p 686]

43. A meeting that must be held by the initial directors of the corporation after the articles of
    incorporation are filed is the _____. [p 686]

44. A person who owns common stock is a _____. [p 687]

45. What is a liquidation preference? [p 688] _____
    _____

46. Why is it a benefit to hold participating preferred stock? [p 688] _____
    _____

47. Repurchased shares are often called _____. [p 689]

48. A _____ is a debt security with a maturity of five years or less. [p 690]

49. Which country will have the largest Internet users in the world by the year 2005? [p 690]
    _____.

50. What is the solution to becoming involved in the Chinese Internet market? [p 690] _____
    _____

Answers to Refresh Your Memory

1. Corporations can only be created according to the laws of the state of incorporation.
    [p 675]
2. A corporation is a legal entity that may sue or be sued in its own name, and enter into and
    enforce contracts as well as hold title to and transfer property. (Answers will vary.) [p 675]
3. Three interesting characteristics of a corporation are that the corporate shares are freely
    transferable, shareholders generally have limited liability, and a corporation can exist in
    perpetual existence unless the duration is stated otherwise in the articles of incorporation.
    (Answers will vary.) [p 675]
4. The classifications of corporations are based upon their locations, owners or purpose.
    [p 677]
5. Private corporations are classified as profit or non-profit. [p 677]
6. Local government corporations are called municipal corporations. [p 677]
7. Professionals such as accountants, doctors and lawyers form professional corporations.
    [p 678]
8. The initials P.C. stand for professional corporation. [p 678]
9. The initials S.C. stand for service corporation. [p 678]
10. A domestic corporation is a corporation in the state in which it was formed. [p 679]
11. A foreign corporation is a corporation in any state or jurisdiction than the one in which it is
    formed. [p 679]
12. An alien corporation is a corporation that is incorporated in another country. [p 679]

13. A novation has the affect of relieving the promoter from liability and rendering the corporation solely liable on the promoter's contract. [p 680]
14. The articles of incorporation are the basic ruling documents of the corporation that must be drafted, filed, and approved by the secretary of state. [p 681]
15. The bylaws regulate the internal management structure of the corporation. [p 684]

Critical Thought Exercise Model Answer

Before a corporation is formed, a promoter takes the preliminary steps in organizing the corporation. The promoter makes contracts with investors and third parties. A promoter may purchase or lease property and goods with the intent that it will be sold or transferred to the corporation when the corporation is formed. The promoter may also enter into contracts with professionals whose services are needed. As a general rule, a promoter is held personally liable on preincorporation contracts. A promoter is not an agent when the corporation does not yet exist. If, however, the promoter secures a contracting party's agreement to only hold the corporation liable, then the promoter will not he held liable for any breach. Additionally, the promoter's personal liability continues even after the corporation is formed unless the promoter gains a release of liability from the third party. It does not matter whether or not the contract was made in the name of, or on behalf of, the named corporation.

Hill was acting as a promoter when he entered into contracts with LandCo, VanTolker, and Dodds. The fact that he signed the contracts as a purported agent of Custom Rides, Inc. will have no effect because the corporation had yet to be incorporated. The employment with Dodds is different than the others because Dodds agreed to seek payment only from Custom Rides, Inc., effectively releasing Hill from any personal liability. Even though Custom Rides, Inc. adopted the contracts executed with LandCo and VanTolker, the lack of a formal novation meant that Hill remained personally liable after incorporation. There could not have been a ratification of the preincorporation contracts because there was no principal to ratify the agent's acts at the time the contract was executed. Therefore, Hill will be personally liable to both LandCo and VanTolker.

Answers to Practice Quiz

True/False:

1. False   There is no federal corporation law that governs the formation and operation of private corporations.
2. True   Specific governmental or political purposes can be met by the formation of government-owned or public corporations.
3. False   Members usually are not liable for the tort committed by its employees or agents.
4. True   Privately owned corporations comprise a large sector of the corporate world.
5. True   A corporation in the state in which it was formed is a domestic corporation.
6. False   An alien corporation is one that is incorporated in another country.
7. True   Corporations may be formed only if the state's statutory formalities are adhered to.
8. False   If a domain name is already being used by another business or individual, the new corporation must choose another name as domain names are afforded intellectual property protection.
9. False   A corporation may not be formed for an unlawful purpose, but, it may be formed for a lawful purpose.
10. True   The bylaws and articles of corporation guide and govern corporations.

11. False   The initial organizational meeting of the corporation's directors is mandatory not optional.

12. False   Shareholders and corporations avoid double taxation by doing business as an S Corporation.

13. False   The filing of the articles of incorporation by the secretary of state is conclusive proof that all conditions of incorporation have been satisfied by the incorporators.

14. False   Common stock is an equity security that acts as the residual value of the corporation and is not given preferences and rights. The stock that gives preferences and rights over common stock is preferred stock.

15. True   Preferred stock may have preferences over various classes of preferred stock.

16. True   Stock that allows the corporation to purchase the preferred stock back at some future date is redeemable preferred stock.

17. False   Treasury shares are stock shares that are repurchased by the company itself.

18. True   Stock options that are granted are usually nontransferable.

19. False   A long-term unsecured debt instrument that is based on the corporation's general credit standing is a debenture. The definition in the question describes a bond.

20. True   Powers beyond express powers that enable a corporation to complete its corporate purpose are implied powers.

21. True   The board of directors usually carries out the liquidation in a voluntary dissolution.

22. True   Criminal penalties may be assessed against corporations in the form of a fine or loss of license, or other sanction.

23. True   Substantial changes in carrying out the initial Model Business Corporation Act were enacted in the Revised Model Business Corporation Act.

24. False   Nonprofit corporations are prohibited from distributing any profit that they make to their members, directors or officers.

25. True   No par shares have no assigned par value and are the most often issued shares by a corporation.

Multiple Choice:

26. C.   Answer C is the correct answer as nonprofit corporations are formed for educational, scientific or religious purposes. Answer A is incorrect as the reasons given for formation are not the reasons individuals would form an S Corporation. S Corporations are formed for a variety of reasons, with a primary one being to avoid double taxation. Answer B is incorrect as public corporations are formed to meet specific governmental or political purposes. Answer D is incorrect as a publicly held Corporation is one with many shareholders whose securities are often traded on a national stock exchange.

27. D.   Answer D is the correct answer as answers A, B, and C are all true statements about professional corporations.

28. D.   Answer D is the correct answer as answers A, B, and C all state true facts regarding the term par value.

29. B.   Answer B is the correct answer as authorized shares are the number of shares provided for in the articles of incorporation. Answer A is incorrect as this answer gives the definition for outstanding shares, not authorized shares. Answer C is incorrect as this provides the definition for treasure shares. Answer D is incorrect as it gives the definition for redeemable stock.

30. A.   Answer A is the correct answer as an agreement between the corporation and the holder that sets forth the terms of the debt security is an indenture agreement. Answer B is incorrect as this gives the definition of a note. Answer C is incorrect as this gives the definition of a bond. Answer D is incorrect based on the reasoning

given above.

31. B. Answer B is the correct answer in that an act that is beyond a corporation's express or implied powers is an ultra vires act. Answer A is incorrect as this gives the definition of implied powers. Answer C and D are incorrect statements of law and are therefore not the right answers.

32. C. Answer C is the correct answer as an involuntary dissolution ordered by the secretary of state is an administrative dissolution. Answer A is incorrect as dissolutions that are recommended by the board of directors are usually voluntary in nature. Answer B is incorrect as involuntary dissolutions by judicial proceedings are judicial dissolutions. Answer D is incorrect based on the reasons given above.

33. D. Answer D is the correct answer as termination with respect to corporations is the ending that results from winding-up the corporation's affairs. Answer A is incorrect as winding-up involves liquidating the corporate assets and it precedes termination. Answer B is incorrect as a judicial dissolution is involuntary and initiated by a judicial proceeding. Answer C is incorrect as a voluntary dissolution is a step toward ending a corporation, but is not the ending itself of the corporation.

34. A. Answer A is the correct answer as a domestic corporation is one in the state in which it is formed. Answer B is incorrect as an alien corporation is one that is incorporated in another country. Answer C is incorrect as a foreign corporation is one in any state or jurisdiction other than the one in which it was formed. Answer D is incorrect as there is no such thing as a promoter's corporation.

35. D. Answer D is the correct answer as answers A, B, and C all list preferences that preferred stock might have.

Short Answer

36. promoter
37. leases, sales contracts and employment contracts.
38. name of the corporation, the number of shares the corporation is authorized to issue and the name and address of each incorporator (answers will vary)
39. The articles of amendment must be filed.
40. An individual or corporation that has the authority to accept service of process on behalf of the corporation.
41. bylaws
42. nonexistence of the corporation
43. organizational meeting
44. common stockholder
45. The right to be paid prior to common stockholders if the corporation is dissolved and liquidated is a liquidation preference.
46. Because it allows the stockholder to participate in the profits of the corporation.
47. treasury shares
48. note
49. China
50. The solution appears to be a large strategic alliance concerning a Chinese-language Web portal supported by investments by U.S. Internet companies.

Chapter 36
DIRECTORS, OFFICERS AND SHAREHOLDERS

Chapter Overview

The previous chapter explored the formation as well as various types of corporations and the characteristics associated with corporations. In this chapter, the rights, duties and liabilities of corporate shareholders, officers and directors are examined, with an emphasis on the differences in the roles and responsibilities of each.

Objectives

Upon completion of the exercises in this chapter, you should be able to:
1. Discuss the function of shareholder, directors, and officers in managing the affairs of the corporation.
2. Explain how shareholders' and directors' meetings are called as well as conducted.
3. Differentiate between straight and cumulative voting for directors.
4. Discuss the agency authority of officers to enter into contracts on behalf of the corporation.
5. Discuss a director's and officer's duty of care and the business judgment rule.
6. Compare how the differences between the management of close corporations and publicly held corporations.
7. Explain the director's duty of loyalty and how it can be breached.
8. Explain a directors' and officers' liability insurance and corporate indemnification.
9. Explain what is meant by the corporate veil or alter ego doctrine.
10. Discuss how electronic communications is now being recognized in Delaware's Corporation Code.

Practical Application

Whether you are a shareholder, a director, officer or a corporate observer, this chapter will provide you with practical information regarding the internal management structure and its direct impact on one another. This knowledge will provide you with the ability to make educated decisions as may pertain to the basic decisions associated with the management of corporations.

Helpful Hints

Just as it takes a village to raise a child, it takes an entire management structure to mold and develop a corporation. If you keep this analogy in mind as you study the key players in its infrastructure, your learning of this area will be rewarding and insightful. Additionally, if you view the shareholders, directors and officers like a pyramid with each having different responsibilities that impact the other tiers, you will begin to better understand their importance in keeping the pyramid in tact in order to avoid corporate collapse. The most important key terms and concepts have been typed in bold in the Study Tips section that follows.

Study Tips

Shareholders

The shareholders hold a significant position in the corporate pyramid, as they are the **owners** of the corporation. They also **vote** on the directors and other important actions to be taken by the corporation, but cannot bind the corporation to any contract.

Shareholder Meetings

Annual shareholder meetings are held to take actions such as the election of director and independent auditors. Note: there are *special shareholder meetings* that may be conducted to evaluate and vote on significant or emergency issues. Examples include potential mergers, or amendments to the articles of incorporation. Attendance at a shareholder meeting may be by a **proxy,** which is another person who acts as an agent of the shareholder. Proxies must be in **writing** and they are **valid** for **11 months.**

As long as a majority of the shares entitled to vote are present, there will be a *quorum* to hold the meeting. An affirmative vote for elections other than the board of directors is required. However, the election of the directors may be by **straight voting** wherein each shareholder votes the number of shares he or she owns on candidates for the directors positions that are open. The method of **cumulative voting** may also be used in voting for the directors. This method entails a shareholder accumulating all of his or her votes and voting them all for one candidate or dividing his or her votes among many candidates. In essence, a shareholder may multiply the number of shares he or she owns by the number of directors to be elected and then vote the entire amount on a single candidate or apportion the product among contenders. This method is good for minority shareholders. *Supramajority voting requirements* can be made thereby requiring a greater than majority of shares to comprise a quorum or the shareholders' vote.

Voting Agreements – The two types of voting agreements to be concerned with are the voting trust and shareholder voting agreements. In a **voting trust** situation, the shareholders transfer their stock certificates to a trustee who is given the authority to vote the shares. In a **shareholder voting agreement**, two or more shareholders agree on how they will vote their shares.

Shareholder's Rights

Right to Transfer Shares

Shareholders have the right to transfer their shares **under Article 8 of the Uniform**

Commercial Code. There are certain restrictions however that the shareholders must be aware of. They concern the right of first refusal and what is known as a buy-and sell agreement. When shareholders do not want certain people to become owners of the corporation, they will often enter into an agreement with another shareholder to prevent new ownership.

The right of first refusal is an agreement that shareholders enter into which grants one another the right of first refusal to purchase shares they are going to sell. Compare this to a buy-and sell agreement whereby the shareholders are required to sell their shares to the other shareholders or the corporation at a price set in the agreement.

Shareholders also have preemptive rights

Preemptive rights give existing shareholders the option of subscribing to new shares being issued in proportion to their current ownership interest. These rights are usually found in the articles of incorporation.

Right to Receive Information and Inspect Books and Records

Shareholders have a right to be up to date about the financial affairs of the corporation and must be given an **annual financial statement**. Further, shareholders have an absolute **right to inspect** the articles of incorporation, bylaws, minutes, and so on within the past three years.

Shareholder Lawsuits

There are two types of lawsuits a shareholder may bring. The first is a **direct lawsuit** against the corporation. The second is a **derivative lawsuit** wherein the directors are empowered to bring an action on behalf of the corporation. If the corporation does not bring a lawsuit, the shareholders have the right to bring it on the corporation's behalf.

Directors

The board of directors makes policy decisions as well as employ the major officers for the corporation. They also make suggestions concerning actions implemented by the shareholders.

Selection of Directors

There are two types of directors, an **inside director** and an **outside director**. An inside director is a member of the board of directors who is also an officer of the corporation. An outside director is a member of the board of directors who is not an officer of the corporation. The **number of directors** is stated in the articles of incorporation, but may be **as little as only one** individual. A **director's term** expires at the next annual shareholders' meeting following his or her election unless the terms are **staggered** so that only a part of the board of directors is up for election each year.

Vacancies and Removal of Directors

Death, illness and resignation are some of the reasons vacancies occur on the board of directors. The vacant position may be filled by the shareholders or the balance of directors. Also, directors may be removed, but only **for cause** and by a vote of the holders of a majority of the shares entitled to vote at the election.

Quorum and Voting Requirement

A quorum is the number of directors required to hold a board of directors' meeting or conduct business of the board.

Committees created by the Board of Directors

Directors may create committees of the board and give certain powers to those committees. Examples of these committees include the executive committee, audit committee, nominating committee, compensation committee, investment committee, and litigation committee.

The **board may not** delegate the power to declare dividends, initiate actions the require shareholders' approval, appoint members to fill openings on the board, amend the bylaws, approve a merger plan that does not require shareholder approval or authorize the issuance of shares.

Compensation and Inspection

Directors may set their own compensation fee. Additionally, directors are required to have access to the books, records, facilities, premises as well as any other information concerning the corporation's formation.

Directors may pay dividends

Dividends are a distribution of profits of the corporation to the shareholders. Directors have the **discretionary power** to pay dividends. If a dividend is to be paid, a date is set prior to the actual payment date called the **record date**. Corporations may use extra shares of stock as a dividend. Stock dividends are paid in proportion to the ownership interests of shareholders.

Officers

Officers have the responsibility of managing the day-to-day operation of the corporation. They also act as agents and hire other officers and employees. The following officers exist in many corporations: president, one or more vice-presidents, a secretary and a treasurer.

Agency Authority of Officers

Officers have the express, implied and apparent authority to bind the corporation to contract.

Removal of Officers

The board of directors may remove any officer unless there is an employment contract to the contrary.

Liability of Corporate Directors and Officers

Directors and officers owe the **fiduciary duties of obedience, care and loyalty.** A director or officer must not intentionally or negligently act outside of their authority. If he or she does, he or she is personally responsible for any resulting damages caused to the corporation or its shareholders. The **duty of due** care involves an officer or directors obligation to discharge his or her duties in good faith and with the care of an ordinary prudent person in a like position would use, and in a manner that is in the best interests of the corporation. Examples of breaches a director or officer will be held personally liable for include the failure to make a reasonable investigation in a corporate matter, or the failure to regularly attend board meetings, or properly supervise a subordinate and failure to keep sufficiently informed of corporate affairs.

The Business Judgment Rule

A director or officer's duty of care is measured as of the time that he or she makes a decision. Honest mistakes of judgment do not render the director or officer liable.

Reliance on Others

A director is not liable if information he or she relied upon is false, misleading or unreliable unless the director or officer has knowledge that would cause his or her reliance to be unwarranted.

Dissent to Director's Action

If an individual director dissents to an action taken by a majority of the board of directors, he or she must either resign or register his or her dissent by placing it in the meeting's minutes, filing a written dissent to the secretary or forwarding his or her dissent by registered mail to the secretary immediately following the meeting.

Duty of Loyalty

Officers and directors are to place their personal interest below that of the corporation and its shareholders. Breaches of this duty include the usurping of a corporate opportunity, self-dealing, competing with the corporation and disgorgement of secret profits.

Liability for Crimes

Officers, directors, employees and agents are personally liable for crimes that are committed while acting on behalf of the corporation. Punishment includes fines and imprisonment.

Liability of Shareholders

Shareholders have limited liability and are liable for the debts as well as obligations of the corporation only to the extent of their capital contribution. Note that a controlling shareholder has a fiduciary duty to monitor shareholders.

Corporate Entity Disregarded

If a corporation is used for improper purposes by a shareholder or many shareholders, the shareholder(s) may be personally liable for the obligations and debts of the corporation. When this is enforced, this is known as piercing the corporate veil. Piercing the veil occurs when a corporation has not been formed with sufficient capital, commingling of personal with corporate funds has transpired or there's been a failure to maintain books and hold meetings.

Refresh Your Memory

The following exercise will enable you to refresh your memory on the rules and principles presented to you in this chapter. Read each question twice and place your answer in the blanks provided. Review the chapter material for any question you miss or are unable to remember.

1. Who is responsible for making policy decisions and employing officers? _____

2. A written document that a shareholder signs authorizing another person to vote his or her shares at the shareholders' meetings in the event of a shareholder's absence is a _____.

3. An exact date in the corporate bylaws that decides whether a shareholder may vote at a shareholder meeting is a _____.

4. If a majority of shares entitled to vote are represented at a meeting either by proxy or in person, there is a _____ to hold the meeting.

5. What is a voting trust? _____

6. Which article of the U.C.C. governs the transfer of securities? _____

7. What rights give existing shareholders the option of subscribing to new shares being issued in proportion to their current ownership interest? _____

8. What right do shareholders have with respect to the books and records of the corporation?
_____

9. What are the two types of lawsuits that shareholders may bring against the corporation? ____
_____

10. What is the function does the board of directors? _____
_____

11. A member of the board of directors who is also an officer of the corporation is an _____
_____

12. A meeting brought by the board of directors to discuss new shares, merger proposals, hostile

takeover attempts is a _____ meeting.

13. The distribution of profits of the corporation to shareholders is known as a _____.

14. What is the date called when a corporation declares a dividend, and sets a date a few weeks before the actual payment called? _____

15. What is the main responsibility of the corporations' officers? _____
_____

Critical Thought Exercise

Ned West was the sole shareholder and president of Westward Co., a corporation that ran truck stops along interstate highways. The corporation did not have its own bank accounts. All business was conducted through West's personal account. All supplies, payroll, debts, and purchases were handled through this one checking account. West also paid all of his personal expenses out of this account. All receipts from the truck stops were deposited into the same account. While the corporation was in business, no directors meetings were ever held. All decisions for the corporation were made solely by West.

For a four-year period, Westward Co. accumulated $187,455 in federal tax liabilities. The government is now seeking to collect the overdue tax payments directly from West. West argues that the government is ignoring his corporate entity.

Can the government pierce the corporate veil in this case and force West to incur personal liability for the taxes owed by Westward Co.?

Answer. _____
_____
_____
_____
_____
_____
_____
_____
_____
_____
_____
_____
_____
_____

Practice Quiz

True/False:

1. ____ The rights of shareholders, directors and officers all differ from one another. [p 699]

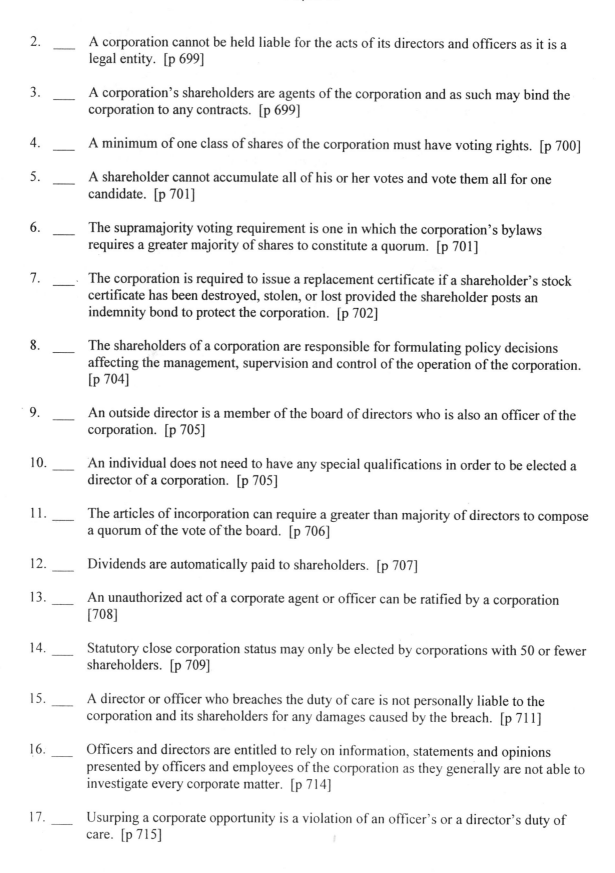

2. ____ A corporation cannot be held liable for the acts of its directors and officers as it is a legal entity. [p 699]

3. ____ A corporation's shareholders are agents of the corporation and as such may bind the corporation to any contracts. [p 699]

4. ____ A minimum of one class of shares of the corporation must have voting rights. [p 700]

5. ____ A shareholder cannot accumulate all of his or her votes and vote them all for one candidate. [p 701]

6. ____ The supramajority voting requirement is one in which the corporation's bylaws requires a greater majority of shares to constitute a quorum. [p 701]

7. ____ The corporation is required to issue a replacement certificate if a shareholder's stock certificate has been destroyed, stolen, or lost provided the shareholder posts an indemnity bond to protect the corporation. [p 702]

8. ____ The shareholders of a corporation are responsible for formulating policy decisions affecting the management, supervision and control of the operation of the corporation. [p 704]

9. ____ An outside director is a member of the board of directors who is also an officer of the corporation. [p 705]

10. ____ An individual does not need to have any special qualifications in order to be elected a director of a corporation. [p 705]

11. ____ The articles of incorporation can require a greater than majority of directors to compose a quorum of the vote of the board. [p 706]

12. ____ Dividends are automatically paid to shareholders. [p 707]

13. ____ An unauthorized act of a corporate agent or officer can be ratified by a corporation [708]

14. ____ Statutory close corporation status may only be elected by corporations with 50 or fewer shareholders. [p 709]

15. ____ A director or officer who breaches the duty of care is not personally liable to the corporation and its shareholders for any damages caused by the breach. [p 711]

16. ____ Officers and directors are entitled to rely on information, statements and opinions presented by officers and employees of the corporation as they generally are not able to investigate every corporate matter. [p 714]

17. ____ Usurping a corporate opportunity is a violation of an officer's or a director's duty of care. [p 715]

18. ___ Officers and directors cannot engage in activities that compete with the corporation unless full disclosure is made and a majority of the disinterested directors or shareholders endorse the activity. [p 716]

19. ___ Shareholders of a corporation have unlimited liability. [p 717]

20. ___ The term piercing the corporate veil refers to the improper use of the corporation by its shareholders. [p 717]

21. ___ Officers and directors may not take advantage of a corporate activity that has not been fully disclosed. [p 716]

22. ___ Many states require a controlling shareholder to monitor shareholders based on his or her fiduciary duty. [p 718]

23. ___ Straight voting refers to when a shareholder gathers all of his or her votes and then votes them all for one candidate or divides them among several candidates. [p 700]

24. ___ Cumulative voting refers to when each shareholder votes the number of shares he or she owns on candidates for each of the positions that are open. [p 700]

25. ___ It is mandatory that the corporation gives written notice of the day, place and time of both annual and special meetings. [p 700]

Multiple Choice:

26. Which of the following is a true statement concerning a supramajority voting requirement? [p 701]
    a. These votes are required to approve mergers.
    b. An amendment must be adopted by the number of shares of the proposed increase.
    c. The articles of incorporation or the bylaws of a corporation can mandate a greater than majority of shares to comprise a quorum or the vote of the shareholders.
    d. All of the above.

27. Which of the following would be a reason for shareholders of the Candy Corporation to bring a direct lawsuit against the corporation? [p 703]
    a. To enforce preemptive rights.
    b. To enforce the right to vote.
    c. To compel payment of declared but unpaid dividends.
    d. All of the above.

28. Which of the following applies to a derivative action brought by a shareholder? [p 703]
    a. A shareholder may bring a derivative lawsuit to compel dissolution of the corporation.
    b. A shareholder may bring a derivative lawsuit to enjoin the corporation from committing an ultra vires act.
    c. Any award from a successful derivative lawsuit goes to the treasury.
    d. If a shareholder is successful in a derivative action against the corporation, the award belongs to that shareholder.

29. Regular meetings of the board of directors [p 706]

a. are called for issuing new shares.
b. are held without notice.
c. are convened for considering proposals to merge with other corporations.
d. are called to adopt maneuvers to defend hostile takeover attempts.

30. Alice and Harvey are on the Board of Directors of the Whizo Corporation. They want to create committees of the board and delegate certain powers to those committees. Which of the following would be the type of committee that Alice and Harvey may create? [p 706]
a. The Compensation Committee
b. The Regular Meeting Committee
c. The Crime Committee
d. None of the above

31. What officers do most corporations have? [p 708]
a. President, vice-president, coordinator
b. President, one or more vice presidents, secretary and treasurer
c. President, vice-president, human resource director, treasurer
d. President, vice-president, secretary and an agent

32. Which of the following expresses the duties that the officers and directors owe to the corporation and its shareholders? [p 710]
a. Duty of obedience, duty to spend, duty of care
b. Duty of loyalty, duty of care, duty to account properly
c. Duty of loyalty, duty of care, duty of obedience
d. Duty of loyalty, duty to make decisions, fiduciary duty

33. Under the business judgment rule, which choice states what the directors or officers are not liable for? [p 711]
a. Usurping a corporate opportunity
b. Self-dealing
c. Honest mistakes of judgment
d. Lending trade secrets to corporate competitors

34. If Frank Smith, a director of the Silly Slime Corporation has usurped a corporate opportunity for himself, what has he done? [p 715]
a. Frank has stolen a corporate opportunity for himself.
b. Frank has purchased a corporate opportunity for himself.
c. Frank has borrowed a corporate opportunity for himself.
d. Frank has transferred a corporate opportunity to himself.

35. Which situation best describes when the court will pierce the corporate veil? [p 717]
a. When the corporation has been formed with thin capitalization.
b. When there has been a commingling of personal and corporate assets.
c. When there has been a failure to maintain corporate books and records.
d. All of the above.

Short Answer:

36. _____ are held to elect directors. [p 699]

37. What types of matters may be discussed at special meetings of the corporation? [p.700]

38. What is the right of first refusal as it pertains to stock? [p 702] _____

39. What is a buy-and-sell agreement? [p 702] _____

40. What types of information are contained in the annual financial statement that is provided to a corporation's shareholders? [p 703] _____

41. Actions that require the shareholders' approval are initiated when the board of directors adopts a _____ that approves the transaction and recommends it to the shareholders for their vote. [p 704]

42. In order to reflect technology, what does the Revised Model Corporations Act provide with respect to directors' meetings? [p 706] _____

43. What type of liability are directors who vote for illegal dividends subject to? [p 707] _____

44. What is a stock dividend? [p 707] _____

45. What type of authority do officers have to bind a corporation to contracts? [p 708] _____

46. Who can remove an officer of a corporation from his or her capacity? [p 709] _____

47. Define the meaning of fiduciary duty. [p 710] _____

48. Tell what D &O insurance is and what its main purpose is. [p 711] _____

49. What does indemnification mean as it applies to the corporation? [p 711] _____

50. When an individual director opposes the action taken by the majority of the board of directors, this is known as [p 714] _____ .

Answers to Refresh Your Memory

1. The directors are responsible. [p 699]
2. proxy [p 700]

3. record date [p 700]
4. quorum [p 700]
5. It is a situation where the shareholders transfer their stock certificates to a trustee who is authorized to vote their shares. [p 702]
6. Article 8 [p 702]
7. preemptive rights [p 702]
8. Shareholders have the right of inspection. [p 703]
9. direct lawsuits and derivative lawsuits [p 703]
10. The board of directors is responsible for formulating the policy decisions that affect the management and control of the operation of the corporation. [p 704]
11. inside director [p 705]
12. special [p 706]
13. dividend [p 707]
14. It is called the record date. [p 707]
15. The main responsibility of the corporations' officers is to manage the day-to-day operations of the corporation. [p 708]

Critical Thought Exercise Model Answer

In corporate law, if personal and company interests are commingled to the extent that the corporation has no separate identity, a court may "pierce the corporate veil" and expose the shareholders to personal liability. West mixed all aspects of his personal business with corporate business. All purchases and payroll checks were made from his personal account. There is no way to separate corporate receipts from West's personal funds. In order to prevent a creditor from "piercing the corporate veil" a sole stockholder needs to careful to preserve the corporate identity. Maintaining separate accounts and detailed records are imperative if corporate identity is to be preserved. West did not attempt to preserve the identity of Westward Co.

Another key factor that favors the government in this case is the failure of Westward Co to hold directors meetings. The failure of the sole shareholder to comply with statutory corporate formalities demonstrates that the corporate form may be a sham. West never consulted with his directors and made all decisions for Westward Co. by himself. When the corporate business is treated in such a careless and flippant manner, the corporation and the shareholder in control are no longer separate entities, requiring the sole shareholder to assume personal liability to creditors of the corporation. West totally ignored the corporate identity and now the government will be allowed to "pierce the corporate veil." West will be personally liable for the corporations tax debt.

Answers to Practice Quiz

True/False:

1. True   Shareholders, directors and officers all have different rights in managing the corporation.
2. False   A corporation can be held liable for the acts of its directors and officers even though it is a legal entity.
3. False   Shareholders are not agent of the corporation and cannot bind it to any contracts.
4. True   A minimum of one class of shares of the corporation must have voting rights.
5. False   A shareholder can gather all of his or her votes and vote them all for one candidate.

6. True   A requirement that a greater than majority of shares constitutes a quorum of the vote of shareholders is a supramajority voting requirement.

7. True   A lost, stolen or destroyed corporate stock certificate must be replaced by the corporate issuance of a replacement certificate.

8. False   The board of directors, not the shareholders, are responsible for formulating policy decisions affecting management, supervision and the operation of the corporation.

9. False   An outside director is a person who sits on the corporation's board of directors but is not an officer of the corporation.

10. True   A person need not have any special qualifications to be elected as a director of a corporation.

11. True   A greater majority of directors can be required in order to constitute a quorum or the vote of the board of directors.

12. False   Shareholders are not automatically paid dividends. Dividends are paid at the discretion of the board of directors.

13. True   A corporation can ratify an unauthorized act by a corporate agent or officer.

14. True   Only corporations with 50 or fewer shareholders may elect the status of a statutory close corporation.

15. False   An officer or director who breaches the duty of care is personally liable to the corporation and its shareholders for any damages caused by the breach.

16. True   Since officers and directors are not able to personally investigate every matter presented to them, they are entitled to rely on information, statements and opinions given to them by officers, employees, lawyers, committees and so on.

17. False   Usurping a corporate opportunity is a breach of the duty of loyalty not a breach of the duty of care.

18. True   Directors and officers cannot encage in activities that compete with the corporation unless full disclosure of the activity is made and there is director or shareholder approval.

19. False   Shareholders have limited liability in that they are liable for debts and obligations to the extent of their capital contribution.

20. True   Piercing the corporate veil refers to the improper use of the corporation.

21. True   In order for an officer or director to take advantage of a corporate activity, there must be full disclosure of that activity.

22. True   Some states require that a controlling shareholder owes a fiduciary duty to monitor shareholders.

23. False   Straight voting is where each shareholder votes the number of shares he or she owns on candidates for each of the positions open.

24. False   Cumulative voting refers to the situation where a shareholder can gather all of his or her votes and vote them all for one candidate or split them among several candidates.

25. True   The corporation is required to give written notice of the day, place and time of annual and special meetings to the shareholders.

Multiple Choice:

26. D   Answer D is the correct answer as answers A, B, and C are all true statements concerning a supramajority voting requirement.

27. D   Answer D is the correct answer as enforcing preemptive rights, enforcing the right to vote and attempting to compel payment of declared but unpaid dividends are all reasons as expressed in answers A, B, and C for the shareholders of the Candy

Corporation to bring a direct lawsuit against the corporation.

28. C Answer C is the correct answer as it is the only true statement that applies to a derivative action brought by a shareholder. Answers A, B, and D are all incorrect as they are all statements that apply to a direct lawsuit, not a derivative lawsuit.

29. B Answer B is the correct answer as it correctly states how regular meetings are held. Answers A, C and D are all incorrect as they refer to special meetings.

30. A Answer A is the correct answer as Alice and Harvey as members of the Board of Directors may create a Compensation Committee provided all of the other board Members if any ratify it. A compensation committee approves management Compensation, including bonuses, salaries, stock plans, fringe benefits, etc. Answers B, and C are incorrect as these type of committees that are usually created by Board of Directors. Answer D is incorrect based on the reasons given above.

31. B Answer B is correct as it properly states the officers that most corporations have. Answer A is incorrect as a coordinator is not an officer. Answer C is incorrect as the human resource director is a member of personnel and not an officer. Answer D is incorrect as an agent is not usually an officer of a corporation.

32. C Answer C is the correct answer as it properly states the duties that officers and directors owe to the corporation and its shareholders. Answer A is incorrect as the officers and directors do not owe a duty to spend. Answer B is incorrect as the officers and directors do not owe a duty to account. Answer D is incorrect as the duty to make decisions may be implied, however, this is too broad of a statement to encompass it in the directors' and officers' duties.

33. C Answer C is correct as the business judgment rule states that the directors or officers are not liable for honest mistakes in judgment. Answers A, B and D are all incorrect as they all are activities for which the directors and officers would be held liable for participating in.

34. A Answer A is correct as the usurping of a corporate opportunity is akin to stealing the opportunity for oneself. Answer B does not state the correct meaning of usurp, nor do answers C and D. Therefore, answers B, C, and D are all incorrect.

35. D Answer D is correct as answers A, B, and C all are situations that describe when the court will pierce the corporate veil and hold the shareholder personally liable for the debts and obligations of the corporation.

Short Answer:

36. Annual shareholders' meetings
37. Only matters stated in the notice of the special meeting may be discussed.
38. An agreement entered into by shareholders that grant one another the right of first refusal to purchase shares that they are going to sell.
39. It is an agreement entered into by shareholders that requires selling shareholders to sell their shares to the other shareholders of the corporation at the price given in the agreement.
40. Balance sheets, income statements and a statement of changes in shareholder equity are the types of information found in an annual financial statement.
41. resolution
42. It permits the board of directors' meetings to be held by way of a conference call.
43. They are subject to joint and several liability.
44. A stock dividend is additional shares of stock paid as a dividend.
45. Officers have express, implied and apparent authority to bind the corporation to contracts.
46. The board of directors may be removed by any officer.
47. The duty of loyalty, integrity, honesty, trust and confidence owed by directors and officers to their corporate employers is what is known as their fiduciary duty.

48. D & O insurance is directors' and officers' liability insurance that a corporation may purchase to defend an officer or director who has been sued in his or her corporate capacity.
49. Indemnification in the corporate sense means that eh corporation as opposed to the officer or director is liable and pays the costs associated with litigation as well as judgments or settlements associated with the lawsuit.
50. dissension

Chapter 37
MERGERS AND TAKEOVERS
OF CORPORATIONS

Chapter Overview

Corporate change is obtained by controlling stockholder votes. Shareholder votes are solicited and voted by proxy. Persons who desire fundamental change in the direction or control of a company often engage in a proxy contest to win over shareholder votes. Another fundamental change may be made by acquiring another company. This may be through a friendly merger of consolidation or by a hostile tender offer. The target company may mount a defense to the takeover. This chapter focuses on all these possible fundamental changes that a corporation may go through.

Objectives

Upon completion of the exercises in this chapter, you should be able to:
1. Explain the process of soliciting proxies.
2. Describe a proxy contest.
3. Understand when a shareholder can insert a proposal in proxy materials.
4. Describe the difference between a consolidation and a merger.
5. Explain the process involved in approving a merger or share exchange.
6. Describe dissenting shareholder appraisal rights.
7. Explain a tender offer.
8. Describe defensive maneuvers to a takeover.
9. Understand the business judgment rule.

Practical Application

For those businesspersons that obtain ownership interests incorporations or choose the corporation as their business form, obtaining or maintaining control of the company is often imperative. It is wise to understand how control of the company may be lost and what efforts can lawfully be made to thwart a proxy battle or hostile takeover.

Helpful Hints

In the corporate environment, mergers, acquisitions, proxy fights, and tender offers are realties that are effectuated only be adhering to the laws and regulations related to these processes and changes. The individual has a greater ability to control their financial stake in a corporation if they understand their rights and duties under the applicable laws. The exercises in this chapter will help you advance your understanding of this area of corporate law.

Study Tips

Before an individual can participate in corporate change and defend their investment, they must understand the major guiding principles and law that controls the areas of proxy fights, mergers, acquisitions, tender offers, and defenses to corporate takeovers. Understanding the following terms and principles is essential to meaningful participation in any of these corporate events. This short outline and glossary of terms is divided into subject areas.

Solicitation of Proxies

proxy voting – shareholders have the right to vote by proxy. A proxy is a means by which a shareholder authorizes another person to represent him or her and vote his or her shares at a shareholders' meeting. This is common in large corporations.

proxy card – a written document signed by a shareholder that authorizes another person to vote the shareholder's shares.

Section 14(a) – of the Securities Exchange Act of 1934 gives the SEC the authority to regulate the solicitation of proxies.

proxy statement – anyone soliciting proxies must prepare a proxy statement that fully describes (1) the matter for which the proxy is being solicited, (2) who is soliciting the proxy, and (3) any other pertinent information.

Section 14(a) prohibits misrepresentations or omissions of a material fact in proxy materials.

proxy contests – when shareholders oppose the actions of incumbent directors and management, they may challenge the management in a proxy contest in which both sides solicit proxies.

reimbursement of expenses – because proxy contests can be very expensive, the incumbent management can obtain reimbursement from the corporation if the contest concerns an issue of corporate policy. The dissenting group can get reimbursed only if it wins the proxy contest.

SEC's proxy rules – shareholders who own less than $5 million in stock of a company may communicate with other shareholders without filing proxy solicitation materials with the SEC. Companies seeking proxies must unbundle the propositions so that the shareholders can vote on each separate issue. Performance charts must be included in annual reports. Companies must provide tables in their annual reports that summarize executive compensation.

Mergers and Acquisitions

Mergers, consolidations, share exchanges, and sale of assets are friendly in nature. Both corporations have agreed to the combination of corporations or acquisition of assets.

merger – occurs when one corporation is absorbed into another corporation and ceases to exist. The corporation that continues is the surviving corporation. The other is the merged corporation. Shareholders of the merged corporation receive stock or securities of the surviving corporation.

consolidation – occurs when two or more corporations combine to form an entirely new corporation. Modernly, consolidations are a rarity.

share exchanges – when one corporation (parent corporation) acquires all the shares of another corporation (subsidiary corporation) and both corporations retain their separate legal existence.

required approvals for a merger – a merger requires (1) the recommendation of the board of directors of each corporation and (2) an affirmative vote of the majority of shares of each corporation that is entitled to vote.

articles of merger or share exchange – must be filed with the secretary of state. The secretary of state will then issue a certificate of merger or share exchange to the surviving corporation. If the parent corporation owns 90 percent of the subsidiary corporation, a **short-form merger** procedure may be followed. Approval of shareholders of neither corporation is required for short-form merger. All that is required is approval of the board of directors of the parent corporation.

sale or lease of assets – a corporation may sell, lease, or otherwise dispose of all or substantially all of its property. Such a sale requires (1) the recommendation of the board of directors and (2) an affirmative vote of the majority of the shares of the selling corporation that is entitled to vote.

Dissenting Shareholder Appraisal Rights

Shareholders who object to a proposed merger, share exchange, or sale or lease of all or substantially all of the property of a corporation have a right to have their shares valued by a court and receive cash payment of this value from the corporation.

Tender Offers

A tender offer is an offer that an acquirer (tender offeror) makes directly to a target corporation's shareholders in an effort to acquire the target corporation. The shareholders of the target make an individual decision about whether to sell to the tender offeror.

Williams Act – regulates tender offers.

leveraged buyout – the tender offeror uses loans to purchase the stock from the stockholders of the target corporation. These loans, called bridge loans, are usually paid back after assets of the target corporation are sold off. Another source of funds for the tender offeror is the sale of junk bonds, which are risky corporate bonds that pay a higher rate of interest. After the tender offer is completed, the acquiring company is saddled with huge debts. When it merges with the target corporation the resulting company's capital structure consists of a low amount of equity and huge amounts of debt.

tender offer rules:
1. offer cannot be closed before 20 days after the commencement of the tender offer
2. offer must be extended for 10 days if the tender offer increases the number of shares that it will take or the price it will pay

3. **fair price rule** stipulates that any increase in price paid for shares must be offered to all shareholders, even those who have already tendered their shares
4. **pro rata rule** requires that shares must be purchased on a pro rata basis if too many shares are tendered.

Section 14(e) of the Williams Act – prohibits fraudulent, deceptive, or manipulative practices in connection with tender offers.

Opposing a Tender Offer

The incumbent management of a target corporation may desire to oppose a tender offer. Management may engage in a variety of activities to impede or defeat the tender offer. Some of these include:
1. **Persuasion of shareholders** – media campaigns used to oppose the tender offer
2. **Delaying lawsuits** – suits filed alleging antitrust or securities violations to buy time
3. **Selling a crown jewel** – selling an asset that makes the target corporation less attractive
4. **White knight merger** – merger with friendly party that will leave target intact
5. **Pac-Man tender offer** – target makes tender offer for the tender offeror
6. **Adopting a poison pill** – strategy built into articles of incorporation, bylaws, contracts, or leases whereby large payouts or termination of contracts become effective if the corporation changes hands
7. **Issuing additional stock** – issuing more stock makes tender offeror buy more shares
8. **Creating Employee Stock Ownership Plan (ESOP)** – block of stock owned by employees is used to oppose acquirer in proxy fight
9. **Flip-over and flip-in rights plans** – allows stockholders to buy twice the value in stock to make company too expensive to buy
10. **Greenmail and standstill agreements** – target pays premium to get back shares from tender offeror

Business Judgment Rule

Fiduciary duty – the duty the directors of a corporation owe to act carefully and honestly when acting on behalf of the corporation

Business judgment rule – a rule that protects the decisions of the board of directors, who act on an informed basis, in good faith, and in the honest belief that the action taken was in the best interests of the corporation and its shareholders.

State Antitakeover Statutes

These are statutes that enacted by state legislatures that protect corporations incorporated in or doing business in the state from hostile takeovers. They are often challenged as being unconstitutional because they violate the Williams Act and the Commerce and Supremacy Clauses of the U.S. Constitution.

Exon-Florio Law

The Exon-Florio Law of 1988, as amended by the Byrd-Exon Amendment of 1992 mandates the President of the United States to suspend, prohibit, or dismantle the acquisition of U.S. businesses by foreign investors if there is credible evidence that the foreign investor might take action that threatens to impair the national security.

Refresh Your Memory

The following exercises will enable you to refresh your memory as to the key principles and concepts given to you in this chapter. Read each question carefully and put your answer in the blanks provided. Review the chapter material for any question you miss or are unable to remember.

1. A _____ _____ is a written document signed by a shareholder that authorizes another person to vote the shareholder's shares.

2. Section _____ of the Securities Exchange Act of 1934 gives the SEC the authority to regulate the solicitation of _____.

3. When shareholders oppose the actions of incumbent directors and _____, they may challenge the management in a _____ contest.

4. Companies seeking proxies must _____ the propositions in the proxy materials so that shareholders can vote on each separate issue.

5. The corporation that continues after a merger is the _____ corporation.

6. A _____ occurs when two or more corporations combine to form an entirely new corporation.

7. A share exchange occurs when a _____ corporation acquires all the shares of the _____ corporation and both corporations retain their separate legal existence.

8. Articles or merger or share exchange must be filed with the _____ ___ _____.

9. If the parent corporation owns 90 percent of the subsidiary corporation, a _____-_____ merger procedure may be followed.

10. A _____ _____ is an offer that an acquirer makes directly to a target corporation's shareholders in an effort to acquire the target corporation.

11. The _____ Act is an amendment to the Securities Exchange Act of 1934 that regulates _____ offers.

12. The _____ _____ rule stipulates that any increase in price paid for shares under a tender offer must be offered to all shareholders, even those who have already tendered their shares.

13. Section _____ of the Williams Act prohibits fraudulent, deceptive, or _____ practices in connection with tender offers.

14. A strategy used by incumbent management to oppose a tender offer is to sell a _____ that makes the target less attractive to the tender offeror.

15. The _____-_____ Law of 1988 allows the President of the U.S. to suspend, prohibit, or dismantle the acquisition of U.S. businesses by _____ _____ if there is credible evidence that the _____ _____ might take action that threatens to impair the _____ security.

Critical Thought Exercise

Blue Cab Co. was merged into Atlantic Cab Corp., with Atlantic being the surviving corporation in the merger. Atlantic did not take over any of the cabs owned by Blue because they were old and in disrepair. Blue Cab was poorly run and owed over $600,000 to Valley Bank for cab purchases. Blue Cab also owed over $60,700 to Fleet Gas Co for fuel purchased by its employees. Blue Cab is owed $43,000 by Broadway Actors Transportation, Inc. (BAT) for limousine services rendered pursuant to a contract. Blue Cab has already commenced suit against BAT for breach of contract. Valley Bank and Fleet Gas brought a suit against Atlantic for payment of the debts. The board of directors of Atlantic refused to honor the debts of Blue Cab because the purpose in taking over Blue Cab was to eliminate a competitor. Atlantic had no desire to acquire the assets of Blue Cab. Co. Atlantic argued that it had never agreed to assume any debt owed by Blue Cab.

What is the effect of the merger and will Valley Bank and Fleet Gas be able to recover breach of contract damages from Atlantic? Can Atlantic maintain the suit against BAT?

Answer. _____

Sample Quiz

True/False

1. ____ A proxy is a means by which a shareholder authorizes another person to vote the shares at the shareholders' meeting as directed by the shareholder. [p 724]

2. ____ In order to act as a proxy, you must be an officer or director of the corporation whose shares are being voted by proxy. [p 724]

3. ____ The Securities Act of 1934 authorized the SEC to regulate the solicitation of proxies. [p 724]

4. ____ If a group desires to solicit proxies to oppose a management action, management has the choice of mailing the proxy material for the dissenting group or providing the dissenting group with a list of stockholders. [p 725]

5. ____ A proxy statement must contain information about who is soliciting the proxy and the number of proxies already solicited on the matter. [p 725]

6. ____ If management desires to solicit proxies from shareholders, it must file the proposed proxy, proxy statement, and other solicitation material with the SEC at least 30 days in advance of the distribution. [p 725]

7. ____ Management is entitled to recover its proxy contest costs for all policy issue contests regardless of which side wins. [p 725]

8. ____ Most shareholders desiring to communicate with other shareholders must file the communication with the SEC even if the shareholder is not seeking a proxy. [p 725]

9. ____ When proxies are solicited, issues must be unbundled. [p 725]

10. ____ No special disclosures are required in annual reports relating to executive compensation packages. [p 725]

11. ____ The SEC has held that cigarette smoking is an area shareholders are entitled to vote, making resolutions opposing tobacco products appropriate for inclusion in proxy statements. [p 726]

12. ____ In a merger, two corporations are combined, with one of the original corporations surviving and the other ceasing to exist. [p 728]

13. ____ In a share exchange, the parent company continues while the other company ceases to exist. [p 729]

14. ____ In an ordinary merger, approval is needed by votes of both board of directors, but shareholders need not approve. [p 729]

15. ____ A short-term merger can be used as long as the number of voting shares outstanding of the surviving corporation increases by less than 20 percent. [p 729]

16. ___ Shareholder appraisal rights may be exercised in mergers, consolidations, short-form mergers, and sales of substantially all the corporate assets not in the ordinary course of business. [p 730]

17. ___ The most direct way to acquire the control of a corporation is through a takeover because no approval is needed from the target corporation. [p 731]

18. ___ A company may take over another corporation by purchasing a sufficient number of the voting shares of the target firm [p 731]

19. ___ A hostile takeover occurs when the management of the firm being acquired opposes the acquisition and a tender offer is made directly to the shareholders of the target corporation. [p 731]

20. ___ Federal law requires no advance notice to the target company before a tender offer is made. [p 732]

21. ___ The fair price rule in the Williams Act requires that tender offers be made for a fair price based upon valuation of the stock. [p 733]

22. ___ A poison pill refers to the management of a target company in a hostile takeover selling off valuable pieces of itself to make itself less attractive to the tender offeror. [p 735]

23. ___ Machine Maker, Inc. issues shares of its stock to its shareholders that may be exchanged for cash in the even of a successful hostile takeover. This is an example of a crown jewel defense. [p 735]

24. ___ A target company may seek an injunction to bar further takeover attempts by another corporation if it can show that the takeover may violate antitrust of securities laws. [p 735]

25. ___ State anti-takeover statutes are aimed at protecting corporations within the state from hostile takeover and are often challenged as being unconstitutional. [p 737]

Multiple Choice

26. Proxy solicitations are regulated by the Securities and Exchange Act of 1934 under [p 724]
    a. Section 10(b).
    b. Section 14(a).
    c. Section 14(e).
    d. Section 16(a).

27. A written document signed by a shareholder that authorizes another person to vote the shareholder's shares is a [p 724]
    a. proxy contest.
    b. proxy statement.
    c. proxy card.
    d. share exchange.

28. A shareholder's proxy can be granted to [p 724]
    a.   only another shareholder.
    b.   officers only.
    c.   officers or directors only.
    d.   anyone.

29. Which of the following states the information that must be contained in a proxy statement? [p 725]
    a.   The matter for which the proxy is being solicited and who is soliciting the proxy.
    b.   The matter for which the proxy is being solicited and an analysis of the likelihood of success of the proxy contest.
    c.   The name of the party soliciting the proxy and an analysis of the likelihood of success of the proxy contest.
    d.   None of the above.

30. Which of the following is one of the rule changes adopted by the SEC in 1992? [p 725]
    a.   Proxies for multiple issues must be unbundled to allow the shareholder to decide separately whether they desire to grant a proxy related to each issue.
    b.   The annual reports of corporations must include detailed information and tables that summarize executive compensation.
    c.   Communications by a shareholder to large numbers of other shareholders no longer must be filed with the SEC if the communication is not soliciting a proxy.
    d.   All of the above.

31. A transaction in which two corporations combine such that afterwards only one corporation still exists and owns all the assets previously owned by both corporations is a [p 728]
    a.   merger.
    b.   consolidation.
    c.   purchase of assets.
    d.   share exchange.

32. A transaction in which two corporations combine such that afterwards neither of the combining corporations continues to exist, but that a third corporation is formed is a [p 728]
    a.   merger.
    b.   consolidation.
    c.   purchase of assets.
    d.   share exchange.

33. What is required in order for a merger to use the short-form procedure? [p 728]
    a.   There must be agreement by both boards of directors to use the short-form procedure.
    b.   There must be an increase of less than 20 percent in the number of shares of voting stock of the surviving corporation.
    c.   There must be ownership by the parent corporation of at least 90 percent of the shares of the subsidiary corporation before the merger.

d. The SEC must approve the use of the short-form procedure.

34. In a typical situation, a shareholder is allowed to exercise a right of appraisal in conjunction with [p 730]
    a. regular mergers.
    b. short-form mergers.
    c. sale or lease of substantially all of the corporate assets.
    d. all of the above.

35. Jungle Corporation purchases a large bloc of shares in Harvest Corporation as its first step in an attempt to take over Harvest. The management of Harvest immediately purchases a similar size bloc of shares in Jungle and notifies it of Harvest's intent to take over Jungle. This defensive tactic is an example of [p 735]
    a. a flip-over plan.
    b. selling a crown jewel.
    c. adopting a poison pill.
    d. a Pac-Man tender offer.

Short Answer

36. What must be in a proxy statement? [p 725] _____

37. What is prohibited by Section 14(a) of the Securities Exchange Act of 1934? [p 725] _____

38. When can a dissenting group get reimbursement for its expenses associated with a proxy contest? [p 725] _____

39. What is a merger? [p 728] _____

40. Describe what happens in a share exchange. [p 729] _____

41. What approvals are required for a regular merger? [p 729] _____

42. When can corporations use the short-form merger procedure? [p 729] _____

43. What is required before a corporation may sell, lease, or otherwise dispose of all or substantially all of its property in other than the regular course of business? [p 730] _____

44. What are dissenting shareholder appraisal rights? [p 730] _____
_____
_____

45. Describe a tender offer. [p 731] _____
_____

46. What is required by the fair price rule? [p 733] _____
_____

47. What is required by the pro rata rule? [p 733] _____
_____

48. What is prohibited by Section 14(e) of the Williams Act? [p 733] _____
_____

49. What is the business judgment rule? [p 735] _____
_____
_____

50. What can the U.S. President do pursuant to the Exon-Florio Law? [p 738] _____
_____
_____

Answers to Refresh Your Memory

1. proxy card [p 724]
2. 14(a), proxies [p 724]
3. management, proxy [p 725]
4. unbundle [p 725]
5. surviving [p 728]
6. consolidation [p 728]
7. parent, subsidiary [p 729]
8. secretary of state [p 729]
9. short-form [p 729]
10. tender offer [p 731]
11. Williams, tender [p 732]
12. fair price [p 733]
13. 14(e), manipulative [p 733]
14. crown jewel [p 735]
15. Exon-Florio, foreign investors, foreign investor, national [p 738]

Critical Thought Exercise Model Answer

A merger involves the legal combination of two or more corporations in a manner that only one of the corporations continues to exist. When Blue Cab merged into Atlantic, Atlantic continued as the surviving corporation while Blue Moon ceased to exist as an entity. After the merger, Atlantic would be recognized as a single corporation, possessing all the rights, privileges, and powers of itself and Blue Cab Co. Atlantic automatically acquired all the assets and property of Blue Cab without the necessity of formality or deeds. The shareholders of Blue Cab receive stock or securities of Atlantic or other consideration as provided in the plan of merger. Additionally, Atlantic becomes liable for all of Blue Cab's debts and obligations. Lastly, Atlantic's articles of incorporation are deemed amended to include any changes that are stated in the articles of merger.

In a merger, the surviving corporation obtains the absorbed corporation's preexisting obligations and legal rights. If the merging corporation had a right of action against a third party, the surviving corporation can bring or maintain a suit after the merger to recover the merging corporation's damages. Atlantic will inherit Blue Cab's right to sue BAT and will be entitled to recover whatever damages Blue Cab was entitled to collect.

Answers to Sample Quiz

True/False:

1. True Voting by proxy is common in large corporations.
2. False The proxy need not be a director or officer.
3. True This is authorized by Section 14(a) of the act.
4. True Management must only make minimal effort to aid the dissenters.
5. False The materials must contain information about who is soliciting the proxy and the matter for which the proxy is being solicited.
6. False The filing must be 10 days in advance of distribution.
7. True The dissenting group must win to get reimbursed.
8. False The new SEC proxy rules adopted in 1992 allow communications without an SEC filing if a proxy is not being sought.
9. True This allows issues to be voted upon separately.
10. False Companies must provide tables in their annual reports that succinctly summarize executive compensation.
11. True Social issues are appropriate for consideration by shareholders.
12. True In a consolidation, both cease to exist.
13. False Both the parent and subsidiary corporations continue to exist.
14. False The approval needed is recommendation by both boards of directors and votes of the shareholders of each corporation.
15. False Short-form mergers can be used when the parent company owns 90 percent or more of outstanding stock of the subsidiary corporation.
16. True If the dissenter is not satisfied with the value placed on shares by the corporation, he or she may petition the court to determine the fair value of the shares.
17. True The tender offer is made directly to the shareholders of the target corporation.
18. True The offer can be made for all or a portion of the shares of the target corporation.
19. True Only the tender offeror's board of directors must approve the offer.
20. True The SEC does not need to be notified either until the offer is made.
21. False the fair price rule states that any increase in the price paid for shares tendered must be offered to all shareholders, even those who have previously tendered their shares.
22. False The poison pill defense refers to strategies built into the target corporation's articles of incorporation, corporate bylaws, or contracts and leases.
23. False This is a poison pill defense.

24. True   These delaying lawsuits create expense and allow time to mount a defense.
25. True   They are challenged as violating the Commerce and Supremacy Clauses.

Multiple Choice:

26. B   this section promotes full disclosure during the proxy solicitation process. Choice A is a section relating to insider trading. Choice C is the section prohibiting fraud in the proxy solicitation process. Choice D relates to a section that prohibits short-swing profits in the sale of securities by insiders.
27. C   The proxy is sent to the corporation and states the shareholder's voting wishes.
28. D   Any person may be authorized to act as a proxy. Choices A, B, and C state choices that may be selected by a shareholder, but they are too restrictive because anyone can be chosen.
29. A   The disclosure must contain these two items. B and C are incorrect because an analysis of the likelihood of success is subjective and is not required. D is not correct because a correct answer is available.
30. D   Choices A, B, and C are all new rules that were adopted in 1992 by the SEC. Therefore, choice D is the correct answer.
31. A   A merger is also used after many hostile takeovers. Choice B is incorrect because in a consolidation neither company survives when a third is formed. Choices C and D are incorrect because both companies continue to exist after a purchase of assets or share exchange.
32. B   Consolidation is correct. This form of business combination is seldom used today. Choice A is not correct because one corporation continues to exist in a merger. Choices C and D are incorrect because both corporations continue to exist when there is a purchase of assets or share exchange.
33. C   All that is required is the approval of the board of supervisors of the parent company as long as the 990 percent condition is met. Choice A is incorrect because no approval is needed from the board of the subsidiary. Choice B is incorrect because this is a condition that negates the need for surviving shareholder approval in a regular merger situation. Choice D is not correct because SEC approval is not needed.
34. D   Appraisal rights apply to mergers, a share exchange, or sale or lease of all or substantially all of the property of the corporation. Objecting shareholders are provided a statutory right to dissent and obtain payment of the fair value of their shares. Choices A, B, and C are correct, but D is the correct answer because all choices are correct.
35. D   In a Pac-Man or reverse tender offer, the target makes a tender offer for the tender offeror. A is not correct because a flip-over allows stockholders to buy twice the value in stock to make the company too expensive to buy. B is not correct because there has been no sale of a valuable asset by Harvest. C is not correct because this was an act by Harvest management, not a strategy built into the articles of incorporation, bylaws, or contracts of Harvest.

Short Answer:

36.   The proxy statement must fully describe (1) the matter for which the proxy is being solicited, (2) who is soliciting the proxy, and (3) any other pertinent information.
37.   Section 14(a) prohibits misrepresentations or omissions of a material fact in proxy materials.
38.   The expenses of the dissenting group are reimbursed only if it wins the proxy contest. If the proxy contest concerns a personal matter, neither side may recover its expenses.

39. A merger occurs when one corporation is absorbed into another corporation and ceases to exist. Title to all assets of the merged corporation passes to the surviving corporation without formality or deeds.

40. In a share exchange, both corporations retain their separate legal existence. The parent corporation owns all the shares of the subsidiary corporation.

41. A merger requires (1) the recommendation of the board of directors of each corporation and (2) an affirmative vote of the majority of shares of each corporation that is entitled to vote.

42. The short-form procedure can be used if the parent corporation owns 90 percent or more of the outstanding stock of the subsidiary corporation. It is a simple procedure because the only approval that is needed is from the board of directors of the parent corporation.

43. It requires (1) the recommendation of the board of directors and (2) an affirmative vote of the majority of the shares of the selling or leasing corporation that is entitled to vote.

44. Shareholders who object to a proposed merger, for example, have a right to have their shares valued by a court and receive cash payment of this value from the corporation.

45. A tender offer is an offer that an acquirer makes during a hostile takeover directly to a target corporation's shareholders in an effort to acquire the target corporation. The shareholders each make an individual decision about whether to sell their shares to the tender offeror.

46. The fair price rule stipulates that any increases in price paid by the tender offeror for shares must be offered to all shareholders, even those who have already tendered their shares.

47. The pro rata rule requires that shares must be purchased on a pro rata basis if too many shares are tendered.

48. Section 14(e) prohibits fraudulent, deceptive, or manipulative practices in connection with tender offers.

49. It is a rule that protects the decisions of the board of directors, who act on an informed basis, in good faith, and in the honest belief that the action taken was in the best interests of the corporation and its shareholders.

50. Under this law, the President may suspend, prohibit, or dismantle the acquisition of any U.S. business by foreign investors if there is credible evidence that the foreign investor might take action that threatens to impair the national security.

Chapter 38

INVESTOR PROTECTION

Chapter Overview

The stock market crash of 1929 motivated Congress to make investor security a priority. Up to this time, fraud and dealing on inside information was rampant. Congress passed two key pieces of legislation in an attempt to remedy the problem. The Securities Act of 1933 requires public disclosure of material information by companies and others who issue securities to the public. The Securities Exchange Act of 1934 was enacted to prevent fraud in the trading of securities, especially insider trading. Additional statutes have been passed by the states. These federal and state statutes are still the cornerstone that forms the protection for investors in securities. This chapter examines these protections.

Chapter Objectives

Upon Completion of the exercises in this chapter, you should be able to:
1. Describe public offerings of securities and registration of those securities with the SEC.
2. Describe the exemptions from registration.
3. Define insider trading violations of Section 10(b) of the Securities Exchange Act of 1934.
4. Explain how tippers and tippees become liable for insider trading.
5. Understand how the SEC is addressing Internet stock fraud.
6. Describe criminal liability for violation of the federal securities laws.
7. Explain the meaning of short-swing profits that violate Section 16(b) of the SEC Act of 1934.
8. Describe investor protection under the Commodity Exchange Act.

Practical Application

This chapter has application from several viewpoints. The investor, which includes individuals, employee groups, and businesses, needs to know the protections that are available under federal state law that prevent fraudulent loss of their investment. Those persons and businesses that issue securities, and the people who work for them, need to know the standards to which the federal government will hold them. Lastly, the unsuspecting investor needs to know what acts may make them part of a fraudulent or criminal transaction so that liability can be avoided. Unless each person familiarizes himself with federal securities law, there is an increased risk of financial loss, damage to their business, and exposure to criminal prosecution.

Helpful Hints

The securities laws are geared to regulating transactions involving the issuance and trading of securities. Focus on the individual transaction or related transactions and the information that was exchanged or withheld as to the particular transaction. It is the improper release or suppression of material information and trading upon that information that triggers the application of the securities laws.

Study Tips

The following terms and sections of the securities laws are key to understanding the material in this chapter. You should develop a working knowledge of these key terms and pay attention to how they are applied by the courts.

security – (1) An interest or instrument that is common stock, preferred stock, a bond, a debenture, or a warrant, (2) an interest or instrument that is expressly mentioned in securities acts, and (3) an investment contract.

Securities Exchange Act of 1934 – A federal statute that primarily regulates the trading in securities.

Securities Act of 1933 – A federal statute that primarily regulates the issuance of securities by a corporation, a general or limited partnership, an unincorporated association, or an individual.

Securities and Exchange Commission (SEC) – A federal administrative agency that is empowered to administer federal securities laws. The SEC can adopt rules and regulations to interpret and implement federal securities laws. Violations of these rules carry civil and criminal penalties.

registration statement – Document that an issuer of securities files with the SEC that contains required information about the issuer, the securities to be issued, and other relevant information.

prospectus – A written disclosure document that must be submitted to the SEC along with the registration statement and given to prospective purchasers of the securities.

prefiling period – A period of time that begins when the issuer first contemplates issuing securities and ends when the registration statement is filed. The issuer may not condition the market by engaging in a public relation campaign during this period.

waiting period – A period of time that begins when the registration statement is filed with the SEC and continues until the registration statement is declared effective. The issuer is encouraged to condition the market during this time.

posteffective period – The period that begins when the registration statement becomes effective and runs until the issuer either sells all of the offered securities or withdraws them from sale.

final prospectus – A final version of the prospectus that must be delivered by the issuer to the investor prior to or at the time of confirming a sale or sending a security to a purchaser.

exempt securities transactions – Transactions that are exempt from registration but must still comply with antifraud provisions of the federal securities laws.

nonissuer exemption – An exemption from registration that permits average investors from registering the resale of their securities because they are not the issuer, an underwriter, or a dealer in securities.

intrastate offerings exemption – An exemption from registration that permits local businesses to raise capital from local investors to be used in the local economy without the need to register with the SEC. The three requirements for this exemption are:
1. The issuer must be a resident of the state for which the exemption is claimed
2. The issuer must be doing business in that state.
3. The purchasers of all securities must be residents of that state.

private placement exemption – An exemption from registration that permits issuers to raise capital from an unlimited number of accredited investors and no more than 35 nonaccredited investors without having to register the offering with the SEC. An accredited investor may be:
1. Any person with a net worth of at least $1 million.
2. Any person who has had an annual income of $200,000 for the previous two years and expects to make $200,000 in the current year.
3. Any corporation, partnership, or business trust with assets of $5 million.
4. Insiders of the issuers, such as officers and directors of corporate issuers and general partners of partnership issuers.
5. Institutional investors such as registered investment companies, pension plans, and colleges and universities.

small offerings exemption – An exemption from registration for the sale of securities not exceeding $1 million during a 12-month period.

restricted securities – Securities that were issued for investment purposes pursuant to the intrastate private placement, or small offering exemption. They cannot be resold for a limited period of time after their initial issue.

Rule 144 – Provides that securities sold pursuant to the private placement or small offering exemptions must be held for one year from the date when the securities are last sold by the issuer.

Rule 147 – Securities sold pursuant to an intrastate offering exemption cannot be sold to nonresidents for a period of nine months.

Rule 144A – The SEC rule permits qualified institutional investors to buy unregistered securities without being subject to the holding periods of Rule 144.

Section 24 of the Securities Act of 1933 – Imposes criminal liability of up to five years prison for violating the act or the rules and regulations adopted thereunder.

SEC actions for violating 1933 act – the SEC may:
1. issue a consent order
2. bring an action seeking an injunction
3. request disgorgement of profits by the court

Section 12 of the 1933 act – Imposes civil liability who violates Section 5 of the act. Under Section 12, a purchaser may rescind the purchase or sue for damages.

Section 11 – A provision of the Securities Act of 1933 that imposes civil liability on persons who intentionally defraud investors who intentionally defraud investors by making misrepresentations or omissions of material facts in the registration statement or who are negligent for not discovering the fraud.

Section 10(b) – A provision of the Securities Exchange Act of 1934 that prohibits the use of manipulative and deceptive devices in the purchase or sale of securities in contravention of the rules and regulations prescribed by the SEC.

Rule 10b-5 – A rule adopted by the SEC to clarify the reach of Section 10(b) against deceptive and fraudulent activities in the purchase and sale of securities.

scienter – means intentional conduct

Regulation Fair Disclosure – Prohibits companies from leaking important information to securities professionals before the information is disclosed to the public.

insider trading – When an insider makes a profit by personally purchasing shares of the corporation prior to public release of favorable information or by selling shares of the corporation prior to the public disclosure of unfavorable information. **Insiders** are:
1. officers, directors and employees at all levels of the company
2. lawyers, accountants, consultants, and other agents hired by the company to provide services or work to the company
3. others who owe a fiduciary duty to the company

tipper – A person who discloses material nonpublic information to another person.

tippee – The person who receives material nonpublic information from a tipper.

Liability Provisions of the Securities Exchange Act of 1934

Section 32 – Makes it a criminal offense to willfully violate the 1934 act or the rules or regulations adopted thereunder.

SEC actions – The SEC may enter into consent orders, seek injunctions, or seek disgorgement of profits by court order.

Insider Trading Sanctions Act – Permits SEC to obtain civil penalty of up to three times the illegal profits gained or losses avoided by insider trading.

Section 16(a) – A section of the Securities Exchange Act of 1934 that defines any person who is an executive officer, a director, or a 10% shareholder or an equity security of a reporting company as a statutory insider for Section 16 purposes.

Section 16(b) – A section of the Securities Exchange Act of 1934 that requires that any profits made by a statutory insider on transactions involving short-swing profits belong to the corporation.

Short-swing profits – Trades involving equity securities occurring within six months of each other.

Commodity Exchange Act (CEA) – Enacted in 1936 to regulate the trading of commodity futures contracts.

Commodity Futures Trading Commission Act amended the 1936 act significantly.

Section 4b of the CEA - Prohibits fraudulent conduct in connection with any order or contract of sale or any commodity for future delivery.

Commodity Futures Trading Commission – Five member federal agency appointed by the President to regulate trading in commodities futures contracts.

Refresh Your Memory

The following exercises will enable you to refresh your memory as to the key principles and concepts given to you in this chapter. Read each question carefully and put your answer in the blanks provided. Review the chapter material for any question you miss or are unable to remember.

1. The _____ ____ _____ _____ is the federal agency that is empowered to administer federal securities laws.

2. A _____ _____ is a document that an issuer of securities files with the SEC that contains required information about the issuer, the securities to be issued, and other relevant information.

3. A _____ is a written disclosure document that must be submitted to the SEC along with the registration statement and given to prospective purchasers of the securities.

4. The _____ _____ is a period of time that begins when the registration statement is filed with the SEC and continues until the registration statement is declared effective.

5. The _____ exemption is an exemption from registration that permits average investors from registering the resale of their securities.

6. The _____ _____ exemption from registration permits local business to raise capital from local investors to be used in the local economy without the need to register with the SEC.

7. _____ securities are securities that were issued for investment purposes pursuant to an exemption. They cannot be resold for a limited period of time after their initial issue.

8. Rule ____ provides that securities sold pursuant to the private placement or small offering exemptions must be held for _____ year(s) from the date when the securities are last sold by the issuer.

9. Section 24 of the Securities Act of 1933 imposes criminal liability of up to _____ years per violation of the act.

10. The SEC is empowered to address violations of the 1933 act by issuing a _____ order, bringing and action seeking an injunction, and requesting _____ of profits by the court.

11. Section _____ is a provision of the Securities Exchange Act of 1934 that prohibits the use of _____ and deceptive devices in the purchase or sale of securities.

12. _____ means intentional conduct.

13. _____ _____ _____, or Reg FD, prohibits companies from leaking important information to securities professionals before the information is disclosed to the _____.

14. The Insider _____ _____ Act permits the SEC to obtain a civil penalty of up to three times the illegal gained or losses avoided by insider trading.

15. Trades involving equity securities occurring within six months of each other are called _____-
_____ profits.

Critical Thought Exercise

Jerry Dallas is a corporate officer for CompuGames (CG), the leading manufacturer of hand-held computer games. The profit margin of CG is greatly impacted by the cost of the microprocessor it purchases for its games from Mini-Micro. Dallas tells his girlfriend, Julie Profit, that she should watch for any announcement of a price increase of 20% or more by Mini-Micro and sell her stock in CG if there is such a large price increase. Profit has a friend, Louis Nooze, who works in the public relations department at Mini-Micro. She asks Nooze to tell her if he hears of an announcement of price increases by Mini-Micro. Two days before a 33% price increase is to be announced by Mini-Micro, Nooze gives the news to Profit. Profit calls her stockbroker and sells all her stock in CG. When the price increase is announced, CG stock falls from $38 per share to $22 per share. By selling her stock before the announcement by Mini-Micro, Profit realizes a profit of $800,000.

If a stockholder initiates a suit against Dallas, Profit, and Nooze, will any of these people be liable for realizing illegal profits based upon insider trading or misappropriation?

Answer. _____

Sample Quiz

True/False:

1. ___ A security may consist of an investment contract. [p 744]

2. ___ The Securities Act of 1933 is a federal statute that primarily regulates the trading in securities. [p 744]

3. ___ The Securities and Exchange Commission can adopt rules and regulations to interpret and implement federal securities laws. [p 744]

4. ___ A registration statement must be filed, but specific contents are not mandatory. [p 745]

5. ___ A prospectus is a confidential document that is filed only with the SEC. [p 745]

6. ___ Securities offering must be written in precise legal language. [p 745]

7. ___ The registration period for securities offerings is divided into four time periods. [p 746]

8. ___ The prefiling period ends when the registration statement is filed. [p 746]

9. ___ The issuer is encouraged to condition the market during the waiting period. [p 746]

10. ___ The posteffective period begins when the registration statement becomes effective. [p 746]

11. ___ The issuer must deliver a final prospectus to a purchaser within a reasonable time after a sale of the security has been confirmed. [p 746]

12. ___ Securities issued by the government and common carriers must comply with all registration requirements. [p 748]

13. ___ Certain transactions in securities are exempt from registration, even if the type of security may not quality as an exemption. [p 748]

14. ___ The Securities Act of 1933 exempts securities transactions not made by an issuer, an underwriter, or a dealer from registration. [p 748]

15. ___ The intrastate offerings exemption requires that the issuer be a resident of the state for which the exemption is claimed, but the purchasers may reside in any state. [p 749]

16. ___ An accredited investor may under the private placement exemption include any person with a net worth of at least $1 million. [p 749]

17. ___ Restricted securities cannot be resold for a limited period of time after their initial issue. [p 749]

18. ___ Securities sold pursuant to an intrastate offering exemption cannot be sold to nonresidents for a period of two years. [p 749]

19. ___ The maximum penalty for each violation of the 1933 act pursuant to Section 24 is two years. [p 751]

20. ___ While the Securities Act of 1933 regulates the original issuance of securities, the Securities Exchange Act of 1934 primarily regulates subsequent trading. [p 754]

21. ___ Manipulative and deceptive practices in the purchase or sale of securities are prohibited by Section 10(b) of the Securities Exchange Act of 1934. [p 754]

22. ___ Rule 10b-5 is a rule adopted by the SEC to clarify the reach of Section 10(b). [p 754]

23. ___ Insider trading occurs when a company employee or company advisor uses material nonpublic information to make a profit by trading in the securities of the company. [p 755]

24. ___ Only officers, directors and employees of a company can be an insider. [p 755]

25. ___ A tipper is not liable for the profits made by a tippee as long as the tipper does not buy or sell any security. [p 758]

Multiple Choice:

26. Securities are defined as: [p 744]
    a. securities such as stocks, bonds, and warrants.
    b. instruments mentioned in securities acts, such as subscription agreements and oil rights.
    c. investment contracts.
    d. all of the above.

27. The securities Act of 1933 primarily regulates [p 744]
    a. short-swing profits.
    b. issuance of securities.
    c. insider trading.
    d. none of the above.

28. Which of the following descriptions does not need to be contained in a registration statement? [p 745]
    a. The securities being offered for sale
    b. The registrant's business
    c. The degree of competition in the industry
    d. The SEC's opinion as to the merits of the securities offered

29. The written disclosure document that must be submitted to the SEC and is given to all prospective investors to enable them to evaluate the financial risk of the investments is called a(n) [p 745]
    a. registration statement.
    b. prospectus.
    c. tombstone advertisement.
    d. offering statement.

30. The time period of the registration process during which the issuer cannot tout the prospectus to potential purchasers is the [p 746]
    a. prefiling period.
    b. waiting period.
    c. posteffective period.
    d. all of the above.

31. Which of the following securities must be registered with the SEC before they can be offered for sale? [p 748]
    a. Securities issued by any government in the United States.
    b. Common stock issued by corporations traded on a national stock exchange.
    c. Insurance and annuity contracts issued by insurance companies.
    d. Securities issued by nonprofit issuers.

32. An exemption from registration that permits local businesses to raise capital from local investors to be used in the local economy without the need to register with the SEC is the [p 748]
    a. nonissuer exemption.
    b. intrastate exemption.
    c. private placement exemption.
    d. small offering exemption.

33. To protect the nontransferability of restricted shares, the issuer must [p 750]
    a. require the investors to sign an affidavit stating that they are buying the securities for investment, acknowledging that they are purchasing restricted securities, and promising not to transfer the shares in violation of the restriction.
    b. place a legend on the stock certificate describing the restriction.
    c. notify the transfer agent not to record a transfer of the securities what would violate the restriction.
    d. all of the above.

34. Vista, Inc. issues stock after making a willful misrepresentation in its registration statement based upon misstatements of material fact concerning the financial health of Vista, Inc. Vista has huge debts that are recorded as assets in its financial statement, which was filed as part of the registration statement. Vista may be exposed to a penalty or remedy pursuant to [p 751]
    a. Section 24 of the Securities Act of 1933.
    b. an SEC consent order.
    c. Section 11 of the Securities Act of 1933.
    d. all of the above.

35. Lansing & Bismarck is a consulting firm that specializes in corporate reorganizations. Toji Bismarck learns that Superior Corp., a pharmaceutical company for whom he is doing temporary work, is about to announce that its scientists have developed a totally effective drug that will both prevent and cure lung cancer. Bismarck tells his wife, Sue, to buy the stock. Sue purchases $10 worth of Superior stock. Sue calls her brother, Ned, the next day. Ned purchases $50,000 worth of Superior stock that immediately climbs to $2.5 million when the drug discovery is announced. Sue's stock climbs to $500. Toji is liable for [p 758]
    a. only the $490 profit made by Sue.
    b. all the profit made by both Sue and Ned, if Ned knew the tip was material inside information.
    c. all the profit made on both Sue's and Ned's trades, regardless of the tippees knowledge.
    d. none of the profits made on the trades because Toji lacked scienter.

Short Answer:

36. What is a security? [p 744] _____

37. What descriptions must be contained within a registration statement? [p 745] _____

38. What is the "plain English" rule adopted by the SEC for securities offerings? [p 745] _____

39. Describe a red herring prospectus. [p 746] _____

40. What are the three time periods during the registrations process? [p 746]
    (1) _____ (2) _____ (3) _____

41. What is a Regulation A offering? [p 747] _____

42. What is a nonissuer exemption from registration? [p 748] _____

43. Who may be an accredited investor under the private placements or small offering exemptions? [p 749] _____

44. What are restricted securities? [p 749] _____

45. How can a small business raise $1 million or less from the public issue of securities? [p 751] _____

46. What must a defendant show to establish a due diligence defense to a Section 11 violation? [p 752] _____

47. What is prohibited by Section 10(b) of the Securities Exchange Act of 1934? [p 754] _____

48. What does Regulation Fair Disclosure (Reg FD) prohibit? [p 755] _____

49. What is required by Section 16(b) of the Securities Exchange Act of 1934? [p 760] _____

50. What does the Private Securities Litigation Reform Act of 1995 provide? [p 761] _____

Answers to Refresh Your Memory

1. Securities and Exchange Commission [p 744]
2. registration statement [p 745]
3. prospectus [p 745]
4. waiting period [p 746]
5. nonissuer [p 748]
6. intrastate offerings [p748]
7. Restricted [p 749]
8. 144, one [p 749]
9. five [p 751]
10. consent, disgorgement [p 751]
11. 10(b), manipulative [p 754]
12. Scienter [p 755]
13. Regulation Fair Disclosure [p 755]
14. Trading Sanctions [p 758]
15. short-swing [p 760]

Critical Thought Exercise Model Answer

Under section 10(b) of the Securities Exchange Act of 1934 and SEC Rule 10b-5, persons may be sued and prosecuted for the commission of fraud in connection with the sale or purchase of any security. The 1934 Act prohibits officers and directors from taking advantage of inside information they obtain as a result of their position to gain a trading advantage over the general public. Section 10(b) of the 1934 act and SEC Rule 10b-5 cover not only corporate officers, directors, and majority shareholders but also any persons having access to or receiving information of a nonpublic nature on which trading is based. The key to liability under Section 10(b) and Rule 10b-5 is whether the insider's information is material. A significant change in a company's financial condition would be material information. The cost of an essential part from a supplier would create that significant change.

Jerry Dallas did not act upon inside information in this case, nor did he act as a tipper. The information he gave was general advice as to the strength of his company and the market factors that affected the price of its main product. All he did was advise Profit to watch for any announcements of a price increase from Mini-Micro. He did not provide any insider information regarding CG. Therefore, Dallas will not be liable for the profit realized by Profit.

To find liability for Nooze, his level of knowledge must be established. Though it appears that he is acting as a tipper, the information that he provided is not being used to trade on Mini-Micro stock. There is no information as to whether Profit told him the purpose of wanting to know when a price increase would occur. Under the tipper theory, however, liability is established when the inside information is obtained as a result of someone's breach of a fiduciary duty to the corporation whose shares are involved in the trading. In this case, Nooze owes no fiduciary duty to CG. There is no proof that his information leak hurt Mini-Micro in any way.

Under a theory of misappropriation, both Nooze and Profit may be liable. The misappropriation theory holds that if an individual wrongfully obtains inside information and trades on it for his or her own personal gain, then the person should be held liable because the individual stole information rightfully belonging to another. Profit and Nooze both knew that they were taking information that was material and belonged to Mini-Micro. Liability should be imposed upon Profit because she traded upon this stolen information. Though Nooze also misappropriated the information, there is a lack of evidence as to his knowledge that it would be used for making a trade of CG stock.

Answers To Sample Quiz

True/False:

1. True   It may also be the typical stock, bond, debenture, or warrant.
2. False   The Securities Exchange Act of 1934 regulates the trading in securities.
3. True   These rules and regulations have the force of law.
4. False   The registration statement must contain information about the issuer, the securities to be issued, and other relevant information.
5. False   The prospectus must be given to prospective purchasers or the securities.
6. False   Securities offerings must be written in plain English.
7. False   It is divided into three time periods: prefiling, waiting, and posteffective.
8. True   The issuer may not condition the market during this period.
9. True   The issuer may also make oral offers to sell and distribute both the preliminary and summary prospectus.
10. True   it runs until the issuer sells all the offered securities or withdraws them from sale.
11. False   The final prospectus must be delivered prior to or at the time of confirming a sale.
12. False   These securities are exempt from registration.
13. True   These transactions are still subject to the antifraud provisions of the federal securities laws.
14. True   Nonissuers, such as average investors, do not have to file a registration statement.
15. False   The purchaser must reside in the same state as the issuer.
16. True   Accredited investors also include persons who earn $200,000 for two consecutive years and expect to make $200,000 in the current year.
17. True   Rule 144 provides that securities so9ld pursuant to the private placement or small offering exemption must be held for one year.
18. False   Rule 147 requires that the securities be held for none months.
19. False   The maximum penalty under Section 24 is five years per violation.
20. True   The 1934 act requires periodic reports to monitor securities transactions.
21. True   It is one of the most important sections in the entire 1934 act.
22. True   Rule 10b-5 is not restricted to purchases of securities of reporting companies. All transfers of securities are covered, even private sales.
23. True   It is illegal because it allows insiders to take advantage of the investing public.
24. False   Other insiders include lawyers and accountants who are hired by the company on a temporary basis and any others who owe a fiduciary duty to the company.
25. False   The tipper is liable for all profits made by the tippee.

Multiple Choice:

26. D   Choices A, B, and C are all forms of securities.
27. B   Requirements that must be followed by issuers of securities are set forth in this act, such as registration requirements. A is incorrect because short-swing profits are covered by Section 16(b) of the 1934 act. C is incorrect because Section 10(b) of the 1934 act covers inside trading. Choice D is incorrect because choice B is available.
28. D   The SEC does not pass upon the merits of the securities offered. Choices A, B, and C must be described in the registration statement.
29. B   The prospectus discloses much of the contents of the registration statement and must have some parts written in plain English. A is incorrect because it is a filing with the SEC that does not require the plain English clarity of a prospectus. C is incorrect because it is only an advertisement telling potential investors where they can obtain a prospectus. Choice D relates to Regulation A offerings and requires much less disclosure.
30. A   The issuer cannot condition the market and run a public relations campaign during this period. Choices B and C are incorrect because the issuer is expected or required to provide a prospectus during these periods. Choice D is incorrect because B and C are incorrect.
31. B   This is a security that is not exempt from registration. Choices A, C, and D are all exempt from registration.
32. B   There is not limit on the dollar amount of capital that can be raised as long as the residence requirements are met. Choices A, C, and D are incorrect because they are not restricted to local activity.
33. D   Choices A, B, and C are all correct statements, making choice D the correct answer. If the issuer has taken these precautions, it will not lose its exemption from registration even if isolated transfers of stock occur in violation of the restricted periods.
34. D   Choices A, B, and C are all possible sources of remedies or penalties for Vista's conduct. Therefore, D is the correct answer. Section 24 imposes criminal sanctions, while Section 11 imposes civil liability. The SEC may also take actions that include filing suit and seeking and injunction, or requesting the court to order disgorgement of profits.
35. C   Toji is liable as the tipper for all profits made by any tippee or remote tippee. Toji's liability is not dependant upon Ned's knowledge of the nature or source of the tip. A is not correct because Toji is liable for the profits of remote tippees. B is not correct because Ned's knowledge is not relevant to Toji's liability. D is not correct because Toji should have known that his tip would be acted upon.

Short Answer:

36.   A security is (1) an interest or instrument that is common stock, preferred stock, a bond, a debenture, or a warrant; (2) an interest or instrument that is expressly mentioned in securities acts; and (3) an investment contract.
37.   A registration statement must contain descriptions of (1) the securities being offered for sale, (2) the registrant's business, (3) the management of the registrant, (4) pending litigation, (5) how the proceeds will be used, (6) government regulation, (7) the degree of competition, and (8) any special risk factors.
38.   Instead of arcane legal language, issuers of securities must use plain English language on the cover page, in the summary, and in the risk factor sections of their prospectuses.
39.   A red herring or preliminary prospectus is used as a sales tool during the waiting period when the issuer is trying to condition the market. It contains most of the information to be contained in the final prospectus except for price.
40.   (1) prefiling period (2) waiting period (3) posteffective period

41. Regulation A permits an issuer to sell up to $5 million of securities during a 12-month period pursuant to a simplified registration process. Such offerings may have an unlimited number or purchasers who do not have to be sophisticated investors.

42. Nonissuers, such as average investors, do not have to file a registration statement prior to reselling securities they have purchased. This is because the Securities Act of 1933 exempts securities transactions not made by an issuer, an underwriter, or a dealer from registration.

43. (1) Any natural person with a net worth of at least $1 million (2) Any natural person who has an annual income of $200,000 for the past two years and expects to make at least $200,000 in the current year (3) Any corporation, partnership, or business trust with assets in excess of $5 million (4) Insiders of the issuers (5) Certain institutional investors

44. Securities that were issued for investment purposes pursuant to the intrastate, private placement, or small offering exemption.

45. It can use the simplified process afforded it under Regulation A by using the Small Corporate Offering Registration Form (SCOR), known as Form U-7.

46. The defendant must prove that after reasonable investigation, he or she had reasonable grounds to believe and did believe that, as the time the registration statement became effective, the statements contained therein were true and that there was no omission of material facts.

47. Section 10(b) prohibits the use of manipulative and deceptive devices in the purchase or sale of securities in contravention of the rules and regulation prescribed by the SEC.

48. Reg FD prohibits companies from leaking important information to securities professionals before the information is disclosed to the public.

49. Section 16(b) requires that any profits made by a statutory insider on transactions involving short-swing profits belong to the corporation.

50. It provides a safe harbor from liability for companies that make forward-looking statements that are accompanied by meaningful cautionary statements of risk factors.

Chapter 39

FRANCHISES AND LICENSING

Chapter Overview

Franchising has become an extremely important method of distributing goods and services to the public. Franchises account for 25% of all retail sales. This method of doing business can have risks for the franchisee, especially when the franchise contract is drafted solely by the franchisor. There bulk of law controlling the area of franchises and franchise agreements comes from contract law (chapters 9-16), sales (chapters 19-22), and intellectual property law (chapter 17). This chapter discusses the creation of a franchise, the rights and duties that arise in a franchise relationship, and the termination of a franchise.

Objectives

Upon completion of the exercises in this chapter, you should be able to:
1. Describe a franchise.
2. List the various forms of franchises.
3. Understand the disclosures required by state and federal disclosure rules.
4. Describe the rights and duties of the parties to a franchise agreement.
5. Explain the various forms of franchise fees.
6. Explain how intellectual property rights apply to franchises.
7. Describe the contract liability of franchisors and franchisees.
8. Understand the tort liability of franchisors and franchisees.
9. Describe the remedies available in conjunction with the termination of a franchise.
10. Describe international franchise formation.

Practical Application

You should be able to understand and analyze the problem areas in franchise formation. This will entail applying contract law principles to the special issues created in a franchise arrangement. Further, you will be able to comprehend the rights and liabilities associated with use of trademarks, service marks, patents, copyrights, trade name, and trade dress as they apply to franchises.

Helpful Hints

The biggest problem areas concerning franchises are in the areas of genuineness of assent, discharge, remedies, and intellectual property. It will be very helpful to review the pertinent chapters presented earlier in this test as part of the overall understanding of franchises.

Study Tips

The study of franchise law requires a basic understanding of the following concepts and principles:

franchise – a business arrangement that is established when one party licenses another party to use the franchisor's trade name, trademarks, patents, copyrights, and other property in the distribution and selling of goods and services.

distributorship franchise – the franchisor manufactures a product and licenses a retail franchisee to distribute the product to the public.

processing plant franchise – the franchisor provides a secret formula or process to the franchisee, and the franchisee manufactures the product and distributes it to retail dealers.

chain-style franchises – the franchisor licenses the franchisee to make and sell its products or distribute services to the public from a retail outlet serving an exclusive territory.

area franchise – the franchisor grants the franchisee a franchise for an agreed-upon geographical area within which the franchisee may determine the location of outlets.

Uniform Franchise Offering Circular (UFOC) – a uniform disclosure document that requires the franchisor to make specific presale disclosures to prospective franchisees.

FTC franchise rule – a rule set out by the FTC that requires franchisors to make full presale disclosures to prospective franchisees.

quality control standards – standards or performance and product quality set forth in the franchise agreement to preserve the franchisor's market name and reputation.

training requirements – employee standards that meet the franchisor's specifications

covenant not to compete – an agreement by the franchisee to not compete with the franchisor for a period of time in a specified area after the termination of the franchise.

franchise fees – fees payable by the franchisee as set forth in the franchise agreement.

initial license fee – a lump-sum payment to obtain a franchise.

royalty fee – fee for use of franchisor's trade name, property, and assistance that is computed as a percentage of the franchisee's gross sales.

assessment fee – fee for advertising and administrative costs.

lease fee – payment for land or equipment leased from the franchisor.

cost of supplies – payment for supplies purchased from the franchisor.

breach of franchise agreement – aggrieved party can sue the breaching party for rescission of the agreement, restitution, and damages.

trademarks – a distinctive mark, symbol, name, word, motto, or device that identifies the goods or products of the trademark owner.

service mark – mark, symbol, name, word, motto, or device that identifies the service provided by the service mark owner.

trade secrets – ideas that make a franchise successful but that do not qualify for trademark, patent, or copyright protection.

tort liability – franchisors and franchisees are liable for their own torts.

independent contractor status – the franchisee is an independent contractor, preventing the franchisor from being liable for the franchisee's torts and contracts.

apparent agency – agency that arises when a franchisor creates the appearance that a franchisee is its agent when in fact an actual agency does not exist.

termination of franchise – the franchise agreement usually states reasons or conditions that allow the franchisor or franchisee to terminate the franchise agreement.

termination "for cause" – termination of franchise agreement for failure to fulfill the duties imposed by the agreement.

wrongful termination – termination of the franchise agreement when cause for such action does not exist.

Refresh Your Memory

The following exercises will enable you to refresh your memory of the principles presented in this chapter. Read each question carefully and place your answer in the blanks provided. Review the chapter material for any question you miss or are unable to remember.

1.   A franchise is established when one party _____ another party to use the franchisor's name, trademarks, patents, copyrights, and other property.

2.   In a distributorship franchise, the franchisor _____ a product and licenses a retail franchisee for _____.

3.   In a _____ _____ franchise, the franchisor provides a secret formula or process to the franchisee, and the franchisee manufactures the product and distributes it to retailers.

4.   In a _____-_____ franchise, the franchisor licenses the franchisee to make and sell its products or distribute services to the public from a retail outlet serving an _____ territory.

5.   The Uniform Franchise Offering Circular is a uniform _____ document.

6.   The FTC franchise rule requires franchisors to make full _____ disclosures to prospective franchisees.

7.   Quality control standards preserve the franchisor's market _____ and _____.

8.   The _____ license fee is a lump-sum payment to obtain a franchise.

9.   A _____ fee is assessed for use of the franchisor's name, property and _____.

10.   An assessment fee is for _____ and administrative costs.

11.   A _____ is a distinctive mark, symbol, name, _____, _____, or device that identifies the goods or products of the owner.

12.   The FedEx on the side of a Federal Express truck is an example of a _____ mark.

13.   _____ _____ are ideas that make a franchise successful but do not qualify for trademark, patent, or copyright protection.

14.   Because the franchisee is an _____ contractor, the franchisor is not liable for the torts or contracts of the franchisee.

15.   _____ _____ occurs when a franchise agreement is terminated by the franchisor without cause.

Critical Thought Exercise

Federal Foods, Inc., runs company stores and sells franchises for its restaurants, known as Yum-Me's. Under the franchise agreement with Federal, each franchisee agrees to hire and train all employees and staff in strict compliance with Yum-Me's standards and policies. Federal employs area supervisors who are responsible for reviewing and approving all personnel actions at any restaurant within the four restaurant chains owned by Federal. This includes comprehensive policies relating to employee hiring, training, discipline, and work performance. As part of the franchise agreement, Federal retains the right to terminate any franchise that violates the rules or policies of the franchisor. In practice, the area managers approve the hiring of whatever employees the franchisee desire and the policies that the franchisee desires to create and implement. The area managers inspect each franchise, dictate the food production method, and enforce customer relations policies that were created by Federal.

Ned, a crew leader at a Yum-Me's restaurant, has repeatedly harassed female employees and customers by making rude and explicit sexual remarks. The franchisee and the on-site manager have done nothing to correct Ned's behavior. Two female employees and three customers have filed suit in federal court against Federal based upon Ned's acts. Federal argues that a franchisor cannot be held liable for harassment by franchise employees. Who should prevail?

Answer. _____
_____
_____
_____
_____
_____
_____
_____
_____
_____

_____

_____

_____

_____

_____

Sample Quiz

True/False:

1. ____ A franchisor and franchisee usually work for the same corporation. [p 768]

2. ____ A franchise is any arrangement in which the owner of a trademark, a trade name, or a copyright has licensed a franchisee to use it in selling goods or services. [p 768]

3. ____ An automobile dealership is an example of a distributorship type of franchise. [p 768]

4. ____ The party who grants a franchise is a franchisor. [p 768]

5. ____ A Coca-Cola bottling franchise is an example of a distributorship franchise. [p 768]

6. ____ Burger King is a chain-style franchise. [p 769]

7. ____ Area franchises are a useful business arrangement for expanding into foreign markets. [p 769]

8. ____ A Uniform Franchise Offering Circular requires the franchisor to make specific disclosures to the FTC. [p 770]

9. ____ There was minimal government regulation of franchising until the 1970s. [p 770]

10. ____ The FTC franchise rule requires the same disclosures to be made by franchisors in all states. [p 770]

11. ____ The most important assets of a franchisor are its name and reputation. [p 771]

12. ____ Despite the franchisee's use of the franchisor's name and reputation, the franchisor has no control over the quality of the franchisee's goods or services. [p 771]

13. ____ Franchisees and their personnel are usually required to attend training programs. [p 772]

14. ____ A franchisor cannot protect itself from a franchisee that opens a competing business in the same area after termination of the franchise. [p 772]

15. ____ Franchisees ordinarily pay a lump-sum fee for a franchise license and separate fees for other products and services obtained from the franchisor. [p 772]

16. ____ A royalty fee is a fee for the continued use of the franchisor's trade name, property, and assistance. [p 772]

17. ___ An assessment fee to cover advertising and administrative costs is one of the typical fees contained in a franchise agreement. [p 772]

18. ___ The lease fee is paid to the third party landlord. [p 772]

19. ___ Each party owes a duty to adhere to and perform under the terms of the franchise agreement. [p 774]

20. ___ Franchisees are prohibited from misusing the franchisor's trademarks and service marks. [p 775]

21. ___ If a franchise agreement deals with the franchisee as an independent contractor, the franchisee and franchisor are not liable for each other's torts. [p 777]

22. ___ Franchisors are usually not liable for the acts of their franchisees, but can be liable if there is an apparent agency. [p 778]

23. ___ The franchisor can terminate the franchisee's agreement only for a legitimate cause. [p 780]

24. ___ Most franchise agreements provide that termination must be "for cause" such as the insolvency of the franchisee or failure of the franchisee to perform under the franchise agreement. [p 780]

25. ___ The Agency for International Development provides financial assistance and incentives to promote franchising to franchisees in developing nations. [p 781]

Multiple Choice:

26. Which of the following is not one of the basic forms of a franchise? [p 768]
    a. Distributorship
    b. Chain-style
    c. Processing plant
    d. Joint venture

27. A business arrangement where one party allows another to use its name, trademark, or sell its products in its business is known as a [p 768]
    a. sole proprietorship.
    b. partnership.
    c. franchise.
    d. joint venture.

28. A franchise agreement involves the licensing to a franchisee of [p 768]
    a. a trade name.
    b. a copyright.
    c. a trademark.
    d. all of the above.

29. An automobile dealership is [p 768]
    a. a chain-style franchise.
    b. a distributorship franchise.
    c. a processing plant franchise.
    d. an area franchise.

30. The party to whom a franchise is granted is the [p 768]
    a. franchisor.
    b. franchisee.
    c. principal.
    d. agent.

31. Bogart enters into an agreement whereby he receives an exclusive territory covering four states in which he is authorized to establish a plant to manufacture Fizzy Beer. After receiving Fizzy's secret formula, Bogart begins making beer. This is a [p 768]
    a. processing plant franchise.
    b. chain-style franchise.
    c. distributorship.
    d. none of the above.

32. For which type of franchise does the franchisee have the right to grant franchises to others within a geographical area? [p 769]
    a. Processing plant franchise
    b. Chain-style franchise
    c. Area franchise
    d. Distributorship franchise

33. The FTC franchise rule requires franchisors to [p 770]
    a. share profits with franchisees.
    b. supply advertising and administrative services to the franchisee.
    c. supply trademarks and secret formulas to the franchisee.
    d. make presale disclosures to prospective franchisees.

34. Which of the following items is generally found in a franchise agreement? [p 771]
    a. Quality control standards
    b. Training requirements
    c. Covenant not to compete
    d. All of the above

35. Which of the following remedies is generally available for breach of a franchise agreement? [p 774]
    a. Damages
    b. Restitution
    c. Rescission
    d. All of the above

Short Answer:

36. What is licensed in a franchise arrangement? [p 768] _____
    _____

37. What is a processing plant franchise? [p 768] _____
    _____
    _____

38. Why is Burger King not a processing plant franchise? [p 769] _____

39. List two hurdles that would convince a company to use franchising in a foreign market instead of company owned stores? [p 769] _____

40. Why are quality control standards important to the franchisor? [p 771] _____

41. Give five examples of a type of franchise fee. [p 772] _____

42. What is the purpose of an assessment fee and what does it cover? [p 772] _____

43. What may an aggrieved party recover in a suit for breach of a franchise agreement? [p 774]

44. What is a trademark and service mark? [p 774] _____

45. What is a trade secret? [p 775] _____

46. What is the name for misappropriation of a trade secret and what is the remedy? [p 775]

47. Why is a franchisor normally not liable for the torts of a franchisee? [p 777] _____

48. What is an apparent agency? [p 778] _____

49. Gives three examples of conduct that would be cause to terminate a franchise agreement. [p 780]

50. What is wrongful termination of a franchise agreement? [p 781] _____

Answers to Refresh Your Memory

1. licenses [p 768]
2. manufactures, distribution [p 768]
3. processing plant [p 768]
4. chain-style, exclusive [p 769]
5. disclosure [p 770]

6. presale [p 770]
7. name, reputation [p 771]
8. initial [p 772]
9. royalty, assistance [p 772]
10. advertising [p 772]
11. trademark, word, motto [p 774]
12. service [p 774]
13. trade secrets [p 775]
14. independent [p 777]
15. wrongful termination [p 780]

Critical Thought Exercise Model Answer

Liability for Ned's acts may be imputed to Federal because of an agency relationship that exists between Federal and the employees of the franchisee. An agency results from the manifestation of consent by one person to another so that the other will act on his or her behalf and subject to the control of the principal, and consent by the agent to so act. An agency agreement may be evidenced by an express agreement between the parties, or it may be implied from the circumstances and conduct of the parties. The principal's consent and right to control the agent are the essential elements of an agency relationship.

The franchise agreement in this case required adherence to comprehensive policies and rules for the operation of the restaurant. Federal enforces these rules and policies by sending area managers to inspect each franchisee. The area managers also approve the hiring and training of each employee. Federal controls the franchisee and the employee's of Yum-Me Restaurant by retaining the right to terminate the franchise agreement. Most importantly, the franchise agreement gave Federal the right to control the franchisees in the very parts of the franchisee's business that resulted in the injuries to the plaintiffs, these parts being the areas of employee training and discipline. Federal, the franchisor, may be held liable under an agency theory for the intentional acts of sexual discrimination by the employee of its franchisee.

Answers to Sample Quiz

True/False:

1. False They are separate business entities.
2. True The licensed property may also include patents and copyrights.
3. True The franchisee serves as a distributor for goods manufactured by the franchisor.
4. True The franchisor is also the licensor.
5. False This is a processing plant franchise. The franchisee is given a secret formula from which it manufactures the product and them distributes it to retailers.
6. True The franchisee makes and sells the licensed product from a retail outlet.
7. True It allows expansion that overcomes government regulation and takes advantage of the franchisee's cultural knowledge.
8. False The disclosures are to prospective franchisees.
9. True California enacted the first state franchise investment law.
10. True This became law in 1979.
11. True Quality standard controls protect these assets.
12. False The quality control standards in the franchise agreement provide protection.
13. True These training requirements can be part of the franchise agreement.
14. False A covenant not to compete can be inserted into the franchise agreement.
15. True This is called the initial license fee.

16. True   It is often computed as a percentage of the franchisee's gross sales.

17. True   It may be billed as either a flat monthly fee of annual fee or percentage of gross sales.

18. False   It is a payment for land or equipment leased from the franchisor.

19. True   Failure to perform is a breach of the franchise agreement.

20. True   These marks must be protected to maintain the public perception of the quality of the goods and services of the franchisor.

21. True   Because there is no agency relationship, neither party is liable for the torts or contracts of the other.

22. True   The apparent agency is created when a franchisor leads a third person into believing that the franchisee is its agent.

23. True   Unreasonable strict application of a just cause termination clause constitutes wrongful termination.

24. True   Difficult situations arise when the cause is debatable, such as failure to meet quality control standards.

25. True   USAID will back up to 50 percent of a loan for a franchisee through a guarantee.

Multiple Choice:

26. D   A joint venture is not an ongoing business. Choices A, B, and C are all franchises.

27. C   The property is used under a license. Choice A has no license arrangement with another business. Choice B is a single business entity, while a franchise involves two businesses. Choice D is not correct because a joint venture is not an ongoing business.

28. D   Choices A, B, and C are all forms of property that can be licensed, making D the correct answer.

29. B   B is correct because in a distributorship franchise, the franchisor manufactures the product and the franchisee distributes the product within a geographical area. This is now automobiles are distributed. A is not correct because the franchisee makes the product in a chain-style and sells it at an outlet. C is not correct because the automobile dealer is not given a secret formula from which to produce cars. D is not correct because the dealership does not set up multiple dealerships within a geographical area as part of the franchise.

30. B   The franchisee receives the license from the franchisor. A is not correct because the franchisor grants the franchise. C and D are not correct because a franchise is not an agency relationship.

31. A   The processing plant franchise involves licensing a formula to allow the franchisee to manufacture and distribute a product to the franchisor's specifications. B is not correct as a chain-style franchise makes and sells products from a retail outlet. C is incorrect because a distributor does not make the product. D is incorrect because A is correct.

32. C   The area franchise gives the franchisee the rights to select the placement and number of franchises within its geographical area. A, B, and D are incorrect because the franchisee in these franchises has no authority to grant an additional franchise to another.

33. D   The full disclosures must have cautionary language concerning risk and facts concerning anticipated profits. A, B and C are not requirements of the FTC rule, but may be part of the duties of a franchisor under specific franchise agreement.

34. D   D is correct because choices A, B, and C are all standard items in a franchise agreement.

35. D   Choices A, B, and C are all possible remedies a party may seek if there is a breach of the franchise agreement. Therefore, D is the correct answer.

Short Answer:

36. The franchisor licenses to the franchisee the use of franchisor's trade name, trademarks, commercial symbols, patents, copyrights, and other property in the distribution and selling of goods and services.

37. A processing plant franchise provides a secret formula or process to the franchisee, and the franchisee manufactures the product and distributes it to retail dealers.

38. A processing plant franchise does not sell the product out of a retail outlet after making it. Burger King not only makes the product, but also serves as the retailer. Therefore, a Burger King franchise is a chain-style franchise.

39. Restrictions in some countries prohibit 100 percent ownership of a business by a foreign investor. Many companies lack the expertise and cultural knowledge to enter many foreign markets. The foreign franchisee would provide national ownership and knowledge of the business and cultural climate in a particular foreign market.

40. The franchisor's most important assets are its name and reputation. The quality control standards set out in a franchise agreement are intended to protect those assets.

41. initial license fee, royalty fee, assessment fee, lease fees payment, cost of supplies payment

42. An assessment fee pays for advertising and promotional campaigns and administrative costs. It is billed either as a flat monthly fee or a percentage of gross sales.

43. The aggrieved party may sue for rescission, restitution, and damages.

44. It is a distinctive mark, symbol, name, word, motto, or device that identifies the goods or services of a particular franchisor.

45. Trade secrets are ideas that make a franchise successful but that do not qualify for trademark, patent, or copyright protection.

46. This misappropriation is known as unfair competition. The holder of the trade secret can sue for damages and obtain an injunction to prohibit further unauthorized use of the trade secret.

47. A franchisee is usually set up as an independent contractor in the franchise agreement. Because there is no agency relationship, the franchisor is not liable for the torts committed by the franchisee.

48. Agency that results when a franchisor creates the appearance that a franchisee is its agent when in fact an actual agency does not exist.

49. nonpayment of franchise fees, failure to maintain quality control standards, misappropriation of a trade secret, and trademark infringement

50. Wrongful termination occurs if a franchise agreement is terminated without just cause.

Chapter 40

EMPLOYMENT AND WORKER PROTECTION LAWS

Chapter Overview

This chapter examines employment contracts and the exceptions to the at-will doctrine that applies to a majority of employment contracts. It also examines the statutes that have been enacted to protect workers. These laws include workers' compensation, minimum wage and overtime pay, occupational safety, pension, immigration, unemployment, Social Security, and other laws that protect employees from unfair treatment.

Objectives

Upon completion of the exercises in this chapter, you should be able to:
1.   Discuss the employment at-will doctrine and the public policy exception to its application.
2.   Describe how state workers' compensation laws function and the benefits that are available.
3.   Explain employer's obligation under OSHA to provide and maintain safe work conditions.
4.   Explain how the Fair Labor Standards Act provides for minimum wage and overtime pay.
5.   Explain when drug and polygraph testing may be used by employers.
6.   Explain the protections provided for employee pensions.
7.   Describe how immigration laws affect employers and employees.
8.   Understand unemployment compensation benefits and Social Security laws.
9.   Describe the rights granted by the Family and Medical Leave Act.

Practical Applications

Upon mastering the material in this chapter, you should be able to recognize the situations where employee rights and protections are applicable and the specific laws that cover a dispute or loss of income. You will understand the limits of the protections and the employee's requirements that must be met to gain protection under the various statutes.

Helpful Hints

Both the employee and employer benefit by a clear understanding of how the various employment protection statutes function. The requirements of some laws apply only to specific employers based upon the qualifying language of the statute. Employees often have requirements of notice and cooperation built into the statute with which they must comply to gain enforcement of their rights. Employers must understand and adhere to the requirements imposed by government regulation in the workplace or they subject themselves to the high costs of law suits and lost production in the workplace.

Study Tips

It is just as important to understand when the employment laws may apply as it is to understand the technical requirements built into the individual statutes. You should develop your understanding of employment laws by organizing the material into general areas.

Employees Protected By Contracts vs. At-Will Employees
An employee who does not have an employment contract is considered an employee at-will. The general rule is that at-will employees can be discharged at any time for any reason. This has been changed by statutes and case law in certain situations. The bulk of this chapter examines the exceptions created to negate the harsh effects of the at-will doctrine.

Statutory exceptions to at-will doctrine
Federal and state statutes protect the overall employment relationship be forbidding discharge in violation of union or collective bargaining agreements. An employer must also refrain from discharging an employee in violation of the Title VII and anti-discrimination laws. When the employee is discharged based upon race, sex, religion, age, handicap, national origin or other protected classifications, the discharge is unlawful, even if the employee is at-will.

Implied-in-fact exception to the at-will doctrine
An implied-in-fact contract is developed by the conduct of the parties. The employer may issue bulletins or manuals that promise continued employment if the company rules are followed. The employer has removed the at-will condition and replaced it with a contractual understanding of the employment relationship.

Public policy exception to the at-will doctrine
An employee cannot be discharged if the discharge violates public policy. Public policy dictates that an employee will not be fired because they serve as a juror, refuse to violate the law, refuse to distribute dangerous products or goods to consumers, or refuse to commit a tort against another person.

Tort exceptions
The employee can sue for damages for wrongful based upon fraud, defamation, or intentional infliction of emotional distress. If the employee is successful in a tort action, he or she may be able to recover punitive damages.

Drug testing of employees
Pre-employment drug testing is generally upheld by the courts. Incumbent employees can be tested when the employer suspects drug use if there is no prohibition of testing in an employee contract. Government employees can be tested whenever their position has an element of public safety. Some statutes require testing when there is an incident or accident, such as a train wreck.

Protective Statutes
The following statutes and legislative schemes protect both substantive and procedural rights of employees in their dealings with employers.

Workers' Compensation Acts
These acts were enacted to compensate employees for injuries that occurred on the job regardless of fault. The amount of compensation payable to the employee is set by statute. Payment under the

workers' compensation statute is the employee's exclusive remedy, meaning that an employee cannot sue their employee when they are injured on the job.

Employee Polygraph Protection Act

The act prohibits most private employers from using polygraph tests. Federal and state governments are not covered by the act. Polygraph tests can also be used by private employers when the employee deals with national defense, public health and safety, drug manufacturing, or is involved in theft or espionage. The act sets up procedures that must be followed or penalties may be assessed.

Occupational Safety and Health Act

The Act was enacted to promote safety in the workplace. It imposes recordkeeping and reporting requirements upon the employer. The enforcement arm created by the act is the Occupational Safety and Health Administration (OSHA). OSHA has adopted regulations to enforce the safety standards created by the act. OSHA may inspect places of employment and cite the employer for violations. OSHA violations carry both civil and criminal penalties.

Fair Labor Standards Act (FSLA)

The FSLA prohibits child labor and establishes minimum wage and overtime pay requirements.

Employee Retirement Income Security Act (ERISA)

ERISA is designed to prevent fraud and abuses associated with private pension funds. Requires that the pension plan be in writing and name a pension fund manager. ERISA dictates how the pension funds can be invested and sets time limits for when pension rights must vest.

Consolidated Omnibus Budget Reconciliation Act (COBRA)

Provides that employee or his beneficiaries must have the opportunity to maintain group health coverage upon dismissal or death due to certain events. Government employees are covered by the Public Health Service Act.

Family and Medical Leave Act

The act guarantees workers unpaid time off for medical emergencies. Applies to employers with 50 or more employees. Employee must have worked for at least one year and performed at least 1,250 hours of work. Covers time off for birth or care of child, serious health condition, and care for spouse, parent, or child with a serious health problem. Employee must be restored to their same or a similar position upon their return.

Immigration Reform and Control Act

Forbids employer from hiring illegal immigrants. Employer must examine documents to determine employees right to work in the country.

Federal Unemployment Tax Act

Employers must pay unemployment taxes to compensate employees during periods of unemployment. Employee does not receive benefits if they are discharged for misconduct or quit without cause.

Social Security

Under the Federal Insurance Contributions Act (FICA) employees and employers make contributions to the Social Security Fund. The funds are used to pay current recipients of Social Security.

Refresh Your Memory

The following exercise will enable you to refresh your memory of the main points given in this chapter. Read the question twice and place your answer in the blanks provided. If you do not remember the principle, go to the next question and come back to the ones you did not answer.

1.   Most employees do not have employment contracts and are considered ___-_____ employees.

2.   Drug testing of incumbent employees by private employers is usually upheld where the employer either has a _____ _____ that an employee is impaired or drug testing is required after an _____ has occurred.

3.   Workers' compensation acts compensate workers and their families if workers are _____ in connection with their jobs.

4.   To recover under workers' compensation, the workers' injuries must have been _____- related.

5.   Workers' compensation precludes an injured worker from suing the _____ for other damages or remedies.

6.   The Employee Polygraph Protection Act prohibits most _____ employers from using polygraph tests.

7.   In 1970, Congress enacted the Occupational Safety and Health Act to promote _____ in the workplace.

8.   The Occupational Safety and Health Act imposes a general duty on an employer to provide a work environment "____ ____ _____ _____" that are causing or are likely to cause death or serious physical harm to his employees.

9.   The Fair Labor Standards Act forbids the use of _____ _____ _____ and makes it unlawful to ship goods produced by businesses that use _____ _____ _____.

10. The FSLA establishes _____ wage and _____ pay requirement for workers.

11. ERISA is a complex act designed to prevent _____ and other abuses associated with _____ pension funds.

12. COBRA provides that an employee of a private employer or the employee's _____ must be offered the opportunity to continue his or her group _____ insurance after the dismissal or death of the employee or the loss of coverage due to certain qualifying events.

13. The Family and Medical Leave Act guarantees workers _____ time off from work for medical emergencies.

14. The Immigration Reform and Control Act makes it unlawful for employers to hire _____ immigrants.

15. To collect unemployment benefits, applicants must be able and _____ for work and be _____ employment.

Critical Thought Exercise

Sid Frost worked as a merchandising supervisor for Global-Mart, Inc., a large discount store employing over 26,000 people. When Frost suffered his third stroke in April 1999, he took leave from work, which was covered by the Family and Medical Leave Act (FMLA) of 1993. The Vice-President of Personnel for Global-Mart approved the leave. Mike Allen, who had been hired only two months after Frost in 1984, temporarily filled Frost's position. When Frost returned to work, he discovered that Allen had been promoted to senior supervisor and given a $7,000 raise. The senior supervisor position is filled from the supervisor classification based upon seniority. Global-Mart refused to allow Frost to return to his position as a supervisor and demoted him to a senior salesman position that required travel away from home on a weekly basis. Six weeks later Global-Mart fired Frost because he was unable to keep up the schedule required by his position and because his expense account was not timely filed by the end of the month.

Frost sues Global-Mart for violation of the FMLA based upon Global-Mart's failure to promote him to senior supervisor or return him to his prior position. Did Global-Mart violate the FMLA?

Answer. _____

_____

_____

_____

_____

_____

_____

_____

_____

_____

_____

_____

_____

_____

_____

_____

Practice Quiz

True/False:

1. ____ An employee who has been wrongfully discharged can only sue his employer for money damages. [p 787]

2. ____ Federal and state statutes restrict the application of the employment at-will doctrine. [p 787]

3. ____ Implied-in-fact contracts develop from the express agreement of the parties. [p 787]

4. ____ The contents of a company bulletin or handbook may be construed as an implied promise that an employee can only be discharged for good cause. [p 787]

5. ____ The most used common law exception to the employment at-will doctrine is the public policy exception. [p 787]

6. ____ Wrongful discharge action cannot be based on tort theories. [p 788]

7. ____ If an employee is successful in a tort action, punitive damages may be awarded. [p 788]

8. ____ *Toussaint v. Blue Cross and Blue Shield of Michigan* held that when an employee inquires about job security and the employer agrees that eh employee shall be employed as long as he does the job, this is not enough to create a contract and the employee may still be discharged at-will. [p 788]

9. ____ Generally, pre-employment drug screening has been upheld by the courts. [p 789]

10. ____ In *Skinner v. Railway Labor Executives Association*, the Supreme Court ruled that postaccident testing was not lawful unless the employer had reason to suspect drug use. [p 789]

11. ____ The U.S. Customs Service can require applicants to submit to drug testing because the job requires that a custom agent interdict illegal drugs, carry a gun, and handle classified material. [p 789]

12. ____ Employers are required to pay for workers' compensation insurance and can not avoid this requirement by setting aside payments in a self-insured account. [p 789]

13. ____ If a worker is dissatisfied with the ruling on his or her workers' compensation claim, they can ask for an appeal with the workers compensation board, but they cannot file suit in a state court seeking workers' compensation benefits. [p 789]

14. ____ Accidents that occur at a company cafeteria or while on a business lunch for an employer are not covered by workers' compensation. [p 790]

15. ____ If an employer intentionally injures a worker during work hours, the employee's remedy is limited to workers' compensation benefits. [p 790]

16. ____ The Employee Polygraph Protection Act does not prohibit the use of polygraph tests on government employees. [p 791]

17. ____ When a private employer administers a polygraph test, they are free to administer the test in the manner they see fit. [p 791]

18. ____ Federal, State and local governments do not have to comply with the Occupational Safety and Health Act. [p 791]

19. ____ OSHA is only allowed to enter a business upon invitation of the employer. [p 791]

20. ____ Under the Fair Labor Standards Act, children ages 14 and 15 may work unlimited hours but only in nonhazardous jobs. [p 793]

21. ____ If an employee works 50 hours one week and only 30 hours the next, he or she is not entitled to any overtime pay because they are only averaging 40 hours per week. [p 793]

22. ____ ERISA requires that all pension plans be in writing and each plan must name a pension fund manager. [p 794]

23. ___ If an employee is killed on the job, the employer must notify the employee's beneficiaries of their right to continue with the company's group health insurance. [p 795]

24. ___ Not only does the Family Medical Leave Act apply to private employers with 50 or more employees, but it also applies to federal, state, and local governments. [p 795]

25. ___ Employers covered by the Family and Medical Leave Act are entitled receive up to 12 weeks of unpaid leave during any 12-month period. [p 795]

Multiple Choice:

26. The termination of an employee will be considered a wrongful discharge if the termination was in violation of [p 787]
    a. a statute.
    b. an employment contract.
    c. public policy.
    d. all of the above.

27. An implied-in-fact contract may be developed from [p 787]
    a. an employee handbook.
    b. public policy.
    c. a written agreement.
    d. a union contract.

28. The termination of an employee because they refused to copy bootlegged CD's would be a wrongful termination because it violated [p 787]
    a. a tort exception.
    b. the implied-in-fact contract exception.
    c. the public policy exception.
    d. a statutory exception.

29. An employee has been wrongfully discharged if the employer caused the termination by [p 787]
    a. committing a fraud against the employee.
    b. intentionally inflicting emotional distress against the employee.
    c. defaming the character of the employee.
    d. all of the above.

30. An employer may not give a polygraph test to an employee if the employer [p 791]
    a. is a landscaping business and the employee reports that the employer is stealing plants.
    b. deals in matters of national security, such as a defense contractor.
    c. provides security services for the protection of public health and safety, such as guarding electrical power plants.
    d. is a drug manufacturer that hires employees that will have access to drugs.

31. The Employee Polygraph Protection Act requires private employers that are permitted to use polygraph testing to follow certain procedures, including [p 791]
    a. allowing the employee to return to the same position with the same pay.
    b. giving notice to the person to be tested.
    c. allowing the employee to maintain health insurance after he is discharged.
    d. giving the employee a hearing in front of an administrative law judge.

32. OSHA standards establish rules pertaining to [p 791]
    a. minimum wage.
    b. amounts of compensation after a work-related injury.
    c. maximum levels for exposure to hazardous chemicals.
    d. age requirements for use of child labor.

33. Employers who establish pension plans for their employees are subject to the recordkeeping, disclosure, and other requirements of [p 791]
    a. COBRA.
    b. ERISA.
    c. FUTA.
    d. FICA.

34. An eligible employee under the Family and Medical Leave Act who takes leave must, upon returning to work [p 795]
    a. accept whatever position is open at the tine.
    b. accept a reduction in pay if someone else has been promoted.
    c. forfeit benefits equal to the value of the leave.
    d. be restored to either the same or an equivalent position with equivalent employment benefits and pay.

35. Social Security benefits include [p 795]
    a. survivors' benefits to family members of deceased workers.
    b. the right to continue group health insurance provided by the employer.
    c. the right to take time off for the birth of a child.
    d. payments for a period of time when the employee is temporarily unemployed.

Short Answer:

36. The courts have held that an _____-___-_____ contract can be created between an employer and employee based upon the conduct of the parties. [p 787]

37. When do the courts usually uphold drug testing of employees who have already been hired by a private employer? [p 789] _____

38. Why were workers' compensation laws created? [p 789] _____

39. What must the employee prove to receive workers' compensation? [p 789] _____

40. List four circumstances when a private employer may give a polygraph test to an employee. [p 791]

_____
_____

41.   Describe four examples of specific duty standards created by OSHA. [p 791] _____
_____
_____
_____

42.   What can OSHA do upon finding a safety violation following an inspection of a place of
      employment? [p 791] _____

43.   According to the Fair Labor Standards Act, what type or work can a child under 14 accept? [p 793]
      _____

44.   If children cannot work in hazardous jobs, who determines what job is hazardous? [p 792]
      _____

45.   To whom may an employer pay less than minimum wage? [p 793] _____

46.   What pension plans are exempt from coverage under ERISA? [p 794] _____

47.   What occurs when an employee has a nonforfeitable right to receive pension benefits? [p 794]
      _____

48.   What is the prerequisite for an employee to be covered by the Family and Medical Leave Act?
      [p 795] _____
      _____

49.   Under the Immigration Reform and Control Act of 1986, an employer must attest to what facts
      before an employee may be hired? [p 795] _____
      _____

50.   How much must a self-employed person contribute to Social Security? [p 797] _____

Answers To Refresh Your Memory

1.   at-will [p 787]
2.   reasonable suspicion, accident [p 789]
3.   injured [p 789]
4.   employment [p 790]
5.   employer [p 790]
6.   private [p 791]
7.   safety [p 791]
8.   "free from recognized hazards" [p 792]
9.   oppressive child labor, oppressive child labor [p 793]

10. minimum, overtime [p 793]
11. fraud, private [p 794]
12. beneficiaries, health [p 794]
13. unpaid [p 795]
14. illegal [p 795]
15. available, seeking [p 797]

Critical Thought Exercise Model Answer

The FMLA guarantees workers unpaid time off work for medical emergencies. There is little doubt that a stroke is a medical emergency and Global-Mart had approved the leave for Frost. The FMLA will apply to Global-Mart because it has over 50 employees. Under the FMLA, the employer must guarantee employment in the same position or a comparable position when the employee returns to work. Employers who violate the FMLA may be held liable for damages to compensate employees for unpaid wages, lost benefits, denied compensation and actual monetary losses up to an amount equivalent to the employee's wages for twelve weeks. The employer may also be required to grant a promotion that has been denied. The restored employee is not entitled to the accrual of seniority during the leave period, however. Frost was not returned to his former position when he returned. He was forced to take a demotion, which required travel. Global-Mart violated the FMLA by demoting Frost. The failure to promote Frost may not be a violation because the promotion was based upon seniority and Frost had less seniority than Allen at the time of the promotion. Therefore, Global-Mart should be ordered to return Frost to his prior supervisor position but will not be required to promote him to senior supervisor. Global-Mart will also be required to pay damages for lost wages during the time Frost was not working die to his firing.

Answers to Practice Quiz

True/False:

1. False   An employee may also sue his or her employer for other remedies such as reinstatement and back pay.
2. True   These statutes include labor laws that forbid discharge in violation of collective bargaining agreements and discharge that is founded upon discrimination that is prohibited by Title VII.
3. False   Implied-in-fact contracts develop from the conduct of the parties, not an agreement.
4. True   The company handbook or personnel policy manual might mention that employees who do their jobs properly will not be discharged.
5. True   An employee cannot be discharged if such discharge violates the public policy of the jurisdiction, such as firing an employee because they fulfilled their jury duty service.
6. False   An employee can sue for wrongful discharge based upon such tort theories as fraud, intentional infliction of emotional distress, and defamation of character.
7. True   In addition to compensatory and incidental damages, an employer may be assessed punitive damages if the conduct is especially egregious.
8. False   A fair construction of this agreement is that the employer has given up his right to discharge at-will without assigning cause and may discharge only for good or just cause.
9. True   While present employees may be protected by their employment from drug testing, job applicants can be required to submit to drug testing as part of the application process.

Chapter 40

10. False   The Court upheld a Federal Railroad Administration rule that requires blood and urine tests of every employee involved in a "major accident" and permits testing of any worker who violates certain safety rules.

11. True   In addition, the testing of off-duty agents is permitted because of the possibility of bribery and blackmail if an agent is using illegal drugs.

12. False   Employers can either pay for the insurance or become self-insured by setting aside payments in a contingency account.

13. False   If the worker disagrees with the agency's findings, he or she may appeal the decision through the state court system.

14. False   These activities are considered to have been done in the course of his or her employment and would be entitled to workers' compensation coverage.

15. False   The employee can collect workers' compensation benefits *and* sue the employer.

16. True   The act only covers private employers' use of polygraph tests.

17. False   The Employee Polygraph Protection Act requires employers to follow procedures such as given notice that the test will be given and using only licensed examiners.

18. True   The act applies only to private employers.

19. False   OSHA is empowered to inspect places of employment for health hazards and safety violations.

20. False   Children ages 14 and 15 may work limited hours in nonhazardous jobs that are approved by the Department of Labor.

21. False   The employee is entitled to overtime pay for each hour worked in excess of 40 hours in a week. Each week is treated separately.

22. True   The plan must be in writing to help avoid fraud and the manager has a fiduciary duty to act as a prudent person in managing the fund.

23. True   The employer must notify the beneficiaries of their rights under COBRA to maintain the health insurance by payment of the premiums.

24. True   Unlike other employee statutes discussed in this chapter, the Family and Medical Leave Act applies to all government employees.

25. True   This 12 weeks of leave can be used for the birth of a child, family illness, or several other reasons set forth in the statute.

Multiple Choice:

26. D   Each choice states a correct source for determining whether or not there has been a wrongful discharge upon the violation of the law associated with that source.

27. A   Answer A is the correct choice because a handbook sets forth the expected conduct of the parties and it is from this conduct that a contract is implied. Choice B is incorrect because is a separate way of avoiding the at-will doctrine that is unrelated to implied-in-fact contracts. Choices C and D are incorrect because they are both express agreements, not implied ones.

28. C   Answer C is correct because discharging an employee because they refuse to violate the law for the employer violated public policy. Answers A, B and D are separate exceptions unrelated to the request of the employer for the employee to do an illegal act.

29. D   Answer D is correct because wrongful discharge can be based on several tort theories. Choices A, B, and C all state tort theories.

30. A   Answer A is correct because a landscaping business does not involve any security or public safety work for which the employer has a genuine safety concern. Choices B, C, and D are incorrect because they are all employment positions that involve issues of public health and safety or national security, thereby allowing the employer to administer a polygraph test.

31. B   B is correct because an employee must be given advance notice when a polygraph test is desired by the employer. Answer A is incorrect because it lists a right granted under the Family and

Medical Leave Act. C is incorrect because it states a right under COBRA. D is incorrect because there is no statutory right to an administrative hearing under the EPPA.

32. C   C is correct because it states one type of safety standard set by OSHA. A is incorrect because minimum wage is set by the Fair Labor Standards Act. B is incorrect because workers' compensation is set by state workers' compensation acts. D is incorrect because child labor laws are set forth in the Fair Labor Standards Act.

33. B   B is correct because the Employee Retirement Income Security Act control all aspects of private pensions created by employers for their employees. A is incorrect because COBRA deals with maintaining group health insurance. C is incorrect because FUTA deals with unemployment compensation. D is incorrect because FICA deals with contributions to Social Security.

34. D   D is correct be cause it is the full statement of what is required when an employee returns from leave under the FMLA. Choice A is incorrect because an employee must be returned to the same or an equivalent position. Answer B is not correct because the employee must be returned to the same level of pay after a leave. C is incorrect because there can be no loss of benefits to an employee who takes a leave under the FMLA.

35. A   Answer A is correct because survivor's rights are part of the compensation plan built into Social Security to help the family of a deceased worker. B is incorrect because continued group health insurance is covered by COBRA, not Social Security. Answer C is incorrect because leave for the birth of a child is covered by the Family and Medical Leave Act. D is incorrect because unemployment compensation is covered by FUTA.

Short Answer:

36.   implied-in-fact

37.   Drug testing of incumbent employees by private employers is usually upheld where the employer either has reasonable suspicion that an employee is impaired or drug testing is required after an accident has occurred.

38.   Before workers' compensation laws were created in response to the situation where the workers and their families were left uncompensated after the employee was injured or killed while during work for the employer. The employee formerly had to sue his own employer for negligence to get any compensation for an injury and if the employer successfully defended against the suit, the employee received nothing. Workers' compensation gives compensation without regard to fault.

39.   The employee must prove that the injury arose out of and in the course of his or her employment.

40.   (1) In matters dealing with the national defense, (2) When employers provide security services that hire employees who protect the public health and safety, (3) When employers are drug manufacturers and distributors that hire employees that will have access to the drugs, and (4) When employers are investigating incidents of theft, embezzlement, espionage, and the like by current employees. The employer must have a reasonable suspicion that the employee was involved in the incident.

41.   (1) Safety requirements for equipment, such as guards on drills and saws, (2) Setting the maximum exposure levels to hazardous chemicals, (3) Regulate the location of machinery and clearance around machinery, and (4) Establish safety procedures.

42.   If a violation is found, OSHA can issue a written citation that requires the employer to abate or correct the situation.

43.   Children under 14 cannot work except as newspaper deliverers.

44.   The Department of Labor determines which occupations are hazardous (e.g., mining, roofing, working with explosives, working with caustic chemicals).

45.   The Department of Labor permits employers to pay less than the minimum wage to students and apprentices.

46. Federal, state, and local government pensions are exempt from ERISA coverage.
47. Vesting
48. To be covered, the employee must have worked for the employer for at least one year and have performed more than 1,250 hours of service during the previous 12-month period.
49. The employer must fill out INS Form I-9, which attests that the employer has inspected documents of the employee and has determined that he or she is either a U.S. citizen or is otherwise qualified to work in the country.
50. Under the Self-Employment Contribution Act the self-employed individual must contribute an amount to Social Security that is equal to the combined amount contributed by the employer and employee under FICA.

Chapter 41

EQUAL OPPORTUNITY
IN EMPLOYMENT

Chapter Overview

Prior to the 1960's, there was little that an employee could do to address discrimination by the employer in regards to hiring, discharge, promotion, pay, and work assignments. Congress addressed discrimination by passing a comprehensive set of law that made it actionable to discriminate against a person because of race, sex, religion, national origin, age, or disability. The interpretation of these federal statutes has created a large body of law that has created a much more level playing field in the workplace. The chapter examines the major legislation and the application of these laws by the courts.

Objectives

Upon completion of the exercises in this chapter, you should be able to:
1. Describe the protection provided by Title VII of the Civil Rights Act of 1964.
2. Identify examples of discrimination based upon race, color, and national origin.
3. Describe conduct that creates sex discrimination, including sexual harassment.
4. Recognize how e-mail may be used as evidence of sexual harassment.
5. Discuss the important protections contained in the Equal Pay Act of 1963.
6. Explain how the bona fide occupational qualification (BFOQ) defense works in discrimination cases.
7. Explain the protections provided by the Age Discrimination in employment Act.
8. Describe the scope of the Americans with Disabilities Act and the protections it affords person with a disability.
9. Define the doctrine of affirmative action and describe how it is used.
10. Describe how the law related to equal opportunity in employment is being applied in Japan.

Practical Application

Antidiscrimination laws set forth mandates for employers and protection for employees that alter the course of conduct of people in the business environment. You should be able to recognize the situations where discrimination is unlawful and instances where a defense to discrimination may apply. This will allow you to make decisions that stay within the requirements set forth by the federal laws.

Helpful Hints

Since most of this chapter concentrates on specific laws and cases that interpret the laws, it is beneficial to know the basic definition or content of each law and understand the examples of how they are applied in the real world. You should focus on the type of conduct that is involved in a situation to determine which area of law is applicable and what actions must be taken to correct the action, if at all possible.

Study Tips

Enforcement of federal antidiscrimination laws

The Equal Employment Opportunity Commission (EEOC) is appointed by the President and is responsible for enforcing the provisions of all the federal laws that address areas of discrimination in the workplace. The EEOC is empowered to not only investigate, but also to issue opinions and directives to offending employers, bring suit against the violator, and even seek injunctive relief to stop the actual conduct that violated a particular law. Though an employee can file suit directly against the employer if the EEOC gives permission, action by the EEOC is the best actions available to force a stop to the illegal conduct.

Title VII of the Civil Rights Act of 1964

Overall, Title VII is the most important piece of legislation ever passed to address discrimination. As such, it provides the authority for the largest number of cases brought to rectify discrimination. The conduct that will trigger a Title VII action will be within the areas of:

- Hiring
- Discharge
- Compensation (rate of pay and classification that affects pay)
- Terms of employment (work schedule, fringe benefits)
- Conditions of the employment (rules, policies and procedures)
- Privileges granted as part of employment (honorary positions, use of company assets)
- Promotion (not promoted when qualified)
- Work assignment (given less desirable assignments that prevent growth)

If any action on the above list is made by an employer based upon a person's race, color, religion, sex, or national origin; or the employee is limited in any way that deprives them of an opportunity based upon race, color, religion, sex, or national origin, a violation of Title VII has been committed.

Title VII applies to:

- employers with 15 or more employees
- employment agencies
- labor union with 15 or more employees
- state and local governments
- most federal employees
- undocumented aliens

Title VII does not apply to:

- Indian tribes
- tax-exempt private clubs

There are two types of discrimination that Title VII addresses:

- Disparate treatment: employer discriminates against individual
- Disparate impact: employer discriminates against entire protected class

Procedure for bringing Title VII action consists of these steps:
- Private complainant must file complaint with EEOC
- EEOC given opportunity to sue on behalf of complainant
- If EEOC chooses not to sue, issues right to sue letter
- Complainant now has right to sue employer

Remedies for violation of Title VII include:
- Recovery by employee of up to two years' back pay
- If malice or reckless indifference to rights is shown, aggrieved party may recover compensatory and punitive damages
- Statutory damages from $50,000 to $300,000 may be awarded depending upon the size of the employer
- Court may order reinstatement, including seniority rights
- Court may issue injunctions to compel compliance

The **Pregnancy Discrimination Act** was added to Title VII in 1978 to forbid discrimination because of pregnancy, birth, or related medical conditions. The effect that pregnancy or giving birth to a new baby may have upon a woman cannot be raised in a job interview or used as the basis for not offering a position. It also forbids the use of pregnancy, giving birth, or a related medical condition, as a basis for making a decision in any of the other employment areas listed above.

Sexual Harassment
Lewd remarks, touching, intimidation, posting pinups, and other verbal of physical conduct of a sexual nature that occur on the job are sexual harassment and violate Title VII. Requesting that an employee has sex with the employer to get hired, receive a promotion, or prevent discharge, are all forms of sexual harassment prohibited by Title VII. When the workplace is permeated with discriminatory intimidation, ridicule, and insult, that is sufficiently severe or pervasive to alter the conditions of the victim's employment and create an abusive working environment, Title VII is violated. In evaluating the severity ands pervasiveness of sexual harassment, a court will focus on the perspective of the victim and ask whether a "reasonable woman" would consider the conduct to be offensive. Evidence of the offending conduct may come from words, physical acts, e-mails distributed within or outside the office, pictures (including material on computers), jokes, threats, and both employer and employee communications. The court will consider the overall effect that several acts have upon the victim.

Defense To Sexual Harassment
An employer may raise an affirmative defense against liability or damages for sexual harassment by proving that:
1. The employer exercised reasonable care to prevent and correct promptly any sexually-harassing behavior, and
2. The plaintiff employee unreasonably failed to take advantage of any preventive of coercive opportunities by the employer or to otherwise avoid harm

Religious Discrimination
Under Title VII, the employer is under a duty to reasonably accommodate the religious observances, practices, or beliefs of its employees if it does not cause undue hardship on the employer.

Defenses To A Title VII Action
Merit. Employers can select or promote employees based on merit. Thus, a promotion can lawfully be based upon experience, skill, education, and ability tests. A test or condition that has no relevance to the position may not be used to prevent a protected class or individual from qualifying for employment.

Seniority. An employer may maintain a seniority system that rewards long-term employees. The system is lawful unless persons in a position of seniority achieved their position through intentional discrimination in the past.

Bona Fide Occupational Qualification. Employment discrimination based on a protect class (such as sex, but other than race or color), is lawful if it is job related and a business necessity. Hiring only women to work in a women's health spa would be legal but hiring only women for a women's clothing store in the mall would be a violation of Title VII.

Equal Pay Act of 1963

Protects both sexes from pay discrimination based on sex. The act prohibits disparity in pay for jogs that require equal skill, equal effort, equal responsibility, or similar working conditions. If two jobs are determined to be equal and similar, an employer cannot pay disparate wages to members of different sexes.

> *Ex:* Sue is paid $8.50 an hour to climb a 30-foot ladder and clean the light fixtures in the ceilings of the employer's warehouses. Mike is paid $14.00 per hour to climb the same ladder and change burned out light bulbs in the same fixtures that Sue is paid to clean. Sue and Mike are doing jobs that require low skill levels and require the same physical risk. The only basis for the disparate pay is the sex of the employees, making this a violation of the Equal Pay Act.

Disparate pay is allowed when it is based upon:
- Seniority
- Merit
- Quantity of quality of product (commissions)
- A differential based on any factor other than sex (shift differential)

Age Discrimination in Employment Act of 1967

The ADEA prohibits are discrimination in all employment decisions, including hiring, promotions, compensation, and other terms and conditions of employment. The Older Worker Benefit Protection Act amended the ADEA to prohibit age discrimination with regard to employee benefits. The ADEA applies to all employees over age 40.

The Americans With Disabilities Act of 1990

The ADA imposes obligations on employers and providers of public transportation, telecommunications, and public accommodations to accommodate individuals with disabilities. Title I of the ADA prohibits employment discrimination against qualified individuals with disabilities in regard to job application procedures, hiring, compensation, training, promotion, and termination. Title I requires an employer to make reasonable accommodations to individuals with disabilities that do not cause hardship to the employer. Employers may not inquire into the existence, nature, or severity of a disability during the application process.

Civil Rights Act of 1866

Section 1981 of this act gives all persons equal contract rights. Section 1981 also prohibits racial discrimination and discrimination based upon national origin. Though most discrimination cased are brought under Title VII, there are two good reasons to bring an action under Section 1981: (1) A private plaintiff can bring an action without going through the procedural requirements of Title VII, and (2) there is no limitation period on the recovery of back pay (claimant can only go back two years under Title VII) and no cap on the recovery of compensatory or punitive damages.

Affirmative Action

This is a policy that provides that certain job preferences will be given to minority or other protected class applicants when an employer makes an employment decision. Affirmative action plans will not be upheld when they discriminate against a majority after past discriminatory practices have already been rectified. Additionally, the courts will not allow employers to give a preference to a minority when another employee is far better qualified for a position.

> *Ex*: Bob is white and has both a master's degree and doctorate in psychology. Bob has 25 years of experience in a supervisory position at Major University Psychological Services Center. Keith is black and only has a bachelor's degree. Keith has worked at Major University for only 2 years and has never held any supervisory position. If Keith is hired as the new director of the entire Psychological Services Center because he is black, Bob will have a cause of action under Title VII for racial discrimination.

Refresh Your Memory

The following exercise will enable you to refresh your memory of the important rules and concepts set forth in this chapter. Read each question twice and put your answer in the blanks provided. Answer the entire exercise, then review questions and the text in areas you did not remember.

1. The _____ _____ _____ _____ is the federal agency responsible for enforcing most federal antidiscrimination laws.

2. Title ____ of the _____ _____ ____ of 1964 was intended to eliminate job discrimination.

3. Title VII applies to employers with _____ or more employees.

4. Title VII applies to any term, condition, _____ of employment including but not limited to hiring, firing, _____, and payment of fringe benefits decisions.

5. _____ _____ discrimination occurs when an employer treats a specific individual less favorably because of their membership in a protected class.

6. If the EEOC refused to file suit on behalf of a claimant, it will issue a _____ to _____ letter.

7. _____ _____ refers to the country of a person's ancestors or cultural characteristics.

8. The Pregnancy Discrimination Act forbids employment discrimination because of pregnancy, _____, or related _____ conditions.

9. Refusing to hire someone unless they have sex with the manager is a form of _____ _____.

10. The frequency and severity of sexual harassment are two factors considered in determining whether the employee is being subjected to a _____ _____ _____.

11. Under Title VII, an employer is under a duty to _____ _____ the religious observances, practices, or beliefs of its employees.

12. Employment discrimination based on a protected class (other than color or national origin) is lawful if it is _____ related and a business _____.

13. The Equal Pay Act forbids disparity in pay for jobs that require equal _____, equal _____, equal _____, or similar working conditions.

14. Persons under age _____ are not protected by the Age Discrimination in Employment Act of 1967.

15. Title I of the ADA requires an employer to make reasonable accommodations to individuals with disabilities that do not cause _____ _____ to the employer.

Critical Thought Exercise

Carol Jones was employed with Richmond Components, Inc. (RCI), an electrical engineering and manufacturing company that supplied parts and guidance system development for the United States Air Force. Jones was a public relations and communications manager for RCI at their facility located on Davis Air Force Base for over nine years. Of the 135 employees at the RCI facility at Davis AFB, only 9 women were in professional positions. Employees in the office where Jones worked used e-mail as the major form of communication between employees. Jones was sent sexually explicit material via e-mail, including pictures that had been downloaded from the Internet. Two male engineers in her work area used semi-nude swimsuit pictures as the screensaver on their computer. Pictures of nude women from magazines were cut out and put in her mailbox with notes, such as, "Will you pose like this for us?" When Jones requested that information for press releases be given to her by a stated deadline, she was told to, "Go have sex and chill out," along with other sexually demeaning comments about her anatomy. When Jones complained to the vice-president in charge of personnel, she was told that she worked in a high-stress 'boys' club" and she had better learn to accept the "give-and-take" environment at RCI. Jones quit her job and filed an action under Title VII. Will she prevail?

Answer. _____

_____

_____

_____

_____

_____

_____

_____

_____

_____

_____

_____

_____

_____

_____

_____

Practice Quiz

True/False:

1. ____ The EEOC is empowered to bring suit to enforce Title VII of the Civil Rights Act of 1964. [p 802]

2. ____ Discrimination based upon race, color, and religion are covered by Title VII, but discrimination based upon sex is covered by Title I of the ADA. [p 802]

3. ____ The requirements of Title VII do not apply to state and local governments and their agencies. [p 802]

4. ____ Any employee of covered employers, except illegal aliens, may bring actions for employment discrimination under Title VII. [p 802]

5. ____ In an action for disparate treatment discrimination, the complainant must prove that he or she applied for and was qualified for the employment position. [p 803]

6. ____ To bring an action under Title VII, a private person must first file a complaint with the EEOC. [p 803]

7. ____ As a remedy for a violation of Title VII, the EEOC may order reinstatement, but it has no authority to grant lost seniority. [p 803]

8. ____ Under title VII, race refers to broad categories such as Black, Caucasian, Asian, and Native American. [p 803]

9. ____ A person cannot claim discrimination under Title VII just because an employer discriminated against them based on their accent. [p 804]

10. ____ Asking a woman during a job interview if she plans on getting pregnant soon is lawful because the employer has the right to know how to schedule his employees' job assignments. [p 806]

11. ____ Conduct must seriously affect the victim's psychological well-being to be actionable as abusive work environment harassment. [p 808]

12. ____ Courts are adopting the reasonable woman standard in analyzing sexual harassment hostile work discrimination cases. [p 808]

13. ____ When asserting an affirmative defense to sexual harassment, the employer must prove that employees were informed of the employer's anti-harassment policy and the complaint procedure put in place by the employer. [p 809]

14. ____ Many religious discrimination cases involve a conflict between an employer's work rule and an employee's religious beliefs. [p 810]

15. ____ An employer may not have to accommodate an employee's request to have Saturday off from work for religious services if the employer has no other employee that can work on that day. [p 810]

16. ___ Employers can not select pr promote employees based on merit if it would mean that a minority employee is denied a job or a promotion. [p 810]

17. ___ To be legal, a bona fide occupational requirement must be job related, but it need not be necessary. [p 811]

18. ___ The Civil Rights Act of 1991 expressly protects U.S. citizens employed in a foreign country by U.S.-controlled employers. [p 812]

19. ___ If a U.S. parent corporation owns a foreign corporation that is incorporated in another country, the foreign-controlled-subsidiary is subject to Title VII because the 1991 act expressly states that discriminatory practices of controlled foreign corporations are presumed to be acts engaged in by the parent corporation. [p 812]

20. ___ If Betty and Joe work for Apex and Betty handles nuclear waste while Joe handles dangerous chemicals, and Joe makes $2 per hour more than Betty, this is a violation of the Equal Pay Act. [p 813]

21. ___ If an employer violated the Equal Pay Act, he must increase the wages of the discriminated-against employee to eliminate the unlawful disparity of wages. [p 813]

22. ___ Under the Equal Pay Act, an employer can pay disparate wages to members of different sexes if the difference is based on a seniority system. [p 813]

23. ___ Under the Equal Pay Act, an employer can pay disparate wages to members of different sexes if one employee works the night shift for which higher wages are paid. [p 813]

24. ___ The Age Discrimination in Employment Act prohibits age discrimination in all employment decisions except the area of promotions, where the employer may consider age in deciding who to promote within the company. [p 814]

25. ___ Under the ADA, an employer may inquire about the applicant's ability to perform job-related functions. [p 814]

Multiple Choice:

26. The enforcement of federal antidiscrimination laws is the responsibility of the [p 802]
   a. OWBPA.
   b. EEOC.
   c. ADEA.
   d. ADA.

27. The definition of what constitutes an "unlawful employment practice" was amended to Title VII by [p 802]
   a. the Equal Employment Practices Act of 1972.
   b. a decision of the United States Supreme Court.
   c. the Americans with Disabilities Act.
   d. the Pregnancy Discrimination Act in 1978.

28. Title VII applies to employers with [p 802]
    a.   8 or more employees.
    b.   12 or more employees.
    c.   15 or more employees.
    d.   33 or more employees.

29. Title VII prohibits discrimination in [p 802]
    a.   hiring.
    b.   promotion or demotion.
    c.   payment of compensation.
    d.   all of the above.

30. To bring an action under Title VII, a private complainant must first file a complaint [p 803]
    a.   in federal district court.
    b.   in the trial court in the state where they reside.
    c.   with the EEOC.
    d.   with the Commerce Department.

31. Conduct that creates a hostile work environment includes [p 807]
    a.   a mere offensive utterance.
    b.   conduct that is sexually offensive, regardless of whether it unreasonably interferes with an employee's work performance.
    c.   conduct that is humiliating.
    d.   all of the above.

32. The standard used by the courts in sexual harassment cases to determine whether certain conduct violates the norms of society is the [p 808]
    a.   reasonable man standard.
    b.   reasonable woman standard.
    c.   reasonable person standard.
    d.   reasonable employee standard.

33. Employers can raise a defense to a Title VII action by showing that the discriminatory conduct was based upon [p 811]
    a.   a merit system.
    b.   a seniority system.
    c.   a bona fide occupational qualification.
    d.   all of the above.

34. Which factor does not justify a differential in wages under the Equal Pay Act? [p 813]
    a.   Protection of a woman's health due to hazardous work conditions
    b.   Merit, as long as there is some identifiable standard
    c.   Quantity or quality of product
    d.   Any factor other than sex, such as night versus day shifts

35. According to the ADA, reasonable accommodations for a disabled employee include [p 814]
    a.   allowing the employee to dictate their work assignment.
    b.   providing part-time or modified work schedules.
    c.   providing another employee to do the work for the disabled employee.
    d.   all of the above.

Short Answer:

36. List the five protected classes under Title VII. [p 802] (1) _____ (2) _____
    (3) _____ (4) _____ (5) _____

37. Name three areas other than hiring, promotion, and compensation that are covered by Title VII.
    [p 802] 1) _____ 2) _____
    3) _____

38. What four things must a complainant prove to show disparate treatment discrimination? [p 803]
    1) _____
    2) _____
    3) _____
    4) _____

39. Disparate impact discrimination is often proven through _____ data about the
    employer's employment practices. [p 803]

40. What two things must happen before a claimant can sue their employer for a Title VII violation?
    [p 803] (1) _____
    (2) _____

41. In Title VII cases involving _____ or _____ _____ to federally protected
    rights, the aggrieved party can recover compensatory and punitive damages. [p 803]

42. If an engineer from India is fired from a company because of his accent, to what type of protected
    class does he belong and why is this the correct protected class to allege in his complaint? [p 805]

43. If a male applicant is not hired by an airline as a flight attendant because "women are more
    compassionate towards passengers," he is a victim of _____ _____. [p 805]

44. Hanging a provocative swimsuit calendar in your office may be _____ _____.
    [p 806]

45. A female plaintiff states a prima facie case of _____ environment sexual harassment when
    she alleges conduct which a reasonable _____ would consider sufficiently severe or
    _____ to alter the conditions of employment and create an abusive _____
    environment. [p 806]

46. Failing to accommodate an employee and forcing him or her to work on their Sabbath when it is not
    necessary is a form of _____ _____. [p 810]

47. Promoting your top salesman, David, to the position of senior salesperson even though Helen has
    worked for you for one year longer is legal because the promotion was based on _____.
    [p 810]

48. Seniority systems are lawful as long as they are not the result of _____ _____.
    [p 811]

49. If two jobs are determined to be equal and _____, an employer cannot pay _____
    wages to members of different sexes. [p 813]

50. The Older Workers Benefit Protection Act amended the ADEA to prohibit _____ discrimination with regard to employee _____. [p 814]

Answers To Refresh Your Memory

1. Equal Employment Opportunity Commission [p 802]
2. VII, Civil Rights Act [p 802]
3. 15 [p 802]
4. privilege, promotion [p 802]
5. Disparate treatment [p 803]
6. right, sue [p 803]
7. National origin [p 803]
8. childbirth, medical [p 805]
9. sexual harassment [p 806]
10. hostile work environment [p 808]
11. reasonably accommodate [p 810]
12. job, necessity [p 811]
13. skill, effort, responsibility [p 813]
14. 40 [p 814]
15. undue hardship [p 816]

Critical Thought Exercise Model Answer

Title VII applies to employers with 15 or more employees. With 135 employees at this facility alone, RCI will be covered by Title VII. Title VII prohibits harassment based upon gender in the workplace. Sexual harassment may be based upon, lewd remarks, touching, intimidation, posting of sexually explicit pictures, and other unwanted verbal or physical conduct that is sexual in nature. Jones will argue that the activities of her co-workers have created a hostile work environment. To determine if the environment at RCI is hostile, a court will look at all the circumstances. These will include the frequency of the discriminatory conduct; its severity; whether it is physically threatening or humiliating, or a mere offensive utterance, and whether it unreasonably interferes with an employee's work performance. The conduct of the male employees at RCI has created a hostile work environment. The acts are frequent and quite severe. Pictures are deliberately put in Jones' mailbox with notes that ask her to pose nude for fellow employees. Jones is berated verbally with sexual statements when she tries to do her job and get information for press releases. She is subjected to the sexually explicit pictures on computers on a daily basis because they have been installed as screensavers. Finally, there was no effort by RCI to stop or correct the harassment. Jones was told to accept it and no action was taken against the offending employees. Jones should prevail on a claim brought under Title VII for sexual harassment.

Answers To Practice Quiz

True/False:

1. True The EEOC is empowered to conduct investigations, interpret statutes, encourge conciliation between employers and employees, and bring suit to enforce the law.
2. False In addition to race, color, and religion, Title VII prohibits discrimination based upon sex or national origin.

3. False   Title Vii applies to state and local governments and their agencies and to most federal government employment.

4. False   Undocumented aliens may bring an action under Title VII.

5. True   Applying for the job and being qualified is one of the four requirements to prove this type of discrimination.

6. True   If the EEOC decides to not sue on behalf of the claimant, the private person may then sue on their own.

7. False   In addition to reinstatement, the EEOC can order that the claimant receive fictional seniority and they can issue injunctions to compel the hiring or promotion of protected minorities.

8. True   Race does not refer to specific ethnic groups. They fall under the national origin class.

9. False   National origin discrimination includes the denial of employment opportunity because an individual has the linguistic characteristics of a national origin group.

10. False   The questioning of a woman applicant about whether she would get pregnant and quit is discriminatory and unrelated to a bona fide occupational qualification.

11. False   There is no requirement that the victim suffer any psychological injury to bring an action for abusive work environment harassment.

12. True   Courts believe that the reasonable person standard is inadequate because it may reinforce the prevailing level of discrimination. Men may find nothing wrong with conduct that violates Title VII.

13. True   In addition to this, the court will consider whether the employer had an anti-harassment policy and whether the employer had a complaint mechanism in place.

14. True   The employer may require that an employee work on their religious Sabbath, raising the issue of whether or not the employer can offer a reasonable accommodation of the employee's beliefs.

15. True   The courts must consider such factors as the size of the employer, the importance of the employee's position, and the availability of alternative workers.

16. False   An employer may hire and promote based upon merit if the merit system is based upon work, education, experience, and professionally developed promotion tests.

17. False   A BFOQ must be both job related and a business necessity.

18. True   The act extended the number of employees covered under discrimination laws by extending protection to U.S. citizens who were working overseas for U.S. companies.

19. True   Employees are protected by Title VII if the foreign corporation they work for is controlled by a U.S. corporation.

20. True   The Equal Pay Act prohibits disparity in pay for jobs that require similar working conditions. Because both Betty and Joe have dangerous work conditions, the employer cannot pay disparate wages to members of different sexes.

21. True   The employer may also have to pay back wages and liquidated damages.

22. True   It is lawful to pay disparate wages to long-term employees as an incentive for them to maintain employment with the employer.

23. True   An employer can pay disparate wages to members of different sexes if the disparity is based upon any factor other than sex, such as shift differentials.

24. False   The ADEA prohibits age discrimination in all employment decisions, including hiring, promotions, payment of compensation, and other terms and conditions of employment.

25. True   The employer cannot ask a job applicant about the existence, nature, and severity of a disability, but he can inquire as to the ability of the applicant to perform the job.

Multiple Choice:

26. B   B is correct because the EEOC is the federal agency that is charged with enforcing federal anti-discrimination laws. Choices A, C, and D are all laws enforced by the EEOC.

27. A   A is the act passed by Congress that amended Title VII. B is incorrect because the definition of unlawful employment practice was added by legislation, not by case decision. Choices C and D

are incorrect because they define discrimination as it pertains to disabilities and pregnancy, but were not the source of the broad language enacted under the EEPA.

28. C   Answer C is correct because it states the threshold number of employees needed to invoke the protection of Title VII. Choices A, B, and D all state incorrect numbers that cannot be located anywhere in Title VII.

29. D   Choice D is correct because choices A, B, and C correctly state areas of employment decisions where discrimination is prohibited by Title VII.

30. C   The claimant must file a complaint with the EEOC first. Only after getting a right to sue letter can the private claimant file suit in state or federal court. Choices A and B are incorrect because the complaint process with the EEOC is a prerequisite to an individual filing suit in a trial court. Choice D is incorrect because the EEOC is part of the Department of Labor.

31. C   Choice C is correct because humiliating acts are the type of conduct that create a hostile environment for the employee. Choice A is incorrect because a single offensive utterance is insufficient. Choice B is incorrect because the conduct did not interfere with work performance. Choice D is incorrect because choices A and B are incorrect.

32. B   B is correct because the courts apply the standard from the perspective of the victim. Choices A, C, and D are incorrect because they would include the perspective of the offending party and considering that perspective would only serve to perpetuate the prevailing level of harassment.

33. D   Choice D is correct because each of the other choices states a valid defense to a claim of discriminatory employment practices under Title VII.

34. A   A is correct because women are entitled to take the same risks at work as men. Choices B, C, and D are incorrect because they state three legal exceptions to the Equal Pay Act.

35. B   B is correct because it would be reasonable to allow an employee to work less hours or during certain times of the day if it did not create an undue hardship on the employer. Answers A and C are incorrect because they would create an undue hardship. Choice D is incorrect because it includes choices A and C.

Short Answer:

36.   race, color, religion, sex, national origin

37.   fringe benefits, job training and apprenticeships, referral systems for employment, work rules, or any other term, condition, or privilege of employment

38.   (1) he or she belongs to a Title VII protected class, (2) he or she applied for and was qualified for the employment position, (3) he or she was rejected despite this, and (4) the employer kept the position open and sought applicants from persons with the complainant's qualifications

39.   statistical

40.   (1) the complainant must file a complaint with the EEOC
      (2) the EEOC must refuse to bring suit and issue a *right to sue letter*

41.   malice, reckless indifference

42.   The discrimination is based upon national origin because speech is one aspect of a person's cultural characteristics, which is part of your national origin.

43.   sex discrimination

44.   sexual harassment

45.   hostile, woman, pervasive, working

46.   religious discrimination

47.   merit

48.   intentional discrimination

49.   similar, disparate

50.   age, benefits

Chapter 42

LABOR RELATIONS LAW

Chapter Overview

When the United States became industrialized in the late 1800's, large corporate employers assumed much greater power than their employees. It was not until the 1930's, during the Great Depression, that state and federal governments began to regulate employment relationships. Legislation granted employees the right to form labor unions and bargain with management for improved working conditions, better pay, and benefits. Further legislation guaranteed the right to strike and picket. This chapter discusses the creation of labor unions and regulation of labor relations.

Objectives

Upon completion of the exercises in this chapter, you should be able to
1. Explain how a union is formed.
2. Describe union elections and the consequences of interfering with union elections.
3. Understand the process of collective bargaining and compulsory subjects of collective bargaining.
4. Explain the mandates of the Plant Closing Act.
5. Describe the difference between union and agency shops.
6. Explain state right-to-work laws.
7. Describe the rights and procedures associated with the right to strike.
8. Describe what constitutes an illegal strike.
9. Describe the right to picket and its limitations.
10. Describe a legal or illegal secondary boycott.

Practical Application

Upon mastering the concepts in this chapter, you should be able to recognize when the conduct involved in a particular labor relationship is legal or illegal. Further, should be able to recognize the general legal principle that applies to a dispute and understand the likely outcome.

Helpful Hints

When there is a labor dispute, emotions are often frayed and the parties are likely to react impulsively. It is helpful to realize that both state and federal governments and the courts have created a large amount of statutory and case law that will dictate the proper conduct of the parties and the consequences of illegal activity. Examine each statute and case closely for the precise conduct that was either condoned or forbidden. By understanding what conduct triggers which rule of law, you will be more effective in your labor relationships.

Study Tips

It is crucial for you to understand the following rules of law and mandates that must be followed when you are involved in a labor action or negotiations.

Norris-*LaGuardia Act.* Made it legal for employees to organize.

National Labor Relations Act. Established the right of employees to form, join, and participate in unions. Placed a duty on employers to bargain and deal in good faith with unions.

Labor-*Management Relations Act.* Expanded the activities that union were allowed to engage in. Gave employers the right to speak out against the unions. Gave the President the right to enjoin a strike for up to 80 days if the strike would create a national emergency.

Labor-*Management Reporting and Disclosure Act.* This act regulates internal union affairs related to union elections, who can hold office, and makes union officials accountable for union funds.

Railway Labor Act. This act allows railroad and airline employees to organize and created a mechanism for the adjudication of grievances.

National Labor Relations Board (NLRB). Appointed by the President, the five members of the NLRB oversee union elections, prevent unfair labor practices, and enforces federal labor laws.

NLRB v. ILA, AFL-*CIO (1985).* This Supreme Court case upheld negotiated contracts that preserved work for the longshoremen. The court felt that allowing the longshoremen to negotiate a contract by which they were required to unload containers that didn't need unloading was beneficial to the national economy and "work preservation" for the longshoremen was a legitimate goal of federal labor policy.

Lechmere v. NLRB (1992). Labor organizers have no right to trespass onto the employer's property to organize the employees when they can have access to the employees via nontrespassory means. Even if it is difficult to contact employees away from work, this does not give the organizers the right to trespass onto the employer's property to pass out leaflets.

NLRB v. Exchange Parts Co. (1964). The Supreme Court ruled that giving increased benefits to the employees on the eve of a union election for the purpose of forming a union was designed to affect the outcome of the election and was therefore, an unfair labor practice.

Plant Closing Act. Requires employers to give their employees 60 days' notice before engaging in certain plant closings or layoffs.

First Nat'l Maintenance Corp v. NLRB (1981). An employer's decision to close a business unit is not part of the terms and conditions that the union can force the employer to negotiate.

Union Security Agreements. If the union obtains a union shop agreement with the employer, all employees must join the union within a certain number of days or they will be terminated. In an agency shop, the employee do not have to join the union, but they have to pay an agency fee equal to union dues.

State Right-*To-Work Laws.* States are free to enact laws that outlaw union and agency shops. Today, there are 21 states that have enacted right-to-work laws.

Refresh Your Memory

The following exercises will enable you to refresh your memory as to the key principles and concepts given to you in this chapter. Read each question carefully and put your answer in the blanks provided. Review the chapter material for any question you miss or are unable to remember.

1. The relationship between employers and employees changed dramatically when the United States became _____ in the late 1880s.

2. As a reaction to employment abuses, workers organized unions to gain _____ strength.

3. Approximately _____ percent of private-sector workers belong to labor unions.

4. In 1932, the _____ Act created the right of workers to organize.

5. The NLRA, also known as the _____ Act, placed an affirmative duty on employers to bargain and deal in good faith.

6. The Labor-Management Reporting and Disclosure Act requires regularly scheduled _____ for union officials by _____ ballot.

7. _____ is the use of economic muscle by unions to preserve jobs that are no longer necessary.

8. The _____ _____ _____ is the group that the union is seeking to represent and must be defined before the union can petition for an election.

9. If employees no longer want to be represented by a union, a _____ election will be held.

10. If union solicitation is being conducted by fellow employees, an employer may restrict solicitation activities to the employees' _____ time.

11. The NLRA makes it an _____ labor _____ for am employer to interfere with, coerce, or restrain employees from exercising their right to form and join a union.

12. The act of negotiating with a union is called _____ bargaining.

13. Under an _____ _____ agreement, employees do not have to become union members, but they have to pay an agency fee.

14. An _____ _____ is when the employer anticipates a strike by some employees and prevents those employees from entering the premises.

15. The action of strikers walking in front of the employer's premises carrying signs announcing the strike is called _____.

Critical Thought Exercise

When the collective bargaining agreement between the United Pickle and Catsup Makers (Union) and Good Foods Company (Good), the Union called for a strike. Picketers were used to walk in front of 27 grocery stores in the greater Cleveland, Ohio area and distribute literature. Some of the picket signs said, "Boycott Pickles and Catsup," and "Don't buy Good pickles here, make them at home." Most signs were pre-printed by the Union and stated, "Boycott All Good Products." The majority of pickles and catsup sold by People's Grocery Store and Larry Supermarket are made by Good. Though customers never saw anyone spray them with catsup, they found their clothing squirted with catsup if they entered People's Grocery Store. Customers refuse to enter People's Grocery and Larry's Supermarket because they feel intimidated and are afraid of the unknown catsup squirter. People's and Larry's file suit in federal court seeking injunctions and damages against Union. Were the activities by the Union illegal?

Answer. _____

_____

_____

_____

_____

_____

_____

_____

_____

_____

_____

_____

_____

_____

_____

_____

_____

_____

_____

Practice Quiz

True/False:

1. ____ Only semiskilled and unskilled worker were permitted to join the American Federation of Labor (AFL). [p 826]

2. ____ During the Great Depression of the 1930s, several federal statutes were enacted giving workers certain rights and protections. [p 826]

3. ____ The power of the courts to thwart peaceful union activity was curtailed by the Norris-LaGuardia Act. [p 826]

4. ____ The right to bargain collectively with employers was granted by the Norris-LaGuardia Act. [p 826]

5. ____ The power of the President to enjoin a strike for up to 80 days was created by the Labor-Management Relations Act, also known as the Taft-Hartley Act. [p 826]

6. ____ Ex-convicts are not disqualified from holding union office. [p 827]

7. ____ The NLRB oversees union elections. [p 827]

8. ____ Managers and professional employees may belong to the same union as the one formed by employees they supervise as long as they work for the same employer. [p 828]

9. ____ If 50% of the employees in the bargaining unit are interested in forming a union, the NLRB can be petitioned to investigate and set an election date. [p 828]

10. ____ If 63 out of 100 employees vote in favor of forming a union, the other 37 employees are left without a bargaining agent. [p 828]

11. ____ Off-duty employees may be barred from union solicitation on company premises. [p 828]

12. ____ Nonemployees cannot enter company premises to solicit membership unless the location of the business and the living quarters of the employees place the employees beyond the reach of reasonable union efforts to communicate with them. [p 828]

13. ____ It is an unfair labor practice for the employer to threaten the loss of benefits if an employee joins the union. [p 829]

14. ____ Where an unfair labor practice has been found, the NLRB may issue a cease-and-desist order of an injunction to restrain unfair labor practices. [p 830]

15. ____ The Plant Closing Act covers employers with more than 25 employees. [p 831]

16. ____ When the union and employer are negotiating, either side can make a "take-it-or-leave-it" proposal if the other side is demanding too much. [p 831]

17. ____ The size and composition of the supervisory force in a company is a compulsory subject of collective bargaining and both sides must negotiate in good faith. [p 831]

18. ____ Employers have no duty to help the union collect union dues. [p 832]

19. ____ If a state enacts a right-to-work law, the employee must join the union if the company employees are represented by a union. [p 833]

20. ____ Once a strike begins, the employer may continue operations by using management personnel and replacement workers. [p 834]

21. ____ During a partial strike, employees continue to occupy the employer's premises. [p 835]

22. ___ Any strike without a 60-day notice is illegal. [p 835]

23. ___ Illegal strikers may be discharged by the employer with no rights to reinstatement. [p 835]

24. ___ A union may discipline members for working for wages below union scale. [p 836]

25. ___ The cost of a minimum-wage employee in Mexico is approximately $4 per hour. [p 837]

Multiple Choice:

26. The act that placed an affirmative duty on employers to bargain and deal in good faith with union was the [p 826]
    a. Norris-LaGuardia Act.
    b. National Labor Relations Act.
    c. The Railway Labor Act.
    d. none of the Above.

27. The Taft-Hartley Act [p 826]
    a. expands the activities that labor unions can engage in.
    b. gives employers the right to engage in free-speech efforts against unions.
    c. gives the President the right to seek an injunction against a strike that would create a national emergency.
    d. all of the above.

28. The Landrum-Griffin Act includes a rule that [p 827]
    a. gives employees the right to form unions.
    b. allows an injunction to be issued to stop unfair labor practices.
    c. makes union officials accountable for union funds and property.
    d. requires a 60-day notice for certain plant closures.

29. The administrative agency created to enforce the Wagner Act (NLRA) is the [p 827]
    a. NLRB.
    b. AFL.
    c. CIO.
    d. Labor Board of Conciliation and Arbitration.

30. Before a union can petition the NLRB for an election [p 828]
    a. it may request that union dues be withheld from employees' wages.
    b. it may compel the employer to sign a collective bargaining agreement.
    c. the employer must give its permission for an election.
    d. the appropriate bargaining unit must be defined.

31. If an employer offers incentive bonuses and increased vacation time to his employees right before an election on the acceptance of a new union, this is [p 830]
    a. within the employer's free-speech rights.
    b. an unfair labor practice.
    c. acceptable under the collective bargaining agreement.
    d. acceptable as long as no threats accompanied the action.

32. The act of negotiating by a union with an employer is called [p 831]
    a. collective bargaining.
    b. picketing.
    c. a wildcat action.
    d. a secondary boycott.

33. Under a union shop agreement, employees [p 832]
    a. do not have to become a union members, but they do have to pay an agency fee.
    b. do not have to join the union or pay any dues if they do not desire, because to force the employee to do so would be illegal.
    c. must join the union and pay dues or they will be terminated from employment.
    d. none of the above.

34. A wildcat strike takes place when [p 835]
    a. striking employees continue to occupy the premises of the employer.
    b. individual union members to out on strike without proper authorization from the union.
    c. employees strike part of the day and work part of the day.
    d. striking employees cause substantial damage to the property of the employer.

35. Picketing is unlawful unless it [p 835]
    a. is accompanied by violence.
    b. obstructs customers from entering the employer's place of business or prevents nonstriking employees from entering the premises.
    c. prevents pickups and deliveries at the employer's of business.
    d. all of the above.

Short Answer:

36. The NRLA is also known as the _____ Act. [p 826]

37. The _____-_____ Act as passed in response to industrywide strikes in the rail, coal, maritime, lumber, oil, automobile, and textile industries between 1945 and 1947. [p 826]

38. The Taft-Hartley Act gives the President the right to seek an _____ against a strike that would create a national _____. [p 826]

39. The Labor-Management Report and Disclosure Act (Landrum-Griffin Act) regulates _____ union affairs and establishes the rights of union _____. [p 827]

40. The three main requirements of the Landrum-Griffin Act are: [p 827]
    (1) _____
    (2) _____
    (3) _____

41. What is the NLRB? [p 827] _____
    _____

42. What are the three main duties of the NLRB? [p 827] (1) _____
    (2) _____ (3) _____

43. What is *featherbedding*? [p 827] _____

44. What is a *bargaining unit*? [p 828] _____
_____
_____

45. Describe where and when these groups may engage in union solicitation activities: [p 828]
fellow working employees _____
_____
off-duty employees _____
_____
union management _____
_____

46. What is an *unfair labor practice*? [p 829] _____
_____
_____
_____

47. What two actions are covered by the Plant Closure Act and when do they apply? [p 831]
_____
_____
_____
_____

48. Name seven things that are proper *compulsory subjects* of collective bargaining. [p 831]
(1) _____ (2) _____ (3) _____ (4) _____
(5) _____ (6) _____ (7) _____

49. When there is a union or agency shop, what is required of employers in regards to dues and fees? What is this requirement called? [p 832] _____
_____
_____

50. What is secondary boycott picketing? [p 835] _____
_____
_____
_____

Answers to Refresh Your Memory

1. industrialized [p 826]
2. bargaining [p 826]
3. 15 [p 826]
4. Norris-LaGuardia [p 826]
5. Wagner [p 826]
6. elections, secret [p 827]
7. featherbedding [p 827]
8. appropriate bargaining unit [p 828]
9. decertification [p 828]
10. free [p 828]

11. unfair, practice [p 829]
12. collective [p 831]
13. agency shop [p 832]
14. employer lockout [p 834]
15. picketing [p 835]

Critical Thought Exercise Model Answer

Picketing is a form of lawful protest that can be undertaken by unions during a strike. The picketing is lawful unless it (1) is accompanied by violence, (2) obstructs customers from entering the employers business, (3) prevents replacement or non-striking employees from entering the premises, or (4) prevents shipments or deliveries from entering of exiting the premises. If the picketing is unlawful for any of these reasons, the employer may seek an injunction to stop the activity. Picketing of the employer's customers or suppliers is known as secondary boycott picketing. Secondary picketing is lawful only if the union pickets the product or service of the employer. The picketing is illegal if it is directed against the business of the customer or supplier who is not involved in the strike. Good Foods can be lawfully struck by picketing the suppliers and customers of Good Foods. Though the Union may picket both People's Grocery and Larry's Supermarket, the picketers cannot ask customers to not enter the stores or refrain from buying goods in the store that are not produced by Good Foods. The picket signs that are being used are legal for the most part. The only sign that creates a problem is the one that says, "Boycott Pickles and Catsup." This sign is not calling for an exclusive boycott of Good pickles and catsup. Both stores could be selling pickles and catsup made by several manufacturers. This would be asking for a general boycott and would be illegal. The other signs are referring to Good Food products and are a proper form of secondary boycott. The squirting of catsup upon the clothing of customers at People's would allow People's to sue Union for the tort of intentional interference with a contractual relationship. An injunction would also issue to stop this from happening again. Failure to honor the injunction would subject the Union to damages for illegal strike activities.

Answers To Practice Quiz

True/False:

1. False   Only skilled craft workers were permitted to join the AFL.
2. True   The statutes were a reaction to employer abuses during industrialization.
3. True   The act made it legal for employees to organize.
4. False   This right was created by the National Labor Relations Act.
5. True   It also expanded the type of union activities that were allowed.
6. False   The Landrum-Griffin Act forbids ex-convicts from holding union office.
7. True   The National Labor Relations Act created the NLRB and gave it the responsibility of overseeing all union elections.
8. False   Section 7 of the NLRA forbids managers from belonging to the same union.
9. False   Only 30% approval within the bargaining unit is needed to petition for an election.
10. False   If the union is approved by a simple majority, the union is certified as the bargaining agent for all 100 employees.
11. True   The employee must be working, but can only solicit during free time.
12. True   An example of this would be a logging camp where the employees never leave work.
13. True   It is illegal for the employer to interfere with, coerce, or restrain employees from exercising their right to form and join unions.

14. True   This is part of the NLRB's enforcement powers under Section 8(b) of the NRLA.
15. False   The Pant Closing Act only applies to employers with 100 or more employees.
16. False   Both sides must negotiate in good faith and the take-it-or-leave-it proposal is interpreted to be an act of bad faith.
17. False   This would be a permissive subject and it is negotiable only if both sides agree to negotiate on the subject.
18. False   Employers are required to deduct union due and agency fees from employees' wages and forward these to the union.
19. False   If a state enacts a right-to-work law, individual employees cannot be forced to join a union or pay union dues.
20. True   This right is guaranteed to the employer by the NRLA.
21. False   This is a sit-down strike. In a partial strike, the employees strike part of the day or workweek and work the other part.
22. True   There is a mandatory 60-day cooling off period.
23. True   Illegal strikers are not protected by the collective bargaining agreement.
24. True   A union has powers to discipline members for several types of conduct.
25. False   The cost of a minimum-wage worker in Mexico, including wages, benefits, and taxes, is less than$1 per hour.

Multiple Choice:

26. B   Choice B is correct as the NLRA was the act that created the duty of good faith bargaining. Choices A, C, and D are labor acts, but they did not address the duty to bargain and deal in god faith.
27. D   D includes all the other choices which are part of the rights set forth in the Taft-Hartley Act. Choices A, B, and C are incorrect because they are included within D.
28. C   C is one of the duties imposed by the Landrum-Griffin Act. Choice A is incorrect because that right is contained in the NLRA. Choice B is incorrect because that rule is also contained in the NRLA. Choice D is incorrect because that rule is contained in the Plant Closing Act.
29. A   A is correct because the NLRB is the administrative body appointed by the president to enforce the NRLA. Choices B and C are incorrect because they are labor unions. Choice D is incorrect because it is a Mexican labor agency.
30. D   Choice D is correct because it states a prerequisite to holding a union election. Choices A, B, and C are incorrect because they describe union activity after the union is formed.
31. B   The correct choice is B because an act that interferes with employees right to form and join unions is an unfair labor practice. Choice A is incorrect because the employer has no right to influence the employees by anything other than words. Choice C is incorrect because the union has yet to be formed, so there can be no collective bargaining agreement and the parties cannot bargain on illegal subjects. Choice D is wrong because illegal persuasion with increased benefits is an unfair labor practice just as much as the use of threats and intimidation under Section 8(a) of the NLRA.
32. A   A is correct because the act of negotiating a contract or collective bargaining agreement is also called collective bargaining. Choices B, C, and D are incorrect because they all relate to strikes and picketing as part of a strike.
33. C   C is correct as it states the correct definition of a union shop. A is incorrect because it states the definition of an agency shop. Choice B is incorrect because it states the rights of the employee in a right-to-work state where union shops are illegal. Choice D is incorrect because a correct choice, C, is available.
34. B   Answer B correctly defines a wildcat strike. Choice A is incorrect because it defines a sit-down strike. Choice C is incorrect because it defines a partial strike. Choice D is incorrect because it defines a violent strike.
35. D   D is correct because choices A, B, and C all state correct examples of illegal picketing.

Short Answer:

36. Wagner
37. Taft-Hartley
38. injunction, emergency
39. internal, members
40. (1) a requirement for regularly scheduled elections for union officials by secret ballot
    (2) a prohibition against ex-convicts and communists from holding union office
    (3) a rule that makes union officials accountable for union funds and property
41. The NLRB is an administrative body comprised of five members appointed by the President and approved by the Senate.
42. The NLRB:
    (1) oversees union elections
    (2) prevents employers and employees from engaging in illegal and unfair labor practices
    (3) enforces and interprets certain federal labor laws
43. The use of its economic bargaining position by unions to preserve jobs that are no longer needed.
44. A bargaining unit is the group of employees that a union is seeking to represent. The group must be defined before a union election can be held. The bargaining unit can be all the employees from the same company, a group within the company, or like employees from several companies.
45. *Fellow employees* can be restricted to solicitation during their free time, such as lunch hours, and can be restricted to nonworking areas such as the cafeteria, restroom, or parking lot. *Off-duty employees* may be barred from union solicitation on company premises.
    Union Management may be prohibited from soliciting anywhere on company property.
46. An unfair labor practice is any act by an employer that interferes with, coerces, or restrains employees from exercising their statutory rights to form and join unions. It is also any act by the union that interferes with a union election, or used coercion, threats, or intimidation to accomplish union goals.
47. Both actions apply only to employers with 100 or more employees and they can be taken only after a 60-day notice to employees. Plant closings are a permanent or temporary shut-down of a single site that results in a loss of employment of 50 or more employees during any 30-day period. Mass layoffs are a reduction of 33 percent of the employees or at least 50 employees during any 30-day period.
48. (1) wages (2) hours (3) fringe benefits (4) health benefits (5) retirement plans
    (6) work assignments (7) safety rules
49. Union and agency shop employers are required to deduct union dues and agency fees from employees' wages and forward these dues and fees to the union. This requirement is calla check-off provision.
50. A type of picketing where unions try to bring pressure against an employer by picketing his or her suppliers or customers. This type of picketing is often used when the employer has no centralized or main office or plant to picket, such as agricultural businesses. Instead of picketing a cotton field, the union may picket the mill where the cotton is sent or a clothing manufacturer that purchases the cotton.

Chapter 43

LIABILITY OF ACCOUNTANTS

Chapter Overview

Accountants can be held liable to both clients and third parties for breach of contract, misrepresentation, and negligence when they fail to properly perform their duties. These duties may include both auditing of financial statements and rendering opinions based upon those audits. Accountants also prepare statements for clients, give tax advice, prepare tax filings, and provide consulting services. In addition to the liability exposure for the common law actions already noted, an accountant may be subjected to liability under securities laws and the tax codes. The material in this chapter will help you examine the liability of accountants and other professionals.

Objectives

Upon completion of the exercises contained in this chapter, you should be able to
1. Define audit and explain the different types of auditor's opinions.
2. Explain the source of an accountant's liability for breach of contract and fraud.
3. Describe an accountant's liability for malpractice.
4. Explain liability under the *Ultramares Doctrine*.
5. Describe the foreseeability standard and accountant liability under the Restatement (Second) of Torts.
6. Outline liability that may be imposed on accountants under the securities laws.
7. Identify accountants' potential criminal liability.
8. Explain the protection of accountants and their clients for their communications.
9. Explain professionals' privilege concerning working papers.

Practical Application

This material will help you determine the duty of care owed by an accountant to a business, thereby allowing you to make an initial determination of whether or not an accountant has fulfilled their duties as required by law. By understanding the conduct that triggers liability for accountants, you will be able to question decisions and procedures that could have far reaching implications for the client and the accountant. Businesses that understand accountant liability will have a better understanding of when they can exercise their business judgment based upon representations and decisions made by their accountants. Likewise, accounts need to be aware of the situations that require them to investigate the information supplied to them by the client.

Helpful Hints

Until you understand the duties that are imposed upon an accountant, you will be unable to determine if they have met their duty of care to the client. Additionally, if you do not understand the duties imposed by statute, you will not know when the accountant has placed the client in jeopardy of civil or criminal liability. In this chapter, focus on the standards that are set and what degree of performance fulfills that standard. Make special note of the trouble areas where mistakes are often made that create liability.

Study Tips

Commence your study of accountant liability closely examining the following standards, types of auditor's opinions, theories of common law liability, theories establishing liability to third parties, sources of statutory liability, and privileges related to accountants' work.

Accounting Standards
Certified public accountants must comply with:
- Generally accepted accounting principles (GAAPs) pertaining to preparation and presentation of financial statements, and
- Generally accepted auditing standards (GAASs) pertaining to audits

Audits and Auditor's Opinions
Audits are the verification of a company's books that must be performed by an independent CPA. Auditors render an opinion about how fairly the financial statements:
- present the company's financial position
- result of operations
- change in financial position

The types of auditor's opinions are:
- *Unqualified opinion–* - The most favorable opinion that the auditor can give. Represents the auditor's finding that the three areas of examination are correct and in conformity with consistently applied generally accepted accounting principles.
- *Qualified opinion* – States that the financial statements are fairly presented except for a departure from generally accepted accounting principles, a change in accounting principles, or a material uncertainty. The irregularity is noted in the auditor's opinion.
- *Adverse opinion* – Determines that the financial statements do no fairly represent the three areas of examination. Usually issued when the auditor determines that the company has materially misstated items on its financial statements.
- *Disclaimer of opinion* – Expresses an inability to draw a conclusion as to the accuracy of the company's financial records. Generally issued when the auditor lacks sufficient information about the financial records to issue an overall opinion.

Theories of Common Law Liability
- *Breach of contract* – an accountant can be held liable for breach of contract and resulting damages when he or she fails to perform as agreed in their *engagement*, or contract.
- *Fraud* – May be found when there is an actual intent to misrepresent a material fact to a client, if the client relies on the misrepresentation. Constructive fraud may be shown if the accountant commits gross negligence in the performance of his or her duties.
- *Negligence* – While performing his or her duties, an accountant must use the care, knowledge, and judgment generally used by accountants in the same or similar circumstances. Failure to fulfill this duty is negligence. An accountant's violation of GAAPs and GAASs is *prima facie* evidence of negligence. An account can be held liable for malpractice if he or she reveals confidential information or the contents of working papers without the permission of the client or pursuant to court order.

Theories of Liability to Third Parties

- *Ultramares Doctrine* – Liability will be imposed only if the accountant is in privity of contract, or a privity-like relationship with a third party. A relationship would occur where a client employed an accountant to prepare financial statement to be used by a third party, such as by a bank to evaluate a client's loan application.
- *Restatement rule* – Liability will be imposed only if the third party's reliance is foreseen, or known, or if the third party is among a limited class of intended, or known, users. This is the rule followed in most states.
- *"Reasonably foreseeable user"* – Liability will be imposed on the accountant if the third party's use of the client's financial statements was reasonably foreseeable.

Sources of Statutory Liability - Civil

- Securities Act of 1933, Section 11(a) – An accountant who makes misstatements or omissions of material facts in audited financial statements required for registration of securities or fails to find such misstatements or omissions may be liable to anyone who acquires the securities covered by the registration agreement. Accountants can assert a due diligence defense and rely upon a reasonable belief that the work was complete and correct. A willful violation of this section is a criminal offense.
- Securities Exchange Act of 1934, Sections 10(b) and 18 – Accountant s are held liable for any manipulative or deceptive practice in connection with the purchase or sale of any security under Section 10(b). Only intentional conduct and recklessness, but not ordinary negligence, violates this section. Under Section 18(a), the accountant may be liable for any false or misleading statements in any application, report, or document filed with the SEC. The accountant can defend against a section 18(a) violation by showing that he or she acted in good faith when making the filing, or the plaintiff in a suit had knowledge of the false or misleading statement when the securities were purchased or sold.

Sources of Statutory Liability – Criminal

- Securities Act of 1933, Section 24 – It is a criminal offense to:
  1. willfully make any untrue statement of material fact in a registration statement
  2. omit any material fact necessary to ensure that the statements made in the registration statement are not misleading, or
  3. willfully violate any other provision of the Securities Act of 1933
- Securities Exchange Act of 1934, Section 32(a) – It is a criminal offense for any person willfully and knowingly to make or cause to be made any false or misleading statement in any application, report, or other document required to be filed with the SEC.
- Racketeer Influenced and Corrupt Organization Act – Securities fraud is defined as a racketeering activity for which 2 or more occurrences qualify as a pattern of racketeering.
- 1976 Tax Reform Act – imposes criminal liability on an accountant for:
  1. aiding or assisting in the preparation of a false tax return
  2. aiding and abetting an individual's understatement of tax liability
  3. negligently or willfully understating a client's tax liability or recklessly or intentionally disregarding IRS rules or regulations
  4. failing to provide a taxpayer with a copy of the return, failing to sign the return, failing to furnish the appropriate tax identification numbers, or fraudulently negotiating a tax refund check

Accountant Privileges

- **Accountant-Client Privilege** – is not recognized by the federal courts, but has been enacted in approximately 20 states where it says that an accountant cannot be called as a witness against a client in a court action.
- **Accountants' Work Papers** – these often include a wide array of notes, memos, calculations, and plans concerning audits, work assignments, data collection, client's internal controls, reconciling reports, research, comments, opinions and information regarding the affairs of the client. Under federal law these papers are subject to discovery. Some states provide work product immunity for accountants, much the same as lawyers, whose work papers on strategy, research, opinions, and trial preparation are not discoverable in a lawsuit involving the client.
- **Ownership of Work Papers** – The accountant is an independent contractor, making the work papers of the accountant his or her property. The accountant does owe the client some rights and duties in regards to these papers, including:
  1. the right to review them upon reasonable notice
  2. the duty to transfer the paper's upon the client's request
  3. the duty not to transfer the papers without the client's permission

Refresh Your Memory

The following exercises will enable you to refresh your memory as to the key principles and concepts given to you in this chapter. Read each question carefully and put your answer in the blanks provided. Review the chapter material for any question you miss or are unable to remember.

1. _____ generate the majority of litigation against accountants.

2. The two uniform standards of professional conduct for accountants are _____ and _____.

3. An _____ _____ is the most favorable opinion an auditor can give.

4. If an accountant fails to fulfill the terms of an engagement, they will be in _____ of contract.

5. _____ _____ occurs when the accountant acts with reckless disregard for the truth or the consequences of his or her actions.

6. For purposes of assigning negligence to an accountant, the accountant's actions are measured against those of a "_____ accountant" in similar _____.

7. The _____ doctrine says that an accountant is not held liable for negligence to a party unless they are in _____ _____ _____.

8. Under the _____ _____, an accountant is liable to any foreseeable user of the client's financial statements when the accountant is negligent.

9. If an accountant engages in _____ or constructive fraud, a third party who relies on the accountant's fraud and is injured may bring a tort action against the accountant.

10. Section 11(a) of the Securities Act of 1933 imposes civil liability on accountant for making misstatements or _____ of material facts in a _____ statement.

11. The Private Securities Litigation Reform Act of 1995 replaced joint and several liability with _____ liability.

12. Section 10(b) of the Securities Exchange Act of 1934 prohibits any manipulative or _____ practice in connection with the purchase or sale of any _____.

13. Section _____ of the Securities Exchange Act of 1934 imposes civil liability on any person who makes any false or _____ statements in any application, report, or document files with the _____.

14. Section 24 of the Securities Act of 1933 makes it a criminal violation to willfully make any _____ statement of _____ fact in a registration statement filed with the SEC.

15. The federal courts _____ discovery of accountants' work papers.

Critical Thought Exercise

BGT Technologies, Inc., issued stock in a public offering that violated federal securities laws due to material misrepresentations and multiple acts of fraud. When it was discovered that BGT has substantially overstated its assets and failed to report debts owed to foreign banks, the SEC commenced an investigation. Kyle Sawyer was a partner in Jones Bateman, an independent certified public accounting firm. Sawyer was responsible for the BGT account and prepared numerous documents as part of the public offering. The documents filed by Sawyer contained the material misrepresentations. The SEC filed a suit against Sawyer and Jones Bateman, charging them with aiding and abetting the securities fraud perpetrated by BGT. Jones Bateman and Sawyer argue that they relied upon the information supplied to them by BGT to prepare the SEC filings. Jones Bateman did not verify or investigate the debt being carried by BGT. Jones Bateman argues that it should not be liable for aiding and abetting the securities fraud by BGT. What is the likely result when the matter is litigated?

Answer. _____

_____

_____

_____

_____

_____

_____

_____

_____

_____

_____

_____

_____

_____

_____

Practice Quiz

True/False:

1. ___ GASSs are the standards for the preparation and presentation of financial statements. [p 842]

2. ___ Pursuant to federal securities law, state laws, and stock exchange rules, an audit must be performed by an independent CPA. [p 842]

3. ___ As part of an audit, a CPA must review the client's financial records, but need not do any independent investigation. [p 842]

4. ___ An adverse opinion is generally issued by an auditor when the financial statements are fairly presented except for a departure from generally accepted accounting principles. [p 843]

5. ___ An engagement is a formal entrance into a contract between a client and an accountant. [p 843]

6. ___ Actual fraud occurs when the accountant acts with "reckless disregard" for the truth or consequences of his or her actions. [p 843]

7. ___ An accountant who does not comply with GAASs when conducting an audit and thereby fails to uncover a fraud or embezzlement by an employee of the client can be sued for negligence. [p 843]

8. ___ Under the *Ultramares Doctrine*, the accountant is liable only for negligence to third parties who are in privity of contract or a privity-like relationship with the accountant. [p 845]

9. ___ Section 552 of the Restatement (Second) of Torts provides a narrower standard for holding accountants liable to third parties for negligence than the *Ultramares Doctrine*. [p 846]

10. ___ Privity of contract is the state of two parties being in a contract. [p 848]

11. ___ If a CPA intentionally falsifies the financial statements of a company to help it obtain a bank loan, the accountant has committed the tort of negligence. [p 849]

12. ___ Section 10A of the Securities Exchange Act of 1994 has removed the dilemma of what to do when the accountant uncovers illegal activities by the client during an audit. [p 849]

13. ___ Accountants are considered to be experts, and the financial statements they prepare are considered an *expertised portion* of the registration statement. [p 849]

14. ___ If an accountant is held to be liable along with four other defendants, the accountant may have to pay the entire judgment because he or she would have joint and several liability. [p 850]

15. ___ Section 10(b) of the Securities Exchange Act of 1934 prohibits any manipulative or deceptive practice in connection with the preparation of an audit. [p 850]

16. ___ The U.S. Supreme Court has decided that only intentional conduct and recklessness of accountants violates Section 10(b) and Rule 10b-5. [p 850]

17. ___ Accountants can be held liable for a Section 10(b) or Rule 10b-5 violation if they aid and abet a fraud that is the basis of the securities violation. [p 851]

18. ___ Section 24 of the Securities Act of 1933 makes it a criminal offense for any person to willfully make untrue statement of any fact in a registration statement filed with the SEC. [p 851]

19. ___ An accountant participates in insider trading in violation of Section 32(a) of the Securities Exchange Act of 1934. The accountant can be punished by fines up to $1 million and imprisoned up to ten years in prison. [p 852]

20. ___ Accountants may be prosecuted under the RICO statute if they engage in multiple acts of securities fraud. [p 852]

21. ___ An accountant may be prosecuted for willful understatement of a client's tax liability, but there is no criminal liability for negligent understatement of the tax liability. [p 852]

22. ___ The U.S. Supreme Court has ruled there is no accountant-client privilege under federal law. [p 852]

23. ___ A work product immunity statute says that an accountant's work papers cannot be used in any court action in the country. [p 853]

24. ___ An accountant has a duty to not transfer the accountant's work papers without the client's permission. [p 853]

25. ___ A client has the right to review the work papers of an accountant who is engaged with the client. [p 853]

Multiple Choice:

26. Standards for the preparation and presentation of financial statements are found in [p 842]
    a. GAAPs.
    b. GAASs.
    c. Greenstein, Logan & Company v. Burgess Marketing, Inc 744 S.W.2d 170 (1987).
    d. The *Ultramares Doctrine.*

27. Standards that specify the methods and procedures that must be used to conduct audits are found in [p 842]
    a. GAAPs.
    b. GAASs.
    c. Greenstein, Logan &Company v. Burgess Marketing, Inc 744 S.W.2d 170 (1987).
    d. The *Untramares Doctrine.*

28. To comply with the standards for the methods and procedures that must be used to conduct an audit, an auditor must [p 842]
    a. review the financial records of the company that is being audited.
    b. check the accuracy of the financial records of the company that is being audited.
    c. conduct a sampling of inventory to verify the figures contained in the client's financial statements.
    d. all of the above.

29. An auditor's opinion that is the most favorable one an auditor can give is a(n) [p 843]
    a. unqualified opinion.
    b. qualified opinion.
    c. adverse opinion.
    d. disclaimer of opinion.

30. An auditor's opinion that is usually issued when the auditor determines that the company has materially misstates certain items on its financial statement is a(n) [p 843]
    a. unqualified opinion.
    b. qualified opinion.
    c. adverse opinion.
    d. disclaimer of opinion.

31. An auditor's opinion which states that the financial statements are fairly presented except for a departure from generally accepted accounting principles, a change in accounting principles, or a material uncertainty, is a(n) [p 843]
    a. unqualified opinion.
    b. qualified opinion.
    c. adverse opinion.
    d. disclaimer of opinion.

32. The most widely followed theory of liability to third parties for negligence by accountants is [p 845]
    a. the *Ultramares Doctrine.*
    b. Section 552 of the Restatement (Second) of Torts.
    c. the foreseeability standard.
    d. GAAPs.

33. Third parties cannot sue accountant s for breach of contract because they are not [p 848]
    a. covered by the *Ultramares Doctrine.*
    b. covered by Section 552 of the Restatement (Second) of Torts.
    c. covered by the foreseeability standard.
    d. in privity of contract.

34. When an auditor discovers an illegal act committed by their clients, pursuant to Section 10A of the Securities Exchange Act of 1994, their first step is to [p 849]
    a. inform the SEC of the auditor's conclusion within one day of discovery.
    b. report the illegal act to the client's full board of directors.
    c. inform the client's management and audit committee.
    d. help the client cover up the illegal act.

35. Civil liability is imposed on any person who makes false or misleading statements in any application, report, or document filed with the SEC by [p 851]
    a. Section 10(b) of the Securities Exchange Act of 1934.
    b. Rule 10b-5 of the Securities Exchange Commission.
    c. Section 18(a) of the Securities Exchange Act of 1934.
    d. Section 32(a) of the Securities Exchange Act of 1934.

Short Answer:

36. What are GAAPs? [p 842] _____

_____

37. What is an *audit*? [p 842] _____

_____

_____

38. When does an auditor give a *disclaimer of opinion*? [p 843] _____

_____

39. What duty is owed by accountants to clients? [p 843] _____

_____

40. An accountant who fails to meet the standard set forth in Question #39 may be sued for _____

_____. [p 844]

41. What are the three major rules of liability that a state may adopt in determining whether an accountant is liable in negligence to third parties? [p 845] (1) _____

(2) _____ (3) _____

42. Describe the *Ultramares Doctrine*. [p 845] _____

_____

_____

_____

43. What conduct produces liability for accountants under Section 11(a) of the Securities Act of 1933? [p 850] _____

_____

44. What is proportionate liability and what is its effect? [p 850] _____

_____

_____

45. Why are accountants vulnerable to a Section 18(A) violation? [p 851] _____

_____

_____

46. How did the decision in Central Bank of Denver, N.A. v. First Interstate Bank of Denver, N.A. affect the liability of accountants under Section 10(b) and Rule 10b-5? [p 851] _____

_____

_____

_____

47. What three things create criminal liability for an accountant under Section 24 of the Securities Act of 1933? [p 851] (1) _____

(2) _____

(3) _____

48. Because securities fraud falls under the definition of racketeering activity, accountants are vulnerable to prosecution under the _____ _____ _____ _____

_____ ____ (RICO). [p 852]

49. Name three specific acts for which an accountant may incur criminal liability under the 1976 Tax Reform Act. [p 852] (1) _____
    (2) _____
    (3) _____

50. Name three rights or duties owed by an accountant to a client in regards to concerning work papers. [p 853] (1) _____
    (2) _____
    (3) _____

Answers to Refresh Your Memory

1. Audits [p 842]
2. GAAP, GASS [p 842]
3. unqualified opinion [p 843]
4. breach [p 843]
5. Constructive fraud [p 843]
6. reasonable, circumstances [p 843]
7. *Ultramares*, privity of contract [p 845]
8. foreseeability standard [p 847]
9. actual [p 849]
10. omissions, registration [p 850]
11. proportionate [p 850]
12. deceptive, security [p 850]
13. 18(a), SEC [p 851]
14. untrue, material [p 851]
15. allow [p 853]

Critical Thought Exercise Model Answer

It has been a much-debated issue whether accountants may be held liable in private actions for aiding and abetting violations of securities laws such as Section 10(b) and Rule 10b-5. The case of *Central Bank v. First Interstate Bank* in 1994 saw the United States Supreme Court rule that private parties could not bring actions against accountants for aiding and abetting violations of Section 10(b) of the 1934 Act. The ruling in *Central Bank* was addressed by Congress when it passed the Private Securities Litigation Reform Act of 1995. The act imposed a new statutory duty on accountants. An auditor must use adequate and thorough procedures in any audit performed by them to detect any illegal acts of customer for whom the audit is being prepared. Any illegality must be disclosed to the company's board of directors, the management audit committee, or even the SEC it the circumstances warrant such action. The act makes aiding and abetting a violation of the Act of 1934 a violation in itself. The Private Securities Litigation Reform Act of 1995 precluded the extension of the ruling in Central bank to SEC actions. Thus, the SEC action against Jones Bateman would be allowed under a theory of aiding and abetting the SEC violations by BGT.

Answers to Practice Quiz

True/False:

1. False   GAAPs are the standards for the preparation and presentation of financial statements.
2. True   The CPA can have no internal relationship with the client.
3. False   The CPA must investigate the financial position of the company, take a sampling of the inventory, and verify information from third parties.
4. False   The adverse opinion is issued when the auditor determines that the company has materially misstated certain items on its financial statements.
5. True   Failure to fulfill the terms of the engagement is a breach of contract.
6. False   This is a definition of constructive fraud.
7. True   GAASs set the standard for the duty of care that must be followed when performing an audit.
8. True   Under this doctrine, the accountant must be aware of the use of the work by the third party.
9. False   The Restatement (Second) of Torts provides a broader standard, which increases accountant liability to third parties for negligence.
10. True   This is a correct definition of privity of contract.
11. False   The accountant has committed fraud. Negligence is an unintentional tort.
12. True   Section 10(A) tells the accountant what steps need to be taken when illegalities are discovered.
13. False   The accountant has special skill and knowledge.
14. False   The accountant would only have to pay for their proportionate degree of liability.
15. False   It prohibits deception in the purchase or sale of any security.
16. True   The Supreme Court rejected negligence as a basis for Section 10(b) and Rule 10b-5 violations.
17. False   The *Central Bank* case removed aiding and abetting as a basis for liability.
18. False   The untrue statement must relate to a material fact.
19. True   This is a correct statement of the maximum punishment for that offense.
20. True   Securities fraud falls under the definition of racketeering activity.
21. False   The accountant may be prosecuted for negligent understatement of a client's tax liability pursuant to the 1976 Tax Reform Act.
22. True   Unlike the attorney-client privilege, accountants have no such privilege in matters that are filed or prosecuted in federal courts.
23. False   These laws are state statutes. The work product immunity rule ahs no application in federal courts.
24. True   This is one of the rights and duties that an accountant must protect in regards to the handling of work papers.
25. True   The client has the right to review his or her accountant's work papers upon reasonable notice.

Multiple Choice:

26. A   A is correct because GAAPs are the generally accepted accounting principle which deal with the preparation of financial statements. B is not correct because GAASs deal with preparation of audits. C is not correct because it is a case that dealt with the failure to follow GAAS. D is incorrect because it is a negligence doctrine.
27. B   B is correct because GAASs are the standards that specify the method and procedures for conducting audits. A is incorrect because it pertains to preparation of financial statements. C is incorrect because if is a case that dealt with the failure to follow GAAS. D is incorrect because it is a negligence doctrine, not a source of accounting standards.

28. D   D is correct because choices A, B, and C are all necessary steps in an audit.

29. A   A is correct because this opinion states that the company's financial statements fairly present the company's financial position. Choice B is incorrect because a qualified opinion notes an exception, departure from accounting principles, or a material uncertainty. Choice C is incorrect because it gives the opinion that there is a material misstatement in the financial records. Choice D is not correct because the auditor renders no opinion due to lack of sufficient information.

30. C   Choice C is issued by the auditor when a material misstatement is found in the financial records of the company. Choice A is incorrect because an unqualified opinion would not be issued if there were anything materially wrong with the financial records. Choice B is incorrect because it only notes a potential problem, not a material misstatement. Choice D is incorrect because no opinion is issued due to a lack of sufficient information.

31. B   B is correct because an exception, departure, or uncertainty, prevent the opinion from being unqualified, but the problems are not serious enough to require an adverse opinion. Choice A is not correct because an unqualified opinion notes no problems. Choice C is incorrect because it reveals a material misstatement in the financial records, not just an exception to or departure from accounting principles. Choice D is incorrect because a disclaimer is made when no opinion is possible due to a lack of sufficient information.

32. A   A is correct because this is the theory applied in a majority of states. Choices B and C are not correct because they are applied in a fewer number of states. Choice D is not correct because GAAPs are used to show negligence, not to extend liability to third parties.

33. D   D is correct because there must be a contractual relationship, or privity, before a party can maintain an action for breach of contract. Choices B, C, and D are incorrect because they state negligence theories and are unrelated to breach of contract.

34. C   C is the correct choice pursuant to Section 10A, which has a three-tier reporting requirement. If the first step is unsuccessful, the auditor must then go to the board of directors. Choice A is wrong because the auditor does not have to report to the SEC until other options are exhausted. Choice B is incorrect because the board of directors does not have to be informed unless the management fails to take timely and appropriate remedial action. Choice D is incorrect because the auditor must act to remedy the illegality by following the mandates of Section 10A.

35. C   Choice C is correct because it imposes civil liability for making false or misleading statements in SEC filings. Choice A and B are incorrect because they relate to actions involved in the purchase or sale of a security. Choice D is incorrect because it deals with criminal liability.

Short Answer:

36.   They are standards for the preparation and presentation of financial statements.

37.   An audit is the verification of a company's books and records pursuant to federal securities laws, state laws, and stock exchange rules that must be performed by an independent CPA.

38.   This opinion is generally issued when the auditor lacks sufficient information about the financial records to issue an overall opinion.

39.   Accountants owe a duty to use reasonable care, knowledge, skill, and judgment when providing auditing and other accounting services to a client.

40.   accountant malpractice

41.   (1) *Ultramares Doctrine* (2) Section 552 of the Restatement (Second) of Torts
      (3) the foreseeability standard

42.   The *Ultramares Doctrine* provides that an accountant is not liable for negligence to third parties unless the plaintiff was either in privity of contract or a pritivy-like relationship with the accountant. Privity of contract would occur if a client employed as accountant to prepare financial statements to be used by an identified third party for a specific purpose that the accountant was made aware of.

43. The accountant is liable for making misstatements or omissions of material fact in a registration statement or failing to find such misstatements or omissions.

44. Proportionate liability replaces joint and several liability and makes a defendant only liable for its proportionate degree of fault. It relieves accountants from being the deep pocket except to the degree of their fault.

45. Section 18(a) imposes civil liability on any person who makes false or misleading statements in any application, report, or document file with the SEC. Because accountants often file reports and other documents with the SEC on behalf of clients, they are vulnerable to liability under this section.

46. The Supreme Court held that defendants could not be held liable for aiding and abetting under Section 10(b) and Rule 10b-5. However, accountants can still be held liable for direct violation of Section 10(b) and Rule 10b-5 caused by their intentional or reckless conduct.

47. (1) willfully make any untrue statement of material fact in a registration statement filed with the SEC, (2) omit any material fact necessary to ensure that the statements made in the registration statement are not misleading, or (3) willfully violate any other provision of the Securities Act of 1933 or rule or regulation adopted thereunder

48. Racketeer Influenced and Corrupt Organizations Act

49. (1) willful understatement of a client's tax liability, (2) negligent understatement of tax liability, or (3) wrongful indorsing a client's tax refund check.

50. (1) right to review the work papers with reasonable notice, (2) duty to transfer the papers upon the client's request, and (3) duty to not transfer the papers without the client's permission

Chapter 44

ADMINISTRATIVE LAW AND
GOVERNMENT REGULATION

Chapter Overview

Administrative agencies that have been established to administer the law have a large and direct impact on the operation of the government, the economy, and businesses. Modernly, we have administrative rules and regulations that cover almost every aspect of a business's operation. The growth in the size of administrative agencies and the rules they create have been staggering. Administrative law functions at the federal, state, and local levels. Understanding the sources and effects of administrative law and being able to function in the administrative law environment is essential for a business if it is going to succeed.

Chapter Objectives

Upon completion of the exercises in this chapter, you should be able to:
1.   Describe government regulation and the source of its authority.
2.   Explain the difference between a regulation and a compensable taking of property.
3.   Explain the functions of administrative agencies.
4.   Understand the major provisions of the Administrative Procedure Act.
5.   Understand the difference among substantive rules, interpretive rules, and statements of policy.
6.   Determine the lawfulness of an administrative search.
7.   Describe the process for administrative agency adjudication of disputes
8.   Explain how administrative agency decisions may be reviewed by the courts.
9.   Understand when the Freedom of Information Act applies.
10. Describe the Government in the Sunshine Act.

Practical Application

Upon mastering the concepts in this chapter, you should understand the basis for the power of administrative agencies, the legality of administrative actions, procedures for challenging administrative action, and the effect of an administrative agency decision. The frontline contact between a business and the government is most often an administrative agency. The regulations and rules that control business behavior are generated and enforced by administrative agencies. The information in this chapter will make it easier for you enforce your rights and meet you obligations under the law.

Helpful Hints

Administrative agencies only have the power granted to them by the branch of government that they serve. As such, administrative agencies are designed to implement the policy of the law as dictated by statute and the Constitution. The Administrative agency must be in compliance with law before it can dictate the conduct of a business or individual. Focus on the parameters of administrative powers to understand when it is necessary to comply with an administrative agency rule or directive and when it is possible to challenge the authority of the agency to act.

Study Tips

It is wise to develop an understanding of the various powers possessed by agencies and the procedural steps that the agency and persons who come before the agency must adhere to. You should then look at the enforceability of agency decisions and a person's right to seek review of an agency decision. Lastly, you need to understand the rules and laws that govern access to agency controlled information.

Government Regulation

General government regulation. Business is subject to general government regulation that applies to many businesses and industries collectively.

Examples:

- Occupational Health and Safety Administration (OSHA) regulates workplace health and safety standards that apply to varied businesses, industries, and occupations. Equipment safety standards are applied equally to coal mines as they are to furniture factories. Work hour regulations apply equally to grocery stores and universities.
- National Labor Relations Board (NLRB) regulates the formations and operation of labor unions. The NLRB will supervise the election of union for garment workers as well as hospital technicians or oil platform maintenance workers.
- Consumer Product Safety Commission (CPSC) establishes safety standards for products sold in this country, whether it is a toy for a child or a microwave oven.

Specific government regulation. Administrative agencies have been created by Congress and the executive branch to monitor specific industries.

Examples:

- Federal Aviation Administration (FAA) regulates only air travel and the airline industry.
- Federal Communication Commission (FCC) is responsible for regulating only federal communications such as radio, television, and telecommunications.
- Office of the Comptroller of the Currency (OCC) regulates national banks.

The Administrative Agency

The theory behind the creation of agencies is that they create a source of expertise in a particular field. Congress and the executive branch are unable to regulate the hundreds of individual industries and specialty areas that are part of our commerce and society. By delegating authority to the experts, the industries and commerce are regulated more efficiently.

federal administrative agencies. The most regulation comes from federal administrative agencies that are either part of the executive branch or independent agencies created by Congress.

state administrative agencies. State agencies enforce state laws and regulations, such as corporations law, fish and game regulations, and workers' compensation law. Local (county and city) agencies closely regulate business, from redevelopment agencies to planning and zoning commissions.

Administrative Law

Administrative law is a combination of substantive and procedural law. Each agency is empowered to administer a particular act or set of statutes. From this foundation, the agency enacts regulations to give effect to the statutes. Part of this body of law is the procedural rules that govern how the agency conducts its business. A prime example of the implementation of administrative law is the Securities and Exchange Commission. They are empowered to administer the Securities and Exchange Act of 1934 and the Securities Act of 1933. To do this, the SEC has developed the SEC Rules. Both sources of law work together to regulate the securities market. This body of law is substantive in nature, with the SEC Rules also providing some procedural guidance.

Federal administrative procedure is controlled mainly by the Administrative Procedure Act (APA). This act set up procedures that federal administrative agencies must follow. Some of the APA rules provide for hearings, rules for conducting adjudicative actions, and procedures for rule making. Administrative law judges (ALJ), who are employees of the agency, preside over administrative hearings and proceedings. The ALJ decides the case and issues a decision in the form of an order.

The power of the agency is restricted to those powers that are delegated to it by either the legislative or executive branch. This is the *delegation doctrine*. The agency has powers from all three branches as it can adopt a rule, prosecute a violation of the rule, and adjudicate any dispute.

Legislative Powers of Administrative Agencies

Agencies are delegated legislative powers that include the following rule making and licensing powers:

- *substantive rule making* – An agency can issue a substantive rule that is like a statute. The rule must be followed and carried civil and criminal sanctions, depending upon the purpose of the rule.
- *interpretive rule making* – An agency can issue interpretive rules that interpret existing statutes. These give notice of how the agency will apply a statute.
- *statements of policy* – These statements announce a proposed course of action that the agency intends to follow.
- *licensing powers* – Statutes often require the issuance of a government license before a person can take action of enter certain business markets. Most agencies have the power to determine whether an applicant will receive a license.

Executive Powers of Administrative Agencies

Executive powers are the powers that administrative agencies are granted, such as the investigation and prosecution of possible violations of statutes, administrative rules, and administrative orders. These powers are often exercised through the use of:

- *administrative subpoenas* – an order that directs the subject of the subpoena to disclose the requested information. Failure to comply with the subpoena may lead to a judicial order for compliance. Further failure to comply with the subpoena, may cause the party to be held in contempt of court.
- *administrative searches* – are physical inspection of business premises. They are considered searches and must comply with the Fourth Amendment, which forbids an unreasonable search and seizure. An administrative search must satisfy the three criteria necessary to make reasonable warrantless inspections. According to the U.S. Supreme Court, these criteria are:
  1. the government has a substantial interest in regulating the particular industry
  2. regulation of the industry reasonably serves the government's substantial interest
  3. the statute under which the search is done provides a constitutionally adequate substitute for a warrant

Judicial Powers of Administrative Agencies

Many administrative agencies have the judicial authority to adjudicate cases in administrative proceedings. The administrative proceeding is initiated by serving a complaint on a respondent, who is the party that is accused by the agency of violating a statute or rule. The respondent must be accorded procedural due process, which requires that the respondent be given (1) proper and timely notice of the allegations or charges, and (2) an opportunity to present evidence in the matter.

At an administrative proceeding, an administrative law judge (ALJ) presides and makes rulings on fact and law without the use of a jury. Both sides have the right to be represented by an attorney, cross-examine witnesses, and produce their own evidence. The ALJ's decision is called an order, which may be reviewed by the agency. Any further appeal is to the appropriate federal of state court.

Judicial Review of Administrative Agency Actions

Most federal and state statutes provide for judicial review of administrative agency actions. If the statute does not contain authorization for judicial review, a party may rely upon the Administrative Procedure Act, which authorizes judicial review for federal administrative agency decisions. Before a petitioner can appeal an action of an administrative agency to a review court, the following conditions must be satisfied:

1. The case must be ripe for review. The petitioner must have standing to sue the agency.
2. The petitioner must have exhausted all administrative remedies. The party must follow agency appeal procedures before a court will agree that administrative remedies have been exhausted by the petitioner.
3. There must be an actual controversy at issue. Under the final order rule, the decision of the agency must be final before judicial review can be sought.

In reviewing the order of the administrative agency, the reviewing court is reluctant to review the factual findings of the agency. The court will look at the following questions:

- Has the agency exceeded its authority as granted by the enabling statute?
- Has the administrative agency correctly interpreted that laws that apply to the agency's action and decision?
- Were there any constitutional violations by the agency during the administrative process?
- Did the agency comply with all procedural requirements of the controlling law?
- Were the agency's actions arbitrary, capricious, or an abuse of its discretion?
- Is the decision of the administrative agency supported by substantial evidence?

Public Accountability of Administrative Agencies

Congress has passed several statutes to make administrative agencies more accountable by subjecting them to increased public scrutiny. These statutes aim to make agency actions and procedures more public in nature and protect people and businesses from overzealous actions by agencies. Four of these Congressional acts are:

- Freedom of Information Act. Requires that federal administrative agencies disclose certain records and documents to any person upon request. No reason for the request need be given. There are exceptions to the act, such as documents that must remain confidential to preserve national security.
- Government in the Sunshine Act. Requires that every portion of every meeting of an agency be open to the public. The public must be given notice of the meeting and informed of the agenda. There are narrowly construed exceptions; such as meetings concerning future litigation and those where criminal acts of an agency target will be discussed.
- Equal Access to Justice Act. Enacted to protect persons from harassment by federal administrative agencies. A private person can sue to recover attorneys' fees and costs associated with repelling an unjustified agency action.
- Privacy Act. Requires that a federal agency maintain only that information about an individual that is relevant and necessary to accomplish a legitimate agency purpose. An individual has the right to inspect and correct the records.

Government Regulation Versus Compensable Taking of Property

The government may exercise its power of eminent domain to obtain ownership of private property for a public purpose. This often happens when agencies seek to revitalize an urban area or the government desires sufficient land for public projects, such as schools, highways, or public access to natural resources (lakes and rivers). The Due Process Clause entitles the owner to bring an action to prevent the taking. Under the Just Compensation Clause of the U.S. Constitution, the government must compensate the owner for any taking by way of eminent domain. The owner may challenge the amount of compensation by asking a court to set the amount. Not all regulation that deprives the owner of use or full value is a compensable "taking." Restricted uses, such as zoning decisions, are not necessarily a taking unless the owner is deprived of all reasonable use.

Refresh Your Memory

The following exercises will enable you to refresh you memory of the key points given to you in this chapter. Read the question twice and place your answer in the blanks provided. Complete the entire exercise, and then review the chapter material you could not remember.

1. Administrative agencies are intended to provide _____ and _____ in dealing with complex commercial organizations and businesses.

2. _____ government regulation applies to many business and industries, such as health and safety standards enforced by OSHA.

3. _____ government regulation monitors specific industries, such as the regulation of television and radio by the FCC.

4. Many administrative agencies are given the authority to adopt _____ and _____ that enforce and interpret statutory law.

5. The majority of federal administrative agencies are part of the _____ branch.

6. The Administrative Procedure Act establishes _____ and _____ requirements for administrative proceedings.

7. When an agency is created, it is delegated certain _____ under the *delegation doctrine*.

8. A _____ regulation is much like a statute.

9. Administrative agencies can issue so-called _____ rules that interpret existing statutory language.

10. _____ powers of administrative agencies give them the power to determine whether to grant or deny a license application.

11. Administrative agencies are usually given _____ powers to investigate and prosecute violations of statutes, rules and orders.

12. The person on whom the complaint is served by an agency is called the _____.

13. _____ due process requires that the statute or rule that the respondent is charged with violating is clearly stated.

14. The _____ ___ ____ _____ Act requires that certain federal administrative agency meetings be open to the public.

15. The _____ _____ Clause mandates that the government pay an owner for their property when it is taken by the government under eminent domain.

Critical Thought Exercise

Macey Resources runs a hazardous waste facility where large quantities of industrial waste are stored, neutralized and packaged for burial once it is dehydrated. A state statute provides that any business that handles more than 5 gallons of hazardous materials in a calendar month is subject to inspection without notice or warrant. Macey's operation includes 300 acres of ponds and transfer machinery. If a pond is not properly maintained, the seepage into the ground water could contaminate a large area with a radius over 15 miles. Within this radius there are numerous housing developments, schools, hospitals, and recreational facilities, including a small lake that is used for fishing, skiing, and swimming. Inspectors from the state and federal environmental protection agencies enter Macey's property without a warrant or any advance notice to inspect the facility and test for hazardous waste seepage outside the drying ponds. The inspectors find numerous violations of state and federal law, including falsification of documents pertaining to disposal of potentially lethal chemicals from a military base. Macey is cited for the violations and is prosecuted by the US Attorney for criminal charges. Macey files motions in the appropriate courts to have the evidence seized by the inspectors suppressed based upon a violation of the Fourth Amendment and failure to procure an administrative search warrant. What is the likely result of such a motion by Macey?

Answer. _____

_____

_____

_____

_____

_____

_____

_____

_____

_____

_____

_____

_____

_____

_____

_____

_____

_____

_____

_____

_____

_____

Practice Quiz

True/False:

1. ___ The establishment of safety standards by the Consumer Product Safety Commission for products sold to consumers is an example of specific government regulation. [p 861]

2. ___ The Poultry Protection Act, as administered by the Department of Agriculture, is an example of general government regulation. [p 862]

3. ___ The Administrative Procedure Act is an act that establishes certain administrative procedures that federal administrative agencies must follow in conducting their affairs. [p 864]

4. ___ Administrative law is composed exclusively of procedural law that is used to implement substantive law taken only from federal statutes. [p 864]

5. ___ An administrative agency can only exercise those powers that are delegated to it. [p 865]

6. ___ Substantive rules issued by administrative agencies do not have the same force of law as a statute that is needed to create civil and criminal liability for violations of the rule. [p 865]

7. ___ Interpretive rules establish new laws, which require public notice and participation. [p 866]

8. ___ Statements of policy announce a proposed course of action that an agency intends to follow in the future. [p 866]

9. ___ In Food and Drug Administration v. Brown and Williamson Tobacco Corporation, the Supreme Court ruled that the FDA had the authority to regulate tobacco as a drug under the authority of the Food, Drug, and Cosmetics Act. [p 866]

10. ___ The investigation and prosecution of violations of statutes, rules, and administrative orders is part of an agency's legislative powers. [p 867]

11. ___ An administrative search is an order that directs the subject of a subpoena to disclose the requested information. [p 868]

12. ___ Most inspections by administrative agencies are considered searches that are subject to the Fourth Amendment of the U.S. Constitution. [p 868]

13. ___ The Due Process Clause of the U.S. Constitution does not apply to administrative adjudication of cases. [p 871]

14. ___ Substantive due process requires the respondent to be given proper and timely notice of the allegations or charges against him or her and an opportunity to present evidence on the matter. [p 871]

15. ___ Substantive due process requires that the statute or rule that the respondent is charged with violating be clearly stated. [p 871]

16. ___ There is no right to be represented by counsel at an administrative adjudication. [p 871]

17. ___ The decision in an administrative adjudication is rendered by the jury. [p 871]

18. ___ The party appealing the decision of an administrative agency is called the petitioner. [p 871]

19. ___ In order for a party to appeal an action of an administrative agency, the case must be ripe for review, meaning that the agency's rule, order, or policy must specifically apply to the party. [p 872]

20. ___ The decision of a federal administrative agency will be reversed unless it was supported by substantial evidence. [p 873]

21. ___ Federal administrative agency employees may be sued based upon their personal liability regarding the actions and decisions they make while performing their agency duties. [p 873]

22. ___ A citizen may obtain records of an agency's personnel practices under the Freedom of Information Act. [p 873]

23. ___ A private party who is the subject of an unjustified federal administrative agency action may sue to recover attorneys' fees and costs. [p 874]

24. ___ Federal administrative agencies can maintain only information about an individual that is relevant and necessary to accomplish a legitimate agency purpose. [p 874]

25. ___ The government may use its military power to acquire private property for a public purpose. [p 875]

Multiple Choice:

26. Regulation of the formation and operation of labor unions in most industries by the NLRB is an example of [p 861]
    a. general government regulation.
    b. specific government regulation.
    c. state government regulation.
    d. local government regulation.

27. The enforcement of the Horse Protection Act by the U.S. Department of Agriculture is an example of [p 862]
    a. general government regulation.
    b. specific government regulation.
    c. state fish and game regulation.
    d. local government regulation.

28. Administrative procedures that federal administrative agencies must follow in conducting their affairs, such as notice and hearing requirements, rules for conducting agency adjudicative actions, and procedures for rule making, were established by the [p 864]
    a. Privacy Act.
    b. Government in the Sunshine Act.
    c. Equal Access to Justice.
    d. Administrative Procedure Act.

29. An administrative agency can [p 865]
    a. adopt a rule or regulation.
    b. prosecute a violation of a rule or statute.
    c. adjudicate a dispute.
    d. all of the above.

30. A federal administrative agency that proposes to adopt a substantive rule must [p 865]
    a. publish a general notice of the proposed rule making in the Federal Register.
    b. give interested persons an opportunity to participate in the rule-making process.
    c. review all written and oral comments.
    d. all of the above.

31. When administrative agencies interpret existing statutory language, they can issue [p 866]
    a. a substantive rule.
    b. an interpretive rule.
    c. a statement of policy.
    d. a final order.

32. Executive powers give an administrative agency the authority to [p 867]
    a. adopt a substantive rule.
    b. adjudicate a dispute over a rule or regulation.
    c. investigate and prosecute a violation of a statute, rule, or order.
    d. interpret a statute as it applies to an industry.

33. Proper and timely notice of the allegations or charges and an opportunity to present evidence on a matter are two requirements of [p 871]
    a. substantive due process.
    b. procedural due process.
    c. substantive rule making.
    d. interpretive rule making.

34. If a person desires to seek review of the decision of an administrative law judge, the first level of appeal consists of a review by the [p 872]
    a. agency for whom the ALJ works.
    b. U.S. District Court.
    c. U.S. Court of Appeals.
    d. U.S. Supreme Court.

35. If Ajax drug company wants to obtain copies of the hearing documents involved with an adjudication involving Zephyr Drug Company and the FDA, they can best force the release of the records of the hearing under the [p 873]
    a. Equal Access to Justice Act.
    b. Government in the Sunshine Act.
    c. Freedom of Information Act.
    d. Privacy Act.

Short Answer:

36. List three agencies that engage in general government regulation. [p 861] (1) _____
    (2) _____ (3) _____

37. What are three requirements or procedural mandates contained in the Administrative Procedure Act?
    [p 864] (1) _____ (2) _____
    (3) _____

38. The _____ says when an administrative agency is created, it is delegated
    certain powers. [p 865]

39. Statutes often require the issuance of a government _____ before a person can enter certain
    types of industries (e.g., operation of banks, television stations, commercial airlines) or professions
    (doctor, lawyer, contractor). [p 867]

40. Judicial enforcement may be sought when a party does not comply with an administrative subpoena
    and the agency can prove that it has _____ _____ to believe the information sought
    will prove a violation of the law. [p 867]

41. List five circumstances under which a search by an administrative agency would be considered
    reasonable within the meaning of the Fourth Amendment. [p 868]
    (1) _____
    (2) _____
    (3) _____
    (4) _____
    (5) _____

42. The person on whom the complaint is served by an administrative agency is called the _____
    _____ [p 870]

43. _____ _____ _____ decide questions of law and fact as they preside over
    administrative proceedings. [p 871]

44. The ALJ's decision from an adjudication states the reasons for the ALJ's decision and is issued in the
    form of an _____. [p 871]

45. The four legislative powers possessed by an administrative agency are: [p 871]
    (1) _____ (2) _____
    (3) _____ (4) _____

46. What three conditions must occur before the decision of an administrative agency can be appealed to
    a court? [p 872] (1) _____ (2) _____
    (3) _____

47. The Freedom of Information Act requires federal administrative agencies to publish agency
    procedures, _____, _____, _____, and other information in the Federal
    Register. [p 873]

48. The _____ Act requires agencies to publish quarterly indexes of certain
    documents. [p 874]

49. A decision by an agency administrator to close meetings to the public because it could be
    embarrassing to the agency for the public to hear the business discussed may violate the
    _____ Act. [p 874]

50. Why does the government have to pay for private property that is obtained by way of eminent domain? [p 875] _____

Answers to Refresh Your Memory

1. resources, expertise [p 861]
2. general [p 861]
3. specific [p 862]
4. rules, regulations [p 864]
5. executive [p 864]
6. notice, hearing [p 864]
7. powers [p 865]
8. substantive [p 865]
9. interpretive [p 866]
10. licensing [p 867]
11. executive [p 867]
12. respondent [p 870]
13. substantive [p 871]
14. Government in the Sunshine [p 874]
15. Just Compensation [p 875]

Critical Thought Exercise Model Answer

Physical inspection of the premises of a business is often crucial to the implementation of lawful administrative regulation by the agency entrusted with monitoring certain commercial activity. Searches by administrative agencies are generally deemed to be reasonable within the meaning of the Fourth Amendment if the business is part of a highly regulated industry where searches are automatically considered to be valid (liquor), or where the business is engages in hazardous activity and a statute expressly provides for nonarbitrary warrantless searches (mines, nuclear power. Evidence from an unreasonable search and seizure may be inadmissible in court depending upon the reasonableness of the search in the particular case. An expectation of privacy in commercial premises is different from, and is less than, expectation in an individual's home. This expectation is made much less is commercial property employed in "closely regulated" industries. Because the owner of the highly regulated business has less of an expectation of privacy, searches that are conducted pursuant to a regulatory scheme do not require a search warrant. The expectation is removed almost totally when the activity is ultra hazardous and highly regulated. Macey, as an operator of a hazardous waste site, would be on notice that a search could take place at any time. He has impliedly waived his Fourth Amendment rights by engaging in this type of business.

Answers to Practice Quiz

True/False:

1. False   This is an example of general government regulation
2. False   Because the act regulates one particular industry, poultry, it is specific government regulation.
3. True   This correctly states the purpose of the APA.

4   False   Administrative law is a combination of substantive and procedural law.
5.   True   This is the delegation doctrine.
6.   False   An administrative substantive rule has the force of law and must be adhered to by covered persons and businesses.
7.   False   They only interpret existing statutory language and are not a new law.
8.   True   They give businesses advance notice of how the agency will proceed on certain issues.
9.   False   The Supreme Court ruled that Congress intended to exclude tobacco products from the FDA's jurisdiction. The Court stated that the FDA had exceeded its authority by misinterpreting the FDCA.
10.   False   These acts are part of an agency's executive powers.
11.   False   This order is an administrative subpoena.
12.   True   The search must be reasonable under the Fourth Amendment to the U.S. Constitution.
13.   False   The agency must afford a party procedural and substantive due process.
14.   False   Notice, hearing, and the opportunity to present evidence are procedural due process rights.
15.   True   It would violate substantive due process if the statute were vague or ambiguous.
16.   False   Both the agency and the respondent may be represented by counsel at a hearing.
17.   False   An administrative law judge renders the decision in the form of an order.
18.   True   The petitioner may appeal the final order of an administrative agency in most cases.
19.   True   The petitioner must have standing to sue.
20.   True   Though most factual determinations of the agency are not overturned, the agency must have substantial evidence to support its decision.
21.   False   Agency employees are immune from lawsuits for personal liability.
22.   False   Personnel records are exempt from disclosure under the Freedom of Information Act.
23.   True   The Equal Access grants this right to Justice Act.
24.   True   The Privacy Act creates this limitation.
25.   False   The power to acquire private property for a public purpose is eminent domain.

Multiple Choice:

26. A   A is the correct choice because the regulation is across numerous industries. Choice B is incorrect because the regulations apply to more than one industry. Choices C and D are incorrect because the NLRB is a federal agency.
27. B   B is correct because the regulation applies to one specific industry. Choice A is incorrect because the act does not apply to numerous industries. Choices C and D are incorrect because they are not a form of federal regulation and the USDA is a federal agency.
28. D   D is the act that set forth the specified procedural requirement for agencies. Choice A is not correct as it concerned the right of an individual to sue an agency for improper action. Choice B is incorrect because it concerned open meetings. Choice C is incorrect because it concerned the limitation upon the type of information that could be retained by agencies.
29. D   D is correct because an agency has all three powers named based upon its legislative, executive, and judicial functions. Choices A, B, and C are incorrect because they eliminate other correct choices.
30. D   D is correct because all the choices are requirements for an agency to adopt a substantive rule. Choices A, B, and C would be incorrect because they are only part of the requirements that are covered by choice D.
31. B   B is correct because and interpretive rule is not a new law, it only interprets existing law. Choice A is incorrect because a substantive rule has the force of a new law. Choice C is incorrect because statements of policy do nothing more than announce a proposed course of action. Choice D is the ruling made by an ALJ at the conclusion of an adjudication.

32. C   C is correct because investigation and prosecution are executive functions. Choices A and D are incorrect because they are legislative functions. Choice B is incorrect because it is a judicial function to adjudicate a dispute.

33. B   B is correct because the basic procedural requirements of due process are notice of the intended government action and the opportunity to present evidence. Choice A is incorrect because substantive due process concerns the requirement that the statute or rule that a person is charged with violating is not vague. Choices C and D are incorrect because they are two legislative functions of an administrative agency not a standard for a fair hearing.

34. A   A is correct because the administrative process is not complete until the agency reviews the decision of the ALJ and issues a final order. Choice B is incorrect because a person must exhaust all administrative remedies before they can file suit in federal district court. Choice C is incorrect for the same reason that B is incorrect with the addition that decisions of the federal district court may be appealed to the U.S. Court of Appeals. Choice D is incorrect because all levels of appeal must be exhausted before a party may petition for review to the U.S Supreme Court.

35. C   C is correct because this act gives public access to most documents in the possession of federal administrative agencies. Choice A is incorrect because this act enables a party to sue for attorneys' fees and costs if they have been the subject of an unjustified agency action. Choice B is incorrect because it concerns open public meetings, not the release of documents. Choice D is wrong because it restricts the retention of information about individuals by an agency and is not concerned with the release or distribution of information.

Short Answer:

36.   NLRB, OSHA, CPSC, SEC are sample choices

37.   notice and hearing requirements, rules for conducting agency adjudicative actions, procedures for rule making.

38.   delegation doctrine

39.   license

40.   reasonable grounds

41.   (1) The party voluntarily agrees to the search (2) The search is conducted pursuant to a validly issued search warrant (3) A warrantless search is conducted in an emergency situation (4) The business is part of a special industry where warrantless searches are automatically considered valid (5) The business is part of a hazardous industry and a statute expressly provides for nonarbitrary searches

42.   respondent

43.   Administrative law judges

44.   order

45.   (1) substantive rule making (2) interpretive rule making (3) statements of policy (4) licensing

46.   (1) The case must be ripe for review. (2) The petitioner must have exhausted all administrative remedies. (3) The decision of the agency must be final before judicial review can be sought.

47.   rules, regulations, interpretations

48.   Freedom of Information

49.   Government in the Sunshine

50.   The Just Compensation Clause of the Constitution mandates that the government must compensate the property owner when it exercises the power of eminent domain.

Chapter 45

CONSUMER PROTECTION

Chapter Overview

Starting in the 1960s and continuing into the early 1980s, federal and state governments enacted numerous statutes in order to regulate the behavior of businesses that deal with consumers. The goal of the legislation was to promote product safety and prohibit abusive, unfair, and deceptive selling practices. This was a drastic change from earlier days when sales to consumers were governed by the principle of *caveat emptor*, which means "let the buyer beware."

This chapter presents the statutes, rules, and cases that allow consumers greater protection and have increased the ability of consumers to sue businesses for damages caused by their dangerous, fraudulent, and deceptive methods. Legal theories have developed in the areas of breach of warranty, negligence, and strict liability. Government mandates and regulation by administrative agencies has mushroomed in the area of consumer protection. These laws and regulations form the consumer protection laws that are examined in this chapter.

Objectives

Upon completion of the exercises in this chapter, you should be able to:
1. ·   Describe the authority and responsibilities of the Food and Drug Administration.
2.   Describe the important regulations pertaining to food and food additives.
3.   Describe the regulation of drugs, cosmetics, and medical devices.
4.   Explain the FDA's food labeling regulations.
5.   Describe the scope of the Consumer Product Safety Act and its effect on product safety.
6.   Describe the regulation of packaging, labeling, and poison prevent labeling.
7.   Explain the meaning of unfair and deceptive practices and efforts to prevent them.
8.   Understand the key elements of consumer credit protection statutes.
9.   Identify the protection provided to credit card users.
10.   Describe the conduct that is prohibited by the Equal Credit Opportunity Act.

Practical Application

Upon learning the main legislative protections for consumers in this chapter, you will understand the duties, obligations, and requirements placed upon businesses when they deal in the manufacture, sale, or distribution of consumer goods or services. This information will allow you to determine your specific rights and obligations whether you are a business that must comply with the law or a consumer who is seeking to enforce a protected right.

Helpful Hints

As with all law, your analysis of a situation must begin with the basis definitions and requirements as contained in the statutes. Once you have that foundation, your focus should turn to the act or nature of the product. By determining where the act or product fits in the legislative scheme of consumer protection, you can alleviate the illegality or enforce the mandates contained in a consumer law. Lastly, many of the statutes require a mental element in combination with the conduct. Examine the intent of the business employee to determine if the statute has been violated.

Study Tips

It is important that you become familiar with the following consumer protections if you are going to be able to analyze actual business situations where the statutes are implicated.

Food, Drug, and Cosmetic Act (FDCA)

This act regulates much of the testing, manufacture, distribution, and sale of foods, drugs, cosmetics, and medical products and devices in the United States. The **Food and Drug Administration (FDA)** administers the act. The FDA implements the FDCA as follows:

- *Regulation of Food* – The FDCA prohibits the shipment, distribution, or sale of aldulterated food, which is any food that consists in whole or in part of any "filthy, putrid, or decomposed substance" that is unfit for consumption. The FDA allows certain amounts of contaminants up to the amount set by their "action levels." For example, tomato juice is allowed to have 10 fly eggs per 3 ½ ounces. Anything below the action level is considered safe to eat.

- **Nutritional Labeling and Education Act** – requires food manufacturers and processors to provide more nutritional information on virtually all foods and forbids them from making scientifically unsubstantiated heath claims. The law requires labels on food items with information on calories, fat, fiber, cholesterol and other substances. The FDA regulations adopted to implement the act, required information on serving size and nutrients. Definitions were developed for *light, low fat*, and *natural*.

- *Regulation of Drugs* – The FDA regulates the testing, licensing, manufacturing, distribution, and sale of drugs. The licensing process is long and thorough. Users of drugs must be provided with a copy of detailed directions that include any warnings and list possible side effects.

- *Regulation of Cosmetics* – The FDA regulations require cosmetics to be labeled, to disclose ingredients, and to contain warnings as to any carcinogenic ingredients. The FDA may remove from the market any product that makes a false claim of preserving youth, increasing virility, or growing hair.

- *Regulation of Medicinal Devices* – The FDA has authority under the Medicinal Device Amendment to the FDCA to regulate medicinal devices, such as heart pacemakers, surgical equipment, and other diagnostic, therapeutic, and health devices. The FDA is empowered to remove quack devices from the market.

- *Other acts and amendments* – The FDA has been empowered by numerous other acts and amendments to the FDCA to regulate pesticides, food additives, color additives, animal drugs and food, biological material (blood, vaccines), food service sanitation, and radiation products (X-ray machines, mircowave ovens, etc.).

United Nations Biosafety Protocol for Genetically Altered Foods

The Biosafety Protocol was passed to resolve a dispute between exporters of genetically modified agricultural products and countries that desired to keep the products out of their country. As a compromise, the 138 countries that signed the protocol agreed to allow the importation of genetically engineered foods as long as they were clearly labeled with the phrase "May contain living modified organisms." This allows consumers to decide themselves whether to purchase altered food products.

Product Safety

The federal government has enacted several statutes that regulate the manufacture and distribution of consumer products. Some of these are:

- The *Consumer Product Safety Act* regulates potentially dangerous consumer products and created the **Consumer Product Safety Commission (CPSC)**. The CPSC is an independent federal agency that is not attached to any department. It interprets the CPSA, conducts research on the safety of products, and collects data and regarding injuries caused by products. The CPSC sets safety standards for consumer products and has the power to compel a manufacturer to recall, repair, or replace a hazardous product. Alternatively, the CPSC can seek injunctions and seize hazardous products. It can also seek civil and criminal penalties.

- *Fair Packaging and Labeling Act* requires the labels on consumer goods to identify the product, the manufacturer, processor, or packager of the product and its address; the net quantity of the contents of the package; and the quantity of each serving. The label must use simple and clear language that a consumer can understand. The act is administered by the Federal Trade Commission and the Department of Health and Human Services.

- *The Poison Protection Packaging Act* requires manufacturers to provide "childproof" containers and packages for all household products.

Unfair and Deceptive Practices

When sellers engage in unfair, deceptive, or abusive techniques, the **Federal Trade Commission (FTC)**, under the authority of the **Federal Trade Commission Act (FTC Act)**, is authorized to bring an administrative proceeding to attack the unfair or deceptive practice. IF the FTC finds a violation under **Section 5 of the FTC Act**, it may order a cease-and-desist order, an affirmative disclosure to consumers, or corrective advertising. The FTC may sue for damages on behalf of consumers in either state or federal court. Improper acts by sellers that are addressed by the FTC include:

- *False and Deceptive Advertising* is prohibited under Section 5 when advertising
  1. contains misinformation or omits important information that is likely to mislead a "reasonable consumer" or
  2. makes an unsubstantiated claim (e.g., "This pain reliever works 50% faster on your headache than our competitors.").

- *Bait and Switch* is another type of deceptive advertising that occurs whena seller advertises the availability of a low-cost discounted item but thenpressures the buyer into purchasing more expensive merchandise. Bait and switch occurs when if
  1. the seller refuses to show consumers the advertised merchandise
  2. discourages employees from selling the advertised merchandise or
  3. fails to have adequate quantities of the merchandise available.

- *Door-to Door Sales* may entail overaggressive or abusive practices. These tactics are handles on a state level where laws give consumers a certain number of days to rescind door-to-door sales, usually three.

- *Unsolicited Merchandise* is handled under the **Postal Reorganization Act**. The act permits persons who have received unsolicited merchandise through the mail to retain, use, disregard, or dispose of the merchandise without having to pay for it or return it.

- *Anti-Spam Statutes* have been enacted by many states to prevent the sending of unsolicited commercial e-mail messages with misleading information in the subject line or transmission path. Courts have held that the benefits of the act outweigh any burden upon commerce.

Federal Consumer-Debtor Protection Laws

The federal government protects consumer-debtors (borrowers) from abusive, deceptive, and unfair practices by creditors (lenders) through a comprehensive scheme of laws concerning the extension and collection of credit. These laws include

- The *Truth-In-Lending Act* requires creditors to make certain disclosures when the creditor regularly
  1. extends credit for goods or services to consumers or
  2. arranges such credit in the ordinary course of their business.

  The TILA is administered by the Federal Reserve Board who adopted a laundry list of disclosures under **Regulation Z**. These disclosures include the finance charge, interest, points, annual percentage rate, due dates of payments, and late payment penalties.

- The *Consumer Leasing Act (CLA)* extended the TILA's coverage to lease terms in consumer leases.

- The *Fair Credit and Charge Card Disclosure Act of 1988* amended TILA to require disclosure of credit terms on credit-and charge-card solicitations and applications. The act requires, in tabular form, disclosure of
  1. the APR
  2. any annual membership fee
  3. any minimum or fixed finance charge
  4. any transaction charge for use of the card for purchases, and
  5. a statement that charges are due when the periodic statement is received by the debtor.

- The *Equal Credit Opportunity Act (ECOA)* prohibits discrimination in the extension of credit based on sex, marital status, race, color, national origin, religion, age, or receipt of income from public assistance programs.

- The *Fair Credit Reporting Act (FCRA)* is located under **Title VI** of TILA. It protects consumers who are subjects of a credit report by setting out guidelines for credit bureaus. The act gives consumers the right to request information on the nature and substance of their credit report, the sources of this information, and the names of recipients of the report.

- The Fair Debt Collection Practices Act protects consumer-debtors from abusive, deceptive, and unfair practices used by debt collectors. The practices prohibited by the FDCPA include:
  1. harassing, abusive, or intimidating tactics (threatening or abusive language)
  2. false or misleading representations (posing as police officer or attorney)
  3. unfair or un conscionable practices (threatening to take illegal action)

  The debt collector may not contact the debtor:
  1. At an inconvenient time
  2. At inconvenient places
  3. At the debtor's place of employment if the employer objects
  4. If the debtor is represented by an attorney
  5. If the debtor gives written notice that the debtor refuses to pay the debt or does not want to have any further contact with the debt collector.

Refresh Your Memory

The following exercises are intended to aid you in refreshing your memory in regards to the important concepts and rules contained in the consumer protection laws that have been presented in this chapter. Answer all the questions in the blanks provided before referring to the chapter material. Review the material for any question that you got wrong or were unable to remember.

1. The FDCA regulates the testing, _____, distribution, and _____ of food, drugs, _____, and medicinal products and devices in the United States.

2. The FDCA prohibits the shipment, distribution, or sale of _____ food.

3. The FDA has issued regulations that require cosmetics to be labeled, to disclose _____, and to contain warnings if they are _____.

4. The FDA is empowered to remove "_____" medicinal devices from the market.

5. To resolve a dispute over genetically modified foods, the United States signed the _____ _____ along with 138 other countries.

6. As part of its powers under the Consumer Product Safety Act, the CPSA is authorized to collect data regarding _____ caused by consumer products.

7. If a consumer product is found to be imminently hazardous, the manufacturer can be required to _____, repair, or _____ the product.

8. The Fair Packaging and Labeling Act requires that a label use simple and _____ language that a consumer can understand.

9. The _____ _____ _____ Act requires childproof containers and packaging for all household products.

10. Federal laws that address unfair, deceptive, or abusive sales techniques are administered by the _____ _____ _____.

11. Advertising is false and deceptive is it contains _____ or omits important information that is likely to mislead a "_____ _____" or makes an unsubstantiated claim.

12. If a person receives _____ merchandise through the mail, they may retain, use, discard, or otherwise dispose of the merchandise.

13. Sending numerous unsolicited commercial e-mail messages that are false and misleading may violate a state's _____-_____ statute.

14. The uniform disclosures required by the Truth in _____ Act and Regulation _____ are intended to help consumers shop for the best credit terms.

15. The ECOA applies to all creditors who extend or arrange credit in the _____ _____ of their business.

Practice Quiz

True/False:

1. ____ The FDCA prohibits the sale of adulterated food, but it doe not regulate the misleading labeling of food. [p 879]

2. ____ Testing of cosmetics is done by the Food and Drug Administration. [p 879]

3. ____ The FDA can obtain orders for the seizure, recall, and condemnation of adulterated food. [p 879]

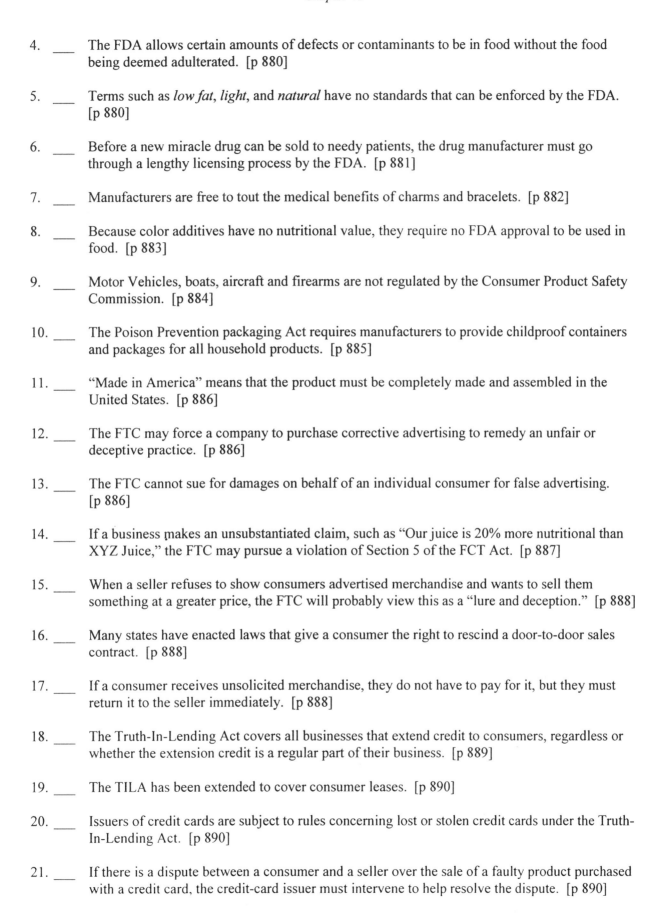

4. ___ The FDA allows certain amounts of defects or contaminants to be in food without the food being deemed adulterated. [p 880]

5. ___ Terms such as *low fat*, *light*, and *natural* have no standards that can be enforced by the FDA. [p 880]

6. ___ Before a new miracle drug can be sold to needy patients, the drug manufacturer must go through a lengthy licensing process by the FDA. [p 881]

7. ___ Manufacturers are free to tout the medical benefits of charms and bracelets. [p 882]

8. ___ Because color additives have no nutritional value, they require no FDA approval to be used in food. [p 883]

9. ___ Motor Vehicles, boats, aircraft and firearms are not regulated by the Consumer Product Safety Commission. [p 884]

10. ___ The Poison Prevention packaging Act requires manufacturers to provide childproof containers and packages for all household products. [p 885]

11. ___ "Made in America" means that the product must be completely made and assembled in the United States. [p 886]

12. ___ The FTC may force a company to purchase corrective advertising to remedy an unfair or deceptive practice. [p 886]

13. ___ The FTC cannot sue for damages on behalf of an individual consumer for false advertising. [p 886]

14. ___ If a business makes an unsubstantiated claim, such as "Our juice is 20% more nutritional than XYZ Juice," the FTC may pursue a violation of Section 5 of the FCT Act. [p 887]

15. ___ When a seller refuses to show consumers advertised merchandise and wants to sell them something at a greater price, the FTC will probably view this as a "lure and deception." [p 888]

16. ___ Many states have enacted laws that give a consumer the right to rescind a door-to-door sales contract. [p 888]

17. ___ If a consumer receives unsolicited merchandise, they do not have to pay for it, but they must return it to the seller immediately. [p 888]

18. ___ The Truth-In-Lending Act covers all businesses that extend credit to consumers, regardless or whether the extension credit is a regular part of their business. [p 889]

19. ___ The TILA has been extended to cover consumer leases. [p 890]

20. ___ Issuers of credit cards are subject to rules concerning lost or stolen credit cards under the Truth-In-Lending Act. [p 890]

21. ___ If there is a dispute between a consumer and a seller over the sale of a faulty product purchased with a credit card, the credit-card issuer must intervene to help resolve the dispute. [p 890]

22. ___ If a person is denied a credit card because of their religion, the consumer may bring a suit against the creditor to recover actual damages. [p 891]

23. ___ Credit reporting agencies may rely upon the accuracy of the information given to them by creditors. [p 891]

24. ___ A debt collector may pretend to be an attorney when trying to collect a debt. [p 891]

25. ___ A debt collector may not contact the debtor if the debtor is represented by an attorney. [p 892]

Multiple Choice:

26. False and misleading labeling of food products is prohibited by the [p 879]
    a. Consumer Product Safety Act.
    b. Fair Packaging and Labeling Act.
    c. Poison Prevention Packaging Act.
    d. Food, Drug, and Cosmetic Act.

27. Food is deemed adulterated if it consists in whole or in part of any [p 879]
    a. filthy, putrid, or decomposed substance.
    b. food that is improperly labeled.
    c. food that does not contain the correct amount in the container.
    d. incorrectly colored or misshaped food.

28. The FDA has the authority to regulate the [p 881]
    a. testing of drugs.
    b. manufacture of drugs.
    c. distribution and sale of drugs.
    d. all of the above.

29. Which item is not regulated by the FDA under the FDCA? [p 882]
    a. Eye shadow
    b. Lipstick
    c. Face soap
    d. Shampoo

30. Tolerances for pesticides used on agricultural products are regulated by the [p 883]
    a. Federal Trade Commission.
    b. Food and Drug Administration.
    c. Consumer Product Safety Commission.
    d. Department of Justice.

31. Because the CPSC regulates potentially dangerous consumer products, it [p 884]
    a. seeks injunctions to stop anyone from making products.
    b. seeks criminal penalties for the manufacture of potentially dangerous products.
    c. issues product safety standards for consumer products that pose an unreasonable risk of injury.
    d. makes private parties file all suits and requests for injunctions.

32. The Fair packaging and Labeling Act requires that a label use [p 885]
    a. simple and clear language that a consumer can understand.
    b. false and misleading information.
    c. highly technical language that is accurate, even if it may be confusing.
    d. unsubstantiated claims if it will increase sales.

33. If a product is assembled in the United States but with primarily foreign parts, it may be labeled [p 886]
    a. "Made in America."
    b. "Made in USA of foreign parts."
    c. "Totally American."
    d. "Mostly American."

34. Which unfair or deceptive sales practice is not regulated by the Federal Trade Commission Act? [p 888]
    a. False and deceptive advertising
    b. Bait and switch
    c. Door-to-door sales
    d. Mailing of unsolicited merchandise

35. If a consumer receives numerous telephone calls from a debt collector in the middle of the night, the consumer may bring an action against the debt collector for violating the [p 891]
    a. Equal Credit Opportunity Act.
    b. Fair Credit Reporting Act.
    c. Fair Debt Collection Act.
    d. Fair Credit and Charge Card Disclosure Act of 1988.

Short Answer:

36. Explain the meaning of adulterated food. [p 879] _____

37. The _____ is empowered to regulate food, food additives, drugs, cosmetics, and medicinal devices. [p 879]

38. What is required of food manufacturers and processors under the Nutrition Labeling and Education Act? [p 880] _____

39. List three examples of "action levels." [p 880] (1) _____
    (2) _____ (3) _____

40. Name three of the FDA requirements for cosmetics. [p 882] (1) _____
    _____ (2) _____
    (3) _____

41. List four types of medicinal devices controlled by the FDCA. [p 882]
    (1) _____ (2) _____
    (3) _____ (4) _____

42. The Biologies Act of 1902 gives the FDA power to regulate biological products, including [p 883] _____
_____.

43. Explain why the United States felt that trade barriers were being used against genetically modified foods and what the United States had to concede to get its exports into foreign countries. [p 884]
_____
_____
_____

44. What are three things that the Consumer Product Safety Commission is empowered to do? [p 884] _____
_____
_____

45. What problem was the Poison Prevention Packaging Act enacted to address? [p 885]
_____
_____

46. What is false and deceptive advertising under Section 5 of the FTC Act? [p 886]
_____
_____

47. Many states have enacted statutes that permit consumers to rescind contracts made at home with _____-____-_____ sales representatives within a _____-day period after signing the contract. [p 888]

48. What can a person do if they receive unsolicited merchandise in the mail? [p 888] _____
_____
_____

49. What items must be contained in a solicitation from a credit card company under the Fair Credit and Charge Card Disclosure Act of 1988? [p 890] _____
_____
_____

50. What happens if a consumer challenges the accuracy of the information contained in their credit file? [p 891] _____
_____
_____

Answers to Refresh Your Memory

1. manufacture, sale, cosmetics [p 879]
2. adulterated [p 879]
3. ingredients, carcinogenic [p 882]
4. quack [p 882]
5. Biosafety Protocol [p 884]
6. injuries [p 884]
7. recall, replace [p 884]

8.   clear [p 885]
9.   Poison Prevention Packaging [p 885]
10. Federal Trade Commission (FTC) [p 886]
11. misinformation, "reasonable consumer" [p 887]
12. unsolicited [p 888]
13. anti-spam [p 889]
14. lending, Z [p 889]
15. ordinary course [p 891]

Answers to Practice Quiz

True/False:

1.   False   The FDCA prohibits the use of false or misleading labels on food products.
2.   True   Under the FDCA, the FDA tests food, drugs, cosmetics, and medicinal devices.
3.   True   This authority extends to drugs, cosmetics and medicinal devices.
4.   True   Until the amount of a contaminant reaches an "action level," the food is still considered safe for human consumption.
5.   False   The Nutritional Labeling and Education Act lead to regulations that were adopted by the FDA that set standard definitions for these terms.
6.   True   The Drug Amendment to the FDCA gives the FDA broad powers to license new drugs that are to be manufactured or sold in the United States.
7.   False   The FDA may remove quack medicinal devices from the market.
8.   False   The Color Additives Amendment of 1968 requires FDA approval of color additives used in food, drugs, and cosmetics.
9.   True   These products are regulated by other government agencies.
10. True   The act is intended to avoid serious injury or death due to mishandling of dangerous products by children.
11. False   The manufacturer may use "Made in America" if 75 percent of the total cost of manufacturing the product are U.S. manufacturing costs or the final product was "substantially transformed" in the United States.
12. True   This is one of the remedies that include issuing a cease-and-desist order or requiring an affirmative disclosure to consumers.
13. False   The FTC may sue in state or federal court to obtain compensation for consumer for any deceptive practice, including false advertising.
14. True   The FTC may seek to halt any false advertising that makes an unsubstantiated claim.
15. False   This type of deception is called a "bait and switch."
16. True   Consumers are usually allowed to rescind these contracts within three days.
17. False   The consumer may dispose of the property as they see fit, without incurring any liability to the seller.
18. False   The TILA does not apply to a creditor unless it extends credit as a regular part of its business.
19. True   The Consumer Leasing Act extended the TILA's coverage to consumer leases.
20. True   They are also subject to rules concerning unsolicited credit cards and faulty products purchased with credit cards.
21. True   This is required under the TILA.
22. True   A consumer may recover actual damages in a civil suit if the card issuer violates the ECOA.
23. False   Under the FCRA, consumer reporting agencies are required to maintain reasonable procedures to ensure the accuracy of their information.
24. False   A debt collector may not make false or misleading misrepresentations under the Fair Debt Collection Practices Act.

25. True   The Fair Debt Collection Practices Act forbids contact by the debt collector with a debtor who is represented by an attorney.

Multiple Choice:

26. D   D is correct because the truthful contents of food labels is controlled by the FDCA. Choice A is not correct because it relates to standards for production and distribution of safe consumer goods. Choice B is incorrect because it relates to information required on labels attached to consumer goods. Choice C is wrong because it relates to the requirement of childproof packaging.

27. A   A is correct because it sets forth a type of substance that is unfit for human consumption. B and C are incorrect because they do not relate to the quality of food. D is incorrect because it involves defects that do not prevent the food from being fit for human consumption.

28. D   D is correct because each of the choices lists a function of the FDFA in relation to the regulation of drugs. Choices A, B, and C would be incorrect individually because it would exclude other incorrect answers.

29. C   C is correct because soap is expressly excluded from regulation under the FDCA. Choices A, B, and D are incorrect because they fit within the FDA's definition of cosmetics that includes substances and preparations for cleansing, altering the appearance of, and promoting the attractiveness of a person.

30. B   B is correct because the FDA regulates numerous products under the FDCA, including pesticides under the Pesticide Amendment of 1954. Choice A is incorrect because it does not create regulations for use of products, but is usually restricted to deceptive and unfair practices. Choice C is incorrect because the CPSC is concerned with the creation of sfe products, not the regulation of their use. Choice D is incorrect because the Department of Justice is concerned with criminal violations, not the regulation of product use.

31. C   C is correct because the CPSC has the responsibility to make sure that potentially dangerous products are made in a safe way so that consumers will not be hurt by products that don't meet minimum safety standards. Choices A and B are incorrect because they are remedies for violations, not a method for dealing with potentially dangerous products. Choice D is incorrect because the CPSC takes action on behalf of consumers.

32. A   A is correct because the label must be easy to understand and not create confusion for the average consumer. B is incorrect because it is the opposite of what is required. Choice C is incorrect because confusing language is prohibited. Choice D is incorrect because unsubstantiated claims are deemed to be deceptive and thus, prohibited, under the FTCA.

33. B   The FTC allows this qualified label when the product does not meet "Made in America" standards. Choice A is incorrect because a product made of foreign parts does not qualify for a "Made in America" label. Choices C and D would be wrong because they are false and misleading.

34. D   D is correct because the mailing of unsolicited merchandise is regulated by the P{ostal Reorganization Act. Choices A, B, and C are all incorrect because they are practices regulated by Section 5 of the FTC Act or by FTC regulations.

35. C   C is correct because the FDCPA protects consumers from abusive, deceptive, and unfair practices used by debt collectors. Choice A is incorrect because that act prohibits discrimination in the granting of credit. Choice B is incorrect because it regulates the accuracy of information retained by credit bureaus. Choice D is incorrect because it pertains required disclosure of credit terms on credit-and charge-card solicitations and applications.

Short Answer:

36. Food is adulterated if it consists in whole or in part of any filthy, putrid, or decomposed substance. Some quantity of contaminants are allowed in food as long as the amount of contaminants does not exceed action limits set by the FDA.

37. FDA

38. They are required to provide nutritional information on virtually all food. This includes the number of calories derived from fat, amount of dietary fiber, saturated fat, cholesterol, and a variety of other substances.

39. (1) 35 fly eggs per 8 ounces of golden raisins (2) two rodent hairs per pound of popcorn (3) 20 insects per 100 pounds of shelled peanuts (4) 20 maggots per 3 ½ ounces of canned mushrooms (5) 10 fly eggs per 3 ½ ounces of tomato juice

40. (1) Cosmetics must be labeled (2) Ingredients in cosmetics must be disclosed (3) Cosmetics must contain warnings if they are carcinogenic

41. (1) heart pacemakers (2) kidney dialysis machines (3) defibrillators (4) surgical equipment

42. vaccines, blood, blood components and derivatives, and allergenic products

43. There was no evidence that the genetically altered foods were unsafe, but foreign countries were prohibiting the importation of these foods into their countries. The United States had to sign the Biosafety Protocol and agree that all genetically engineered foods would be clearly labeled with the phrase "May contain living modified organisms."

44. The CPSC is empowered to adopt rules and regulations to interpret and enforce the CPSA, conduct research on the safety of consumer products, and collect data regarding injuries caused by consumer products.

45. Because children suffer serious injury or death when they open household products and inhale, ingest, or otherwise mishandle dangerous products, the act was enacted to require manufacturers to provide "childproof" containers and packages for all household products.

46. It is advertising that contains misinformation or omits important information that is likely to mislead a "reasonable consumer" or makes an unsubstantiated claim.

47. door-to-door, three

48. They can retain, use, discard, or otherwise dispose of the merchandise without incurring any obligation to pay for it or return it.

49. The written solicitation must contain the APR, any annual membership fee, any minimum of fixed finance charge, any transaction charge for use of the card for purchases, and a statement that charges are due when the periodic statement is received by the debtor.

50. The agency may be compelled to reinvestigate. If the agency cannot find an error despite the consumer's complaint, the consumer may file a 100-word statement of their version.

Chapter 46

ENVIRONMENTAL PROTECTION

Chapter Overview

With great increase in population growth, urbanization, and all forms of industry, our desire for higher profits, more products, and technological advancement lead to damage to the environment on a worldwide basis. In an effort to curtail the damaging effects of pollution, the federal government and states have created environmental protection laws that apply to all businesses and individuals. This chapter examines the efforts of the government to contain the levels of pollution that is still being made, while cleaning up huge amounts of pollution and hazardous waste that have been dumped into the environment.

Objectives

Upon completion of the exercises in this chapter, you should be able to
1.   Identify when an environmental impact statement is needed and what it must contain.
2.   Describe the mandates of the Clean Air Act.
3.   Explain the effluent water standards of the Clean Water Act.
4.   Understand what technologies must be installed to prevent air and water pollution.
5.   Explain how environmental laws regulate the use of toxic substances.
6.   Understand the environmental laws that regulate hazardous wastes.
7.   Describe Superfund law and how it authorizes the government to recover the cost of cleaning up hazardous waste sites.
8.   Explain the scope of the Endangered Species Act and how it protects threatened species and their habitats.
9.   Describe criminal sanctions for polluters.
10. Understand the North American Commission on Environmental Cooperation and how it monitors transborder pollution.

Practical Application

Upon mastering the concepts in this chapter, you will understand the theory and application of environmental protections laws. You will recognize when an action violates one of the laws and the remedies for the violation.

Helpful Hints

With all of the different regulations that have been enacted to curtail pollution and its effects upon the environment, it is helpful if you organize your analysis of any situation based upon the type of damage done or the segment of the environment that is at risk. This will lead you to the correct statute or regulation for guidance as to how the situation will be handled by the appropriate agency or the courts.

Study Tips

You should organize your study of environmental protection by looking at the areas of the environment that are protected. Examine the laws and cases within the areas of air, water, toxic and hazardous substances, nuclear waste, endangered species, and noise.

Under the common law, both an individual and the government could bring a suit for negligence. The individual could bring an action for private nuisance and the government could maintain an action against a polluter for public nuisance. This was a very ineffective way of controlling pollution. With the creation of the Environmental Protection Agency (EPA) by Congress in 1970, the federal government had a vehicle for implementing and enforcing federal environmental protection laws. The EPA can make rules, adopt regulations, hold hearings, make decisions, and order remedies for violation of federal environmental laws. The EPA can also initiate judicial proceedings against violators.

The National Environmental Policy Act was created in 1969. Under this act, an environmental impact statement must be prepared to assess the adverse impact that any legislation or federal action will have upon the environment. This study is required before the project or legislation can be approved. Each state has a similar statute.

Air Pollution

- The *Clean Air Act* provides comprehensive regulation of air quality in the United States. It directs the EPA to establish national ambient air quality standards (NAAQS) for certain pollutants. There are primary levels to protect humans and secondary levels to protect vegetation, climate, visibility, and economic values. The states are responsible for enforcing these levels. The Clean Air Act regulates both stationary (manufacturing plants) and mobile (automobiles) sources.
- *Nonattainment areas* are regions that do not meet air quality standards. Deadlines are established for areas to meet attainment levels. States must submit compliance plans that
  1. identify major sources of air pollution and require them to install pollution control equipment
  2. institute permit systems for new stationary courses
  3. implement inspection programs to monitor mobile sources

  States that fail to develop and implement a plan are subject to the following sanctions:
  1. loss of federal highway finds
  2. limitations on new sources of emissions (prohibits new construction of industrial plants in the nonattainment area)
- The *Clean Air Act Amendment of 1990* allows companies to trade sulfur dioxide emissions (the pollutant that causes acid rain). Companies still face strict quotas, but they are free to satisfy their limits by buying pollution credits from other companies. These credits are actually traded on the Chicago futures market.
- *Toxic air pollutants* cause serious illness or death to humans. The EPA must identify toxic pollutants, set standards for these chemicals, and require stationary sources to install equipment to control emissions of toxic substances. These standards are set without regard to technological or economic feasibility.
- *Indoor air pollution* is a serious problem that is not regulated. Some buildings have air that is 100 times more polluted than the outdoor air. This is caused mainly by tightly sealed buildings and exposure to indoor chemicals and construction materials.

Water Pollution

Any person who wants to discharge pollution into water must obtain a permit from the EPA. This permit system is called the National Pollutant Discharge Elimination System (NPDES). The EPA can deny a permit or set restrictions as to amount and frequency of discharge.

- The *Clean Water Act* has been updated and amended several times from 1948 to 1987. Pursuant to the act, the EPA has established water quality standards that define which bodies of water can be use drinking water, recreation, wildlife, and agricultural and industrial uses.
- The Clean Water Act authorizes the EPA to establish water pollution standards for **point sources** of water pollution, which are stationary sources of pollution such as paper mills, manufacturing plants, electric utility plants, and sewage plants. The EPA sets standards for technology that must be used and requires dischargers of pollution to keep records, maintain monitoring equipment, and keep samples of discharges.
- The Clean Water Act prohibits **thermal pollution** because it damages the ecological balance and decreases oxygen in a waterway.
- The Clean Water Act forbids the filling or dredging of **wetlands** unless a permit has been obtained from the Army Corps of Engineers. Wetlands include swamps. Bogs, marshes, and similar areas that support birds, animals, and vegetative life.
- The *Safe Drinking Water Act* authorizes the EPA to establish national primary drinking water standards. The act prohibits dumping of waste into wells.
- The *Marine Protection, Research, and Sanctuaries Act* requires a permit for dumping waste and foreign material into ocean waters and establishes marine sanctuaries as far seaward as the Continental Shelf and in the Great Lakes and their connecting waters.
- The Clean Water Act authorizes the U.S. government to clean up **oil spills** within 12 miles of shore and on the Continental Shelf and to recover the cleanup costs from responsible parties.
- The *Oil Pollution Act of 1990*, which is administered by the Coast Guard, requires the oil industry to adopt procedures that can more readily respond to oil spills.
- The United Nations Conference on the Law of the Sea (LOS Convention) established a 200-mile exclusive economic zone (EEZ) for coastal nations. This convention grants sovereign rights to coastal nations to explore, exploit, conserve, and manage living resources in their EEZs. The coastal nations have the right to board and inspect ships, arrest a ship and its crew, and instigate legal proceedings against violators of its EEZ rights.

Toxic Substances

Many of the chemicals used for agriculture, mining, and industry contain toxic substances that cause birth defects, cancer, and other health-related problems. Because of the grave danger posed by these chemicals, the federal government has enacted legislation to regulate their use.
- The *Insecticide, Fungicide, and Rodenticide Act* requires pesticides, herbicides, fungicides, and rodenticides to be registered with the EPA. The EPA may deny, suspend, or cancel the registration if it finds that the chemical poses an imminent danger. The EPA sets standards for the amount of residue that is permitted on crops sold for human and animal consumption.
- The Toxic Substances Control Act requires manufacturers and processors to test new chemicals to determine their effect on human health and the environment before the EPA will allow them to be marketed. The EPA requires special labeling for toxic substances and may limit or prohibit their manufacture and sale. A toxic substance that poses an imminent hazard may be removed from commerce.

Hazardous Waste

Solid waste may cause of significantly contribute to an increase in mortality or serious illness or pose a hazard to human health or the environment if they are not handled properly. These wastes consist of garbage, sewage, industrial discharge, and old equipment. If these wastes are mishandled they can cause air, water, and land pollution. They are regulated as follows:
- Congress enacted the *Resource Conservation and Recovery Act* to regulate the disposal of new hazardous waste. The act authorizes the EPA to regulate facilities that generate, treat, store, transport, and dispose of hazardous wastes. Any substance that is toxic, radioactive, or corrosive

or can ignite is a hazardous material. Hazardous wastes are tracked and regulated from the moment they are created to the time of their final disposal or storage.

- The *Comprehensive Environmental Response, Compensation, and Liability Act*, which is known as the "**Superfund**" gave the federal government a mandate to deal with years of abuse and neglect in the disposal of hazardous waste. The EPA is required by the Superfund to:
    1. identify sites in the United States where hazardous wastes have been disposed, stored, abandoned, or spilled, and
    2. rank these sites regarding the severity of the risk they pose.

The sites with the highest ranking are put on a National Priority List. The sites on this list receive first priority for cleanup. Studies are conducted to determine the best method for cleaning up the waste site. The Superfund provides for the creation of a fund to finance the cleanup of sites. The EPA can order a responsible party to clean up a hazardous waste site. If the party fails to do so, the EPA can clean up the site and recover the cost from any responsible party under a theory of strict liability. The cost of cleanup can be recovered from:
1. the generator who deposited the wastes
2. the transporter of the wastes to the site
3. The owner of the site at the time of disposal
4. the current owner and operator of the site

The Superfund contains a right to know provision that requires businesses to:
1. disclose the presence of certain listed chemicals to the community
2. annually disclosure emissions of chemical substances released into the environment , and
3. immediately notify the government of spills, accidents, and other emergencies involving hazardous substances.

Nuclear Waste

Nuclear power plants create radioactive waste that maintains a high level of radioactivity for a very long period of time. Two federal agencies monitor and regulate nuclear energy in the United States.

- The Nuclear Regulatory Commission (NRC)regulates the construction and opening of commercial nuclear power plants. The NRC monitors the plants and may close an unsafe plant.
- The EPA sets standards for allowable levels of radioactivity in the environment and regulates the disposal of radioactive waste. The EPA also regulates thermal pollution caused by the nuclear power plants and emissions and uranium production.

Endangered Species

The Endangered Species Act protects endangered species and threatened species of animals. The EPA and the Department of Commerce designate critical habitats for each endangered and threatened species. Real estate or other development in these habitats is prohibited or severely limited. In addition to the Endangered Species Act, there are numerous other acts that protect migratory birds, eagles, horses, burros, marine mammals, and fish.

Noise Pollution

Noise pollution is created by planes, automobiles, manufacturing plants, construction equipment, audio equipment, and the like. Because noise pollution has a direct impact on humab health, the federal government has addressed the need to decrease noise pollution.

- The Noise Control Act authorizes the EPA to establish noise standards for products sold in the United States. The EPA and Federal Aviation Administration jointly establish noise limitations for airplanes. The Department of Transportation and EPA regulate noise from trucks, railroads, and interstate carriers. The Occupational Safety and Health Administration (OSHA) regulates noise levels in the workplace.
- The Quiet Communities Act authorizes the federal government to provide financial and technnical assistance to state and local governments to help control noise pollution.

Transborder Pollution

When another country is the source of pollution in an affected country, the countries must deal with transborder pollution. The regulation of this type of pollution depends upon the existence of a treaty between the offending and affected countries. The United States had several treaties with Canada and Mexico to address many transborder pollution issues. The whole issue of transborder pollution and regulation of global pollution is in its infancy.

Refresh Your Memory

The following exercise will enable you to refresh your memory of the principles given to you in this chapter. Read the question twice and place your answer in the blanks provided. If you do not remember the answer, go on to the next question and finish the exercise. After reviewing the chapter material again, retake this exercise.

1. Under common law, a private party could bring a civil suit based on _____ _____ to recover damages from a polluting party.

2. The _____ _____ _____ coordinates the implementation and enforcement of the federal environmental protection laws.

3. The National Environmental Policy Act requires that an _____ _____ _____ be prepares for all proposed legislation and major federal action that significantly affects the quality of the human environment.

4. The _____ _____ _____ was enacted in 1963 to assist states in dealing with air pollution.

5. The Clean Air Act directs the EPA to establish _____ _____ ____ _____ _____ for certain pollutants at two different levels: primary and secondary.

6. Industrial plants, oil refineries, and public utilities are examples of _____ sources of air pollution.

7. Regions that do not meet air quality standards are designated _____ _____.
8. The Clean Air Act Amendments of 1990 allows companies to trade _____ _____ emissions which are responsible for acid rain.

9. EPA standards for toxic substances are set without regard to _____ or technological feasibility.

10. Indoor air pollution, or _____ _____ syndrome, is caused by a combination of airtight buildings and exposure to chemicals and construction materials.

11. The Clean Water Act authorizes the EPA to establish water pollution control standards for _____ sources of water pollution, such as paper mills, mines, and manufacturing plants.

12. The Clean Water Act authorizes the U.S. government to clean up oil spills within ____ miles of the shore and on the _____ Shelf.

13. _____ _____ are chemicals used for agricultural, industrial, and mining uses that cause injury to humans, birds, animals, fish, and vegetation.

14. The Resource Conservation and Recovery Act defines _____ _____ as a solid waste that may cause or significantly contribute to an increase in mortality or serious illness or pose a hazard to human health or the environment if improperly managed.

15. The Endangered Species Act requires the EPA and the Department of Commerce to designate _____ _____ for each endangered and _____ species.

Critical Thought Exercise

The citizens of Marzville, Ohio became concerned when they started noticing very high rates of death and birth defects in the community. The Friends of Marzville (FOM), an environmental investigated the situation and it was discovered that a hazardous waste disposal site in Marzville had polluted the ground water with very high levels of carcinogenic chemicals. Fast Dump, who had purchased the land from Wow Chemical Company, runs the disposal site. Wow chemical had operated a chemical manufacturing facility at the site from 1951 to 1982. Wow Chemical dumped hundreds of thousands of gallons of chemicals and contaminated water into open pits and into a drainage pip that emptied into the Marzville Creek, which in turn emptied into Marzville Lake. Fast Dump takes in solid and liquid waste from numerous sources, including the Tripp Trucking, a hazardous waste transportation company who has the exclusive contract to haul all the hazardous waste for the huge, multinational petrol-chemical corporation, Chemkill.

What relief can FOM seek for the citizens of Marzville? Who may be liable for the horrible situation in Marzville and the massive cleanup that is needed?

Answer. _____

_____

_____

_____

_____

_____

_____

_____

_____

_____

_____

_____

_____

_____

_____

_____

_____

_____

Practice Quiz

True/False:

1. ____ The purpose of an environmental impact statement is to provide enough information about the environment to enable the federal government to determine the feasibility of a project. [p 898]

2. ____ Primary levels for ambient air quality standards refer to those levels that are safe for vegetation, climate, matter, visibility, and economic values. [p 898]

3. ____ Although the EPA establishes air quality standards, the states are responsible for their enforcement. [p 898]

4. ____ Automobile and other vehicle emissions are considered mobile sources of air pollution under the Clean Air Act. [p 899]

5. ____ States must submit Clean Air Act compliance plans that identify major sources of air pollution and require them to install pollution control equipment. [p 900]

6. ____ Asbestos, mercury, benzene, and vinyl chloride have been listed as hazardous solid waste under Section 112 of the Clean Air Act. [p 901]

7. ____ The EPA must reach a determination of what amount of a toxic substance is "safe" and then set emission standards at that amount. [p 901]

8. ____ The government has not adopted any regulations governing indoor air quality. [p 902]

9. ____ Any person who proposes to discharge pollution into a waterway must obtain a permit from the EPA. [p 902]

10. ____ Dischargers of pollution are required by the Clean Water Act to keep samples of all discharges. [p 903]

11. ____ Thermal pollution upsets the ecological balance in a waterway by decreasing the oxygen content of the water. [p 904]

12. ____ The Clean Water Act forbids the filling or dredging of wetlands unless a permit is obtained from the EPA. [p 904]

13. ____ The Safe Drinking Water Acts authorize states to establish primary drinking water standards. [p 904]

14. ____ There is no limitation or permit required for dumping wastes out in ocean waters. [p 904]

15. ____ The Oil Pollution Act of 1990 requires the oil industry to adopt procedures that can readily respond to oil spills. [p 905]

16. ____ The Oil Pollution Act of 1990 requires that all new oil tankers have a triple-thick hull design. [p 906]

17. ____ The Law of the Sea Convention gives coastal nations a 12-mile exclusive economic zone off their shores. [p 906]

18. ___ Pesticides must be registered with the EPA before they can be sold. [p 907]

19. ___ The EPA can ban a toxic substance if it poses even the slightest possibility of harming humans or the environment. [p 907]

20. ___ Hazardous waste is defined as any offensive substance that is stored or processed in a landfill. [p 908]

21. ___ Only those persons who are disposing of hazardous waste need a permit from the EPA. [p 908]

22. ___ The federal government has no jurisdiction over underground storage facilities, such as gasoline tanks at gas stations. [p 908]

23. ___ Intentional dumping of sewage into a waterway is only punishable by a civil penalty under the Clean Water Act. [p 908]

24. ___ The current owner-operator of a hazardous waste disposal site can be held liable for cleanup costs assessed by the EPA even though the hazardous waste in question was dumped years before the current operator owned the facility. [p 909]

25. ___ Companies are required to report their environmental liabilities in their financial statements. [p 910]

Multiple Choice:

26. At common law, the government could bring a lawsuit against a polluter based upon a theory of [p 897]
    a. private nuisance.
    b. public nuisance.
    c. violation of the Clean Air Act.
    d. volation of the Clean Water Act.

27. Air pollution is caused by [p 898]
    a. mobile sources.
    b. stationary sources.
    c. both mobile and stationary sources.
    d. none of the above.

28. Under the Clean Air Act, the EPA establishes primary and secondary levels of allowable pollution. These standards are called [p 898]
    a. adverse impact.
    b. national ambient air quality standards.
    c. pollution credits.
    d. the National Pollutant Discharge Elimination System.

29. The trading of pollution credits is allowed under the [p 900]
    a. Clean Air Act Amendments of 1990.
    b. Clean Water Act.
    c. River and Harbor Act.
    d. Safe Drinking Water Act.

30. If a company is unable to comply with the standards set by the EPA for vinyl chloride emission levels because the expense of compliance would bankrupt the company, the EPA standards under the Clean Air Act [p 901]
    a. may be disregarded.
    b. only have to be complied with to the degree that they do not create an undue hardship.
    c. only need to complied with to the degree of the company's present ability.
    d. must be fully complied with without regard to economic or technological feasibility.

31. Pursuant to the Clean Water Act, the EPA has established water quality standards that define which bodies of water can be used for [p 902]
    a. public drinking water.
    b. recreation and propagation of fish and wildlife.
    c. agricultural and industrial uses.
    d. all of the above.

32. Under the Clean Water Act, dischargers of pollution are required to [p 903]
    a. pay a "use fee" each time they discharge pollutants.
    b. keep records.
    c. maintain monitoring equipment.
    d. keep samples of discharges.

33. The Clean Water Act does not regulate [p 904]
    a. thermal pollution.
    b. national primary drinking water standards.
    c. wetlands.
    d. oil spills.

34. The operator of a hazardous waste disposal site will have to clean up contamination caused by improper dumping of hazardous waste over 30 years ago by a previous owner of the waste site pursuant to the [p 909]
    a. Toxic Substances Control Act.
    b. Insecticide, Fungicide, and Rodenticide Act.
    c. Resource Conservation and Recovery Act.
    d. Comprehensive Environmental Response, Compensation, and Liability Act.

35. Under the Endangered Species Act, a wildlife form may be declared threatened or endangered by [p 911]
    a. the EPA.
    b. the Department of Commerce.
    c. the secretary of the interior.
    d. the Endangered Species Commission.

Short Answer:

36. Congress created the Environmental Protection Agency to coordinate the implementation and _____ of the federal environmental _____ laws. [p 897]

37. An environmental impact statement must address what five things? [p 898]
    (1) _____ (2) _____
    (3) _____ (4) _____
    (5) _____

38. What are the two levels of standards for national ambient air quality standards and what do they protect? [p 898] (1) _____
    (2) _____

39. What is a state implementation plan under the Clean Air Act? [p 898] _____
    _____

40. What can the EPA do if the pollution control equipment on a manufacturer's now cars do not meet EPA emission standards? [p 900] _____
    _____

41. What is the National Pollutant Discharge Elimination System? [p 902] _____
    _____

42. What are wetlands? [p 904] _____
    _____

43. What is the purpose of the Marine Protection, Research, and Sanctuaries Act? [p 904] _____
    _____
    _____

44. Under the Clean Water Act, where can the U.S. government clean up oil spills? [p 904]
    _____
    _____

45. What are exclusive economic zones? [p 906] _____
    _____

46. What is required by the Toxic Substances Control Act? [p 907] _____
    _____
    _____

47. What type of facilities is the EPA authorized to regulate under the Resource Conservation and Recovery Act? [p 908] _____
    _____

48. What is noise pollution? [p 913] _____
    _____
    _____

49. Who is responsible for controlling noise pollution in the workplace? [p 913] _____
    _____

50. What is transborder pollution? [p 913] _____

Answers to Refresh Your Memory

1. private nuisance [p 897]
2. Environmental Protection Agency [p 897]

3.　environmental impact statement [p 898]
4.　clean Air Act [p 898]
5.　national ambient air quality standards [p 898]
6.　stationary [p 899]
7.　nonattainment areas [p 900]
8.　sulfur dioxide [p 900]
9.　economic [p 901]
10.　sick building [p 902]
11.　point [p 903]
12.　12, Continental [p 904]
13.　toxic substances [p 906]
14.　hazardous waste [p 908]
15.　critical habitats, threatened [p 911]

Critical Thought Exercise Model Answer

Congress enacted the Comprehensive Environmental Response, Compensation, and Liability Act, also known as the "Superfund," which gave the federal government the authority and duty to deal with hazardous wastes that have been dumped, spilled, or abandoned in such a manner that a serious risk to public health has been created. The EPA is responsible for identifying the hazardous waste sites in need of cleanup and coordinating the studies to determine the best way to handle the situation. The EPA has the authority to clean up hazardous sites quickly to prevent explosion, contamination of drinking water, or other imminent danger. Because the drinking water of Marzville is contaminated, the city will be entitled to priority over other cleanup sites. The EPA can order a responsible party to clean up a hazardous waste site. If that party fails to do so, the EPA can clean up the site and recover the cost of cleanup. The Superfund imposes strict liability for all those involved in use of the site. The EPA can recover costs from (1) the generator who deposited the waste, (2) the transporter of the waste to the site, (3) the owner of the site at the time of the disposal, and (4) the current owner or operator of the site. Liability is joint and several, meaning that any party who is at fault even to the slightest degree will be responsible for the entire cleanup. In the Marzville situation, Wow Chemical is liable as the original owner at the time the chemicals were dumped. Chemkill is liable as a generator of waste and Tripp Trucking is liable as the transporter of the waste to the facility. Lastly, Fast Dump is liable as the current operator. The Superfund law applies retroactively, so acts of dumping at the Marzville site that took place at the site prior to 1980 are still covered. Of course, the application of the Superfund law only applies to the cost of cleanup. Any party damaged by the hazardous waste dumping can still pursue their own suit under applicable tort theories.

Answers to Practice Quiz

True/False:

1.　True　The EIS is also used as evidence in court whenever a project is challenged as violating the NEPA.
2.　False　Primary levels refer to protecting human beings.
3.　True　The federal government does have the right to enforce the standards if the states fail to do so.
4.　True　Air pollution controls must be installed on these mobile sources.
5.　True　They must also institute permit systems for new stationary sources and implement inspection programs to monitor mobile sources.
6.　False　They are listed as toxic substances.

7. False — After the "safe amount is determined, the EPA must then set emission standards accordingly to provide for an "ample margin of safety."
8. True — No standards exist for this type of pollution.
9. True — The EPA can deny or set restrictions on such permits.
10. True — They are also required to keep records and maintain monitoring equipment.
11. True — It also causes harm to fish, birds, and animals that use the waterway.
12. False — The Clean Water Act forbids the dredging or filling of wetlands without a permit from the Army Corps of Engineers.
13. False — The EPA decides the standards for minimum quality of water for human consumption. [p 46-8]
14. False — The Marine Protection, Research, and Sanctuaries Act requires a permit for dumping waste into ocean waters.
15. True — The act was in response to the devastating damage caused by the Exxon Valdez.
16. False — The requirement is for a double-hull design for all new tankers.
17. False — The LOS Convention gives coastal nations sovereign rights in a 200-mile zone.
18. True — Registration is required by the Insecticide, Fungicide, and Rodenticide Act.
19. False — The chemical must pose an imminent hazard or unreasonable risk before it can be prohibited by the EPA.
20. False — Hazardous waste is defined by the RCRA as a solid waste that may cause or significantly contribute to an increase in mortality or serious illness or pose a hazard to human health or the environment if improperly managed.
21. False — Under the RCRA, anyone who generates, treats, stores, or transports hazardous waste materials must obtain a government permit to do so.
22. False — Under the RCRA, the EPA is authorized to regulate underground storage facilities.
23. False — Illegal dumping of sewage is punishable as a criminal violation of the Clean Water Act. [p 46-12]
24. True — The EPA can recover the cost of cleanup from the generator who deposited the wastes, the transporter of the wastes, the former owner of the facility, and the current owner of the facility.
25. True — In 1992 the SEC adopted regulations that made disclosure of environmental liabilities in the financial statement of the company mandatory.

Multiple Choice:

26. B — B is correct because public nuisance actions must be brought by a governmental entity. A is incorrect because this action can only be maintained by a private person. Choices C and D are incorrect because they are not common law tort theories.
27. C — C is correct because both mobile sources (automobiles) and stationary sources (manufacturing facilities) are sources of air pollution. Choices A and C are only partially correct. Choice D is wrong because a correct answer is available.
28. B — B is correct because ambient levels set the amount that exists overall that is unhealthy for humans, vegetation, etc. Choice A is incorrect because adverse impact relates to an environmental impact statement which is not a standard, but an individual report. Choice C is not correct because pollution credits refers to the amount of pollution that a business can use or trade. Choice D is incorrect because NPDES refers to water pollution, not air pollution.
29. A — A is correct as under this act, as a business may purchase credits from another company that is not polluting as much as they are allowed. Choices B, C, and D are incorrect because they all relate to water, not air, pollution.
30. D — D is correct because economic hardship does not excuse compliance with Section 112 of the Clean Air Act as it pertains to toxic air pollutants. Choices A, B, and C are all incorrect because they allow for less than complete compliance.

31. D D is correct because all of the choices are bodies of water that are defined by the EPA pursuant to the Clean Water Act. Choices A, B, and C are not correct because they only state one of the bodies of water.

32. A A is correct because a use fee is not part of the legislative scheme. Choices B, C, and D are incorrect because they are all requirements under the Clean Water Act.

33. B B is correct because national primary drinking standards are regulated by the Safe Drinking Water Act, not the Clean Water Act. Choices A, C, and D are not correct because they are all areas regulated by the Clean Water Act.

34. D Choice D created the Superfund, which requires the current operator to pay cleanup costs for past improper dumping. Choices A, B, and C do not pertain to the cleanup of hazardous waste sites.

35. C Choice C is empowered to declare a species either endangered or threatened. Choices A and B are required to designate critical habitats once a species is put on the endangered or threatened list, but the list is created by the secretary of the interior. Choice D does not exist.

Short Answer:

36. enforcement, protection

37. (1) describe the affected environment (2) describe the impact of the proposed federal action on the environment (3) identify and discuss alternatives to the proposed action (4) list the resources that will be committed to the action (5) contain a cost-benefit analysis of the proposed action and alternative actions

38. (1) primary- to protect human beings (2) secondary – to protect vegetation, climate, visibility, matter, and economic values

39. The SIP sets out how the state plans to meet the federal air quality standards that is being required by the EPA for the state.

40. The EPA can require the automobile manufacturer to recall and repair or replace pollution control equipment that does not meet EPA emission standards.

41. It is a permit system that requires any person who proposes to discharge pollution into the water to obtain a permit from the EPA.

42. Wetlands are areas that are inundated or saturated by surface water or ground water that support vegetation typically adapted for life in such conditions.

43. It extended environmental protection to the ocean. It requires a permit for dumping wastes and other foreign materials into ocean waters and establishes marine sanctuaries.

44. The government can clean up oil spills in ocean waters within 12 miles of the shore and on the Continental Shelf.

45. They are 200-mile zones along coastal nations within which the coastal nation has sovereign rights to explore, exploit, conserve, and manage living resources.

46. It requires manufacturers and processors to test new chemicals to determine their effect on human health and the environment before the EPA will allow them to be marketed.

47. The EPA is authorized to regulate facilities that generate, treat, store, transport, and dispose of hazardous wastes.

48. It is unwanted sound from planes, manufacturing plants, motor vehicles, construction equipment, stereos, and the like that causes loss of hearing, loss of sleep, depression, anxiety, and other emotional and psychological symptoms and injuries.

49. The Occupational Safety and Health Administration regulates noise levels in the workplace.

50. Transborder pollution is pollution that originates in an offending nation and travels into the affected nation.

Chapter 47

ANTITRUST LAW

Chapter Overview

After the Civil War, America changed from an agricultural to an industrialized nation. Freedom of competition took a huge blow with the formation of powerful business trusts that monopolized large segments of the country's economy. The anticompetitive practices of these large corporate enterprises resulted in monopolies in the oil, gas, sugar, cotton, and whiskey industries. Congress then stepped in and passed antitrust laws to limit the anticompetitive behavior of powerful trusts. The laws were written in general language, much like the Constitution, so that they could be applied to a broad range of activity and have the ability to respond to economic, business, and technological changes. This chapter examines the antitrust laws that strive to preserve freedom in the marketplace.

Objectives

Upon completion of the exercises in this chapter you should be able to
1. Explain the purpose of antitrust laws and describe the federal antitrust statutes.
2. Apply the rule of reason and the per se rule to identify unreasonable restraints of trade.
3. Describe horizontal and vertical restraints of trade that violate Section 1 of the Sherman Antitrust Act.
4. Explain acts of monopolization that violate Section 2 of the Sherman Antitrust Act.
5. Describe the scope of Section 7 of the Clayton Act as it relates to mergers.
6. Apply Section 5 of the Federal Trade Commission Act to antitrust cases.
7. Explain how antitrust laws prohibit unfair and deceptive conduct over the Internet.
8. Explain the exemptions from antitrust laws.

Practical Application

As seen in the application of antitrust laws in the case of *United States v Microsoft Corp.*, antitrust laws remain a vital part of the federal government's enforcement of freedom of competition. Whether it is the small investor, consumer, or business partners of large corporations, anticompetitive behavior can still damage many economic interests. When corporations are allowed to dominate large segments of the economy, their failure is more devastating because there is a void that is unfilled by an able competitor. The government will continue to examine each merger, acquisition, and anti-competitive contract through the scope of the federal antitrust laws. Our economy depends upon their existence and enforcement.

Helpful Hints

There can be no meaningful discussion of antitrust law until you understand the mandates of the major federal antitrust laws and the activities that trigger their application to the conduct of an individual, small business, or corporation. Examine each act individually and pay close attention to the type of conduct that it prohibits. Then focus on the types of activity that have triggered federal intervention in the past. This will make you better able to predict what type of behavior will be called into question in the future.

Study Tips

An organized examination of the individual antitrust laws and acts forbidden by the important sections is key to your understanding of antitrust law. You need to understand the general proposition or prohibition of each section and the specific practice or activity that violates the section.

Enforcement of Antitrust Laws

Government actions – Enforcement of antitrust laws is divided between the Antitrust Division of the Justice Department and the Bureau of Competition of the Federal Trade Commission (FTC). The Sherman Act is the only major act with criminal sanctions. The government may seek civil damages, including treble damages for antitrust violations. The courts can also order divestiture of assets, cancellation of contracts, liquidation of businesses, any other reasonable remedy that will effectuate freedom of competition.

Private actions – Any private person who suffers antitrust injury to his or her business or property can bring a private civil action against the offenders. They may recover treble damages, costs of suit, and attorneys' fees.

Section 1 of the Sherman Antitrust Act

Section 1 outlaws restraints of trade. To determine the lawfulness of a restraint, the court applies the *rule of reason* and the *per se rule*.

Rule of Reason – The Supreme Court held that only unreasonable restraints of trade violate Section 1. The courts examine the following factor when trying to apply the rule of reason:

- The pro- and anticompetitive effects of the challenged restraint
- The competitive structure of the industry
- The firm's market share and power
- The history and duration of the restraint
- Other relevant factors

Per Se Rule – Some restraints are automatically a violation of Section 1 and no balancing of pro- and anticompetitive effects is necessary. Once a restraint is characterized as a per se violation, there is not defense or justifications for the restraint. If a restraint is a not per se violation, it is examined under the rule of reason.

Horizontal Restraints of Trade

A horizontal restraint of trade occurs when two or more competitors at the same level of distribution enter into a contract, combination, or conspiracy to restrain trade. These horizontal restraints include:

- *Price-Fixing* – Occurs where competitors in the same line of business agree to set the price of the goods or services they sell: raising, depressing, fixing, pegging, or stabilizing the price of a commodity or service. Price-fixing is a per se violation.
- *Division of Markets* – Occurs when competitors agree that each will serve only a designated portion of the market. It is a per se violation to enter into a market-sharing arrangement that divides customers, geographical area, or products.
- *Group Boycotts* – Occurs when two or more competitors at one level of distribution agree not to deal with others at another level of distribution.
- *Lawful Horizontal Agreements* – Some agreements at the same level are lawful, such as trade association rules, exchanging non-price information, and participating in joint ventures. These horizontal restraints are examined using the rule of reason.

Vertical Restraints of Trade

A vertical restraint of trade occurs when two or more parties on different levels of distribution enter into a contract, combination, or conspiracy to restrain trade. The Supreme Court has applied both the per se rule and the rule of reason in determining the legality of vertical restraints of trade under Section 1. These vertical restraints include:

- *Resale Price Maintenance* – Occurs when a party at one level of distribution enters into an agreement with a party at another level to adhere to a price schedule that either sets or stabilizes prices.
- *Nonprice Vertical Restraints* – These restraints are examined using the rule of reason. They are unlawful if their anticompetitive effects outweigh their procompetitive effects. Nonprice vertical restraints occur when a manufacturer assigns exclusive territories to retail dealers or limits the number of dealers in a geographical area.

Defenses to Section 1 of the Sherman Trust Act

- *Unilateral Refusal to Deal* – A unilateral choice by one party to refuse to deal with another party does not violate Section 1 as long as there was no action by two or more parties in concert. This rule is known as the **Colgate doctrine**.
- Conscious Parallelism – This defense applies if two or more firms act the same but no concerted action is shown.
- Noerr Doctrine – Under this doctrine two or more persons may petition the executive, legislative, or judicial branch of the government or administrative agencies to enact laws or take other action without violating antitrust laws.

Section 2 of the Sherman Act

Section 2 prohibits the act of monopolization and attempts or conspiracies to monopolize trade. To prove a violation of Section 2, requires showing that the defendant possesses monopoly power in the relevant market and is engaged in a willful act of monopolization to acquire or maintain the power. The court will examine the following elements and defenses in determining the existence of a Section 2 violation:

- *Defining the Relevant Market* – This requires defining the relevant product or service market and geographical market. The relevant market generally includes substitute products or services that are reasonably interchangeable with the defendant's products or services. The relevant geographical market is defined as the area in which the defendant and its competitors sell the product or service.
- *Monopoly Power* – This is the power to control prices or exclude competition measured by the market share the defendant possesses in the relevant market.
- *Willful Act of Monopolizing* – A requires act for there to be a violation of Section 2. Possession of monopoly power without such act does not violate Section 2.
- *Defenses to Monopolization* – Only two defenses to a charge of monopolization have been recognized:
    1. innocent acquisition (acquisition because of superior business acumen, skill, foresight, or industry)
    2. natural monopoly (a small market that can only support one competitor)
- Attempts and Conspiracies to Monopolize – A single firm may attempt to monopolize. Two or more firms are required for a conspiracy to monopolize.

Clayton Act Section 7

Section 7 provides that it is unlawful for a person or business to acquire stock or assets of another where in any line of commerce or in any activity affecting commerce in any section of the country, the effect of such acquisition may be substantially to lessen competition or to tend to create a monopoly. In order to determine whether a merger is lawful under Section 7, the court must examine the following elements:

- *Line of Commerce* – Determining the line of commerce that will be affected by the merger involves defining the relevant product or service market. It includes products or services that consumers use as substitutes. If an increase in the price of one product or service leads consumers to purchase another product or service, the two products are substitutes for each other. The two products are part of the same line of commerce because they are interchangeable.
- *Section of the Country* – Defining the relevant section of the country consists of defining the relevant geographical market that will feel the direct and immediate effects of the merger.
- *Probability of a Substantial Lessening of Competition* – If there is a probability that a merger will substantially lessen competition or create a monopoly, the court may prevent the merger under Section 7.

In applying Section 7, mergers are generally classified as one of the following:

- *Horizontal Merger* – A merger between two or more companies that compete in the same business and geographical market. The court uses the presumptive illegality test for determining the lawfulness of horizontal mergers. Under this test the merger is illegal under Section 7 if:
  1. the merged firm would have a 30 percent or more market share in the relevant market and
  2. the merger would cause an increase in concentration of 33 percent or more in the relevant market.

  Other factors are also considered such as the past history of the firms involved, the aggressiveness of the merged firms, the economic efficiency of the proposed merger, and consumer welfare.
- *Vertical Mergers* – A vertical merger is a merger that integrates the operations of a supplier and a customer. In a backward vertical merger, the customer acquires the supplier. In a forward vertical merger, the supplier acquires the customer. Vertical mergers do not increase market share but may cause anticompetitive effects.
- *Market Extension Mergers* – A merger between two companies in similar fields whose sales do not overlap. They are treated like conglomerate mergers under Section 7.
- *Conglomerate Mergers* – Are mergers between firms in totally unrelated businesses. Section 7 examines the lawfulness of such mergers under the following theories:

  The **Unfair Advantage Theory** holds that a merger may not give the acquiring firm an unfair advantage over its competitors in finance, marketing, or expertise.

  The **Potential Competition Theory** reasons that the real or implied threat of increased competition keeps businesses more competitive. A merger that would eliminate this perception can be enjoined under Section 7.

  The **Potential Reciprocity Theory** says if Company A, which supplies materials to Company B, merges with Company C (which in turn gets its supplies from Company B), the newly merged company can coerce Company b into dealing exclusively with it.
- *Defenses to Section 7 Actions*

  The **Failing Company Doctrine** – Under this defense, a competitor may merge with a failing company if:
  1. there is no other reasonable alternative for the failing company
  2. no other purchaser is available
  3. the assets of the failing company would disappear from the market if the merger did not proceed

  The **Small Company Doctrine** – Two small companies are permitted to merge if it would make them more competitive with a large company.

- *Hart-Scott-Rodino Antitrust Improvement Act* – Requires certain firms to notify the FTC and the Justice Department in advance of a proposed merger. Unless the government challenges the proposed merger within 30 days, the merger may proceed.

Section 3 of the Clayton Act – Prohibiting Tying Arrangements

Section 3 prohibits tying arrangements involving sales and leases of goods. Tying arrangements are vertical restraints where a seller refuses to sell one product to a customer unless the customer agrees to purchase a second product from the seller. The defendant must be shown to have sufficient economic power in the tying product market to restrain competition.

Section 2 of the Clayton Act – Price Discrimination

Section 2(a) prohibits direct and indirect price discrimination by sellers or a commodity of a like grade and quality where the effect of such discrimination may be to substantially lessen competition or to tend to create a monopoly in any line of commerce.

- *Elements of a Section (2)a violation* - To prove a violation of Section 2(a), the plaintiff must show sales to two or more purchasers involving goods of like grade and quality that results in actual injury.
- *Indirect Price Discrimination* – This is a form of price discrimination (favorable credit terms, reduced shipping charges) that is less readily apparent than direct forms of price discrimination.
- *Defenses to Section 2(a) Actions* – There are three statutory defenses:
  Cost Justification A seller's price discrimination is not unlawful if the price differential is due to "differences in the cost of manufacture, sale, or delivery" of the product. Quantity or volume discounts are lawful to the extent they are supported by cost savings.
  Changing Conditions Price discrimination is not unlawful if it is in response to "changing conditions in the market for or the marketability of the goods." Reduction in price of winter coats would be lawful when the spring line of clothing comes out.
  Meeting the Competition A seller may engage in price discrimination to meet a competitor's price.

Section 5 of the Federal Trade Commission Act

Section 5 prohibits unfair methods of competition and unfair or deceptive acts or practices in or affecting commerce. Section 5 covers conduct that (1) violates any provision of the Sherman Act of the Clayton Act, (2) violates the spirit of those acts, (3) fills the gaps of those acts, and (4) offends public policy, or is immoral, oppressive, unscrupulous, or unethical, or causes substantial injury to competition or consumers.

Section 5 of the FTC Act and the Internet

Section 5 prohibits unfair and deceptive acts affecting commerce. When Internet site operators use deceptive methods to capture Internet traffic, such as disguising the true nature of their site, this practice violates Section 5. The FTC used Section 5 to shut down the "page-jacking" and "mouse-trapping" used by Internet porn sites.

Exemptions From Antitrust Laws

Statutory exemptions include labor unions, agricultural cooperatives, export activities of American companies, and insurance business that is regulated by a state. Other statutes exempt railroad, shipping, utility, and securities industries from most of the reach of antitrust law.

Implied exceptions are given by federal court decision. Two such exemptions include professional baseball and the airline industry.

State action exemptions are economic regulations, such as utility rates, mandated by state law. Though it is a form or price-fixing, the states and utilities are not liable under for anti-trust violations.

Refresh Your Memory

The following exercise will enable you to refresh your memory on the rules of law and principles presented to you in this chapter. Read each question twice and place your answer in the blanks provided. Review the chapter material for any question you miss or are unable to remember.

1. The Sherman Act is the only major antitrust act with _____ sanctions.

2. Section 1 of the Sherman Act prohibits contracts, combinations, and conspiracies in _____ of trade.

3. The rule of _____ holds that only _____ restraints of trade violate Section 1 of the Sherman Act.

4. A _____ restraint of trade occurs when two or more competitors at the same _____ of distribution enter into a contract, combination, or conspiracy to restrain trade.

5. Horizontal _____ _____ occurs when the competitors in the same line of business agree to set the price of goods or services they sell.

6. Competitors that agree that each will serve only a designated portion of the market are engaging in _____ of markets, which is a _____ _____ violation of Section 1.

7. A _____ _____ occurs when two or more competitors at one level of distribution agree not to deal with others at a different level of distribution.

8. _____ _____ _____ is a per se violation of Section 1 that occurs when a party at one level of distribution enters into an agreement with a party at another level to adhere to a _____ schedule that either sets or stabilizes prices.

9. Section 2 of the Sherman Act prohibits the act of _____ and attempts or _____ to monopolize trade.

10. A merger is illegal if it will lessen the competition in any _____ of commerce.

11. A _____ _____ is a merger between two or more companies that compete in the same business and _____ area.

12. A _____ _____ merger is a merger between two companies in similar fields whose sales do not overlap.

13. The _____ _____ _____ is a defense to a Section 7 violation under the Clayton Act that allows two or more _____ companies to merge without liability if the merger allows them to compete more effectively with a large company.

14. The Robinson-Patman Act prohibits price _____ in the sale of goods.

15. Quantity or volume discounts are lawful under Section 2 of the Clayton Act because of the _____-_____ defense.

Critical Thought Exercise

When the partners of The Four Brothers Pizza Shoppe terminated the partnership, they divided the greater Chicago area into four parts and agreed to restrict the geographical area within which each would advertise and deliver pizzas. Two years later one partner filed suit against the other three alleging in part that the restriction on advertising and delivery area was a per se violation of the Sherman Act. Was the agreement made as part of a breakup of a partnership that divided a city into geographical areas for advertising and delivery a violation of antitrust law?

Answer. _____

_____

_____

_____

_____

_____

_____

_____

_____

_____

Sample Quiz

True/False:

1. ____ A private person may recover treble damages in an action under the Clayton Act. [p 919]

2. ____ The rule or reason holds that any restraints of trade violate the Sherman Act. [p 920]

3. ____ A horizontal restraint of trade occurs when two companies at different levels of distribution enter into an agreement to restrain trade. [p 921]

4. ____ Price-fixing agreements occur between sellers. Agreements between buyers are not price-fixing restraints of trade under the Sherman Act. [p 921]

5. ____ Price-fixing is a per se violation of Section 1 of the Sherman Act. [p 921]

6. ____ Division of markets is a restraint of trade for which a court will apply the rule of reason to determine if it is an unlawful restraint. [p 922]

7. ____ A group boycott would occur if a group of television manufacturers agreed not to sell their products to certain discount retailers. [p 923]

8. ____ A vertical restraint of trade occurs when tow or more parties on the same level of distribution enter into an agreement to restrain trade. [p 925]

9. ___ A bicycle manufacturer that sells its product only to retailers that agree to sell them at the prices set by the manufacturer is engaged in resale price maintenance, a per se violation of Section 1 of the Sherman Act. [p 925]

10. ___ Nonprice restraints are unlawful if their anticompetitive effects outweigh their procompetitive effects. [p 927]

11. ___ Trade associations can help avoid antitrust liability be not discussing or exchanging price information about current or future sales to customers. [p 927]

12. ___ A unilateral refusal to deal is not a violation of Section 1. [p 927]

13. ___ Conscious parallelism is when two or more firms act the same but no concerted action is shown. [p 928]

14. ___ To prove a violation of Section 2 of the Sherman Act, the government need only prove that a defendant possesses monopoly power in the relevant market. [p 928]

15. ___ The relevant geographical market, for Section 2 analysis, is defined as the area in which the defendant and its competitors sell the product or service. [p 928]

16. ___ For an antitrust action to be sustained, the defendant must possess monopoly power in the relevant market. [p 928]

17. ___ There are only two defenses to a charge of monopolizing: innocent acquisition and competitors' incompetence. [p 929]

18. ___ Section 7 of the Clayton Act only applies to stock and asset mergers. [p 930]

19. ___ If ABC Beer, a beer that is sold nationally, desires to merge with Little Beer, which is sold in Ohio, Indiana, and Michigan, the relevant geographical market for this merger will be the entire United States because ABC is a national beer. [p 931]

20. ___ The test for determining the lawfulness of horizontal mergers is the "substantial lessening of competition" test. [p 931]

21. ___ If a regional furniture manufacturer in Los Angeles merges with a regional furniture manufacturer in Boston, and their sales do not overlap, this is a vertical merger. [p 932]

22. ___ The unfair advantage theory holds that a conglomerate merger may not give the acquiring firm an unfair advantage over its competitors in finance, marketing, or expertise. [p 933]

23. ___ Tying arrangements involve the seller's refusal to sell a product unless the customer purchases a second product. [p 934]

24. ___ A violation of Section 2(a) of the Clayton Act for price discrimination must involve goods of like grade and quality. [p 936]

25. ___ If a strawberry broker sells berries to six stores for the same price, then reduces the price for store seven because the fruit is starting to spoil, this is not a price discrimination violation of Section 2(a) of the Clayton Act. [p 936]

Multiple Choice:

26. Section 1 of the Sherman Act outlaws certain [p 920]
    a. restraints of trade.
    b. monopolization.
    c. mergers.
    d. tying arrangements.

27. Courts analyze a price-fixing allegation under the [p 921]
    a. rule of reason.
    b. per se rule.
    c. innocent acquisition rule.
    d. natural monopoly standard.

28. Which of the following is not a horizontal restraint of trade under the Sherman Act? [p 925]
    a. Price-fixing
    b. Division of markets
    c. Resale price maintenance
    d. Group boycott

29. When two or more competitors at one level of distribution agree not to deal with others at another level of distribution, this is a restraint of trade known as [p 923]
    a. price-fixing.
    b. division of markets.
    c. resale price maintenance.
    d. group boycott.

30. Which of the following is a defense to a Section 1 violation? [p 927]
    a. Innocent acquisition
    b. Unilateral refusal to deal
    c. The failing company doctrine
    d. Meeting the competition

31. Section 2 of the Sherman Act prohibits [p 928]
    a. restraint of trade.
    b. mergers.
    c. monopolization.
    d. tying arrangements.

32. The power to control prices or exclude competition measured by the market share the defendant possesses in the relevant market is [p 928]
    a. price-fixing.
    b. a tying arrangement.
    c. the unfair advantage theory.
    d. monopoly power.

33. A conglomerate merger may be enjoined under the [p 933]
    a. unfair advantage theory.
    b. potential competition theory.
    c. potential reciprocity theory.
    d. all of the above.

34. The protection of quality control coupled with a trade secret may save a [p 935]
    a. tie-in arrangement.
    b. price-fixing arrangement.
    c. division of markets arrangement.
    d. resale price maintenance arrangement.

35. Price Discrimination is allowed under Section 2 of the Clayton Act is the defendant can show [p 936]
    a. a cost justification.
    b. changing conditions.
    c. it is just meeting the competition.
    d. all of the above

Short Answer:

36. What can the government do if a Sherman Act antitrust violation is established? [p 919]

37. What factors does the court examine when applying the rule of reason? [p 920] _____

38. What is the per se rule? [p 921] _____

39. Explain the meaning of price-fixing. [p 921] _____

40. What was the price-fixing found to exist in United States v. Brown University? [p 925]

41. Describe resale price maintenance. [p 925] _____

42. Describe an example of a nonprice vertical restraint. [p 927] _____

43. Describe an example of the doctrine of conscious parallelism. [p 928] _____

44. For the purpose of analyzing a Section 2 violation of the Sherman Act, what is a relevant geographical market? [p 928] _____

45. Name two defenses to a monopolization charge and give an example of each. [p 929]
    (1) _____
    (2) _____

46.	What test does the court apply to determine the relevant product or service market in Section 7 analysis under the Clayton Act? [p 930] _____

_____

_____

47.	Explain the difference between a forward vertical merger and a backward vertical merger. [p 932] _____

_____

48.	What is a conglomerate merger? [p 933] _____

_____

49.	If two companies are proposing a merger, what must they do to comply with the Hart-Scott-Rodino Antitrust Improvement Act? [p 934] _____

_____

50.	If a doctor charges one patient $200 for the same procedure as she charged another patient only $55, is this price discrimination a violation of the Robinson-Patman Act? [p 936] _____

_____

Answers to Refresh Your Memory

1.	criminal [p 919]
2.	restraint [p 920]
3.	reason, unreasonable [p 920]
4.	horizontal, level [p 921]
5.	price-fixing [p 921]
6.	division, per se [p 922]
7.	group boycott [p 923]
8.	Resale price maintenance, price [p 925]
9.	monopolization, conspiracies [p 928]
10.	line [p 930]
11.	horizontal merger, geographical [p 931]
12.	market extension [p 932]
13.	small company doctrine, small [p 934]
14.	discrimination [p 935]
15.	cost-justification [p 936]

Critical Thought Exercise Model Answer

Society's welfare is harmed if rival businesses are permitted to join in an agreement that consolidates their market power or otherwise restrains competition. The types of trade restraints that Section 1 of the Sherman Act prohibits are generally divided into horizontal and vertical restraints. A horizontal restraint is any agreement that in some way restrains competition between rival businesses competing in the same market. These agreements include price fixing, group boycotts, and horizontal market division. It is a per se violation of Section 1 of the Sherman Act for competitors to divide up territories or customers. The effect of the agreement between the four former partners is to say, "That will be your market and this will be mine." The agreement to limit advertising and delivery to different geographical areas was intended to be, and was in practice, an agreement to allocate markets so that the per se rule of illegality applies.

Answers to Sample Quiz

True/False:

1. True   They may also recover costs and attorneys' fees.
2. False Only unreasonable restraints of trade violate Section 1 of the Sherman Act.
3. False The two companies must be on the same level of distribution.
4. False While most price-fixing occurs between sellers, an agreement among buyers to set the price they will pay for goods of services is also price-fixing.
5. True   There is no justification for or defense to this activity.
6. False Division of markets is a per se violation of Section 1.
7. True   This would be two or more competitors at one level of distribution agreeing not to deal with others at a different level of distribution.
8. False They would be on different levels of distribution in a vertical restraint of trade.
9. True   This is a form of vertical price-fixing.
10. True   The rule of reason is applied to this type of restraint.
11. True   They can also avoid liability by not agreeing to share or split customers or geographical areas or operate only during agree-upon hours.
12. True   This is because there is no concerted action with others.
13. True   There is no Section 1 violation because each firm is acting on its own.
14. False It must also be proven that the defendant engages in a willful act of monopolization to acquire or maintain the power.
15. True   This may be a national, regional, state, or local area, depending on the circumstances.
16. True   Monopoly power is the power to control prices or exclude competition.
17. False While innocent acquisition due to superior business acumen is a defense, the only other defense is that of natural monopoly, caused by the market only being to support one competitor.
18. False Section 7 applies to all methods of external expansion, including technical mergers, consolidations, purchases of assets, subsidiary operations, and joint ventures.
19. False The relevant geographical market is the area that will feel the direct and immediate effects of the merger. The area of the three states is the geographical market.
20. False The presumptive illegality test is applied to horizontal mergers.
21. False This is a market extension merger.
22. True   The rule is intended to prevent wealthy companies from overwhelming the competition in a given market.
23. True   This is a vertical trade restraint and was one of the allegations against *Microsoft*.
24. True   To avoid this rule, sellers sometimes try to differentiate identical or similar products by using brand names.
25. True   This is an example of the changing conditions defense to a Section 2(a) violation.

Multiple Choice:

26. A   A is correct as Section 1 prohibits different types of horizontal or vertical restraints of trade. Choice B is prohibited by Section 2. Choice C is prohibited by Section 7 of the Clayton Act. Choice D is prohibited by Section 3 of the Clayton Act.

27. B   There is no justification or defense to price-fixing. Choice A is incorrect because it requires a balancing test that allows for justification. Choices C and D relate to Section 2 violations.

28. C   Choice C is a vertical restraint. Choices A, B, and D are incorrect because they are all horizontal restraints of trade under Section 1.

29. D   D is correct because it correctly defines a boycott. Choices A, B, and C are not correct because they do not involve a refusal to buy or sell goods or services.

30. B   It is a defense because it does not involve a concerted action between two or more parties. Choice A is a defense to a Section 2 monopolization charge. Choice C is a defense to a charge under Section 7 or the Clayton Act. Choice D is a defense to a price discrimination charge under Section 2 of the Clayton Act.

31. C   Section 2 prohibits the act of monopolization and attempts or conspiracies to monopolize. Choice A is prohibited by Section 1 of the Sherman Act. Choice B is prohibited by Section 7 of the Clayton Act. Choice D is prohibited by Section 3 of the Clayton Act.

32. D   Choice D is correct because monopolization power is controlling the two key aspects of the market: prices and competition. Choice A is a restraint of trade, not a part of analyzing a monopoly. Choice B relates to a violation of the Clayton Act, not Section 2 of the Sherman Act. Choice C is relates to conglomerate mergers.

33. D   All three choices are correct theories under which a conglomerate merger may be enjoined.

34. A   This is lawful in situations where there is a legitimate reason for the tying arrangement. Choices B, C, and D are per se violations for which no justifications are allowed.

35. D   Choices A, B, and C are all correct statements of a defense to price discrimination under Section 2 of the Clayton Act.

Short Answer:

36.   The government can seek criminal sanctions. It can also seek civil damages, including treble damages. Broad remedial powers allow the courts to grant orders for divestiture of assets, cancellation of contracts, liquidation of businesses, and licensing of patents.

37.   The court will examine the following factors: The pro-and anticompetitive effects, the competitive structure of the industry, the firm's market share and power, the history and duration of the restraint, and other relevant factors.

38.   A rule that is applicable to those restraints of trade considered inherently anticompetitive.

39.   Price fixing occurs when competitors in the same line of business agree to set the price of the goods or services they sell. It is accomplished by raising, depressing, fixing, pegging, or stabilizing the price of a commodity or service.

40.   The trading of information and agreements to offer scholarships only to specified students constituted price-fixing by explicitly fixing the amount of scholarship money applicants were paid to attend the school.

41.   A per se violation of Section 1 occurs when a party at one level of distribution enters into an agreement with a party at another level to adhere to a price schedule that either sets or stabilizes prices.

42.   It includes a situation where a manufacturer assigns exclusive territories to retail dealers or limits the number of dealers that may be located in a certain territory.

43.   An example would be if two competing manufacturers of a similar product both separately reach an independent decision not to deal with a retailer. There is not violation of Section 1 because each of the manufacturers acted on its own.

44.   It is the area in which the defendant and its competitors sell the product or service. This may be a national, regional, state, or local area, depending on the circumstances.

45.   (1) innocent acquisition (for example, acquisition because of superior business acumen, skill, foresight, or industry), (2) natural monopoly (for example, a small market that can only support one competitor, such as a small-town newspaper).

46. The courts apply the functional interchangeability test. Under this test, the relevant line of commerce includes products or services that consumers use as substitutes. If two products are substitutes for each other, they are considered as part of the same line of commerce.

47. In a backward vertical merger the customer acquires the supplier, while in a forward vertical merger the supplier acquires the customer.

48. It is a merger that does not fir in the other categories of mergers and involves a merger between firms in totally unrelated businesses.

49. They are required to notify the FTC and the Justice Department in advance of a proposed merger.

50. No, because Section 2 of the Clayton Act does not apply to the sale of services.

Chapter 48

PERSONAL PROPERTY
AND BAILMENTS

Chapter Overview

Property would have little if any value if the law did not protect the rights of owners to use, sell, dispose of, control, and prevent others from trespassing upon their property. Property may be either real property (buildings and land) or personal property. In this chapter we examine the types of personal property, the methods of acquiring ownership in personal property, and property rights in mislaid, lost, and abandoned property. The chapter then discusses bailment of property, situations where possession of (but not title to) property is delivered to another party for transfer, safekeeping, or use. The typical rental of equipment is a bailment.

Objectives

Upon completion of the exercises in this chapter, you should be able to
1. Define personal property.
2. Describe the methods for acquiring ownership in personal property.
3. Describe how ownership rights are transferred by gift.
4. Understand how title to personal property is acquired by purchase, production, accession, and confusion.
5. Apply the rules relating to lost, mislaid, and abandoned property.
6. Define ordinary bailments and list the elements of a bailment.
7. Describe the rights and duties of bailors and bailees.
8. Explain bailee liability for lost, damaged, or destroyed property.

Practical Application

Businesses are constantly transferring ownership of personal property or creating personal property for sale. Additionally, temporary use of property, whether by borrowing or renting, is a common commercial practice. The material in this chapter has valuable application to everyday business practices. Knowledge of the rights and duties relating to ownership and bailment of personal property helps anyone to make informed and reasoned choices when deciding how to deal with a personal property issue.

Helpful Hints

Once it is determined that something is personal property, it is wise to focus on the treatment of the property to determine who has rights in it and what duties may have arisen in regards to the property. The circumstances under which possession of property is accomplished from person to person or business to business will determine who may ultimately be responsible for damage to or loss of the property. The law differentiates the rights of people depending upon how they came into possession of the property and the circumstances surrounding the acquisition of possession.

As you study this material, look at the status of the property as it changes possession. This will guide you in applying the correct law to solve a personal property issue.

Study Tips

In order to answer questions or resolve disputes relating to personal property, it is wise to examine personal property from the perspective of creation and acquisition, transfer by gift, temporary or permanent loss, and rights and duties associated with bailments. The following terms and rules of law are essential to that understanding.

Acquiring Ownership in Personal Property
The methods for acquiring personal property are:
- *By Possession* – Property can be acquired by capturing it.
- *By Purchase or Production* – The most common way to obtain property is to purchase it. Production is another common method. A manufacturer who turns raw materials into a product acquires ownership of the product.
- *By Gift* – A gift is a voluntary transfer of property without consideration. The person making the gift is the donor and the person receiving the gift is the donee. The three elements of a valid gift are:
    1. **Donative intent** For a gift to be effective, the donor must have intended to make a gift.
    2. **Delivery** Delivery must occur for there to be a valid gift. Delivery can either be physical or constructive (giving title documents to a car).
    3. **Acceptance** This is usually not a problem unless the gift is refused.

  Gifts *inter vivos* are made during a person's lifetime while a gift *causa mortis* is made in contemplation of death. Gifts causa mortis can be revoked up until the time of death. ***Uniform Gifts to Minor Acts*** allow adults to make irrevocable gifts to minors. The custodian of the gift has broad discretionary powers to invest the money or securities for the benefit of the minor.
- *By Will or Inheritance* – If a person who dies has a valid will, the property is distributed to the beneficiaries, pursuant to the provisions of the will.
- *By Accession* – Accession occurs when the value of personal property increases because it is added to or improved by natural or manufactured means.
- *By Confusion* – Confusion occurs if two or more persons commingle fungible goods. The owners share ownership in the commingled goods to the amount of the goods contributed.
- *By Divorce* – Parties obtain property rights in the property of the marital estate.

Mislaid, Lost, and Abandoned Property
People find property belonging to others and ownership rights to the property differs depending on whether the property was mislaid, lost, or abandoned. These are the rules that apply to property in those categories.
- *Mislaid Property* – Property is mislaid when the owner places it somewhere and forgets it. The owner will probably return when it is discovered that the property was mislaid. The owner of the property where it was found has the right to take possession. The owner of the premises becomes an involuntary bailee and must take reasonable care of the property until it is reclaimed. The typical situation for this is when a patron leaves their glasses or jacket at a business.

- *Lost Property* – Property is lost when the owner negligently, carelessly, or inadvertently leaves it somewhere. The finder of the property takes title against the world except the true owner. The finder must make efforts to return the property.
- *Abandoned Property* – Property is classified as abandoned if the owner discards the property with the intent to relinquish his rights in it or he gives up all attempts to locate lost or misplaced property.
- **Estray Statutes** – most states have an estray statute, which dictates what the finder of lost or misplaced property must do to acquire title to the property. This usually includes turning the property over to the police, giving notice that the property was found, and waiting for a time period to pass. The finder can then claim ownership.

Bailments

A bailment is a transaction where the owner transfers his or her personal property to another to be held, stored, delivered, or for some other purpose. Title to the property remains in the owner. The owner of the property is the bailor and the party who received the property is the bailee.

- There are three essential elements that must be present to create a bailment:
    1. Only person property can be bailed.
    2. There must be delivery of possession which also involves two elements:
        (i) The bailee has exclusive control over the personal property
        (ii) The bailee must knowingly accept the personal property.
    3. There must be a bailment agreement, which may be either express or implied.

Ordinary Bailments

There are three classifications of ordinary bailments. The importance of these categories is that they determine the degree of care owed by the bailee in protecting the bailed property. The three categories are:

- Bailments for the sole benefit of the bailor are gratuitous bailments that benefit only the bailor. The typical gratuitous bailment involves the bailee watching the bailor's property as a favor without compensation. The bailee only owed a duty of slight care. As long as the bailee is not grossly negligent, no liability will be incurred for loss or damage.
- Bailments for the sole benefit of the bailee are gratuitous bailments for the sole benefit of the bailee. This is the typical "borrowing the lawnmower" situation. The bailee owes a duty of great care. The bailee is responsible for even the slightest negligence.
- Mutual benefit bailments are made for the benefit of both the bailor and bailee. The bailee has a duty of reasonable care, making the bailee liable for any goods that are lost, damages, or destroyed because of his or her negligence. This is the typical paid storage or valet parking situation.

Special Bailments

Special bailees include common carriers, innkeepers, and warehouse companies. In addition to the rules applicable to ordinary bailees, they are subject to the special liability rules contained in Article 7 of the Uniform Commercial Code (UCC).

- Common Carriers – These bailees offer transportation to the public. They include airlines, railroads, bus companies, trucking companies, and public pipeline carriers. The delivery of goods to a common carrier creates a mutual benefit bailment. Unlike an ordinary bailment, common carriers are held to a duty of strict liability. If goods are lost, damaged, or stolen, the common carrier is liable even if it was not at fault. The liability of airlines for lost luggage is limited to $1,250 per piece of luggage for a domestic flight.

- Warehouse Companies - These bailees contract for the storage of goods for compensation. They are held to a duty of reasonable case. They are not liable for the negligence of others that causes loss or damage.
- Innkeepers – An innkeeper owns a facility that provides lodging for compensation. Under common law, innkeepers are held to strict liability for the loss or damage to the property of guests. Most all states have innkeepers' statutes that limit the liability of innkeepers. To limit their liability, the innkeeper must provide a safe and make guests aware of its availability for their use.

Documents of Title

A document of title generally serves as a receipt for the goods, establishes the terms of the bailment contract, and evidences title to the goods. It is evidence that the holder of the receipt is entitled to receive, hold, and dispose of the document and the goods that it covers.

- Warehouse Receipts – This is a written document issued by a warehouseman. It contains the terms of the bailment. The warehouse has a lien on the goods until all expenses incurred have been satisfied.
- Bill of Lading – This document of title is issued by a carrier when goods are received for shipment. Bills of lading are issued by common carriers, contract carriers and others engaged in the business of transporting goods. A through bill of lading provides that connecting carriers may be used to transport the goods. The original carrier is liable to the bailor for loss or damage caused by the connecting carrier.

Refresh Your Memory

The following exercise will enable you to refresh your memory of the principles presented to you in this chapter. Read each question twice and place your answer in the blanks provided. Complete the entire exercise, and then review the chapter material for any question you miss or are unable to remember.

1. A person can acquire ownership of a wild animal by _____ _____ of it or _____ it.

2. The most common method of acquiring title to personal property is by _____ the property from its owner.

3. A _____ is a voluntary transfer of property without consideration.

4. A gift _____ _____ is a gift made during a person's lifetime that is an _____ present transfer of ownership.

5. If a person dies with a valid will, the property is distributed to the _____. If there is not will, the property is distributed to the _____ as provided for in an inheritance statute.

6. _____ occurs when the value of personal property increases because it is added to or improved by natural or _____ means.

7. Property is _____ when its owner voluntarily places the property somewhere and then inadvertently forgets it.

8. The finder of _____ property obtains title to the found property against everyone except the _____ owner.

9. _____ statutes permit the finder of lost or misplaced property to obtain title to the property if they follow the procedure set forth in the statute.

10. Property is _____ if the owner discards the property with the intent to relinquish his or her rights in it.

11. A _____ is a holder of goods who is not a seller or a buyer, but to whom possession of the property has been entrusted by a bailor.

12. To create a bailment, the bailor must deliver _____ of the goods to the bailee.

13. Bailments for the sole benefit of the bailor are _____ bailments for which the bailee owes only a duty of _____ care.

14. Common carriers are held to a duty of _____ _____.

15. A _____ _____ _____ is a document of title that is issued by a carrier when goods are received for transportation.

Critical Thought Exercise

Tom Cruel, chairman of the Central Republican Committee for Rashaw County, was transporting a valuable painting in his trunk to a friend's home where it was to be displayed during a fundraiser. Cruel stopped at the country club for lunch and left his Mercedes in the care of a parking attendant who worked for Jiffy Parking Service, Inc. The attendant left the key box unattended while taking a break. The car and its contents were stolen. The car was recovered by police using a global positioning system, but the trunk was empty upon its return. Cruel was missing the painting worth $30,000, a golf bag and clubs valued at $1,400, and a CD case containing 120 music compact discs worth an estimated $1,500. Cruel has filed suit against Jiffy for the value of all the items taken from the trunk, including the painting. Is Jiffy liable to Cruel? If so, for which stolen items must it pay damages to Cruel?

Answer. _____

Sample Quiz

True/False:

1. ___ Tangible property includes stock certificates, bonds, and copyrights. [p 947]

2. ___ Taking possession or capturing property is the most common method of acquiring property. [p 948]

3. ___ A constructive delivery will be found for a gift when the key to a safe-deposit box where the gift is located is handed over to the donee. [p 949]

4. ___ A gift cause mortis is made during a person's lifetime and is an irrevocable present transfer of ownership. [p 949]

5. ___ The Uniform Gift To Minors Act is used by adults whenever they want to give a gift of any type of personal property to a minor. [p 950]

6. ___ If a person dies without a will, their property will be distributed to the beneficiaries. [p 951]

7. ___ A business owner who has an addition built on his building acquires ownership by accession. [p 951]

8. ___ If an improvement is made to the owner's property by mistake and the improvement cannot be removed, the owner obtains title to the improvement but must pay for it. [p 951]

9. ___ Confusion occurs if two or more persons commingle fungible goods. [p 951]

10. ___ The owner of premises where personal property is mislaid is entitled to take possession of the property against all except the rightful owner. [p 952]

11. ___ The finder of lost property obtains title to such property against the whole world except the true owner. [p 953]

12. ___ Most estray statutes allow the finder to retain the found property while searching for the true owner. [p 953]

13. ___ If an owner of mislaid or lost property gives up any further attempts to locate the property, the property is abandoned. [p 953]

14. ___ In a bailment, the owner of the property is the bailee. [p 954]

15. ___ A bailment is different than a sale or a gift because title to the goods does not transfer to the bailee. [p 954]

16. ___ Only personal property can be bailed. [p 955]

17. ___ To have a delivery, the property must be put in the possession of the bailee, but the bailee does not have to knowingly accept the personal property. [p 955]

18. ___ A bailment for a fixed term terminates at the end of the term or sooner by consent of the parties. [p 955]

19. ___ When a bailee is requested to care for property as a favor, this is a mutual benefit bailment. [p 957]

20. ___ The bailee in a gratuitous bailment owes a duty of ordinary care. [p 957]

21. ___ In a bailment for the sole benefit of the bailee, the bailee owed a duty of great care. [p 957]

22. ___ If you rent a cement mixer from an equipment rental company, you have probably entered into a mutual benefit bailment. [p 957]

23. ___ In a bailment for the sole benefit of the bailee (borrowing a lawnmower), the bailor must notify the bailee of any known defects in the bailed property. [p 958]

24. ___ Common carriers are not liable for the loss, damage, or destruction of goods caused by their ordinary negligence. [p 959]

25. ___ Domestic airlines have limited liability for lost luggage under the Civil Aeronautics Act of 1938. [p 962]

Multiple Choice:

26. Animals and minerals are [p 947]
    a. real property.
    b. a fixture.
    c. tangible property.
    d. intangible property.

27. Which of the following is method of acquiring ownership in personal property? [p 948]
    a. By possession
    b. By purchase or production
    c. By gift
    d. All of the above

28. A gift made in contemplation of death is a gift [p 949]
    a. inter vivos.
    b. causa mortis.
    c. by will or inheritance.
    d. by accession.

29. When a person cuts a car in half, adds a middle section, and creates a limousine, he has acquired ownership to the limousine by [p 951]
    a. purchase or production.
    b. gift.
    c. confusion.
    d. accession.

30. If Dave hangs his jacket in a coatroom at a restaurant and forgets to take it home, his jacket will be considered [p 952]
    a. mislaid property.
    b. lost property.
    c. abandoned property.
    d. intangible property.

31. If Sue put her purse on the top of her car and it is blown off the roof as she drives to work, the purse is [p 953]
    a. mislaid property.
    b. lost property.
    c. abandoned property.
    d. intangible property.

32. When a co-worker leaves their car at your house while on vacation, this is a [p 957]
    a. bailment for the sole benefit of the bailor.
    b. bailment for the sole benefit of the bailee.
    c. mutual benefit bailment.
    d. gift.

33. A bailment cannot exist without [p 955]
    a. personal property.
    b. delivery of possession.
    c. a bailment agreement.
    d. all of the above.

34. In caring for the goods that are shipped with it, a common carrier is held to a duty of [p 959]
    a. slight care.
    b. reasonable care.
    c. strict liability.
    d. ordinary care.

35. A document of title is used to [p 960]
    a. serve as a receipt for the goods.
    b. establish the terms of the contract between the parties.
    c. evidence title to the goods.
    d. all of the above.

Short Answer:

36. What is tangible property? [p 947] _____

37. What are seven ways to acquire personal property? [p 948] _____

38. What three elements must be shown to prove a valid gift? [p 949]
    (1) _____
    (2) _____
    (3) _____

39.   What is mislaid property? [p 952] _____
_____

40.   Most states have an estray statute that permits a finder of lost or misplaced property to clear title to the property (and become the new owner) if [p 953] _____
_____
_____
_____

41.   Describe what makes property "abandoned." [p 953] _____
_____
_____

42.   What is a bailment? [p 954] _____
_____
_____

43.   What must a bailee do at the termination of a bailment? [p 956] _____
_____

44.   Give an example of a bailment for the sole benefit of the bailee. [p 957] _____
_____

45.   What sort of duty of care is owed by someone who borrows a power tool from a neighbor? [p 957]
_____

46.   What is a mutual benefit bailment? [p 957] _____
_____

47.   When are warehouses liable for loss or damage to the bailed property? [p 959] _____
_____

48.   What is an innkeeper? [p 959] _____

49.   What must an innkeeper do to take advantage of an innkeeper's statute? [p 959] _____
_____
_____

50.   What is a document of title? [p 960] _____
_____

Answers to Refresh Your Memory

1.   taking possession, capturing [p 948]
2.   purchasing [p 948]
3.   gift [p 949]
4.   inter vivos, irrevocable [p 949]
5.   beneficiaries, heirs [p 951]

6.   accession, manufactured [p 951]
7.   mislaid [p 952]
8.   lost, true [p 952]
9.   estray [p 953]
10.   abandoned [p 953]
11.   bailee [p 954]
12.   possession [p 955]
13.   gratuitous, slight [p 955]
14.   strict liability [p 959]
15.   bill of lading [p 961]

Critical Thought Exercise Model Answer

For liability to be created, a bailment must exist. A bailment is created when personal property is delivered into the possession of a bailee by a bailor for a stated purpose for some period of time. The bailee has the right of exclusive possession, but the bailor retains ownership of the bailed property. Delivery may be accomplished by actual physical delivery of the property or constructive delivery of an item that gives control of the property, such as delivery of a car key to a parking lot attendant. By delivering his car key to the employee of Jiffy Parking, Cruel created a bailment agreement. Mutual benefit bailments are bailments that benefit both parties. The bailee (Jiffy) owes a duty of reasonable care to protect the bailed goods. The bailee is liable for any goods that are lost, stolen, damaged, or destroyed because of his or her negligence. The law presumes that if bailed property is lost, damaged, destroyed, or stolen while in the possession of the bailee, it is because of lack of proper care by the bailee. They typical commercial bailment where someone pays to have his property watched for a fee is this type of bailment. A bailee accepts responsibility for unknown contents of a bailed automobile when the presence of those contents is reasonably foreseeable based on the factual circumstances surrounding the bailment of the automobile. It cannot be said that a country club parking attendant should reasonably foresee the presence of a valuable painting in a member's car trunk. Unless the bailee accepts possession of the property, either expressly or impliedly, there can be no bailment. Therefore, Jiffy Parking had no duty of care to protect the painting in the trunk. The other items lead to a different result. It is quite foreseeable that a club member would have golf clubs in his trunk. Additionally, car owners often have cases to carry an assortment of music for them to play in their car. Jiffy Parking will be liable to Cruel for $2,900, the cost of the golf clubs and compact discs.

Answers to Sample Quiz

True/False:

1.   False   Stocks, bonds, and copyrights are intangible property.
2.   False   Purchasing is the most common method of acquiring property.
3.   True   Control has been given to the donee by delivering the key.
4.   False   A gift cause mortis is a gift made in contemplation of death.
5.   False   This statute applies only to gifts of money or stock.
6.   False   If a will does not exist, the property is distributed to the heirs by statute.
7.   True   Accession can be by natural or manufactured means.
8.   False   The owner does not have to pay for the improvement.
9.   True   The owners share ownership in the proportion of the goods contributed.
10.   True   The owner of the premises becomes an involuntary bailee.
11.   True   The lost property must be returned to its rightful owner if they are located.

12. False   Most statutes require that the property be turned over to a government agency.
13. True   Anyone who finds this property acquires title to it.
14. False   The owner is the bailor.
15. True   Instead, the bailee must follow the bailor's directions concerning the goods.
16. True   Real property cannot be bailed.
17. False   The bailee must knowingly accept the personal property.
18. True.   This is the typical rental of equipment situation.
19. False   This is a bailment for the sole benefit of the bailor.
20. False   The bailee only owes a duty of slight care.
21. True   The bailee is liable if they are even slightly negligent and the property is damaged, lost, or stolen.
22. True   You have the benefit of using the equipment and the company receives the benefit of compensation.
23. True   The bailor is not liable for defects that could have been discovered through reasonable inspection.
24. False   Not only are they liable for negligence, they are strictly liable for all damage.
25. True   Airline liability for lost luggage is limited to $1,250 per piece of luggage.

Multiple Choice:

26. C   Tangible property includes physically defined property. A is incorrect because real property is land. Choice B is incorrect because a fixture is personal property that has become real property by being permanently attached to land. Choice D is incorrect because intangible property represents rights that can't be reduces to a physical form, such as a copyright.
27. D   D is correct because all three choices are methods for acquiring personal property.
28. B   The gift may be revoked anytime before death. Choice A is incorrect because this is an irrevocable gift that does not contemplate death. Choice C and D are incorrect because they are not types of gifts.
29. D   When goods are improved by manufacture, this is accession. A is incorrect because production is from scratch, and the limousine was added to an already existing piece of property. Choice B is incorrect because there is no indication that the limousine was given to the new owner. Choice C is incorrect because this is not a fungible good that has been commingled.
30. A   Property that is voluntarily placed somewhere and then inadvertently forgotten is mislaid property. B is not correct because lost property is carelessly left somewhere, not intentionally placed somewhere. C is incorrect because Dave had no intent to relinquish his ownership rights. D is incorrect because a coat is physical property, not representative of some other property.
31. B   Sue has negligently let the purse be blown off and it is now in an unknown location. A is incorrect because Sue did not intentionally place her purse in the road. C is incorrect because she did not intend to relinquish her ownership interest in the purse. D is not correct because the purse is tangible property.
32. A   The co-worker is the bailor and is the only one receiving a benefit from this bailment. B is incorrect because there is no benefit to the bailee in this situation. C is incorrect because there is no benefit for the bailee, nor is there any compensation involved. D is not correct because the co-worker did not intend to pass title by leaving the car.
33. D   Choices A, B, and C are essential elements of a bailment. D is therefore correct.
34. C   A common carrier is liable regardless of fault if the goods are lost, damaged, or stolen. Choice A only applies to a gratuitous bailment. Choices B and D are the same, and both standards do not apply to common carriers or innkeepers.
35. D   Choices A, B, and C are all correct uses for a document of title, making D the correct answer.

Short Answer:

36. It is all real property and physically defined personal property such as buildings, animals, minerals, automobiles, and equipment.
37. capture or possession, purchase or production, gift, will or inheritance, accession, confusion, divorce
38. (1) donative intent (2) delivery (3) acceptance
39. Property is mislaid when the owner voluntarily places the property somewhere and then inadvertently forgets it.
40. (1) The finder reports the found property to the appropriate government agency and turns over possession. (2) Post notices describing the lost property. (3) A specified time passes without the rightful owner claiming the property.
41. Property becomes abandoned if an owner discards the property with the intent to relinquish his or her rights in it or an owner of mislaid or lost property gives up any further attempts to locate it.
42. A transaction where an owner transfers his or her personal property to another to be held, stored, or delivered. Title to the property does not transfer.
43. The bailee is obligated to do as the bailor directs with the property. Usually, the bailee is obligated to return the identical goods bailed.
44. A typical situation would be where the bailor is watching the property as a favor.
45. This is a bailment for the sole benefit of the bailee, which requires a duty of great care.
46. A bailment for the mutual benefit of the bailor and bailee. It is typified by the equipment rental agreement. The bailee owes a duty of ordinary care to protect the bailed property.
47. Warehousers are liable only for loss or damage to the bailed property caused by their own negligence. They owe a duty or reasonable care.
48. An innkeeper is the owner of a facility that provides lodging to the public for compensation.
49. The innkeeper can avoid liability if a safe is provided in which the guests' valuable property may be kept and the guest was aware of the safe's availability.
50. It is a negotiable instrument developed to represent the interests of different parties in a transaction that uses storage or transportation between the parties.

Chapter 49

REAL PROPERTY

Chapter Overview

In the Western world, we have come to value real property more than most any other possession. To the ownership of land attaches wealth and influence in western society. More importantly, the privacy rights associated with property ownership are assigned great personal worth and psychological value. Even in the face of government power, we proclaim, "A man's home is his castle." In this chapter we focus on the legal rights associated with ownership, occupation, use, and transfer of real property.

Chapter Objectives

Upon completion of the exercises contained in this chapter, you should be able to
1. Describe the different types of ownership interests in real property.
2. Describe ownership interests in surface, subsurface, and air rights.
3. Describe a life estate.
4. Identify and explain the future interests of reversion and remainder.
5. Explain the different types of joint tenancy.
6. Describe the difference between separate property and community property.
7. Understand how property can be acquired by adverse possession.
8. Explain recording statutes.
9. Distinguish between easements appurtenant and easements in gross.

Practical Application

Upon mastering the concepts in this chapter, you should be able to recognize how a piece of real property is held by the owner and what affect that has upon its use, transfer, and value. As an example, real estate that has an easement attached to it is worth less because another party has the right to use the property for their own purposes as specified in the easement. When the property is transferred to another owner, that owner may have to accept the easement, depending on whether legal requirements have been met.

Helpful Hints

There are many rules created by common law, statute, and current case law. A logical order can be created to this large volume of law if you focus on the creation of the right in the land, its transfer, and perfecting the right by giving notice to the rest of the world. When you are faced with a real property problem, you need to know how the person or company obtained its interest in the real property, what rights go with that interest, if any other party claims a joint interest in the same property, and how that interest is protected or sold to another. Unlike personal property that is usually not granted to a beneficiary until a will becomes effective, the transfer of an interest in real property may be dictated by the language and conditions contained in the deed. It is often necessary to look backwards in the line of owners to determine who will own the interest in the future.

Study Tips

The following outline will help you create a mental checklist of the main issues and rights involved in ownership and transfer of rights in real property. This "checklist" is constantly trying to answer the following questions:

- Is this real or personal property?
- In what form is the reap property currently owned?
- Does anyone hold a future interest in this land?
- Does anyone a co-owner of this real property?
- Was there a legal transfer of an ownership interest?
- Was the transfer of the ownership interest property recorded by deed?
- Does anyone own a nonpossessory interest in this real property?
- Is any legal action being taken against the real property?

Nature of Real Property

Real property is the land itself and any buildings, trees, soil, minerals, timber, plants and other things that are permanently affixed to the land. Any building or permanent structure that is built upon the land becomes part of the real property. The owner of the property also owns the subsurface rights to any minerals, oil, gas, or other commodity that may be under the surface. These subsurface rights may be sold separate from the rest of the real property. Both natural and cultivated plants are part of the real property. They become personal property if the owner severs them from the land. Items that are permanently affixed to the land or a building become part of the real property if they cannot be removed without causing substantial damage to the realty. A regular refrigerator would remain personal property and may be removed when the realty is sold. A built-in commercial refrigerator becomes a *fixture* and is sold with the realty.

One other type of property is the air space above the surface of realty. This space may be sold or leased separate from the realty like a subsurface right.

Ownership Rights

The ownership rights one possesses in real property is called an estate in land. An estate is defined as the bundle of legal rights that the owner has to possess, use, and enjoy the property. The type of estate an owner possesses is determined by the deed, will, lease or other document that created or transferred ownership rights.

- A *freehold estate* is an estate where the owner has a present possessory interest in the real property. Two types of freehold estates are estates in fee and life estates.
  - A *fee simple absolute* is a type of ownership of real property that grants the owner the fullest bundle of legal rights that a person can hold in real property.
  - A *fee simple defeasible* grants the owner all the incidents of a fee simple absolute except that it may be taken away if a specified condition occurs or does not occur.
  - A *life estate* is an interest in land for a person's lifetime. Upon that person's death, the interest will be transferred to another party.

Future Interests

A person may be given the right to possess property in the future rather than in the present. The two forms of future interests are:

- *Reversion* – A right of possession that returns to the grantor after the expiration of a limited or contingent estate.
- *Remainder* – If the right of possession returns to a third party upon the expiration of a limited or contingent estate.

Concurrent Ownership

The forms of co-ownership or concurrent ownership are

- *Joint Tenancy* – Upon the death of one owner, the property passes to the other joint tenants automatically. This is called the right of survivorship.
- *Tenancy in Common* – The interest of a surviving tenant in common passes to the deceased tenant's estate and not to the co-tenants.
- *Tenancy by the Entirety* – This form can only be used by married couples. This also has a right of survivorship, but unlike a joint tenancy, one tenant cannot sell their interest in the realty.
- *Community Property* – None states recognize community property rights. Upon the death of one spouse, one-half of the community assets automatically pass to the surviving spouse. The other half passes by will or by the state's intestate statute.
- *Condominium* – A form of ownership in a multiple-dwelling building where the purchaser has title to an individual unit and owns the common areas as a tenant in common.
- *Cooperative* – A form of ownership of a multiple-dwelling building where a corporation owns the building and the residents own shares in the corporation.

Transfer of Ownership of Real Property

An owner may transfer their interest in realty by one of the following methods:

- *Sale* – This is the passing of title from a seller to a buyer for a price. It is also called a conveyance.
- *Tax Sale* – The government may obtain a tax lien against property for unpaid property taxes. If the lien remains unpaid, a tax sale is held to satisfy the lien.
- *Gift, Will, Inheritance* – These forms of transfer involve granting title to another without the payment of any consideration.
- *Adverse Possession* – When a person openly possesses the property of another, they may acquire title if certain statutory requirements are met. The owner must have notice that his or her land is being wrongfully possesses and take no steps to eject the adverse possessor.

Deeds and Recording Statutes

Deeds are used to convey property by sale or gift. The seller or donor is called the *grantor*. The buyer or recipient is the *grantee*. A *warranty deed* has the greatest number of warranties or guarantees. The *quitclaim deed* provides no protection for the buyer, granting only whatever interest the grantor possesses.

A *recording statute* provides that copies of the deed and other documents, such as mortgages and deeds of trust, may be filed with the *county recorder's office* to give constructive notice of the ownership to the world. Recording statutes are intended to prevent fraud and to establish certainty in the ownership and transfer of property.

A seller has the obligation to transfer *marketable title* to the grantee. Marketable title means that the title is free from encumbrances, defects in title, or other defects that would affect the value of the property.

Nonpossessory Interests

Nonpossessory interests exist when a person holds an interest in another person's property without actually owning any part of the property. The three nonpossesory interests are

- **Easements** – An easement is a given or required right to make limited use of someone else's land without owning or leasing it.

  Easements may be **expressly** created by
  1. *grant* – where the owner gives another party an easement across his or her property
  2. *reservation* – where an owner sells his or her land but keeps an easement on the land

  Easements may be **implied** by
  1. *implication* – where an owner subdivides a piece of property with a well, path, road or other beneficial appurtenant that serves the entire parcel, or by
  2. *necessity* – where a landlocked parcel must have egress and ingress

- There are two types of easements
  1. Easements Appurtenant – A situation created when the owner of a piece of land is given an easement over an adjacent piece of land.
  2. Easements in Gross – An easement that authorizes a person who does not own adjacent land the right to use another's land. Examples include easements granted for power lines, telephone lines, gas lines, and cable lines.

  The easement holder owes a duty to maintain and repair the easement.

- **Licenses** – A license grants a person the right to enter upon another's property for a specified and usually short period of time. A ticket to a football game gives you a license to use a seat in the stadium for a period of time.

- **Profit** – Grants a person the right to remove something from another's real property.

Refresh Your Memory

The following exercise will enable you to refresh your memory on the rules of law and principles presented to you in this chapter. Read each question twice and put your answer in the blanks provided. Review the chapter material for any question that you miss or are unable to remember.

1. Houses, farms, and buildings are all forms of _____ property.

2. Real property includes items of personal property, called _____, that are affixed to real property.

3. Rights to minerals and other things under the surface of land are called _____ rights.

4. A person's ownership rights in real property are called an _____ _____ _____.

5. A _____ _____ _____ is the highest form of ownership of real property.

6. An estate that may be taken away if a specified condition occurs or does not occur is a _____ _____ _____.

7. A _____ is a right of possession that returns to the grantor after the expiration of a limited or _____ estate.

8. A _____ _____ is a form of co-ownership that includes the right of survivorship.

9. A _____ or _____ is the most common method of transferring ownership rights in real property.

10. A _____ is a transfer of property from one person to another without exchange of money.

11. _____ _____ is when a person who wrongfully possesses someone else's real property obtains title to that property if certain statutory requirements are met.

12. _____ are used to convey real property by sale or gift.

13. A grantor has the obligation to transfer _____ title or good title to the grantee.

14. An _____ is an interest in land that gives the holder the right to make limited use of another's property without taking anything from it.

15. A _____ _____ gives the holder the right to remove something from another's real property.

Critical Thought Exercise

Jim Lewis and Dale Tingle decided to form a partnership for the purpose of entering the restaurant business. Prior to forming the partnership, Lewis and Tingle purchased a large Victorian house in Sacramento with the idea that they would convert the first floor into a restaurant and the upper floors into office space. Lewis contributed $90,000 to the purchase and Tingle contributed $10,000. Lewis and Tingle took title as joint tenants with the right of survivorship. The partnership was formed five months later and the Sacramento property was converted into a restaurant and offices as planned. When Lewis and Tingle purchased another house in Davis, California, they took title as tenants in common. Tingle contributed $100,000 as the down payment for the Davis property. When the partnership was dissolved, the court ordered that both properties be sold. Lewis was given a reimbursement for the Sacramento property in the amount of $80,000. The Davis property was sold for $320,000 and the proceeds of the sale were divided equally between Lewis and Tingle. Did the court divide the proceeds from the sale of the two properties properly?

Answer. _____

_____

_____

_____

_____

_____

_____

_____

_____

_____

_____

_____

_____

_____

_____

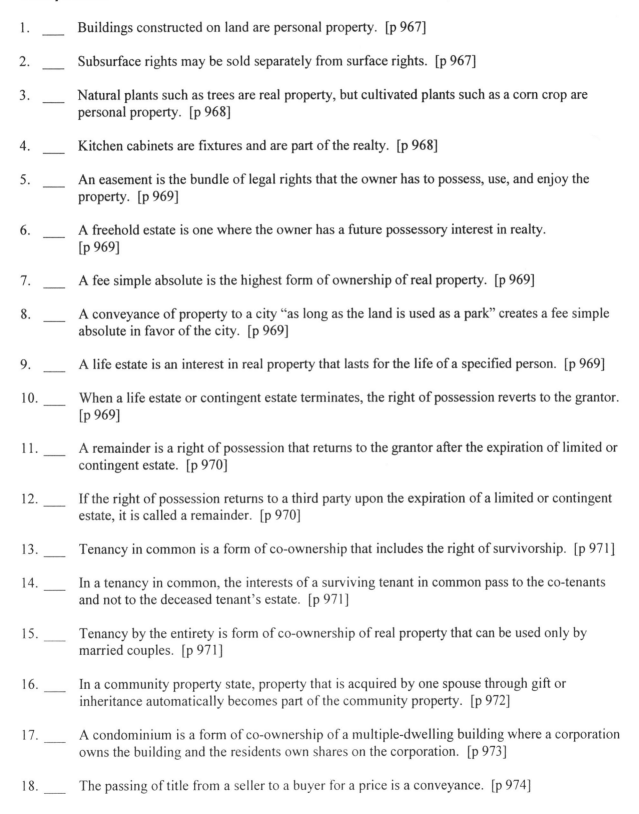

Practice Quiz

True/False:

1. ___ Buildings constructed on land are personal property. [p 967]

2. ___ Subsurface rights may be sold separately from surface rights. [p 967]

3. ___ Natural plants such as trees are real property, but cultivated plants such as a corn crop are personal property. [p 968]

4. ___ Kitchen cabinets are fixtures and are part of the realty. [p 968]

5. ___ An easement is the bundle of legal rights that the owner has to possess, use, and enjoy the property. [p 969]

6. ___ A freehold estate is one where the owner has a future possessory interest in realty. [p 969]

7. ___ A fee simple absolute is the highest form of ownership of real property. [p 969]

8. ___ A conveyance of property to a city "as long as the land is used as a park" creates a fee simple absolute in favor of the city. [p 969]

9. ___ A life estate is an interest in real property that lasts for the life of a specified person. [p 969]

10. ___ When a life estate or contingent estate terminates, the right of possession reverts to the grantor. [p 969]

11. ___ A remainder is a right of possession that returns to the grantor after the expiration of limited or contingent estate. [p 970]

12. ___ If the right of possession returns to a third party upon the expiration of a limited or contingent estate, it is called a remainder. [p 970]

13. ___ Tenancy in common is a form of co-ownership that includes the right of survivorship. [p 971]

14. ___ In a tenancy in common, the interests of a surviving tenant in common pass to the co-tenants and not to the deceased tenant's estate. [p 971]

15. ___ Tenancy by the entirety is form of co-ownership of real property that can be used only by married couples. [p 971]

16. ___ In a community property state, property that is acquired by one spouse through gift or inheritance automatically becomes part of the community property. [p 972]

17. ___ A condominium is a form of co-ownership of a multiple-dwelling building where a corporation owns the building and the residents own shares on the corporation. [p 973]

18. ___ The passing of title from a seller to a buyer for a price is a conveyance. [p 974]

19. ____   If a person dies without a will, his or her property is distributed to the heirs as stipulated in the state's intestate statute. [p 974]

20. ____   The party who transfers an ownership interest in real property is the grantee. [p 976]

21. ____   A recording statute requires that a mortgage or deed of trust be recorded in the county recorder's office of the county in which the real estate is located. [p 976]

22. ____   A party who is concerned about his or her ownership rights in a parcel of real property can bring a tort action to have a court determine the extent of those rights. [p 977]

23. ____   Marketable title means that the title is free from any encumbrances, defects in title, or other defects that are not disclosed but would affect the value of the property. [p 978]

24. ____   The only two ways to create an easement is by grant or reservation. [p 979]

25. ____   A license grants a person the right to enter upon another's property for a specified and usually short period of time. [p 979]

Multiple Choice:

26. Which of the following is real property? [p 967]
    a. The tables and chairs in a restaurant
    b. A portable hot tub
    c. A camper in which a family is living
    d. An in-ground swimming pool

27. The rights to natural gas under Sue's home are her [p 967]
    a. easement rights.
    b. profit.
    c. personal property.
    d. subsurface rights.

28. An estate that may end upon the occurrence of a condition is a [p 969]
    a. fee simple absolute.
    b. fee simple defeasible.
    c. reversion.
    d. life estate.

29. If a grantor conveys property "to Ann Brown for life," the grantor's retained interest in the property is called a [p 970]
    a. reversion.
    b. remainder.
    c. life estate.
    d. tenancy in common.

30. Larry conveys real property to "Jim Smith and Greg Brown, as joint tenants, with the right of survivorship." If Smith dies, his interest in the property will pass to [p 971]
    a. Smith's heirs.
    b. Smith's beneficiaries under his will.
    c. Brown.
    d. the state where Smith resided when he died if he did not have a will.

31. Larry conveys Blackacre to "Jim Smith and Greg Brown, as tenants in common." Jim Smith has a will that leaves his entire estate to Ned Green. If Smith dies, his interest in Blackacre will pass to [p 971]
    a. Smith's heirs under the state's intestate statute.
    b. Green.
    c. Brown.
    d. none of the above.

32. The owner of a condominium [p 973]
    a. has title to their individual unit.
    b. owns the common areas as tenants in common with the other owners.
    c. may sell or mortgage their unit without the permission of the other owners.
    d. all of the above.

33. Fred wants to convey Whiteacre to Sue without making any representations or incurring any liability. The best protection for Fred would be to convey Whiteacre by way of a [p 976]
    a. warranty deed.
    b. quitclaim deed.
    c. quiet title action.
    d. gift.

34. Gus has a home on a 10-acre parcel that he subdivides into two 5-acre parcels. Gus builds a new house on the subdivided parcel. The only way for the new homeowner to get to the main road is to drive across Gus's parcel. The new homeowner has acquired an [p 979]
    a. easement by express grant.
    b. easement by implication.
    c. license.
    d. profit a'pendre.

35. The government must compensate a property owner when the government takes his or her property by eminent domain under the mandate of the [p 980]
    a. Just Compensation Clause.
    b. action to quiet title.
    c. Statute for the Regulation of Open Property.
    d. profit a'pendre.

Short Answer:

36. Things such as radio towers, bridges, and grain silos are considered _____ property. [p 967]

37. Give four examples of things that may be removed from the earth or sold as part of an owners subsurface rights. [p 967] _____

38. Give four examples of things in a home that are fixtures and cannot be removed upon a sale of the real property. [p 968]_____

39. Three types of estates are [p 969] 1) _____
    2) _____ 3) _____

40. A life estate that is measured in the file of third party is an [p 969] _____.

41. The interest that the grantor retains for him- or herself or a third party is a [p 970] _____ _____.

42. Name and define two future interests. [p 970]
    1) _____
    2) _____

43. What is a joint tenancy and how should it be created in a deed? [p 971] _____
    _____
    _____

44. What can a tenant in common do with their property without the consent of the other co-owners? [p 971] _____

45. What is a cooperative? [p 973] _____
    _____

46. What is the closing in a real estate sale? [p 974] _____
    _____

47. What is a gift? [p 974] _____

48. What is adverse possession? [p 975] _____
    _____

49. What is a marketable title? [p 978] _____
    _____
    _____

50. What is an easement? [p 978] _____
    _____
    _____

Answers to Refresh Your Memory

1. real [p 967]
2. fixtures [p 968]
3. subsurface [p 967]
4. estate in land [p 969]
5. fee simple absolute [p 969]
6. fee simple defeasible [p 969]
7. reversion, contingent [p 970]
8. joint tenancy [p 971]
9. sale, conveyance [p 974]
10. gift [p 974]
11. adverse possession [p 975]
12. Deeds [p 976]
13. marketable [p 978]

14. easement [p 978]
15. profit a'pendre [p 979]

Critical Thought Exercise Model Answer

The deed to the Sacramento property created a joint tenancy in the real estate. When a joint tenancy is created, each tenant acquires an equal right to share in the enjoyment of the land during his or her lives. A joint tenancy confers equivalent rights on the tenants that are fixed and vested at the time the tenancy is created. These do not change just because an additional agreement is executed to form a partnership. Once a joint tenancy is established between two people and a partition action is undertaken to divide the property, each person owns a one-half interest and they are entitles to one half of the total proceeds without reimbursement for an unequal down payment. When parties hold property as tenants in common, each tenants share is fully divisible and fully transferable to a purchaser or an heir upon death. The Davis property was subject to equitable adjustments for the large down payment made by Tingle. When the property is sold, the court must determine the percentage of equity that is attributable to the original down payment. Tingle will be entitled to a substantially greater share of the proceeds from the Davis property. However, the court may consider the Davis as just one asset in the partnership. The adjustments to the division of the proceeds will consider the partnership contributions and assets as a whole.

Answers to Practice Quiz

True/False:

1. False   Buildings are real property.
2. True   Owners may sell mineral rights, oil rights, etc., without selling their surface land.
3. False   All plant life and vegetation are considered real property.
4. True   They cannot be removed without causing substantial damage.
5. False   This is the definition of an estate.
6. False   A freehold estate is a present possessory interest in realty.
7. True   This is because it grants the owner the fullest bundle of legal rights that a person can hold in real property.
8. False   This conditional conveyance creates a fee simple defeasible.
9. True   When the specified person dies, the property reverts to the grantor or the grantor's estate or other designated person.
10. True   This is called the right of reversion. It need not be stated in the conveyance.
11. False   This is a reversion, not a remainder.
12. True   The person who is entitled to the future interest is called a remainderman.
13. False   Joint tenancy includes the right of survivorship.
14. False   In a tenancy in common, the interest passes to the deceased tenant's estate.
15. True   It also carries with it the right of survivorship for the spouse.
16. False   Gifts and inheritance remains the separate property of spouse who received it.
17. False   This is the definition of a cooperative.
18. True   It is also called a sale.
19. True   A person must have a will to give property to specific beneficiaries.
20. False   This is the definition of a grantor.
21. True   This gives notice to the world as to the claimed ownership of that realty.
22. False   This is a quiet title action.
23. True   The best way to be sure that one has obtained marketable title is to obtain title insurance from an insurance company.

24. False   An easement may also be created by implication or necessity.
25. True   A typical license is a ticket to a sporting event or play.

Multiple Choice:

26. D   An in-ground pool cannot be removed without causing substantial damage to the property. Choices A, B, and C are all portable and their movement or removal will not damage the land.
27. D   The owner or land owns the rights to whatever is under the surface of his or her land, including minerals, gas, and oil. A is incorrect because an easement is a right to use or cross another person's land. B is not correct because a profit is the right to remove something from another person's land. C is not correct because gas and minerals are a form of real property until they are removed from the land.
28. B   This fee is signified by use of language such as "so long as" and "until." Choice A is an estate that cannot be terminated or taken away. Choice C is the right that the grantor has after a limited or contingent estate ends. Choice D is not terminated by a condition, but by the end of the life of a specified person.
29. A   A reversion is a right of possession that returns to the grantor at the expiration of a limited estate. The life estate in Ann Brown is a limited estate. Choice B is not correct because the remainder is an interest held by a third person, not the grantor. Choice C is not correct because the grantor will obtain the property in fee simple absolute. Choice D is incorrect because this is a form of co-ownership, not a future interest.
30. C   Under the right of survivorship, the interest of the deceased tenant passes to the surviving tenant. A and B are incorrect because the interest will not pas to Smith's heirs or beneficiaries. D is incorrect because the only way the interest will pass to the state is if there is no right of survivorship combined with a lack of any heirs or beneficiaries.
31. B   Green will receive the interest in Blackacre because Smith's interest may be passes through a will. A is incorrect because Smith has a will and did not die intestate. C is incorrect because a tenancy in common does not have a right of survivorship. D is incorrect because B is a correct answer.
32. D   D is correct because A, B, and C are all rights of a condominium owner.
33. B   A quitclaim deed provides the least amount of protection for the buyer (and is thus, best for Fred) because the grantor conveys only whatever interest he or she has in the property. A is not correct because a warranty deed contains the greatest number of warranties. C is incorrect because it involves a lawsuit when there is a dispute over the title to a parcel of real estate. D is incorrect because even a gift must be deeded.
34. B   It is implied by Gus's action that he would allow the new owner to have a driveway across his property. A is incorrect because Gus never expressly granted the right to cross his land to the new owner. C is not correct because a license is usually for a short specified period of time. D is incorrect because nothing is being removed from Gus's land.
35. A   If the owner is not satisfied with the government's offer for compensation, the owner may bring an action to have a court determine the amount of compensation. B is not correct because it is an action to settle ownership of property, not the compensation to be paid by the government. C is not correct because it concerns ownership rights in Germany. D relates to compensation for taking something (timber) from the owners land.

Short Answer:

36.   real
37.   oil, gas, coal, gold

38. carpeting, doors, lights, sinks, cabinets
39. fee simple absolute, fee simple defeasible, life estate
40. estate pour autre vie
41. future interest
42. 1) A reversion is a right of possession that returns to the grantor after the expiration of a limited or contingent estate.
    2) A remainder is when the right of possession returns to a third party upon the expiration of a limited or contingent estate.
43. It is a form of co-ownership that includes the right of survivorship. It is created when the property is conveyed "to Mike and Sue as joint tenants, with the right of survivorship."
44. A tenant in common may sell, give, devise, or transfer his or her interest in the property.
45. A cooperative is a form of co-ownership of a multiple-dwelling building where a corporation owns the building and the residents own shares in the corporation.
46. It is the finalization of a real estate sales transaction that passes title to the property from the seller to the buyer.
47. A gift is a transfer of property from one person to another without exchange of money.
48. It is when a person who wrongfully possesses someone else's real property obtains title to that property if certain statutory requirements are met.
49. It is title that is free from any encumbrances or other defects that are not disclosed but would affect the value of the property.
50. An easement is a given or required right to make limited use of someone else's land without owning or leasing it.

Chapter 50

LANDLORD-TENANT RELATIONSHIPS

Chapter Overview

The average business does not have the resources to buy land and build its store, offices, manufacturing facilities, or other commercial facilities. Renting or leasing real property is a necessary part of doing business. This chapter covers law in the areas of contracts and real property that relate to the landlord-tenant relationship. It also discusses the regulation of land use by the government.

Objectives

Upon completion of the exercises in this chapter, you should be able to
1.   Describe the various types of tenancy.
2.   Identify the landlord's duties under a lease.
3.   Understand a tenant's duties under a lease.
4.   Describe how federal law in the areas of fair housing and disabilities regulates real estate.
5.   Explain how tort liability arises for landlords and tenants.
6.   Describe how a lease can be terminated.
7.   Explain how restrictive covenants restrict the use of land.
8.   Describe public and private nuisances.
9.   Understand how zoning laws regulate the use of land.
10.   Describe the acquisition of property by the government by the use of eminent domain.

Practical Application

Upon learning the objectives in this chapter, you should understand the duties and rights of landlords and tenants in the common leasing of real property. Failure to meet the duties imposed at common law and by statute may cause a tenant to lose their tenancy. A landlord who violates their duties is subjected to damages and sanctions. A businessperson who is leasing a storefront or commercial building must understand the restrictions on the use of the building and what affirmative tasks must be undertaken to keep them out of breach of contract.

Helpful Hints

It is important that you learn the terminology associated with the rights and duties that arise from the landlord-tenant relationship. In each lease of real property, whether you are the landlord or the tenant, you must understand your obligations and know how those obligations are created in a written lease. You must also understand the obligations that are created by statute and remain in effect even if they are not included in the lease. As you examine each right and duty, determine the type of land use that is proper and improper in each situation.

Study Tips

A landlord or tenant can have obligations created by the lease, by statute, or by common law doctrines such as negligence. Examine each of these areas individually to discover the specific rights and duties that are created for the landlord and tenant.

Landlord-Tenant Relationship

This relationship is created when the owner of a freehold estate transfers a right to exclusively and temporarily possess the owner's property. The tenant receives a leasehold estate.

The types of tenancy are:

- *tenancy for years* – a tenancy created when the landlord and the tenant agree on a specific duration for the lease.
- *periodic tenancy* – a tenancy created when a lease specifies intervals at which payments are due but does not specify how long the lease is for.
- *tenancy at will* – a lease that may be terminated at any time by either party.
- *tenancy at sufferance* – a tenancy created when a tenant retains possession of property after the expiration of another tenancy or a life estate without the owner's consent.

Duties Owed by the Landlord

The landlord has the following duties:

- *duty to deliver possession*
- *duty not to interfere with the tenant's right of quiet enjoyment* – the law implies a covenant of quiet enjoyment in all leases. The landlord may not interfere with the tenant's quiet and peaceful possession, use, and enjoyment of the leased premises.
- *duty to maintain the leased premises* – the landlord must comply with the requirements imposed by building and housing codes. Under an implied warranty of habitability, the leased premised must be fit, safe, and suitable for ordinary residential use.

Duties Owed by the Tenant

A tenant owes the landlord the duties agreed to in the lease and any duties imposed by law. These include:

- *duty not to use leased premises for illegal or nonstipulated purposes*
- *duty not to commit waste* – waste occurs when a tenant causes substantial and permanent damages to the leased premises that decreases the value of the property and the landlord's reversionary interest in it.
- *duty not to disturb other tenants* – a landlord may evict the tenant who interferes with the quiet enjoyment of other tenants.

Tort Liability of Landlords and Tenants

Landlords and tenants owe a duty of reasonable care to third parties not to negligently cause injury to them. The landlord also owes this duty to the tenant.

Transferring Rights to Leased Property

Landlords may sell, gift, devise, or otherwise transfer their interests in leased property. The new landlord cannot alter the terms of an existing lease.

The tenant may transfer his or her rights under a lease to another by way of an assignment. The new tenant is the assignee and is obligated to perform the duties that the assignor had under the lease. The assignor remains responsible for his or her obligations under the lease unless released by the landlord.

If a tenant transfers only some of his or her rights under the lease, it is a sublease. The sublessor is still responsible under the lease and the sublessee does not obtain any rights under the original lease.

Land Use Control

Land use control is the collective term for the laws that regulate the possession, ownership, and use of real property. Forms of land use control include:

- *private nuisance* – a landowner or tenant who is affected in the use and enjoyment of real property by the use of adjoining or nearby property may bring a private nuisance action for damages.
- *restrictive covenants* – this is a private agreement between landowners that restricts the use of their land. They are often used by residential developers and condominium buildings to establish uniform rules for all occupants.
- *public nuisance* – this is a nuisance that effects or disturbs the public in general.
- *zoning* – zoning ordinances are local laws that are adopted by municipalities and local governments to regulate land use within their boundaries. Zoning ordinances are adopted and enforced to protect the health, safety, morals, and general welfare of the community. A landowner may obtain a variance that permits a type of building or use that would not otherwise be allowed by a zoning ordinance.

Refresh Your Memory

The following exercise will enable you to refresh your memory of the principles given to you in this chapter. Read the questions twice and place your answer in the blanks provided. Review the chapter material for any question you miss or are unable to remember.

1. A landlord holds a _____ estate that he or she can transfer to a tenant for their use.

2. The tenant's interest in property is called a _____ _____.

3. The rental agreement between the landlord and tenant is called the _____.

4. When the landlord and tenant agree on a specific duration for the lease, it is a tenancy _____ _____.

5. A _____ tenancy may be terminated by either party at the end of any payment interval.

6. A lease that may be terminated at any time by either party is a tenancy _____ _____.

7. An unlawful detainer action is undertaken by a landlord to _____ a holdover tenant.

8. The law implies a covenant of _____ _____ in all leases.

9. _____ or _____ codes impose specific standards on property owners to maintain and repair leased premises.

10. The implied warranty of _____ provides that the leased premises must be fit, safe, and suitable for ordinary residential use.

11. Waste occurs when a tenant causes _____ and _____ damage to the premises.

12. A tenant owes a duty not to disturb the _____ and _____ of he leased premises by other tenants.

13. An _____ is a transfer by the tenant of his or her rights under a lease to another.

14. A _____ _____ is a private agreement between landowners that restricts the use of their land.

15. A _____ is an exception that permits a type of building or use in an area that would not otherwise be allowed by a zoning ordinance.

Critical Thought Exercise

The City of Peaceful Meadows has numerous historical districts and expensive housing. The architecture is classical with almost no use of neon signs in commercial areas. As the city grows and new commercial areas are developed on streets that intersect with the interstate freeway on the edge of town, the city council is becoming increasingly alarmed with the increase in large electric signs and the typical glass and metal construction used by fast food restaurants and chain stores. Peaceful Meadows passes a zoning ordinance that forbids electrical signs over five feet by eight feet in size and limits the use of neon to the face of opaque signs that must be mounted flush with the ground. The style of the signs must be in conformance with the classical architecture of Peaceful Meadows. Three large chain restaurants desire to place 70-foot tall signs on the property where they are constructing restaurants near the freeway. They also desire to build their restaurants in the style that they always use in other communities because these "cookie-cutter" plans are efficient and economical to build. The Planning Commission of Peaceful Meadows rejects the permits for all signage and building plans proposed by the three restaurants. The restaurants apply for a variance to allow them to avoid the restrictive zoning law. These variance applications are also denied. The restaurants file suit and allege that the zoning ordinance creates an undue hardship and prevents then from making a reasonable use of their land. They also complain that the zoning ordinance is unfairly applied to them due to the numerous other restaurants that already have very tall signs and cheap unsightly construction.

Is aesthetic zoning lawful as used by the City of Peaceful Meadows?

Answer. _____

Sample Quiz

True/False:

1. ___ A tenant holds both possession and temporary title to property under a leasehold. [p 987]

2. ___ The owner who transfers the leasehold estate is called the lessee. [p 987]

3. ___ Most statutes of fraud require written leases for periods of time longer than a year. [p 987]

4. ___ In a tenancy for years, property is leased for a specific duration of time. [p 988]

5. ___ A tenancy for years terminates when one party gives notice to the other party. [p 988]

6. ___ A month-to-month tenancy is a type of tenancy for years. [p 988]

7. ___ A periodic tenancy is created when a lease specifies intervals at which payments are due but does not specify how long the lease is for. [p 988]

8. ___ A periodic tenancy automatically terminates at the end of the payment interval. [p 988]

9. ___ If a tenant dies during a periodic tenancy, the lease immediately reverts back to the landlord. [p 988]

10. ___ A tenancy at will may be terminated at any time by either party. [p 988]

11. ___ When a tenant retains possession of property at the end of his or her tenancy, a tenancy at will is created. [p 988]

12. ___ A tenant at sufferance is a trespasser. [p 988]

13. ___ Because a tenant at sufferance has no legal right to possession of the property, most states allow the landlord to take immediate possession of the property without the need for court process. [p 988]

14. ___ The Civil Rights Act does not regulate the sale or transfer of real property. [p 989]

15. ___ A person who leases a single-family dwelling and does not own more than three single-family dwellings is not prohibited from discriminating in their advertisement to rent the dwelling. [p 989]

16. ___ A landlord may not enter leased premises unless the right is specifically reserved in the lease. [p 989]

17. ___ The law implies a covenant or quiet enjoyment in all leases. [p 989]

18. ___ An unlawful eviction requires the landlord to actually evict the tenant by physically preventing him from possessing the leased premises. [p 989]

19. ___ States and municipalities have enacted housing codes that require property owners to maintain and repair leased premises. [p 990]

20. ___ An implied warranty of habitability requires that leased premises must be fit, safe, and suitable for ordinary residential use. [p 990]

21. ___ Waste by a tenant does not include ordinary wear and tear. [p 992]

22. ___ In a Net, Net, Net Lease, the landlord is responsible for paying the property taxes, utilities, and insurance. [p 993]

23. ___ A tenant owes a duty of utmost or great care to persons who enter upon the leased premises. [p 993]

24. ___ If a landlord transfers complete title to the leased premises, the existing lease is cancelled and the tenant must negotiate with the new owner for a new lease. [p 994]

25. ___ Excessive noise or pollution caused by a manufacturing plant would be examples of a public nuisance. [p 996]

Multiple Choice:

26. Larry rents a storefront in the mall for the Christmas season from October 1st through December 31st. This is an example of a [p 988]
    a. tenancy for years.
    b. periodic tenancy.
    c. tenancy at sufferance.
    d. tenancy at will.

27. Larry leases a storefront in the mall and agrees to pay $1,600 per month, due by the 10th of each month. This tenancy is a [p 988]
    a. tenancy for years.
    b. periodic tenancy.
    c. tenancy at sufferance.
    d. tenancy at will.

28. Larry rents a storefront in the mall for the Christmas season through December 31st. As of January 5th, Larry has not moved out of the store. This tenancy is a [p 988]
    a. tenancy for years.
    b. periodic tenancy.
    c. tenancy at sufferance.
    d. tenancy at will.

29. A tenancy at will [p 988]
    a. continues for the duration of the lease and then terminates automatically without notice.
    b. continues from payment interval to payment interval.
    c. continues at the will of the parties and may be terminated by either party at any time with adequate notice.
    d. arises when a tenant wrongfully occupies real property after the expiration of another tenancy or life estate.

30. Kyle, a landlord, has always rented his apartments to female schoolteachers. Kyle believes that schoolteachers, especially women, are neat and quiet and make the best tenants. Does Kyle have the right to discriminate against others in favor or female schoolteachers in this manner? [p 989]
    a. Yes, because Kyle owns the premises and is free to contract with whomever he pleases.
    b. Yes, because Kyle is free to rent his freehold estate to anyone he desires.
    c. No, because there is no proof that schoolteachers are neat.
    d. No, because Kyle is prohibited by the Civil Rights Act from discriminating against tenants on the basis of their sex.

31. A landlord's promise that he or she will not interfere with the tenant's quiet and peaceful possession, use, and enjoyment of the leased premises is a(n) [p 989]
    a. implied warranty of habitability.
    b. duty to deliver possession.
    c. warranty of title.
    d. covenant of quiet enjoyment.

32. The Country Inn rents efficiency suites by the day, week, and month. The Inn has staircases and steps leading into all suites as part of its Victorian architecture. The Inn tells all disabled persons that it is unable to accommodate physical handicaps. The policy of the Country Inn [p 990]
    a. is lawful because private businesses do not have to accommodate handicapped persons.
    b. is lawful because an owner may design their hotel to fit their own style and budget.
    c. is unlawful because the Americans with Disabilities Act prohibits discrimination on the basis of disability in places of public accommodation operated by private entities.
    d. is unlawful because it violates the Fair Housing Act.

33. Dave rents a storefront for his laundromat and the apartment underneath the store. The apartment is below street level and Dave's bathroom floods when the washing machines are in heavy use. The failure of the landlord to rectify this plumbing problem is a breach of the [p 990]
    a. duty to deliver exclusive possession.
    b. covenant of quiet enjoyment.
    c. implied warranty of habitability.
    d. duty to not commit waste.

34. A transfer by a tenant or his or her entire interest under a lease to another is [p 994]
    a. a delegation.
    b. a sublease.
    c. an assignment.
    d. a breach of contract.

35. Sue purchases a lot in a housing development. Her deed contains a building height restriction that prohibits any structure taller than one story. Sue builds a two-story house on her lot. The building of this house by Sue is a [p 996]
    a. private nuisance.
    b. violation of the restrictive covenant.
    c. public nuisance.
    d. variance.

Short Answer:

36. Give two examples of a tenancy for years [p 988] _____

_____

37. What must a landlord do to remove a holdover tenant? [p 988] _____

_____

38. What can a tenant do if a landlord refuses to cure a defect that causes a constructive eviction? [p 989] _____

39. What factors are considered in deciding whether a barrier to accessibility for a disabled person must be removed by the owner of an old building that was built before the ADA was enacted? [p 990]

_____

_____

_____

40. What is the implied warranty of habitability? [p 990] _____

_____

41. What may a tenant do if a landlord fails to maintain or repair leased premises and it affects the tenant's use and enjoyment of the premises? [p 991] _____

_____

_____

_____

_____

42. When does a tenant commit waste? [p 992] _____

_____

_____

43. What are four of the most common types of commercial leases? [p 993] _____

_____

_____

44. What level of care must a tenant use towards a visitor to the leased premises? [p 993] _____

_____

45. How may a tenant be liable for rent after he or she has assigned the lease to a third person? [p 994]

_____

46. What remedy does the landlord have if a sublessee fails to pay rent? [p 995] _____

_____

47. What is land use control? [p 995] _____

_____

48 Give three examples of a public nuisance. [p 996] _____

_____

49. What is the purpose of a zoning ordinance? [p 997] _____

_____

50. What is a variance? [p 998] _____

_____

Answers to Refresh Your Memory

1. freehold [p 987]
2. leasehold estate [p 987]
3. lease [p 987]
4. for years [p 988]
5. periodic [p 988]
6. at will [p 988]
7. evict [p 988]
8. quiet enjoyment [p 989]
9. building, housing [p 990]
10. habitability [p 990]
11. substantial, permanent [p 992]
12. use, enjoyment [p 992]
13. assignment [p 994]
14. restrictive covenant [p 996]
15. variance [p 998]

Model Answer to Critical Thought Exercise

Municipalities may enact zoning ordinances pursuant to their police power as reserved to them by the Tenth Amendment. Zoning ordinances may (1) designate the type of land use allowed in an area (residential, commercial, industrial), (2) restrict the height, size and locations of buildings, and (3) establish aesthetic requirements or restrictions for signs and exteriors of buildings. The owner who wishes to use his land for a use different from that contained in a zoning ordinance may request a variance. The landowner must prove that the ordinance causes an undue hardship by preventing the owner from making a reasonable use or return on investment. Zoning laws are applied prospectively; allowing uses in existence at the time the ordinance is passed to continue. Modifications or renovations often trigger a requirement that the nonconforming use be terminated. A city's planning commission may legally act to protect the character and stability of its neighborhoods. The city may consider what effect any variance may have upon surrounding properties and the overall zoning plan for the city. If a zoning ordinance is enacted pursuant to the city's police power to protect its residents' health, safety, and welfare, then it will be deemed a lawful exercise of constitutional power. The ordinance in Peaceful Meadows was enacted to preserve the quality of the community and to protect the value and use of property in the city. The ordinance only required that the restaurants conform to aesthetic requirements. The ordinance did not prevent the building of the restaurants or the use of signs to announce the location of the restaurants. The restaurants were not deprived of the use of their land and may still obtain a reasonable return on their investment. The zoning ordinance in Peaceful Meadows does not create an undue hardship and is therefore lawful in both design and application.

Answers to Sample Quiz

True/False:

1. False   The tenant has a nonfreehold estate and does not hold title to the property.
2. False   The landlord is the lessor.
3. True   This is a type of contract that cannot be performed within one year.
4. True   This may be for a week, month, year, or other period of time.

5. False   A tenancy for years terminates automatically, without notice, upon the expiration of the stated term.
6. False   This is a periodic tenancy.
7. True   This period is normally monthly with rent due on a specific day each month.
8. False   A periodic tenancy is terminated at the end of an interval with proper notice given by either party.
9. False   The lease transfers to his or her heirs for the remainder of the current payment interval.
10. True   No notice was required at common law, but most states now have notice periods.
11. False   This is a tenancy at sufferance.
12. True   This is not a true tenancy, but merely possession of the property without right.
13. False   The owner must go through unlawful detainer proceedings to regain possession.
14. False   The Fair Housing Act prohibits racial discrimination in all transfers of real property.
15. False   To qualify for this exemption, the lessor cannot use a real estate broker of advertise in a discriminating manner.
16. True   This is part of the landlord's duty to deliver exclusive possession.
17. True   The landlord may not interfere with the tenant's quiet and peaceful possession, use, and enjoyment of the leased premises.
18. False   The landlord may also constructively evict the tenant by causing the premised to become unfit for the intended use.
19. True   Housing codes set minimum standards regarding heat, water, lights, and other services.
20. True   Examples of uninhabitability would be rodent infestation, leaking roofs, and unworkable bathroom fixtures.
21. True   Normal soiling of the carpet, faded paint, and sun-damaged drapes are examples of ordinary wear and tear.
22. False   The tenant is responsible for paying these costs in addition to the rent.
23. False   The tenant owes a duty of reasonable care.
24. False   The property is subject to the existing lease and the new landlord cannot alter the terms of the lease.
25. True   These nuisances harm the public and are not restricted to any particular landowner.

Multiple Choice:

26. A   This tenancy is for a specific duration, so it is a tenancy for years. B is incorrect because the tenancy has a set expiration date. C is incorrect because the tenant is not occupying the store without permission. D is incorrect because the tenancy may not be terminated prior to the expiration date.
27. B   This tenancy has not expiration date and rent is payable in set intervals. A is incorrect because the lease has no expiration date. C is incorrect because the tenant is not a trespasser. D is incorrect because the periodic rent payments will require adequate notice for termination.
28. C   By staying past the expiration of the lease, Larry has become a trespasser and now has a tenancy at sufferance. A is incorrect because the tenancy for years expired on December 31st. B is incorrect because the lease has a termination date. D is incorrect because even a tenancy at will involves mutual consent for the tenant to occupy the premises.
29. C   C states a correct definition of a tenancy at will. A is incorrect because it defines a tenancy for years. B defines a periodic tenancy. D defines a tenancy at sufferance.
30. D   The Fair Housing Act makes it unlawful for a party to refuse to rent or sell a dwelling to any person because of his or her race, color, national origin, sex, or religion. A, A and C are incorrect because the mandates of the Fair Housing Act control the renting of property.
31. D   The covenant is broken if the landlord interferes with the tenant's use and enjoyment of the property. A is incorrect because it relates to maintaining the premises is a safe, fit, and suitable condition. B is incorrect because it relates only to the duty to turn over possession and does not

relate to continued use. C is incorrect because it relates to the landlords right to transfer possession, not interference with possession.

32. C The ADA requires facilities to be designed, constructed, and altered in compliance with accessibility requirements. A is incorrect because the ADA applies to private businesses. B is incorrect because the ADA has design and construction guidelines that must be followed. Choice D is incorrect because accommodations for disabilities are not covered by the Fair Housing Act.

33. C Leased premises must be fit, safe, and suitable for ordinary use. The flooding of the bathroom makes the apartment unusable. A is incorrect because possession has been delivered but the condition of the premises are not suitable. B is incorrect because there is no outside interference with possession or use of the premises. D is not correct because waste applies to damage by tenants.

34. C The assignee acquires all the rights that the assignor had under the lease. A is not correct because a delegation only transfers the duties under a contract. B is incorrect because a sublease only transfers part of the rights under a lease. D is incorrect because a tenant may assign their rights under a lease unless it is expressly prohibited in the lease.

35. B A restrictive covenant is an agreement between private landowners that restricts the use of their land. The height restriction was implemented by private agreement. A is not correct because the house is not a nuisance since it does not make entry onto another's land. C is not correct because for the same reason as B and because there is not harm caused to others. D is not correct because the restrictive covenant was contained in a private agreement and no government permission was sought for an exception to a zoning law.

Short Answer:

36. Renting an office for five years, renting a vacation home for the summer, renting a room for one week

37. The landlord must go through legal proceedings, called an unlawful detainer, to remove the holdover tenant. A few states allow the landlord to use self-help to evict a holdover tenant if force is not used.

38. The tenant may (1) sue for damages and possession of the premises, or (2) treat the lease as terminated, vacate the premises, and cease paying rent.

39. With respect to existing buildings, architectural barriers must be removed if such removal is readily achievable. In determining when an action is readily achievable, the factors to be considered include the nature and cost of the action, the financial resources of the facility, and the type of operations of the facility.

40. A warranty that provides that the leased premises must be fit, safe, and suitable for ordinary residential use.

41. The tenant may (1) withhold from his or her rent the amount by which the defect reduced that value of the premises to him or her, (2) repair the defect and deduct the cost of repairs from the rent due for the leased premises, (3) cancel the lease if the failure to repair constitutes constructive eviction, or (4) sue for damages for the amount the landlord's failure to repair the defect reduced the value of the leasehold.

42. Waste occurs when a tenant causes substantial and permanent damage to the leased premises that decreases the value of the property and the landlord's reversionary interest in it.

43. Gross lease, net lease, double net lease, and triple net lease

44. The tenant owes a duty of reasonable care to persons who enter upon the leased premises.

45. The assignor remains responsible for his or her obligations under the lease unless specifically released by the landlord. If the assignee fails to pay rent, the assignor will be liable.

46. Because there is no legal relationship between the landlord and the sublessee, the landlord must seek the rent from the sublessor.

47. Zoning ordinances are adopted and enforced to protect the health, safety, morals, and general welfare of the community.

48. Noise from a manufacturing plant or nightclub, fumes from a business, odors from a livestock yard, pollution from a manufacturing plant.

49. An exception that permits a type of building or use in an area that would not otherwise be allowed by a zoning ordinance.

50. Uses and buildings that already exist in the zoned area that are permitted to continue even though they do not fit within the new zoning ordinance.

Chapter 51

INSURANCE

Chapter Overview

The potential risk of loss that a business or individual faces due to death, fire, or injury may be staggering. Insurance is a crucial part of business planning. This chapter examines the insurance contract, types and uses of insurance, defenses used by insurance companies to avoid liability, and secondary liability for losses. The businessperson should understand the types of insurance coverage that are necessary for the proper protection of personal and business assets.

Objectives

Upon completion of the exercises in this chapter, you should be able to:
1. Describe the essential parts of an insurance contract.
2. Understand the meaning of an insurable interest.
3. Describe various types of life, health, and disability insurance.
4. Describe the parameters of fire and homeowners coverage.
5. Explain uninsured motorist and no-fault insurance.
6. Understand the various forms of business insurance.
7. Explain the coverage provided by an umbrella insurance policy.
8. Describe an insurance company's duty to defend its insured.
9. Describe the defenses used by insurance companies to avoid liability.

Practical Application

Even the most successful business has limited resources. This chapter will help you develop a greater understanding of the role that insurance plays in the overall business plan and estate planning of the individual. By understanding the coverage provided by different insurance products, you can make an informed decision as to the type and amount of insurance that is needed to achieve business and personal goals that have been set. Just as import is an understanding of your rights as an insured and the potential defenses that an insurance company will use to avoid paying a claim.

Helpful Hints

You should examine insurance products and incorporate them into any business plan and personal estate plan. When a businessperson is making a decision as the type and amount of coverage needed, he or she must first determine the asset or risk for which protection is needed. The coverage must then be matched to that risk. The needs of a business will vary depending upon the type of business activity, product produced or sold, importance of key personnel, and exposure to liability based upon the risk created by the business to its employees and members of the general public.

Study Tips

In order to accomplish their business goals, each businessperson should understand the important points contained in the following outline. This laundry list of insurance terms and principles is indispensable.

Regulation of the Insurance Industry

Each state has enacted statutes that regulate the insurance industry that operates within the state. State regulation covers all aspects of insurance company incorporation, licensing, oversight, termination of business, and the licensing of agents and brokers.

Insurance Contracts

- The *insurance contract* is a form of third party beneficiary contract, as was discussed in Chapter 15. The insurance contract, or *policy*, is purchased by the *insured* who pays premiums to the insurance company or *insurer*. The policy is usually sold by an *agent* who works for the insurance company or by an *insurance broker* who represents several insurance companies and is the agent of the insured.
- *Mandatory provisions* are required by statute and must be included in each policy. If mandatory provisions are omitted from the contract, they will still be implied. Examples of these provisions include coverage for certain losses and how limitations on coverage must be worded in the contract.
- The *effective date of coverage* is the first date when the insurer becomes obligated to pay for any loss suffered by the insured. This effective date may be when the application and first premium are paid, when a physical exam is passed, or when a broker obtains the insurance.
- Modification of an insurance contract by the parties is usually accomplished by adding an *endorsement* to the policy or by executing a document called a *rider*.
- A person must have an insurable interest in anything he or she insures. For life insurance, a person must have a familiar relationship or an economic benefit from the continued life of another. For property insurance, anyone who would suffer a monetary loss from the destruction of the property has an insurable interest in that property.
- Coverage is limited by deductible clauses and exclusions from coverage.

Life Insurance

- *Life insurance* is a form of insurance where the insurer must pay a specific sum of money to a named **beneficiary** upon the death of another. There are numerous life insurance products, including whole life, limited-payment life, term life, universal life, and endorsement and annuity. The amount of **premiums** for a policy depends upon factors such as availability of a cash or surrender value, and the period over which premiums will be paid.
- *Key-person life insurance* is often purchased by business owners to finance **buy-sell agreements** upon the death of one of the owners of the business. If an insured owner dies, the insurance proceeds are paid to the deceased's beneficiaries. The deceased's interest in the business then reverts to the other owners of the business according to the terms of the buy-sell agreement. This allows a business to continue upon the death of an owner and prevents the beneficiaries from selling off the assets of the business.
- A *double indemnity clause* stipulates that the insurer will pay double the amount of the policy if death is caused by accident or criminal agency.
- *Exclusions from coverage* in many policies include death caused by military actions, executions by government, accidents in private aircraft, and suicide within one or two years.

Health and Disability Insurance
- *Health insurance* can be purchased to cover the costs of medical treatment. Plans vary from health maintenance organizations with low deductibles and co-payments to self-funded plans that have high deductibles, but have greater freedom in choosing doctors and much lower monthly premiums.
- *Disability insurance* provides a monthly income to an insured who is unable to work due to a non work-related disability.

Fire and Homeowners Insurance
- A standard *fire insurance policy* protects real and personal property against loss resulting from fire and certain related perils. Most policies provide for replacement cost insurance that pays the cost to replace the damaged or destroyed property at its current cost.
- A *homeowners policy* covers personal liability in addition to the risks covered by the fire insurance policy. The homeowners policy covers losses from a much wider range of causes, including negligence and theft.
- A *residence contents broad form* policy covers losses incurred by renters for damage or destruction to their possessions.

Automobile Insurance
Many states have mandatory automobile insurance statutes. Proof of insurance is required to be kept on file with the state department of motor vehicles. The basic types of automobile insurance are:
- *Collision insurance* insures the owner's car against the risk of loss or damage. The premium varies depending upon the amount of deductible paid towards any loss by the car owner.
- *Comprehensive insurance* insures an automobile from loss or damages from causes other than collision, such as fire, theft, hail, falling objects, earthquakes, floods, and vandalism.
- *Liability insurance* covers damages that the insured causes to third parties. This coverage usually has a limit for injury to each person in an accident, a limit for the total bodily injury for all persons injured, and a limit for property damage.
- *Medical payment coverage* covers medical expenses for the driver and his or her passengers who are injured in an accident.
- *Uninsured motorist coverage* provides coverage to the driver and passengers who are injured by an uninsured motorist or hit-and-run driver.
- *No-fault automobile insurance* has been enacted in some states. Under this system, a driver's insurance company pays for any injuries he or she suffered in an accident, no mater who caused the accident. Claimants may not sue to recover damages from the party who caused the accident unless the injured party suffered serious injury.

Business Insurance
The owner of real property and a business should purchase several types of insurance in addition to liability and fire insurance. These additional types of insurance include:
- *Business interruption insurance* that pays for lost revenues during the period a business is rebuilding after a fire or some other event.
- *Workers' compensation insurance* pays for injuries and lost wages of employees who are injured on the job. This insurance is mandatory in most states.
- *Fidelity insurance* covers the employer against losses caused by employee theft or fraud.

- *Directors' and officers' liability insurance* protects directors and officers from liability for their negligent actions that they take on behalf of the corporation.
- *Product liability insurance* protects against losses incurred by manufacturers and sellers for injuries caused by their defective products.

Other Types of Insurance

Some special types of insurance that a particular business or individual may desire include:

- *Professional malpractice insurance* which covers the injuries caused by professionals, such as doctors, lawyers, accountants, and architects, resulting from the negligent performance of their duties.
- *Title insurance* protects against defects in title and liens and encumbrances that are not disclosed on the title insurance policy. A lender often requires this insurance before it will fund a loan.
- *Credit insurance* may be purchased by either the creditor or debtor to protect against the debtor's inability to pay a debt. It usually consists of credit life insurance or credit disability insurance.
- *Marine insurance* protects owners and shippers against loss or damage to their ships and cargo.
- *Group insurance* is an insurance that is sold to all the members of a single group, often all the employees of one employer, union, or professional association.
- *Umbrella insurance* coverage pays only if the basic policy limits of a liability policy have been exceeded. This insurance is inexpensive and often extends coverage to $5 million.

Performance of Insurance Contracts

The parties to an insurance contract are obligated to perform the duties imposed by the contract. The duties of the insured are:

- *Duty to pay premiums* – the insured must pay the agreed-upon premiums. Many policies include a grace period during which an insured may pay an overdue premium.
- *Duty to notify insurer* – the insured must notify the insurer after the occurrence of an insured event.
- *Duty to cooperate* – the insured must cooperate with the insurer in investigating claims made against the insurer.

The duties of the insurer are:

- *Duty to defend* – the insurer has a duty to defend against any suit brought against the insured that involves a claim within the coverage of the policy.
- *Duty to pay insurance proceeds* – the insurer's primary duty is to pay legitimate claims up to the policy limit.

Defenses of the Insurer

The most common defenses that may be raised by the insurer to avoid liability are:

- *Misrepresentation and concealment* – the insurer may avoid liability if: 1) the applicant makes a material misrepresentation in the application that is relied upon by the insurer in deciding whether to issue the policy, or 2) the applicant concealed material information from the insurer. Many states have enacted incontestability clauses that prevent insurers from contesting the statements in an application after a number of years.
- *Breach of warranty* – the insured may be required to make affirmative or promissory warranties that certify that facts or conditions are true, such as there being no known structural defects in a building, or that facts will continue to be true while the policy is in effect. The breach of these promises by the insured will relieve the insurer of liability.

Subrogation

If an insurance company pays a claim to an insured for liability or property damage caused by a third party, the insurer succeeds to the right of the insured to recover from the third party.

Refresh Your Memory

The following exercise will enable you to refresh your memory on the important principles presented to you in this chapter. Read each question twice and place your answer in the blanks provided. Review the chapter material for any question you miss or are unable to remember.

1.   Under an insurance contract, the insurance company is the insurer who _____ the insurance coverage.

2.   An insurance _____ usually works exclusively for one insurance company.

3.   An _____ is an addition to an insurance policy that modifies it.

4.   Before a person can purchase insurance, they must have an _____ _____ in the insured item or person.

5.   _____ clauses provide that insurance proceeds are payable only after the insured has paid a certain amount of the damage or loss.

6.   _____ life insurance is issued for a limited period of time with premiums payable and coverage effective only during this term.

7.   The _____ is the person who is to receive the insurance proceeds of a life insurance contract when the insured dies.

8.   The standard fire insurance policy protects the homeowner from loss caused by _____, lightning, _____, and water damage.

9.   An insured may wish to obtain insurance for specific valuable items under their homeowners policy. This is accomplished by adding a _____ _____ _____.

10. A policy called the _____ _____ _____ _____ covers the renters' possessions against the same perils as a homeowners policy and personal liability coverage.

11. _____ insurance is a form of property insurance that insures an automobile from loss or damage from causes other than collision.

12. _____ insurance covers damages that the insured causes to third parties.

13. _____ insurance protects an employer against the dishonesty and defalcation of employees, such as embezzlement of money from the business.

14. The insurer had a duty to _____ against any suit brought against the _____ that involves a claim within the coverage of the policy.

15.   A _____ is a representation of the insured that is expressly incorporated in the insurance contract.

Critical Thought Exercise

The five partners in the law firm of Higgins & Ford, LLP, purchased a $500,000 life insurance policy on the life of each partner from Celestial Insurance. The firm was listed as the beneficiary. On the application forms, the relationship pf the beneficiary to the insured was listed as "business/family association." The period of contestability was two years. Three years after the policy on the life of Victor Ford was purchased, Mr. Ford died in an automobile accident. Celestial refused to pay on the policy and filed suit in a federal district court against Higgins & Ford, seeking to have the policy declared void *ab initio* (from the beginning) on the ground that the law firm lacked an insurable interest.

Does the misleading statement regarding the relationship with the insured by the beneficiary or the lack of a personal relationship with Victor Ford prevent Higgins & ford from having an insurable interest?

Answer. _____

_____

_____

_____

_____

_____

_____

_____

_____

_____

_____

_____

_____

_____

Sample Quiz

True/False:

1.   ___   The party who pays a premium to a particular insurance company for insurance coverage is the insurer. [p 1003]

2.   ___   An insurance agent is an independent contractor who usually represents a number of insurance companies. [p 1003]

3.   ___   If state mandatory provisions are left out of an insurance contract, the contract will be interpreted without them. [p 1003]

4.   ___   An applicant who applies for insurance from an insurance company's agent is usually covered from the moment he or she submits the application and pays the first premium. [p 1004]

5.   ___   An endorsement is an addition or modification to an insurance contract. [p 1004]

6. ___ An insurable interest must be based upon a close family relationship, not a business relationship. [p 1004]

7. ___ Only the owner of real or personal property has an insurable interest in the property. [p 1004]

8. ___ The owner of a life insurance policy is the person who contracts with the insurance company and pays the premium. [p 1006]

9. ___ The owner of a life insurance policy, not the insured, has the power to name the beneficiary of the insurance proceeds. [p 1006]

10. ___ The use of key-person insurance and buy-sell agreements is a valuable tool to protect a business in the event of the death of partner or indispensable officer of a company. [p 1006]

11. ___ Under a double indemnity clause, the insurer will pay double the amount of the policy if the insured dies of a sudden illness, such as a stroke or heart attack. [p 1006]

12. ___ Disability insurance payments made to an insured are usually based on the degree of disability. [p 1007]

13. ___ A standard fire insurance policy protects the insured against loss to real and personal property caused by fire or acts of the insured that damage property of a third party. [p 1007]

14. ___ A property owner who buys a homeowners policy does not need a separate fire insurance policy. [p 1008]

15. ___ Specific valuable items, such as an expensive painting, are covered from loss under a homeowners policy. [p 1008]

16. ___ A homeowners policy provides comprehensive liability insurance for the insured but a rider is needed to extend coverage to cover the damage caused by family members. [p 1008]

17. ___ Damage to renters' personal property is covered by the landlord's homeowners policy. [p 1008]

18. ___ Automobile collision insurance pays for damage caused of the insured's car is struck by another car. [p 1010]

19. ___ Comprehensive automobile insurance covers an automobile from loss or damage from causes other than collision. [p 1010]

20. ___ Automobile liability insurance covers damages that a third party causes to the insured. [p 1010]

21. ___ All states have enacted legislation that compensates employees for work-related injuries for which employers may purchase workers' compensation insurance. [p 1011]

22. ___ To purchase marine insurance the insurer must be the owner of the vessel. [p 1012]

23. ___ An insured must file a written claim called a proof of loss with the insurer to fulfill his or her duty to cooperate. [p 1014]

24. ___ The insurer's duty to pay insurance proceeds includes a duty to investigate claims and make reasonable efforts to settle disputed claims. [p 1014]

25. ___ Incontestability clauses are state laws that prevent insurers from contesting statements made by insureds in applications for insurance after the passage of a stipulated number of years. [p 1014]

Multiple Choice:

26. The regulation of the insurance industry was granted to the states and insurance companies were exempted from federal antitrust laws by [p 1003]
    a. the Commerce Cause of the U.S. Constitution.
    b. the federal insurance code.
    c. insurance company self-regulation.
    d. the McCarran-Ferguson Act.

27. Which of the following statements is accurate? [p 1003]
    a. Insurance brokers work for an individual insurance company.
    b. Insurance brokers are independent contractors who represent a number of insurance companies.
    c. Insurance agents represent multiple insurance companies.
    d. Insurance agents and brokers are both independent contractors.

28. An applicant who applies for property or liability insurance from an insurance broker is usually not covered until [p 1004]
    a. the broker accepts the first premium payment.
    b. the broker accepts the application from the applicant.
    c. the broker obtains the insurance from an insurance company.
    d. the insurance company receives the first premium at its headquarters.

29. Mary is a partner in a very successful accounting firm, is married, and has two children. Who has an insurable interest that would allow them to purchase life insurance if Mary is the insured? [p 1004]
    a. Mary's husband
    b. Mary's children
    c. Mary's partners in the accounting firm
    d. All of the above

30. The type of life insurance that has a cash value that grows at a variable interest rate is [p 1005]
    a. universal life.
    b. whole life.
    c. term life.
    d. limited-payment life.

31. Small businesses, such as partnerships, limited liability companies, and close corporations, often purchase _____ life insurance on the owners of the business. [p 1006]
    a. whole
    b. key-person
    c. universal
    d. term

32. To protect against the risk of loss caused by property damage by the insured or members of the insured's immediate family, the insured should have [p 1008]
    a. standard fire coverage.
    b. a personal articles floater.
    c. liability coverage.
    d. residence contents broad form coverage.

33. To protect against the risk of loss caused by theft of his or her vehicle, and insured should purchase [p 1010]
    a. automobile collision insurance.
    b. automobile comprehensive insurance.
    c. automobile liability insurance.
    d. automobile medical payment coverage.

34. Which of the following is an insurance policy that provides coverage beyond the basic policy limits of the insured's other insurance policies? [p 1013]
    a. Title insurance policy
    b. Credit insurance policy
    c. Group insurance policy
    d. Umbrella insurance policy

35. Which of the following is not a duty of an insured under an insurance contract? [p 1013]
    a. Duty to pay insurance proceeds
    b. Duty to pay premiums
    c. Duty to cooperate
    d. Duty to notify insurer

Short Answer:

36. Give four different examples of an effective date for an insurance policy. [p 1004]
    (1) _____
    (2) _____
    (3) _____
    (4) _____

37. What is an insurable interest? [p 1004] _____

38. What is the difference between universal and term life insurance? [p 1005] _____

39. What are five steps to follow when purchasing key-person life insurance? [p 1006]
    (1) _____
    (2) _____
    (3) _____
    (4) _____
    (5) _____

40. What is a double indemnity clause? [p 1006] _____

41. What is the difference between health insurance and disability insurance? [p 1007] _____
_____
_____
_____

42. What are three things covered by liability coverage under a homeowners policy? [p 1008]
   (1) _____
   (2) _____
   (3) _____

43. Who can purchase identity fraud insurance and what does it cover? [p 1010] _____
_____
_____

44. List four standard types of coverage that an automobile owner may purchase? [p 1010]
   (1) _____ (2) _____
   (3) _____ (4) _____

45. Five types of business insurance that a business may purchase in addition to property and fire insurance are: [p 1011] (1) _____ (2) _____
   (3) _____ (4) _____ (5) _____

46. Why may a business want to purchase marine insurance? [p 1012] _____
_____

47. Give an example of how an umbrella policy works [p 1013] _____
_____
_____
_____
_____
_____

48. What is an insurer's duty to defend? [p 1014] _____
_____
_____

49. What is an incontestability clause and how is it applied? [p 1014] _____
_____
_____
_____

50. Explain how the doctrine of subrogation is applied. [p 1016] _____
_____
_____
_____

Answers to Refresh Your Memory

1.   underwrites [p 1003]
2.   agent [p 1003]
3.   endorsement [p 1004]
4.   insurable interest [p 1004]
5.   Deductible [p 1005]
6.   term [p 1005]
7.   beneficiary [p 1006]
8.   fire, smoke [p 1007]
9.   personal articles floater [p1008]
10. residence contents broad form [p 1008]
11. comprehensive [p 1010]
12. liability [p 1010]
13. Fidelity [p 1011]
14. defend, insured [p 1014]
15. warranty [p 1015]

Critical Thought Exercise Model Answer

A person must have an insurable interest in anything he or she insures. If there is no insurable interest, the contract is treated as a wager and cannot be enforced. In the case of life insurance, a person must have a close family relationship or an economic benefit from the continued life of another to have an insurable interest in that person's life. An insurable interest may be based upon a business relationship. Higgins & Ford not only had a business relationship with Ford, but as a partner in the firm, Higgins & Ford derived an economic benefit from the continued life of Victor Ford. His death created an economic loss for Higgins & Ford, especially if his partnership interest was subject to attachment by creditors. Because the policy was not void *ab initio* and because the period for contesting the policy had passed under the contestability clause, Celestial may not now challenge the terms of the policy or the extent of Higgins & Ford's insurable interest.

Answers to Sample Quiz

True/False:

1.   False   The insured purchases the insurance and pays the premiums.
2.   False   The insurance broker is an independent contractor.
3.   False   The mandatory provisions will be implied in every contract.
4.   True   The agreement may even be oral, but the agent usually issues a written binder.
5.   True   An endorsement or rider control over conflicting provisions or previous endorsements or riders.
6.   False   An insurable interest may also be based upon a business relationship, such as the creditor who has an insurable interest in a debtor.
7.   False   For example, mortgagees, lienholders, and tenants have an insurable interest.
8.   True   This may be a business or person separate from the insured and beneficiary.
9.   True   A son may be the owner and beneficiary of a policy where his father is the insured.
10. True   The proceeds of the insurance policy are used to pay the beneficiaries of the deceased and the ownership interest of the deceased reverts to the other partners or owners.
11. False   A double indemnity clause applies in cases of death by accident.

12. True   The monthly payments provide income to an insured who is disabled.
13. False   A standard fire insurance policy does not carry personal liability coverage.
14. True   A homeowners policy includes both personal liability and fire coverage.
15. False   A personal articles floater is needed in addition to the homeowners policy to cover specific valuable items.
16. False   A homeowners policy covers the insured and family members.
17. False   A renter must purchase residence contents broad form coverage to cover their personal property.
18. True   Coverage applies even if the insured's car is parked at the time of the collision.
19. True   These other causes include fire, theft, storms, falling objects, vandalism, floods, earthquakes, and riot.
20. False   Liability insurance covers damages that the insured causes to third parties.
21. True   This insurance covers employees who are injured within the scope of their employment.
22. False   Shippers may also purchase marine insurance to cover the risk of loss to their goods during shipment.
23. False   A proof of loss is filed to fulfill the insured's duty to notify insurer promptly of claims.
24. True   Insurers that do not pay legitimate claims are liable for breach of contract and may also be liable for tort damages.
25. True   This clause counteracts the defense of misrepresentation and concealment.

Multiple Choice:

26. D   This act was passed by Congress to expressly remove the insurance from federal regulation under the Commerce Clause. A is incorrect because the Commerce Clause favors federal regulation. B is not correct because there is no federal insurance code. C is incorrect because the government regulates the insurance industry, not by the industry itself.

27. B   The insurance broker is the agent for the insured and sells insurance for different companies. A is not correct because a broker is not an employee of any one insurance company. C is not correct because an agent works for one company exclusively. D is incorrect because an insurance agent is not an independent contractor.

28. C   The broker does not work for an individual company, so he or she must contact one or more companies to see who will underwrite the policy. A, B and D are incorrect because they are all events that do not trigger coverage.

29. D   Each of the parties has an insurable interest because they have a close family relationship or an economic benefit from the continued life of Mary. A, B, and C are not correct because they disregard other correct choices.

30. A   Universal life combines features of both term and whole life. B, C, and D are not correct because they do not involve an investment portion that is invested at a variable interest rate.

31. B   Combined with a buy-sell agreement, this insurance protects the business in the event of the death of an owner. A, C, and D are types of life insurance, but they are not the category of insurance that the question calls for. The key-person insurance may be one of the other three choices, (i.e., the company could buy whole life on a company owner.)

32. C   Liability coverage protects against injury or damage caused by the insured or his immediate family to the person or property of third parties. A is not correct because fire insurance does not protect against injury to the property of third parties unless the insured property is damaged first. B is not correct because it protects against loss or damage to the insureds property. D is not correct because this protects against the loss or damage to the insureds personal property when the insured is a renter.

33. B   Comprehensive coverage protects against non-collision losses such as damage or loss from theft, storms, earthquakes, and vandalism. The other types of coverage so not specifically protect against loss from theft.

34. D   An insurer will issue an umbrella policy if the insured has purchased a stipulated minimum amount of coverage on another policy, usually a homeowners policy. A is incorrect because it pertains to protection against defects in the title to real estate. B is not correct because if protects a creditor against default by a debtor. C is incorrect because it provides health insurance coverage for members of a single group.

35. A   The duty to pay insurance proceeds is a duty owed by the insurer to the insured. B, C, and D are all duties owed by the insured.

Short Answer:

36.   (1) Homeowner insurance bought through an agent is effective when the application is submitted with the first premium payment.
(2) Property of liability insurance bought from a broker is effective when the broker obtains the insurance.
(3) Life insurance may only become effective upon the passing of a physical exam.
(4) Insurance from a vending machine is effective when the receipt is received from the machine.

37.   An insurable interest is a personal interest in the item or person based upon a family, economic, or ownership interest in the person or property.

38.   Term life insurance is effective for a limited period of time and only pays the face value of the policy while universal life combines features of whole life and term life, giving a set face value that is increased by an investment portion of the premium with no set time for expiration of the policy, as in whole life.

39.   (1) The owners must agree upon the dollar value of their ownership interests in the business.
(2) The owners must execute a buy-sell agreement among themselves and the company.
(3) The company then purchases key-person life insurance from an insurer in the amount specified in the buy-sell agreement.
(4) The company must pay the premiums on the policies when due.
(5) When the owner dies, the company must submit a claim and pay the beneficiaries.

40.   A clause that stipulates that the insurer will pay double the amount of the policy if death is caused by accident.

41.   Health insurance pays for the costs of medical treatment, surgery, and hospital care while disability insurance pays for lost income and provides a monthly payment when the disabled person cannot work.

42.   (1) Persons injured on the insured's property.
(2) Persons injured by the insured or immediate family members away from the property.
(3) Property damaged by the insured or members of the immediate family.

43.   Any person who has a homeowner's or renter's insurance policy may purchase identity fraud insurance for a small additional premium. The new coverage pays the expenses a victim has in clearing their name and correcting their financial records. It covers attorney's fees, phone and mail costs, lost wages, and the cost associated with applying for new loans.

44.   (1) collision insurance (2) comprehensive insurance
(3) liability insurance (4) medical payment coverage

45.   (1) business interruption insurance (2) workers' compensation insurance (3) fidelity insurance (4) directors' and officers' liability insurance (5) product liability insurance

46.   If the business engages in shipping of goods by ship or other vessel, the marine insurance will cover the risk of loss to their goods during shipping. Marine inland insurance may be purchased for shipping that uses inland waters such as rivers and lakes.

47.   If a homeowner has liability insurance that pays up to $500,000 for each insured event and an umbrella policy for $5 million of coverage, and a family member negligently causes $3 million in

damages to a hotel that is burned down, the liability policy will pay the first $500,000 of the damages and the umbrella policy will cover the remaining $2.5 million in damages.

48. The insurer has a duty to defend against any suit brought against the insured that involves a claim within the coverage of the policy. The insurer must provide and pay for lawyers and court costs necessary to defend the lawsuit. If the insurer fails to defend, it will be liable for any judgment, attorney's fees, and litigation costs.

49. It is a clause that prevents insurers from contesting statements made by insureds in applications for insurance after the passage of a stipulated number of years. If an applicant denied ever using drugs when they are actually an addict and then died six years later of an overdose, the insurance company would be forbidden from claiming that the insured misrepresented and concealed information on the application to avoid paying the claim by the beneficiary.

50. If an insurance company pays a claim to an insured for liability or property damage caused by a third party, the insurer succeeds to the right of the insured to recover from the third party.

Chapter 52

WILLS, TRUSTS, AND ESTATES

Chapter Overview

Wills and trusts are the two main ways that a person disposes of their assets prior to or upon their death. These assets may include business ownership, intellectual property, stocks and bonds, real estate, and personal property. A person who dies intestate, or without a will, will have his or her estate distributed according to a state statute. A trust may be created before death so that property may be held and managed for the benefit of another.

Objectives

Upon completion of the exercises in this chapter, you should be able to:
1. Describe the requirements for making a valid will.
2. Understand how a will can be revoked.
3. Describe holographic and noncupative wills.
4. Explain the types of gifts that can be contained in a will.
5. Understand the principles of abatement and ademption.
6. Explain *per stirpes* and *per capita* distribution of an estate.
7: Describe the effect of simultaneous death of beneficiaries.
8. Explain the effect of the execution of mutual wills.
9. Describe the application of an intestacy statute.
10. Explain the probate process.
11. Describe the formation and functioning of a trust.

Practical Application

When a businessperson acquires assets, it is wise to know how those will be distributed upon their death. The fruits of years of hard work may be wasted if a person does not take adequate steps to preserve their estate and ensure that the estate will be distributed as they wish. As discussed in Chapter 51, insurance, especially key-person insurance, is an integral part of the estate planning process. A business may have to be dissolved if the owners do not take estate planning into account.

Helpful Hints

The main purpose of entering into business is to acquire wealth and provide the necessities of life for yourself, family, and others that depend upon you. Regardless of the amount of current assets held by a person, everyone should have an estate plan. It may be as simple as a will or may involve complex estate planning with the use of trusts, tax consultation, and use of joint tenancy. If an estate plan is in place, it will provide the distribution of assets as desired by the businessperson even if the assets grow or change. Periodic updates of the estate plan are advisable.

Study Tips

In order to make informed judgments involving estate planning, the individual should understand the following principles law relating to wills and trusts.

Requirements for Making a Will

A will is a declaration of how a person wants his or her property distributed upon death. The person who makes this testamentary disposition of property is called the testator or testatrix. The persons designated to receive the property are the beneficiaries.

Every state has a Statute of Wills that sets forth the requirements for a valid will. They are

- Testamentary capacity – the testator must be of legal age and of sound mind
- Writing – the will must be in writing except for noncupative wills
- Testator's signature – the will must be signed at the end.

Attestation by Witnesses

Wills must be attested to by two or three objective and competent persons. The person need not live in the same state, but all the parties must be present when the will is attested to by all witnesses and signed by the testator.

Changing the Will

Wills may be changed by a codicil, a separate document that must be executed with the same formalities as a will. The codicil must incorporate by reference the will it is amending by referring to the testator by name and the date of the previous will. The codicil and will become one document that is read as a whole.

Revoking a Will

Any act that shows a desire to revoke a will shall be deemed a revocation. Making a new will, burning, tearing, or crossing out the pages are all forms of revocations. Wills may also be revoked by operation of law, such as when people get divorced or a spouse is convicted of the murder of the other spouse.

Special Types of Wills

- *Holographic will* are entirely handwritten by the testator, dated, and signed. They need not be witnessed.
- *Noncupative wills* are oral wills made before witnesses during a final illness. They are sometimes call deathbed wills.

Types of Testamentary Gifts

- A gift or real property is a *devise.*
- A gift of personal property is a *bequest* or *legacy.*
- *Specific gifts* are specifically named items of personal property, such as a ring.
- *General gifts* do not specify the source, such as a cash gift.
- *Residuary gifts* are established by a residuary clause that leaves the portion of the estate left over after all distributions and costs are satisfied.

Ademption and Abatement

- *Ademption* – the beneficiary receives nothing when the testator leaves a specific gift and that gift is not in the testator's estate when he or she dies.

Chapter 52

• *Abatement* – if the testator's estate is not large enough to pay all of the devises and bequests, the doctrine of abatement applies. If the will has general and residuary gifts, the residuary gift is abated first. If the will only has general gifts, each gift is reduced proportionately.

Per Stirpes and Per Capita Distribution

When the will leaves the estate to the testator's lineal descendants, it will be distributed either per stipres or per capita.

- *Per stirpes* – the lineal descendants inherit by representation of their parents.
- *Per capita* – the lineal descendants equally share the property of the estate without regard to the degree of relationship to the testator. Children share equally with grandchildren.

Videotaped and Electronic Wills

Electronic wills and videotaped wills do not have any legal force by themselves. A written will is still required. The videotaped or electronically recorded will can be used to supplement the written will to show that the testator had testamentary capacity.

Reciprocal Wills

Reciprocal will arise where two or more testators execute separate wills that make testamentary dispositions of their property to each other on the condition that the survivor leave the remaining property on his or her death as agreed by the testators.

Undue Influence

A will may be invalidated if it was made as a result of undue influence upon the testator. Undue influence occurs when one person takes advantage of another person's mental, emotional, or physical weakness and unduly persuades that person to make a will. The persuasion by the wrongdoer must overcome the free will of the testator.

Murder Disqualification Doctrine

Most state statutes and court decisions provide that a person who murders another person cannot inherit the victim's property.

Intestate Succession

If a person dies without a will, or a will fails for some legal reason, the property is distributed to his or her relatives pursuant to the state's intestacy statute. Relatives who receive property under these statutes are called heirs. If there are no heirs, the property escheats (goes) to the state.

Probate

Probate is the process of a deceased's property being collected, debts and taxes being paid, and the remainder being distributed. A personal representative must be appointed to administer the estate. If the person is named in a will, they are called an executor. If the court appoints the representative, they are an administrator. A probate proceeding is administered and settled according to the state's probate code. Almost half of the states have adopted most or all of the Uniform Probate Code.

Living Wills

People who do not want their lives prolonged indefinitely by artificial means should sign a living will that stipulates their wishes before catastrophe strikes and they become unable to express it themselves.

Trusts

A trust is a legal arrangement established when one person, the settlor or trustor, transfers title to property to another person to be held and used for the benefit of a third person. The property held in trust is called the trust corpus or trust res. Trusts often give any trust income to an income beneficiary and the corpus is distributed to a remainderman upon termination of the trust. There are several kinds of trusts.

- **Express trust** – A trust created voluntarily by the settlor. Express trusts are either:
  - *inter vivos trust* – a trust that is created while the settlor is alive
  - *testamentary trust* – a trust created by will
- **Implied trust** – A trust that is implied by law or from the conduct of the parties. These trusts are either:
  - *constructive trust* – an equitable trust that is imposed by law to avoid fraud, unjust enrichment, and injustice
  - *resulting trust* – a trust created by the conduct of the parties
- **Charitable trust** – created for the benefit of a segment of society or society in general
- **Spendthrift trust** – designed to prevent a beneficiary's personal creditors from reaching his or her trust interest
- **Totten trust** – created when a person deposits money in a bank in their own name and holds it as trustee for the benefit of another

Refresh Your Memory

The following exercises will enable you to refresh your memory as to the key principles and concepts given to you in this chapter. Read each question carefully and put your answer in the blanks provided. Review the chapter material for any question you miss or are unable to remember.

1. Every Statute of Wills requires that the testator have _____ capacity.

2. Wills must be _____ to by two or three objective and _____ persons.

3. Wills may be changed by a _____.

4. A _____ will is entirely handwritten by the testator, dated, and _____.

5. A gift in a will of personal property is a _____ or _____.

6. _____ occurs when a specific gift is not in the testator's estate when he or she dies.

7. When distribution of property takes place _____ _____, the lineal descendants inherit by representation of their parents.

8. A will may be invalidated if it was made as a result of _____ _____ upon the testator.

9. If a person dies without a will, their property will pass by _____ _____.

10. A personal representative who is appointed in a will to administer an estate through probate is called the _____.

11. People who do not want to be kept alive by artificial means may execute a _____ will.

12. Property held in trust is called the trust _____ or trust _____.

13. An _____ _____ trust is an express trust created while the settlor is alive.

14. A _____ trust is created by a will.

15. A _____ trust is created when a person deposits money in a bank in their own name and holds it as trustee for the benefit of another.

Critical Thought Exercise

Fanny York was unmarried and had no children. Her will made the following bequests: (1) all of the stock she owned in AOL to her friend Betsy Petersen, (2) all of her stock in Lucent Technologies to her great niece, Molly Burke, (3) her entire doll collection to be sold and the proceeds to be held in trust for the benefit of her two cats, Elmo and Fred, and (4) the residue to Teen Recovery. When the value of her stocks dropped sharply in 2002, York sold the stock and placed the proceeds in separate bank accounts. A piece of paper with Petersen's name is put inside the savings book for the account started from the proceeds from the sale of the AOL stock. Another savings book has a piece of paper with Burke's name on it. The balance of this account came from the sale of the Lucent stock. When York dies in November 2002, Teen Recovery requests that the entire estate, including the proceeds from both savings accounts, be granted to it. Teen Recovery also requests that the proceeds from the sale of the dolls be given to it because the cats are not human and should not be considered a legitimate heir.

Should the probate court give the proceeds from the bank accounts to Burke and Petersen? Should the court uphold the trust for the benefit of Elmo and Fred?

Answer. _____

_____
_____
_____
_____
_____
_____
_____
_____
_____
_____
_____

Practice Quiz

True/False:

1. ___ A will is a declaration of how a person wants his or her property distributed upon death. [p 1022]

2. ___ The persons designated to receive the property under a will are the testators. [p 1022]

3. ___ A will may be signed at any point in the will if there is an attestation clause. [p 1022]

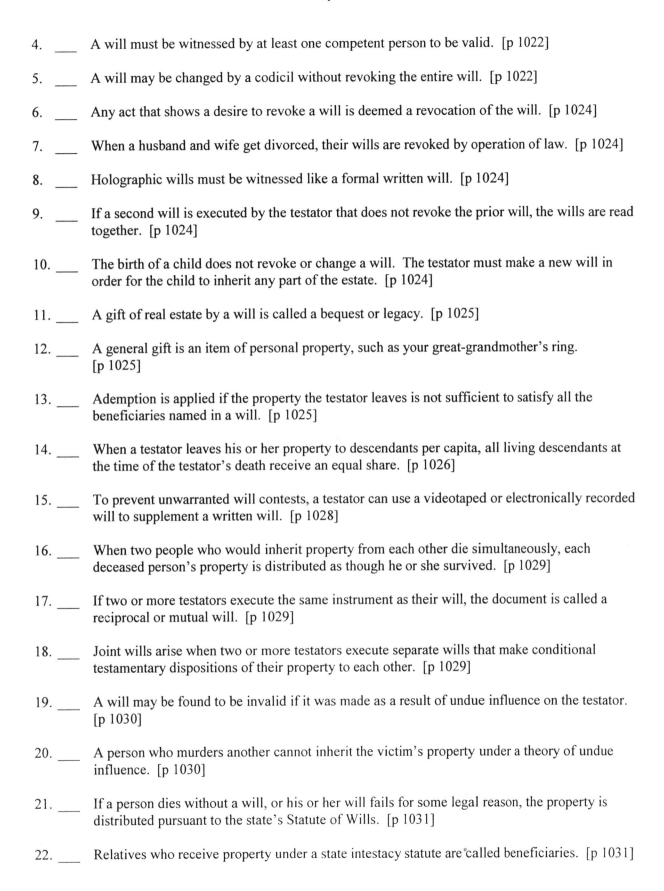

4. ___ A will must be witnessed by at least one competent person to be valid. [p 1022]

5. ___ A will may be changed by a codicil without revoking the entire will. [p 1022]

6. ___ Any act that shows a desire to revoke a will is deemed a revocation of the will. [p 1024]

7. ___ When a husband and wife get divorced, their wills are revoked by operation of law. [p 1024]

8. ___ Holographic wills must be witnessed like a formal written will. [p 1024]

9. ___ If a second will is executed by the testator that does not revoke the prior will, the wills are read together. [p 1024]

10. ___ The birth of a child does not revoke or change a will. The testator must make a new will in order for the child to inherit any part of the estate. [p 1024]

11. ___ A gift of real estate by a will is called a bequest or legacy. [p 1025]

12. ___ A general gift is an item of personal property, such as your great-grandmother's ring. [p 1025]

13. ___ Ademption is applied if the property the testator leaves is not sufficient to satisfy all the beneficiaries named in a will. [p 1025]

14. ___ When a testator leaves his or her property to descendants per capita, all living descendants at the time of the testator's death receive an equal share. [p 1026]

15. ___ To prevent unwarranted will contests, a testator can use a videotaped or electronically recorded will to supplement a written will. [p 1028]

16. ___ When two people who would inherit property from each other die simultaneously, each deceased person's property is distributed as though he or she survived. [p 1029]

17. ___ If two or more testators execute the same instrument as their will, the document is called a reciprocal or mutual will. [p 1029]

18. ___ Joint wills arise when two or more testators execute separate wills that make conditional testamentary dispositions of their property to each other. [p 1029]

19. ___ A will may be found to be invalid if it was made as a result of undue influence on the testator. [p 1030]

20. ___ A person who murders another cannot inherit the victim's property under a theory of undue influence. [p 1030]

21. ___ If a person dies without a will, or his or her will fails for some legal reason, the property is distributed pursuant to the state's Statute of Wills. [p 1031]

22. ___ Relatives who receive property under a state intestacy statute are called beneficiaries. [p 1031]

23. ___ If a deceased has no will and no surviving relatives, the deceased property escheats to the state. [p 1031]

24. ___ A will is probated to establish its validity and to carry out the distribution of the estate. [p 1032]

25. ___ The settlor is the person who creates the trust by transferring the res to the trustee. [p 1034]

Multiple Choice:

26. The person who makes a will is the [p 1022]
    a. testator.
    b. executor.
    c. beneficiary.
    d. administrator.

27. The person who receives property upon administration of a will is the [p 1022]
    a. testator.
    b. executor.
    c. beneficiary.
    d. administrator.

28. Which of the following is not a requirement to form a valid will? [p 1022]
    a. The testator must have testamentary capacity.
    b. The will must be in writing.
    c. The testator must sign the will.
    d. An attorney must prepare the will for it to comply with the Statute of Wills.

29. A will that meets the requirements of the Statute of Will is called [p 1022]
    a. a holographic will.
    b. a formal will.
    c. a noncupative will.
    d. none of the above.

30. A separate instrument that must be executed to amend a will is called a [p 1022]
    a. trust.
    b. holographic will. ·
    c. codicil.
    d. attestation.

31. Which of the following will not revoke a will? [p 1024]
    a. Divorce
    b. A child being born after the will has been executed
    c. A subsequent will that revokes all prior will and codicils
    d. The testator burning the will in her fireplace

32. If Mary leaves $5,000 to Nancy in her will, this gift is a [p 1025]
    a. general bequest.
    b. general devise.
    c. specific bequest.
    d. specific devise.

33. When a testator leaves a specific devise of property to a beneficiary, but the property is no longer in the estate when the testator dies, the beneficiary receives nothing under the principle of
    a. abatement.
    b. ademption.
    c. intestacy.
    d. per capita distribution.

34. When an 88-year-old man leaves all of his property to the lawyer who drafted his will and ignores numerous blood relatives, a probate court will likely invalidate the will [p 1030]
    a. under the murder disqualification doctrine.
    b. because of the lack of proper attestation.
    c. because of undue influence.
    d. unless it is a holographic will.

35. A trust created by will that comes into existence when the settlor dies is a(n) [p 1034]
    a. charitable trust.
    b. Totten trust.
    c. inter vivos trust.
    d. testamentary trust.

Short Answer:

36. What are the three main requirements of a valid will? [p 1022] _____
    _____

37. What is attestation? [p 1022] _____
    _____

38. Define a codicil. [p 1022] _____
    _____

39. List three ways a will may be revoked. [p 1024] (1) _____
    (2) _____ (3) _____

40. What is required for a valid holographic will? [p 1024] _____
    _____

41. What is a residuary gift? [p 1025] _____
    _____

42. When does abatement apply? [p 1025] _____
    _____

43. Explain per stirpes distribution. [p 1026] _____
    _____
    _____

44. Can a videotaped will substitute for a written will? [p 1028] _____
    _____

45. When does undue influence occur in the execution of a will? [p 1030] _____
_____
_____

46. Explain the possible distribution of a person's estate if they have not executed a valid will. [p 1031] _____
_____
_____

47. What is the purpose of a living will? [p 1032] _____
_____

48. Who can be the beneficiary of a trust? [p 1034] _____
_____
_____

49. How does a person create a trust? [p 1034] _____
_____
_____

50. When may an embezzler become a trustee? [p 1035] _____
_____
_____

Answers to Refresh Your Memory

1. testamentary [p 1022]
2. attested, competent [p 1022]
3. codicil [p 1022]
4. holographic, signed [p 1024]
5. bequest, devise [p 1025]
6. ademption [p 1025]
7. per stirpes [p 1026]
8. undue influence [p 1030]
9. intestate succession [p 1031]
10. executor [p 1032]
11. living [p 1032]
12. corpus, res [p 1034]
13. inter vivos [p 1034]
14. testamentary [p 1034]
15. Totten [p 1035]

Critical Thought Exercise Model Answer

If a testator leaves a specific gift of property to a beneficiary, but eh property is no longer in the estate of the testator when he or she dies, the beneficiary receives nothing. This is called the doctrine of ademption. When York sold the stock and opened the two savings accounts, this was an ademption. The stock was a specific gift. Though York may have been trying to preserve the value of the bequest by selling the stock when their values fell significantly, there isn't sufficient proof that York wanted to create a separate gift of money. Petersen and Burke may argue that by putting their names with the savings books, York created Totten trusts for them. However, there is no indication that York held the funds in trust for them. The trust that is to be created for the benefit of the two cats is lawful. In addition to people, trusts may be created for the benefit of animals, groups, social causes, the environment, or any other lawful purpose. As long as a trustee is named and there is a way of fulfilling the testator's wishes, courts have upheld trusts that were created for the care and maintenance of pets. The court should find that the specific gifts to Petersen and Burke were revoked by the sale of the stock and the funds in the accounts are now part of the residue that goes to Teen Recovery.

Answers to Practice Quiz

True/False:

1. True   A will has no legal effect until the death of the testator.
2. False   Beneficiaries receive property under a will.
3. False   The will must be signed at the end to prevent fraud.
4. False   Depending upon the state, a will must be witnessed by at least two or three persons.
5. True   The codicil must be executed with the same formalities as a will.
6. True   This act may be tearing, burning, or defacing the will.
7. True   Those portions not disposing of property to the spouse remain valid.
8. False   A holographic will need not be witnessed.
9. True   Any conflicting provisions are controlled by the second will.
10. False   The newborn is entitled to receive his or her share of the parents' estate as determined by state statute.
11. False   It is called a devise.
12. False   This is a specific gift.
13. False   This is the definition of abatement.
14. True   All descendants receive and equal share regardless of their degree of relationship to the testator. Children must share equally with all relatives.
15. True   The videotaping should involve a reading of the will by the testator and the asking of questions to show the testator's sound mind.
16. True   It is a question of inheritance that is decided by the Uniform Simultaneous Death Act.
17. False   The document is a joint will.
18. False   These wills are joint or reciprocal wills.
19. True   The undue influence is usually established by circumstantial evidence surrounding the making of the will.
20. False   This rule is not undue influence, but the murder disqualification doctrine.
21. False   The property is distributed pursuant to the state's intestacy statute.
22. False   They are called heirs.
23. True   In-laws do not inherit under most intestacy statutes, so a daughter- or son-in-law does not receive the inheritance of their deceased spouse.
24. True   A specialized court, called a probate court, supervises the administration and settlement of the estate.
25. True   The trustee has legal title to the trust corpus, and the beneficiary has equitable title. [p 1034]

Multiple Choice:

26. A A few states still maintain the additional designation of testatrix for a female testator. B is not correct as the executor is the person named in the will to serve as personal representative for the administration of the will. C is not correct because the beneficiary receives the property upon disbursement. D is incorrect because the administrator is the personal representative who is appointed when an executor is not named in the will.

27. C The beneficiary may be a person, organization, or institution. A, B and D are incorrect as defined in Question 26.

28. D A person may prepare their own will. Choices A, B, and C are all requirements to form a valid will.

29. B The requirements for a formal will must be followed without exception. Choices A and C do not meet all the formal requirements, lacking either attestation or a writing. Choice D is not correct because a correct choice, B, is available.

30. C A codicil must be executed with the same formalities as a will. A is not correct because a trust is a legal arrangement for holding property by one person for the benefit of another. B is not correct because it is an informal will in the testator's own handwriting. D is incorrect because the attestation is the action of a will be witnesses, not an amendment to the will.

31. B The birth of a child after a will has been executed does not revoke the will but does entitle the child to receive his or her share of the parents' estate as determined by state statute. A is not correct because divorce revokes and disposition of property to the former spouse. C is not correct because a properly executed subsequent will revokes a prior will if it specifically states the testator's intention to do so. D is not correct because any act that demonstrates an intent to revoke the will serves as a revocation.

32. A General gifts doe not identify the specific property from which the gift is to be made, such as a cash amount that can be paid from any source. B is not correct because a devise related to real property. C is not correct because a specific gift refers to a specifically named piece of property. D is not correct because a specific devise is a gift of a particular piece of real property, not cash.

33. B The gift lapses and is not granted from other estate assets. A is not correct because abatement is a method for dividing an estate that does not have enough assets to satisfy all the gifts and taxes. C is not correct because intestacy applies when there is no will. D is not correct because per capita distribution is a method for dividing the estate equally among all the living descendants.

34. C The large benefit to the beneficiary with such an easy opportunity to exert influence is strong evidence of undue influence. A is incorrect because no one was murdered. B is not correct because the presence or lack of an attestation clause does not prevent undue influence. D is not correct because undue influence can be used whether there is a formal will or a holographic will.

35. D The danger of waiting until death to create a trust by will is that the trust will be deemed invalid if the will that creates the trust is invalid. Choices A and B are forms of inter vivos trusts that are created during the settlor's lifetime. Choice D is incorrect for the same reason, as it is created during the settlor's lifetime, not upon his or her death.

Short Answer:

36. testamentary capacity, a written will, testator's signature
37. The action of a will be witnesses by two or three objective and competent people.
38. A separate document that must be executed to amend a will. It must be executed with the same formalities as a will.
39. (1) divorce (2) an act by the testator that destroys the will (3) execution of a subsequent will that expressly revokes all former wills and codicils
40. The will must be entirely in the testator's own handwriting, dated, and signed by the testator.

41. A gift of the estate left over after the debts, taxes, and specific and general gifts have been paid.
42. When the testator's estate is not large enough to pay all the devises and bequests.
43. In per stirpes, the lineal descendants (grandchildren and great-grandchildren of the deceased) inherit by representation of the parent. They split what their deceased parent would have received. If their parent is alive, they receive nothing.
44. The videotaped will is not valid by itself, but it can be used to supplement the written will to demonstrate the testamentary capacity of the testator.
45. Undue influence occurs when one person takes advantage of another person's mental, emotional, or physical weakness and unduly persuades that person to make a will.
46. If a person dies without a will, their property is distributed to his or her relatives, called heirs, under the state's intestacy statute. If there are no surviving relatives, the deceased's property goes to the state.
47. People who do not want their lives prolonged indefinitely by artificial means may execute a living will that stipulates their wishes before catastrophe strikes and they become unable to express it themselves because of an illness or an accident.
48. The beneficiary can be any identifiable person, animal, charitable organization, or other institution of cause that the settlor chooses. A group or entire class of persons, such as "all my grandchildren" can be named.
49. A trust document states that the settlor shall deliver the property that comprises the res or corpus to a named trustee, along with legal title, to be held for the benefit of the named beneficiary. The trustee may manage and invest the corpus and is responsible for distributing the income and corpus as directed by the trust instrument.
50. The property or money that an embezzler takes may be invested in another business or piece of real estate. If so, a court may impose a constructive trust under which the embezzler, who hold title to the property, is considered a trustee who is holding the property in trust for the rightful owner.